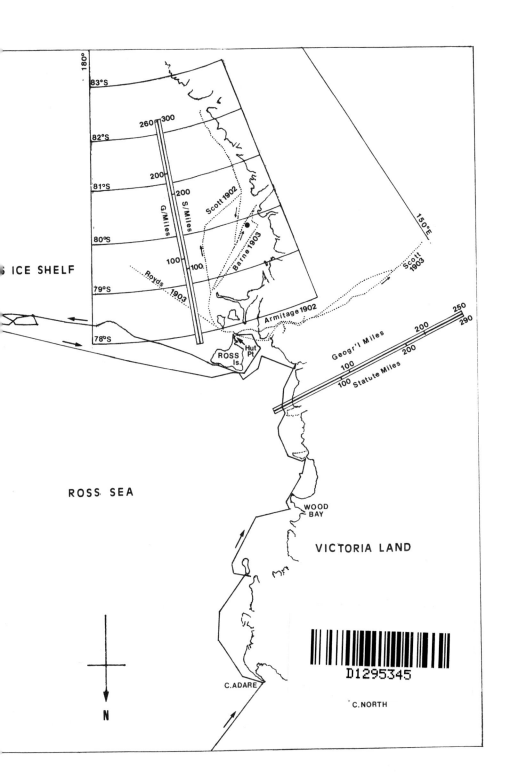

ANTARCTICA UNVEILED

DISCOVERY IN WINTER QUARTERS, 1902. Contemporary painting by marine artist Harold Whitehead showing Scott's ship with Observation Hill in the background. Reproduced by kind permission of Brian Sims, great-nephew of Leading Stoker Thomas Whitfield RN of the ship's company.

ANTARCTICA UNVEILED
Scott's First Expedition
and the Quest for the Unknown Continent

DAVID E. YELVERTON

WITH A FOREWORD BY HRH PRINCE PHILIP, DUKE OF EDINBURGH
AND AN INTRODUCTION BY ROBERT SWAN, OBE

UNIVERSITY PRESS OF COLORADO

Copyright © 2000 by David E. Yelverton
International Standard Book Number 0-87081-582-2

Published by the University Press of Colorado
5589 Arapahoe Avenue, Suite 206C
Boulder, CO 80303

The University Press of Colorado is a cooperative publishing enterprise supported, in part, by Adams State College, Colorado State University, Fort Lewis College, Mesa State College, Metropolitan State College of Denver, University of Colorado, University of Northern Colorado, University of Southern Colorado, and Western State College of Colorado.

The paper used in this publication meets the minimum requirements of the American National Standard for Information Sciences—Permanence of Paper for Printed Library Materials. ANSI Z39.48-1984

Library of Congress Cataloging-in-Publication Data

Yelverton, David E., 1922–
    Antarctica unveiled : Scott's first expedition and the quest for the unknown continent / David E. Yelverton ; with a foreword by HRH Philip, Duke of Edinburgh ; introduction by Robert Swan.
      p. cm.
    Includes bibliographical references (p.).
    ISBN 0-87081-582-2 (alk. paper)
    1. British National Antarctic Expedition (1901–1904) 2. Antarctica—Discovery and exploration. 3. Scott, Robert Falcon, 1868–1912—Journeys—Antarctica. 4. Discovery (Ship). I. Title.

G850 1901 .D68 Y45 2000
919.8'904—dc21   00-055198

Designed by Laura Furney
Typeset by Daniel Pratt

09 08 07 06 05 04 03 02 01 00   10 9 8 7 6 5 4 3 2 1

In undying memory of Léonie
who gave up much so this story might be told
only to fall victim to cancer just as the first draft was completed.
There is not a man in the saga this book unfolds
who would not have been proud to display the cheerful
and selfless courage with which she faced her last ordeal.

Commander Robert F. Scott RN at
Lyttelton, New Zealand, in 1901. Cour-
tesy, Scott Polar Research Institute,
Cambridge.

CONTENTS

ILLUSTRATIONS

BUCKINGHAM PALACE.

This fascinating book could be described as long overdue. The drama of Captain Scott's death and the failure of his party to return after reaching the South Pole has completely overshadowed the remarkable achievements of his first expedition ten years earlier.

The author has been at pains to set the planning and execution of this first of Scott's expeditions against the state of knowledge of the Antarctic at the time. It is only when seen in this context that the true value of the expedition can be assessed. It was the first to penetrate the interior of Antarctica, it produced the first firm evidence of the existence of an Antarctic continent, and it effectively located the South Magnetic Pole. Indeed, it discovered more about Antarctica than six other expeditions that went south at the dawn of the 20th century.

The book also gives convincing answers to a number of questions about personalities, relationships, the process of decision-making and the sheer difficulties of human existence in such a challenging climate. It is a work of painstaking scholarship and meticulous research.

—HRH THE DUKE OF EDINBURGH

ACKNOWLEDGMENTS

Without the practical aid of, and time generously given by, Dr. Colin Bull, veteran Antarctican glaciologist and Ohio State University administrator; William J. Mills, keeper and librarian at the Scott Polar Research Institute of Cambridge University; and Dr. David M. Wilson FZS, great-nephew of Dr. Edward A. Wilson of Antarctic fame, it is unlikely that I would have succeeded in drawing together into a readable narrative the multitude of facts about the expedition related in this book. To them I owe an immeasurable debt, as I do to my late wife Léontine (Koopmann)—Léonie to all her friends—without whose untiring support and enthusiasm this book would never have been written.

Of inestimable value, too, has been the friendship, encouragement, and practical help given without stint by New Zealand Antarctic historian and honorary fellow of Canterbury University, David L. Harrowfield. Polar Medal holders Cdr. Angus B. Erskine RN (rtd); Dr. Margaret A. Bradshaw, geologist and president of the New Zealand Antarctic Society; and John M. Alexander, Scott Base commander in 1990–1991, have contributed more than most could wish for to the construction of this history.

Acknowledged with particular gratitude must also be the kindness of HRH Prince Philip, Duke of Edinburgh, in writing the foreword, as also that of Robert Swan OBE, who has contributed the introduction.

New Zealanders David Geddes, operations manager, and Chris Rudge, former information officer, of Antarctica New Zealand, and mountaineer Peter Braddock took photographs that were invaluable to understanding the topography and course of the expedition, as did John Alexander, who led three companions (Phil Clarke, Peter Harding, and Tracy Clare) to the summit of Mount Heine on White Island and thereby helped establish the route followed by Ernest Shackleton on the first ascent of that summit with Edward Wilson and geologist Hartley Ferrar. Alexander's dramatic aerial photo, reproduced here, well portrays the daunting nature of the Descent Glacier, traversed on the first ascent of the Ferrar and Upper Taylor Glaciers.

Others whose encouragement over many years has done much to sustain my efforts at the most difficult stages of research and writing include the late Sir Peter Scott; Lady Philippa Scott; the late Lord Edward Shackleton; Lord Kennet of the Dene, son of Lady Kathleen Scott; Evelyn Forbes, daughter of Hartley Ferrar; Major General Patrick Cordingley of Gulf War fame; Nigel de N. Winser, deputy director of the Royal Geographical Society in London, together with Gwen Lowman, deputy editor of the society's journal, and Peter K. Clark, the society's former keeper of collections; polar historian Ann (Savours) Shirley, whose transcript of Edward Wilson's diary, published by Blandford Press, greatly simplified the study of that unique document; Dr. Peter Wadhams, former director of the Scott Polar Research Institute, and his wife; and John C. Parsloe, national secretary of the New Zealand Antarctic Society.

Over many years Robert K. Headland, well-known authority on polar history, curator and archivist at the Scott Polar Research Institute, and Christine Kelly, archivist at the Royal Geographical Society, bore the brunt of a multitude of inquiries in an era of severely limited staffing, and their unflagging interest did much to smooth the assembly of the bulk of information contained in this account. That process was also assisted materially by David M. Rootes, executive director of the polar logistics and support company Poles Apart.

Others who contributed valuable advice and help include Simon Barnes; the late John Bentley, who served on the 1925–1927 Discovery (Oceanographic) Expedition; Cdr. F. R. Brooke RN (rtd) and Wing Cdr. J. R. Claydon RNZAF (rtd) of the Commonwealth Trans-Antarctic Expedition; the late Captain William R. Colbeck; Alan J. Clark, deputy librarian at the Royal Society; Anthony Colwell; Brian G. Cox, honorary curator emeritus of the Blandford Forum Museum Trust; David J. Erskine-Hill; Jim Ghinn of CCS Photoprinters of Wimborne, Dorset, who produced the outstanding color photographs reproduced in this book; Dr. John Goodge of Southern Methodist University, Dallas;

William A. Howatson-Heald, whose father served on both of Scott's expeditions; Richard G. McElrea, the Christchurch, New Zealand, coroner and founding chairman of the Antarctic Heritage Trust; the late William J. McGregor, retired ship's master of RRS *Discovery* at Discovery Point, Dundee; Dr. David Meldrum of the Scottish Marine Biological Association; Rupert Neeland of Messrs. Christie's; Robert Nisbet; Baden N. Norris, Antarctic curator of the Canterbury Museum, New Zealand, and Joan M. Woodward, photographic archivist there; John G. Scott, grandson of the Royal Marine Gilbert Scott who served throughout the expedition; Deirdre Shepherd, librarian at Antarctica New Zealand; Brian Sims, great-nephew of Thomas Whitfield, a leading stoker aboard *Discovery*; Messrs. Sotheby and Co.; Drs. Bernard Stonehouse and Charles Swithinbank of the Scott Polar Research Institute; and Anthony P. Theelke.

Finally, thanks are also due in full measure to Cheryl Carnahan, whose patient editing of the manuscript improved the text, eliminated inconsistencies, and contributed to accurate notation of many source references.

In acknowledging the greatly appreciated help of all those mentioned here, I do not imply their approval of, or agreement with, conclusions expressed in this history of Scott's first expedition, which are entirely my own.

—DAVID E. YELVERTON FRGS
Hitchin, Hertfordshire

INTRODUCTION

This book tells the extraordinary story of triumph over setbacks that characterized the first expedition to penetrate the Antarctic continent, which conceded barely a toehold to six other expeditions that went south at the dawn of the twentieth century.

Robbed of time to prepare and train by an Admiralty jealous of civilian control of what was, to all intents and purposes, a naval expedition, and subject to Treasury parsimony that scarcely funded the cost of the special ship required for magnetic research, Scott and the men of the 1901–1904 British National Antarctic Expedition had to improvise under budgetary constraints unknown to the men of the parallel German expedition, which was funded almost entirely by their government.

It was all the more surprising, therefore, that Scott's first expedition discovered more about the unknown continent's interior than any of the other expeditions. Frustrated as Scott's hopes of reaching the South Pole were (nowhere was doing so among the expedition's official aims), Scott nevertheless brought back evidence that convinced the scientific establishment of the existence of an Antarctic Continent rather than a collection of islands, and that was the greatest prize at stake for scientists and geographers alike.

The sledge journeys into the heart of Victoria Land and Ross's great ice barrier, discovered sixty years before, also effectively located the "lost" South Magnetic Pole, so vital to southern trade route navigation in the decades before the satellite era began. All of this was accomplished with the loss of only one life, and that through an understandable mistake identified here for the first time (seven died on the other expeditions, of which only one death was accidental).

Not only do we learn what Scott and his men did but also why. The book's almost three-dimensional account, which will ring true to those who have traveled in the footsteps of Antarctic pioneers, reveals the often fraught realities that shaped Scott's decisions. It challenges even the most experienced polar traveler to assert, without hindsight, that he or she would have acted differently, given what Scott knew at the time.

Basing his account almost entirely on original sources, the author reveals the expedition as anything but the prisoner of outdated naval tradition. Rather it was the belief, held by some leading geographers, that Victoria Land had a west coast, with the possibility that it was part of a polar archipelago, that shaped Scott's handling of the expedition. The methods he adopted were almost entirely those expounded by the famous Norwegian explorer Nansen, who described the expedition's results as "magnificent."

The author refutes many widely accepted impressions of Scott as a leader, as well as the alleged animosity between Shackleton and him during, and immediately after, the expedition. He also provides a lesson on how easy it is to misinterpret diaries. Scott is shown to have been in favor of using dogs, having based the numbers he took on those taken by Nansen on his North Pole attempt over much worse surfaces. Anything but the martinet some have branded him, and in contrast to his personal aversion to seal meat, Scott is revealed, in his first report from New Zealand, as determined from the start to accustom everyone to a "so essential" diet of seal and penguin meat.

Not just the story of Scott's exploits, largely obscured in public perception by the tragedy that overtook him a decade later, this book also tells for the first time the full story of lesser-known sledge journeys that were epics of discovery in their own right.

The expedition's subsequent treatment at the hands of the scientific establishment is shown to have been largely based on an extraordinary mistake by the Meteorological Office, which Scott recognized but did not live to see publicly questioned. Vital specimens that demonstrated that Antarctica was once part of the Gondwana supercontinent remained unexamined for nearly a quarter of a century, an omission that played its part in Scott's death.

We learn more about the role of many ordinary sailors who became seasoned Antarctic travelers and mountaineers, helping to open the door to a century of scientific research that today yields environmental information of value to everyone on this planet.

With this book's many insights into a historic British achievement, I believe we can arrive at a fairer estimation of its ranking in the annals of twentieth-century exploration than it has been accorded in the last twenty years.

—ROBERT SWAN OBE
Barras, Cumbria

PROLOGUE

PROPHETS BEFORE THEIR TIME
Fathers of the Conquest of Antarctica

In 1849 a young graduate named Georg Neumayer became assistant to the physics professor at the university in Munich.[1] He began studying the conclusions of Alexander von Humboldt and Carl Friedrich Gauss on terrestrial magnetism, so vital to compass navigation, and made up his mind to devote his career to that science. He soon realized that the polar regions, the "home" of the magnetic poles, were the only areas lacking observations to substantiate the formula Gauss had devised to predict the forces of the earth's magnetic field anywhere on the surface of the globe.

As a result, Neumayer began to read the reports of the recent British, American, and French Antarctic expeditions.* Inspired by Ross's assertions that much remained to discover in the far south, he made exploration of the Antarctic his life's goal.

Failing to get into the Austrian Navy after acquiring a Mate's certificate, Neumayer set off for Australia, arriving in 1852 with the aim of joining the navy there. When his application was rejected, he tried his luck in the Bendigo gold diggings. Unable to strike it rich, he eked out a living teaching navigation to sailors who had followed the lure of gold, and he eventually worked his way back to Germany in 1854.

---

* Led, respectively, by Sir James Clark Ross RN, Lt. Charles Wilkes USN, and Commodore Jules-Sébastien Dumont d'Urville, exploring south of the Antipodes in 1839–1842.

CLEMENTS R. MARKHAM. In 1855, age 25, when he was in the Indian Civil Service. The magnetic spell of polar exploration had been implanted in his soul when he served as a naval cadet aboard HMS *Assistance* in the 1850–1851 search for Sir John Franklin. Reproduced from Markham, Sir A. H., *The Life of Sir Clements R. Markham KCB, FRS* (London: John Murray, 1917).

In Munich Neumayer's luck changed when he met Alexander von Humboldt and Justus von Liebig, the chief scientific adviser to King Maximilian II, father of Ludwig II, the patron of Wagner. Doubtless steered by the two great scientists, Neumayer submitted a paper to the king on the advantages to Antarctic research of studying terrestrial magnetism at Melbourne, and the enlightened Bavarian king provided the funds that built and staffed the Flagstaff Observatory. Neumayer was its first director in 1856.

Nine years later, back in a Germany moving from confederation to

GEORG NEUMAYER. In 1849, age 23, as a young gradu-
ate. Inspired by the achievements of Sir James Clark
Ross and the great German pysicist Johann Carl
Friedrich Gauss, he made the study of Antarctic ter-
restrial magnetism his life's work. Reproduced from
Neumayer, Georg von, *Auf Zum Südpol* (Berlin: Vita
Deutches Verlagshaus, 1901).

the national unity he strongly believed in, Neumayer made his first
appeal for Antarctic exploration to be renewed and a central oceanographic institution to be established. At home his Antarctic proposals
fell on deaf ears, but later he won the backing of the Academy of
Sciences in Vienna for an expedition to the McDonald Isles to observe the transit of Venus across the sun's disc (due to occur in 1874).
The scheme was dropped when the Franco-Prussian War broke out
but was revived in 1871, only to be canceled when its principal spon-
sor, Austrian Arctic explorer Vice Adm. Wilhelm Tegethoff, died in
April of that year. This ended Neumayer's only chance of going to the

Antarctic, for by the time his ideas bore fruit he was too old to accompany the expedition he had dreamed of for so many decades.

But the appeal to prospects of national greatness through fostering maritime enterprise that the pursuit of oceanography would serve led in 1876 to the founding of the Deutsche Seewarte, the maritime observatory at Hamburg that became the premier European oceanographic institute and won the admiration of all who studied the oceans. Neumayer was appointed director, a post he held until 1903.

Fourteen times over twenty-five years at major scientific and geographic congresses Neumayer appealed in vain for an Antarctic expedition. Finally, the sixth International Geographical Congress in London in 1895 generated the will that would turn hopes into action for this by now elder-statesmanlike figure and his English and Scottish counterparts, Sir Clements Markham and Sir John Murray.

In contrast to Neumayer, the young Clements Markham,[2] born in 1830, did get into the Royal Navy as a cadet in 1844, only to become disillusioned with the severe discipline a year later.* Despite being promoted in 1847 to Midshipman of the Foretop and winning the devotion of the hundred men under his command, his interest turned to geography and discovery. Two years of increasing frustration followed before opportunity in those fields opened in early 1850. Lt. Sherard Osborne, a messmate from Markham's first ship, got him posted, still as midshipman, to HMS *Assistance*, bound for the Arctic in search of Sir John Franklin.

After narrowly escaping destruction in the ice before the summer was out and wintering with six other ships in the Barrow Strait, Markham had his first experience of sledging during the 1851 searches. The prospect of returning to humdrum duties, and the extreme disciplinary regimes absent on the Arctic expedition, triggered his departure from the navy.

Armed with £500 from his father, Markham set off to search for the origins of the Incas. Three years later, in 1855, the results of his lone expedition to Peru won him election to fellowship in the Royal Geographical Society and a job in the India Office. There his extraordinary exploit, smuggling the jealously guarded quinine plant out of Peru to establish it in India for the prevention of malaria, was followed in 1863 by his appointment as honorary secretary of the society.

---

* The fifteen-year-old lad had joked publicly about a navigational error by the naval instructor. As a consequence, he had been reported on a trumped-up charge. He had then dared to protest to the captain when a petty officer, disrated for drunkenness, was sentenced to thirty-six lashes for a second offense.

Permanently infected by his friend Osborne with a thirst for polar exploration, interrupted only by a stint as official geographer in the 1868–1869 Abyssinian campaign, Markham campaigned for ten years to bring about the naval Arctic expedition of 1875–1876, led by Sir George Nares, during which Markham's cousin (and later biographer) established a new farthest-north record. Markham went as a guest aboard HMS *Alert* as far as Godhaven, halfway up the west coast of Greenland. In July 1875 he returned in the supply ship, which narrowly escaped disaster when holed by an uncharted rock.[3]

In the wake of his cousin's achievement, the seeds of Markham's interest in Antarctic exploration first bore fruit at an Aberdeen meeting of the British Association for the Advancement of Science (BAAS) in 1885. A committee of eight, including Markham, was appointed to press the government to pursue research in the Antarctic. With his enthusiasm freshly stirred, Markham was already shaping the concept of a naval expedition when, on a visit to the West Indies squadron in 1886, he first encountered Midshipman Robert Scott and mentally registered him, among others, as potential officer material for its execution.

The committee's first initiative had been to approach the state governments in Australia for support for Antarctic research. The only serious response came from Victoria, which offered £5,000 if the British government would do likewise. All this came to nothing in 1887, when the Treasury refused to consider the idea.

Markham turned to the public arena. He wrote an article on the need for Antarctic research for the London *Graphic*.

After serving twenty-five years as secretary of the RGS, Markham retired from that post. The campaign for Antarctic exploration was dead by the end of the 1880s. But Markham's election as president of the society in November 1893 reopened the way to practical action in pursuit of the one great geographical problem he passionately believed Britain could and should solve: Did an Antarctic continent exist?

Murray, his Scottish ally on the BAAS committee, emerged as the third great nineteenth-century progenitor of what was to be twentieth-century action to resolve the questions posed by the Antarctic, for it was he who opened the door for Markham to gain support from the scientific establishment. Murray had returned in 1876 from the globe-circling *Challenger* voyage as a convinced advocate of further Antarctic exploration. That inspiration had come during the ship's brief push southward in the unusually favorable 1874 season when it became the first steam vessel to cross the Antarctic Circle, reaching 66°40S. Commanded by Captain Nares (before his recall in January

1875 to lead the Arctic expedition), the ship had encountered ice-free seas after emerging from the pack on February 16. However, Nares's orders precluded further progress southward, and the expedition could only bring back tantalizing rock samples of continental origin, dredged up from the ocean floor.

Murray was appointed to direct the gigantic task of producing the fifty royal quarto volumes of the *Challenger* reports, seven of which he wrote himself. He paid for many of the volumes out of his own pocket as government departments began to quibble about the cost. When the volumes were completed in 1895, he was elected a fellow of the Royal Society; the following year he was appointed a knight of the Order of the Bath.

Markham's first act as president of the RGS had been to invite Murray to speak at the society's November 23, 1893, meeting. Advocating that a party of well-equipped observers should winter on the Antarctic mainland because nothing was known of the physical characteristics of the ice sheet or the land it covered, Murray emphasized that meteorological observations in the Antarctic were key to understanding the world's climate.

Going on to describe the *Challenger* expedition's possible proof of the existence of a continent near the Pole, Murray was able to add the contributions of two commercial expeditions that had returned the same summer from the Weddell Sea. Several men from those 1892–1893 voyages were soon numbered among the pioneers of the new century, their apprenticeship served amid the Antarctic ice aboard four small whalers out of Dundee and the sealer *Jason*, sent out by Christen Christiansen of Sandefjord at the mouth of Oslo Fjord.[4]

One of the men, William Spiers Bruce, surgeon and naturalist aboard the *Active*, was in the audience that November night and heard Murray relate that bottom samples Bruce had obtained from near the shore of the Antarctic Peninsula contained rocks of continental origin. Murray also described how Norwegian Captain Carl Anton Larsen, commanding the *Jason*, had landed on Seymour Island and picked up fossil shells closely resembling examples known in Britain and South America, which first established the geological age of that land. Not quite fairly, Larsen was credited with obtaining the first proof of the existence of sedimentary rock in Antarctic land, when in fact the American Dr. James Eights had found a piece of fossil wood in the South Shetlands on the Palmer-Pendleton expedition of 1829–1831, a discovery until then widely ignored in Europe.[5]

However, although Larsen's contact with Fridtjof Nansen (he had transported Nansen's party to Greenland in 1888 for the first crossing of the southern part of that vast ice cap) had given him insight into the importance of scientific observation, the Dundee whalers were sent on a strictly commercial search for bowhead whales, rich in valuable whalebone for ladies' corsets and by then almost obliterated in their usual haunts off Greenland. As a result, the scientists complained that their objectives were subordinated to the commercial goals of the expedition. This gave Markham and Murray solid evidence, in time for the RGS meeting, to support their contention that only a naval expedition would meet the aims of the scientists and geographers.

Addressing the November meeting, Murray put the size and scope of the required expedition into sharper focus. He urged that it should comprise two ships at least 1,000 tons each (the *Challenger* was over 2,300 tons) and should extend for three southern summers and two winters, with "largely civilian" parties of ten men each to be left at Bismarck Strait and McMurdo Bay* during both winters, with the ships replenishing their stores over the intervening summer and bringing the men back the third summer. He argued that these two bases would provide simultaneous observations at two widely separated points.

Only one expedition was living up to Murray's ideals: it was Nansen's, locked in the ice and drifting in the *Fram* across the Arctic Ocean. Paying tribute to it and similar future ventures, Murray went on:[6]

> A few months ago I bade good-bye to Nansen (aboard his ship) and said I expected within 2 years to welcome him on his return from the Arctic; but I expressed some doubt if I should again see the *Fram* [Markham was, but Murray was not, numbered among the few who believed Nansen would succeed in his plan to drift across the Pole locked in the ice and emerge near Greenland].[†] "I think you are wrong" was the reply. "I believe you will welcome me on this very deck, and after my return from the

---

* Bismarck Strait on the western side of the Antarctic Peninsula, named by German sealer Edouard Dallmann in 1874, lies at 65°S and was believed to lead eastward through to the Weddell Sea. McMurdo "Bay," more imagined than seen by Sir James Ross during his sensational discoveries south of New Zealand fifty years before, lay in 77°S.

† In a report on the 1875–1876 expedition, Markham had concluded that water flowed across the North Polar Sea from the Eastern to the Western Hemisphere (PRGS: 21/6 September 1877). Nansen had not seen that report when he independently came to the same conclusion. When he learned of it after his return, he emphasized that Markham had been the first to recognize the basis for the *Fram*'s drift plan (GJ 26/1: July 1905).

Arctic, I will go to the South Pole, and then my life's work will be finished." This is a spirit we must all admire. I feel it deserves and is most likely to command success. All honour to those who venture into the far north, or far south, with slender resources and bring back with them a burden of new observations. A dash to the South Pole is not what I now advocate, nor is it what British science desires. It demands rather a steady continuous, laborious, and systematic exploration of the whole southern region.

There is no reason to think this view was not shared by Markham, albeit with more emphasis on geographical discovery than Murray perhaps meant to imply.

Neither Markham nor Neumayer could know that within two years the gateway to action would at long last start to open. For different reasons, each man passionately believed in the benefits of Antarctic exploration, and Murray's speech illuminated the common ground between them.

The map he exhibited—with detailed exceptions, it was little different when the new century dawned—showed that geographically the exploration of this huge part of our planet was centuries out of step, but this time it would take more than a few voyages by a Vasco da Gama or Columbus. More than twenty-five expeditions, spread over sixty years, were needed to reveal the shape of the land hidden in this last blank space on the map of the globe.

For their part in the genesis of those expeditions, von Neumayer, Markham, and Murray—all men of the nineteenth century and prophets before their time—must surely be regarded as the first of the twentieth-century Antarctic pioneers. How the convictions they faithfully pursued were translated into two great national expeditions, and the British one led by Scott became the first to establish the existence of the unknown continent, is the story unfolded in this book.

ANTARCTICA UNVEILED

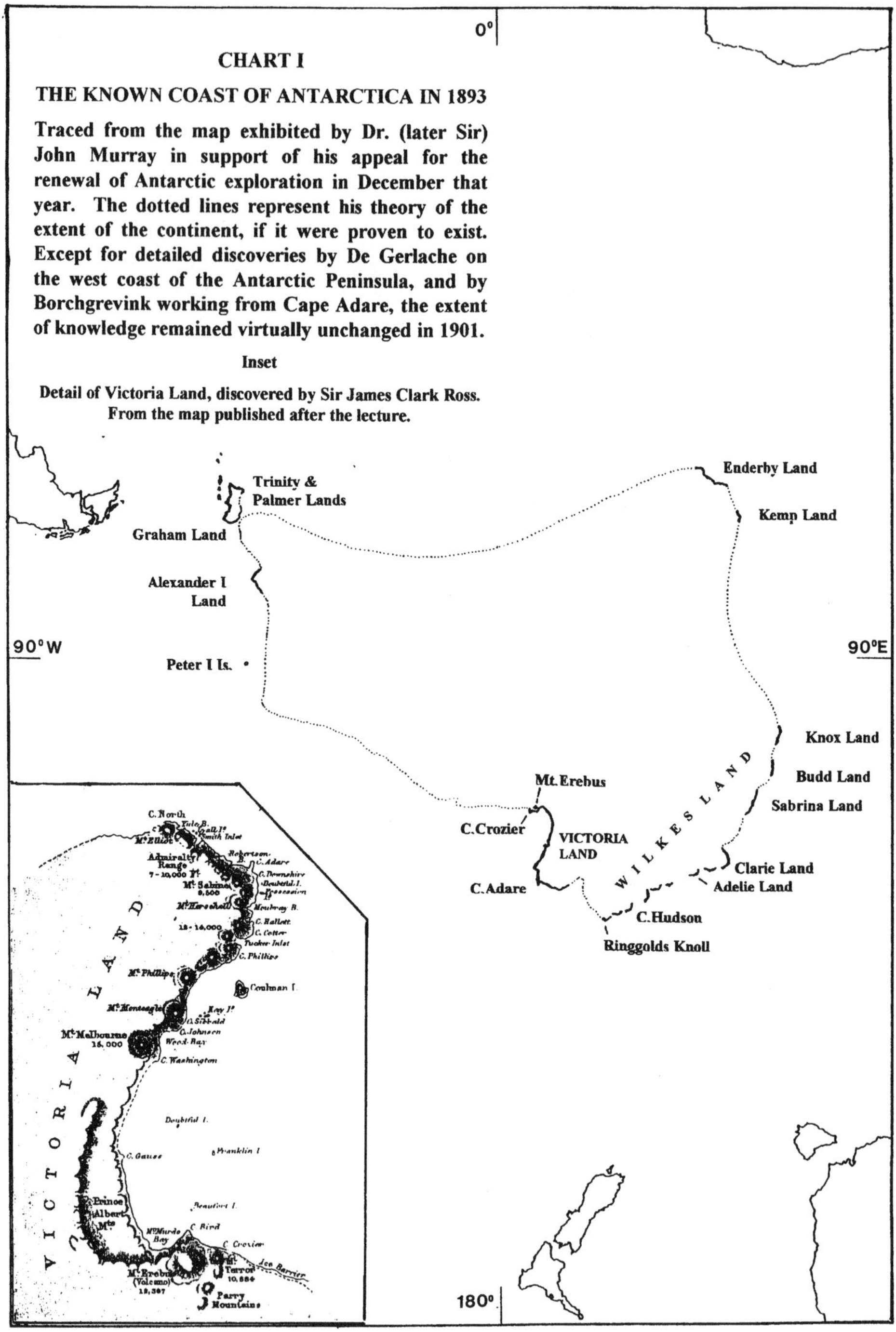

CHART I

THE KNOWN COAST OF ANTARCTICA IN 1893

Traced from the map exhibited by Dr. (later Sir) John Murray in support of his appeal for the renewal of Antarctic exploration in December that year. The dotted lines represent his theory of the extent of the continent, if it were proven to exist. Except for detailed discoveries by De Gerlache on the west coast of the Antarctic Peninsula, and by Borchgrevink working from Cape Adare, the extent of knowledge remained virtually unchanged in 1901.

Inset

Detail of Victoria Land, discovered by Sir James Clark Ross.
From the map published after the lecture.

0°

Enderby Land

Kemp Land

Trinity & Palmer Lands

Graham Land

Alexander I Land

90° W

90° E

Peter I Is.

Knox Land

Budd Land

Sabrina Land

Mt. Erebus

C. Crozier

VICTORIA LAND

C. Adare

W I L K E S L A N D

Clarie Land

Adelie Land

C. Hudson

Ringgolds Knoll

Inset labels

VICTORIA LAND

C. North
Terra B.
Mt. Elliot
Smith Inlet
Admiralty Range
7 - 10,000 Ft.
Robertson
C. Adare
Mt. Sabine
8,500
C. Downshire
Doubtful I.
Mt. Herschell
Possession
Moubray B.
Mt. Phillips
12 - 14,000
C. Hallett
C. Cotter
Tucker Inlet
C. Phillips

Coulman I.

Mt. Monteagle
Cap. I.
Mt. Melbourne
16,000
Mt. Sibbald
C. Johnson
Wood Bay
C. Washington

Doubtful I.

C. Gauss

Franklin I.

Prince Albert Mts.

Beaufort I.

McMurdo Bay
C. Bird
C. Crozier
Mt. Erebus
(Volcano)
12,367
Mt. Terror
10,884
Ice Barrier
Parry Mountains

180°

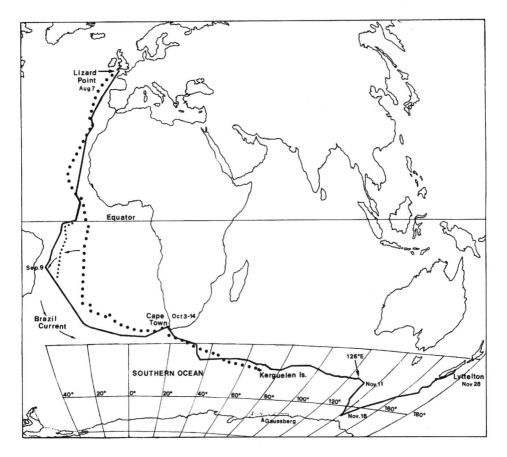

CHART II

DISCOVERY -- MISTRESS OF THE SOUTHERN SEAS

The Courses of the British and German Ships to their Magnetic Bases.

From the Cape *Discovery* took nine days less than the German ship to reach the Kerguelens. Discounting the magnetic meridian detour to the ice, her time from the Cape to New Zealand was equivalent to about thirty-five days compared to forty-nine days by the relief ship. That season the *Penrhyn Castle*, a typical commercial square rigger bound for Chile in ballast, with fourteen thousand square feet of canvas, took fifty days from 20°E to the meridian of Lyttelton.

Ships' Courses: ━━━━━ *Discovery* ＊＊＊＊   Course possible and position reached by Sep.9 if *Discovery*
            ● ● ● ● *Gauss* had been able to sail within 6 points (67.5°) of the wind.

ARRIVAL DATES AND ACTUAL SAILING TIMES IN DAYS EN ROUTE

		Lizard Point *	to	Equator	to	Cape Town arr.	dep.	to	Kergu-elens	to	126°E	to	Lyttelton
Discovery	1901	Aug. 7	23	Aug. 31	55	Oct. 3	Oct.14	15	Oct.29 *	12	Nov.11 *	=8	Nov.28
Gauss	1901	Aug. 20	36	Oct. 1	84	Nov. 23	Dec. 7	24	Dec.31				
Morning	1902	Jul. 3	33	Aug. 3	75	Sep. 29	Sep.29	15	Oct.14 *	18	Oct.31 *	16	Nov.16

The Germans' time from Equator to Cape was lengthened by calms and an extensive sounding program.

(* = Date crossing meridian)

CHART III

SUMMARY OF RELEVANT ENTRIES IN
THE DECK AND OFFICIAL LOGS,
ROYDS' DIARY, AND SCOTT'S ACCOUNT

Passages in bold emphasize periods of Scott's presence on the bridge during embayment crisis

JANUARY 31

±1800:   With sea clear to the horizon from NE through W, **Scott** instructs Barne follow coastal ice edge, **goes below after some 35 hours on bridge**.

1920:   Reaching farthest east, Barne finds "ship embayed." Alters course to "S30W" magnetic (approximately NW true).

2000-2115: Shackleton passes through wide lead to emerge in "large bay", follows edge round "in search of opening"

±2340:   **Scott back on bridge** when Royds comes up to take over middle watch. Royds finds Shackleton explaining situation. **Scott** points out apparent exit from bay on bearing "N25E" magnetic, (approximately EbyS true), **then goes below**.

FEBRUARY 1

0123:   Royds arrives at Barne's cul-de-sac of previous evening, informs Scott, alters course 15 points to port.

0300:   **Scott on bridge again**, points out channel on port bow, apparently leading to open water beyond ice on starboard bow. **Scott goes below**.

0320:   Royds reaches berg where ship watered, finds channel blocked, turns NW (true), and hands over to Barne at 0400 hrs.

±0600:   Barne records "strong ENE [true] set [in current]." Armitage takes over from Barne, just after Barne finds way south blocked.

0730:   **Scott arrives on bridge;** is surprised to find Armitage lost. Neither man can recognise way out, nor, despite N5E (true) course, that it cannot be ahead. Sends for Royds who, "purely by luck", sees they are "going wrong." Scott (and evidently Armitage too) are unconvinced.

0850:   Royds finally persuades Scott to turn SE (true) across bay. Reaching the coastal ice again, Shackleton, now on watch, turns ship to SW (true).

1035:   Shackleton reaches "watering place of yesterday", finds exit channel open.

****

Sources: Deck and Official Logs (RGS Antarctic Archive 21/1 and 21/4)
Royds' Diary (SPRI ms 654/1), Scott (1905) v.I pp188-190

CHART III

ESCAPE FROM A "VERY NASTY POSITION"

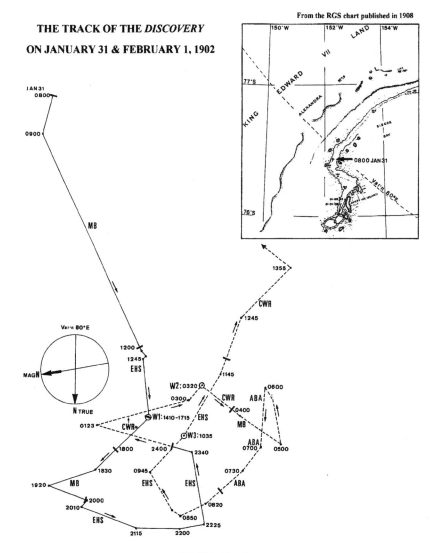

THE TRACK OF THE *DISCOVERY*

ON JANUARY 31 & FEBRUARY 1, 1902

From the RGS chart published in 1908

NOTES & LEGEND

Ship's track plotted according to courses recorded in the Deck Log, without taking account of ice movement in the strong ENE current Barne recorded. For the period between 1715hrs on Jan.31 and Noon on Feb.1 the ship's speed was not recorded, and the track plotted assumes a 3-knot average for that time. In reality, by the time the ship made her second circuit round the 'bay' in the pack, it was almost certainly several miles NE of its first location.

━━ = Track on Jan. 31, 1902. ▬ ▬ ▬ = Track on Feb. 1, 1902.   ▌ = Watch Change.

W1 = Berg where Ship watered on Jan.31
W2/W3 = 2nd and 3rd occasions Ship was at same point.

Officers on Watch: ABA = Armitage; MB =Barne; CWR = Royds; EHS = Shackleton.

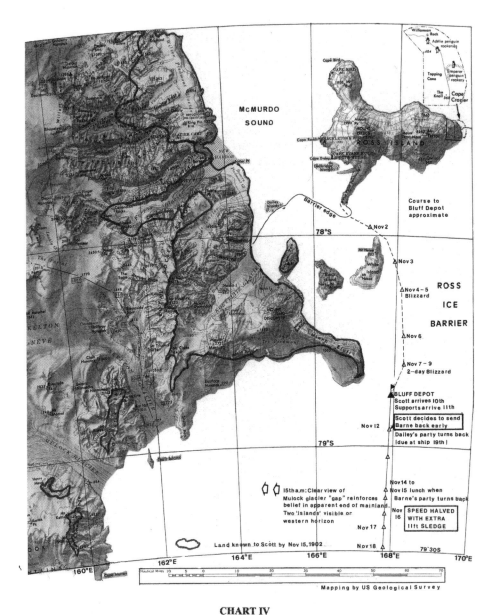

McMURDO
SOUND

ROSS ISLAND

Course to
Bluff Depot
approximate

Barrier edge

78°S

△Nov 2

△Nov 3

△Nov 4 – 5
Blizzard

ROSS

ICE

BARRIER

△Nov 6

△Nov 7 – 9
2-day Blizzard

▲ BLUFF DEPOT
Scott arrives 10th
Supports arrive 11th

Scott decides to send
Barne back early

Nov 12   △   Dailey's party turns back
(due at ship 19th)

79°S

Nov 14 to
△ Nov 15 lunch when
15th a.m: Clear view of   Barne's party turns back
Mulock glacier "gap" reinforces
belief in apparent end of mainland.   Nov   SPEED HALVED
Two 'islands' visible or   16   WITH EXTRA
western horizon   11ft SLEDGE

Nov 17 △

Land known to Scott by Nov 15,1902   Nov 18 △   79°30S

162°E   164°E   166°E   168°E   170°E

160°E

Nautical Miles 10   5   0   10   20   30   40   50   60   70   80

Mapping by US Geological Survey

CHART IV

THE SCENE OF SCOTT'S CRITICAL CHANGE OF PLAN

CHARTS V & VI

THE SOUTHERN SLEDGE JOURNEY ROUTE
from the
BLUFF DEPOT TO SCOTT'S FARTHEST SOUTH

Chart V

From the Mina Bluff Depot in 78°45S to Depot "B" in 80°29S
November 12 to December 14, 1902
Also showing the approximate return route to the Bluff

Chart VI

From Depot "B" to Farthest South in ±82°11S
December 16 to 31, 1902
also showing probable return route to January 6, 1903

and

marked up to show the orientation of (A thru C) three historic
sketches by Dr. Edward Wilson, that appeared in the *South Polar
Times* in June 1903, and (D) Shackleton's photo of the coast of
Cape Wilson that the three men tried unsuccessfully to reach, all of
which serve to locate camps on the final leg of the journey south

together with

a plate relating those pictures to the relevant map abstract
reproduced at larger scale.

Mapping by US Geological Survey
Times at camps are approximate, and camp dates reflect arrival
time.

NOTES ON ROUTE PLOTTED IN CHARTS V & VI

The outward route charted by Lt. Mulock in 1908 is suspect: (a) because it does not marry up with camp positions on the final leg of the outward journey that are established by the orientation of sketches made by Wilson (shown at A thru C on Chart VI) and the crucial panoramic photos taken by Shackleton at the Dec. 28, 1902 camp, and (b) because it places Depot "B" beyond the rifts curving southeast of Cape Selborne instead of almost a mile short of their eastern margin.

Wilson's diary is the only one that records all but two of the daily mileages and, plotted on the courses charted by Mulock, they would put the deopt in 80°34S and, similarly, beyond the rifts.

For the depot to be west of the rifts' present position in 80°30S would require them to have moved over five miles further from the coastin the sixty-odd years preceding the US Geological Survey map date. Present-day glaciological knowledge makes that extremely unlikely.

Scott's 80°30S midnight sight an hour after starting south from the deopt (making one mile an hour according to Wilson). That, together with Scott's and Wilson's accounts of the first day's travel northward form the depot, with the two men pulling 525 lbs and Shackleton seriously ill, make it highly unlikely the depot was further south than 80°29S.

Adjustments to daily mileages needed to make the track and camp positions on Charts V and VI fit the parameters here mentioned, and the evidence of Wilson's *South Polar Times* sketches, do not exceed 7%. That figure is well within the likely inaccuracy inherent in the sledgemeter readings in the soft snow conditions, which they encountered for much of the journey. Appendix VII adds further explanation of the basis for the camp positions shown.

Distances to camps at the start of the return journey are scarcely reliable, as the sledgemeter broke down on January 9, 1903. It must have been in a far-from-optimal condition for several days before that. While the return course plotted by Mulock equates roughly to the orientation of Wilson's Jan. 20 Byrd Glacier sketch in the *South Polar Times*, it fails to accord with that of his Jan. 25 panorama, or the Jan. 27 (noon) photo Shackleton took of the lunch camp on the approach to the Bluff.* The probable course shown on Chart V is plotted to equate to the evidence these pictures provide.

---

* Facing p. 114 in vol. II of Scott's *The Voyage of the* Discovery.

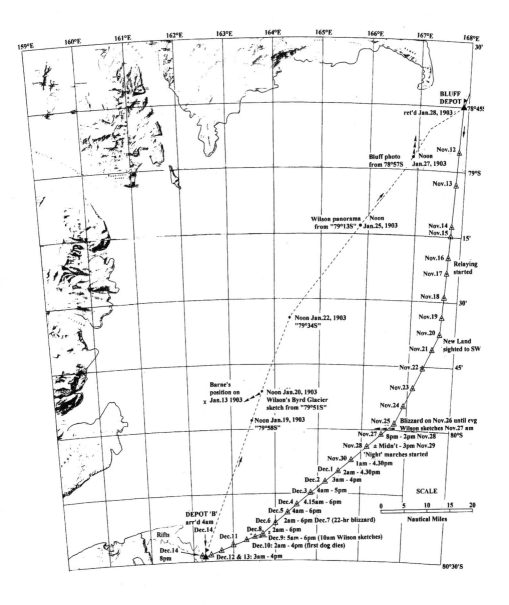

CHART V

THE SOUTHERN JOURNEY

FROM THE BLUFF DEPOT TO DEPOT B: NOVEMBER 12 TO DECEMBER 14, 1902

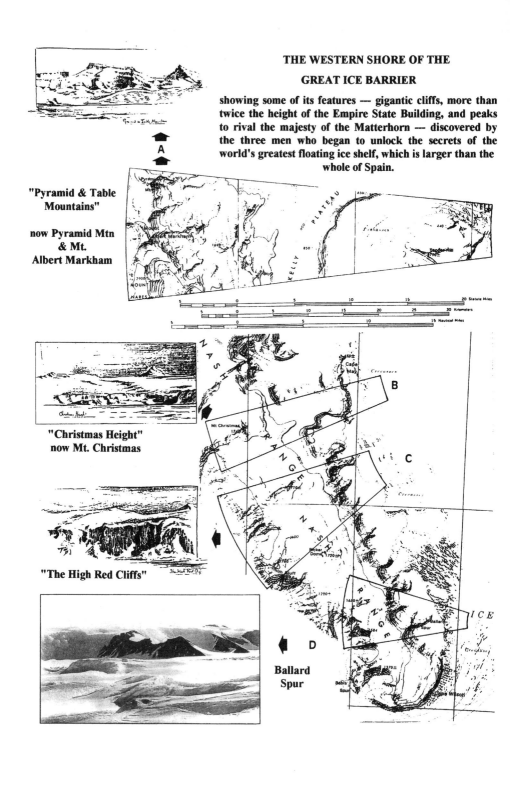

THE WESTERN SHORE OF THE
GREAT ICE BARRIER

showing some of its features — gigantic cliffs, more than twice the height of the Empire State Building, and peaks to rival the majesty of the Matterhorn — discovered by the three men who began to unlock the secrets of the world's greatest floating ice shelf, which is larger than the whole of Spain.

"Pyramid & Table Mountains"

now Pyramid Mtn & Mt. Albert Markham

"Christmas Height" now Mt. Christmas

"The High Red Cliffs"

Ballard Spur

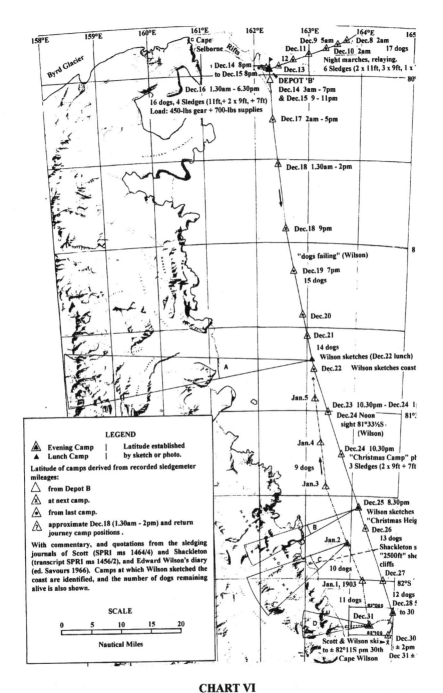

CHART VI

THE SOUTHERN JOURNEY

FROM DEPOT B TO FARTHEST SOUTH & FIRST DAYS OF THE RETURN

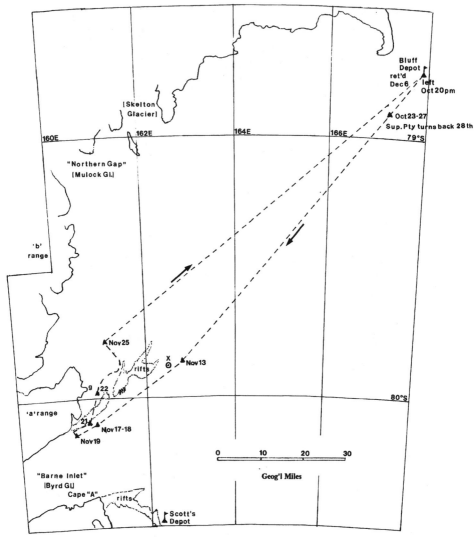

CHART VII

BARNE'S SECOND SEASON JOURNEY TO THE BYRD GLACIER IN 1903

An approximate reconstruction of his route from the accounts in his diary and report to Scott, plotted on map outline traced from a US Geological Survey Map

x = Farthest point reached on January 13, 1903 on first sledge journey.

g = Where pink and grey granite erratics were picked up from the Barrier surface offshore, little heeded evidence of the continental character of the coast Barne had discovered.

'a' range is Britannia Range; 'b' range is Conway Range; Cape 'A' is Cape Selborne

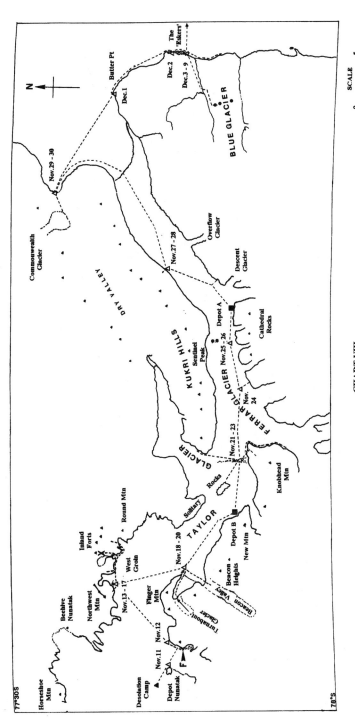

CHART VIII

FERRAR'S EPOCH-MAKING JOURNEY

F   Where fossilised vegetable matter was first found on November 12, 1903.

X   Where sandstone rocks containing fossilised *Glossopteris indica* v. Schimper leaves were collected on November 16, 1903.

△   Campsites showing dates (as 'nights of') spent at each.

••••   Line of glacier movement markers set out on first ascent of glacier.

SCALE

0   5

Naut. Miles

CHART IX

CAPE CROZIER IN 1902 - 3

Showing Barrier & Sea Ice situation as
described in the contemporary Journals
and Reports

Δ   Wilson's camps in 1903.

x   Site of Wilson's stone shelter, built
on what is today named Igloo Spur,
during his midwinter visit to the
emperors' rookery in 1911.

G   Glacier that stopped the first
message party in March 1902.
Skelton and Edgar Evans reached
the message post on Oct.11, 1902 by
bypassing it on the sea ice.

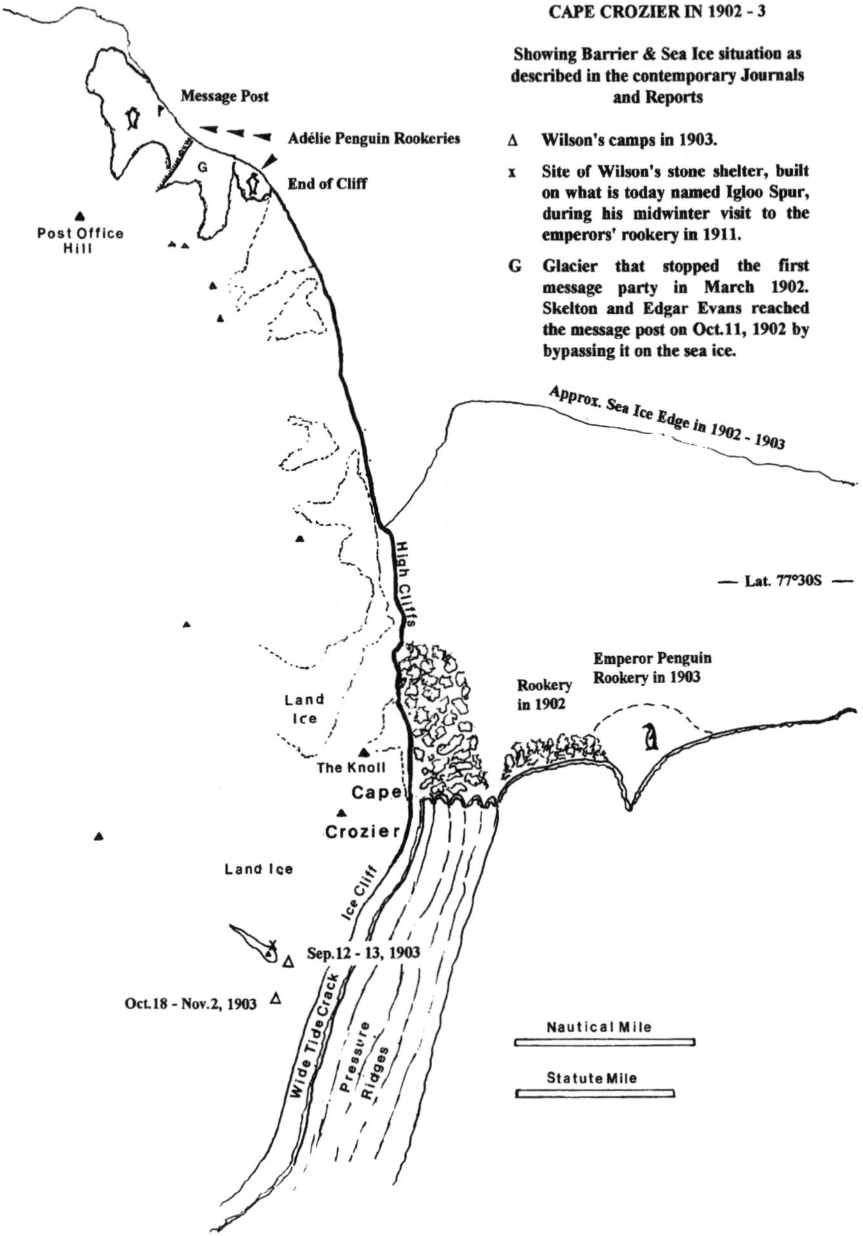

Message Post

Adélie Penguin Rookeries

End of Cliff

Post Office
Hill

Approx. Sea Ice Edge in 1902 - 1903

— Lat. 77°30S —

High Cliffs

Land
Ice

The Knoll

Cape

Crozier

Land Ice

Ice Cliff

Rookery
in 1902

Emperor Penguin
Rookery in 1903

Sep.12 - 13, 1903

Oct.18 - Nov.2, 1903

Wide Tide Crack

Pressure
Ridges

Nautical Mile

Statute Mile

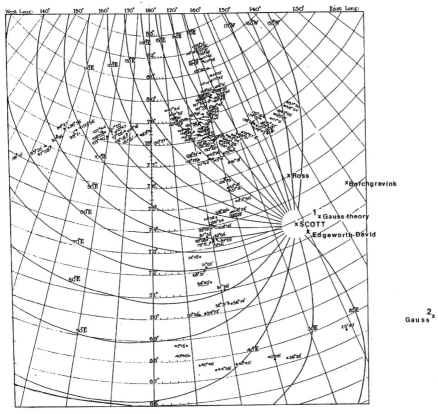

West Long.: 140° 150° 160° 170° 180° 170° 160° 150° 140° 130° East Long.:

Chart I. Lines of equal magnetic declination.
From observations made by the Officers of the National Antarctic Expedition, 1902-1904.
By Commander L. W. P. Chetwynd, Royal Navy.

CHART X

THE TRACKING OF THE SOUTH MAGNETIC POLE

A chart in the Scientific Report on Physical Observations showing the location of the South Magnetic Pole established by Scott, for the first time from adequate land-based observations, crucially those on his western summit journey in 1903. Also shown are the positions calculated theoretically by Carl Friedrich Gauss (#1) some eighty years before Scott's expedition, and (#2) recalculated by him from reported observations before the departure of the 1839-42 expeditions, along with those calculated from observations on Ross's and Borchgrevink's expeditions. Compared to the definitive position established in 1909 by Prof. Edgeworth David's sledge party on Shackleton's expedition, the accuracy of Scott's result, within 40 miles of the actual position, and numerous observations away from volcanic areas, was crucial to the reconstruction of the southern hemisphere magnetic map, so vital to navigation.

PART 1

PRELUDE TO ACHIEVEMENT
The Anguished Fulfillment of a Dream

1

SCIENCE AND THE DREAM OF DISCOVERY
The Genesis of a National Epic

When John Murray addressed the RGS meeting in November 1893, almost nothing was known about the Antarctic. There had been positive sightings of land along only around 13 percent of the circumference of the Antarctic Circle, most in the quadrant south of Australia and New Zealand.

The coast Sir James Clark Ross discovered in 1841 lay almost 300 nautical miles beyond the Antarctic Circle and at the eastern end of that quadrant. It ran 360 miles further southward in a continuous chain of mountains to the point where Ross conjectured that it turned east toward the smoking volcano he named after his ship, HMS *Erebus*.*

Around 350 miles northwest of the majestic peaks backing Cape Adare, at the northern end of the chain, supposedly lay Ringgold's Knoll, the easternmost 1840 sighting by the U.S. Exploring Expedition under Lt. Charles Wilkes. That fact remained in dispute because Ross sailed close by two years later without seeing a sign of land.

Further to the west lay Adélie Land, also discovered in 1840 by the French expedition under Admiral Dumont d'Urville. From that point almost due south of Tasmania, Wilkes's less disputed sightings were strung along the Antarctic Circle 900 miles westward.

---

* Geographical or true nautical miles are used except where noted because they equal minutes of latitude (e.g., 60 miles = 1° Lat.). As such, they better quantify progress southward, the initial goal of all the expeditions.

There were just two earlier sightings further west—Kemp Land and Biscoe's Enderby Land south of Africa—then nothing until the Antarctic Peninsula, still ill defined after 80 years of commercial voyages in quest of seals and whales. Between there and Enderby Land, James Weddell had reached 74°15S in 1823 without sighting land. For nearly 9,000 miles around the Antarctic Circle, no sign of a coastline had been seen.

The great question for Murray's audience and for scientists throughout Europe was what these scattered sightings represented. Were they mere islands or fragments of the mythical seventh continent? Ross had never landed, and he concluded that the mountains he saw were volcanic. Only the Frenchman's granite specimens from off-shore islands and rocks of continental origin dredged up just outside the Circle by HMS *Challenger* in 1874 hinted at the presence of a continent somewhere toward the South Pole.

But if that was the bait to attract scientific establishment support, even such a sensational discovery as a seventh continent was unlikely to excite government interest. On the other hand, questions of national interest *were* invoked by the unresolved navigational problems that abounded in the Southern Hemisphere for the maritime trade Britain dominated.

The annual change in the direction the compass needle points can be determined by an observatory in the area, but at those then existing closest to the Antarctic (Cape Horn, the Cape of Good Hope, and Melbourne) little change was occurring. Reports from the southern ocean, where the Cape Horners plied, suggested the compass variation from true north was changing rapidly. The weather that far south often prevented ships from verifying their compass observations by astronomical sights, with the result that many went miles out of their optimal routes. And for lack of observations in the far south, the method of calculating the positions of the magnetic poles and hence of the earth's magnetic field, devised by German mathematician Carl Friedrich Gauss, could not be verified for the Southern Hemisphere. As Georg Neumayer put it, the world had lost track of the South Magnetic Pole since Ross had established its approximate position. Gauss's formulas could no longer be used to calculate the compass variation in the far south.

A further question was posed by the magnetic storms that disturbed the compass needle in the southern ocean. The storms occurred most frequently south of Australia, where two regions of maximum magnetic force had been found, whereas there were virtually no such regions south of Cape Horn. That fact, and the as yet barely understood subject of atmospheric electricity, could probably be clarified by intensive observations in the Antarctic.

These issues, so vital to Britain's maritime trade, attracted the support of the Navy Hydrographer's Department. The Germans, too, already in open competition for empire, saw the finding of the lost magnetic pole as vital to their shipping interests.

But Markham also realized that the support of the Royal Society (in which Murray and the Hydrographer Admiral Wharton were prominent figures) was vital to Treasury support. Lack of data from the polar region prevented a proper understanding of other Southern Hemisphere phenomena, such as the behavior of tides, ocean currents, glaciers, and weather, all of which were of prime interest to the Royal Society.

A great argument was raging between meteorologists, who thought the permanent low pressure that prevailed in the "roaring forties" extended to the South Pole, and others who believed the Pole was surrounded by a vast anticyclone, from which winds blew outward to the ring of low pressure prevailing in the southern ocean. For the latter, Ross's records of a gradual rise of his barometers south of 75°S had provided the first evidence. Whatever the truth, all agreed that Antarctic weather exercised a dominant influence throughout the Southern Hemisphere.

Because of its known connection with the shape of the earth, gravity measurement in the region would benefit the science of geodesy. The calculation of the length of a degree of latitude was uncertain that far south, where the amount of flattening of the globe around the pole was unknown. Thanks to new German pendulum apparatus, gravity measurement in the Antarctic had become a practical proposition, and that could also bring a better understanding of the interrelation between the earth's gravity and its magnetic field.

In the field of biology, practically nothing was known about the distribution of plankton, key to the ecological chain supporting the southern whales, already of interest as decimated northern populations ceased to support the industry.

Geologists, divided on the nature of the last Ice Age, saw the Antarctic as the key to resolving that mystery. They erroneously believed the Greenland ice sheet did not flow out into the sea, not even in the narrow sound separating it from northern Canada. Ice sheets that had been seen in the Antarctic certainly did so, however, and no one knew why. The key to the shaping of Europe in the Ice Age might lie in the answer to that question—and so, as a joint delegation of the societies would later put it to the government, might the key to the origin of life on earth. Then as today, for scientists of many disciplines, such a goal would justify any mission into the unknown.

As Markham saw it, the geographical discovery of the distribution of land and water in the Antarctic was the key to settling these debates once and for all.[1] Above all, the question of the existence or otherwise of an Antarctic Continent was the common denominator that linked the scientists of the Royal Society to the geographers of the Royal Geographical Society in a common dream of discovery. It was potentially a formidable alliance.

2

THE LONG ROAD TO FINANCE

Imperial Edict and Treasury Parsimony

In July 1895 most leading exponents of the geographical sciences met in London for the 6th International Geographical Congress, with Sir Clements Markham in the chair as president of the host society. At his invitation, Georg Neumayer (by then, as a privy councillor, von) was the principal speaker on Antarctic exploration. During the ensuing discussion the president of the Paris Geographical Society proposed that a provisional committee be appointed to draw up a resolution on the best steps to be taken to advance Antarctic discovery. It was Markham's prerogative as president of the congress to nominate the committee. In doing so he remarked prophetically, "I always prefer a committee of one whenever really substantial work has got to be done." Much as he must have hoped, the congress voted in favor of the resolution drawn up by the committee, chaired by Neumayer, "that . . . the exploration of the Antarctic Regions is the greatest piece of geographical exploration still to be undertaken. That in view of the additions to knowledge in almost every branch of science which would result from such a scientific exploration the Congress recommends that the scientific societies throughout the world should urge in whatever way seems to them most effective that this work should be undertaken before the close of the century."[1]

Neumayer outlined a German plan for an expedition, with two exploring ships, to establish a magnetic observatory on land within the Antarctic Circle and settle the major geographical question as to whether there was a continent or an archipelago around the South

Pole. His long campaign in Germany had at last produced some action at a Bremen Geographical Society meeting three months before, when a committee had been set up with Neumayer as chairman to determine the size, cost, and aims of a national expedition. The committee, however, was no more immediately effective than Sir Clements's first RGS Antarctic Committee whose two-ship, three-year plan the RGS Council had adopted on February 12 the previous year. Nor, for that matter, was the resolution at the London meeting, although it could claim to have played its part in the genesis of four other expeditions* and it triggered the cooperation and competition between the two great national enterprises that in the end helped Markham and Neumayer get the government support so vital to their success. (It was almost four years before sufficient funds were forthcoming in either country to allow ship procurement to proceed.)

Markham's first gambit was again to approach the First Lord of the Admiralty in the marquess of Salisbury's third Conservative government, but on November 11, 1895, the First Lord declined to receive a deputation, as his mind was made up against a government expedition.[2] The next month the RGS Council was undecided about backing a private expedition, and in January 1896 even the society's Expeditions Committee declared itself opposed to an expedition.

That summer, when Fridtjof Nansen and Hjalmar Johansen had appeared like ghosts from the north at the Jackson-Harmsworth (farthest-north attempt) expedition base in Novaya Zemlya, Markham and his wife, Minna, set off for Norway. There on September 9 they saw the triumphant return of the *Fram* to Oslo and dined at the palace after the investiture of Nansen, Otto Sverdrup, and Colin Archer, the ship's designer, as knights of the Order of St. Olaf.[†] The next day Nansen showed Markham around the *Fram*.[3]

---

* The resolution helped Lt. Adrien de Gerlache gain the support of the Royal Belgian Geographical Society. His expedition sailed from Antwerp in 1897 but never reached its destination in Victoria Land, becoming marooned in the pack for a year after making striking discoveries on the west coast of the peninsula. It also enabled Carsten Borchgrevink to gain the patronage of Sir George Newnes for his Southern Cross expedition, which sailed in 1899 for the same destination, and directly inspired the Swedish expedition led by Dr. Otto Nordenskjöld that left Gothenburg for the Weddell Sea in October 1901, as well as the Scottish National Antarctic expedition led by William Bruce that followed in its wake a year later.

† Nansen was dubbed Knight Grand Cross, Sverdrup and Archer Knights Commander.

Meanwhile, the German Joint Antarctic Committee had met twice and was still undecided on the scope of the expedition to recommend. Neumayer was urging a two-ship expedition. Erich von Drygalski, the thirty-two-year-old Berlin geography professor who had led an expedition to Greenland and was destined to be chosen as leader of the forthcoming expedition, argued for one ship on the grounds that, as in Wilkes's expedition, the second ship would simply hinder the first because of the need to keep in touch.

Markham had to wait until November 1896 before feeling comfortable approaching the First Lord of the Admiralty again. This time the result was more favorable. Markham sought help in-kind rather than cash, but because of the growing naval threat from Germany the First Lord could offer neither men nor ships. However, he expressed interest, and after an invitation to dinner to meet Nansen in London in February 1897, he agreed to give Markham a letter defining the limits of Admiralty help.

The letter was duly forthcoming on April 6, 1897. Armed with this offer of all available information, the loan of instruments, and their lordships' "great interest" in the project, Markham carried the day at the RGS Council meeting six days later and was authorized to issue an appeal for funds.

That same month, at the German Joint Committee meeting at Jena, a two-ship plan was proposed with a somewhat optimistic cost estimate of £47,500. The decision was taken to try to raise funds from the public through the country's major centers of learning. A three-man Action Committee was formed, and Drygalski was asked to lead the expedition. As in England, the Germans faced an uphill struggle to gain popular support, and nearly two years later subscriptions still totaled only £2,000.[4]

Despite authority to appeal to the public for funds, Markham struck out yet again for government support. First he approached the Australian colonial state premiers, who were in London in July 1897 for Queen Victoria's Diamond Jubilee. Only the Victoria government responded, offering £1,000. Undeterred by the small response, Markham began to look around for ships in Norway and started to develop a plan for the expedition. He then made what he later described as a serious mistake, again approaching the Royal Society for help.*

---

* In 1893, after the meeting addressed by Murray, he had invited the Royal Society to join in, but without telling him the society had made an unsuccessful unilateral approach to the government, only informing him of its failure a year later.

But the continental examples and the story unfolding in London show that, short of royal patronage—and in England perhaps even with it—the support of the senior scientific institution was indispensable for obtaining government money, which Markham rightly judged would in the end be the making of the expedition. This time, more promisingly, the Royal Society organized an Antarctic meeting for February 1898, at which Murray gave what amounted to his 1893 speech, now entitled "The Advantages of an Antarctic Expedition." Even the hydrographer, Admiral Wharton, supported the proposal, which was once more for a naval expedition with a budget of £150,000.[5]

That same month the German Joint Antarctic Committee adopted Drygalski's single-ship plan and appointed him leader, unanimously declaring that the expedition could not succeed without the active cooperation of the navy. So the head of the Naval Department at the German Admiralty was approached. He immediately took in hand the design of the ship and the preparation of estimates, and Drygalski found three shipyards willing to tender.

The estimates, ready in July, totaled £150,000 for a two-ship plan, £60,000 for a single-ship expedition, and £75,000 for the plan eventually adopted, with one ship supported by two colliers to take supplies to the advance base in the Kerguelen Islands. These estimates formed the basis of an appeal to the kaiser, and the slow process of government approval began.

With the Belgian expedition missing in the Antarctic, the sailing of Carsten Borchgrevink's expedition, under British colors, in the *Southern Cross*[6] helped to arouse German public interest. By October 1898 Neumayer had the home affairs minister as an ally.[7]

In England, having formed a Joint Antarctic Committee in April of that year, the two societies once again approached the government, this time writing directly to the prime minister. Within a month the reply came that Lord Salisbury could hold out no hope of government help.

Turning again to the RGS Council, Markham persuaded the council to authorize an appeal for £50,000, toward which the society would donate £5,000, about a third of its capital. The appeal was issued in July, and Markham traveled to Berlin to dine with Baron Friedrich von Richthofen, president of the Berlin Geographical Society (Gesellschaft für Erdkunde) who introduced him to Drygalski. At that dinner the seeds of cooperation between the two expeditions were sown.

Back in London, a second circular to the society's fellows in November 1898 brought further contributions, boosting the total fund to £14,000. That was seven times what the Germans had raised, although, as Markham knew, they had their navy and government ministers actively behind them.

The fund in London could have been more had the Royal Society taken steps, as Markham and the RGS had done, to raise support. In fact, not one penny came from the Royal Society other than small personal gifts from some of its officers. This lack of support proved to be a mistake, for it ultimately cost the society virtually all say in the organization of the national expedition.

Within the space of a month, in the spring of 1899, the fortunes of both expeditions changed dramatically. In March a London businessman, Llewellyn Longstaff, hearing that the expedition might have to be abandoned for lack of funds, asked Markham if £25,000 would enable it to set out. Five days later the promise of funds was sealed over tea. The way was suddenly open for action.[8] Markham's diary began to hum with daily activity increasingly concerned with the new ship, for his attempts to find an existing ship suitable for the planned magnetic work had failed. At Markham's invitation, however, the Prince of Wales had agreed to become patron, and his son, the future King George V, became vice patron two days later. The vital doors were opening.

Later that month Neumayer's committee at last received the indispensable sanction from the kaiser, stating that the entire cost of the expedition would be met from the national budget. Assured that the expedition would start, Richthofen immediately wrote to Markham and Murray, as well as to the U.S. Navy Office, seeking their cooperation in scientific observations simultaneous with those planned for the German expedition.

Drygalski's appointment as leader of the expedition was confirmed in the official announcement shortly afterward, and the detailed design and procurement of the German ship got under way. By July, naval headquarters had inquiries out to six firms seeking tenders by November for a ship to be built from timber supplied from seasoned navy stocks. At the same time, the first instruments were ordered with the aid of the Royal Prussian Institute, and the expedition route was settled.

In London on April 18, Markham drafted an appeal to the prime minister and the chancellor, which, after approval by the Joint Committee, was signed by some of the leaders of British science, headed by Lord Lister as president of the Royal Society, and more than forty others ranging from the Astronomer Royal to university vice chancellors. The appeal gave an estimate of £100,000, requested support of £60,000 spread over four years, and referred to the Reichstag having been asked to vote £50,000 in support for the German expedition on top of what was euphemistically called a "large" public subscription. "On grounds of policy alone," ran the letter, "we submit that this is not the time for our country, so long the mother of discovery and of maritime enterprise, to abdicate her leading position." It concluded with a request that the ministers receive a deputation to supply any further information required.

The First Lord of the Admiralty, Arthur Balfour, standing in for the Chancellor, received the deputation on June 22. After speeches by Markham and four others setting out the maritime and scientific advantages, Balfour replied that he believed the Chancellor would give large financial support and in words that showed how he had been impressed by the arguments put forward, added his view that:

> it would not be creditable to an age which, above all other ages, flatters itself that it is scientific, if we were . . . to acquiesce in the total ignorance which now envelops us with regard to so enormous a portion of the southern hemisphere of our planet.[9]

That night Markham described it as "all very satisfactory" in his diary after Balfour had been toasted at the Geographical Club anniversary dinner at the Ship Inn in Greenwich.

Eleven days later, on July 3, Lord Lister received a letter from the Treasury promising a grant of £45,000 spread over four years, providing an equal amount was forthcoming from other sources "to enable the scheme to be efficiently carried out."[10] The amount was £15,000 less than the two societies had asked for, and another £3,000 would have to be found to match the grant. With no offer forthcoming from the Royal Society, the RGS was forced to sell off further investments to raise the money, bringing its contribution to half of the society's assets. It was less comfortable than the Germans' situation, but at least an expedition could start. Four years bar a month from the passing of the resolution at the last international congress, the breakthrough had come, in time for Markham's sixty-ninth birthday.

Markham headed for the next international congress in Berlin at the end of September, where the dual triumph of their long effort allowed Markham and Neumayer to announce that their expeditions were assured. The mantle of Ross in pursuit of scientific information vital to navigation on the grand scale would be carried to the Antarctic, this time by leaders from two nations soon to be deadly rivals for domination of the seas.

Their patrons now had to decide how the expeditions should go and where they should go.

3

SHIPS FOR DANGEROUS WATERS
Birth of the Discovery and the Gauss

In both countries procuring a ship or ships had rightly been seen as the first priority, and as early as August 1897 Markham was in Sandjefjord in the Oslo Fjord looking for a whaler, the cheapest solution to the transport problem. But the delicate nature of instruments the scientists would demand for magnetic measurements afloat, with their embargo on steel bolts in the ship's construction within a large radius of the position of the instruments, soon ruled out that economy.

Six months after Markham began his search and long before funds were assured, the Germans had decided in favor of building a ship. In England, Markham felt unable to make that decision until March 1899, when Llewellyn Longstaff's promise had at last ensured that a British expedition would set sail.

Immersed in the efforts to raise money and clear that no existing whaler could meet the magnetic requirements, Markham had turned his attention to the old HMS *Discovery*, Nares's ship on the 1875–1876 British Arctic Expedition. He had just learned that the ship would need new boilers and that the last survey had revealed some rot[1] when the Longstaff offer changed everything.

That very evening Markham wrote to Sir William White, assistant controller at the Admiralty, about having a new ship built.[2] Sir William replied that he believed one could be built cheaply in Milford Haven or other British ports where wooden shipbuilding lingered on but that seasoned wood would be difficult to get. Urging Markham to have a design prepared by a naval architect, Sir William added, "No doubt you could obtain without difficulty full particulars of the *Fram* for your guidance," suggesting that the Admiralty's chief constructor, William E. Smith, who had been trained in wooden shipbuilding, could undertake the job in his spare time.[3]

Markham replied the next day, proposing to approach the *Fram*'s designer, Colin Archer in Norway, but before the newly convened ship subcommittee met at his house on April 10, Sir William replied, sincerely hoping Sir Clements would reconsider his proposal "to go to Norway for the building of [the] vessel. Colin Archer is no doubt a man of great skill and large experience, but it would be a matter for great regret that a ship to carry a British Antarctic expedition should be built outside these islands."[4]* Allied to his prediction about the shortage of seasoned timber,[5] which would have unwelcome consequences later, Sir William's patriotic instinct effectively prohibited employment of the prestigious designer of Nansen's ship and, hence, of the stocks of seasoned timber he would have used.

Smith was duly called in. Meeting again on April 26, the committee unanimously decided the ship should be built along the lines of HMS *Discovery*, the surviving drawings of which had arrived that day. Unfortunately, they were not the working drawings hoped for when Markham and Admiral Sir Leopold McClintock first talked to Smith on the 17th. There was only a profile, a midship section, and deck and hold plans.[6] So what had been going to entail a few alterations to working drawings became a major design project. That situation, however, did allow some features of the *Fram* to be adopted.[7]

Presented with the outline drawings at the April 26 meeting, the chief constructor brought up the matter of the *Fram*'s design, but the ship's hull cross-section was rejected as unsuitable for the tempestuous seas of the southern ocean.[†] However, Archer's approach to the stern design, protecting the rudder, was adopted.[8] The recent merchant ship practice of two topsails per mast, more economical in man-

---

* These facts refute the implication in an article in the February 1980 *Mariner's Mirror* that Markham insisted on a new ship and believed that only the navy was competent to design it (vol. 66, pp. 68–70: A.G.E. Jones: "The Steam Yacht Discovery," republished 1992 by Caedmon of Whitby in "Polar Portraits," a collection of papers by the same author).

† Only the month before, the scientific journal *Nature* had reported Drygalski as saying that because of the stormy nature of the southern seas, the lines adopted in the construction of the *Fram* would not be suitable for the German ship, with seaworthiness being the first requirement (Nature vol. 59, p. 442: 3.9.1899).

power, was also adopted, as was the raking forward of the stem (bow) to facilitate the bow rising on the ice and breaking it, as in ice-breaking vessels.

Compared with the German ship, which had 325 HP engines and, although intended to carry 400 tons of coal could only take 363 on its final leg to the Antarctic,[9] the British ship would be built with 450 HP engines and a coal capacity of 335 tons. The ship was bark rigged (two square-rigged masts, the third, the aft "mizen" mast, rigged fore and aft), whereas the German ship was a barkentine (only the foremast square rigged and, in its case, with a fifth royal sail above the topgallant).

Compared with Nares's ship, the sail area was barely increased (to about 8,700 square feet), and Scott eventually criticized that decision. However, as Smith explained after the expedition returned, doing so would have required tauter rigging, with greater risk of spars carrying away when colliding with ice. And the taller masts required would have meant longer ropes that would be harder to handle when coated with freezing water.[10]

The *Gauss*, which had 11,000 square feet of sails (compared with the *Fram*'s 6,000), had to have its topmasts stepped down and yards cockbilled* when there was danger of collision with heavy ice. Concern for protection of men on deck led to the increase (to 4'9") in the height of enclosed rail (topside) around the upper deck of the British ship. That, in turn, added to the problem, also related to the lack of sail area, that arose from the large amount of gear and boats to be carried above deck and the adoption of the old HMS *Discovery*'s mast location plan. Together, these features led to complaints that the ship would not sail close to the wind, a vital asset in dodging ice. This must have been a characteristic of the old HMS *Discovery*, but it would not have been remembered by Markham or any other member of the committee, for none of them had sailed aboard the ship in 1875.

Even if Smith did point out the consequence of the masts being stepped that far back, he would have emphasized the advantage that the mainmast would be more than 30 feet from the magnetic laboratory and thus could be supported with wire rigging. The price to be paid was the consequent need for weather helm, for it tended to turn the bow into the wind. The rudder, set to counter this, then acted as a brake on the ship's speed under sail.

---

* Angled at about 45° to lower the center of gravity and hence the strain on the mast.

Original ⅛th scale model of *Discovery* supplied by the Dundee Shipbuilders Company and now in the collection of the Royal Geographical Society, London.

Facing page: Views of the top deck. Note the aft-facing compass binnacle on the bridge with voice tubes to the engine room and the quartermaster controlling the helmsmen at the wheel in the stern. The companionway to the crew's quarters can be seen abaft the foremast. The parrels holding the yards, two of which later fractured, are clearly seen in the same picture. In the stern view, the braces by which the deck watch controlled the set of the yards can be seen leading through blocks mounted on bumpkins extending from the deck rails ("topsides," as they were called). The main hand pump can be seen on the port side of the engine room, and the cover of the well through which the screw was raised shows immediately aft of the wheel. The donkey boiler stack can be seen on the starboard side of the forecastle, with the anchor windlass it drove situated between the anchors, ahead of the galley ventilation hatch and stack. Courtesy, the Royal Geographical Society.

Smith at first positioned the captain's cabin aft of the engine room because of the magnetic requirement. But the committee had stipulated accommodation to the standard aboard small warships, and that required a covered companionway to the wardroom, which had to pass through coal bunker space, with the cabin having its own stove. Both features transgressed the first priority: maximum coal economy and capacity. The only way out was to increase the ship's length by 10 feet, which further reduced maneuverability in ice.

The *Fram*'s stern design, which protected the rudder, was adopted but was changed to incorporate the rounded form found so effective by smaller gunboats in heavy seas. The wheel was situated right aft to enable the helmsman to keep an eye on the sails. Sharply criticized by

the Dundee whalers, the design proved a resounding success in the "roaring forties" and further south.[11] Bilge keels were considered initially because they "would add largely to the comfort of those on board" by reducing rolling, but they were later rejected because of the danger of the ship getting entangled in the ice.[12]

The designers in Berlin took the same view as those in London, and there were no bilge keels on the *Gauss*. Instead, recognizing that the ship's rounded form amidships (a compromise between the *Fram*'s wedgelike shape and the conventional, which they adopted in combination with bow and stern sections more like the *Fram*'s) would provoke additional rolling, they chose an unconventionally broad beam for the ship. Comparison of the two ships' dimensions shows this clearly. *Discovery*'s beam was 34 feet for a waterline length of 172 feet, *Gauss*'s 37 feet for a 151 foot length. Whereas the worst rolling aboard *Discovery* invariably occurred when the sails were furled in heavy cross seas, Drygalski would speak of the deck of his ship as almost constantly swept with huge waves and "heavily rolling and pitching."[13]

When it came to speed, both nations considered their ships primarily as sailing ships with auxiliary engines for navigation in ice, because safety and economy dictated minimum use of coal on the voyages. So they placed little emphasis on outright speed. Under steam, *Discovery* reached nearly 9 knots on trial, unladen except for ballast, so something less was to be expected when the ship was fully laden. Off Yarmouth on the voyage to London, Markham described the ship as steaming at 7 knots "easily."[14] At Kiel the *Gauss* met its specified speed of 7 knots under steam in the calm waters of the harbor, but at sea with even a light roll and pitch the ship could attain only 5 to 6 knots at most.[15]

Markham's ship, for he became the registered owner although it really belonged to the RGS, was also the faster under sail. The ship logged 191 miles on a day's run with a force 4 to 5 wind on the port quarter on August 20 1901, compared with only 144 miles achieved by the *Gauss* on September 10 under virtually identical conditions as the latter followed *Discovery* southward through the Atlantic.

So in terms of speed, the British had more than an edge over the Germans. Thus, although the *Gauss* was more maneuverable, it availed them little. But although conditions in the engine rooms in the tropics were more or less equally unbearable, with temperatures of 140°F and worse (147°F) in the German ship, *Discovery* had an extra drawback in terms of lack of comfort. Commenting on the insulation, Reginald Skelton, the chief engineer, wrote Smith after the first winter in the Antarctic: "One item entirely wrong with this ship is that the ship's side is not lined in the living spaces . . . the bedding of the bunks is frozen to the ship's side and large lumps of ice appear on the ends of the bolts."[16]

Clearly, the opinion had prevailed that the sides of *Discovery* were thick enough to make such insulation unnecessary. That mistake could have been avoided three different times, but by the time Scott—listening to Nansen—recognized the problem, the ship was half built, and cost precluded the remedy.

Evidently, Nansen had not mentioned the outer wall insulation when he showed Markham the *Fram,* but he did give details of it in his book *Farthest North,* published in London in 1898, adding: "One of the greatest difficulties of life on board ship which former Arctic expeditions had had to contend with, was that moisture collecting on the cold outside walls either froze at once or ran down in streams into the berths . . . it was not unusual to find the mattresses converted into solid masses of ice."[17]

Markham had not wintered in the Arctic, but the memory of those cold cabin walls ought to have been in the minds of the other nine members of the ship committee, all of whom had been members of one of those expeditions. When they met on September 25, 1899, they approved Smith's drawings the day before Markham arrived in Berlin for the International Geographical Congress.

The Germans, however, had insulated the outer walls of the cabins aboard their ship, whose sides were 2 inches thicker than *Fram*'s at cabin level and, like *Fram,* had triple planking compared with double in the British ship. Markham must have been reminded of that when reading the specifications of the German ship Drygalski had handed him on October 1, 1899.[18]

However, back in London, Markham went over Smith's drawings of the *Discovery* with him, and the point about the cabin wall insulation must have escaped the attention of both men. Thus the third chance to include it slipped away.

In the British ship, the cabins were to be heated by two stoves in the wardroom around which they were ranged, whereas in the German ship they were heated by steam piping designed to give 50°F when the temperature was 25°F outside, using the auxiliary boiler. Theoretically practicable because of the greater coal capacity, that luxurious facility proved unusable when the realities of coal consumption began to dominate the Germans' fate in the Antarctic. In practice, anthracite stoves in the passageways succeeded in holding the temperature there and, thanks to snow banked against the ship, even on the windward side, up to the freezing point.[19]

But there were no complaints about the temperature aboard *Discovery*, either, only about the stoves smoking and the condensation from lack of insulation in the cabins. These were small blemishes on the record of a ship that served the expedition well.

Almost a year after the ship committee first met, the ship's keel was laid, and shortly afterward Markham chose *Discovery* as its name.[20] Two years to the day after Longstaff had sealed his promise, the ship rode down its Dundee slipway into the waters of the Tay, launched by Lady Minna Markham just twelve days before the German' ship *Gauss* first slid into the waters of Kiel Harbour.

4

PREORDAINED STRATEGIES
The Shaping of the British and German Plans

The approach to the all-important decision as to where the British and German ships were to head had begun many years earlier. In Germany, Neumayer's passionate interest in obtaining the proof of Gauss's theories by measuring magnetic forces in the Antarctic had shaped a strategy for their expedition long before the 1895 congress opened the way for it to happen. He wanted the expedition to set up an observatory west of the magnetic pole, with another on the coast discovered by Ross to the east—a wish that also lay behind the early arguments about needing two ships.

But it was a two-way dream of discovery that settled the route for the German attack. Like Wilkes, Drygalski believed the coast would prove to be continuous from Wilkes's "Termination Land," the Americans' most westerly sighting in 97°37E, to John Biscoe's and Peter Kemp's sightings over a thousand miles to the west. Neumayer held that a sea between them ran far toward the Pole and connected up with the Weddell Sea. Almost certainly, he based that belief on the claim by American sealer Benjamin Morrell to have sailed through open seas south of Biscoe's and Kemp's tracks.[1]

From these two aims sprang the idea of a thrust almost directly toward the magnetic pole from South Africa, with the Kerguelen Islands as an advance magnetic station conveniently near the great-circle course. Such a plan could yield both the long-sought observations on the unknown side of the magnetic pole as well as major discoveries in the great gap between Wilkes's and the earlier British sightings.

In 1896 the *Fram*'s return added to Neumayer's theory the dramatic chance that a similar drift, perhaps across the Pole itself, could emerge in the Weddell Sea. This swung the balance in favor of choosing the quadrants either side of the Greenwich Meridian for the German expedition.

The decision neatly avoided a potential clash for Markham, who had first begun to think through the options for the British expedition in Norway after winning the RGS Council's support in 1897. He had independently arrived at a preference for the other two quadrants (either side of the 180° meridian, which ran through the Ross Sea). The two concepts undoubtedly fused into mutual accord at a dinner with Richthofen and Drygalski in July the following year.

Richthofen turned that accord into a formal proposal as soon as the kaiser sanctioned the expedition in April 1899, when he also put forward the concept of simultaneous magnetic and weather observations by the expeditions and observatories throughout the world. The sweeping aim was nothing less than the construction for the first time of weather and magnetic force maps for the entire Southern Hemisphere. The entire plan was ratified at the Berlin congress six months later, when Markham outlined the potential of each quadrant and a committee of four scientists from each country was set up to coordinate the program of observations.[2]

Whereas Neumayer's primary interest in the magnetic work had immediately directed German intentions to almost a single point, Markham had to determine the most promising sector for the British expedition from half of the Antarctic's circumference. The field open to him extended from a point southwest of Perth to Bellinghausen's Peter I Island three-quarters of the way across the Pacific.

Looking at the probable harvest of knowledge from two possible routes, Markham saw the first, westward from Cape Adare (170°E), as potentially resolving the question left unanswered by d'Urville and Wilkes—namely, whether their sightings had been parts of a continuous coastline or merely isolated islands. However, Markham had to acknowledge that pack ice threatened access to the coast over the entire route.[3]*

The second route, eastward from Cape Adare, offered more dramatic possibilities. Markham assumed that steam would enable the

---

* The following four paragraphs summarize, with quotations, Markham's handwritten "Plan of the Expedition," drafted, according to his diary, in the course of December 1-4, 1900.

pack to be forced a month sooner than the early January passage, which had been possible for Ross under sail alone. If the ship would "at once proceed to the most eastern point reached by Ross along the Barrier . . . the pack [there] may not be impenetrable in December, when . . . most important discoveries will be made to the eastward, especially if the land beyond the barrier turns to the south with an eastward face, and this offers a navigable channel along its shore."

Markham had some grounds for hoping that might be so, for both Ross at Victoria Land* and in 1894 Larsen in the Weddell Sea had found ice-free passage along east-facing shores (although the Norwegian was eventually stopped by ice just beyond the 68th parallel). If it proved otherwise, he thought McMurdo "Bay" would offer a safe place for wintering the ship, from where he envisaged journeys south and west and exploration of the volcanic area itself. He believed it was "the route which offers the best prospect of securing the main objects of the expedition with the best chances of complete success and the minimum risk."

In the 1,500-mile sector between Ross's farthest-east point and the Russians' discoveries (Alexander I Land and Peter I Island) west of the Antarctic Peninsula, he thought a steam vessel might penetrate the pack and reach land, but "not without considerable risk." For the British, he concluded, the route should be the one "*leaving least to chance, and running the least risk*" (my italics), and that was certainly eastward from Cape Adare, but only beyond Ross's farthest point if there was no risk of entrapment.

Caution would be the hidden hallmark of Markham's direction of the entire expedition, allied to a confidence in the leader he chose that would be the envy of any person leading an expedition for the first time today. It was Murray (by then Sir John), however, who first publicly described a plan for the British expedition when he addressed the Royal Society Antarctic meeting in February 1898, advocating a base at Cape Adare for one or two winters with sledging excursions toward the interior. That Murray's address departed little from Markham's strategy was apparent from the unqualified support Markham gave Murray's ideas in the discussion that followed, although he would probably have supported any speaker who favored an expedition at that stage.[4]

---

* The modern designation of Ross's "South Victoria Land" is adopted from here on.

SIR JOHN MURRAY, KCB, 1900. Photographed on September 1, 1900, on his last sounding expedition to Loch Leven. Photo published in the *Scottish Geographical Magazine* and reproduced courtesy, the Royal Scottish Geographical Society.

But by October 1898 Murray, writing in support of the expedition in the *Scottish Geographical Magazine*, showed he had reverted to his original 1893 idea of two bases on opposite sides of the continent, the first south of Peter I Island, with a thrust toward the Pole from there while the ship went on to establish the second between Cape Adare and Cape North, with another sledge journey from there to the Pole by way of the magnetic pole.[5] The divergence of view between these two great campaigners was already emerging, and the first hint of a rift came when Markham described his erstwhile ally as "very noisy and dictatorial; [of] no use" at a meeting in April 1899.[6] However, it was not until the Berlin congress in September of that year that Murray's change of outlook was spelled out as widely different from Markham's thinking.

In the discussion after Markham's paper, Murray declared that in his view the first expeditions should be mainly oceanographic; a "thorough exploration of the ocean around the Antarctic continent . . . would show the points from which the exploration of the continent itself might be attempted with the best prospect of success."[7] This foreshadowed the parting of the ways. Within two months Murray had resigned from the Joint Committee and was championing the Scottish National Antarctic Expedition proposed by William Bruce.

The conflict between Markham's interest, inspired by an insatiable thirst for geographical discovery, and Murray's, primarily oceanographic, robbed Markham of an ally who could probably have assured the unity of the two great London societies at the time it was most needed. Their disunity, when detailed plans and staff were discussed, dangerously delayed decisions and left the British expedition's commander with only a handful of men and little more than eight months to organize everything except the negotiating and accounting for the ship purchase.

The trouble surfaced when the Joint Committee met on October 27, 1899, and Markham presented his evaluation of the routes, which he had polished in the light of the Berlin agreement with the Germans. The first meeting convinced Markham that nothing would be accomplished working through the committee, which would, he expostulated, "strangle the expedition with red tape."[8] The break came after Markham's proposal for a four-man Executive Committee to replace the larger one was carried a week later over much hostility from Murray and Hydrographer Admiral Wharton.

At much subsequent cost to the expedition, the Joint Committee declined to vote itself out of existence. The new committee was charged with submitting a plan and instructions to the commander, as well as formulating the composition of the executive and staff, for approval by the Joint Committee. After that, it was to appoint the executive and scientific staff, subject again to final approval by the larger committee. This was almost what Markham had wanted, and he and Adm. Sir Vesey Hamilton were to represent the RGS. Inexplicably, the Royal Society nominated an Oxford professor of zoology who specialized in the mimicry of butterflies as its senior representative! He was paired with Capt. Thomas H. Tizard, navigator of the *Challenger* twenty-five years before and now Assistant Hydrographer, predictably a mere spokesman for Wharton. The scene was set for conflict before the committee even met.

Markham was firmly in favor of the ship wintering at a safe anchorage in the Antarctic, just as many navy ships had done in their most successful Arctic exploits. But no one knew whether a safe harbor

SIR CLEMENTS R. MARKHAM, KCB. President of the Royal Geographical Society and guiding light of the British expedition (probably taken in 1905). Photo Thomson, reproduced from Mill, H.R., *The Siege of the South Pole* (London: Alston Rivers, 1905).

could be found, so an either/or compromise was necessary. With cost considerations complicating the choice, it took Markham until June 9, 1900, to persuade the Executive Committee to approve a broad, three-season plan.

In the first season the ship would determine whether there was a suitable harbor for wintering the ship or a site for landing a shore party on the coast from McMurdo Bay to Cape Adare. Following that, the ship would explore westward toward Wilkes's and d'Urville's discoveries before returning to Melbourne for the winter. Then in the second season the ship would either support exploration from the discovered harbor, wintering the ship there to return by way of the

PROF. DR. GEORG VON NEUMAYER. Privy councillor and
director of the Deutsche Seewarte at Hamburg at the
time of the German expedition, which he had campaigned
so long to bring about. Reproduced from Neumayer,
Georg von, *Auf Zum Südpol* (Berlin: Vita Deutches
Verlagshaus, 1901).

Falklands in 1904, or land a shore party and explore beyond the eastern end of the barrier discovered by Ross, returning to Melbourne and
picking up the party in January 1904 before returning home by way of
the Falklands.[9]

However, by December 1900 the shore party option had to be
abandoned, for the funds would not cover a three-season plan unless
something was cut.[10] The total cost had risen to £95,000 against the
£91,000 available.

The two committees approved the new estimate, but the plan was
once more in the melting pot, for as the Hydrographer pointed out,

the landing party idea dictated a third season, which could now be afforded only if the shore party was cut out.[11] What he proposed instead was little more than a sea exploration, much like Murray's proposal at the Berlin congress the year before. This did not constitute the great breakin Markham had in mind.

Also, assuming a winter harbor could be found quickly, Markham believed that wintering the expedition in the Antarctic meant the ship could also explore during the first navigable season and that, thus, the whole company, not just a small party, could be ready for sledging before the next navigable season started. "A small party could not do a tenth of the work [of] the whole force," he wrote in the plan he drafted on December 1, a mere seven months before the expedition was scheduled to sail.[12] Wintering the ship opened the maximum opportunity for extensive discovery of the interior by several parties working in different directions, albeit in only one area of the 6,000-mile coastal span of the two quadrants chosen.

But by then risk loomed large in the region of Markham's highest hopes of new discovery east of Ross's barrier. De Gerlache's Belgian expedition had returned in 1899 with two of the crew bereft of reason and others in poor shape after being trapped in the ice for a year near the 90°W meridian. A year later, Borchgrevink, in the *Southern Cross*, had been stopped by ice before reaching the eastern end of the barrier, just as Ross had been. That left the coast of Victoria Land, with the possibility of a suitable harbor in 77°S at McMurdo "Bay" as the favorite sector for a wintering harbor.

Opportunely, Borchgrevink had reported finding a "splendid winter harbour"[13] in Wood Bay with an easy route to the interior.[14] Louis Bernacchi, his physicist, had substantiated that report when he met Markham on November 15, subsequently saying there was no more than a hundred feet to climb and a very gradual gradient "to the great snowcap."[15] From that moment on Wood Bay, little short of 75°S, waxed large in Markham's hopes, for the meteorologists had demanded a base that far south to resolve their much disputed theory about an anticyclone over the Pole.

Curiously, the new plan, foreshadowing the subsequent course of the British expedition, was not unlike the old one in its retention of the either/or, ship wintering, or landing party options. But equipment and stores for either option had to be carried in the ship from the start, and the exploration westward from Cape North was now definitely subject to funds being available for the third, 1903-1904 season.

The official record has it that Markham's new plan was unanimously approved by the Executive Committee "as altered after careful consideration."[16] The great difference was that the landing party had disappeared and the draft plan now looked like this:

1901 voyage	Magnetic observations continuously throughout voyage and south of 40°S with soundings and dredging whenever opportunity occurs
1901–1902 season	Eastward along and beyond ice barrier, with sledge journey south from its edge
1902 winter	Winter between Wood Bay and McMurdo Bay, setting up magnetic base
1902–1903 season	October–December: Sledge journey south and geological exploration to west January–March: Magnetic work on board and explore westward from Cape Adare if time allows
1903 winter	If funds for two years only: Return via Falklands with magnetic survey and soundings in southerly latitude across Pacific ("any danger of being beset must be avoided")
1903–1904 season	If funds for three years: Proper exploration west from Cape Adare or such other exploration as the commander may decide on in consultation with the director of the civilian scientific staff

Markham had the plan he believed would steer the expedition to the two places with the greatest potential for the dramatic sledge journeys of discovery he dreamed of seeing accomplished. Getting the man he believed could carry the plan through had been an even longer process. Scott now held the rank of commander and since October had been very much privy to the plan and its potential costs, but the road to his appointment had been paved with obstacles.

5

OVERTURE TO FAME
Scott's Journey to Experience

The press announcement at the end of March 1899, on the strength of Longstaff's gift, quickly produced the first volunteers from the ranks of aspiring junior naval officers. Lt. Charles Royds, distantly related to Markham and destined to become the British ship's first lieutenant, came for tea with the Markhams on April 3. Not until June 5, however, did Markham encounter the man he wanted to command the expedition. Walking home from an RGS Council meeting presided over by the Prince of Wales, he met Robert Falcon Scott, a thirty-one-year-old torpedo lieutenant aboard the Channel Squadron flagship HMS *Majestic.* Scott, described years later by Ernest Shackleton as "the most daring man I ever knew,"[1] promptly volunteered to command the expedition for which Markham had at last obtained solid financial backing.

Markham knew something of Scott's abilities from 1887, when he was a guest of the commodore of the West Indies Squadron. Markham had then ranked Scott sixth on a list of potential commanders after a captain and four commodores, all of whom were now, twelve years later, too old. Markham even believed Ross, Franklin, McClintock, and Nares had been too old at the time of their polar exploits.

That left Scott at the head of the list when Balfour gave the delegation the green light on June 22, 1900. With friends in high places in the naval hierarchy, Markham had little doubt the Admiralty could be persuaded to release Scott when the government gave its formal backing to the expedition. But it took almost a year to get Scott appointed and yet more time to get him released.

Markham's letters to Scott before July 1, 1899,[2] show that he immediately took up Scott's candidacy with the Appointments Subcommittee, where he encountered opposition that delayed the appointment until May the following year. According to Markham, Sir George Nares wanted his own son to be appointed, and Sir William Wharton wanted one of his own men, although the most eligible, Capt. Mostyn Field, was forty-four and did not want the position. For three months nothing moved until Markham got back from the congress in Berlin.

Markham had his two naval volunteers, but with the Admiralty's attention fixed on the Boer uprising the question was, would they be released? Without informing the subcommittee, Adm. Sir Anthony Hoskins and Markham's cousin (the retired admiral) Sir Albert H. Markham were enlisted to campaign for naval officers to lead the expedition.

Markham pressed his preference for Scott on his cousin,[3] but at the end of March 1900, when he finally heard from Sir Anthony, he was told that the navy would release a commander and a lieutenant and no more.[4] The telegraph cables were ringing with messages from China where the first missionary victim of the Boxer Rebellion had been murdered on January 11. No names were mentioned in the letter, so Markham wrote to the First Lord, proposing Scott and Royds.[5]

Six days later the secretary of the Admiralty announced the appointment of Scott to command the expedition and of Royds as his chief assistant.[6] They would be released from duty on August 1.

Markham's announcement of the appointments provoked a storm in the Executive and Joint Committees. He did not overcome their opposition until a special committee of naval members of the larger committee finally gave way on May 24. Wharton's candidates—the first not fit enough and the second too old, as Markham put it in his diary—were outvoted 7 to 2 in favor of Scott.[7]

Despite Markham's best efforts, a year had been wasted as far as Scott's appointment and the time available for his training were concerned. The person who knew how to accomplish what Scott was appointed to do was the Norwegian Fridtjof Nansen, thirty-nine years old and the acknowledged master of polar travel—first to cross the Greenland icecap and hero of the *Fram*'s drift across the north polar sea to reach the farthest north in 1895, only recently bettered by a few miles by the Italian Duke of Abruzzi. Beside Nansen's exploits, the crossing of Spitsbergen's main island by Sir Martin Conway and even the Jackson-Harmsworth expedition would have appeared small in their potential for lessons applicable to exploring the vastness of the Antarctic. Accessible experience with clothing, sledges, dogs, and skis lay with the Scandinavians, so conveniently near compared with Canada and Greenland, and the British (and the Germans) naturally gravitated to Norway for advice and supplies.

Markham's annual vacations in Norway had brought him into contact with Dr. Johan Hjort, who with Nansen had forged new techniques that placed the Norwegians at the forefront of oceanography as well as of polar exploration. Not surprisingly, Markham's first action after Scott's release was to send for him to come over to Norway. Markham had sailed for Oslo (known then as Christiania) on June 29 and early in July wrote to Scott to tell him he had been onboard the Norwegian state-owned oceanographic ship *Michael Sars* and realized how old-fashioned the Hydrographer's department was in the practice of oceanography.[8] He urged Scott to come in September when the ship was going for a demonstration cruise with Drygalski aboard. In the end, this timetable clashed with Scott's magnetic course at Deptford, under Capt. Ettrick W. Creak, director of compasses in the navy, arranged for by the Executive Committee in Markham's absence. Scott finally reached Oslo on October 9, 1900, and was met at the Grand Hotel by the father of the expedition.

Scott paints a graphic picture in his journal of the deluge of facts and advice he faced during that crowded tour. In its pages can be seen the origin of many features of the subsequent expedition and its equipment. Through it rings a receptiveness that, even if heightened by the attraction of a new life after many years of regimented routine, foreshadows Scott's fascination with the scientific puzzles of the far south. They would engrave their spell on his personality as deeply as the sense of adventure must have animated his audacious proposal to Markham at 21 Eccleston Square the previous year. Scott was taken to Vokskollen, a new private health hydro 1,640 feet above Oslo on Bogstadvannet Lake where Sir Clements and Lady Minna were staying, and his journal-cum-notebook starts the next day.[9]*

Scott plunged into daylong discussions with Nansen and Hjort aboard the *Michael Sars*. Hjort agreed to get dredges and trawls made

---

* The account in this chapter is based on Scott's journal in the Scott Polar Research Institute archives (ms352/2 BJ). Where no source reference is indicated, quotations are from that document. The text makes clear the date on which he wrote each one. Italics in quoted passages are mine; underlining is Scott's. His occasional understandable spelling errors in names have been corrected.

to his design for the British expedition. Over dinner that evening, Scott tapped Nansen's views on subjects more immediate to the expedition's main goal.

Sketches in the journal illustrate how Nansen's ideas on the insulation of living quarters differed sharply from the 1½-inch asbestos behind paneling being considered for the British ship. "He thinks asbestos [is] not good enough . . . [I need to] go into this with Smith thoroughly," Scott wrote, but it became irrelevant when the shortage of money became critical after his return. However, his sketch of Nansen's suggested arrangement of wardroom ventilation mirrors almost exactly depicts the scheme adopted aboard *Discovery*.

Scott had wanted to take 30-foot whalers, according priority to seaworthiness in Antarctic seas, as opposed to Nansen's concern that they should be 20 feet long and thus easier to get ashore.[10] Back in London Scott compromised, and *Discovery* eventually sailed with a cutter (left in New Zealand) and five 26-foot whalers, which were sufficient to carry the ship's company.[11]

Nansen suggested that Scott meet with the duke of Abruzzi, whose expedition had just topped Nansen's farthest north by 20 miles. "It appears many deals might be done," Scott noted that night, "as he was extremely well supplied with sledges etc." Scott later marked this entry "no good" when he discovered that everything had been left in the north, as the entry two days later reveals.

Scott met with Markham again, and a revealing journal entry showed that before the expedition Scott was in favor of dogs, the resistance coming from Markham. "In the evening . . . [we] discussed dogs. He is evidently yielding, and we must do something in this line very shortly."*

Scott's trip on the *Michael Sars* the next day quickly demonstrated that the winch design and installation planned for the *Discovery* needed modification. He immediately wrote to Smith and Skelton to have its manufacture stopped until he got back to England with plans Hjort had given him.

Nansen agreed with Reginald Koettlitz's ideas that scurvy was caused by ptomaine poisoning[†] of tinned foodstuffs and made notes on

---

* Markham appears to have forgotten that his Arctic hero Sir Francis Leopold McClintock's article in the *Antarctic Manual* had described two of his journeys, one of 1,000 miles with six dogs when "men and dogs worked harmoniously together for . . . nearly 80 days" and the other of 420 miles in 25 days with fifteen dogs in temperatures averaging –35°C (Murray [1901]: pp. 301–302).

† Salmonella poisoning.

Nansen's suggestion for detecting this problem by sampling a percentage of tins supplied. The journal does not mention Nansen referring to the need for fresh food. But the Norwegian's words "meat is too precious onboard" in the 1898 English edition of his book *Nansen's Farthest North*[12] and frequent references to hunting seal and reindeer suggest he must have spoken of the value of fresh meat, even though he wrote of tinned dried vegetables and bread as the prime defense against scurvy.[13] Later, Scott read the message of the importance of fresh meat on the Belgian expedition in Frederick A. Cook's *Through the First Antarctic Night*, and even before reaching the Antarctic he would show that he had thoroughly grasped that lesson.

Scott learned that Nansen thought Borchgrevink had been supplied with domestic dogs bought on the streets of Archangel, which were "probably useless." As a result, no attempt was made to acquire Borchgrevink's dogs, which had been let loose on Native Island, off New Zealand's Stewart Island.

There is no word in the journal about the food for the dogs that would play such a damaging role in the expedition to come. The food consisted of dried fish, and Nansen's book on the *Fram*'s drift shows that Nansen must have recommended it[14] because the man who brought him his West Siberian dogs had fed them dried fish during the three-month journey to meet the *Fram* south of Novaya Zemlya.

Scott asked for twenty West Siberian Ostiak dogs of the type used by Nansen on his journey to the farthest north then achieved at 86°13½N on April 8, 1895. Twenty seems a very small number. But although the potential cost may have caused restraint, the number did have a practical basis. Nansen had used twenty-eight dogs to haul three sledges at the start of a journey estimated to last a hundred days. The dogs were expected to last up to eighty days. Nansen and his companion took a thirty-day supply of food and planned to kill dogs progressively over the ensuing fifty days, feeding the carcasses one by one to the remaining dogs until there were none left for the final twenty days.[15]

If dogs were going to be used, it would be on the Southern journey that Scott wanted above all to undertake himself. At that time it seemed likely that a southward-running coast would be discovered beyond Ross's farthest east or that the ship would be able to winter in McMurdo "Bay," as Nansen believed. In that case, there were to be journeys to the east and south over the barrier, which Borchgrevink had shown to present a smooth surface for sledging, and one to the west through the mountains into the interior of Victoria Land. The western route would probably be unsuitable for dogs, given Nansen's experience in which progress was down to 4 miles a day when the going was rough but as many as 21 miles a day could be gained where the snow lay over smooth ice.

The journal gives no hint of Scott's arithmetic, and he never mentions the Pole. Nansen's twentieth dog was shot on the seventy-fifth day of his journey, but that time would barely suffice to get to the Pole and back if the dogs continuously achieved Nansen's best daily mileage. In opting for twenty dogs, Scott can only have assumed that the smooth barrier surface would make a higher daily mileage feasible. However, in the end the price quoted allowed twenty-two dogs to be ordered.[16]

Scott's final entry on the twelfth was about the unsettled question of his second in command: "must sound Brooks and select [a] man then see Douglas and point out importance to Navy—then for last man [who was to be Ernest Shackleton] let matters take their course, also Armitage if Admiralty does not rise." Scott had not yet met Albert Armitage who had at first declined Markham's offer of the position[17] but then, on Markham's second attempt on May 27, accepted subject to his wife's agreement.[18] Markham insisted that Armitage meet Scott before formally accepting,[19] but Armitage was sailing for China aboard the P&O ship *Malta* on May 29. When he returned in September, Markham was in Norway and Scott on the course at Deptford, so it had been impossible for them to meet before Armitage sailed again, this time not returning until early December.

Lt. Martin Leake from one of Scott's former ships had turned up out of the blue to visit Markham on May 27, the day he wrote to Armitage.[20] Three days later Scott heard that Armitage had accepted the renewed offer, and on June 1 he attended the Executive Committee meeting that agreed to recommend Armitage as his second in command.[21] Markham read Leake's application, along with those of two other naval lieutenants, to the committee. The fact that he knew Leake undoubtedly prompted Scott to call at Markham's home the next day to ask if he could be appointed to the post instead of Armitage.

Markham must have deferred to Scott for the time being, because at the June 8 committee meeting Armitage's appointment was "deleted for the present."[22] That move left the door open both ways, but clearly by October Markham had persuaded Scott that Leake was not the man for the job, and nothing more is heard of his application. After Scott and Armitage finally met in December, there is evident relief in Markham's mid-January diary entry that "Scott and Armitage get on capitally."[23]

On October 13 the subject of wintering the ship in the Antarctic came up: "Very wet day. Started fine and walked with Sir Clements and discussed possibility of wintering in open water in large bay*–Sir C. expounded much of interest in regard to northern movements with Nansen's chart . . . all very interesting–Winter Quarters *must* be found."

The meeting with the Italian explorer took place the next day, but the hoped-for chance of buying dogs and equipment cheaply was quickly dashed. In any event, the tents were much too heavy and provided no lessons for the British expedition:[†]

> Oct. 14th . . . started to see Duke of Abruzzi at Victoria Hotel. A spare clean looking individual, well dressed and with very nice manners–showed us photographs of Stella Polaris in ice–she [was] pushed on to and crushed against ice foot–quarters were taken up on ice and journeys by sledge started–farthest north: the travelling, by photograph, very good–on the whole it must have been good–padding of ship a good bit of work, photographs excellent, *tents heavy, not much to be learnt here,* and nothing to be got [e.g., for the British expedition] as all dogs were shot and stores etc. left in the North [my italics].
>
> Duke of Abruzzi spoke about sledge runners–said they came to the conclusion that stout wood runners was best [solution]. . . . Duke also mentioned much work done with guncotton. . . .
>
> Met Nansen on way down . . . talked more about thermometers and necessity of having exact measurement of sea depths. . . .
>
> Looked over plans of ship [*Discovery* plans]–pointed out difficulty of working Hjort's nets. Of course it can be done if we set our minds to it.

Their conversation covered oceanography, instruments, the specifications of *Discovery,* and footwear, with Scott later noting Nansen's recommendation of Komager (waterproof Laplander boots with soles of undertanned oxen or seal hide and lined with senne grass).

> All these matters must be very carefully considered with the clothing. Nansen says take lots of moccasins sledging. Foot covering is certainly the most important consideration on such occasions.
>
> Oct. 15th. Left Volkskollen, came to Grand Hotel . . . found Nansen, Hansen and 2 Germans Drs. Philippi and Vanhöffen, the latter an old-

---

* Undoubtedly because McMurdo Bay was envisaged as a wide-sweeping bay. Borchgrevink's expedition had not sighted it, so Ross's description was all they had to go on.

† Clearly Scott's words "not much to be learnt here" referred to the heavy tents and not to the expedition as a whole, as claimed by Huntford (1979: p. 140) in support of his disparaging aspersion that "Scott gives the impression of not really wanting to learn."

ish looking man but the former spritely enough. Hjort joined us and we [lunched] together . . . went with Nansen and Germans to Christiansen's shop. Saw sledge, ski, and other articles.

All sledges seem to be made of ash–ski of ash, American hickory, maple, elm–latter liable to warp–Nansen gave many hints . . . explained his steel knees [triangular brackets reinforcing sledge framework joints] as greatly strengthening the sledge structure–he is dead against many-man sledges and rather for single or double.

Nansen pointed out that McClintock's six-man sledges weighed 90 pounds against the 12 pounds of a one-man sledge to his design and advised cladding the runners with thin nickel-plated steel, known as "German Silver," with wooden underrunners for working on ice. Scott, far from being the naval diehard unwilling to learn, put all this into practice but felt it was safer to "have sledges of all sorts [sizes]. . . . Everything depends on the nature of the country." In the event, he took 11-foot and 9-foot sledges for six-man teams and 7-foot sledges,* often used for instruments but suitable for three-man teams, and had the German Silver put on in the Antarctic as Nansen advised.

Scott also accepted the argument in favor of harnessing dogs alternately on either side of a single sledge trace rather than employing the Inuit or Eskimo "fan" traces Nansen had used in 1895, and he made a note to suggest getting Eskimo dogs from the Hudson Bay Company. Nansen had wanted Greenland or Hudson Bay dogs for the *Fram* expedition, but the obstacles to procuring them had proved insuperable.[24] Nansen was also "very doubtful" over the volume of petroleum needed for a dynamo–undoubtedly this was the origin of the decision by Scott and Drygalski to adopt windmill power for their dynamos.

At this time there was no shortage of conflicting advice regarding skis to confuse Scott's appreciation of their merits for sledge hauling. In Cook's book he read: "For mere pleasure journeys they [e.g., skis, or snowshoes as he and others called them] proved in every way superior to the Canadian rackets [snowshoes] and other patterns; but where it became necessary to pull sledges over rough paths, the other kind were better."[25] And as Crichton-Somerville, a practiced skier with twenty-five years' experience, wrote to Markham: "They could be useful . . . for light work over soft snow [but] are of no use for men who have to drag."[26]

That point would be echoed two years later when Scott and Wilson, with the remnant of their dog team failing and Ernest Shackleton

---

* One can be seen in the display at Discovery Point, Dundee.

a sick man, found that in soft snow they could not "put the same weight on the traces as we do on foot."[27] And a decade after that, the experience was repeated in even more threatening circumstances when champion Swiss skier Xavier Mertz, alone with Mawson and the remaining six dogs pulling Mawson's sledge after their companion had vanished in a bottomless crevasse, found he could not pull his lighter sledge on skis.[28]

Nansen must have told Scott and Markham a different story, for he had written of his 1888 crossing of Greenland (without dogs): "Lest any reader should be led to believe . . . that our skis were of little or no use to us, I ought perhaps to state . . . that without their help we should have advanced very little . . . skis are considerably better than Indian snowshoes even for hauling purposes . . . for 19 days continuously we used our ski from early morning till late in the evening, and the distance we thus covered was not much less than 240 [statute] miles" [out of 270].[29] Yet there was also Nansen's qualification of their merits in his account of the *Fram* expedition: "One cannot have them properly fastened on when one has to help the dogs at any moment" on uneven snow-covered ice.[30]

Although Crichton-Somerville's misinformed views and Nansen's qualification of the merits of skis were certainly relayed to Scott by Markham, he did not hesitate to employ them once he was ashore in the Antarctic, even including sledge hauling on skis in the sports events held before the winter set in. Although the sports were run for morale's sake, the inclusion of those races as well as downhill and flat ski races demonstrated Scott's keenness to encourage their use.[31]

On October 16 Scott set off early to meet the now famous designer of the *Fram*: "Oct. 16th. Got up 6.30. Started for Larvik. Found Colin Archer at station an older man between 60 and 70—very quiet in manners talked of boats in general—had lunch with him, a son and daughter—both bright nice looking people—son very silent. After lunch discussed desultory matters and rather wasted time" [e.g. not discussing points of immediate relevance to Scott].*

Discovery was already half built, so there was not much scope for suggestions from Archer on the fundamental design, but clearly Scott

---

* In the context of what could still be adopted in the design and equipment of *Discovery* that had been discussed over lunch, the words "rather wasted time" clearly do not indicate a disregard for Archer's opinions, as alleged by Huntford (1979: p. 141). Given Scott's attitude toward Abruzzi's achievement, already cited, the case for Scott having "closed his mind to the experience of Polar explorers" is discredited.

had hoped to get some important hints from his host about details where there was still room for change without heavy expense. The notes he wrote that evening show that Scott's mind was open to anything Archer had to say. He was still concerned about light boats and cabin insulation. Archer agreed about the kayaks, but in discussion about the proposed layer of asbestos under the upper deck in the ship's specification, Archer believed two layers with an air space between them would be much better.

Inevitably, talk turned to further comparisons between the British and Norwegian ships. Archer had doubts about the strength of the British ship: "[He] pointed out framing of *Fram* and its strength . . . [but] acknowledged three layers of beams made a difference" [*Fram* had two].

Scott made a note that Royds would have to go to Dundee in November to address matters affecting the working of the ship. Reginald Skelton, the chief engineer Scott had recruited before setting off for Norway, would look after the machinery. By the end of the next day, Scott had seen cookers. The price made Scott determine to have them made in England from the sketch in Nansen's book. Primus stoves, too, could be bought in London.

Finally, he saw Hjort again and got the winch design ultimately adopted for *Discovery*, as the note that day (October 17) shows: "Had a long yarn with Hjort—much he said was practicable, some not . . . idea of separating the winches for sounding and large work seems excellent. The wire in 2,000 fathom lengths [3,650 meters] is very good . . . advises gallows to which I agree" [to raise and lower nets instead of using the ends of the yards].

Scott asked Nansen to arrange with Christiansen for a six-man sledge, a dog sledge, two pairs of skis, one elm, one ash, and a set of dog harnesses. Money was the arbiter again: "Nansen evidently fears man will stick in price—this must be as it may—there seems no other way of getting these things." Most of the needed items would have to be made in England.

That evening he had to rush away after supper—"Nansen full of expressions of wish to help in every way"—and caught the night train ("2nd class 43 Kroner") for Copenhagen, arriving 5:30 P.M. the next day. The next morning, the 19th, Scott first ordered samples of pemmican and butter as supplied to Nansen for the *Fram*. Going to Prof. Cornelius Knudsen's factory, from which the British Admiralty occasionally bought equipment, he ordered various instruments for the expedition including the self-registering block and reel that would be used for sounding through the sea ice around winter quarters.

Introduced to two experienced captains in the Greenland Survey Service, Scott mentioned the size of the crew proposed for the *Discovery*, and the two men immediately criticized that number. Clearly, it had produced a similar reaction in Norway, for he wrote that evening: "Had a long yarn on various matters. What was principally brought to my notice and serious consideration is that the crew is ridiculously large in the eyes of all foreigners. This point is again and again driven home—*"the crew must be largely reduced."*

The crew, or "working complement," envisaged for the British ship had indeed grown inexorably. Whereas the *Gauss* was to be crewed by thirty officers and ratings and the *Morning* by twenty-eight, including two teenage midshipmen, when Scott had first arrived in London he found on June 8 the Executive had agreed to a total of forty-one for his ship on June 8[32] and that on June 21 the ship subcommittee had even proposed forty-two.[33]

By the time *Discovery* sailed in August 1901, Scott had brought the crew down to thirty-five, including himself, but in practice the working complement was thirty-four since Armitage could command the ship. He had wanted to cut one of the four stokers and one of the three assistant stewards.[34] Fortunately, in light of conditions experienced on the voyage, the four stokers were retained. Naval tradition in the subcommittee must have overruled him on the question of stewards, in part because of the incorporation of a separate chief petty officers' mess for the carpenter, bosun, chief steward, and engine room artificer. The extra stewards and the second cook—wisely included in light of subsequent events—accounted for the four extra crew compared with the *Gauss*.*

Scott's crew, with its few extra men and twelve-strong deck crew, could hardly be described as excessive considering the scale of operations eventually undertaken, the prospect of casualties, and the uncertainty as to whether the ship would be forced to leave a shore party in the Antarctic to achieve any land exploration at all during the first season. Alternating deck watches of six seamen (of whom two could be needed at the helm) were barely enough aboard *Discovery* nearly twenty-five years later when, with six-strong watches and once more headed for the Antarctic, the ship was, in the words of John Bentley, the senior cadet midshipman aboard, "if anything undermanned, particularly in very bad weather of which we had more than our share. . . . In

---

* See Appendix 3 for a comparison of the working complements of the British and German ships.

very bad weather or in an emergency, the cry would be 'All hands on deck,' and it meant just that. The sailmaker, carpenter, cook, etc. would all help but would not be called upon to go aloft."[35]

The risks involved with smaller watches can literally be felt in Gerald Doorly's description of rounding the Cape in heavy weather on the 1902 voyage in the *Morning* with its watches of five seamen (evidently the two young midshipmen were not assigned to deck duties under ordinary conditions). Awakened at midnight by a heavy lurch of the ship, Doorly found the twenty-one-year-old second mate, Sub-Lt. Teddy Evans (later Lt. Evans of the *Broke*)—with no sail training since leaving the *Worcester* five years before—trying by himself to haul in one of the t'gallant yard braces. Of the five men on the deck watch under Evans, one man was on lookout and one on the wheel. Doorly sent two men to let go the halyards and so saved the masts from being broken and carried overboard, putting the fifth man to help with the wheel. He had to call all hands, and it took four or five men to brace the yard round and spill the wind out of the sail. The yard would not come down until they had done that, despite the halyards that held it up being loosed, such was the force of the wind.[36]

On October 20 Scott took the train to Berlin, reading Dr. Frederick Cook's account of De Gerlache's Belgian exedition on the way: "Oct. 20th: Left Copenhagen 10.20—arrived Berlin 8.30 P.M., nothing very eventful—read Cook's account—they must be a poor lot except Lecointe who alone appears to have had some grit—the food seems to have been very bad." As harsh as his judgment was of men in advanced stages of malnutrition, Scott would not forget the lesson behind his comment on the food. Lecointe's book eventually made clear that what lay behind Scott's comment on the food was De Gerlache's refusal to allow seal meat to be served—"what would the press say when it got out that they had eaten seals!!" he had said to Lecointe in justification of his refusal.[37]

But the evidence about scurvy Scott read on his long train journey was far from straightforward. The word *scurvy* does not appear in Cook's book, in which he uses the term *polar anaemia*, the main symptoms of which were not those habitually characteristic of the dreaded disease. For Scott, the one clue in the book was the description of swollen ankles in the July epidemic and the effectiveness of fried penguin and seal steaks in combating the condition after De Gerlache had been overruled. The other customary symptoms—swollen gums and stiff joints—are never mentioned in the book. Contrary to Roald Amundsen's assertion more than a quarter of a century later,* Cook's account creates the impression of no concerted attempt to amass a stock of seal meat before pushing into the area of greatest risk of being ensnared by the ice—there are only five mentions of capturing seal for food during the time in the ice.[38]

Despite the fact that Nansen and Johansen were perfectly fit after eighty-seven days without fresh food,[39] Scott took Cook's message to heart and mounted a deliberate campaign to build a stock of seal meat as soon as he reached the Antarctic coast. Even before arriving in New Zealand, he insisted that everyone accustom themselves to penguin meat when the opportunity presented itself at the sub-Antarctic Macquarie Island.

Cook's book, almost uniquely frank in describing the collapse of morale among the members of the Belgian expedition, leaves his reader with an impression of pervasive dissension and suspicion when things began to go wrong, which somewhat detracts from the discoveries and fine scientific observations he describes. In what was clearly a straight transcript of Cook's diary entry for July 12, 1898, Scott read: "There has, however, been one among us who has not fallen into the habit of being a chronic complainer [about symptoms of illness]. This is Captain Lecointe. The captain has had to do the most trying work . . . with frosted fingers, frozen ears, and stiffened feet, but with characteristic good humour he has passed these discomforts off."[40] Steeped in a naval tradition which held that the crew of a ship survived or sank together, and with a ready appreciation that the dangers of the Antarctic were fully as demanding as those of battle, Scott's journal comment exposed for the first time the priority he would give to morale and loyalty in his selection of officers and approval of scientists for the British expedition. This priority revealed itself again during his first year in the Antarctic in his reaction to men who complained.

The next day (October 21) Scott met the leader of the German expedition. Like Nansen, Drygalski along with Vanhöffen had experience sledging in the north, although 600 miles south of Nansen's latitudes. They had wintered at 70°27N in Disko Bay on the west coast of Greenland on the Berlin Society's 1892–1893 expedition, which Drygalski had led, principally to study glaciation. In the spring of 1893 the two men, in addition to some smaller trips, had made two longer sledge journeys along the coast—the first 100 miles south-

---

* In his 1927 autobiography *My Life as an Explorer* (p. 27), Amundsen referred to "a great number" of seals and penguins he and Cook had killed.

ward, the second a month-long effort reaching as far as 73°N.

"Monday Oct. 21st Berlin (Palast Hotel): Eventful day. Met Von Drygalski—showed me plans of ship and discussed many matters. . . . On to lunch and to Richter thermometer maker. Afterwards back here and more discussion over my plans." Listing the division of work adopted by Drygalski, Scott later followed it in principle, although not to the letter. Opposite he listed Drygalski's polar clothing as a suit of furs for all, as well as sealskin trousers, worn with a "blouse with head cover" made of wolfskin for the officers and reindeer skin for the men. Everybody was to have woolen caps, 7 woolen suits (4 of Icelandic wool), 3 waistcoats, 6 vests, 9 long woolen pants (3 of Icelandic wool), and 18 pairs of stockings. Curiously, footwear was not mentioned. Then came the revelation that Drygalski enjoyed an enviable advantage that Scott, whose every move was subject to approval by cumbersome committees, immediately saw as vital to his chances of getting the British expedition organized on time: "Two points of great personal interest transpired (i) he has emancipated himself from all control, (ii) he has refused to be subject to any orders."

That day in Berlin Scott went on to talk about the British expedition plan, with Drygalski agreeing "in the main" and expressing his "certainty" (underlined by Scott) that they would be able to winter in McMurdo Bay. His views also accorded well with Markham's on the necessity of absolute discretion for the commander once in the Antarctic. As Scott recorded: "His principle is to be prepared for all things and [to] do that which is possible."

However, that did not make Scott averse to instructions, as he wrote after the expedition: "There is no doubt as to the wisdom of leaving to the commander of an expedition the greatest possible freedom of action, so that at no time may his decision be restricted by orders which could not have been conceived with a full knowledge of the conditions. But instructions for the conduct of an expedition may serve a most useful purpose . . . [if] they contain a clear statement of the relative importance of the various objects for which the expedition is undertaken."[41]

Scott's last two days in Berlin were largely taken up with a visit to the Royal Prussian Institute at Potsdam and a tour of instruments to be used on the German expedition, critically including the Eschenhagen magnetographs that would also have to be operated according to a complicated program on his own expedition. The following afternoon he caught the 2:30 P.M. train for England, arriving at Liverpool Street at 9:00 A.M. on October 24.

He went to see Markham straightaway, rightly awed with the enormity of the task that remained if the ship were to sail by the end of July as intended. "Fully impressed him with our backwardness. Suggested calling on Rücker," he wrote in the last entry in the journal. The next day Scott had the "long talk with Rücker" that paved the way for the freedom of action Rücker would help Markham win for him at the Joint Committee meeting on November 20.

The first year of the new century was nearly gone, and just seven months remained to organize everything. It all had to be done by written or face-to-face communication, for the telephone scarcely existed and already-stretched funds put a brake on the use of the telegraph.

Those months were so crowded for a man whose companions were, for the most part, not even available, that his journey to Norway would prove Scott's only chance to learn the many skills that lay so completely outside his previous experience, and that learning occurred by word of mouth only, except in the case of the oceanography aboard the *Michael Sars*. It was hardly surprising that many details of the *Discovery* Expedition mirrored the advice he received from Nansen during that short stay in the great explorer's country. However, the task Scott now faced was soon to be complicated rather than helped by the return to England of the geologist Markham had backed for the position of chief scientist—and little more than two months hence it would be complicated to an extent that would bring Scott to the point of resigning.

6

DISPUTED AMBITIONS
Gregory and the Leadership Challenge

Alongside Markham's campaign for Scott's appointment ran the long saga of the first director of the Civilian Scientific Staff, which began when Dr. John W. Gregory of the Natural History Museum approached Markham on October 12, 1899, for a reference in support of his application for chair of geology at Melbourne University.[1] Probably influenced by the fact that at that time Melbourne was to be the base from which the ship would sail to the Antarctic, Markham was led to consider that Gregory might be a suitable candidate for the second-most-important post on the expedition.[2]

In contrast to Scott's candidacy this one provoked no hostile reaction, for by coincidence, at the first meeting of the Executive Committee on November 10, when the question came up, Prof. Edward Poulton suggested Gregory as a candidate. Markham, knowing Gregory had walked 30 miles across Spitsbergen with Sir Martin Conway in difficult conditions in 1896, had consulted Sir Martin and Dr. John Scott Keltie (later secretary of the RGS). Finding them in favor, he voted for Gregory. When Gregory declared his interest, Markham discussed the expedition with him at length on November 24, 1899.

But in outlining his ideas on the course of the expedition, Markham had opened a door to a dispute that nearly destroyed the expedition before it had even left England. As soon as he was on his way to Australia, Gregory wrote a letter in which he suggested that he, as chief scientist, should lead a six-man-strong sledge party with dogs from Ross's McMurdo Bay to the magnetic pole and thence southward to return through the mountains to the shore hut maintained by two sailors in their absence. This was to occur in the second season, for he saw the ship first exploring westward from Cape Adare, landing where possible for ski training before landing the shore party, then carrying out oceanography in the second summer, and finally picking the party up in 1904.[3] Initially, by its expression as a preference of what he later insisted on to the point of resignation, Gregory's letter (dated January 19, 1900) masked the incompatibility of his outlook with the concept of a *Challenger*-type organization intended for the expedition.

Markham, in his seventieth year, was ill when the letter reached Poulton, who circulated it to his Executive Committee colleagues. The crucial words were "The scientific staff will, *I presume*, be under the command of the scientific head; its members will report to him, and he will make all necessary arrangements with the captain *for work on board* (my italics) and will be allowed considerable influence in the selection of the scientific staff."

This was entirely compatible with the position on the *Challenger*, which governed Markham's approach to the definition of the post and would for the same reason hardly have excited opposition from Captain Tizard or the Hydrographer, Admiral Wharton. But Gregory's belief, expressed in the same letter, that the landing party should be run by the scientific staff and that in the event of a naval party also landing, the scientific leader should have "at his absolute disposal" sledges, dogs, and two good sailors makes it hard to understand why Markham wrote to Gregory on March 16 informing him that his letter of January 19 had been approved.[4]

Markham's concept was radically different from Gregory's, foremostly in determining that operations should be commanded by a naval officer and reasoning that more could be accomplished if the ship could spend the first winter frozen in at McMurdo Bay. Markham was fully recovered by that time, and his failure to respond to Gregory's ideas, so sharply at odds with his own, was less strange only than his lack of comment at the Executive Committee meeting on June 8, 1900, three days after reading in a second letter that Gregory had concluded from the February 15 cable[5] that the committee had agreed with his January 19 letter "in which I had suggested the names of the staff *and the conditions under which I was willing to accept the post*" (my italics).[6]

The committee threw out Gregory's idea of winter exploration by ship, with its implicit risk of losing the ship and stranding the shore party. Curiously, the new plan[7] retained the either/or, ship wintering, or landing party options, although equipment and stores for either option now had to be carried in the ship from the start, and the exploration westward from Cape Adare was definitely subject to funds being available for the third, 1903–1904, season.

Thus, on December 5, 1900, when Gregory arrived at Liverpool, nothing in the plan conflicted outright with his idea that a shore party should be landed. He had gone straight to Dundee and met Scott for the first time, promptly lending him a copy of his letter from the previous January.

Scott returned it without adverse comment, for it had only expressed an opinion that it might be better if the scientific director commanded any shore party,[8] and he would have seen such matters as being within Markham's province. To have objected to the letter would hardly have been an auspicious start to working with the man he would have to cooperate with in so many areas.

Back in London the two men attended the RGS Council dinner on December 10. Both must have been made aware of the new plan for the first time that week, for on the fifteenth Scott reported to Markham that Gregory was "wanting to be put ashore with a landing party."[9]

Gregory repeated the request in a letter to Markham. His demand was not very strident: "If the ship winters in McMurdo Bay, then the difference is a matter of detail," he wrote,[10] referring to what he had written back in January.

Markham responded immediately with an invitation to discuss the subject at length with him and Scott the next day.[11] Both Scott and Gregory were then present at the December 19 Executive Committee meeting to consider the new plan.

Gregory revived the question because of a subtle change from the June plan. In that plan the Victoria Land coast was to be searched for suitable sites for either wintering the ship or landing a shore party, and the decision would be made on return to Melbourne as to which course would be followed. Now, however, the relevant paragraph read: "It will be for the Commander of the Expedition to decide, with knowledge acquired on the spot, whether he will seek for the best available winter quarters for the ship; or whether he will establish a station for a landing party and return with the ship."[12]*

---

* Mirrored here also were the words Drygalski was writing at about the same time in an article on the German expedition for the scientific journal *Nature*: "What will actually be done must naturally be decided on the spot" (1.2.01: p. 319). Drygalski supported Markham's views on not tying the expedition leader too closely to a plan.

However, in the printed version of the plan presented to the meeting, which approved it without alteration, Markham had changed the wording to read:[13]

> Much must be left to the discretion and judgement of the commanding officer, *in consultation with the chief of the civilian scientific staff,* as regards procedure in carrying out the plan of operations, and full confidence must be placed in his combined energy and prudence. It is impossible to give instructions of a more detailed character in . . . circumstances respecting which nearly total ignorance prevails. . . . The details must be left to the leader to whom the very responsible work of conducting the operations has been entrusted (my italics).

That, however, was not enough for Gregory, and on January 7, 1901, he sent Scott a draft of what he thought the instructions to the scientific director should be. According to Gregory,[14] Scott rejected the draft, but there must have been some rapprochement because Markham received a letter from Scott a week later saying he had smoothed things over with Gregory.[15] Yet the next day Scott told Markham that Gregory was causing difficulties about his position on the expedition.[16]

Gregory wrote to Markham that he was dissatisfied with his position as explained by Scott,[17] so when Markham had translated the plan into draft instructions[18] he sent a copy of those for the scientific staff director to Gregory, only to have them rejected. Markham requested a statement of just what Gregory wanted, and he received a draft on January 22 that indicated that Gregory wanted virtually to command the expedition and to have sole charge of all shore operations.[19] This was the first rumble of the storm to come.

Markham immediately rejected Gregory's demands, and at the Executive Committee meeting on January 30 the instructions for the commander and the scientific director, as drafted by Markham, were approved despite Gregory's sudden refusal to accept anything less than command of the expedition, with Scott as master of the ship.[20] By that time Markham knew Gregory was clandestinely hatching support in the Royal Society, for on January 27 Poulton had approached Armitage to see if he would command the ship in the event of Scott's resignation![21] Rejected indignantly by Armitage, Poulton then persuaded certain Royal Society members of the Joint Committee to draft alterations to the instructions without calling on the expedition secretary, Cyril Longhurst, to record their decisions, which he was supposed to do at every meeting concerning expedition business.

These alterations were then tabled without notice at the next Joint Committee meeting on Friday, February 8. In the ensuing furious argument, described by Markham as "a regular bear garden,"[22] the RGS representatives were able to force an adjournment until the twelfth.

Markham's report of the meeting left Scott so depressed that he wrote Armitage the next day, saying he could see "no way out but resignation."[23] However, on February 10 Armitage has it that he and Markham persuaded Scott that all was not lost.[24]

It could hardly have been a foregone conclusion to Sir Clements, for with four members of his team unable to attend,[25] the Royal Society had a majority of fifteen to twelve before discussion even began. Seconded by the Hydrographer, who in the December discussions of the Executive Committee had been diametrically opposed to a shore party, the modified instructions placed Gregory in command of shore operations and relegated the ship to getting his party there and back, although the decision as to whether a place was safe for landing was to be Scott's alone. Either way, the ship was not to winter in the Antarctic.

Before that (according to Armitage*), Markham had alluded to Poulton's approach to Armitage, and Poulton then insisted on reading a letter he had received from Markham, which Markham regarded as private. That and an offensive personal remark by *Challenger* physicist James Y. Buchanan were too much for Markham, who justifiably stormed out of the meeting.[26]

When it came to the vote, Nares, with Arctic admiral Pelham Aldrich and two others from the RGS team, deserted Markham, so the alterations were carried by a still larger majority. Poulton and Sir Archibald Geikie were deputed to express the hope to the waiting professor that he would not resign.

But Markham was not to be beaten. Inviting the Royal Society treasurer, Alfred B. Kempe (later a KC)—"a sensible friendly man"—to discuss the impasse, he wrote out a conciliatory proposal to lay the groundwork for peace. Markham marshaled his allies at the RGS council meeting the following Monday. His meeting with Kempe bore fruit at

---

* Armitage's description of events, written almost twenty-five years later (Armitage [1925]: pp. 138–139), described how Scott had given his "word of honour" that he would not divulge the existence of the letter and then appears to imply that Scott broke his word by divulging it to Markham, who "related the story of the letter" at the Tuesday meeting. But it is scarcely credible that its existence was not brought up when the two men met at Markham's home. And whatever Armitage's ideas about the letter's confidentiality, it was hardly the height of loyalty to conceal its message of trouble brewing, given what had taken place at the Friday meeting.

the next two meetings of the Joint Committee.[27] A number of the changes were watered down. On March 18 Markham received Sir Michael Foster's announcement that the Royal Society was ready to approve the instructions.

After traveling to Dundee for the launch of the *Discovery*, Markham worked up an "Antarctic Memoir"[28] that minced few words in its assault on the landing party scheme and won him the council's backing on March 28: "Both navigable seasons would be wasted in landing and embarking Dr. Gregory . . . the great sum expended on the ship would be wasted and the expedition would be a fiasco. Any old whaler would do as well for the Professor's passenger ship." He also distrusted the experience of the nominated shore party, comprising Gregory, a physicist, a doctor, and five men: "Little could be done . . . by so small a party, quite inexperienced and ignorant of the management of dogs and of driving sledge dogs, for which practise is essential. If there is a landing party, it should be commanded by Mr. Armitage . . . who is well versed in dog driving, with the experience of four sledging seasons."

Redrafting the instructions and a résumé of the reasons for rejecting the offending proposals, Markham headed a three-man delegation with Sir George Goldie and Admiral McClintock for the RGS. They met the Royal Society delegation, which included Kempe, on April 12 and, spearheaded by a forthright speech by Sir George, ended up with an agreement that the Royal Society would return the altered instructions as rejected. The Joint Committee would convene on Friday, April 17, when the two societies' representatives would vote to set up a six-man Select Committee.

With Sir George standing in for Markham, the motion was carried, with Poulton and Buchanan the sole dissenters. The Select Committee duly met on May 6, and once more Goldie carried the day on the crucial question: Scott would be the one to decide whether the ship wintered or landed a shore party. A telegram was sent asking Gregory if he agreed, and when, as expected, he replied in the negative, adding in a second cable that he "could not be responsible for the scientific work under such an arrangement," that was taken to imply his resignation.[29]*

---

* Gregory remained on good terms with Scott. Just before the expedition sailed from New Zealand the following December, his mother-in-law told the Melbourne correspondent for the *Sphere* that Gregory had no quarrel with Scott, and she thought such stories had been fabricated by people with an ax to grind. That meshed with the journalist's impression of Scott, whom he had met and felt was

When the instructions were at last approved two weeks later, they were little different from those Markham had first drafted back in December.[30] The entire debilitating diversion from the business of organizing the expedition, which nearly robbed it of the man chosen to lead it, had effectively removed the man who would have been Scott's most influential aide at the most crucial stage of procurement.

Back at the beginning of December, armed for the first time with a free hand and a budget, Scott had only a bare eight months left to get the expedition ready to sail. On hand in London and able to help were only the expedition secretary, Cyril Longhurst, and Markham himself, with Koettlitz working from Dover on the food and medical requirements. Skelton and Royds would be in Scotland for at least three months, and the expedition biologist and zoologist were studying the Borchgrevink collections at the Natural History Museum. Armitage had not even been safely recruited.

It would be a race against time.

---

the sort of man any reasonable person ought to get on with (SPRI 1329: 12.18.01 letter to Mrs. Gregory). Scott was still writing to Gregory in a friendly vein during and after the return of the expedition, and Gregory's review of Scott's book in 1906 contained no criticism of Scott (*Nature*: 1.25.06).

7

ROSS'S SUCCESSORS PREPARE

The Road to Cowes

When Scott stepped into his temporary office at the RGS building at No. 1 Savile Row on August 1, 1900, his principal aide was still Markham, who was away in Norway. There was just a year to go before the expedition, and apart from Skelton, who would go straight to Dundee to supervise construction of the ship's machinery as soon as he was freed from his ship, only the expedition secretary, Cyril Longhurst, was there to help, and he also had to do the work for all the committees. Royds was still aboard HMS *Crescent* on a visit to Canada, and Lt. Michael Barne would not return from the China station until seven months later when the Boxer Rebellion was quelled. Like Skelton, he had been selected from officers from Scott's ship HMS *Majestic* who had volunteered when they heard of Scott's appointment.*

Neither Reginald Koettlitz, away in Brazil, nor Thomas V. Hodgson, who was curator of Plymouth Museum and had to give reasonable notice, could free themselves until November. Armitage was en route to the Far East and would not return until December.

In contrast, Drygalski had been in unfettered command of preparations for around three months. Even before that time, thanks to the kaiser's unequivocal edict fifteen months earlier, he had ordered most of the instruments (almost all available domestically) along with his

---

* If Scott "enjoyed no confidence in his person, as distinct from obeisance to his rank," as Huntford alleged (1979: p. 148), it is hardly likely that fellow officers would have volunteered to serve under him.

observation balloon outfit, which Sir Joseph Hooker had advised both expeditions to take. Four scientists were working directly for him. Ernst Vanhöffen, the biologist, with Nansen's help, was in Denmark and Norway buying sledges, skis, and dog harness. Surgeon Hans Gazert was in Munich studying bacteriology and helping Drygalski evaluate and purchase provisions, while the geologist, Emil Philippi, was gaining deep-sea dredging experience off the coast of Scotland. Friedrich Bidlingmaier, the magnetician, was in Potsdam studying under Prof. Eschenhagen, inventor of the self-recording variation instruments that would be used. The captain of the ship was aboard a whaler gaining experience in the northern ice region, something Armitage, the prospective navigator of the *Discovery*, already had in good measure. The chief engineer was at Friedrichshafen learning how to use balloons.

In September Royds joined Scott on the compass magnetics course at Deptford and then went to Scotland to supervise the shipbuilders' work on everything connected with the sailing of the ship. By January 1901 he was even further from Scott, learning about meteorology in winter conditions at the observatory on the summit of Ben Nevis. He returned on February 2 and left immediately for a magnetic course at Kew Observatory.[1]

Scott, Armitage, Barne, and the physicist also had to attend those courses. In contrast to the Germans, all of the training had to be squeezed into the last nine months before the expedition sailed. That in turn meant that much administrative work would fall on Scott's desk that might otherwise have been shared.

It was not that Markham had not tried to complete the staff or had failed to give polar experience proper priority. The scientific appointments were still subject to approval by his distant correspondent in Melbourne. Alfred Harmsworth had made Koettlitz's participation, like Armitage's, a condition for his gift of £5,000 to the expedition fund. That accorded well with Markham's polar experience criterion, and despite Gregory's recommendation of another doctor who had no experience he chose Koettlitz, who was Gregory's second choice.[2] For the same reason he had also at first proposed William Spiers Bruce as oceanographer and chief assistant instead of Hodgson, whom Gregory had suggested. Markham was unaware when he wrote to Gregory[3] that Bruce, who had given up waiting after hearing nothing since a brief acknowledgment of his application a year earlier, was on the brink of announcing his own expedition.[4]

Instead of Gregory's nominee, Markham had proposed David Wilton as zoologist, lately on the Jackson-Harmsworth expedition to

Franz Josef Land with Koettlitz, Bruce, and Armitage. But Gregory attached more importance to scientific than to polar experience, rejecting Wilton and Bruce on the grounds that the scientific results of the Jackson expedition had been "meagre."[5]*

Markham's unexplained omission of Gregory's chosen physicist, Professor Miers, caused Gregory to recommend Professor Pollock, professor of physics at Sydney University,[6] and he was offered the position after the Joint Committee had agreed at the June 15 meeting. Nearly three months passed before they learned that Sydney University had refused to grant Pollock leave to join the expedition,[7] so the Joint Committee was again asked for a recommendation.

The appointment was stalled until the committee met on November 20, when once again no recommendation emerged. Finally, Professor Schuster, a member of the magnetic subcommittee liaising with the Germans, came up with the young physicist George Clarke Simpson. Scott took to him immediately. Like Scott and all the other officers and scientists taken on except Barne, Simpson had to take a medical examination at the Admiralty on January 4, 1901.

Markham believed the expedition must have two doctors,[8] which opened the way for the twenty-eight-year-old medical graduate who became the most famous of the Antarctic doctors. Edward Wilson had turned up for his interview with his arm in a sling a week before Scott set off for Dundee on November 30. A pricked finger had turned septic. The finger had been operated on, and neither he nor Scott knew he would develop an abscess in December and need another operation to remove it before attending the medical board. Scott's first reaction to the man who would play such a major role in his future can be guessed from the fact that his appointment ran from the day of the interview.[9]

Although Wilson's arm was still in a sling, the Admiralty medical board passed him, subject to a final examination on July 13. Either because of that proviso or because Wilson told him about the tuberculosis he had recovered from in 1899, Scott approached Wilson's doctor who replied that although he hadn't been consulted about the poisoned arm he saw no problem on that score, adding, "It is with regard to his constitution and previous illness that I can speak and I believe he would be quite fit for the expedition."[10]

---

* This was scarcely the "summary" rejection (implicitly by Markham) inferred by Huntford (1985: p. 81).

Despite having told Scott, Wilson never mentioned the tuberculosis to the board until he had passed the final examination in July, when his conscience made him turn back into the room and tell them about it. The ensuing X ray showed traces of scars in his lungs, and the board advised against his going on the expedition. By that time it would have been hard to find another surgeon, let alone one who was also a gifted artist and ornithologist, and Scott set so much store in the qualities he had seen in the man that he was prepared to take him if he took responsibility for any consequences regarding his health.

Edward Wilson, who a mere twenty months earlier sat down and gasped for breath before reaching the 8,000-foot contour in the valley above Davos and nearly killed himself in a fall above Fluela Pass, joined the *Discovery* on August 5, 1901. Little did he think that less than a decade hence he would stand at the Pole with the man under whom he now sailed.[11]

But if Scott had gained a kindred spirit on the expedition by that decision, he lost another when the January 4 medical board's reports reached him, for they had thrown out the physicist, George Simpson. A week later he wrote to Professor Schuster who had recommended Simpson:[12]

> I very much regret to tell you that Simpson has failed his medical examination . . . the medical board pronounced him unfit, but the cause seemed to indicate that an operation might put him right. However it appears that even if an operation were performed, no medical man could prophesy that he would be thoroughly serviceable; under the circumstances we have, very reluctantly, to dispense with his services. Personally I am very disappointed as I thought him an exceedingly nice fellow. For the short time he has been with us he has displayed great energy and much tact . . . [he] would have been in every way fitted for the work.*

Before the decade was out, Scott enrolled Simpson as meteorologist for his second expedition.

A new candidate was hastily found. With Gregory's approval, the expedition at last had a young physicist, William Shackleton from the Solar Physics Laboratory, after the Executive Committee agreed to his appointment on January 30, 1901.

Two months previously, with October and November largely taken up with the visit to Norway and Berlin, revising estimates, and win-

---

* Scott would not have written this if Simpson were a man to whom he had "taken a personal dislike," as alleged in Huntford (1979: p. 143).

ning his case for untrammeled command, Scott, according to Markham, had received little or no help from the official subcommittees; in fact, the meteorological and oceanographic committees had just had their first meetings.[13] Not until January 11, barely more than six months before the expedition was to sail, did the Geological and Physical Geography Sub-Committee meet and come to the weighty conclusion that the objects of the expedition should be to establish whether a continent or an archipelago existed in Antarctica and to explore the geological history of any land there.[14] The contrast with Neumayer's and Markham's detailed counsel to the expedition leaders hardly needs emphasis!

As Scott set off for Dundee on November 30 to meet Gregory for the first time, the questions of the second in command and the ship's third officer were still unresolved. Armitage, whose acceptance had been made provisional on his agreement after meeting Scott, went to see Markham the day Scott returned from Scotland.[15] Markham wrote in his diary, "seems willing to accept the conditions but wishes first to have a talk with Scott."

Twenty years later Armitage would claim he had made it a condition that "if possible," he was to be landed with a surgeon, eight men, dogs, and supplies for two years with no restriction on his sledging.[16] In the context of a general complaint that the agreement had been broken, he wrote that Scott had asked him to waive the condition when they reached the Antarctic, which was logical as by then it had become possible for the whole expedition to remain there, and the result would have been to return the expedition to the split leadership that Armitage was "absolutely against."[17]

Although Markham still favored Armitage as leader of a shore party if the ship did not winter,[18] the facts previously related make it extremely unlikely that the "if possible" referred to any other situation than that of the ship being unable to winter. Armitage, though, met Scott before the year was out and was on the payroll from January 1, 1901.[19] In his own words: "I was charmed with him from the start. . . . I never met a more delightful man than Scott to work with . . . never did I admire Scott so much as in the way he handled his old advisers and organised matters generally."[20]

After Gregory's arrival, his increasing involvement in the controversy over his position appears to have limited his practical contribution to trying to get prices for every item on a list of scientific equipment he had drawn up.[21] On January 2 he had sent Scott a supplementary list, saying he still hadn't completed the estimates for the first list.[22]

While in England, Gregory's opinions of Scott contrasted sharply with his subsequent high regard for Scott's achievements. Further, despite not having completed estimates he could have organized from Australia many months previously, Gregory also accused Scott of being behind with "his departments."[23]

Gregory had brought a £280 quote for the main hut. Its specification had been drawn up by his Australian subcommittee, based on the design of Peary's Anniversary Lodge in the far north of Greenland's west coast (±77°40N 68°W) on his second 1893–1895 expedition but with wall insulation suggested by Australian experience in the design of frozen meat warehouses.[24]* With the £220 estimated to equip it and Koettlitz's quote of £50 for the observation huts, the total was splendidly less than the £2,000 allowed in the estimate. The big hut, 37 feet square, was ordered after Gregory returned to Australia, but some modification must have been decided on—possibly that of the wall insulation—for the contract was agreed at a price of £335. After the later addition of the veranda on three sides, the final unfitted cost was £360.[25]

Gregory had done something else that immediately benefited Scott. In light of his impending return to Australia, he had proposed the appointment of George Murray, head of the Botanical Department at the Natural History Museum, as his deputy until the ship reached Melbourne.

Scott at last had a senior scientist at his side—a man of decision who quickly made the sort of progress it must be assumed could have been achieved long since had the scientific director not been on the other side of the world. Murray had been directing the compilation of the Antarctic Manual, a guide for the scientists on the expedition, and his opinion of Scott contrasted sharply with that of Gregory. The high regard he had for Scott and Armitage showed clearly in the letter he wrote to the RGS librarian, Dr. Hugh Robert Mill, on his return from Dundee: "in 1¼ days I have settled the deck plan for winches, reels, sounding gear, trawling and dredging gear, special tow netting and thermometer and water bottle gear, and the fittings for the Biological and physico-chemical workshop. Many matters which would have taken weeks of committees (joint and disjointed) Scott and I have settled quietly greatly to *Gregory's* advantage [his emphasis]. Scott

---

* Scott's misconception, born of poor communications from Gregory, has persisted through to Huntford's acceptance that it was a bungalow more suited to outback use (1979: p. 153).

is a good chap and a first class organiser. I think he will go all the way and Armitage too."[26]

That was on February 24. Two days later he wrote that he had "a budget from Gregory . . . instructing me to do things I have already been to Dundee and done differently and better. Oh Lord! What an expedition, but order will come."[27] The "budget" was clearly the long-overdue estimate and final list of equipment required, and George Murray must get the credit for organizing the procurement of most of the laboratory and scientific equipment on it.

Just over a week earlier, on February 17, Ernest Shackleton had been appointed third officer, the only officer appointed without an interview, thanks to the recommendation of Llewellyn Longstaff, whose son Shackleton had met on one of his voyages to South Africa. It was a practical recommendation because apart from Scott and Armitage, he was the only officer with any experience in square-rigged ships. However, Shackleton would not be free to join the group until July.

Of the others so far recruited, only Armitage had been available during January and February. Royds' meteorological training at Ben Nevis in January was followed by a month's training at Kew.[28] Barne, training at Ben Nevis in February, then had to attend the compass course at Deptford, as did all the ship's officers. They were barely all freed from training when Scott and Royds had to set off northward, accompanied by the Markhams and Armitage, for the launch of the ship, which went off without a hitch on March 21. One quaint mis-understanding arose. *Lloyds Weekly* announced three days later that *Discovery* had been launched for William Bruce's Scottish National Antarctic Expedition![29]

Royds and Skelton stayed on to supervise the installation of the engines and rigging. The hemp rope rigging of the foremast had just been started. As Scott had found out too late, this was something else the ship subcommittee had not tackled since it had been set up in the spring of 1899. The last rope was finally dispatched on March 30, and then only after a telegram from Scott produced action.[30]

At this stage, with Hodgson on an oceanographic cruise on the *Michael Sars*, Scott had to send Armitage to Norway to chase orders placed with suppliers there. Although the pattern sledges and skis had been shipped to England in January, Scott had clearly found it im-practical to get more made in England, and Armitage was instructed to obtain the remainder.

The question of fur clothing had been posed back in November, when Koettlitz had first sought a quote. The shadow of cost by then overhung everything, and the quote seemed so high that Scott first checked with Crichton-Somerville to see whether Müller was the best supplier.

Getting the required confirmation as late as January 28,[31] Scott had to accept the quote on the basis of a "satisfactory reduction" on account of quantity, because the skins had to be bought by the supplier at the February sales in the north of Norway where the best skins from the autumn cull would be available. Following Drygalski's precedent, Scott had ordered thirty-six outfits of reindeer skin and fifteen of wolfskin for the officers and scientists.[32]

When Armitage got to Oslo, he took up the question of cost with Müller, who refused to reduce the price. However, he offered to pay the freight if the Wilson Line declined to carry the clothing to London free of charge.[33]

Obtaining the supply of dogs had also been taken on by Armitage. Back in November, Koettlitz had approached David Wilton, who had given him an estimate for West Siberian Ostiak dogs of the type Nansen had used. In January Scott had placed the order with Wilton, at first asking him to hire a Russian to escort the dogs to Melbourne by fast mail steamer.

Wilton advised against doing that and offered to escort the dogs as far as London, where they were to be transferred to a barge and thence to the London Zoo. But the cost involved (Wilton's fare and similar expenses) forced Scott to decline the offer.* Later he recruited Isaac Weller, a merchant seaman from Whitstable, to escort the dogs to Melbourne and take charge of them in the Antarctic. The waiving of quarantine regulations in Melbourne was another of the multitude of details Scott had to arrange from the expedition office. He and expedition secretary Cyril Longhurst had set up headquarters in two rooms at the London University building on January 15.[34]

Early in April Wilton wrote Armitage in Oslo that he had heard Alexander Trontheim was buying 400 dogs for an American expedition and taking them to Archangel (if only the British expedition had such backing, Armitage must have thought).[35] Wilton hoped to get Trontheim to buy the extra dogs, and then Wilton would go to Archangel and pick out the best 22 for Scott.[36] A month later Scott sent Wilton 600 rubles (the pound sterling was equal to 9.37 silver rubles), saying he had arranged for the dog biscuits, collars, and chains to be

---

* Contrary to the implication in Huntford (1979: p. 146), Wilton, by then committed to Bruce's expedition, could not have accompanied the dogs to the Antarctic.

sent to the vice consul at Archangel and was applying to the Russian Embassy for duty exemption.[37]

By that time Scott had Barne's help, along with that of the young physicist William Shackleton, to whom he had delegated the collecting of books for the expedition.[38] At this late stage he had to try to fill the senior crew posts himself in anticipation of the Admiralty agreement to release a naval crew, for which Sir Anthony Hoskins had been steadily lobbying.

Scott was hoping to get Frederick Dailey from HMS *Ganges* as carpenter, and when the Admiralty letter arrived consenting to release twenty-three ratings[39] he already had James Dellbridge, one of Skelton's engine room artificers from HMS *Majestic*, on the books, along with a civilian cook, Sydney Roper, who had won a silver medal in a national cooking competition. The day after the letter arrived, Royds, at last returned from Dundee, was dispatched to Chatham, the Channel Fleet base, to seek out further suitable volunteers.

The supply of the balloon now became urgent. Markham had first inquired for one in January. The city importer quoted the reasonable price of £270 for a German balloon that had achieved a good record with the Berlin Aeronautical Society over a four-year period. The price, however, excluded the gas and cylinders to hold it, for which Markham had been trying to find a supplier.[40]

Progress with the search stalled while the Gregory crisis ran its course. Scott tried first to get Sir Clements and the new president of the Royal Society, Sir William Huggins, to sign a request to the War Office for loan of an outfit. When the refusal came four days later,[41] Scott and Markham decided to appeal through the *Times* for £1,200 after getting a quote from the Army Balloon Factory at Aldershot. The resulting quote was whittled down to £1,388 for two 8,000 cubic foot balloons and seventy cylinders 9 feet long by 9¾ inches diameter, containing enough gas for four ascents.

That late decision added more last-minute training to the crowded month before they sailed. Ernest Shackleton, Reginald Skelton, and William Heald spent July 25 at Aldershot making 1,000-foot ascents. William Lashly, a leading stoker with a noted mechanical bent, was the only one who could be spared for a week's course. But the balloons and cylinders were ready in time, unlike a large amount of stores that had to be shipped out by liner to Melbourne.

May had also seen the conclusion of the lengthy business of agreeing on the coordinated program of weather and magnetic observations to be undertaken by the British and German expeditions, with a number of observatories scattered over the globe, including a new one at Christchurch in New Zealand, for which the instruments had to be bought and tested at Kew. The most positive step forward, however, had been the successful trial of the *Discovery* on May 14, attended by Royds and Skelton. The splendid performance of the ship's engine was reflected in the fulsome report in the next day's *Dundee Advertiser.*

Leaving the Camperdown Dock, the ship was steamed four times over the measured mile off Arbroath, twice with and twice against the tide. The mean speed was almost 9 knots, against the expected 7. Lightly ballasted, the propeller had not been properly submerged, and an extra knot was optimistically added to expectations.[42]

The pity was that *Discovery* was never to be tested under sail until the ship was on the way to South Africa. Theoretically, *Discovery* had been designed to make 8 knots under sail, and plans for the voyage out were laid on that basis. Had funds been ampler, the crew might have been mustered aboard before the voyage to London, on which the ship's sailing ability would have emerged in a very different light and the alteration of plan, with its attendant extra cost that left 1,100 cases of stores and the dogs to be shipped from Melbourne to New Zealand, might have been avoided.*

By the end of the month Markham was on his way to Dundee again, Scott having gone ahead, preparatory to taking possession of the now completed ship and steaming it down the east coast with a scratch crew to London. On May 30 they were shown the working of various machinery. When lifting the propeller was demonstrated, disaster was narrowly avoided. Lifting the propeller and screw had not been included in the trials, and Markham's diary gives a dramatic description of the accident that nearly killed Scott before the expedition even started.

Royds took everyone to see the demonstration, the propeller being lifted by tackle from the spanker boom. Suddenly, the iron hook broke in two and the 2½-ton screw crashed down, the block hitting the deck exactly where Scott had been standing a few seconds before. The ship's designer, William Smith, had moved Scott away just in time.

Discovery had to go back into dry dock, as the screw was jammed in its lifting shaft. Fortunately, the stern post and rudder mechanism proved undamaged, and two days later the screw was in place once

---

* The number of cases is deceptive as a guide to the volume of those stores, because everything had to be packed in boxes weighing no more than about 56 pounds for easy handling aboard *Discovery* and when landing them in the Antarctic.

more. By June 3 all was ready for the departure, and Markham went onboard with Scott, Armitage, Royds, Skelton, George Murray, and Hodgson. Markham slept in Scott's cabin, and the next day they steamed out of the Tay bound for London, passing Yarmouth about 11 A.M. on the 5th when, as he wrote in his diary, the ship was steaming at 7 knots easily.

Markham agreed with Murray and Scott that he should ask Sir William Huggins to appoint Murray as scientific director to replace Gregory.[43] Later that month the RGS Council confirmed support for his appointment, but Murray was refused leave of absence for more than the period needed to enable him to sail with the ship to Melbourne.[44]

After midnight the group stopped at Gravesend to await daylight and in the morning moved up the river to tie up in the East India Export Dock (on which Poplar Power Station later stood), just east of the Blackwall Tunnel. It was June 6, a day less than eight weeks ahead of sailing.

The crew was still anything but complete, and with Gregory's resignation a geologist also had to be found. With only twenty-three volunteers authorized from the Channel Fleet, Scott had to find eight men from elsewhere—a sailmaker, an artificer to stoke and work the donkey boiler and engine that drove the capstan and windlass, a ship-wright (carpenter's mate), an assistant cook, an assistant steward, and three seamen.

Royds recommended offering the second cook's job to Charles Clarke from Aberdeen, the cook at the Ben Nevis Observatory, and he was quickly recruited. Inquiries through the Dundee shipbuilders led to shipwright James Duncan (age thirty-one) and two seamen, John D. Walker (twenty-five) and James Masterton (thirty-three), all from Dundee and with experience aboard whalers in the northern ice fields.[45] Duncan possessed double potential, for he had worked for the ship-builders throughout the construction of the ship.[46] The floating maritime population in London dockland yielded sailmaker Hugh Miller, donkeyman William Hubert, junior steward Albert Dowsett, and a Brixham seaman, John Mardon.

Finding an experienced geologist ready to go at such short notice had been another matter, and the only practical recommendation was of a Cambridge graduate from Belfast who had just taken his honors exam in natural science, Hartley T. Ferrar (twenty-two). Markham was impressed with Ferrar when he came to lunch at Eccleston Square on July 21.[47]

Other problems diverted attention from the main task of chasing supplies and getting them packed and stowed aboard the ship. A week after the ship docked, Treasury requirements for detailed accounting came home to roost, and after a week's midnight-oil burning by Scott and Longhurst and a visit to the Admiralty with a Treasury representative, the subject was straightened out only with the aid of a clerk from the Treasury—belated help indeed compared with the government backup accorded to Drygalski in Berlin.

Social events began to multiply, with benefactors of the expedition inevitably feeling entitled to see the ship and others wanting to entertain the officers. These interruptions got so bad that Scott complained to Markham, but with little effect.[48] Lunches and dinners proliferated, but one such interruption was worthwhile because Scott and most of the crew met Henryk Arctowski after listening to his lecture on the Belgian expedition.

Colin Archer and others were being shown the *Discovery* one day when Reginald Skelton discovered a leak under the forward end of the engine bed. For the second time the ship was hurried into dry dock, and after five days all was apparently put right. Some thought the leak had been caused by the accident in Dundee, but Skelton believed the ship's timbers had shrunk. If he was right, this was the first serious consequence of the lack of seasoned timber Sir William White had warned Markham about two years before.[49]

Royds resumed loading stores and coal on July 11. In the end, 300 tons of coal were aboard. Because the beams made it difficult to trim, it had taken two-and-a-half days to load 240 tons into the main bunker (through canvas chutes passing through the wardroom). The rest went into the "pocket" bunkers either side of the engine room.

The men were all aboard by July 1, although they did not sign the crew agreement until July 27. On the morning of the 15th, Markham heard from the king's secretary that the king wanted to inspect the ship on the 23rd or 24th. Two days later, however, he was told the inspection would have to take place at Cowes on August 5. There was nothing to do but accept the delay, which was welcome news to the packers sweltering in the holds of the ship and particularly to Edward Wilson, who was about to get married.

On July 15, the day before Wilson's wedding, the bishop of London held a service aboard ship for the whole company. Markham presented Wilson with a three-tier silver dessert stand with an inscription saying it was a present from his companions aboard the ship for his wedding the next day at St. Mary Magdelene Church in Hilton in

Officers and scientists with expedition secretary aboard *Discovery* on July 17, 1901, the day after Edward Wilson's wedding. *Left* to *right* in the front row: George Murray, Cdr. Scott, Lt. Armitage, Lt. Royds; back row: Dr. Wilson, William Shackleton, Lt. Barne, Cyril Longhurst (expedition secretary), Lt. Shackleton; Eng. Lt. Skelton, Thomas Hodgson, Reginald Koettlitz.

Inset (*left*) Louis Bernacchi, who replaced William Shackleton as physicist; (*right*) Hartley Ferrar, who joined a week later as geologist after Professor Gregory resigned. Courtesy, the Scott Polar Research Institute, Cambridge.

Cambridgeshire. Two days later he brought his bride, Oriana, to see the ship before going for an all-too-short honeymoon stay in Pinner. He and the other scientists and officers were photographed onboard, and all must have seemed well on that sunny day.

But a row was in the offing that involved one man in the photo. William Shackleton, the physicist, had an argument two days later with Armitage and Royds about the arrangement of stores in the holds within a 30-foot radius of the magnetic laboratory.[50] He was probably right, but for Scott it was another episode in a chapter of incidents that, according to George Murray, made the young physicist steadily more unpopular with his colleagues.[51]

Scott got Murray to take up the question of a replacement, but dismissal at this stage could open the way for an action for damages. By good luck the dental examinations everyone had to undergo were under way,[52] and Scott got an adverse report on Shackleton's teeth on the 21st, which allowed him to write a letter of dismissal.

The luckless physicist rushed to his dentist in Yorkshire, who wrote a report saying his teeth were all right. Armed with that, he appealed to Professor Rücker but met with little sympathy. Referring to Shackleton in a letter to Kempe as a "silly fellow" who gave him the impression that he "had not been easily handled,"[53] Rücker advised Shackleton that it was better for him to be left behind on account of his teeth; any other reason would leave a black mark against him. In the end, Shackleton accepted £50 as compensation.

Markham realized that the only practical candidate to replace Shackleton was Louis Bernacchi, at that time in London. Further, Bernacchi would have to stay behind to learn how to use the Eschenhagen magnetographs not yet delivered to Kew for testing. Scott and Markham wrote him on July 24. Bernacchi asked Keltie, the new RGS secretary, about the status of William Shackleton's appointment. Only when he received an assurance from Scott that Shackleton's dismissal was final did Bernacchi accept on July 27.[54]

He was instructed to report to the observatory at Kew on August 15. However, the Eschenhagen instruments had arrived from Potsdam without detailed literature, so he had to go to Potsdam and try to get back by the 15th.[55] In the end, he traveled with the instruments to Marseilles to board a liner for Melbourne.

Ferrar had to take over the analysis of sea water on the voyage out, which required that Mill go along to Madeira to show him how to do it.

All was ready by noon on July 31. Markham and Lady Minna; Scott's mother and one of his sisters; Sir George Goldie, the man who had won the battle over the instructions to Scott; and several relatives of the officers came onboard with the designer of the windmill-driven generator.

Discovery emerged from the lock gates on the tide and passed downriver to cheers from the training ship *Worcester*, so familiar to Armitage and the naval officers, dropping off all guests except for Markham and the generator supplier at Greenhithe. Markham slept in Murray's cabin that night. Scott promoted Armitage to acting senior lieutenant and Ernest Shackleton to acting lieutenant, for Markham had secured him a commission in the Royal Naval Reserve.[56] Scott's black Aberdeen terrier, Scamp, and Armitage's white samoyed, Vyncka, were in kennels under the starboard bridge ladder along with three kittens, one black and two tabbies. The next evening they anchored off the pier in Stokes Bay at what is now the southern end of Gosport.

The following morning, August 2, they started the process of swinging the ship to establish the compass variation. Induced by the mass of steel aft in the engine room, it changed when sailing in different directions.

Ernest Shackleton's fiancée, Emily Dorman, was at the Anglesey Hotel with Scott's younger sisters.[57] Edward Wilson and his bride would not arrive until the 3rd—with her help he was completing the illustrations of seals in the Southern Cross Expedition's natural history reports prepared from what had survived of Hanson's notes. Going out to the ship on the 4th, Wilson got leave to stay another night onshore, leaving early next morning to board the ship at 8 A.M. August 5. With Admirals McClintock and Markham, Sir Allen Young, Longstaff, and Scott's mother also aboard, Armitage then took *Discovery* over to Cowes.

In perfect weather the king and queen came aboard before midday with their twenty-three-year-old daughter Princess Victoria and the usual retinue including Captain Lambton, commanding the paddle-driven royal yacht *Osborne*. Sir Clements introduced Scott and Longstaff, and Scott presented the officers and scientists. The king then inspected the men drawn up on the port side amidships, going on to inspect the living quarters and laboratories and everything on the upper deck. All were then drawn up on the starboard side for an address by the king, who turned to Scott at the end and, fishing the decoration out of his tails pocket, pinned the badge of a member of the newly founded Royal Victorian Order on Scott's tunic. After the royal departure, guests were allowed to come on board. The staff signed the visitors' book in the royal yacht before returning for lunch.

The inexorable demands of the Treasury meant there was work to be done on the accounts even at that last minute, and Markham was tied up the entire afternoon with Longhurst in the Marine Hotel, coming back for the evening and not returning ashore again until after midnight. Even if he did suffer from occasional painful attacks of gout, nobody could deny the energy of the man in his seventy-first year who had brought it all about. The next day he was scheduled to leave for Norway where he would search for a relief ship, for which he had already been raising money. Once there, he would still find time to walk with his wife up to 40 miles a day.

In the morning Scott and Murray went ashore to breakfast with Markham. Relatives and fiancées came aboard for one last visit, and *Discovery* steamed off, soon to be overhauled and forced to stop in the path of a yacht race so the First Sea Lord could come aboard to wish them luck.

All too soon they were abreast of Yarmouth, and mothers and sweethearts had to get into the launch that was following them. With Oriana Wilson in a gray dress and black summer hat among the others waving handkerchiefs until they could hardly distinguish the men aboard, *Discovery* steamed off past the Needles and into the sunset—the first proud ship to sail south in the new century's assault on the still mysterious Antarctic. For Markham more than anyone there that day, it was the fulfillment of a dream.

PART 2

SCOTT'S OPENING CAMPAIGN

*In Pursuit of the Great Enigma:
Antarctic Continent or Archipelago?*

8

A RACE AGAINST TIME

The Voyage to New Zealand

At 7 A.M. Wednesday, August 7, 1901, with *Discovery* about 8 miles beyond Start Point, First Lieutenant Charles Royds was on the bridge for the morning watch.* Giving the order to the helmsman in the stern, he turned the ship's bow southward and had the spanker (fore-and-aft gaff sail) hoisted on the mizen mast to catch what little wind there was on that hot summer day. Little more than an hour later, when Michael Barne had taken over, the last sight of England slipped below the horizon as *Discovery* steamed toward Madeira, the first port of call. There the ship would fill up with coal and disembark Dr. Hugh Mill, aboard to organize the physicist's work, which Louis Bernacchi would have handled on the voyage.

The weather those first eight days made it a "regular yachting trip" for Royds.[1] Not even the 31° roll to port worried him as *Discovery* ran into a northwesterly swell in the Bay of Biscay. There was "no jerk at the finish, just a quiet roll and everything remained in its place." When Mill returned, he told assembled members of the RGS that "*Discovery* proved a particularly comfortable ship, for her rolling was remarkably

---

* The "first" watch started at 8 P.M. (8 bells, 1 bell following at 8:30 P.M., 2 bells at 9 P.M., and so on until 8 bells rang the start of the next watch). The "middle" watch started at midnight and the "morning" watch at 4 A.M. The rest of the day was divided similarly into "forenoon" watch until noon, "afternoon" watch until 4 P.M., and, on the voyage to the Cape, a single "dog" watch until 8 P.M. Royds took the morning and dog watches, Barne the forenoon and first, and Ernest Shackleton the nighttime middle watch and the afternoon watch.

easy compared with most steamers of her size."[2] Koettlitz and Reginald Ford, acting chief steward, were the only men who were seasick.

There was more than enough to do with everything to practice for the oceanographic work and getting the meteorological observations routine established. Much of the equipment needed for the scientific work was difficult to find in the holds, because late deliveries had prevented optimum stowage arrangements. With a large proportion of officers' time taken up with entertainment for and by backers, actual and potential, and the work involved in kiting out the ship, the whereabouts of stores in the holds was known principally to Chief Steward Edward Else. He, however, had been forced to stay behind to take charge of the 1,100 cases of supplies that were to follow by steamer to Melbourne, mostly because of late deliveries but also, surprisingly, because more could not fit into the holds.[3] As Scott later recorded and Bernacchi found when he reached Melbourne,[4] Else's paperwork was in a totally muddled state, which made it even more difficult to find any item.[5]

Now at sea, Scott found that the emergency rations had been put into the main hold instead of up in the more accessible carpenter's and engineer's store where they could be retrieved quickly in the event of having to abandon ship. Everything was rearranged in short order.

They could not, however, keep all of the tinned foodstuffs outside the 30-foot radius around the magnetic observatory.[6] There were probably at least 3,000 cases aboard Discovery, and two-thirds of those would have contained tinned food.[7] It was likely this problem that had provoked William Shackleton's argument with Royds that led to the physicist's dismissal. In practice, the positioning of the tins made measurements tricky to take but did not seriously undermine the magnetic results.[8]

As aboard the Gauss, the handling of the oceanographic gear and tow nets, slung out as soon as they entered the Bay of Biscay, had to be learned from scratch, using extra men on deck by day and night. At eight o'clock each morning Royds came off watch and worked on deck straight through until he went back on watch again at 4 P.M.[9]—a 16-hour day embracing the lion's share of the meteorological observations using a large array of instruments.

Drygalski described the Germans' first efforts as a succession of mishaps.[10] The Germans' kites, like the British, came to grief, and meteorological instruments were lost or damaged.[11]

In the biological laboratory, under the starboard wing of the bridge, Hodgson worked on preserving specimens from the tow-net hauls, and Wilson made the sketches for him. The charts of the clockwork graphs registering atmospheric pressure, temperature, and humidity had to be marked in pencil at noon Greenwich Mean Time because of the changing ship's time. Four types of thermometers under the bridge were read and recorded hourly. The readings were then verified by a separate operation of a sling hygrometer and an aspiration psychrometer.

Hourly, too, a canvas bucketful of water was hauled up to the bridge so the sea's surface temperature could be recorded. Ferrar recorded its density, as well as the amount of carbonic acid gas in the atmosphere. The rainfall gauge, lashed on top of the hydrogen cylinders on the weather-side aft deckhouse, had to be moved to the other deckhouse every time the ship changed tack. This was going to be anything but a yachting holiday.

By the afternoon of Monday, August 12, west of Lisbon, the northeast trade wind, blowing since the day before, had reached a steady force 3 when a gust suddenly broke the main-mast lower topsail yard's parrel (which allowed the yard to swivel and run up and down the topmast). Nothing crashed to the deck, for the yards were held up by the "lifts" (ropes and chains handled from the foot of the masts), but confidence about what would happen in the stormy southern ocean waters was shaken, especially when the corresponding parrel on the foremast was later found to be cracked around the neck. The crew made up a temporary lashing and steamed on to sight Madeira at noon on the 14th, stopping that evening to practice using the sounding winches for the first time and to carry out a deep-sea temperature station. The sounding went off well, as did the deep-water temperature reading and water sampling using the one Pettersen-Nansen water bottle provided by the Admiralty.[12]

The continuous work that first week, so different from normal naval routine, helped break the ice. As the diaries of William Lashly and Thomas Williamson testify, the crew was kept advised of such things as noon position and mileage made every twenty-four hours.

As to the staff, Mill later said, "I was never in pleasanter company." The scientific work had obviously been aided by that unusual feature that distinguished Scott from most naval officers. "The essentially scientific turn of [his] mind," Mill wrote to Markham, "impressed me strongly, and the rapidity with which he mastered the detail . . . was remarkable."[13] He added, "There has not been a jarring note anywhere," acknowledging Scott's contribution to the general atmosphere aboard by adding, "his quiet firmness and tact [in command] are equally striking."

However, long before they let go the port anchor in Funchal Harbor that night, Scott had begun to grapple with an unforeseen problem that would affect the success of the entire first season in the Antarctic. With farther to sail than the Germans to reach the Antarctic, he had been dismayed at the time it was taking to get to Madeira. Scott had been led to expect more than the 7 knots *Discovery* achieved under steam and sail in the force 3 NE winds the British had encountered. Like Scott, the Germans, leaving Kiel a few hours later that very morning, were destined to discover that the *Gauss* would manage only a disappointing 7½ knots under sail in a force 7 NE wind.[14] That night Skelton recorded the British ship's average as less than 6½,[15] and they had been steaming on all but the first day.

The plan when *Discovery* left Cowes was to sail from New Zealand for the Antarctic on December 4. Economy dictated that the major part of the voyage would have to be done under sail alone. The engines had to be conserved for the Antarctic, and the number of stokers was inadequate for steaming for weeks on end. But now it was obvious that under sail the ship would only reach a "respectable speed" with "nearly a gale of wind" blowing, as Scott put it in a letter to Markham. And by that he cannot have meant less than force 7 and more likely the force 8 that the Beaufort scale described in those days as a "near gale" (today "fresh gale"), with wind speeds of 34–40 knots (39–46 mph).

Scott ascribed this situation to the ship's "terribly small" sail area. But the *Gauss*, with over 25 percent more sail and favorable winds (mostly force 4 to 7) took two-and-a-half days more than the British ship to cover the same distance to Madeira. And a year later, the *Morning*, with a typical whaler's spread of canvas, could do no better than 7 knots under sail in a force 7 northeasterly.[16] Aboard *Discovery* a collective optimism had clearly led everyone to expect more.

The reality Scott now faced, and he had long seen it in the offing, was that ninety days remained to reach New Zealand by mid-November—the latest date that would allow them to achieve anything that first season. Of the ninety days, five would be needed for the diversion toward the magnetic pole. There had to be a week at the Cape of Good Hope to compare the magnetic instruments with those at the local observatory and to take on coal and provisions. To that another week was needed at Melbourne for similar comparisons, as well as taking on the dogs and stores shipped out by other ships, together with the shore hut and Australian tinned meat.

With a day lost to weld the parrels, Scott could see that the sailing time was down to seventy days for the 12,000 or so miles to Lyttelton. And the "stations" for sounding and deep-sea water sampling and temperature readings, for which the ship had to be held almost stationary for up to four hours, depending on the depth, had to be fitted into that time as well.

Without any delays, the ship would have to average over 7 knots, and clearly *Discovery* would not have a chance to do that until they picked up the westerlies almost as far south as the Cape of Good Hope and more likely not until they sailed into the "roaring forties" after the South African visit. Scott sat down the next morning at Funchal to write that 6¾ knots was the best average to be hoped for. Most of the oceanographic work would have to be abandoned. "Murray takes it extraordinarily well. He is perfectly excellent as a messmate and as a director."[17]

His doubts were reinforced as they left the next day, August 16, under sail alone for the first time. That evening Ernest Shackleton wrote in his diary, "We found the ship steered badly, there being too much sail aft and not enough forward."[18] The weather helm was having a serious effect on the ship's speed.*

The Germans were suffering the same problem. The foremast in their ship had to be stepped further back than optimum because of the enormous mass of strengthening "deadwood" in the bow, and much weather helm had to be used under sail, partly for that reason and partly because of the resistance of the upper works toward the stern when sailing close to the wind.[19]

Aboard *Discovery*, Skelton was ordered to start the engines again at 4 A.M. on the 17th.[20] For a brief while they enjoyed a stiff breeze and the ship managed 9 knots, flanked by schools of bonito chasing flying fish that skimmed clear of the surface in hundred-yard flights. The noon-to-noon run of 191 miles was encouraging, but then the engine had to be shut down to clean boiler tubes.

They took the opportunity to try out the trawl, but it promptly collapsed in its frame.[21] Despite having been obtained in Norway and based on the *Michael Sars* pattern, it was evidently not suitable for towing at any sort of speed, and after experiments with canvas and wood frames for the nets, Scott designed a net that successfully towed

---

* In those days this characteristic was referred to as lee helm, because the helmsman put the tiller of an open boat over to leeward to turn the rudder toward the weather.

at more than 9 knots. From then on, Murray and Hodgson were assured of a continual supply of specimens for study.

By that time, the work had been organized on a systematic basis, running to a routine inscribed in the Order Book by Murray and Scott. A weekly slide lecture for the men was started with "immediate excellent effect." Murray was obviously pleased by the "gratifying questions" after the lectures. He was also impressed with the way Scott and Royds became "miraculously expert" in the use of the microscope.[22]

But the favorable wind did not last. On August 22, as they approached the Canaries, it shifted dead against them. As *Discovery* steamed on with sails furled, night temperatures in the cabins soared into the 80s (Fahrenheit). What it was like in the stokehold can be gauged from the diary of one of the seamen mustered to help there: "I did not exactly volunteer to be roasted alive: it's true she was built to keep the heat in, and to find that out you only have to go down in the bunker in the tropics."[23] For the next six days the temperature there was never less than 140°F.[24] The Germans experienced even worse temperatures in their stokehold, which reached 149°F.

On Friday, August 23, the British ship was steaming between Senegal and the Cape Verde Islands when someone found 2 feet of water, black and stinking, slopping about in the forward holds.* These holds extended for 45 feet between the first and third watertight bulkheads. The water unquestionably came from a new leak, because during the search for some of the stores no one had observed undue levels of bilge water in the holds.

The *Discovery* was not alone in springing a leak. One was also discovered aboard the *Gauss* when it neared Madeira a week later. It had first appeared, and then as mysteriously disappeared, before the ship left Kiel. In this case the trouble lay in the more usual trouble spot close to the sternpost, and for seventeen days before reaching Cape Town, the crew had to pump out every hour.[25]

Aboard the British ship Scott[26] and Skelton[27] noticed what may have been an essential clue: the greenheart planking just above the waterline was shrinking because of the heat of the tropical sun. If that wood could shrink, so equally could the main timbers of the ship. The source of the water in the holds did not become completely clear even after the ship had been dry-docked in New Zealand, but the symp-

---

* Scott speaks of 2 feet of water (RGSAA 12/1/5). Wilson recorded 6 feet in the main hold (SPRI WD: 8.23.01), but Armitage (Armitage 1905: p. 19) says only the bottom layer of cases was immersed, so Scott's report is undoubtedly correct.

toms then revealed indicated that the price was beginning to be paid for the lack of seasoned timber.

In the holds the bottom layer of cases, stacked three deep, was covered with black slime, with large numbers of tins rusted through.[28] Ernest Shackleton was put in charge of restowing, and, aided by Barne and Wilson, work went on around the clock bringing the stores up to the top deck. Everything smelled very unpleasant until the holds were pumped out and disinfected and the cases decontaminated. Scott and Armitage joined in the work of cleaning the stores and moving them down to the mess deck, where they gradually filled every available space until Duncan completed a new floor in the holds four days later.

Much food had to be jettisoned. Wilson, put in charge of the scientific and wine stores either side of the fresh water tanks, finally got them straight again on August 30.

That night they were barely 60 miles from the equator, and the usual festivities were launched by one of the senior petty officers, William Macfarlane, dressed as a triton with a false beard. He "boarded" the ship and announced through a megaphone that tomorrow Neptune would christen anyone who had not crossed the line before.

With Shackleton on the bridge next morning, the watch hoisted the flags for *Discovery*'s identifying letters SMLF as they passed an Italian square-rigged four-master, the *Giobatta Repetto*, on the opposite tack. Then the usual hilarious ordeal began for the initiates.

Hodgson, christened "Muggins" since declaring he had found some sea animal with an unpronounceable name that sounded like Muggins, along with Wilson, Ferrar, and eight crewmen, made up the victims. Before the customary shave and ducking by Macfarlane and fellow tritons (Leading Seaman Arthur Pilbeam and Able Seaman Frank Wild), Neptune in the person of Petty Officer David Allan and his "wife," merchant seaman John Mardon, arrived with his court, singing sea shanties with the aid of two bottles of whisky quickly passed around the comic team of eleven men. For the men, it was the high point in a relaxed regime.

The aftermath, however, fractured the amicable atmosphere that evening. The party turned sour on the mess deck, with four men in particular involved in what must have been abusive diatribes against officers and quartermasters.* "There were rows in the evening," as Hodgson put it, with Mardon becoming "very loquacious and critical."[29]

---

* Three of the first class petty officers (Allan, Kennar, and Macfarlane) were rated quartermasters and took charge of the helmsmen in difficult weather conditions.

The next morning Walker fainted on duty in the stokehold where the boilers were not yet let down. Wilson, called out at 6 A.M., found that his thumb had been bitten through to the bone by Duncan during a drunken fracas.[30]

After the service that Sunday, September 1, Scott called a general assembly. Hodgson recorded the subsequent statements: "Mardon is discharged and to be handed over to the authorities at the next port . . . a matter of reform required is language, which is a trifle tall on the lower deck. Duncan, Walker and Page had to toe the line subsequently."*

This was the first occasion when Scott had to apply formal discipline. Even though Mardon had been "under the influence," few could blame Scott for seizing the opportunity to recruit a replacement at Cape Town less likely to argue with orders in the Antarctic, where other men's lives might be at risk. As it was, although Mardon had clearly broken mercantile law, Scott relented when they reached Cape Town and simply discharged him without handing him over to the police.[31]

Years later Shackleton, leading his own expedition, would take the same line in just as firm a way when two men in his party, shipwrecked on the ice, were reprimanded for refusing an order.[32] Nothing in Scott's handling of the Mardon case suggests that he was any more of a martinet than Shackleton or any other officer could be when discipline was threatened, a point demonstrated again at Cape Town.

But behind the comedy on the deck as they crossed the line and its aftermath, other events quietly unfolded that had as much effect on the first season as if they had taken place in the Antarctic. Nature had begun to steal precious days with the head winds of the past week, but at least it now produced the customary SE trade wind. Still under steam, Armitage gave the order to change course 23° to the west, heading the ship decisively toward the Brazilian coast.[33]

The equator-crossing ceremony over and the wind a steady force 3, the engines were shut down for the bearings to be adjusted. They were in a shocking state according to Skelton, who had not had a chance to dismantle them before they sailed.

For the second time Michael Barne stood on the bridge and found the ship wouldn't hold the course at any speed worth counting. Not only did he have to ease the ship away another 2° to the west, but it began to make four times as much leeway, pushed sideways by wind

---

* To "toe the line" was the vernacular for being brought before the commanding officer for sentence.

and current so it was advancing 10° west of the intended course. Just as his watch was ending, the wind shifted back to due south and, except for a couple of hours that evening, remained that way until the following night.

The best *Discovery* would sail was 7 points off the wind, with a whole point (11¼°) of leeway when the wind blew with any sort of strength, so they had to sail nearly at right angles to the wind, 87° from it, compared with a commercial square-rigger's 70°. The ship could do nothing but carry them due west.[34] And that was by no means all the ship's fault. With the coal down to about 100 tons and around 35 tons of stores traveling to Melbourne by liner instead of in the holds[35]*, *Discovery* must have been nearly 17 inches higher out of the water than when it had sailed from Madeira, with the inevitable increase in leeway that would entail.

Keeping the engines going had saved them from the effects of the southerly wind for the past week. Now for every day needlessly sailed west instead of southwest, they would have to sail an extra day eastward.

After thirty-one hours the wind again backed to the more customary SE, and they could resume their progress southwestward. The wind blew steadily for nine days—on just one day it was force 6, but too often it was only 3 or 4. Coal was already so reduced that they decided to use candles for lighting despite the fact that the auxiliary boiler was piped up to the steam-driven dynamo.[36]

By September 9, six days behind schedule counting the day lost for repairs at Madeira, the wind was still in the southeast. They would be forced still further to the southwest instead of to the south, as they needed. Just sixteen days remained for them to reach Cape Town by the planned date of September 25. It might take ten days at the present speed to reach the strong westerlies in 35°S, and at 8 knots it would then take thirteen more days to reach the Cape six days late. Scott had no alternative but to ask Armitage to cut the corner, as much as that might cost in coal consumption.

It is hard to see why Scott didn't abandon the planned visit to South Trinidad on that southeastward push, although it only cost them about eight hours' steaming. The visit did yield several new species for the scientists, including the small petrel named after Wilson.

After nine days the bid to reach the Cape on time was lost. Only 35 tons of coal remained, and still they hadn't found the NW wind that ought to have been blowing down the track they steered.[37]

---

* Including the dogs' dried fish sledging food and Spratts biscuits.

Only on September 27, when they reached the Greenwich Meridian, did they finally pick up the outright westerlies, although they were only force 5 to 6 instead of the usual force 7 to 8 encountered on the threshold of the "roaring forties." Well before Scott sat down to write his report, he had resigned himself to arriving eight days late, on October 3. That meant pushing the departure from New Zealand back to December 12, and with possibilities of further delay at and after the Cape, he made up his mind to cable for authority to cut out the call at Melbourne.

For George Murray, who had "done so much to establish the happy relations existing between all aboard," as Scott wrote in the report,[38] the delay raised a difficult question about whether he could get back to London from Lyttelton by the time his leave of absence expired:[39]

> Here we are south of the Cape and on 11°W. I see no prospect of getting there until about Oct. 4th though our last run under sail almost beat our best under steam. We have only 4 days of coal and must do a lot of sailing. It is settled we go to Lyttelton direct from the Cape. I shall look the matter up—I may be able to get home sooner via San Francisco [e.g., across the United States]. . . . I went into times and distances in the evening and it is plain I must return from the Cape . . . we are so late that stopping to trawl or dredge is out of the question, and there is no sense in my going on. Moreover someone must see to the relief ship and get home by November. The Captain, Armitage and I held a council and we decided I [will] go home.

To Hodgson, however, Murray gave the omission of Melbourne as the reason for his return,[40] but he had given a different reason to Scott. "He is dead keen on running *the second ship* [my italics], and this is the sole reason for his going," Scott wrote to Markham.[41]*

When he got back to London, Murray told both stories. To a colleague in the Royal Society he gave the expiring leave as the sole reason for his return,[42] whereas to Markham he said "that his sole reason for coming home was to help with the second ship."[43] But as Markham added in his letter to the Royal Society treasurer on November 9, "He has a wild idea of going out . . . as chief person, combining a sledging expedition with the relief."

The winds continued to give the crew of the *Discovery* halfhearted support, and they had to get up steam once more the day before they

---

* These documents give no hint of a quarrel with Scott mentioned in an unsourced assertion by Huntford (1979: p. 148). The fact that they had been forced to abandon the oceanographic work was largely responsible for the total specimens collected comparing unfavorably with other contemporary expeditions.

arrived at Cape Town on October 3, with just 30 tons of coal left. However, before Scott had finished his report, he realized that *Discovery* had done rather well: "On the 26th it blew very fresh with a heavy sea and I am pleased . . . that the ship proves very stiff and an excellent and most comfortable sea boat . . . taking all things into consideration I think she has done as well as could be expected for a vessel of her type."[44]

A year later it would take the *Morning* seventy-five days to cover much the same distance and course as against his ship's fifty-five. *Discovery* had certainly done as well as could be expected.

Two days before they reached Cape Town, everyone was busy papering ventilators and cracks in the wardroom floor while the canvas chutes were installed through the hatches in the ceiling and floor in readiness for coaling operations.[45] As they rounded the corner into Table Bay to see the "tablecloth of cloud," as Edward Wilson put it, rising to dapple the peaks of Table Mountain, a pilot met and guided them to a coaling berth in a town that had just been placed under martial law following the appearance of Afrikaaner guerrillas not far from the outskirts. It was no place to do the work the ship needed to refit it for the voyage to New Zealand, but fortunately the British admiral had offered full facilities at the Simonstown naval base on the other side of the cape. The offer did not extend to coal, which, however, the Union Castle Line had offered to supply at cost price (30 shillings per ton free-on-board, against the 72 shillings the Germans would have to pay for the 70 tons they required). So the next day Skelton, helped by two of his leading stokers, Arthur Quartley and William Page, supervised the loading of 230 tons while Dellbridge worked on the engines and Hubert kept steam up on the boilers.

However, in the relaxed half-voluntary code of discipline aboard, alcohol again became freely available. At the end of the day Skelton recorded, "I had great trouble with some of my men—in fact throughout the ship the men were unsatisfactory—chiefly owing to the fact that their friends would bring them drink."[46] By that evening, according to him, Hubert and Page were drunk and incapable, Page had been "grossly insubordinate" to Dellbridge, and Lashly was on the sick list. Scott, pleased with the crew, had written in his report that "the men have given great satisfaction with the one exception of the merchant seaman Mardon." But he had unwittingly contributed to more trouble by agreeing to advance wages to the men totaling £140.[47]

Two days after they reached the Simonstown base, Skelton brought Page and Hubert up before Scott.[48] Page, there for the second time, would normally have expected to be discharged to serve a naval detention sentence ashore. But instead, Scott simply stopped the two men's shore leave, pay, and rum allowance.

Scott needed another stoker, and a total of three deck seamen had to be recruited, for besides the two merchant navy men John Waterman, one of the naval seamen, would have to be discharged. He had been isolated in the sick bay for some time with syphilis.

Markham, with a practical tolerance born of his contact with the navy, wrote Scott five weeks later that he was "sorry for young Waterman: his mother is a nice woman at Beverley, and he has written of his regret at having to leave the ship."[49] The seaman's words show that Scott's shipboard regime was hardly the morale-sapping straitjacket some who met him took it to be.

Drygalski was in as much trouble with his crew. The second bosun, a seaman, and the cook had appointed themselves spokesmen for a discontented faction after the engine room leak had become serious. On arrival at Cape Town, they had demanded that the crew be paid off unless the ship was dry-docked. The only dock was occupied, and waiting was out of the question, so the three ringleaders were let go and another man was discharged at his request. Two others were discharged "for minor misdemeanours."[50] Discipline aboard the German ship was, if anything, stricter than that applied by Scott and his officers.[51]

For Scott, there was still the problem of the shore party, which, if landed, would leave the ship undermanned, for only five men had been allowed by the Admiralty. Weller would bring the number up to six when he joined with the dogs in New Zealand. That left Scott two short of the eight men needed.

The laboratory assistant, Job Clarke, who also acted as the warrant officers' mess steward, was the only other man discharged. So Scott needed to recruit seven men and, understandably, if six of them could be naval men, so much the better. The laboratory assistant could be a civilian.

Despite the war situation, the admiral produced three seamen, a stoker, and a royal marine. That left Scott to find two men. If he could get a civilian for the laboratory and a merchant seaman to make up the deck watches, then one of the naval seamen could join the shore party, as could the marine, Pte. Gilbert Scott, when he was released from steward's duties by the arrival of Chief Steward Edward Else.

The Union Castle Line produced and highly recommended a volunteer seaman, Robert Sinclair. Like the other new recruits,* he was paid 1 shilling and 6 pence per day. Horace Buckridge, an Australian, volunteered to fill the laboratory post without pay but was taken on at £5 per month.[52]

The ship had come around to Simonstown in the night after the coaling was done, in the roughest spell the crew had experienced so far. Steaming with all sail furled on a heavy swell from the wide Atlantic, the ship rolled 37° each way. The previous worst had been 33° on September 26, when the wind had broken a topgallant clewline (rope holding the lower corner of the sail).

It was a notorious stretch of sea for any ship emerging from the shelter of Table Bay, as the *Gauss* would experience two months later with the frequent crash of breaking glassware sounding in the laboratory.[53] In *Discovery*'s cabins objects flew about that had not stirred since leaving England, and even the upright piano was flung on its face. This was a foretaste of what was to happen as they sailed across the westerlies on the last leg to New Zealand.

Unlike Melbourne and Christchurch, the Cape Town magnetic observatory was adversely affected by the town's electric trams, so Armitage, Barne, and the two professors worked in a tent on the plateau behind the town on the Cape of Good Hope peninsula. They could work only by daylight, partly because of the guerrilla situation, so the work took ten days instead of a week, which did not appear to matter much now that they were cutting out the Melbourne call. This allowed more time for work on the ship. The rigging was entirely reset, the engines overhauled, and the deck and sides recaulked above the waterline, and divers scraped weed and barnacles from the hull below.

By Sunday, October 13, the scientific collections from the nets and from South Trinidad were packed for Murray to take home, and the last letters were posted. All that day and the next morning *Discovery* lay out in the bay being swung for compass variation before full speed ahead was rung at 1:05 P.M. and they steamed past cheering ranks on the warships, bound for some of the stormiest seas in the world and their first encounter with the ice.

They were twelve days behind the intended departure date, but the chart of their course shows that not only had they saved the week at Melbourne, but to run up there from 50°S would have cost them two days. Theoretically, therefore, nine of the twelve days could be

---

* See Appendix 2.

afforded, although Scott and Armitage must have known that the battle to reach their destination by mid-November was already lost. With 3,800 miles "running the easting down," as the Cape Horners called it, averaging, say, 7 knots, and 3,300 miles sailing across the prevailing winds (including the 600 miles due south in 130°E) at, say, 6 knots at best, they would need forty-six days for the voyage. That meant a November 28 arrival at Lyttelton. Eight knots achieved on the fast leg would only save them three days. The diversion toward the magnetic pole to measure the intensity and dip of the earth's magnetic force along the line of zero compass variation would be all they could afford outside the business of getting there as fast as possible.

After four days they reached the 40th parallel, where freighters usually found the winds they needed. There, for just one morning, a good westerly breeze allowed them to shut off the engines. The next day the wind veered to the northeast, and they had no alternative but to steam further south.

With the north wind rising to force 7 in the early hours of October 21, they made their best twenty-four-hour run so far with 203 miles by noon that day, but at a price. As Thomas Williamson wrote of their first extreme roll, which dipped the clew of the mainsail into the sea as they changed course, "whilst wearing ship she rolled 44° which is a terrible amount . . . sometimes actually frightening me."[54] He had been flung from one side of the deck to the other.[55] The sea kept the decks awash with 2 or 3 inches of water, flung the drawers out of the chest in Scott's cabin, and upset the india-rubber baths in others. Wilson, suddenly ending up in the scuppers, was unperturbed, as he recorded that evening: "Many funny things happen in these happy times . . . and the condition can hardly be called one of comfort, though it certainly isn't one of danger . . . the worse all this gets, the more we all enjoy it . . . the crockery is fast disappearing in small pieces. . . . There were three seas coming at us from opposite quarters, and very little wind to steady us, hence our rolling."[56]

The mileage for the first seventy-two hours under sail alone was disappointing, with the wind constantly changing. However, after passing 30 miles north of the Crozet Islands, hidden in the mist of snow and sleet, they began a series of encouraging runs aided by a NW gale that carried them almost 800 miles eastward over the next four days.

The noon log reading registered 217 miles on the 27th through seas the irrepressible Wilson described as:[57]

> Absolutely magnificent, often 30 ft from crest to hollow, and sometimes even 40 ft . . . each one looks as though it must come right over the ship

and swamp her, but she just lifts to them in the most wonderful buoyant manner, and ships an occasional green sea, and otherwise nothing but spray . . . though we are going at nine knots an hour or more . . . these enormous masses of water are continually catching us up and passing us . . . every hour or so up comes a bitterly cold snowstorm, which whitens our sails and rigging . . . with the water a deep rich ultramarine to lapis lazuli with white streaks of foam . . . we are blowing a regular gale and yet so "dry"—forgive the expression, for we are wet through all day . . . our ship is surprising everyone by its seagoing excellency, its only drawback being that it rolls persistently and heavily.

The rolling was the only thing Wilson complained about. It was at its worst in confused or cross swells and, above all, when these were combined with calms. That, too, was the experience aboard Cape Horners, on one of which Shackleton had served his apprenticeship in 1891–1894. Running before the wind with bare yards squared, as *Discovery* clearly did sometimes during those gales, also exacerbated the rolling, as it deprived the ship of the steadying effect of the sails.[58]

The great advantage Scott's ship enjoyed was that it could keep going in such weather, and with minimum work aloft to shorten sail, only the main and foresail had to be furled. The ship's commercial contemporaries, still in the majority in those tempestuous latitudes, frequently had to lie to. Shortened down to little more than one topsail, they would keep the bow 2 or 3 points from the wind. Rising to the "graybeards," the bow lessened their impact when breaking across the deck amidships, as they invariably did when the ship was heavily laden. In effect, they would sail slowly backward before the wind.

The rounded stern saved *Discovery* from that situation but could not prevent the risk of the rudder being smashed sideways, which would sweep the ship around beam-on to wind and sea. That was the "broached to" fate so feared by the heavily laden commercial square-riggers. It exposed them to the broadside assault of a 50-foot wave crashing across the deck and carrying everything overboard before it. They always bent on old patched sails in such conditions, for if the sails were suddenly reversed by the wind ("caught aback") and didn't blow out, the masts might be broken with disastrous results.

The next day aboard *Discovery* a huge wave swept the stern around, threw the three men on the wheel to the deck (two would have been thrown right over it), and then crashed onboard.* James Duncan

---

* This narrow shave definitely sprang from the quartermaster not having applied the wheel brake (Armitage 1905: p. 25).

described the wave as "towering" up to the upper topsail.[59] Scott, Barne, and Wilson found themselves hanging on for grim life as the water rushed over them, submerging Scott on the lee side of the bridge for many seconds until the ship rolled straight again. Wet through from necks to sea boots, they all burst out laughing. "And they call it a 'dry' ship," Wilson expostulated in his diary that night.[60]

Armitage didn't think it was funny to find himself in 2 feet of water in the magnetic laboratory below the bridge, with notebooks and instruments awash. Fortunately, he had the window open and not the door. The wardroom was drenched, the mess deck flooded, and the drowned galley fire gushed steam. The winter clothes, just brought up from the hold, were soaked where they lay, awaiting distribution. Happily, nothing disastrous had happened aloft, despite the fact that all the sails were new.

By then *Discovery* had often had 3 or 4 inches of water slopping to and fro on the deck, but the crews of the ship's commercial contemporaries were also frequently working in as many feet of water.[61] The *Gauss* had encountered its first severe gales on the last leg to the Cape, rolling on its beam ends, but the ship's worst experience was to come as it pushed south from Heard Island the following February, shipping enormous seas fore and aft that had the seamen working up to their chests in water.[62]

Discovery was passing its first real test with flying colors, as Scott later wrote:[63]

> [It was] the first real test of the ship's seaworthy qualities and it is pleasing to record that she proves entirely satisfactory from this important point of view. She rises easily and lightly to the heaviest seas, is wonderfully stiff under canvas and surprisingly dry . . . a wonderfully good sea boat to the great credit of her designer, as this point might easily have been overlooked in an attempt to follow the lines of modern polar ships and in forgetfulness of the extreme difference of sea conditions in these southern latitudes to those . . . in the north. . . .
>
> A good sea boat is usually what seamen call "lively" and the *Discovery* proves anything but an exception to the rule; she is tossed about like a cork . . . and we have recorded rolls up to 47°. The heavy motion does not cause the discomfort that might be expected, but it adds difficulties to much of the work, and the "lurching" . . . is especially disadvantageous to the magnetic observations.

The lurching Scott referred to was in no way unusual in the commercial sailing ships,[64] and *Discovery* was far from fully laden, having already used up about 50 tons of coal. It also seems likely that there was more volume than weight in the holds.

DISCOVERY IN THE WESTERLIES. A typical day in the southern ocean "running the Easting down" to the magnetic meridian. In just such conditions the rounded stern, so decried by the whaling fraternity in Dundee, saved *Discovery* from being pooped as each huge wave overtook the ship. Some of the gas cylinders for the balloon, each 9¾ inches in diameter, can be seen on the roof of the starboard after deck house, used as a store. The port side deck house contained the ammunition magazine and the signal locker. Courtesy, the Royal Society.

On the afternoon of October 29, after passing about 80 miles
north of the Kerguelen Islands, the wind moderated a little.* Having
averaged more than 8½ knots for three days, they found themselves
achieving 10 knots when the wind got up to force 9 the next day. They
were being overhauled by waves more than 40 feet high running from
the northwest at 220-foot intervals.[65]

This was to be the last gale to help them on their way, and it drove
them another 800 miles eastward in four days, with a record twenty-
four-hour run of 223 miles logged at noon October 31. As a reminder
of the dangers the crew faced in such conditions, they passed the body
of a sailor floating in the water. "Poor fellow," wrote Armitage, "perhaps he had been torn from his floating home by some huge wave or
had fallen from aloft as he endeavoured to furl a sail."[66]

By the next evening the wind had gone, and steam was raised once
more. The time had come to edge southward—they were slightly more
than a quarter of the way around the globe, and from nearly 47°S
latitude course was set for the center of maximum intensity of the
earth's magnetic force, then at 52°S 131E, south of Australia. From
there the plan was to steam almost due south to the ice to record
changes in magnetic force and dip as they approached the magnetic
pole. Scott expected to reach 65°S.[67]

With little help from the sails, it was November 12 before they
could turn south, with topgallant yards lowered to minimize strains
on the masts in collisions with ice. Once more the strong WSW swell
set the ship rolling, and in the night a heavy swell toppled some oil-
skins stacked against an oil lamp not firmly secured, starting a fire. As
dangerous as that was in a wooden ship, the fire drill they had practiced in the Atlantic put a speedy end to it.[68]

Cloud cover meant their farthest south as they met the ice on the
16th could only be estimated by dead reckoning, but the excitement
of their first sight of the pack is more than apparent from the diary
excerpts Scott included in the report he wrote as they approached
New Zealand:[69]

> Nov.16th . . . Fast ice seen about 10 A.M. and amid much excitement we
> watched small pieces of decayed drift ice gradually growing in size and
> number and assuming more fantastic shapes. . . . The intense blue of the
> small sea-swept holes and caverns [in the small floes that were big enough
> to produce severe shocks if not avoided] was noticed with delight. . . . At

---

* The *Gauss* would take twenty-four days to reach the islands from the Cape,
compared to the fifteen days *Discovery* took.

4 P.M. a strong ice blink was observed to the left and right and a line of white ahead and in half an hour we had run into a loose pack of drift ice, amongst which were occasional small fragments of glacier ice showing blue and heavy in contrast. . . . After hoisting the whaler, filled and wore ship and stood on into the pack. At 8 P.M. it became thicker and at 9 we were in a close pack of pancake ice. . . . Shortly after, our way was stopped. Sails were furled and steam put on the engines. DR [dead reckoning] lat 62.50S long 139.40E . . . slowly circled round and headed northwards.

Time was against them, and with the essential magnetic readings achieved, Scott had to resist the temptation to follow the ice edge trending away to the southeast. It took them five days, all but one under steam, to reach Macquarie Island, where they stopped for four hours and increased the number of bird specimens to fifty. Hodgson, Skelton, and PO Jacob Cross were kept busy skinning the birds as soon as Wilson had made watercolor illustrations of the heads and feet, which he had to do rapidly before the color faded. The skins would be sent to London for taxidermy at the Natural History Museum.

Among the carcasses were a number of king penguins, and as Scott reported: "The opportunity was taken of serving out the flesh of the penguins for food. I had anticipated considerable prejudice on the part of the men to this form of diet *which it will so often be essential to enforce* [my italics] and was agreeably surprised to find that they were by no means averse to it. Many pronounced it excellent, and all seemed to appreciate the necessity of cultivating a taste for it. I found no prejudice more difficult to conquer than my own."[70*]

Scott had from the start been alive to the need for fresh meat in the diet in the Antarctic, and here for the first time he exhibits the personal aversion to the taste that had deterred so many and with such disastrous consequences on the Belgian expedition. Scott was not going to allow that same fate to occur when his expedition reached the Antarctic.

Another day's steaming was needed before they picked up a WNW wind that let them use the sails again. Two more days brought them in sight of Auckland Island, 270 miles south of New Zealand. Passing north of the island, they soon found themselves being driven uncomfortably close to a lee shore by a rising gale. As Scott put it in the report he was compiling:[71]

---

* This extract from his report expressly contradicts the theory expressed by Huntford (1979: p. 164) that Scott took the scurvy threat "less seriously than Amundsen."

We were glad to get clear of the north end [of the island] before the full force of a strong gale [force 9] developed. It blew hard during the night and the morning [November 26], a very heavy and uncomfortable sea, but we were able to hold our course within 2 points under topsails and easy steam. The ship lurched heavily in the morning and an angle of 56° was recorded on the clinometer.* Wind and sea dropped rapidly in the evening of the 26th, sails were furled and the course set for Cape Saunders Light which was sighted in the evening of the 27th.

By that time they had only about 70 tons of coal aboard, and the less weight below, the more the gear stowed on deck had raised the center of gravity. The coal usage would have already raised the ship a foot compared with the draft it drew on leaving the Cape. It is hardly surprising, then, that in such a gale and beating across a heavy NW sea, "as big a sea as one ever comes across, I am told by the officers,"[72] as Wilson put it, *Discovery* would register the most extreme roll so far. The next morning, Friday, November 28, Scott completed his report:[73]

This morning the breeze came fair from the SE and under steam and sail we have made such excellent progress that we should be off Lyttelton tonight. . . . Throughout the voyage we have lost neither a sail nor a rope yarn nor have we had any accident to the considerable amount of top hamper that is by necessity secured above the upper deck. For this satisfactory state of affairs I would submit that the greatest credit is due to . . . Mr. Skelton [chief engineer] Mr. Royds [first lieutenant], Mr. Feather [boatswain], Mr. Dailey [carpenter], and Mr. Dellbridge [engineer artificer].

As they dropped anchor in the darkness that night, Scott and his crew—mostly novices in sail apart from himself, Armitage, Royds, Shackleton, and the Dundee men—had surmounted their first hurdle. Besides achieving the first magnetic survey in a wooden ship since Ross's survey sixty years before along the southern trade routes, they had mastered the control of a brand new ship in seas that had sunk many a vessel twice the size of *Discovery*.

They had made it from the Cape in forty-six days. Earlier that year the Welsh Castle Line's *Penrhyn Castle*, 238 feet long with 28,000 square feet of canvas and making 12 or 13 knots in the westerlies on the same route but bound for Chile with 900 tons of ballast aboard, had taken fifty days to pass the meridian of New Zealand. And that ship had made no detour to the south. The tortoise had indeed beaten the hare.

It was a fine start to Scott's first command.

---

* The statement in a February 1980 *Mariner's Mirror* article (vol. 66: pp. 68–70) that Scott never mentioned such an extreme roll is clearly incorrect.

9

TO THE THRESHOLD OF DESTINY
Passage to a Frozen World

As well as they had done, Scott was under no illusion about the amount of work to be tackled before they could sail for the Ross Sea.[1] He faced three problems, of which the worst was the water leaking into the ship that now required an hour of hand pumping daily to keep the level below the floor installed in the holds. Matters had taken a bad turn after they had pushed into the ice, when the bow compartment began to flood from a leak somewhere among its massive timbers.

With the possibility that no safe harbor would be found for wintering the ship and having to leave a shore party, and with the working complement for the return in that case not yet up to the safe minimum, he could ill afford such a commitment of the crew's time in normal seas, let alone in the ice-ridden waters they would have to work through beyond Ross's farthest east. They could only dry-dock the ship, despite the volume of stores waiting to be loaded. The Harbour Board quickly came to the rescue—Discovery could enter its dry dock on Tuesday, December 3.

The next problem faced him on the quay side, and the decision to dry-dock the ship opened the way to resolving it. All the stores shipped from England and Melbourne were there, including the unassembled magnetic huts. Like the tallies of stores already aboard, the paperwork for everything was Else's responsibility and in just as bad a state.[2] On the brink of such a voyage into the unknown, to be unsure about supplies was as dangerous as any hazard, so Scott ordered Shackleton to have the holds cleared and retallied.³ With shore leave due, work on sails, rigging, and a multitude of other overhauls meant casual labor had to be hired. This became the first of a new wave of contingency costs not foreseen in the estimates that would affect crucial decisions later.

The shore party problem immediately worsened. The old trouble with alcohol had exploded the day the ship berthed. Royds graphically described the situation that day: "[The ship was] crowded with visitors after tieing up at 1 pm [November 29]. . . . Employed till midnight in seeing our drunken sailors over the side. Every man had been collared and taken to have a drink . . . the consequence is 'Blind-oh.'"⁴

He was up until 3.30 A.M., as there was "not a single sober man onboard." Skelton was similarly appalled: "The men have been behaving very badly . . . up to now, there has been a great deal of fighting and drunkenness and I hope two of the seamen will be discharged . . . the stokers with the exception of Page and Hubert behave very well."⁵

By the time the ship entered dry dock, things had reached such a pitch that after Able Seaman Baker had come close to blows with Quartermaster Kennar, Royds had all the men assembled on the mess deck at 9 A.M. and had Scott give them a dressing down. He wheeled the defaulters up in front of Scott, but no one was discharged, for Scott's hand was tied by the legal position under the Merchant Shipping Act and there was no guarantee he could get replacements of better quality.

The situation was beyond Royds's usual experience in the navy, where disciplinary measures could be enforced at virtually every port at which a warship might call: "It is awful and men are asking to leave the ship and in fact are all very unsettled. How I wish they would keep away from the drink as they are excellent whilst at sea, but when in harbour they forget themselves."⁶ Three days later Royds noted that Baker and Sinclair and even the first class petty officer, William Smythe, were absent all day: "I have very little doubt that [Baker and Sinclair] mean to run . . . we put the police on their tracks."⁷ But Sinclair, who was well liked, came back, and by the 9th Smythe had reappeared, too. Despite that, the decision was made to discharge Smythe and Baker to the Australian cruiser HMS *Ringarooma*—"it will be a very good thing as they have both caused a lot of discontent onboard," Skelton wrote.⁸

Scott would again be three short for the deck watches if eight of the men had to be left ashore for want of a safe harbor for the ship. So

SOME OF THE CREW AT LYTTELTON IN 1901. *Left to right* on Mizen Boom: ABs Vince, Peters, Wild, PO Evans, ABs Walker, Heald, Sailmaker Miller, PO Macfarlane, Carpenter Dailey, 2nd Engr. Dellbridge; *Left to right* on Poop Deck: Cpl. Blissett, AB Sinclair, Ldg. Stoker Page, ABs Dell, Weller, Ldg. Stoker Quartley, PO Smythe, AB Williamson, PO Allan, Ldg. Seaman Pilbeam. Courtesy, the Scott Polar Research Institute.

Smythe was kept on and reported to the Admiralty for disrating to able seaman. Only one replacement could be found—Thomas Crean, an Irish bluejacket from County Kerry. He was released from the *Ringarooma*, and Scott was now just one short of the required strength. When Baker had not returned three days later, he was officially reported as a deserter.[9]

Once the ship was in dry dock, one of the most experienced Christchurch shipwrights, H. J. Miller, was put in charge, with Dailey assigned to monitor the search for the leaks. Almost immediately, as the water was pumped out of the dock, water spurted out of wormholes in the outer greenheart sheathing.[10] Unfortunately, Dailey had not been present at the London dry-docking and so was ignorant of the pinholed character of greenheart. As Edwin Bate, the London societies' overseer during the ship's construction, knew, the sheathing was not designed to keep water out, only to protect the outer planking.

Miller's men were therefore set to scraping off all the coal-tar coating to see if there were more pinholes. Hundreds more came to light and were laboriously plugged. That and the recementing of the heads of the 10-inch "dumps" (nails) that held the sheathing to the planking, which also dripped water, contributed to solving the hold leaks. The real cause, however, was almost certainly poorly seasoned oak used in the main frames, as predicted by Sir William White.[11]

The elm planking was almost certainly the Canadian "rock" elm habitually used in wooden ship construction, but the oak in the frames had to be seasoned for ten years or shrinkage was to be expected in the built-up frames, as well as in the planking behind the sheathing, unless the elm had been matured for some time. This combination added up to a potential for bending the long rivetlike bolts and, of course, for shrinkage, which would leave the bolt loose and break the seal between frame and planking and lining, which was 3½-inch pitch pine that was also liable to shrink and warp.

But to Dailey and the readers of his reports, including Scott and, six weeks later, Markham, it looked like shoddy workmanship and poor supervision by Bate, whom both Smith and Richard Green, the London shipbuilder who had tackled the first leak, held responsible. When challenged the following February, Bate replied that he had tested hundreds of fastenings daily and had ordered the contractor to replace any loose ones before cementing.[12]

Practically speaking, there was no time to start a wholesale removal of the planking or lining, and the only thing to do was to stop up everything that might be letting water in. Surprisingly, although clearly for want of time, the coaltar coating was not replaced.[13]

Everything was done by December 11, and the next day the ship was afloat once more and towed over to its berth, where 235 tons of Westport coal were loaded until late that evening, bringing the total in the bunkers up to 285 tons. For the next four days, restowing and rerigging were in full swing. The engine room leak had been fixed, but to everyone's disappointment the bow compartment was leaking again the morning after the ship was back in the water. Then water was found in the main hold again, but Royds found that it was from a leaking flange on the sea suction to the main hold, almost certainly meaning the salt waterline to the galley pump. He thought it accounted

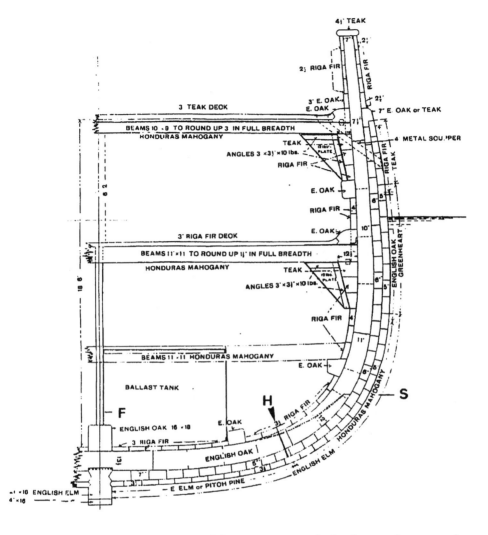

CROSS-SECTION OF THE DISCOVERY, showing bilge construction and other features that suggest the probable cause of the leak that developed in the hold. Excerpt from drawings originally appended to tender inquiry and later published with the text of a lecture given at the April 12, 1905, meeting of the Institute of Naval Architects by the designer, William E. Smith CB, superintendent of contracts at the Admiralty.

Key: F=level of floor installed in the holds after water to that depth was discovered after leaving Madeira; H=position of 1.25-inch dia. hole 18 inches deep found full of shavings during the dry-dock inspection in New Zealand; S=bilge level.

Construction materials shown are those originally specified in the tender inquiry. Frames were eventually fabricated from Scottish oak, with beams of Russian oak and, in some instances, pitch pine. Outer planking was Canadian rock elm below the waterline, pitch pine above. Ice sheathing down to bilge level was greenheart aft of and ironbark forward of the forecastle break, with sheathing continued to keel (believed in rock elm, although no positive statement to that effect survives). Design draft was 16 feet 2 inches amidships.

for the original leak, but had that been the case it would have been spotted when the holds were cleared in the Atlantic.[14]

Back in dry dock six days later, loose fastenings holding the bow plates once more cast suspicion on the builders, but the Dundee Shipbuilding Company later pointed out that Bate had insisted on the bow plates being fixed hard up against the plate protecting the stem instead of being half an inch clear of it, as was usual in whalers. That would have exposed the plates to undue shocks in their first encounter with ice. Bate had clearly had no experience building ships for work in ice.[15]

Miller, as enthusiastic as any for the expedition's success, wanted to have another try, but Scott could not afford the time. Further, apart from the considerable cost, the situation was "not now serious as the amount of water made can be pumped out daily in 10 minutes and the stores stowed in the compartment are not susceptible to damage from water."[16] Yet it cannot have been too comfortable a feeling to be setting off to actually break through the ice if that much damage could result from having barely entered it on the way to New Zealand.

Scott, however, had less to worry about than Captain Ruser aboard the *Gauss*. The engine room leak, having been eliminated in dry dock without identifying its source, reappeared undiminished the day before the ship sailed from Cape Town. Three times a day, all the way to the Antarctic, the Germans were condemned to pump their ship out.[17]

Aboard *Discovery* the cook, Sydney Roper, and the assistant steward, Albert Dowsett, had been discharged the day they arrived. "They were very poor men and I believe scoundrels, certainly the [steward] was," Skelton recorded the day the ship entered dry dock.[18] A thirty-six-year-old Tasmanian cook, Charles Brett, was engaged, and later the son of a Christchurch banker, Clarence Hare, just twenty-one, became the youngest member of the expedition, replacing the discharged steward. There was one more loss when the sailmaker had to be left behind for health reasons.[19]

On December 21, after a service led by the bishop of Christchurch, they steamed out to the cheers of spectators packed on the quay and on every vantage point, escorted by the *Ringarooma* and a gunboat. Three of the sailors climbed to the mast crosstrees, and one, Charles Bonner, who was extremely popular, took a bottle of whisky aloft with him and, alas, climbed above the crow's nest to the very top of the mainmast. He lost his footing and was killed instantly when he struck the winch house roof headfirst.

The escorting ships were signaled to stop cheering, and the cruiser went ahead to arrange the funeral at Dunedin, where, at Port Chalmers, the crew members were to pick up as much coal as they could squeeze in, generously donated by a local businessman. Captain Rich, commanding the *Ringarooma*, released a volunteer seaman, Jesse Handsley, to replace Bonner, but after the naval men had returned from the funeral, carried out with full naval honors, they found that Sinclair, who had been well liked by his naval messmates, had once again vanished. Scott learned that he had held himself responsible in part for Bonner's death and declined to have him reported to the port superintendent or the police.[20]

It was Christmas Eve, and nothing could be done to replace him. They would, after all, be two short for the shore party, for with Weller occupied with looking after the dogs, Joyce and Crean, recruited for it, had to be assigned to deck duties on the voyage south. If the ship did not winter in the ice, they could hardly be spared for the shore party that would have to be left behind.

In almost every other respect, the work in New Zealand had gone without a hitch. Bernacchi and Armitage had worked on calibrating the magnetic instruments in the new observatory built at Markham's and Professor Rücker's instigation. The other scientists had received invaluable help from the leading scientists at the Canterbury Museum to familiarize themselves with what was known of sub-Antarctic birds, plants, and microorganisms. And the hospitality extended to everyone had been boundless.

There was no way to surmount the great shortage of space aboard ship. Of the three years' provisions intended, a four-months' supply had to be left behind for the relief ship, or for *Discovery* if it had to return, to bring down the following season. And there was no space for any of the huts below deck. The huts, which weighed at least 30 tons, ended up on the after-skid beams above the engine room between the two boats, increasing the potential for rolling with such a weight far above the waterline.

Fifty gas cylinders and 1,500 (imperial) gallons of kerosene* in 6-gallon cans were on deck. With 40 of the 45 tons of coal loaded at Port Chalmers also on deck, the ship, which had left Lyttelton drawing 18 feet 8 inches astern, was even lower in the water as a tug took it in tow for the first few miles. The ship had just 9 feet freeboard amidships—Scott believed that was safe for survival, but many a prayer must

---

* The American term *kerosene* is used throughout when referring to paraffin.

have been raised for a gale-free passage through the stormy latitudes they had to traverse.

However, the weather posed none of the feared problems. Instead, it was actually too calm, eating into the vital coal stock for thirty-six hours before they reached the 59th parallel where the first icebergs could be expected. There fog shrouded everything as they sailed cautiously at 5 knots, with doubled lookouts straining to sound the alarm at the first hint of a berg looming in the mist. Even the birds disappeared.

Despite the lack of sun and postponement, by common accord, of Christmas festivities, everyone's spirits had revived enough for the New Year to be welcomed with suitable libations. Although lime juice had failed to prevent two men's deaths on the Jackson-Harmsworth expedition, Koettlitz had allowed himself to be influenced by Nansen's inclusion of the juice in the rations on the *Fram* expedition, recommending the purchase of 156 gallons. Consequently, the punch in the wardroom had to be made from whisky and lemon essence, for Koettlitz's recommendations had not included lemon or orange juice, and those fruits had not been among the many gifts from Christchurch people squeezed in when the stores were restowed.

On January 2, 1902, the men of *Discovery* were among the first bergs, sailing beneath clear blue skies. They had started down the 170°E meridian, on which lay Scott's first objective, Borchgrevink's hut at Cape Adare, where the first messages for the relief ship would be left. Deflected eastward when the wind turned to the southwest on December 30, they crossed the Circle early on Friday, January 3, a good 250 miles out of the most direct way but still ahead of the Germans, then only at the Kerguelen islands.

A few hours later they were running into loose pack ice, from 1 to 5 feet thick, surprisingly smooth-topped and with less snow on it than the pack they had seen on the way from the Cape. The ship advanced through open leads, occasionally having to drive into heavier pack, which gave "some good blows," as Duncan put it.[21] They stopped, with Scott's approval, to put out a boat and shoot their first seals. Wilson's interest was in the skins as specimens for museums, which he would preserve in brine-filled casks, but Scott also wanted to take every opportunity to lay up the meat for the winter.

With the temperature just below freezing, the upper deck became a regular butcher's shop that morning as the sheep were slaughtered and their carcasses hung in the rigging to freeze. In the afternoon it was the seals' turn, Wilson having shot the first, a crab-eater, in the morning and five more added by the end of the day. Wilson and Walker, the Dundee seaman from the training ship *Mars*, were joined by Cross and Weller in the grisly task of cutting them up. Sunday the 5th was decreed a holiday, which they kept as Christmas Day amid much larger floes under gray skies with mist obscuring the view. It was not enough, however, to stop Scott and Skelton shooting two more seals. The life-saving larder was growing apace.[22]

The level surface presented a fine opportunity for everyone to try out their skis: "Officers, staff and men staggering about in all directions, everyone thoroughly enjoying it," as Wilson put it. By the end of the afternoon many were becoming sufficiently confident to participate in impromptu races, which helped to generate a jolly atmosphere for the evening festivities when everyone congregated on the mess deck for a singalong. Wilson distributed cards from his bride and gave the warrant officers a box of crackers. Eventually, the men sang a song, finishing with a cheer. "We cheered back and then served out another tot of rum," Royds recorded in his diary.[23]

Only 35 miles were gained by noon the next day, and by then the ice had become too thick for progress to be made with the power produced by one boiler alone. So while steam was gotten up on the second boiler, they watered ship. The photo taken that day of Scott and Koettlitz out on skis shows the ice must have been at least 10 feet thick. Yet the floes cracked easily enough once the ship got on the move again.

They had been eating seal since the first captures and that day had seal liver for breakfast and seal steak for dinner,[24] but with doubtful expressions of pleasure, as Scott later admitted, for Armitage, Koettlitz, and Bernacchi had not yet taught the cook how to get the foul-tasting fat out of the meat. However, a few days later, Thomas Williamson wrote in his diary, "I reckon we are just about getting used to seal flesh now, which is not so bad when one has made a few attempts."[25] Scott had certainly taken the lessons of the Belgian expedition to heart.*

At last, after the slowest spell of all in the ice, a breeze sprang up during the evening of the 7th, and they could see a dark band above the horizon that signaled clear water in the offing. Two more seals were brought aboard before the ship emerged from the ice the next

---

* Shackleton, who was put in charge of the commissariat the day they reached Cape Adare, was alleged to have told his navigator aboard the *Quest* twenty years later (Worsley 1931: p. 277) that he had difficulty persuading Scott to have seals shot for food, but that hardly equated with what had gone on up to that time.

morning to cross the 70th parallel . By noon they were counting their luck beneath a brilliant sun in a clear blue sky with all trace of the ice below the horizon astern—they had gotten through in four days.

They had obtained one or two specimens of Emperor and Adélie penguins on the way through the pack ice, but now shoals of the latter disported themselves in the blue water as the great Admiralty Range rose above the horizon ahead. They were steaming on one boiler again to husband their coal and with all sails bar the mainsail set.

By midnight the sun was dipping over the mountains in a beautiful semisunset effect. Mount Sabine was right ahead.[26] The highest of all the peaks ahead and over a hundred miles distant, the mountain had clouds about its summit that were bathed in golden sunlight. It appeared to be just a few miles away in the clear atmosphere.

By morning, however, they were facing a second belt of thick pack near the point at which the peninsula joined the mainland southeast of Cape Adare. It took them all day to work along it and around the Two Sisters Rocks,* standing sentinel off the cape itself. They dropped anchor off the south edge of the triangular beach, almost a mile long, on the west side of the cape. Opposite the ship stood Borchgrevink's huts among uncountable myriad penguins.

Scott had sat down to write the report to the presidents of the two societies that he would leave, along with his and others' letters home, in a zinc cylinder in the hut. This was the first of six points where he had promised to try to leave news of their whereabouts and intentions.† "We are now within 6 miles of Cape Adare having forced our way through the pack southwestward," Scott wrote that evening. "We have barely expended our deck cargo of coal and our bunkers are completely full . . . a number of seals have been killed in the pack and have been served out as rations. They prove excellent eating and I propose to lay in such a stock as shall provide us with fresh food throughout the winter should we remain in the ice."[27]

As the others gazed at the coast of the land whose secrets they had come to unveil, Scott's mind was already filled with the future, his first goal achieved in a surprisingly easy conquest of the pack. Leaving Royds in charge of the ship, the boat carrying him and all the others from the wardroom grounded on the beach, and Scott stepped ashore on the threshold of the land he was to emblazon so indelibly with his name.

---

* One has disappeared, probably weakened by frost and then destroyed by an iceberg.

† Dismissed by Thomson (1977: p. 62) as "surrealist farce . . . not much more informative than 'Kilroy was here.'"

10

GATEWAYS TO THE UNKNOWN
The Search for a Foothold

Markham's original plan had emphasized exploration beyond Ross's farthest east and envisaged a direct passage to arrive there in December. But the instructions* in Scott's desk in his day cabin had diluted that goal to simply establishing whether land existed to the east of the Great Ice Barrier. Effectively, reaching that area in December had been out of the question since the late arrival at the Cape. Scott had therefore committed himself, in a December 17, 1901, letter from New Zealand,[1] to first examining the coast, from Cape Johnson at Wood Bay to Cape Crozier at the western end of the barrier. He would try to leave messages giving their intentions for the relief ship at Cape Adare, Possession Island, Coulman Island, Wood Bay, Franklin Island, and Cape Crozier.

Several of the instructions would fully justify that course. The emphatic injunction to establish a magnetic base in Victoria Land (clause 7) was coupled with instructions to examine the coast (clause 16) and to make an advance into the western mountains (clause 18). Above all, the injunction (clause 19c) that any landing party could only be left ashore between Wood Bay and Cape Crozier meant Scott first had to sail down this coast to see if any location was feasible, preferably south of Wood Bay (clause 10).[†]

---

* See Appendix 1.

[†] These clauses contradict the assertion in Huntford (1979: p. 152) that Scott ignored an instruction from Markham to set up winter quarters in Robertson Bay behind Cape Adare.

Here at Cape Adare was the first opportunity for land-based magnetic readings, and as Bernacchi, Armitage, and Barne set about that task, the other scientists scoured the rookeries and escarpment for every kind of specimen—animal, plant, and mineral. Bernacchi, the young "veteran" of the *Southern Cross*, landed with Koettlitz, Barne, and Hodgson to deposit the zinc cylinder containing Scott's report and everyone's letters home in the hut he had lived in just three years previously. After showing the group where everyone had slept and ate, he led them up the scarp to Nicolai Hanson's grave a thousand feet up the peninsula.

On board once more, the anchor was weighed at 3 A.M., and they steamed out through a line of grounded bergs. As they turned southeast and pushed into the line of pack they had come through on the way in, it suddenly compacted and, bearing down on them at 4 to 5 knots on the incoming tide, forced them back toward the bergs.[2]

Amid the windless stillness of a perfect summer scene, broken only by the throb of the engines and the grinding of the floes, the Antarctic sprang its first trap, threatening to drive the ship to destruction on the immovable cliffs of caverned ice that drew inexorably closer. With Armitage directing from the upper topsail yard,[3] the struggle went on for four hours, steadily losing ground until—barely in time—the tide slackened, leads appeared in the floes, and *Discovery* began at last to draw away from disaster. This was the first warning that despite the notional horsepower of the ship's engines, treacherous traps existed off that coast in even the most serene conditions.

The crisis had been made worse at first by Scott's decision to run on one boiler to save nearly 2 tons of coal a day. Despite the scary experience, that economy was so paramount that once clear of the pack he felt constrained to have the second boiler shut down again. The pack moved steadily northward up the coast, keeping them 15 miles east of the Possession Islands, and they had no choice but to make for the next letterbox at Coulman Island. It took them forty-eight hours to get into the lee of the island against a rising wind that backed into the southwest and then, on January 14, built up to hurricane force, pushing them back into the ice north of the island. Raising steam on the second boiler once more, the engines, to everyone's relief, held the ship against the 90 mph wind throughout the night. Those asleep were constantly awakened by collisions with the ice.

By the next afternoon it was just calm enough for Scott to make a difficult landing in a considerable swell. Small floes were jostling the boat[4] as he got ashore with Ferrar, Dailey, Cross, Duncan, and the message post at Cape Wadworth, where the *Southern Cross* party had landed to leave their message. Their message post was still standing.

Wilson remarked with irritation in his diary after the Coulman Island landing that "the captain is strangely reticent about letting a soul on the ship know what even his immediate plans are."[5] He had learned of the landing only at the last minute.

Intent on steaming down the coast, Scott stood the ship across the strait to Ross's Cape Jones and came upon barrier ice, a new experience for everyone except Bernacchi. Gigantic walls as high as the mastheads towered before them as they entered the bay Borchgrevink had named after Lady Newnes, looking to Armitage as though they would endure to the end of time.

About 3 miles into the narrowing channel between the barrier and the cape, another channel less than a mile wide ran WSW into the ice cliff. A short way in, smooth sea ice was speckled with a hundred or so seals and a small group of twenty Emperor penguins disconsolately moulting. Scott ordered the crew to slaughter and skin as many as possible. As Scott later wrote:* "We resolved to turn night into day, and although it was 10 P.M. start about our work at once . . . not a pleasant task, but one we regarded as very necessary—namely that of adding to our larder sundry joints of seal. We felt fairly confident of finding a wintering spot before the season closed, but we had no guarantee that we should find seals in its vicinity, and it seemed the wisest plan to get them whilst we could."[6]

By 2:30 A.M. they had killed around thirty seals and a dozen penguins. Wilson saw that several penguin corpses were drifting away on a small floe and, with Scott's permission, went off with Ferrar to chase it. Within an hour they got the birds back to the floe where Jacob Cross and Isaac Weller were at work. That, too, broke away.

The watch officer saw them but said nothing, thinking the ship could catch them and take them onboard. Four chilling hours later the lightly clad men were picked up, and the next officer on watch, after an encounter with an unusually disgruntled Wilson, received the full brunt of the captain's displeasure when Scott came on deck.

---

* It was at this time that Scott is alleged by Huntford (1985 #2: p. 85) to have conceded to Shackleton's demand that seal should be put on the menu. But Skelton's diary records that seal was on the menu from January 5 onward, remarking on the 6th that it was "very fair eating, just like beefsteak" after seal steak was served for breakfast in the wardroom (SPRI 972 1.15.02 and 342/1/1: 1.6.02).

Moving out of Lady Newnes Bay, they found the direct way south barred by pack and had to go around the north of the island again, only to find the pack astride their course to Wood Bay. Seal carcasses were still being cut up and hung in the rigging as the coasts of the bay rose above the horizon beneath the cloud-topped 9,000-foot Mount Melbourne. The pack, 7 feet thick, stopped them 20 miles short of Cape Johnson on January 18.

This first gateway to the interior had loomed large in Markham's hopes ever since Bernacchi had described a very gradual gradient to the icecap after Borchgrevink's return.* It was not to be, however, for to wait for the ice to clear might spell the end of all other exploration that season. Scott could only steam away around Cape Washington, telling everyone they would return.†

From there on everything was going to be new. Ross, from as much as 75 miles out, had seen the mountain peaks and endorsed the 1846 map of his discoveries "line of coast not distinguishable from its great distance." Now, in perfect clarity, the coast unrolled before them, with Wilson sketching as they went—sometimes on deck, sometimes in the crow's nest with Shackleton. "The coastline south of C. Washington runs back into a deep bay and then turns directly to the south," Scott wrote, "in places fringed by an ice foot, while in others bare rocky slopes descend to the water's edge."[7] Describing foothills in the foreground and, higher up, a range of lesser mountains joining Mount Melbourne to the tabular giant he later named after Nansen, Scott then speaks of the 15-mile-wide glacier with a beehive-shaped rock nunatak sticking out of the middle of the mass of ice sweeping down from the horizon, depicted in Wilson's sketch of the Reeves Glacier. All of this accords well with what is known today about the coast down to Evans Coves, named seven years later after the captain of Shackleton's ship, the *Nimrod,* and visible at the right of Wilson's picture.

"And now," Scott wrote, "as we skirted the ice foot on our right, we found ourselves suddenly brought up in a curious inlet with ice walls on every side, and were obliged to turn and retrace our steps for

---

* See Chapter 4.

† Frank Plumley's 15.1.02 diary entry at Lady Newnes Bay, referring to the seals "which we intend burying for winter use," shows everyone knew of the intention to winter. If any of the merchant navy men were under the impression that they had signed on for a single round-trip, they cannot have read the preamble to the crew agreement they signed, by which they agreed "to serve on board . . . for any period up to 5 years" (PRO: BT100/145).

some way when, still keeping the icewall on our right, we found ourselves going due east away from the land."[8] They had come to an ice
barrier 60- to 150-feet high stretching 30 miles out to sea in a southeasterly direction, which the *Southern Cross* had encountered on February 8, 1900, without recognizing what it was, having been forced away
eastward before reaching its end.

Their achievement during those two splendid days was learning
the true form of the coastline from Cape Washington southward,
rightly named after Scott, and by rounding the end of it, discovering
that Borchgrevink's "barrier" was in reality an enormous ice tongue,
subsequently named after Drygalski.

South of the tongue the smoking cone of Ross's Mount Erebus,
120 miles away, rose above the horizon. Blocked on its way north, the
pack kept them 30 miles from the coast until they were twice that
distance further south. Here they were able to steer gradually southwest until they encountered the nose of another ice tongue, later named
after Nordenskjöld. It too projected seaward 30 miles from the mountains but seemed far wider at its base.

Twenty miles beyond it, they sighted a dark cliff against white
snow slopes, at last promising some sort of an inlet. The thrust of the
instructions was to establish and conduct explorations from a magnetic base hereabouts, regardless of what happened further east. With
the longer sledging season possible if the ship could stay there, Scott
felt this first hopeful-looking place had to be investigated, even at the
cost of much time pushing in through the coastal pack, which suddenly appeared thicker than any so far seen. It took twenty-three hours
to reach the entrance to the inlet, where the character of the ice changed
abruptly.

Smooth, thin, recently formed, and cracked in a regular pattern,
the ice told of placid sheltered water in the lee of its steep southern
shore, broken at one place by a glacier running from behind the bluff
cliff they had seen from far out to sea. That cliff proved to be a shoulder jutting out to the northwest, which they named Discovery Bluff.
Scott led a party including Koettlitz, Wilson, and Shackleton across
to an ice foot about 1½ miles beyond the cliff and never more than 20
feet wide. Rounding a cape a few hundred yards further on, there
before them was a perfect harbor running in southwest another 1½
miles to a glacier, with the steep rock above them, facing northwest,
kept bare of snow by the warmth of the afternoon sun.

That accounted for the orange-colored lichen and real moss
Shackleton found, to Koettlitz's delight, populated by the same minute

insect (*collembola*) Kløvstad of the *Southern Cross* had found but existing here over 400 miles further south.[9] Koettlitz explained that this suggested that the land had been connected to other continents in about the Cambrian Period, when the earliest forms of life developed, more than 570 million years ago.*

As soon as the party returned Scott announced that the harbor was suitable for wintering the ship. Stoker Frank Plumley recorded that night that "the exploring party reported it suitable for winter quarters, so if we do not find better we shall come back there for the winter."[10] As they pushed out through the pack, lit by the midnight sun, Scott felt the problem was resolved—they had a harbor just 5 miles short of the 77th parallel to fall back to.

After reaching open water on the morning of the 21st, the pack once more prevented them from approaching the shore. Scott, anxious to find a more southerly harbor, scanned the coast through binoculars and spotted another inlet 40 miles further south of Granite Harbour, as they had named the first from the preponderance of that rock on its shores. For several hours they tried to get closer, but the ice was 12 feet thick.[11]

Reluctantly turning away, they pushed on through thin pack until Scott could see around the southern extremity of Mount Erebus. At first it appeared there was no land south of the volcano and that the newly discovered western mountains, running south from Granite Harbour, terminated at the conical mountain later named after the ship, with nothing between there and the volcano except a small patch like a distant island. Four hours later the hope of finding a strait leading southward was dashed when the apparent island was joined by several hilltops. These broadened out until they appeared to be connected to form the end of the bay. Fifty miles from the ship, and only 10 miles from where Ross had placed the coast joining Erebus to the mainland, the hills varied in height from 2,300 to 3,200 feet. Modern maps show how they could have appeared continuous that day.

The ice blocked further progress, and it was time to head east. Scott had found two harbors, and assuming there would be coastal ice in the spring, they could reach the lower parts of the ridge up what looked like very gentle slopes.

Rounding Cape Bird at midnight, Scott made straight for Cape Crozier, the last of the prearranged message points. They had followed

---

* Specimens are now known from a billion years ago.

the coast closely, and the planned diversion to Franklin Island was out of the question.

Scott wrote his dispatch in the morning and, like the others, wrote a letter home. The unknown beyond Ross's farthest east awaited them, and no one could guarantee the relief ship would reach them.

In the dispatch, addressed to the presidents of the two societies, Scott made his intention very clear. "We found on the west coast of [McMurdo Bay] two excellent harbours. They are, respectively, in 76°55S and 77°30S approximately. It is my intention to return to one of these spots for the winter, preferably the southern. I shall now proceed along the Great Barrier and endeavour to explore its eastern extremity."[12]

Heaving to after dinner that evening about 4 miles northwest of Cape Crozier, Armitage stayed aboard to swing the ship along with Hodgson, who worked the dredge as the ship swung around. Scott and all the other staff were rowed ashore by seven seamen in one of the whalers, accompanied by instruments for Bernacchi and Barne to take magnetic readings, two message cylinders, and a post.

Despite the shelter promised by three stranded bergs, they approached with caution to avoid capsizing the boat. At the right moment the order to pull hard rang out, and as the boat was carried in on the wave, everyone jumped out and the boat was dragged onto the beach at the cost of a lot of waterlogged feet.

Scott, Royds, and Wilson pushed through the massed Adélie penguins and struggled up a 35° scree slope, the kind where the foot slips back one step for every two ascended, to the 1,350-foot summit of the old volcanic cone behind the eastern end of the beach. There they stood, the first men to see the southern coast of the Erebus-Terror massif and to look out over the vastness of the barrier from such a height. Stretching away to a featureless horizon under the midnight sun, it was like a silken sea frozen into unnatural stillness. From here it looked like the gateway to the south.

The departure from the beach was even trickier, and they managed it only with Barne jumping into the icy water to keep the stern to the waves. Wilson returned with an albino penguin caught by one of the seamen. He got to bed at 3 A.M., only to be awakened three hours later as they came abreast of Cape Crozier.

As they steamed past the blood-red cliff, which the barrier edge squeezes past in a chaos of ice, Wilson was too cold to sketch, standing there in pajamas and a coat. The barrier front proper, little more than 60 feet high as they started along its face, alternately freshly fractured and weathered according to how long ago a berg had calved from it, did not yet strike Wilson as particularly impressive. To Scott, however, there was a historic question to settle.

On January 28, 1841, Ross had sailed past this spot about 8 miles off the barrier, compelled by the lack of steam power to keep a safe distance. From the crow's nest aboard HMS *Erebus* he had seen what he took to be continuous mountains stretching south of the island, and he named them the Parry Mountains. Scott was aloft in the crow's nest in good time to see them, if they existed. Fully 40 feet above and less than a quarter of a mile from the barrier surface, Scott looked southwest, with the sun well away to the east and illuminating the scene from behind his left shoulder. There, to his surprise, he saw in the distance the bare tops of hills protruding above the horizon and realized they must be the crests of those he had seen from McMurdo Bay, as he still thought it to be.

On his second voyage, in February 1842, Ross had been within 1½ miles of the barrier face at his farthest east and found it 107-feet high, "less than half its height at C. Crozier,"[13] which he had never approached closely. Scott, in trying to account for the error by the otherwise meticulous observer, later reasoned that Ross must have taken any peaks visible above the barrier's top as necessarily of great height.[14]

That alone could have led to the illusion, without even taking account of elevation by mirage. Sixty-one years later, Scott still took the crests as part of land joining Erebus to the new mountains at the southwest of McMurdo Bay, but in less than a month they were named (from east to west) White, Black, and Brown Islands. They probably deserve to be known as the Parry Islands.

By the end of the day, a hundred miles farther east, all aboard were marveling at the grandeur of the barrier's ramparts as they rose to 240 feet, towering over their ship as it steamed not more than 300 yards from their silent hugeness.[15] Here they found it was 12 miles north of the position the *Southern Cross* had reached in mid-February two years earlier. Stopping to make the first of a series of thrice-daily soundings to establish whether the barrier was afloat, they found bottom at 480 fathoms, twelve times the thickness of the ice above the surface. Even with the evidence of grounded icebergs, where the part above water was about a seventh of that below, only when they could moor to its edge would they accept that the barrier was afloat, at least along its northern edge.

From its high point, the barrier dropped steadily throughout the second day until it was no more than 15 feet high a few miles before they reached the 180° meridian. Sounding as they went, sometimes as close as 100 yards, the ship and its crew were never more than 2 miles from the face. The barrier had curved south until the 179°E meridian, where they reached 78½°S with the barrier face 30 miles south of its position when the *Southern Cross* had made its second close approach two years before.

As they advanced and compared their course with Borchgrevink's, it appeared that a 25- or 30-mile strip of barrier about 150 miles long had broken away during the past two years. Borchgrevink had found the barrier's northern edge in much the same position as in Ross's day. The third day they passed between about fifty bergs and the barrier. Two others still near the face had so obviously just broken away that there could be little doubt they were steaming past the birthplace of huge numbers of the Ross sea icebergs.

As they entered an 8-mile-wide channel south of what looked like a very long berg, the weather had become so misty that it wasn't until they spotted lower ice ahead that they realized they were in a cul-de-sac and had to turn back along its north face at 5 A.M. As they emerged and tried to turn around the snout of what was really just an ice tongue, an ENE gale arose, against which the engines could make no headway. Shutting them down, Scott then tried tacking seaward under sail but soon had to give up and let the ship be driven 30 miles westward and far off the barrier before the gale eased. Back near the barrier face, they found the wind had increased the westerly current to about 5 knots. By the time they were back at the ice tongue early on the 28th, two whole days had been written off, and more coal had been expended running the second boiler.

By noon the barrier face had risen to 150 feet, towering once more above the masts. A maze of bergs forced them away northward, where the ship was engulfed by fog. When they were able to get back close again, they soon passed an opening just east of the 167°W meridian. Once again it ran in with a slight easterly slant but this time with a sharp-pointed ice peninsula 90 feet high jutting out from its southern face.[16] Wilson thought its north cape was 200 feet high. With the sunlight falling against its far side, cracks and caves in its north face gleamed with a bright blue that quickly had him sketching.

This was the second new feature to break the otherwise continuous face of the barrier. It was less awesome than he had expected: "One begins to think there is something stupendous about it after all," he wrote that evening.[17]

That night, while many were asleep, the ship entered the inlet from which Borchgrevink had sledged south to 78°50S. The chart shows it as a small cove about 1½ miles long at the southeast corner of a wider bay. That tallies well with the description in shipwright Duncan's diary, which makes it clear that everyone realized its significance.[18] The fog entirely hid the next inlet, later the scene of the dramatic meeting with the *Fram* during Scott's second expedition.[19]

By noon on January 29 they were past and just south of Ross's farthest east on his 1842 voyage, where he had recorded the appearance of land to the south. Look as they might, there was no sign of it, but all day they had a sense of impending change as the barrier edge turned north. At last, at about 8 P.M., where it turned eastward for 5 miles, now only about 50 feet high, the surface sloped upward so much that there could be little doubt that there was land underneath the ice. Scott, paraphrasing his diary, described how the skyline was so vague that the instruments could not register its height, despite the evening light coloring the nearer slopes a bright orange with deep blue and purple shadows, as Wilson remembered.

Armitage remembered the slopes as running up to about 500 feet. That and the 100 fathom sounding right in the bay with overturned bergs, bearing streaks of earth on their exposed keels, added up to a certainty that they had discovered the eastern flank of the barrier. Ferrar immediately put off in a boat and got samples of the earth. Aboard the ship Hodgson, after several disappointing hauls earlier in their eastward voyage, at last dredged up "the most wonderful collection of starfish, sea urchins, polyzoa, and crustaceans, delicate things reminiscent of tropical seas, but all living at a temperature of 29°F."[20]

Maddeningly, the fog got worse and obscured everything for almost twenty-four hours, as they groped northward along what was clearly an ice foot, occasionally glimpsing ice-clad domes that had to be supported by land. At last, at 8:40 P.M. on January 30, just as the wardroom dinner bell sounded and while Scott, Armitage, Koettlitz, and Royds were still on the bridge, there was the solid black rock they had strained to catch sight of all day. It was jutting through the snow slopes of a group of hills about 2,000 feet above them. Although they were there a month later than originally intended, they had answered the first great question.

That morning the edge of the ice foot had turned abruptly east, and they were now at 155°W, a hundred miles further east than Ross had penetrated. The view was still restricted, but no pack ice was visible seaward. The sounding showed bottom at 88 fathoms, which by midnight had increased to 265 as the fast ice, now 7- to 8-feet thick, forced them steadily away from the newly discovered land, later named after the king.

Having discovered the land, Scott had to make some attempt to find a harbor somewhere along it. Although he had expressed the intention of returning to one of the harbors found in McMurdo Sound, Markham had written of an equally strong preference for winter quarters being set up "in the unknown eastern region" as an alternative to Wood Bay.[21] In spite of the ship's triple beams, it had evidently been accepted from the start that the *Discovery* had to winter in a place sheltered from the enormous pressures generated by the pack when it met an immovable shore.

By the evening, ice standing 8 feet above the water was looming on the port beam as they steamed on in a wide channel between it and the land ice.[22] The daylit night became foggier by the hour, and although glimpses of rock were seen once or twice, all signs of land had vanished by morning.

Scott, who had been on the bridge all night, had to wait until 5 P.M. on the 31st before the sun came out. By then they had almost completed three hours' work watering the ship. They had tied up near a prominent iceberg at the edge of the fast ice, which had proved encouragingly easier to dig out than the stubbornly hard stuff off the Victoria Land coast. Pushing off at 5:15 P.M., they got out of the channel into a sheet of water open to the horizon except for the ice edge to starboard, which carried on as far as they could see to the northeast.[23]

Still following it in the hope that there would be an opening to the south or that more land would appear, Royds handed over to Barne at 6 P.M. for the second dog watch. It seems from Scott's account that it was at this time, after twenty-three hours on the bridge, that he first went below to catch up on sleep, because he describes the course as northerly at the time.[24]

Nothing in the ship's situation suggested it was in any danger at that time.* Ninety minutes later, however, the way was barred at the head of a narrowing bight in the ice, and Barne altered course 15 points to port to follow the ice edge west by north. This was the

---

* The ship was certainly not ringed with icebergs, as suggested by Huntford when asserting that Scott ought to have remained on the bridge (1985 #2: p. 59). Scott's order to carry on following the fast ice edge northeastward can hardly be described as risky or rash when no pack was visible to the northwest.

beginning of a twelve-hour period that transformed the first great success into a situation fraught with danger.

Taking over the first watch at 8 P.M., Shackleton found he could
resume the northeast course, but now again in a channel with floe ice
to port. Within ten minutes there was only one way to go—once more
to the west. "Entered a large opening and proceeded in search of exit
at other end—proved to be a large bay," he wrote at 8:10 P.M. in the deck
log, adding later, "Altered courses in search of opening on farther side."[25]

Just over two hours later, the far end of the "bay" forced him to
alter course southward. When Royds came up from his cabin at 11:40
to take over the middle watch, Scott was already on the bridge. After
Shackleton had explained the situation, Scott made out what he took
to be the exit. Having pointed it out to Royds as he took over, Scott
then went below. Royds goes on to record how at "about 1:30 A.M.
[on February 1—the deck log entry is 1:23 A.M.] I saw there was something wrong, so informed the captain and altered course 16 points
[180°]."[26] The deck log differs, showing a 15-point course change to
get out of the self-same cul-de-sac where Barne had "found [the] ship
embayed" and recorded a change of course to S30W (mag) the previous evening.[27]

Royds's version of events shows that in Scott's account, written
three years later, he did not do justice to himself by suggesting that
after first going below he did not come on deck again until the ship
was on its way around in a circle for the second time, about 7 A.M. on
February 1. Royds makes it clear that Scott was not only on the bridge
at midnight but was back again at 3 A.M. and was still there an hour
later: "At 3 A.M. we came up to the floe from which we had watered
the afternoon of yesterday, and it had drifted in the meantime north
about 5 miles. Seeing clear water on the starboard bow he [Scott] told
me to make for it, the entrance [to the clear water] being on the port
bow. Then I left the deck at 4:00."[28]

Scott once more went below but only snatched another three
hours' sleep, for by 7.30 A.M. he was on the bridge again arguing with
Armitage, who had relieved Barne.[29] Neither knew where they were,
so Royds was summoned to the bridge.

Barne clearly had the ship well started on a second tour of the
icebound bay, this time in a clockwise direction:[30]

> At 7:30 there was a panic, and I was sent for hurriedly as it appears that
> Barne, finding no clear water, had turned and was in reality going back
> into the bay again. There was much swearing as to the way out, which was
> the berg we had watered close to, etc., but I saw at once *purely by luck* [my

emphasis] that we were going wrong and at last managed to convince the Captain, so we again turned back and at last got out of what at one time looked a very nasty position.

As Scott explained, with young ice forming it was necessary to keep the ship moving.[31] If he betrayed some agitation it was because no one yet knew how ice behaved that far south in the Ross Sea, and there was a strong ENE set in the current, threatening to sweep ice and ship away to the fate the Belgians had suffered.[32]

Only later did Scott discover that at that season in that area they were more likely to be carried out to sea to be released as the pack broke up. Had they known that at the time, the freezing over of this now-enclosed water would not have appeared so menacing. Combined with the evident disappearance of the entrance to the channel they had entered through, the experience would have been traumatic for a highly experienced commander, let alone a man under firm instructions to avoid having his ship become trapped in the ice like De Gerlache's *Belgica*.[33]

A few hours before, nothing had suggested danger, even though Scott had written that he did not want the relief ship to follow further than Borchgrevink's Bight.[34] The fact that once out of the channel there had been no sign of ice to port suggested that they had passed between a large mass of pack and the fast ice edging the shore, and the set of the current would have argued against pack sweeping in from the northwest.

Now, suddenly, the Antarctic had sprung its second trap, and if they couldn't find a way out it looked as though the aims of the expedition would come to naught. Everywhere the men on the bridge could see in the patchy visibility, the ice presented the same unchanging barrier to escape.

Chart 3, based on the deck log, shows it was not until 8:50 A.M. that Royds could convince Scott, and for that matter Armitage, who had been on the bridge since 6 A.M., that they ought to turn back. He was right, and at 10:35 A.M. they were at a berg close to the original watering place. There they found the channel they had entered by, and it was still open. "Altered course S50E [S30W true] left bay in which new ice was forming," Shackleton wrote in the deck log.[35]

Still in the channel at noon on February 1, they probed several ways that promised an escape to the northwest, from where they might press eastward again, but they all led nowhere. With the wind getting up from the east and a clearing sky, and prompted also by the fear that the McMurdo harbors might be frozen up, too,[36] Scott made his decision:

they would return to Granite Harbour or, better still, to the opening they had seen about 35 miles south of the harbor.

That evening, with the sun behind the newly discovered hills, Wilson sketched for a watercolor that best portrays the promise that led Scott to determine to return to the area.[37] He could not know that he would not see the coast again.

With exploration to the east blocked, Scott was now able to settle the future of the expedition. The next day he met with all the officers and gave them the outline plan for the next two seasons on the assumption that they would be allowed to do more exploration in the second season rather than sail straight home via Cape Horn. When he had diffidently confessed his lack of a plan to Nansen,[38] Scott knew, as Drygalski did, that he could not make a plan until he got to the Antarctic, and he must have known that the plan would depend on two things—whether he found a safe harbor or shore for a landing party (virtually synonymous) and what would come of the eastward exploration.

As soon as the safe harbor was found, everyone knew of his intention to winter there if nothing better could be found to the east. The "exploring party reported it [Granite Harbour] suitable for winter quarters, so if we do not find better we shall come back there for the winter," Plumley had written the evening they steamed away from the harbor.[39] With all possibilities closed to the east, Scott outlined what he had clearly been thinking out since the discovery of Granite Harbour, remembering, of course, that the instructions virtually prescribed the plan for him.

After wintering in the most southerly harbor feasible in McMurdo Bay, sledge parties were to go in three directions. The main one would go south, with *Discovery* waiting for its return. The other two were to explore the immediate neighborhood of McMurdo Bay and Mounts Erebus and Terror. That would take care of the main instruction about what to attempt if the ship could stay in the south.*

When the relief ship arrived, it would find the message they had left and come into the bay to find them either at Granite Harbour or at the more southerly point. Then Scott would redeem his pledge to Armitage that he could lead a major sledge journey. Immediately on its arrival, the relief ship would land Armitage and a party at Wood Bay to sledge to the magnetic pole, waiting there to pick them up and take them back to New Zealand.

---

* See Appendix 1, clause 18a.

When the three sledge parties returned, *Discovery* would explore the coast westward from Cape Adare and run back to Lyttelton. After refitting there in the winter of 1903, the ship would break through the pack once more, steam straight for the land they had just discovered, "and spend the whole summer working it out," to use Wilson's words. Running out of the ice in March 1904, they would return home via Cape Horn.[40]

The plan made sense to Scott's audience, for Royds praised it as excellent as he wrote in his diary that evening.[41] The whole concept must have been based on the relief ship coming south as early in the season as *Discovery* had intended to. William Colbeck, already Markham's chosen captain back in September, was to bring the ship out through the Suez Canal if necessary to maintain that timetable.[42]

If Armitage's party did anything in the spring, they would have to be back before the ship arrived, which in the light of their experience should be before the end of December. With more powerful engines than *Discovery*, Scott had no reason to think the *Morning*, designed by Svend Foyn, the Norwegian whaling explorer, would not get through the pack as easily as he had. A week should see Armitage ashore at Wood Bay, with ten weeks to accomplish the 300-mile round-trip to the magnetic pole.[43]

The next evening, February 3, they ran into a narrow inlet the fog had hidden on the way east. About 2 miles wide with walls 90 to 140 feet high, the inlet ran 12 miles into the barrier.[44] At the end it turned westward into a valley where its edge dropped to the level of the rail amidships, about 12 feet above the water.[45] Running away west was a crack with forty or fifty seals scattered along it.

Here, Scott decided, was the chance to use the balloon to explore the extent of the barrier at this end and to see if there was a sign of land further to the southeast, as well as to stock up with seal meat. All this justified a day's delay, despite the fear that the McMurdo harbors might freeze up. Armitage got permission to take a sledge party southward, provided he was back within twenty-four hours.

The haste with which Armitage was able to get the necessary equipment together and leave within thirty minutes was a tribute to the considerable order Shackleton had achieved during the restowing at Lyttelton. However, in the rush to get away a tent was left behind, so five of the six men in the party shared a three-man tent on the barrier that night. Armitage and Cross each weighed 14 stone, so Bernacchi slept outside, leaving the three seamen, Jesse Handsley, Thomas Crean, and Ernest Joyce, to squeeze in with the two heavyweights.

The balloon party under Skelton spent the evening getting the equipment ready for an ascent in the morning, and almost everyone else got some exercise on skis or playing football on the ice. Ferrar took Williamson and set off around the end of the creak to head 10 miles eastward in search of land or traces of earth.[46]

Later, when everyone was onboard again, with emergency stores out on the ice for the shore party in case the ship had to put to sea to avoid incoming pack, they all came rushing on deck when the ship jerked violently with a tremendous scrunching sound as a small iceberg ground its way along the starboard side, tearing off part of a sheathing plank. Shackleton, for one, never forgot that narrow shave. Despite the ship being moored to the northern side of the inlet, the small "growler," 20 feet wide, had come in from the sea and was swung toward the ship on the incoming tide. It just missed the bow and, coming to a stop, everyone tried vainly to push it away with poles. That was a forlorn hope. Had it struck square on, the growler was heavy enough to have crushed the ship. Eventually, as the tide receded, it headed toward the ship once more and, after grinding along the side again, left the inlet. Clearly, this was no harbor to winter in and was none too secure for even a short stay.

Meanwhile, Armitage and Bernacchi, on skis with the four other men pulling the sledge, had disappeared to the southwest over the southern ridge of the shallow valley from which the inlet opened. The party found themselves in another wide valley about 120 feet deep running east-west, with a crevasse along it about 5 feet wide in which they found seawater about 40 feet below the ice surface. Climbing out over the far rim, they advanced about 5 miles on the level, then crossed another similar valley and camped at 8:45 P.M. With 200 pounds on the sledge, Cross and the three men had averaged about 3½ mph, although no sledge meter was fitted to confirm it. The object was clearly to examine the barrier and take magnetic readings well away from ship and land, not to break records. The temperature had been a comfortable 10°F during the day. With the thermometer barely above 0°F that night, Bernacchi slept quite comfortably outside on snow banked against a sastrugi ridge, which says a lot about the clothing they took.

Next morning, leaving Joyce and Crean to pack up the sledge, the others set off southward on skis, passing over more plateaus and valleys for about 11 miles when Handsley, not yet very adept on skis and delaying them, was sent back to join the others at the camp. Armitage and his two companions went on to reach a point he reckoned was 3 miles beyond the 79th parallel.

They must have been pleased to think they were the first men to reach that far south. However, Armitage was measuring from the ship, and later he corrected their reach to 78°34S, 29 miles further north. Had they really been 3 miles beyond 79°S that morning, they would have skied a total of 36 miles in 2¼ hours, an unlikely performance with a novice skier in the party, let alone taking account of their stopping to calculate the height of a ridge with the theodolite, which they did at least once.[47] Despite Armitage's experience, Scott was evidently right when he wrote "at this time we were very prone to exaggerate our walks."[48]

They could see nothing of land when they turned at 8:45 A.M. After a mile they saw the balloon going up, and picking up the three men at the camp, they were able to steer directly for the ship, getting in at 2:15 P.M.

There, Scott himself had made the first ascent in the balloon. Daring as usual, he had insisted on being the first despite having had no training. After a somewhat hesitant start, with instructions shouted from the ground, he had gotten the balloon up to about 600 feet, only to be somewhat disappointed by the poor visibility on distant horizons.

After Scott was safely down, they found the balloon would not lift two men because of the weight of the 1-inch dredging wire rope they were using. So Shackleton had to go up alone with the quarter-plate camera to take the first Antarctic aerial photos. William Heald then took the balloon up for a third ascent before the lunch break.[49] Afterward, the wind got up and tore the fabric, so further ascents were abandoned, which was a good thing because the valve was found to be damaged, as though to confirm Wilson's worst fears about a "business" he regarded as "an exceedingly dangerous amusement in the hands of such inexperienced novices."[50]

Regarding viewing the surface of the barrier, everything was flattened out, and Armitage's party on skis had actually learned much more about it. Nevertheless, the photo taken by Shackleton shows the surface was far from level at the horizon, and what Scott took for clouds through his binoculars looks convincingly like a very solid "hump" at the top right-hand corner of the picture, which faces SSW. They were, in fact, a good 70 miles west of the mainland heights, so it was little wonder they were flattened into a featureless whiteness to the east.

While Dailey and Duncan moved more than 200 cases to one of the engine room bunkers to make a workshop in the forecastle store forward of the galley, all the others had been sent to kill and skin seals, visible up to 3 miles away. They got about twenty-four carcasses aboard that afternoon, with some seals herded back and killed beside the ship.[51]

Steaming out at 7:30 P.M. that evening, they hoisted sail to save their coal, running westward in temperatures dropping to 5°F. The wind blew off the barrier, coating the rigging with hoarfrost, which made Scott fear they might already be too late to get into the harbor. As Mount Terror came into sight, the sails and ropes were stiff with ice, and a freezing fog developed that had the hands struggling to brace the yards around and steer away from hidden danger. Once into the lee of the mountain, however, the wind dropped and the fog cleared.

Under steam once more, they rounded Cape Bird and headed directly for the New Harbour inlet, as they later named it, only to be stopped by the pack 8 miles short of its entrance.[52] They could have reached it, but from that short distance it looked like less of a safe haven than when seen from far off, so with open water to the south, Scott decided to follow the ice edge, hoping for a yet more southerly harbor.

This time the sky cleared, and the whole scene became brilliantly clear. Beyond the inlet a huge range of mountains opened out before them, dominated by a 15,000-foot peak (later named Mount Lister) and running south to join up with the conical mountain (Mount Discovery) they had seen on January 21.

In 77°47S they came to fast ice, worn into fantastic shapes by water courses and covered with black volcanic sand from which vertical slabs of ice stood out and barred any route for a sledge. The dredge was put out, bringing up a rich haul for Hodgson. After landing to examine the strange icescape, they followed the ice edge eastward. By 8 P.M. it became apparent that there was nothing between what was soon to be called White Island and the southern arm of Mount Erebus.

McMurdo Bay had become McMurdo Strait, not, alas, with a navigable seaway to the south but with glistening ice sloping up eastward to the great highway to the south that Scott, Royds, and Wilson had seen from the hill near Cape Crozier. Two hours more brought them to a promontory jutting westward from the line of hills extending south from Erebus. Approaching the point slowly, the bow grounded gently a short way off the shore. The south side was blocked with ice, so after backing off, Scott decided to tie up to the ice in the bay on its northern side, promptly named Arrival Bay. Around the other side was "the most perfect little natural harbour imaginable," as Wilson described it.[53]

It was 11 P.M. on Feb.8 when they moored, and Ferrar set off immediately for the conical hill toward the southern end of the cape. Climbing to the top of what was soon to be known as Observation Hill, he saw for the first time positive proof that Mounts Erebus and Terror were on an island and were not joined to the mainland.[54]

Exploring the little peninsula the next morning, they found an even deeper bay in its south shore and realized that the shallow water off the point probably protected it from invasion by icebergs. The sea ice was cracking in all directions, with thousands of seals scattered over the surface. That was a promising sign that there would be no lack of these animals in the coming winter. Scott and Skelton walked 10 miles out the next day to round the southern cape that stood between the ship and the limitless barrier. It was flatter by far than its eastward end had appeared, and they could see all the way to the eastern end of Ross Island.

Even as they moved about that morning, Nordenskjöld's Swedish expedition aboard the *Antarctic* came in sight of Snow Hill Island. His party wintered there, in 64°22S, after abandoning its third attempt to find a safe haven further south on the western side of the Weddell Sea. Their ship had been repulsed by the ice in 66°10S and everywhere else Nordenskjöld had tried, as Markham had predicted. Drygalski, aboard the *Gauss*, was still southward bound at the 61st parallel, not even in sight of his goal.

As though to confirm the superiority of the bay on the south side, Scott's ship broke away from the ice in Arrival Bay, and they moved around to tie up to the sea ice south of the point. With frequent interruptions to keep the ship in one place, they began to unload and erect the main and magnetic huts.

It was February 17 when the sea ice finally vacated the bay and *Discovery* could at last tie up to the ice foot, about 10 feet high, with the bow to the east. Drygalski was still not in sight of land.

Four nights later Capt. Hans Ruser, on the bridge of the *Gauss*, blanketed by a blinding blizzard, struggled for four desperate hours to escape from encircling ice and was finally trapped as irrevocably as the Belgians had been. The Germans' were marooned 50 miles from the coast they had discovered the day before.

Halfway between them and the Swedish expedition's six-man shore party under Otto Nordenskjöld, 840 miles farther from the Pole on the opposite side of the world, Markham's strategy had placed Scott, with his forty-seven men, at the gateway to an apparently unobstructed highway to the south.

11

AN ICY APPRENTICESHIP
A Disastrous Start

Scott had the advantage of position and numbers. However, with an untrained force, Scott realized that during the remainder of the season, everyone needed to gain experience sledging. Armitage's experience sledging was inferior to Nansen's on the Greenland ice cap, but his 300-mile journey with Frederick Jackson around the two western islands of the Franz Josef Land group did arm the British expedition with northern experience equal to that of the Germans and Swedes.

Other than Armitage, no one had actually used any of the sledging equipment or, except for Weller, acquired any experience using dogs. Scott saw the initial tasks for that season as learning to use the dogs and giving everyone a chance to gain some experience sledging. The latter could be accomplished by two sledge journeys—one to deposit news of their whereabouts at the mail post west of Cape Crozier, the other to establish a first depot on the route to the south.

That was dependent on learning what lay beyond the islands directly south of them. Their summits would be far higher than the balloon could ascend. A journey to climb the highest could not await trials with the dogs, so Scott allowed Barne and Shackleton to toss a coin for the privilege of leading the three-man party that would have to take the "pram," a collapsible dinghy, in case the sea ice broke away and marooned them beyond the as yet unknown edge of the barrier. Shackleton won, and Wilson and Ferrar were assigned as his companions.

Before the other sledge journeys, however, the method of dog driving had to be settled. Some of the dogs had been moved to kennels onshore, to the relief of seamen assigned to keep the decks clean.[1] The dogs were being used to draw timbers up to the hut site on sledges with hand rails for the driver to hold on to at the back. That led to arguments between Armitage and Bernacchi about how to get the best out of the dogs.

The outcome of a competition was sadly revealing. At first, neither man could get his sledge started. Eventually, Bernacchi, who argued for the gentle touch rather than the whip, romped away, only to lose control and be left running behind as the sledge went up the ski slope. Despite his experience, Armitage, using coercion, never even got his dogs to trot. He was probably already predisposed in favor of ponies, at least for the barrier surface the southern party had in prospect, writing after the expedition that "Siberian ponies would do better than dogs, from what I have experienced with both animals in the North."[2]

The dogs were of the same type as those used by Nansen, but Scott realized for the first time that Wilton had chosen animals of three distinctly different pedigrees, hardly a good omen for inexperienced drivers, given their tribal nature.[3]

The three bound for the easternmost island, christened White Island, which appeared to have the nearest and highest summit, did not see much of the trials, as they were packing gear and practicing pitching their tent. On February 17, the first day Scott felt sure the ship would not be driven out to sea again, the hut construction was sufficiently advanced for him to release men for sledging preparations. Three men were assigned to pull Shackleton's sledge, topped with the pram, through the gap between Crater Hill and Observation Hill, ready for the start the next morning.

As though to confirm Scott's insistence on the pram, it suddenly began to blow hard from the north after dinner, and the stern hawser snapped, letting the ship swing away from the ice foot. The anchor held, as did the sides of the still roofless main hut, sheltered by the higher ground behind it. As the wind increased to gale force, men still working there were hastily brought off by boat. With the gale still blowing the next day, the White Island party's start was postponed until the 19th.

Perversely, after the three men had started for the island, a sharp wind sprang up from the south at lunchtime, and the ship was soon bumping against the ice in an alarming manner. Raising steam and moving the ship away, the men saw a mass of ice approaching from the south, threatening to crush the ship against the shore, but at the last

SHACKLETON'S FIRST SLEDGE. *The 11-foot sledge Shackleton, Wilson, and Ferrar used for the historic first journey to White Island. Three of the seamen pose in front of Observation Hill before pulling it through "the Gap" to the sea ice at its eastern end. As yet unsure about the behavior of the ice beyond the hill, Scott had insisted they take the pram in case the ice broke out and they were cut off. Shackleton's flag flies ahead of Ferrar's (amidships) and Wilson's, a custom dating from the Navy's Arctic exploits when they were found useful for identifying parties at a distance. They proved equally useful in the Antarctic with its frequent wind-driven shoulder-high drift. Courtesy, Canterbury Museum, Christchurch, New Zealand.*

moment it veered away. The ship would clearly not be secure until it was frozen in, and in the meantime it had better be kept offshore. The situation hardly boded well for the small party on the other side of the cape.

Shackleton and his sledgemates had started in fine weather, dragging their heavy load and imagining their objective to be 10 miles distant at most. Stopping for 20 minutes for lunch at 2 P.M., the three were engulfed in a drift as the gale swept over them, happily without carrying away the ice. Totally unaware that the distance was twice what they had estimated, they struggled on for nine hours against the stinging drift. Wilson afterward described their experience:[4]

> At 11:30 P.M. the wind was worse than ever and we were all simply done, so we decided to camp at once and wait until the wind dropped. Up to this time Shackle's face had suffered most from the cold. His cheek was

constantly going dead white in one place, and Ferrar's nose went too. My face wasn't troubled, but the moment we halted and started to unpack, though we were all doing things as energetically as they could be done, the cold and the snow drift and the wind were so bad that we all began frostbites. Shackle's ears went as well as his face and the whole of the back of one hand. Ferrar's nose went and then he was safe with the cooking stove as soon as we had got the tent up, an awful business in such weather, as it flapped about in our hands like a handkerchief.

However we dug out our trench and shoved the poles into the flapping business, and then while one of us sat on the edge, the other put blocks of ice on it. Shackle and I managed this. We then stayed the tent by rope to the sledge and boat, unpacked our food bag, and all our furs and floor cloth and bundled them all into our little tent. It was a crowded place! Then we had time to look at our frostbites. Shackle's ear was badly blistered and his hand was still all white. We rubbed it until it had got painful and then it blistered and was very sore the next few days. My fingers were all white on the backs and tips, but soon came round and didn't blister, but my big toe was gone again and was now like a little balloon of blister.

We got our foot gear off. The ski boots were frozen to the socks, so that both came off in one and it took us all we knew the next morning to tear the socks out. The sweat of one's feet had lined the boots with ice. We got into our long fur boots and our feet began to get comfortable. Then we got our supper cooked, hot cocoa and pemmican and biscuit and jam and butter, and then we began to get our furs on, an awful job in a small tent, but it was too bad to go outside, as our furs would have been filled with drift in no time. The other two were bricks to me now. They dressed me first, as I was constantly getting cramp in the thighs whenever I moved, and having dressed me, they put me on the floor and sat on me while they dressed each other. At last we were all in our wolfskins . . . and settled off to sleep huddled together to keep warm. We lay on our Jaeger blouses, but the cold of the ice floor crept through and the points of contact got pretty chilly. We put Ferrar in the middle and though that was the warmest place, he was coldest during the night. I think he was most done up. Shackle and I both slept fairly well, until at 1:30 the wind dropped and though of course it was midnight, it was a beautiful still clear bright morning with a wonderful pink glow all over Erebus and Terror. And there lay our blessed island still a long way off, so we slumbered again until 3:30 A.M. and then turned out, packed our camp and started trudging again towards the island.

Not realizing they had crossed from sea ice to barrier ice, they dragged the boat on the sledge until they pitched camp at 7:30 A.M., 2 miles short of the island, and they slept the sleep of exhaustion until 4 P.M. After a meal and a round of compass angles by Shackleton, they roped up and got ashore to reach the summit of the highest crater (now called Mount Heine) at midnight. Bitterly cold, they found the tea half frozen in the water bottles they carried inside their tunics but were saved from a thirsty descent by some fruit syrup that hadn't frozen.

On their way up to the icily cold 2,300-foot vantage point, where Wilson began to sketch, the view that had first met their eyes beyond the shoulder of "Island II," as he dubbed it (later named Black Island), would change the course of the expedition. Away to the southwest were new mountains, seemingly ending in the same limitless barrier that stretched away to the horizon in that direction. And from this highest point they could see the barrier was unbroken to the south beyond what was clearly only a mountainous finger of land stretching southeast from Mount Discovery—a highway to the Pole with, as Wilson saw it, "no Antarctic continent at all."[5]

For all the cold and unfavorable light, Wilson's sketch was wonderfully clear. The sun had just set due south of them (it had first dipped below the horizon only two nights before) and, aided by a splendid memory, Wilson combined what they could see with the by then invisible view beyond the second island.

Ferrar estimated the "new mountain range" to be about 120 miles (140 statute miles) distant.[6]* Most of the intervening coastline was hidden behind Black Island, and at that early stage, with nothing properly positioned on a chart, Wilson's disorientation was betrayed by his diary entry that evening in which he described the sun as setting beyond the western ranges, in contradiction to his own sketch. The idea that the coast they could see extended westward rather than southward created an impression, just eighteen days after Scott had first announced his broad plan, that would add a new dimension to that plan and tax to the limit the manpower he could deploy.

They were back at their tents for hot bacon and cocoa at 2:30 A.M. and slept until midday. A 2½-hour walk then took them to the gap between White and Black Islands that afternoon. From that vantage point there seemed no reason for not taking the shortest route to the

---

* The latest American maps show that at midnight the northeast face of Mount Keltie, the highest mountain in the Conway Range, would have been in deep shadow and thus have presented just such a dark cone-shaped silhouette as depicted in Wilson's sketch. The faint island south of the mountain must therefore have been the Mount Chalmers–Mount Willis ridge in 79°22S, which is just about as distant as Ferrar estimated.

THE VIEW THAT RESHAPED THE EXPEDITION. Edward Wilson's sketch, dated February 20, 1902, the day the three members of Ernest Shackleton's sledge party to White Island were the first to see what lay beyond the skyline visible from Observation Hill near the ship. Ostensibly the view from Mount Heine at the northern end of the island, it was in reality a combination of the view south from there with that to the southwest from the southern slopes of Mount Hayward (Crater II). The prominent peak in the "New Mountain Range" can have been none other than Mount Keltie. Modern maps show its northeastern face, in shadow when Wilson sketched around midnight, would have presented just such a dark conical profile. The faint "island" south of it must therefore have been the Mount Chalmers–Mount Willis ridge, about 120 geographical miles away in 79°22S. Courtesy, the Scott Polar Research Institute.

end of the Bluff when it came to sledging south. Camping there for an uneasy night, with the southeast wind threatening to blow their tent away, a nine-hour march with one stop for lunch brought them to water a few miles from their starting point.

The boat proved too small to carry the sledge, so they had to drag it around the ice edge to the point on the north side of the gap, where they dumped everything except their personal kit. From there, in half an hour the trio was back at the ship, at 10:30 P.M., where they enjoyed the luxury of a hot bath.

With the road to the south now clear, their short journey had made equally certain to Scott that the point of the Bluff (later Minna Bluff) would be a convenient place for a first depot. It was a ready-made goal for a second training journey. While Scott led the first party to leave news of their whereabouts at the Cape Crozier letterbox, a second could usefully take some provisions to the Bluff.

The day the three men returned, the roof had been completed on the main hut. Like the walls and floor, the roof was double, with felt interlining, and needed Duncan and four seamen to fix it by sections. As in Peary's Anniversary Lodge, the idea was that the "veranda" would be walled in with provision cases and snow banked around them. On February 23 Duncan's team began putting in the thirteen posts to support the overhanging edges of the roof, and more men worked at landing eight months' stores for use if the ice broke and the ship was forced to put to sea.

By that time, Armitage and Bernacchi were helping Duncan put up the larger magnetic hut, 75 yards further up the slope. The hut was 11 feet 6 inches square, and it was ready by the 27th, with accurately plumbed brick piers supporting an oak bench for the Eschenhagen magnetographs and their lamps. There were four instruments, three for each of the "elements" (vertical, horizontal, and total intensity) of magnetic force and one to record the temperature. Each moved a mirror to project a pencil beam onto the clockwork-driven photographic paper roll and so provided a continuous record of the variation of each of the values.

Also installed was the seismograph, designed by the famous physicist Professor Milne, whom Bernacchi had visited briefly at his home on the Isle of Wight. It was an incredibly delicately balanced 6-foot-long horizontal pendulum supported on *Discovery's* most bizarre piece of cargo, an 18-inch glazed drainpipe 3 feet long, set into the frozen soil so that it extended 19½ inches above floor level. A kerosene lamp projected light through a hole in the tip of the arm, downward onto its own clockwork photographic paper roll. There was also an electrometer for measuring electricity in the atmosphere. This was particularly for use during the appearance of auroras, which began their fantastic displays as soon as darker nights set in.

The magnetographs only recorded the variation of the forces, not the absolute values, so instruments to measure those were installed in the smaller hut, 25 yards further up the slope. Its front and back had to be aligned to face exactly east and west, and the sides and roof had observatory-like apertures with sliding doors for the transit telescope to rate the chronometers, because the most exact record possible of the time of observations was required.

Bernacchi succeeded in making his first records with the magnetographs on the March 1 "term day." On the term days he and all cooperating observatories, along with magneticians Bidlingmaier and Bodman on the German and Swedish expeditions, would also make simultaneous observations of the absolute measurements according to Greenwich Mean Time. They had to repeat them on the first and fifteenth days of succeeding months. With the second hut not complete until March 18, the first absolute measurements had to be made in the magnetic laboratory aboard ship.

All these delicate measurements relied on an even temperature, and many gallons of kerosene would be used in the attempt to keep it so when there was no snow to bank around the hut's walls. On April 12 Wilson noted that the snow that fell never amounted to much. At Hut Point, in contrast to the other expeditions using similar huts, there was only old crystalline snow swept along when the wind blew, but as yet none that accumulated.

The ski slope had become so icy by February 26 that most of the men had stopped using it. When Scott went out the next day for a run, an exposed ridge, or "sastrugi," caught one of his skis and twisted his knee so badly that his leg had to be put in a splint.

With Armitage required at base to assist with the observations for aligning the instruments in the huts and fixing the accuracy of the clocks by the stars, Royds's appointment to lead the Crozier Party was inevitable. Skelton, Barne, and Koettlitz with eight men and eight dogs would make up the party, and preparations were already in full swing. Koettlitz lectured the men on avoiding frostbite, as Scott resigned himself to inaction.[7]

By March 3 the four sledges were packed, and the next day, with eight other men helping, Royds's party had to get them up and over the stony 800-foot plateau flanking the north of the gap and down to the ice, which by now was broken back north of the point where the pram had been left on the return from White Island. More dogs were harnessed for the drag up the slope, but over the bare ground at the top the sledges had to be carried. The whole process took five hours but, eager to press on, they hitched the sledges in pairs, an 11-foot one towing a 7-foot sledge pulled by four dogs and six men, helped at first by an extra man until they were well beyond the 10- to 15-foot high pressure ridges close to the shore.

Despite nearly 32° of frost and their internal clocks still attuned to northern seasons so that they had been molting since February 20, the dogs pulled well, barring "some fights and a little trouble with the seals,"[8] but the force 3 wind from the east left Barne's ear frostbitten by the time they stopped for tea at 6 P.M. Camping at 8:15 that evening, Royds reckoned they had done 11 miles, for there were no sledgemeters to measure distances covered. Everyone was suffering from cramps, and they had gotten into drifted snow.

Royds, Koettlitz, and Wild were in the first tent, with Quartley, Vince, and Weller in the second, the men sleeping in their reindeer suits (the officers wore wolfskin) because the three-man sleeping bags had proved too small.[9] Cooking was a slow business for Barne's team, for the tent cooker was broken. His tentmates were Skelton and the young Clarence Hare. The fourth tent held PO Edgar Evans, stoker Frank Plumley, and AB William Heald. By that time Barne's team had five dogs, for "Maggie" had refused to turn back after the pull over the hill. Royds's team had four.

In the morning everyone was very stiff—the tent temperature had been 5°F in the night. It was a splendid, calm, sunny morning, but they now faced the problem of pulling the sledges through snow a foot deep. Although soft, it was of the gritty character so prevalent in the Antarctic, so that by the afternoon the dogs were licking their sore feet every time the sledge halted. The first evening they had refused to eat anything, so it was little surprise that with the terrible drag of the snow, the dogs as well as the men were exhausted by 5:45 P.M. after only 6 miles, as Royds estimated it. Some of the dogs had bleeding feet, but they ate their daily ration of two dog biscuits and half a dried fish.[10] Royds noticed that they preferred the fish that evening.

As temperatures fell to -22°F, small frostbites appeared, not least because the men had worn their ski boots throughout except for Quartley, who had changed into finesko when his feet got too cold. On Thursday the 6th, the snow became deeper still, and the best they could manage was 4 miles in six hours of going. Despite the dogs' efforts, about which they had no complaint, everyone was exhausted. Weller collapsed across the sledge when they stopped, breaking the sling thermometer.

On Friday the going grew even worse, with their legs sinking 18 inches into snow. They had entered an area of calms from which the snow was evidently never evicted by gales. By noon they were so far down in a hollow that they could see no land, not even the summit of Mount Erebus. Royds had been making for land, and they were crossing a series of ridges running parallel to the south coast of the island. By 5:30 P.M. they were 2 miles from the cliffs on the coast but so exhausted that Royds called it a day and camped. He didn't even record the distance for the day, spent dragging their loads up and down with rests every twenty minutes. Exhausted as they were, their sleep was disturbed during the night by avalanches falling over the cliffs with a thunderous roar.

Writing to Scott that evening, Royds described their position as located at the foot of hill between Mounts Erebus and Terror. That would have placed them about 20 miles as the crow flies from their start point, with 30 miles to go to Cape Crozier and then having to find their way to the rookery where the mail post stood. They had three weeks' rations, and at the present rate eleven of the twenty-one days would be gone before they reached the cape, more if the weather did not hold.

The only option was for Barne to take the men and dogs back with three sledges while Royds, Skelton, and Koettlitz went ahead on skis with one small sledge. Writing an order to Barne, Royds unfortunately ended it with the instruction: "You are to use your own discretion about the route, remembering that the way by the nunatak is not known, whilst you know that should the ice be still fast, you are certain of making the land by the way we came."[11] The nunatak he referred to was Castle Rock, the most prominent feature about 4 miles along the ridge running north from the bay where the ship was anchored.

After a day's rest, on March 9 the two parties started off in opposite directions. From the angles Barne recorded that evening, he reckoned his party had retreated about 8 miles, finding the snow deeper as they got nearer to the land. Their experience that day led to the birth of multisledge trains, for they found the three sledges, one behind the other and pulled by all the men and dogs, were easier to pull than two sledges had been with six men and six dogs.

But the cost was evident, for the next morning Vince was coughing up blood and complaining of breathlessness. Despite this, Barne led the party on for 7½ hours, not counting lunch and tea breaks. The group covered about 11 miles and arrived at the small bay under Castle Rock on the evening of the 10th. Twenty minutes before they camped, Wild convulsed with cramps and had to be carried on one of the sledges.

Trouble had begun even earlier when they found the one pricker they had for the two primus cookers was broken. They couldn't even have a cup of tea or any hot food until they reached the ship, which, however, scarcely looked like a serious matter at this stage, with no sign of the weather breaking.

The slope looked gentle to the top of the peninsula, with its table-like plateau to the ski slope above the ship. In fact, it was far gentler than the climb from their starting point (it became a recognized route to the barrier on Scott's second expedition), and that persuaded Barne to opt for the Castle Rock route after he had taken Evans and Heald over and found there was no tide crack to stop them from getting onto the land.

After a night when the temperature dropped to −31°F, someone got the second cooker going enough to melt snow for a cup of water but not enough to make tea or to cook anything.[12] Barne ordered them all to put on ski boots, which everyone did except for Hare and Vince whose boots were frozen so hard they could not get them on. Evans managed to put his on only by leaving off his second pair of stockings. Shortly before 10 A.M. they started up the gently terraced slope and reached the top about half a mile south of the rock. At that point the weather, so miraculously fine for the past seven days, broke with a southeast wind, soon engulfing the whole ridge in flying drift.

Barne just had time to take the bearing of Crater Hill and to notice some rock protruding above the drift somewhat to their right before everything was blotted out. It took at least half an hour's blind traveling before they reached shelter, if it could be called that, as the tents were in ever-increasing danger of being blown away while they ate a cold lunch. Totally unaccustomed to mountaineering and thinking they were close to the ship, Barne felt the safest thing would be to leave the equipment and slog on foot to the ship without the hindrance of any load, taking the dogs with them.

It was 2:15 P.M. when they started to take down the tents and at least quarter of an hour more before they were ready to go. Within "a few yards," as Hare put it, they found themselves "on a steep icy slope" and, despite being supported between Heald and Weller, he slipped from their grasp and vanished down the slope.[13] Still not understanding that the slope was on the seaward side of the crest, Barne told the party to spread out across their line of advance to increase Hare's chances of finding them when he caught up.

This maneuver placed even more of the party on the slope, and in a moment Evans had slipped and slid out of sight. Barne sat down and slid after him, thinking to help him back up the slope. Seconds later he found himself accelerating down an ever-steepening gradient until he was miraculously stopped by a snowbank. To his great relief Evans appeared, and a few seconds later Quartley slid into the bank in a whirl of drift. They found themselves unable to climb back up the slope, and like Hare, who was fruitlessly blowing his whistle in the shrieking fog of snow not very far from them, Barne decided to try to get back to the sledges. Meanwhile, the five men at the top of the slope shouted in vain every time the wind momentarily decreased. The temperature was about −18°F.

When no one appeared after a long while, Wild, the leading spirit of the party, as Scott put it, persuaded the uneasy group to head for the ship. With Vince between him and Plumley and still totally unaware of the cliffs at the bottom of the slope, he led the party off in the supposed direction of the ship.

Before long, as Plumley related, "all five of us slipped and went sliding down to the edge of the precipice bringing up on some soft snow. Poor Vince having fur boots on was not able to stop himself and went over into the sea directly under us . . . we were within a few feet of the edge."[14]

Scott must have had great difficulty piecing together what had happened, for whereas Armitage,[15] Wilson, and Ferrar all repeat Plumley's story, Wild's version was reported three different ways. Quartley, in his account to Skelton, added further variations from Hare's and Plumley's stories, relating that the whole party was walking down a slope when Hare slipped and implying that they had camped no great distance from Castle Rock.[16]

Scott relates that Wild told him the party was descending diagonally when they came suddenly to the cliff edge and Wild shouted to them to stop.[17] All succeeded except for Vince and a dog.

Duncan, who must also have heard the story directly from Wild, left yet another account: "proceeding further along the slope . . . they proposed to slide down . . . after going some way they began to lose control . . . all of a sudden Wild shouted for them to hold on he seeing clear water ahead it was with great difficulty and by straining every nerve they got stopped. Vints being unable to [stop] went further on and suddenly disappeared."[18] Royds relates that only Vince slipped, dragging Wild with him to within barely a foot of the edge.[19]

Of the survivors, Wild alone had some nails in his boot soles, and it was only the sheath knives that enabled them to struggle, foothold by foothold, up the terrifying climb to safety. Plumley described the climb as a fearful struggle, with the men digging their knives into the ice. (Duncan speaks of them crawling on hands and knees.) Reaching the top, Wild kept the party to stony ground and, finding a familiar rock near the ski slope, the four exhausted men groped their way down, clambering over the ship's rail at 8:15 P.M., over five hours after their ordeal began.

Met by Shackleton, Wild asked if any of the others had returned, and on being told they had not he replied, "then they are all gone." That news struck everyone like a thunderbolt, for Wild was too exhausted to add that the party had separated, and it was at first taken that of all those who had set off with Royds, only these four had survived.[20]

Soon thereafter, Barne and his two companions heard the ship's siren as they regained the crest of the ridge. Unable to ascend directly, they had found the cliff edge 5 yards below their snowbank and realized for the first time they were on the west side of the peninsula. Following the cliff edge northward, they had seen the sea where the cliff was at its lowest and shortly afterward had been able to climb up to the ridge.

THE WESTERN SHORE OF HUT POINT PENINSULA–SCENE OF THE TRAGEDY ON MARCH 11, 1902. The picture shows the shore from Castle Rock to the second crater and the suddenly steepening slope Barne's party faced as they negotiated the northwest shoulder of the crater. Beyond it can be seen the summit of the third crater, in the lee of which they had pitched the lunch camp. Panorama taken by Chris Rudge when information officer of the New Zealand DSIR Antarctic Division, now Antarctica New Zealand. (*Right*) "DANGER SLOPE," picture of the second crater and scene of the accident taken from the *Discovery* 2 miles offshore on March 13, 1902, published in Captain Scott's *The Voyage of the Discovery*. The line of the ice cliffs, much higher in Scott's day, corresponded with that of the lower outcrops visible in the panorama. In both pictures X marks the probable site of Vince's fatal accident. The dotted lines on the 1902 picture represented Scott's understanding of (*left*) the point to which Evans, Barne, and Quartley slid, which cannot have been many yards from where the same snow bank saved Hare, and (*right*) the route Wild claimed he had led his party, with an asterisk marking Scott's understanding of the scene of the accident. Clearly the version of events related in Scott's book stemmed entirely from Wild's account. However, one of the party (Frank Plumley) recorded that they had all slipped soon after starting again when the others had not reappeared. It is clear that their slide was stopped by the same snowbank that saved the others.

Hare could not stand on the slope because of the wind, but he managed to crawl up to the ridge where, like the others, he began to search for the sledges. Blown off the top of a hill, he found three of the dogs curled up in the snow and set off with one of them. He was the only survivor who knew nothing of the sea at the bottom of the slope he had climbed, and blundering onto it once more, he again lost his footing.

At some point in his slide he must have passed out, for he remembered nothing more until he awoke half covered with snow, the dog emerging from a nearby drift. Hare could see that they were halfway down the slope ending in a cliff above the sea. He didn't realize that it was Thursday, March 13.[21]

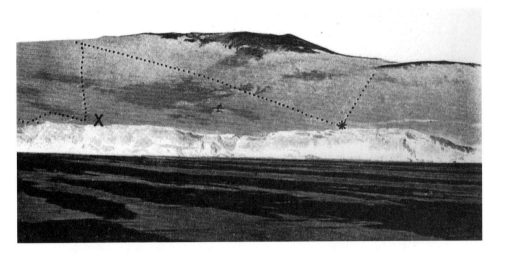

On the Tuesday evening when Wild's party had come aboard, Scott, with his leg still in a splint, could only wait while Armitage, with Wilson, Ferrar, Wild, and twelve other men, set off to search for the missing men. Shackleton made a dangerous boat journey to search the base of the cliffs in case Vince or any of the four others had fallen onto sea ice at the foot of the cliffs.

The search party was some way along the ridge, checking the lee side of every rock protrusion, when Barne's trio loomed out of the drift. According to Wilson they could barely speak intelligibly, and one was talking outright gibberish. Ferrar, who was more familiar with the lay of the land than anyone, set off to take them back to the ship, arriving after midnight. It was 2 A.M. before the main party returned. They had found the sledges and four dogs at the north end of the fourth rocky outcrop along the ridge, but it was far too dangerous to search the slope for Hare.

After some sleep, Wilson led a second party in colder but slightly better conditions. Anyone not on the move in ski boots would soon have frostbitten feet, so sending Ferrar, Hodgson, Feather, and four other men back with the sledges, Wilson, with Bernacchi and Cross roped up and wearing crampons, began to search the dangerous slope. The drift had been only knee-high on the summit plateau, but as soon as they were a few yards down it rose to shoulder-level and threatened to blank everything out, so Wilson called off the search. The three men returned to a somber evening aboard the ship, everyone feeling sure that Clarence Hare had lost his life.

In the morning it was still blowing hard when Ferrar went on deck at 10:15 A.M. to find three men looking at a man coming down the hillside. Like Scott, who was heard to say "thank God one of my boys has returned," Wilson felt as though Hare had come back from the dead. And indeed it was Hare and, as the men who ran to greet him found, without a trace of frostbite! Barne, who had lost his gloves in his fall, was in imminent danger of losing many of his fingers. Evans was in the sick bay with his ear half the size of a cricket ball. Wilson could scarcely believe Hare had not been injured during his ordeal. He insisted on defrosting Hare for seven hours in the magnetic laboratory where there was a settee,[22] raising the temperature gradually from −16°F to +34°F before moving him to join Evans, where he made a complete and rapid recovery.

Apart from the loss of some fingernails, Barne's hands had recovered enough after twelve days to allow him to write his report to Scott, concluding by "taking the full responsibility for this sad occurrence, for which I am entirely to blame."[23]

Scott did not criticize Barne in his book and in his official report went out of his way to quote extenuating circumstances in excusing Barne and to praise his subsequent sledging leadership. Mentioning only that "he imagined himself much closer to the ship than he was," Scott suppressed a passage in Barne's report that reveals his failure to grasp the relation of the summit craters and peaks to the safe plateau and the dangerous seaward slopes.[24] The plateau could be seen clearly from the sledge route, and previously, as the ship had first approached Hut Point, he must have been able to see the dangerous seaward slopes.

Hare gave a clue as to where some of them thought they were when he wrote in his diary on the 15th, describing how "Mr. Barne was leading steering by compass and shortly we reached the foot of a hill which was taken to be Crater Hill."[25] As they had sledged for barely forty minutes from Castle Rock, the 3-mile trip to Crater Hill was scarcely in question in those conditions.

Piecing the diary descriptions together against the view southward from Castle Rock, it is clear they had come to the hill immediately north of the second crater.[26] The suppressed passage in his report shows that Barne was under the impression that the next hill lay "between ourselves and the top of the ski-run" and had determined to "go round this hill, leaving it on our left,"[27] a decision that becomes intelligible only in the light of the map he drew after he had recovered. He used

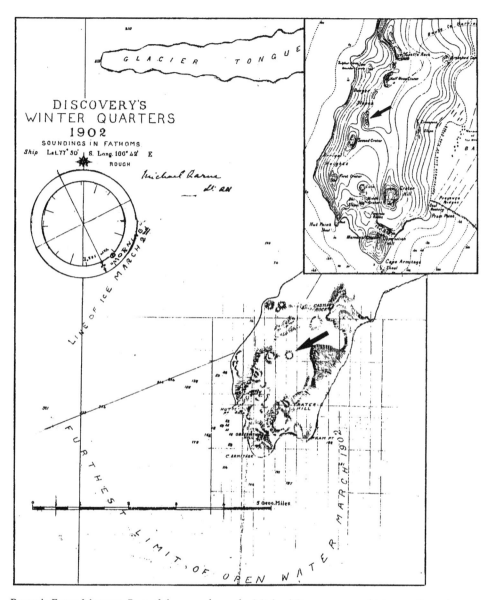

BARNE'S FATAL MISTAKE. *Part of the map drawn by Michael Barne to record his soundings during the winter of 1902–1903. The arrow added here highlights the position he thought the third crater occupied, thus believing it was safe to pass on its west side. Inset: Part of a 1913 map by Frank Debenham showing the true position of the crater (arrowed). Courtesy, the Royal Geographical Society.*

that map to record his soundings through the sea ice that winter. It shows that he thought the hill was in the middle of the safe plateau! The men's impression that they were sheltering behind Crater Hill also accounts for Wild's readiness to move toward the fatal slope on the right side of the hill.

The picture taken from Castle Rock (see p. 163) clearly shows the much steeper slope that faced anyone starting to pass around the seaward flank of the second crater. It also reveals the rocky outcrop that saved the lives of all except George Vince.

The picture in Scott's book, taken two days after the tragedy,[28] shows that in 1902 the fatal cliff began at the outcrop and was thus far higher than the present ice cliff. The ice cover of the slopes has obviously thinned to reveal the outcrop.

But the two pictures also show that when *Discovery* first approached Arrival Bay 2 miles further south, no one could have seen the hill immediately north of the crater, and Barne would have formed his mistaken impression of its position from the view from Crater Hill and on the outward stages of the fatal journey. On such impressions had hung the life of the Antarctic's first victim in the new century.

After Hare's return, the ship was taken to search the coast in the faint hope that Vince might have landed in soft snow on fast ice. No such ice was found, and the one consolation to all that night, for he was missed as the ever-cheerful soul of the party right up to the moment of his death, was that oblivion must have engulfed him within a few seconds in those icy waters.

If an air of sadness hung in the messes, the atmosphere was brightened below deck by the electric light that had been switched on four days after the Crozier Party started. It did not dispel the anxiety for the three men still out, though.[29] The day of the fatal accident, they had made their first attempt to cut across the eastern slopes of Mount Terror to the penguin rookery and, foiled by crevasses, got the sledge down to the barrier again and moved on nearer the cape. That evening they got within 3 miles of it, but the snow built up to 6 inches thick on their skis as the fringe of the fatal blizzard nearly prevented them from finding their camp again.[30]

They tried twice more over the next two days, getting beyond the cape but failing to find the rookery. It was too cold to wear ski boots, and Skelton's fineskos were almost worn out. Food was running short, and Royds, content that a practical route had been found, abandoned further attempts to find the rookery. It took them five days to get back. Shackleton was sent out with a party to meet them. He was evidently very cautious in the wake of the drama, for Ferrar complained in his diary about being "annoyed at the supervision I received from Shackleton."[31]

As they came around the north side of Crater Hill, leaving the sledges near Pram Point, the ship was anchored 130 yards from the shore, where the dogs were chained up outside their kennels. That had come about because when the eight surviving dogs had all returned they were regarded as strangers, and two were set upon and killed by their mates. With the loss of the one that had followed Vince over the cliff, the expedition's vital traction power was down to twenty dogs before a single depot was laid for the great Southern journey.

Even if the dogs' efforts had been futile in the deep snow south of the volcanoes, the White Island journey had shown that they would likely do well out on the barrier, where the surface was hardened by the wind. On the Crozier journey the dogs had pulled well, even though the men had helped, just as they had when Armitage had made his 300-mile sledge journey with Frederick Jackson around the main western islands of Franz Josef Land in 1897.

That was the only journey Armitage had made with dogs, and the two men had started out with twelve and the remaining Siberian pony. Although fed bear meat, seven of the dogs had died. His two other much shorter journeys had been made with ponies, drawing sledges in trains hitched behind each other. Scott adopted this practice as he set off with the dogs for the Bluff at the end of the month, aiming to give as many others as possible a chance to experience at first hand the problems they would face when the serious sledging began in the spring.

Scott had waited nine days to be sure the ice would not break out again before he could remove so many men from the crew. When Royds's party returned on the 19th, they had been collected in a whaler. Only by March 24 was the ice thick enough for anyone to walk to the shore. The delay gave time for Royds's suggestions to be implemented. Boxes were made for the cookers, kerosene tins, instruments, and lamps—in fact, for anything that might break. The cloth was reinforced at the tents' apexes.

Royds's party had used sledges with wooden runners, and they had not run well in the tracks pressed down by the leading sledge. So Duncan was put onto covering the runners with German Silver (nickel-plated steel), also setting out to cover twenty-three pairs of skis as well in an effort to stop them from clogging with snow.[32] The question of load arrangement on the sledges needed rethinking, especially with the large quantity of stores to be hauled to the point of the Bluff that had been seen by the White Island Party.

By the time the eight sledges were ready on Good Friday, March 28, it was very late in the season. Even so Scott, only mobile again shortly before Royds's return, had gone through the gap the day before to be sure the ice was firm enough at Pram Point. He found it was, but to reach it there was an 11-foot drop to its surface, preferable, however, to lugging the loads over the shoulder of Crater Hill.

The sledges were taken through the next day, and a ramp was cut to get them down to the sea ice. The start was postponed until the following Monday, when the two sledge trains were finally pulled away from the ice foot at noon. The snow-free surface soon revealed itself to be anything but slippery. The smooth ice was sprinkled with "flowers" of salt extruded from the ice as it froze and so increased the friction for the sledge runners and discomfort for the dogs' feet.

Armitage had been put in charge of organization, and, according to him, Scott had insisted that the stores be left in their packing cases.[33] That was a fairly understandable safety precaution, as they were to remain in the open 50 miles to the south through a winter of which no one had any experience in those latitudes.

Curiously, in the light of Royds's experience and his own with Jackson, Armitage was against having men pull with the dogs.[34] Scott had to admit in the end that he was right, but Jackson's words were oddly at variance with Armitage's claim that the dogs didn't pull as well: "There is a popular picture of dog-driving of a man seated on a sledge twirling a long whip around his head and careering gayly along at a rate of ten or twelve miles per hour behind a team of dogs. This unfortunately is anything but a true one. We never think of riding upon a sledge, but are more than contented if it can be kept in motion at a slow walk by the united effort of the animals and ourselves."[35]

The four-sledge trains, each pulled by nine dogs, were led by Scott and Armitage, Wilson traveling with Scott and Ferrar with Armitage. Feather and Dellbridge headed up the three petty officers, Allan, Macfarlane, and Smythe, with Williamson, Walker, and Blissett, to make up six men to each train.[36] Including the depot supplies, each train weighed about a ton.

The weather was very different from what Royds had experienced, his party having suffered just one night of extreme cold when the thermometer bottomed out at −44°F. Royds had faced into a force 4 wind for just four hours; now there was a cutting wind in their faces from the start, with the temperature down to −36°F and lower. The dogs, in the early stages of molting on the Crozier journey, were a sorry sight, with the remaining hair coming out in handfuls and the new coats scarcely grown.

During the first night nobody got much sleep, because the dogs were howling all night on account of the cold.[37] Some of the dogs refused to pull, and others, Scott reckoned, were not exerting more than a 50-pound pull, so the twelve men ended up dragging more than 300 lbs each. Besides feeling the cold, many of the dogs suffered from sore feet.[38] The resulting speed was excruciatingly slow, and it took nearly six hours to reach the edge of barrier ice just after sunset, a distance of as many miles. There they were able to find snow to melt for cooking, and the temperature fell to -42°F as they got into their "furs."

Instead of the wolfskin fur suits Royds and his two companions had slept in, the officers were trying out reindeer skin outfits comprising a jacket with hood that fastened to half a sleeping bag instead of trousers for their legs. The outfits had worked well when they had practiced getting into them, but here in howling winds amid hard-frozen snow it was like taking part in a potato sack race on a skating rink, with the added hazard that once a man had fallen, the skins were so hard that it was difficult to get up again. In the tent they were also infinitely clumsy to get into.*

The officers' usual wolfskin furs had been manageable at the February temperatures encountered on the way to White Island. Now they found the reindeer outfits "simply awful . . . once in one can do nothing but lie as one falls," as Wilson wrote.[39] No wonder Scott's irritation with "our ill-made fur clothing" surfaced in his account,[40] for these suits were what Nansen had advised, and they had been made in Norway. But at least the men kept warm, although they were damp from condensed perspiration. On this trip the men were trying out the three-man sleeping bags, and they complained bitterly of the cold.[41] "Tried to sleep without success," wrote Duncan later, recording -47°F.

The next day the wind had diminished, and the temperature was quite warm, at 8°F to start with but down to -42°F again when they camped after making only 3½ miles. Unable to move in the violent wind the next morning, they advanced another 2 miles after lunch, with the temperature always -40°F or lower.

Both Armitage and Scott saw that it was impossible to go on, and after a miserable night they dumped four sledges with 2,000 pounds

---

* Their design, attributed to unnamed experts by Huntford (1985 #2: p. 68), had, of course, originated in Norway.

of stores and faced north for home. The dogs raced back, needing no help from the men, and they reached the ship by 6 P.M., traveling by sea ice all the way, to find the temperature there had never dropped below -12°F.

Wilson thought it had been so severe a test that if they had gone on the men "might easily have lost a foot or two,"[42] for they had needed much supervision to avoid injury as it was. Beyond question it was an unfair test of the dogs, exposed to those temperatures in their advanced stage of molting.

At least the food had provoked no complaints. Duncan described the first evening's supper of the Copenhagen Beauvais Company's pemmican and a rasher of bacon, with wholemeal biscuits and cocoa, as very enjoyable. Breakfast consisted of pemmican, biscuits, and tea, and for lunch they had the sweeter American pemmican with bacon, biscuits, and cocoa. The Danish pemmican was 50 percent lard, 30 percent beef, and 20 percent water.[43]

After their return it was too late to organize a training run for Kennar and the other six seamen or for those in the engine room, who had been dismantling the engines after Skelton's return. If the price of experience had been bitter, at least they had learned in the actual conditions they would face—better in the end than if the expedition had been delayed a year to allow everyone to practice in Norway or Switzerland. Even if a year's delay could have been afforded, that had been ruled out by the agreement on synchronized magnetic observations.

Just about everything except the cookers and sledges would have to be modified. But at least they had the ship, with ample men and ample resources, which would hardly have been the case with a landing party stuck in the 37-foot-square hut. It was time to organize for winter.

12

INTO A DARKENED WORLD
First Winter at Hut Point

No one had wintered that far south before, and if the temperature had plummeted to -40°F in March, what might it reach in mid-winter? As they were to discover, though, condensation would be the greater problem.

Scott's first concern, however, was for fresh meat. His men were not going to suffer the "polar anemia" that had overcome De Gerlache's men on the Belgian expedition. In late February they had begun killing seals at the barrier edge, at first losing some to skuas when they did not immediately drag them to the ship. Now in April parties were out building up the larder whenever weather permitted. Six were killed on the 5th, and Hare recorded several teams out on the 13th, with seal meat on the menu twice a week. Lashly wrote of "seal every other day."[1]

A seal provided two meals for the entire complement, so counting three meals a week from March to August, thirty-nine seals would see them through. After the Lady Newnes Bay cull they had a stock of around sixty, with probably fifty left at the beginning of March when six weeks remained before the sea froze and the seals disappeared. As things turned out, Wilson was able to find seals as late as the end of May, so there was no problem keeping up the ration. With the mutton on Sundays, four meals of fresh meat a week seemed a satisfactory diet.

As April wore on, the impact of the winter climate was surprisingly less than expected in the brightly lit living quarters aboard the motionless ship. Cold meals on some days were tolerable, giving the cooks a respite. As in the wardroom, a single stove was found adequate in the crew's quarters. Whether that was really the case or was partly by choice because the French-designed army stoves smoked is unclear. Duncan described the stoves as heartbreaking after sweeping the flues on June 7. The stoves would not draw whenever there was any southing in the wind, which occurred on more than half of the days in winter. Royds attributed the trouble to the elbows in the flues.[2]

In the wardroom cabins the temperature could be kept up to 60°F, but at floor level it was a different matter. The mess deck was covered with linoleum, but the cork flooring in the cabins had not even survived the voyage to New Zealand.[3] Nor had the caulking in the deck, which continued to drop into the coal bunker below because of the shrinkage of the Riga fir planking. There had been no money to spare for that caulking in Christchurch.[4]

Similar problems had occurred on the German ship, where the felt insulation under the linoleum flooring soon became damp and smelly, having to be jettisoned before they reached Madeira. In the tropics the deck caulking had also dropped into the main bunker, and from then on coal dust had seeped into some of the cabins aboard the *Gauss.*

Wilson seldom felt any discomfort in his Russian felt boots, although the water can froze in his cabin. The Germans' cabin temperatures regularly fell to -32°F until their windmill-driven electric lighting failed as a result of ineffective voltage regulation. The kerosene or blubber lamps, which they then had to use, improved the ambient temperature somewhat. Scott tolerated the temperature by sitting at his desk with his feet in a box of sennegrass. For some inexplicable reason, no one had shut the door between the stokehold and the bunker or closed the ventilators. At last, on June 11, he got Duncan to fix felt beneath the floor of his night and day cabins and to close the watertight doors and ventilators.[5]

Duncan had to start fixing felt in Ferrar's cabin as early as April 29 to defeat the dripping from frozen lumps of condensation on the cemented-in heads of the hull bolting. The same operation followed in Armitage's cabin, the sick bay, and Royds's cabin, all on the port side of the ship.

The Germans escaped that problem because of the triple external planking and the pitch and ground cork filling (as in the *Fram*) between the frames, even though some of the pitch had been lost. It had melted in the tropics, where it had continually choked the bilge pump intake strainers, finally blocking the engine room ventilators when most needed.[6]

Matters improved in July, when the snow reached deck level on the starboard side. Cabins on the port side remained exposed, because the wind sculpted a 12-foot-wide canyon in the snow that elsewhere built up to gunwale level by the end of the winter. The outlet in the seamen's "head" had frozen up, so Duncan had to build a lavatory for the men on the starboard side.

Everyone had cold baths until early May. After that, officers and men enjoyed the luxury of a hot bath weekly, the men using the officers' rubber portable baths on Fridays. Wilson was the "fresh-air fiend" of the wardroom, arguing with Armitage and Koettlitz about opening the skylight and dubbing them "these stuffy Arctic explorers." He could not imagine how Nansen had tolerated it with an average temperature over 70°F in the smaller quarters aboard the *Fram*.[7]

Wilson did admit that if the cabins were what he called reasonably cool, condensation increased. When they started using the forward stove (because the aft one was beginning to burn out because it was bronze), he felt "nearly cooked," as the forward one was nearer his cabin.[8] After the temperature reached 77°F one night, Wilson finally won the argument and persuaded Scott to post an instruction that the skylight should be opened if the temperature rose above 60°F.

For Skelton's men, working in the engine room overhauling the engines, things were anything but warm. More than a yard from the stove the thermometer read 0°F most days, but by June 15 Plumley wrote that they did not notice it much.

The dreaded darkness unquestionably affected morale. The sun disappeared on April 23, but it was still just light enough to work outside on May 13.[9] The awning had been fixed up on April 7. It was like a marquee, extending from the forecastle break to the winch house and providing a totally enclosed area 78 × 33 feet. Duncan described the awning as a "great success,"[10] but it cut out the daylight through the skylights and ports in the upper deck.

At first that loss was compensated by the electric light, which had been commissioned on February 27[11] but was not turned on permanently until April 2. Eleven days later someone forgot to feather the blades when the wind got up, and they were soon bent. Although Skelton's men repaired them in three days, the stiffest gale yet collapsed the entire head on May 2, and from then on they relied on oil lamps and candles.

THE WINDMILL BROKEN AFTER THE FIRST GALE. The picture shows how the boats were put out on the ice 100 yards from the shore to clear the way for erecting the winter awning, for which some marquee-type supports are already in place. Courtesy, the Royal Society.

Some of the lamps were of the American Hitchcock patent design with no chimney, the draft created by a clockwork fan, but, as ever, money had restricted the number bought. Scott had one given to him for his cabin, but Wilson and others bought theirs in Cape Town.[12] Scott recorded that the lamps used 35 gallons of kerosene a week, so a third of the 1,500 gallons brought south must have been used up before the main sledging season started.

Outside, the moon soon demonstrated that the Antarctic winter was not all darkness. By May 23 the moon shone like daylight. Two evenings later it was so brilliant that Duncan and two companions set off to go around the peninsula, which, surprisingly, they still believed was an island. Realizing there was no way around beyond Castle Rock, they followed the coast back and were able to climb up to it near the slopes Barne and his companions had crawled up in the blizzard. They got back safely along the summit plateau, and, getting onboard at 11:40 P.M., received the sort of telling off the foolish escapade deserved.

With the moon waning quite rapidly after that, the first onset of real darkness soon "proved very trying" to some, according to Hare, who recorded some "unnecessary unpleasantness" caused by a few being "short-tempered and quarrelsome," as well as "a few fights." He had the common sense to add, "These little troubles we may expect—no expedition has been without them."[13]

Although the moon again lit up the mountains like daylight by June 12 and shone for twenty-four hours on the 22nd,[14] its departure on the 25th heralded a week of "pitchy dark," as Wilson described it, coinciding with two successive blizzards. These events quickly affected morale. Although Royds wrote on June 18 that the men were nothing if not cheerful, he had to add, "but say what you like, the absence of the sun has and must have a depressing effect."[15] By the last day of the month, Hare wrote "that all were sick and tired of continual darkness."

There was an hour's twilight at midday June 30, and a week later Duncan, speaking of more twilight every day, commented that everything was going smoothly. The returning light had a great deal to do with it. When the days were not thickly overcast, which they rarely were that month, the light from the fiery orange glow on the northern horizon built up until it lasted nearly six hours on the 29th. There was good daylight by mid-August, and the sun finally reappeared on the 22nd after 123 days of no sun.

It was surprising how many days allowed skiing and walking. Time and again Duncan and others went out on skiing excursions, and Wilson and Shackleton visited the thermometer they had installed on the top of Crater Hill. Of the 123 days in the four months to the end of August, about half were calm or only moderately windy, but the calmer it was the lower the temperature would drop. Only 34 days were bad enough to prevent voluntary excursions from the ship.

Two storms in May and another in July produced winds of 75 to 100 mph. During the last, when the average wind speed for 2 days was 75 mph, it blew at not less than 85 mph for twelve hours, and the two-hourly readings at the weather station 60 yards astern of the ship had to be omitted at night for the first time. They had been carried on during eight previous blizzards, but now everyone except Bernacchi was forbidden to leave the ship, and he had to crawl all the way to and from the nearer magnetic hut.

In such storms one could be lost twenty paces from the ship, and the noise was such that it was impossible to hear someone shouting directly into one's ear. Onboard the fires had to be doused, as drift soon blocked the flues. Fortunately, the galley was not affected, so the men could at least have hot food, sitting in thick coats until the wind dropped the second evening. They emerged to find that the forward end of the awning had ripped open, and snow was packed close to its apex. The dogs were dug out, but the boats were buried.

The boats had been put out 100 yards from the 10-foot-high ice foot below the main hut to get the awning up, as had always been the practice—without mishap—on many Arctic expeditions.[16] Scott came to bitterly regret that he had not heeded Bernacchi's advice that snow piling up around them would sink the sea ice, allow water to flow over it, and freeze the boats into a solid block. The rescue of the boats never prevented anyone from going sledging, as a basic complement had to be left aboard to handle the ship when the ice went out the following summer. And there were enough men to start on the boat recovery without interfering with the preparations for the sledging.

By the end of August it was clear they would have to wait for the summer temperatures to melt the ice to recover the boats. As things turned out, even by mid-December the ice had not melted, and they had to resume the operation. With much damage from blasting and sawing, the job of extricating the boats took until January 19.

During the winter the minimum temperatures had been down to –47°F, but apart from the coldest day, August 7, when they experienced –62°F, –22°F was more usual, and the southerly blizzards would push the mercury up to –4°F. Moonlit football had been enjoyed on three days around mid-June, even when the thermometer stood as low as –35°F.

But if temperatures during the day were tolerable in a climate where dryness makes it appear less cold, there was little comfort at nighttime when taking readings, replenishing the glycerin-based ink, or changing the paper charts on the recording instrument drums at the farther weather station 150 yards astern of the ship.[17] Excruciating was the word that most accurately described the sensation, however high the temperature, when a gale of wind was hurling a drift past the watchkeeper, no higher than shoulder level if he was lucky, as he hung on to the line that guided him to the instruments.

Every two hours around the clock someone had to get out along the guide rope to take ten different readings by the light of a far from reliable lamp. Ordinary hurricane lamps proved useless, and Skelton came to the rescue with a new design. The bulk of the work fell on Royds, who took the readings from 10 A.M. to 10 P.M. and kept the records. The other officers, including Scott, took them by turn every eleventh night from midnight to 8 A.M.

Barne was in charge of tide gauges, depth soundings, and, above all, sea temperatures when the opportunity occurred, mostly in conjunction with Hodgson's operations. Those involved cutting through the ice, often near a seal hole over which they would build an igloo. They would operate a dredge by cutting a slot in the ice between two holes, dropping the wire through attached to the dredge, and letting the slot freeze over. The dredge would then be hauled from one hole to the other, often with results that fascinated Hodgson, especially on July 4, when he found an unknown ten-legged sea spider in the dredge. Until then, every known example had only eight legs.

For Bernacchi it was a lonely life on the term days, isolated around the clock in the farther magnetic hut, known as the "Absolute" hut. Like Cross and others working at the main hut, when drift blotted everything out survival depended on never losing one's grip on the guide rope. From the ship to the Absolute hut, the rope was almost 300 yards long.

In the larger magnetograph hut he had to keep the oil stove filled and daily top up the lamp that provided light for the photographic traces through the four mirrors on the Eschenhagen instruments, as well as the seismograph lamp—all delicate enough work in the comfort of a warm observatory, because accidental movement of a lamp or an instrument could send the traces off the edge of the paper. He also had to rewind the clockwork as fast as possible to minimize the break in the records.

Weekly at first and then on the term days each month, he had to make hourly observations of the absolute magnetic values, supplemented by 180 readings at twenty-second intervals during a different hour on each of those days. The Eschenhagen paper roll gear in the larger hut had to be altered to run at accelerated speed during those selected hours. In that routine there was little to excite his enthusiasm other than the occasional wild swing of a trace on the 20-cm-wide roll. His enthusiasm was sparked, though, when the seismograph, started on March 14, recorded a full-blown earthquake on May 26. It was the submarine earthquake that devastated Guam, 6,000 miles away. Later, working in a partitioned-off corner of the shore hut, he and Skelton made the first-ever Antarctic pendulum observations for determining gravity. That process had normally required laboratory conditions for the maintenance of low vacuum and extreme chronometer-accuracy measurement.

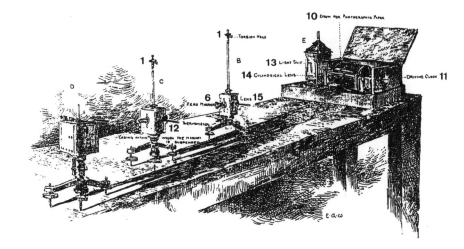

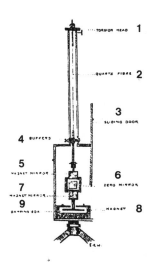

THE ESCHENHAGEN MAGNETOGRAPH. Wilson's sketch for the *South Polar Times*. Recently invented in Germany, the magnetograph represented a huge gain in ease of adjustment and repair, as well as portability, compared with the bulky separate instruments previously required for recording changes in the horizontal and vertical forces of the earth's magnetic field. Given those and the variation from true north of the horizontal, the strength and direction of the field could be measured. The component instruments were set up in the first magnetic hut, 75 yards up the slope from the main shore hut, with the heavy stone table set on brick piers. The drum carried a photographic paper strip 48 cm long and revolved once in 24 hours, recording light from the lamp E reflected from mirrors in the housings B, C, and D. A shutter rose each hour to interrupt the zero mirror beam and so recorded the time. Instrument B measured the change in variation and the temperature, whereas changes in the horizontal and vertical force were measured by instruments C and D. The absolute values were measured by instruments in the second magnetic hut, further up the slope.

Key: (1)=torsion head, (2)=quartz fiber, (3)=sliding door, (4)=buffers, (5 and 7)=magnet mirrors, (6)=zero mirror, (8)=magnet, (9)=damping box, (10)=drum for photographic paper, (11)=driving clock, (12)=thermometer, (13)=light slit, (14)=lamp's cylindrical lens, (15)=lens in each housing.

Except in the galley, no such inexorable demands governed the mess deck, where initially the crew worked mostly on maintenance once the huts were completed. Until sledging preparations started, the men's afternoons were free, and when weather allowed they skied over the sea ice or walked or played football. Late in May Wilson—like Koettlitz, involved in medical inspections that brought him into repeated contact with many of the men—was confident that they were "all merry and find plenty of games and occupations."[18]

Duncan, James Dell, and Hare played the mandolin and George Croucher the accordion. *Shovehapenny* and draughts tournaments were interspersed with whist and other games. Wild received one of the small silver expedition medals for defeating the others at draughts. The medals had been struck in anticipation of the need for such diversions, as well as sports, to maintain morale.

The degree to which morale was dependent on entertainment was apparent when, in early June, Duncan complained that nothing had been organized since Royds's slide show and singalong on May Day.[19] Preparations began a few days later for a play gotten up by Barne with nine parts, all requiring makeup and costumes from the theatrical kit donated in London. And everyone started making decorations for the Midwinter Day party that was to be their Christmas, because so many would be sledging on Christmas Day.

June 23 began with smoked herring for breakfast, followed by finishing the paper chains and lanterns and the individual set pieces on each of the six mess tables. At 12:30 the officers toured them. Scott congratulated everyone on the show, which included an extraordinary illuminated carved ice centerpiece on one table. They distributed presents and cards from Royds's mother and Wilson's bride before the Christmas lunch that started with real turtle soup, substituted ham for turkey, accompanied by a bottle of Bass ale, and finished up with plum pudding, brandy sauce, and a tot of rum. A few skied around the point as far as Castle Rock while others slept it off, and the evening was rounded off with a singalong.

The play, *Ticket of Leave*,[20] in which Wild played the leading man with Buckridge and Gilbert Scott as the ladies, was presented to loud applause on the stage Duncan had built in the main hut. Three weeks later Royds began to organize another show. With lectures by Hodgson and Ferrar, there were no more grumbles in Duncan's diary except when all were kept waiting under the awning longer than usual during the Sunday inspection of the ship on August 3. For his part, Royds later wrote that whereas "several of the officers used to go and sit and talk to [the] men for hours together and so . . . kept in touch with them," he did not believe more was needed to amuse the men, "as they have been able to [keep amused] without outside help, which to my mind is far better."[21]

The roll call on Sunday mornings was part of the naval routine Scott maintained and applied to everyone, even though the service held on the mess deck was not compulsory, as Duncan recorded several times. Even if some missed it, Plumley spoke for many when he wrote, "We are not all angels, but I think the greater part of us enjoys it."[22] If to civilians the code of discipline that encompassed the Sunday routine appeared strict, other naval rules such as restrictions on smoking were relaxed, and the men were free to smoke at any time in their quarters.

There were only three cases in which Scott applied a heavy hand that first year. Despite Shackleton's relaxed control of the commissariat department, by the time they reached Hut Point Brett, the thirty-six-year old cook, was tired of the routine that kept him in the galley all day. The next morning he refused to report for duty and was hauled up in front of Scott. Scott did not tolerate a refusal to obey an order any more than Shackleton did, and the cook was sentenced to be put in irons until he agreed to resume duty. They were not secured to anything, and he was able to get out of them and throw them overboard. After that, he was handcuffed and lashed to the windlass in the forecastle, but again he escaped.[23] He seems to have been recaptured, as Ferrar described him as being released at 6 P.M. that same evening.*

The subsequent incidents concerned a man who continued to smoke during the Sunday service. He does not appear to have suffered more than a telling off that few would disagree with. The only other man to fall foul of the code was the donkeyman, William Hubert. In Bernacchi's words, he was "not made for polar exploration."[24] Early in May Hubert asked to see Scott and in a truculent manner produced a piece of the cake served for tea, asking, "D'you call this cake?" Scott immediately sent for a piece of the cake served in the wardroom, which was identical to that for the men. Hubert's punishment was severe according to Bernacchi, writing thirty-five years later, although none of the seamen mentioned it in the diaries known to have survived.

---

* As Plumley's diary (SPRI: ms. 972) makes clear, there is no basis for the claim by Huntford (1979: p. 153, and 1985 #2: p. 86) that he was chained "on" deck. Although the forecastle was none too warm, it would have received some heat from the galley below.

MEMBERS OF THE CREW, SEPTEMBER 30, 1902. *Above*: Mess no. 1. Front (*left to right*): William Smythe, Arthur Pilbeam, John Walker, Thomas Williamson; back (*left to right*): Jesse Handsley, Ernest Joyce. *Below*: Mess no. 2. Front (*left to right*): Arthur Quartley, William Hubert, Frank Plumley, Thomas Whitfield; back (*left to right*): William Lashly, William Page. Courtesy, the Royal Geographical Society, London.

MEMBERS OF THE CREW, SEPTEMBER 30, 1902. *Above*: Mess no. 3. Front (*left to right*): Edgar Evans, David S. Allan, James Duncan; back (*left to right*): Jacob Cross, William Macfarlane, Thomas Kennar. *Below*: Mess no. 4. Front (*left to right*): Frank Wild, George Croucher, William Peters, Thomas Crean; back (*left to right*): William Isaac Weller, William Heald, James Dell. Courtesy, the Royal Geographical Society, London.

MEMBERS OF THE CREW, SEPTEMBER 30, 1902. No. 5 (galley) mess. Front (*left to right*): Henry Brett, Gilbert Scott, Horace Buckridge, Clarence Hare; back (*left to right*): Arthur Blissett, Charles Clark. Courtesy, the Royal Geographical Society, London.

Health, so frequently a barometer of morale, could hardly have been better. The day before the "Christmas" lunch, Wilson recorded only one man on the sick list, saying, however, that it was a case of "real illness." Koettlitz and Wilson took the man's swollen legs to be symptoms of scurvy, dreaded among sailors at that time.[25]

However, Scott revealed in his July 17 journal entry that it was not scurvy: "The [second] case of sickness was that of Crean." Scott goes on to describe his swollen legs: "He is now quite recovered, and the doctors are quite reassured that it was not scurvy but due to some obstruction which they cannot at present place—they think however that he ought not to go sledging, which is a loss for our parties."[26]

The first case of illness had been psychological. Smythe, whom Ferrar had encountered "in a state" on the evening of June 16,[27] had, as Scott related, been suffering from "depressed spirits . . . the doctors had told the men his blood was below average but not below normal. His weight had also gone down; the men chafed him, he took it in the wrong way, and an extra tot of rum was [all that was] needed for his outburst. The remedy was simple—I had a talk with him . . . [and] have given him one or two special tasks as though he were selected on his merits for them. The cure is complete and he is now in as good spirits as any of the rest."[28] Scott's response was far removed from that of a martinet.

Regarding the diet, the menus quoted by Hare on the last day of August show that there was still enough seal meat to support three meals weekly, although the stock was almost depleted. In both wardroom and mess deck the food was surprisingly varied:[29]

Monday	Breakfast—porridge, curry and rice, cold meat, cocoa or coffee Dinner—soup, tinned boiled ham, potatoes, turnips, fruit pie
Tuesday	Breakfast—porridge, tinned salmon, cocoa or coffee Dinner—soup, roast seal, potatoes, peas, ginger pudding
Wednesday	Breakfast—porridge, minced collops (tinned savory mincemeat), cocoa or coffee Dinner—soup, beef pie, potatoes, haricot beans, prunes and rice
Thursday	Breakfast—porridge, sardines on toast, cocoa or coffee Dinner—soup, seal steaks, potatoes, carrots, milk pudding
Friday	Breakfast—porridge, curry and rice, cocoa or coffee Dinner—soup, cold tinned meat, potatoes, haricot beans, stewed fruit
Saturday	Breakfast—porridge, rissoles, cocoa or coffee Dinner—soup, seal, potatoes, parsnips, roly-poly pudding
Sunday	Breakfast—porridge, cold tongue, tinned salmon, cocoa or coffee Dinner—soup, fresh mutton, potatoes, peas, plum pudding

The New Zealand mutton was so popular that Scott wished they had more: "One improvement would certainly be acceptable, that is more mutton and with one of our smaller holds fitted for cold storage it would have been possible." He went on to explain that the temperature in the compartments under the mess deck had fallen little below 41°F.[30]

The potatoes were dried, and they were the only item everyone criticized, apart from the taste of the seal meat. The problem was the cook, who was too lazy to prepare seal in a palatable manner, from late May onward never attempting anything other than frying it.[31] It was, however, by no means universally condemned in the diaries so many of the crew and officers kept.

On the mess deck the men had porridge only three times a week and ate dried potatoes or tinned vegetables for their midday meal. For tea the wardroom had sardines, bread, and jam daily, with cakes on alternate days, and the men had salmon or sardines three times a week and cheese and jam daily. Every man had splendidly fresh bread, baked daily by the assistant cook, Charles Clarke.[32]

By that time the alternating pattern of blizzard and calm, moonlight and total darkness held no terror for Scott and his forty-six companions. Properly provisioned except for fresh vegetables or the as yet unknown vitamins that could replace them, they had emerged virtually unscathed from the four darkest months of the year. An examination by Koettlitz on August 2 had revealed no traces of scurvy.[33] Scott could rest assured that he had avoided the fate of the men aboard the *Belgica.**

Sledging preparations had been under way since June 27,[34] and all was now ready for the depot and Crozier journeys that would serve as the final trials for clothing and gear, so essential to the key journeys into the unknown that were the main planks in Scott's plan. But before even those trials, the harnessing of the dogs had to be decided upon. Only three dogs (Boss, Vic, and Wolf) had not pulled well when Scott tried them out on August 2. Three others had needed a touch of the whip. But the dogs had gnawed through their harness, so Feather had contrived a new arrangement that was ready by the last day of the month. Scott opened the spring season two days later with a short trip northward along the coastal ice to test it out.[†]

Little did anyone know when the party returned on September 5 that the Southern Depot journey, on which he would set off twelve days later, would radically change the plan developed in early June and tax Scott's equipment and seemingly overample force to the hilt.

---

* If Crean had been suffering from scurvy caused by the winter diet, his condition would have worsened a month later, but it had not. That and Koettlitz's August 2 findings clearly disqualify assertions (as in Huntford 1979: p. 166) that vitamin C deficiency was already rife by midwinter.

† The new design was tried on August 31, after which Scott's journal recorded that fifteen dogs pulled 900 pounds. Five days later, after the 10-mile test run northward begun on September 2, Wilson recorded that the harness worked well, but the wire had badly chafed the dogs. Scott's journal had it that the traces chafed. So they decided to revert to hemp rope. The experiment had certainly not occupied "much of the winter" or sprung from any theoretical rejection of the harnesses bought by Wilton, as asserted by Huntford (1979: p. 164). On the Southern Depot journey, Wilson's December 2 diary entry once more referred to many dogs being badly chafed by the "harness," despite the reversion to hemp.

13

THE BEST-LAID SCHEMES . . .
The Birth and Compromise of Scott's Plan

Scott outlined his plans for the coming season in greater detail even
before Crean's symptoms had begun to worry the doctors in June.
The plan up to the arrival of the relief ship revolved around the Southern journey "as far south in a straight line on the Barrier as we can [go],
reach the Pole if possible, or find some new land," wrote Wilson.[1] All
the dogs would be used, and Scott would take one or two companions. He wanted Wilson to go, believing it essential to have a doctor
in the party. Wilson strongly advised taking a third man in case one
became ill, and their preference lay with Shackleton, despite Wilson's
misgivings about his health.

Barely a month later Wilson wrote, "For some reason I don't
think he is fitted for the job. The Captain is strong and hard as a
bulldog, but Shackleton hasn't the legs that the job wants; he is so
keen to go, however, that he will carry it through."[2]

As originally planned, the party was to leave at the beginning of
November, and, to conserve the dogs' energy, most of their provisions
would be carried by men and transferred to them, in part at the Depot
Scott still intended to establish off the Bluff and finally 50 miles south
of there in 79°30S. Mention of the Pole as the target 630 miles further south, making the round-trip 1,480 miles to be accomplished in
ninety-two days, must have been based on the assumption that the
barrier surface might extend all the way to the Pole. This would require a daily average of over 16 miles, and the entire plan was clearly an
extrapolation of the two-man Nansen precedent, the great explorer

having set off with Johansen and their dogs from the *Fram* to cover 300 miles less. So the estimate was not unreasonable if one took into account the better traveling offered by the barrier surface compared with the rough sea ice Nansen had encountered.

Barne was to lead the support party, which would start off first and wait at the first depot until Scott's party arrived. The dog sledges would then go on for 50 miles and wait for Barne, with some of the men, to bring the second load for transfer to them. While waiting for Barne's return, Royds would take a party to deposit the dispatches at the Crozier letterbox, and then, when they were both back at the ship, Armitage would lead the other main early-season thrust, taking Barne and Ferrar to survey the coast westward from the Bluff that Wilson and Shackleton had seen from White Island.

That journey was a major addition to the program, and Scott can have thought it possible only by revising his estimate of the relief ship's arrival. Previously, the relief ship was to take the Magnetic Pole Party, leaving *Discovery* to await Scott's return by the end of January. Now Armitage was to undertake this extra journey before the *Morning* arrived. Then, while he led the Magnetic Pole Party from Wood Bay and returned north in the *Morning*, Scott would explore westward from Robertson Bay in *Discovery* and, as before, return independently to New Zealand. That would complete everything the instructions had required except serious exploration east of the Barrier. This was how matters stood on June 12.[3]

In a debate on navigation on July 1, Scott revealed his intention, if allowed a third season, to run down the 107°W meridian in Cook's tracks and use the westward current to explore along to the land they had discovered east of the Barrier and then return home by way of the Falklands. Royds was sure they would be ordered home immediately once they reached New Zealand.

They believed two months would suffice for the preparations, with what was needed to alter the clothing and reinforce the tents, so a start on that work was not imperative until June 27. The sailors' training in sail repair proved invaluable in altering by hand all the "fur" suits-cum-sleeping bags that had proved so unmanageable on the abortive autumn journey. Although the three-man sleeping bags had proved chilly for the men on that trip, the alternative of one-man bags for all involved so much weight that everyone except officers, scientists, and others in their tents would have to use the three-man bags.

The shortage of money had been behind the decision not to use young animal skins, which would have made the bags warmer and lighter. The quotation from Müller of Dramman (see Chapter 7) had been so costly that despite Scott's provisional acceptance of it in time for the supplier's journey north to the February sales,[4] the Norwegian had ignored his insistence on the use of young animal skins The thirty-six suits and twenty sleeping bags, as well as the 100 unsewn skins, were all from older animals. Müller had never replied to Scott's request for a quantity discount, and whether he had never bought the more expensive skins or had sold them to others, by the time he received Scott's telegraphed confirmation order it was too late for Armitage to reject anything when he reached Norway, and the better skins had ended up in other hands.

Off and on, men were working on the clothing until the middle of August. In early July Duncan had started cladding the sledge runners with German Silver to overcome the traction problems encountered on the Crozier journey. By July 22 men began to prepare food bags, which had to be made and then filled with a week's rations for three men. The bags were carried in larger canvas "tanks," with dimensions dictated by the sledge packing arrangement.

The ration per man was a little over 33 ounces per day of dried food, and of that about 12 ounces was biscuit, which required wooden cases to protect it from knocking to bits on the move.* So a food bag for the week would weigh about 55 pounds. Sixteen pounds of that was ship's biscuit, which went into Venesta wood boxes containing a three-week supply. With the packing totaling 22 pounds, a week's rations for three weighed 77 pounds gross, so the food for the men on the Southern journey would add up to 1,000 pounds, or nearly half a ton. The depots would contain just 15 percent of that amount. No wonder Scott needed all the dogs!

Sixteen puppies had been born during the winter, and knowing the dogs would not return from the Southern journey, Scott was evidently banking on the puppies to do some useful work even that first year. When two died on October 26 after all the puppies had become sick, apparently from eating some waste thrown overboard by Hodgson, Scott wrote in his journal, "Wilson administered castor oil with good result and I hope we shall lose no more."[5]

To save space, most of the sledges had not been assembled, and building them up went on under Duncan's command starting on

---

* The 21 ounces excluding the biscuit was food from which most normal water content had been removed. In everyday terms it represented 44 ounces plus 12 ounces of biscuit, or a daily ration of 3½ pounds of food per man.

August 9, no less than half the crew being put on that at one stage. Although one watch had been diverted to dig out the boats after the great July blizzard, everything except Duncan's work on the German Silver shodding was ready by the end of August.[6] A few days earlier Scott had conducted some trials with 600-pound loads on shod and unshod sledges. Four men could not move the sledge with wooden runners, but two men easily pulled the one Duncan had clad with German Silver. The point was proved, and all the sledges would run with the metal cladding. Two days later Scott briefed the crew on the sledging plans, precautions, and care of the gear. By September 1 everything was ready for the dog trials.[7]

Throughout the preparations the sledging plans had slowly been crystallizing as the results of more calculations by Scott and Wilson emerged. In mid-July Wilson had been hard at work on sledge loads and food rations. The plan was for the dogs to be killed progressively to feed the remainder. Wilson was "having to arrange daily food to the ½ oz for 3 months. No simple job. Also one dog lasts 17 dogs how many days? One dog lasts 16 how many, and so on till 1 dog lasts 4 dogs how many days? And then by the grace of God we shall be nearing our first depot and not much more than a week or two from home."[8]

Fortunately, Wilson had taken notes on sledge loads from Nansen's *Farthest North,* one of the books Scott found missing from the expedition library.[9] It is inconceivable that Markham, an admirer of Nansen, had not suggested the book to William Shackleton* when he had called on him for advice, and yet somehow the book had not been obtained. Fortunately, the purchases and gifts had included Drygalski's and Nansen's books on their exploits in Greenland.[10]

By the end of August, the date predicted for the arrival of the *Morning* had been moved forward to mid-January, and the start was set for mid-October to allow them to get back by the earlier date.[11] Based on what they had experienced in *Discovery,* arriving in McMurdo Sound on January 21 and beating a way in to Granite Harbour, mid-January must have seemed realistic. The ice might break and allow *Discovery* to get away two weeks earlier for the Wilkes Coast exploration, but that was far from certain.

The relief ship's arrival in mid-January would also allow an earlier start for Armitage's magnetic pole journey, because the ice in Wood

---

* The young physicist, no relative of Ernest Shackleton, given the job of assembling the library (as mentioned in Chapter 7) before his disqualification in July 1901 following an adverse dental health report.

Bay that had stopped them on January 18 had been firm enough for a landing to be made that early in the month. The time allowed for the journey under the first plan had looked desperately short, given the need to break through the mountains. The journey westward from the Bluff would be led by Barne.

Perhaps Bernacchi had voiced doubts about the ascent from Wood Bay. In reality, he was less sure of its ease than he had appeared in his lecture to the RGS, which Scott had attended in March the year before. Then he had described it as a fairly easy access to the "great snow cap,"[12] but in his introduction to the scientific report on the magnetic observations published after the expedition, he spoke of "considerable difficulties on account of the lofty mountain ranges that may have to be crossed; but at Lady Newnes Bay the mountains are comparatively low."[13] The late January start previously envisaged would not have allowed a return earlier than the end of March, and Scott's sledging experience at that time of year had hardly been a good omen for Armitage's return through the mountains.

For one or both of these reasons the plan had been changed to allow Armitage to start without waiting for the *Morning,* and by August 22 the crew knew that the party, with Koettlitz as doctor, and ten men would head "northwest," as Duncan wrote that day, to find another way through the mountains to the magnetic pole: "This is to be a big job as it will be mountainous work."[14] Strictly speaking, the place due northwest from the ship was Granite Harbour, which Royds had described as "a very good place for making inland."[15] If Scott and Armitage had it or somewhere further north in mind, the men would have had to sledge straight across the sound on the sea ice. But Scott knew the ice was not solid enough, writing, "if only the western route was fully open from here what great hopes we could weave for the western parties, but every glance across the strait reveals the long shadow so ominously showing that decayed ice impossible for the traveller."[16]

Setting off for the dog harness trials on September 2 in semiblizzard conditions, with four sledges drawn by four dogs each, for Scott the question of small versus large teams was quickly settled in favor of a single large team when the two teams began fighting. Rearranged after the tangle had been separated, the two double-sledge trains reached Turtle Rock before the weather forced them to camp. That night the Southern journey trio shared a tent for the first time, with Skelton, Ferrar, and Feather in the other tent. In little better weather they followed the coast to the base of the glacier tongue the next day and traced its 15- 20-foot edge along to camp after another blizzard thwarted an attempt to cross it. On the 5th, leaving Feather to guard the dogs and pack up the sledges, they got over the tongue and took a closer look at the islands later named after Dellbridge.

They soon found the sea ice was recent, with open water right up to the western shores. That ruled out the new plan for Armitage. There could be no sledging across McMurdo Sound to Granite Harbour, let alone to the glacier beyond the Drygalski Ice Tongue. The route through the mountains would have to be found further south.

The trip showed that the harnesses were satisfactory, but the dogs had gnawed at the traces, and some had to be muzzled. The traces would have to be remade using wire. Even the reluctant dogs proved teachable on that trip "and did good work eventually."[17] Scott was satisfied that their capacity for work "had been abundantly proved."[18] With just eighteen left, for one had died on July 6, that was good news for the Southern journey. The dogs had covered slightly more than 37 miles. The trip had also served to test the new sledgemeters Skelton and his men had made, using spare recorders from recording blocks used for the oceanographic work.

One thing remained to be settled: Would it be possible to head for the Bluff by the shorter route between White and Black Islands, or would they have to take the longer route out on the barrier to the east of White Island to avoid insuperable crevasses? Scott would take Barne and Shackleton and some dogs to find out, which would also give Barne a chance to learn the terrain for his Depot Party.

At this stage Barne's party was to start at the beginning of October, and Scott was to time his start so as to catch them at "the farthest point arranged," where they would establish a second depot. Scott's September 12 journal entry finished with the confident remark, "If with the dogs we can get a clear three months beyond the furthest depot the main party can establish I shall be more than satisfied."[19]

First, however, there was the new problem of how to get through the formidable mountains to the west by a route farther south than previously envisaged and approachable over the sea ice. There were two possibilities: the gap between Mount Discovery and the new range dominated by Mount Lister, which Scott favored, and the inlet due west 30 miles south of Granite Harbour, which Armitage thought was more promising.[20]

Scott knew the magnetic pole journey ranked high with Markham, and Drygalski might even now be setting out on his. Two parties would have to be dispatched straightaway. Royds would take the southwest route and Armitage the western one.

THE VIEW LOOKING SOUTHWEST FROM CASTLE ROCK (situated 4 miles north of Hut Point). The prominent mountain in the center of the picture–taken about 11 P.M.–is Mount Discovery with Brown "Island" to its immediate west. It was toward the gap between them, much more apparent from Observation Hill near Hut Point, that Royds's Southwest Reconnaissance Party set off on September 10, 1902. Moraine debris prevented them from getting close enough to see that the so-called island was in fact joined to Mount Discovery. The rounded summit of Mount Morning can be seen behind Brown Island. Both form part of the right bank of Koettlitz Glacier, which Royds hoped would lead to the interior of Victoria Land. On the horizon at the extreme left of the picture is Black Island, which appears at the right side of Wilson's February 20, 1902, panorama, composed from sketches drawn on the way to and at the summit of Mount Heine. Photographed by and reproduced courtesy of Dr. David Meldrum of the Scottish Marine Biological Association.

Royds had his men and equipment ready in four days. Koettlitz and Lashly shared his tent and used one-man sleeping bags, and Evans, Wild, and Quartley were in the other, sharing a three-man bag. Scott handed Royds his orders on the evening of September 9. He was to probe the southerly route to the interior of Victoria Land and allow Koettlitz to study the geology and ice formations.[21] The orders to Armitage were similar, but failing a practical route directly west he was to examine the apparent fjord they had been unable to reach in the ship on February 8 (New Harbour) and study as much of the coastline as possible.

Leaving the morning of September 10, Royds led the first sledge party to set out in the Antarctic that spring, pulling two sledges linked together with one behind the other and weighing 840 pounds, a load of 140 pounds per man. One of Skelton's new sledgemeters was attached to the rear sledge to measure their progress. Heading for the gap between Black and Brown Islands, more or less directly toward Mount Discovery, they were soon traveling on rough ice covered with grit and stones. That night none of the party could sleep; the temperature plunged to -47°F and was 9° colder the following night.

Royds separated the sledges in an attempt to travel faster, but soon they were capsizing as fog thickened and hard ridges in the surface caused by the wind (*sastrugi*) became more pronounced. On the third day, in such poor light that they could hardly see the bottom of the next furrow, the leading 12-foot sledge broke loose. Royds narrowly avoided serious injury as it struck his ankle and then broke its bow against the next ridge. When the fog lifted they could see they were still 4 miles from the western corner of Black Island, with the way ahead barred by moraines built of massive granite blocks. They had traveled just 16 miles, about halfway to the apparent gap between Mount Discovery and Brown "Island."

The only thing Royds could do was turn east and go around the other end of Black Island. The German Silver had split on one of the runners because not enough nails had been used, and it had to stripped off with the inevitable extra drag on surfaces only occasionally of polished ice. It took two-and-a-half days for the 15-mile trip eastward to the gap between White and Black Islands.

By lunchtime on the 16th they could just see the shoulder of Mount Discovery when they were engulfed by a violent blizzard from the southwest. In no time the second tent collapsed. After a struggle to get it up again and to stay both tents to the sledges, Royds ordered everything necessary for a prolonged stay to be moved inside. In the course of this, Lashly's sleeping bag was suddenly taken by the wind, vanishing into the whirling whiteness.

When all were inside, Royds and Koettlitz had to sit the entire afternoon with their backs to the canvas to prevent it from flapping to pieces. With no sign of the sleeping bag in the morning, the only option was to retreat. Not less than 8 miles on their way they came across the sleeping bag, and shortly afterward they sighted Scott's Depot Party coming toward them.

Armitage and Barne, with ten men, had gone out on the last day of August to bring in the cases abandoned during the abortive autumn attempt. Now Scott, with Barne, Shackleton, and thirteen dogs, had set off to sledge a smaller load of provisions to the Bluff (about 500 pounds gross).[22] That Wednesday evening the two parties camped about 5 miles apart, going in opposite directions. Getting off to sleep in the dark, for there were still only twelve hours of daylight, Royds was awakened by an even more violent blizzard at about 2:30 A.M.

Shortly afterward, Scott also awoke to find himself lying in the open, with no sign of the tent, in zero visibility. After a few bewildered moments he realized that he had slid out from under the bottom edge of the tent, and he managed to claw his way back in. This was the beginning of a hideous ordeal that, with two momentary remissions allowing food to be fetched from the sledge, went on for fifteen hours, with the three holding on to the tent skirting with increasingly frostbitten hands.

At last, at about 6 P.M. they found that two biscuit boxes, each weighing about 43 pounds, would hold the tent down, and they could attend to their hands. "An inspection of hands showed that we had all been pretty badly frost-bitten, but the worst," wrote Scott, "was poor Barne, whose fingers have never recovered from the accident last year, when he so nearly lost them. To have hung on to the tent through all those hours must have been positive agony to him, yet he never uttered a word of complaint."[23] Royds's party had only been able to reach their food bags in the second lull. The wind was in the NNW when they turned in, so they faced the tent flaps south. That meant the ventilators faced south, too, so their tents had gradually filled with snow.

When the storm petered out with a few last gusts around midnight, everything in Scott's tent was half full of frozen slush. Their trousers were frozen stiff, and there was a unanimous vote to go back the 14 miles to the ship to dry everything out before starting again. Following Royds's party, which got aboard for breakfast, Scott's party arrived after lunch, having, in his words, "accomplished nothing except the acquisition of wisdom" at the hands of Antarctic weather.[24]

The smallest mistakes had foiled both missions. Lashly, on his first sledge trip with no experience of the force of a blizzard, had put his sleeping bag down beside the tent to go back to the sledge for more gear, and in a second a gust had whisked it away as though it were a feather, when it cannot have weighed much less than 20 pounds by that time. Scott and his companions, all with some experience with autumn weather conditions, had failed to pile enough snow on the tent skirt. No one made that mistake again.[25]

As Royds stepped aboard, Armitage, Ferrar, Heald, and Walker were 3 miles from New Harbour, as they had named the inlet they were heading for, having set off from their camp 500 feet up the snow-covered piedmont slope at the base of the 4,000-foot hills bounding its south shore. The day of the blizzard (September 18) they were fog-bound, and with the men suffering from painful legs for the past four days and Walker complaining that his ankle felt as though it was sprained, Armitage had decided to limit the next day's work to a short journey on skis as far as New Harbour, leaving Cross and Gilbert Scott at the camp.[26]

The excursion revealed the road to the interior. When the ship had gotten within 8 miles of the inlet the previous February, all that could be seen was a glacier-filled fjord with a mountain at its head. Now, rounding the shoulder above Butter Point (not yet named), they could see that the glacier did not end at the 8,000-foot mountain with a knoblike head about 25 miles from them but was joined by a wide glacier flowing in from its northern flank.

Most of the first 10 miles was filled with chaotic glacier ice "like a cemetery. Huge masses broken and fissured, standing up to a height of 50 feet, mixed with rubble. . . . Many erratics of great size are poised on these masses. Moraines like shot rubbish heaps are scattered here and there, 10 to 60 feet in height."[27] Skiing down to the ice below them, they were able to move up the valley along a channel of smooth ice cut by the heat of the sun between the glacier ice and the wall of the valley.

After 4 miles or so, Ferrar was so exhausted that Armitage sent him back to the camp with Heald and pressed on with Walker. As soon as they started off, a furious wind began to swirl down the valley, and the temperature plunged nearly 10 degrees to -45°F. After another 3 miles it was clear that they would be caught out in very dim light if they did not turn back. Still 3 miles from the glacier surface proper, they saw no other way to reach it and so came away with the conviction that there was no route for sledges through that lowest part of the valley.[28]

By the time they got back to the east-facing slope of the camp it was 1 A.M., and in the twilight Walker spotted two sets of footprints. Concluding from their direction that Heald and Ferrar must be lost, the two men followed the prints 3 miles beyond the camp and back again, arriving at 5 A.M., twenty-one hours after setting out with just some chocolate and biscuit for food. Not far from the camp they were met by Cross and Scott, who had begun to fear for their safety.

ARMITAGE'S WESTERN RECONNAISSANCE PARTY READY TO START ON SEPTEMBER 11, 1902. Armitage (*second from right*), with PO Jacob Cross beside him in the lead and Royal Marine Gilbert Scott to his right, stand ready ahead of Hartley Ferrar, flanked by AB William Heald (*left*) and Dundee seaman John Walker. All are harnessed to the 11-foot sledge towing the 7-footer behind it, with one of the two new sledgemeters fabricated during the winter. The picture shows how the snow had built up on the lee side of the ship, helping starboard cabin insulation, in contrast to cabins on the port side. The "Gap" is visible beyond the funnel. This picture formed the basis of the design of the British Polar Medal, first awarded on the return of the expedition. Courtesy, the Royal Society.

The two lost men had returned just three hours earlier, and it was soon clear that Heald had saved Ferrar's life. After refusing to let him lie down several different times, he at last agreed to Ferrar's request for half an hour's sleep, but he woke him after five minutes, saying the half-hour was up.[29] Twice more the young geologist had laid down and gone to sleep from sheer exhaustion, and each time Heald had succeeded in waking him and getting him on the move again until at last they saw the lantern Cross had put up on a bamboo.

After a meal the entire party slept right through the 20th and, waking to a fine morning, set off at 11 A.M. on the 21st to look at the Blue Glacier, as Armitage named it that day. To Armitage it appeared to run down from the mountain they had seen at the head of the New Harbour glacier and to connect by way of a pass with the main glacier, later named after Ferrar.

They got the sledges onto Blue Glacier for a better view, but the way down was another matter, and by 10 P.M. on the 22nd they were still 700 feet above sea level. It took them all the next day to reach sea level, with several sledge capsizes along the way. The diversion had been well worthwhile, because what they had been able to see tended to confirm Armitage's guess that there was a pass over 2,000 feet above where they had gotten onto the glacier.

After visiting the westernmost of the Dailey Islands on the 24th and finding moss growing under 6 inches of snow, Armitage became so alarmed about the condition of Ferrar and Heald, whose symptoms were now plainly those of scurvy, that he determined to cover the 20½ miles to the ship with just two breaks for meals.

Koettlitz was away, as was Scott, when they reached the ship at 6 A.M. on September 26, so Wilson examined the whole party that evening. Heald's condition was the worst of all, and Ferrar's legs were swollen up to his groin. Wilson told only Armitage and Royds of his findings, which Royds found "astounding . . . when one thinks of the fresh meat, both mutton and seal, which has been constantly provided throughout the winter."[30]

Wilson reexamined the six men again the next afternoon, having read everything he could on the subject of scurvy. The symptoms were showing up in all of them, and Wilson detected that even Walker's sprained ankle, which had been very painful again on the march back, was really caused by the same malady.

After a consultation that evening,[31] Wilson, Armitage, and Royds determined that a more liberal diet was needed, with first priority given to increasing the ration of fresh seal meat. Armitage described the measures they took in a report he wrote two days before Scott returned:[32]

> Immediately that Dr. Wilson informed me that in his opinion scurvy had made its appearance amongst the Ship's Company in the persons of my sledge-party, I consulted with Lieut. Royds and Dr. Wilson as to the best measures to adopt to prevent its spread. Our conclusion was:—1st. Fresh meat daily. 2nd. A liberal diet in every way. 3rd. Every possible means to be taken to ensure warm dry quarters. 4th. To render the daily lives of the Ship's Company as cheerful as possible.
>
> Lieut. Barne proceeded to Pram Pt. and brought in seal-meat. I instructed Mr. Ford to give all hands fresh seal-meat for dinner every day. To place Lime-juice on the Messes tables for dinner each day. To give all hands oatmeal porridge for breakfast each morning, as well as meat. To see that their jam supply was liberal, and extra bottled fruit served out. To give them potatoes and vegetables freely.

I had the Cook before me, and told him that, now that Sledging Parties were going out I desired him to make use of his really important position; that I required the seal meat to be cooked in as variable and appetising a manner as possible. That the potatoes should be dished up differently and made more palatable, as well as the vegetables, and I took the liberty of informing him that *on his efforts in this direction would depend the return of his bonus* [my italics].

The 28th was a Sunday, and already the prospect of recovering pay, forfeited previously when the cook refused duty, was having its effect. The food, which as usual included mutton as the main dish, "could not have been better cooked," as Armitage put it.[33]*

By Tuesday Wilson had discovered that the forehold had become a stinking mess of seal blood through the cook's practice of thawing out the seal carcasses in the galley without attempting to stop the blood from draining through the floor hatchway. This was yet more evidence in support of Scott's description of the cook's habits as "dirty." A month before that everyone had become ill from the soup, and someone discovered he had prepared it in a dirty pan.[34]

Matters were made worse by the rising temperature, which melted the bilges. Everything above and below the forward hold floor had become a malevolent breeding ground for bacteria, so Wilson had the entire area scrubbed and disinfected.[35]

On October 2 Koettlitz returned after being out nine days with Bernacchi and Dailey. Because Royds had been unable to detect any promising route to the interior, the three men had been right around Black Island and established that there was no viable route near Mount Discovery.

The next day the two doctors examined the entire ship's company, but apart from Ferrar and Heald, Koettlitz regarded the symptoms he found as "only slight" and believed they "will, I hope, quickly disappear if fresh seal meat is made the staple meat diet for every member of the expedition," as he wrote in his report that evening. They had found twelve men with "slight congestion" of the gums, two more with decidedly unhealthy-looking gums, and only two with scorbutic symptoms in their legs.[36]

---

* Clearly, the improvement had been wrought by the prospect of the restored bonus and not solely because of better treatment, as Huntford implied (1979: p. 166), quoting Ferrar's opinion, although the young geologist was not present at Brett's dressing down by Armitage.

The next evening Scott's party arrived back, the essential Bluff Depot established at last. He had started on September 24 with the sixteen dogs that remained, for by that time two more had been lost. Many of the men had been made responsible for feeding a dog apiece and often took them out for walks or ski runs. Two taken out by a party of men a fortnight previously had been allowed to run off and had never returned.[37]

Barne's hands needed a long time to recover, so Scott had taken Feather in his place. They had picked up the loads dumped 14 miles out and gone on to complete 23 miles the first day. The next day's progress was very different. With a sharp southwest wind in their faces, the dogs refused to pull until it eased, and they had gained barely more than 10 miles when they camped a little beyond the ridge between White and Black Islands. Heading out southeast to clear the Bluff, *sastrugi* running directly across their course limited their advance to 15 miles. Although encouragingly near the point of the Bluff, they found a forest of cracked ice cones between them and their goal. Turning away east, with the mounds growing ever higher and denser, they were soon grappling with a chaos of broken ridges, eventually almost 30 feet high.

Pinned down by a blizzard on the 28th, they started off next morning in a flat calm, Scott leading ahead of the dogs. Shackleton and Feather led the dog teams in Scott's tracks as he probed a zigzag path across snow-bridged crevasses. Feather, immediately behind him, suddenly disappeared with a shout as his lead dog tried to cut a corner and pulled him off balance. The snow collapsed under him, and in a second he was dangling in a crevasse. For a terrible moment Scott thought the bosun was lost. When they had hauled him up, they could see that one of the traces had been cut through. It was a narrow shave.

After that they joined all four sledges in train behind the sixteen dogs.* Even so, thirty minutes later the rear sledge disappeared and brought the whole train to an instant halt. The sledge could not be lifted bodily, so Feather, with great sangfroid considering his narrow

---

* Huntford (1979: p. 167) asserted that the single-team multisledge train was the product of "Scott's theories," ignoring both the fact that it had worked well on this journey and the real cause of the decision. His first experiments with single-sledge teams were clearly based on Nansen and Johansen's three single-sledge teams arrangement (with Johansen controlling two single-handedly) on their North Pole attempt.

escape, volunteered to be let down to unpack the sledge in midair until it was light enough to haul up.

Traveling 9 miles on September 30, they finally got clear of the crevasses before camping for lunch. Heading southwest for the afternoon run, after 6½ miles they arrived at a point in exact line with the last prominent cone on the Bluff and the summit of Mount Discovery. There, 8 miles southeast of the Bluff, they established the depot, safe in the knowledge that it could be found as long as one could see its flags over the drift on a bad day. They cached six weeks' provisions for three men and 150 pounds of dog food, enough to keep the dogs going for somewhat longer.[38]

Clearly the route to the depot had to be east of White Island, and that was the way they had returned, taking only three days for the 67 miles (77 statute miles), which was hardly surprising given the light load and the dogs' innate readiness to pull when homeward bound. After the three men had relaxed over a hearty dinner, Armitage and the two doctors gave Scott the devastating news of the scurvy outbreak. The mid-October start was doomed, for it would be foolhardy to begin the main sledge journeys until all trace of the disease was eliminated.

Before Scott had set out, fifteen men had been named for the support party, and ten were to go with Armitage and Koettlitz.[39] That left ten men for the skeleton crew, enough to avoid having to take any of those worst hit by the symptoms and just enough to man the ship if the ice broke up before the support party got back, which was extremely unlikely.

Even if Koettlitz was confident about fresh meat being the answer to the problem of scurvy, for all the doctors knew in those days the cause might have been an infection or food poisoning or even the damp living conditions, rife since condensation problems had returned with the higher temperatures. A big drive was begun to eliminate the dampness. The main hold was cleaned up, and 3 inches of bilge water was pumped out after the stores had been put on deck to dry out.[40]

The seal meat, served three times a week throughout the winter, had run out as early as a week before Armitage's party had set off, according to Bernacchi,[41] although Scott recorded that it lasted a week longer.[42] With the now daily consumption, the seal meat from new catches ran out again on Monday, October 6, but two seals appeared on the ice close to the ship the next day. They kept the ration going for four days. However, when no more had appeared by Wednesday, it was clear that they would have to hunt further afield.[43] Wilson and

Barne set out on Thursday with all the dogs and four sledges, heading directly for the glacier tongue 8 miles to the north. Taking Cross, Walker, Weller, and Dell, they were aiming to bring back three complete sledge loads, cutting the seals up as they were killed.

The 1,000 pounds of seal they brought in on Sunday morning enabled the ration to be stepped up to twice daily, and all tinned meat was stopped. No one had enjoyed the seal dishes during the winter, and at first there were a few glum looks on the mess deck. However, by October 20, when the mutton was finished, the preparation of the seal had improved so much that no one missed the mutton.[44]

When the sealing party returned Heald's leg was getting worse, and Wilson was still writing of patients in the plural. The intensive diet of seal and the general cleanup had not helped. Wilson was baffled: "It seems almost necessary to fall back on the tinned foods for explanation" (the salmonella poisoning theory).[45]

It was obvious that they could not start before the end of the month and that they would have to carry seal meat. There were now eighteen dogs again, as the missing two had been found on September 28, but even Bernacchi's former *Southern Cross* dog Joe would have to be commandeered. Scott and Wilson had to work out the loads and stages again.

The need for the original thrust southwest from the Bluff had also resurfaced, with an added dimension. As Scott had told them when he returned, the mountains Shackleton and his companions had seen in that direction from White Island now looked like the southern end of Victoria Land, with the barrier surface extending around it and away to the northwest.[46] At the lunch camp on September 30 he had noted: "It is clear that the main land mass ends with the Western ranges whose western slopes again descend to barrier or sea level. A faint shadow to the South of the new land indicates yet another small isolated patch of rock."[47]

Scott's conclusion that day would have a momentous effect on the great Southern journey he had so thoroughly planned. Bernacchi believed there was now more evidence for "an archipelago of islands than a great continent."[48] That conclusion only lent more weight to the Southern journey, dull as it might be in Wilson's opinion, foreseeing weeks of travel over a featureless barrier.

Discussing the new choice of routes to the South Magnetic Pole, Armitage evidently still favored the mountain route as the more direct and as a shortcut if there were a coast on the other side of the moun-

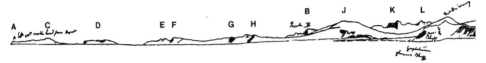

THE ANTARCTIC'S CRUCIAL DECEPTION. The view looking westward from Bluff Depot, which, taken with Wilson's view from White Island, convinced Scott he was looking at the end of South Victoria Land when he first established the depot on September 30, 1902. Michael Barne's December 31, 1902, sketch of the view from Bluff Depot shows how its position aligned with the last peak on the bluff and that of Mount Discovery. When he turned back from 79°12S with his Southern Support Party, Scott instructed him to lead his Southwest Party on a course for the farthest point visible to the south (A), and on New Year's Day, 1903, he set out on its bearing of N92½°E (S66½°W true). Photos taken in January 1991 from 79°S 164°E show that the point can only have been the last peak in the Conway Range in 79°25S, within 3° of his reading, a deviation easily accounted for by the volcanic nature of the Mount Discovery area. Poor visibility must have masked the summit of Mount Harmsworth and much of the skyline between (F) and (H), no doubt also causing Barne to show the Worcester Range linked to Mount Morning by a ridge that does not exist. Barne's B is Mount Cocks, C=Mount Keltie, D=Mount Kosko–Mesa group, E=Mount Dawson-Lambton and 2,391 m peak, F=Mount Speyer, G=south wall of Mount Northcliffe, H=great buttress on north flank of Delta Glacier cwm, J=Mount Morning, K=Mount Huggins, L=Mount Rücker and ridge to Salient Peak. With grateful acknowledgment to David (Dave) Geddes, late of Antarctica, New Zealand, whose photos, referred to above, enabled all of the features in this historic sketch to be identified. Courtesy, the Scott Polar Research Institute.

tains, as the new discovery suggested. So the two men settled on that route. Armitage would take the glacier route, and Barne, after his return from the south, would take a party to explore westward from the Bluff, leaving extra supplies at the Bluff Depot so more could be carried south for Scott's party.

Scott recalculated everything and had the details ready for Wilson to check by October 15.[49] The final decision came four days later. Whereas previously he had envisaged a second depot, the fact that no one could start much before the end of October meant the two parties would have to travel together once the dogs had caught up with Barne's party, which would start two days earlier on October 30.

Armitage's numbers had been increased, doubtless because of the mountainous route he had chosen. As a result, Scott had confined his own supporting party to twelve men, including Barne, giving them a week to get to the depot. Five days after that he would[50]

Send 6 of the 12 back carrying the remaining 6 on for another 10 days, so that we can make our final departure with the full weights from the point this [e.g., the Second Support] party can reach in 20 days [round-trip from the depot] and we must return for relief to the [Bluff] depot, which by that time should be replenished with the small amount of stores we shall need to bring us in . . . if all goes as I expect, Barne after returning to the ship, will come again to replenish the depot and explore on to the westward. Armitage will go west and endeavour to cross the range . . . and, if he is able, return around the Bluff.

Barne would use the Bluff Depot to deposit supplies for his last leg back to the ship, allowing that much more to be carried on to the point they could reach by November 20.

George Mulock's charts (published in 1908) show the end of the Bluff in 78°42S, and modern surveys confirm that finding. That put the depot in 78°45S, about 67 miles out from the ship, so Scott was assuming an average of over 9½ miles per day by the man-hauling party to enable them to reach it by November 5. If, taking the progressive lessening of the load as the safety margin, he assumed the same daily average for the fifteen days beyond the depot, that meant he was count-ing on starting with a full load from about 81°S. Allowing a day (No-vember 21) for a transfer of stores, another at the depot on the way back, and conservatively assuming an extra mile per day on the return, Barne should have been back at the ship on December 11. That would allow a start for the southwest on, say, December 18.

As to the Southern Party, there was no more mention of 3 months from the support party's farthest. Although the *Discovery* could wait for the party until mid-February, the experiences the previous Febru-ary meant there had been no question of a return after the end of January. So they would have ten weeks.

Starting from 81°S on November 22 and similarly allowing twenty days from there back to the ship, for they might well be man-hauling by that time, they would have to be back at the same point by January 11, a round-trip of fifty days. If, subtracting a week for bad weather, Scott believed a daily 15 miles southward was possible with the full complement of dogs, he could only have hoped for 85½°S at the most. That required almost 11 miles a day on the return, with most of the dogs having been killed by the time they were back at 81°S. It is more likely he accepted 85°S as a realistic goal. It wasn't the Pole or even as close to the earth's axis as Nansen had reached, but it would be halfway to the center of that final blank white circle that appeared on most maps. As Drygalski had predicted, the cold light of experience and observation on the spot had pointed the way to a plan, which no amount of theory at home could have done.

Adding the seal meat to the rations had caused a problem. The raw meat was three-quarters water, but some experiments cooking it in margarine had successfully reduced the weight by 57 percent. They reckoned they needed 140 pounds of meat, and that amount was rendered down to 60 pounds. In the end they took more and, after Barne turned back, had 70 pounds with them. It was nearly as concentrated as the pemmican. They could not know that the overcooking to drive out the water also drove out most of the vitamin C.[51]

Before Armitage set off and preferably before Scott started south, someone had to deposit the message for the *Morning* at the Cape Crozier letterbox. Royds was unhesitatingly allowed to take the men regarded as the epitome of reliability and strength after the abortive southwest reconnaisance journey once Koettlitz and Wilson declared them free of scurvy. Lashly could turn his hand to anything and, like Evans, was distinguished for his "great strength and good nature." Quartley was the most powerful man onboard, and Wild had won his spurs on the first fatal Crozier Party.[52] Unknown to Wilson or any who waved them off, their journey would yield the naturalist's prize Wilson was so keen to find and would start a quest that would be resolved only when he made the same journey, at dead of the winter night, a decade later.

Pulling two 11-foot sledges on skis, Royds's party reached a 1,000-foot pass in the far slopes of Mount Terror on Friday, October 10, after a week's traveling during which night temperatures were regularly -40°F, dipping one night to -58°F. That was the lowest temperature ever experienced by a sledging party. Royds had injured his ankle, so Skelton and Evans set off the next afternoon in fine, calm conditions and reached the mail post rookery in two-and-a-half hours.

After fixing the vital message tube, they saw three Emperor penguins about 500 yards out on the frozen Ross Sea and noticed a regular track along the shore that did not come from either of the Adélie rookeries. The next day, Sunday, October 12, Skelton set off at 10 A.M. with Wild and Quartley to find out if there was a way down to the barrier from the Mount Terror slopes. Foiled at first, they turned north until they came to a bare cliff and, looking down, saw about 300 Emperor penguins. Skelton had time to take five photos before the approach of bad weather forced a hasty retreat to camp. Because no Adélies had yet appeared at Hut Point, he was convinced they had discovered the Emperors' breeding place. Proving that would require another visit.[53]

FIRST-EVER PHOTO OF AN EMPEROR PENGUIN CHICK. Taken by Reginald Skelton at the Cape Crozier rookery on October 18, 1902. Edgar Evans (*left*) and American Leading Stoker Arthur Quartley look on. Courtesy, the Royal Society.

The blizzard that started that evening trapped them for five days, during which they could prepare only one hot meal. Otherwise they existed on biscuits, sugar, cold Bovril (a concentrated beef extract drink), and chocolate.

Released from their cramped prisons—the snow pressed on the walls of the tents until they could hardly move—on the morning of Saturday the 18th, Royds, Lashly, and Wild went to examine the pressure ridges, some over 50 feet high, while Skelton, Quartley, and Evans set off to reach the Emperors. The birds were still there, massed in what was certainly their rookery—the first ever discovered. The men brought back three young birds (which did not survive). There were many dead chicks and no sign of eggs, so if those were to be found the place would have to be visited earlier in the season.

Leaving camp on the 19th, the party was back at the ship on the 24th without a suspicion of scurvy, despite their ordeal.[54] Scott could leave with the assurance that the *Morning* would know where to find them.

On the last day of October he drafted his orders to Armitage and Barne, as well as to Royds, who would remain in charge of the ship while the three parties were away. At Wilson's request that final plan, encapsulated in an attachment (which has not survived) to Scott's last sledging order, included another Cape Crozier journey to acquire an Emperor's egg and a freshly hatched chick, if possible, for the Natural History Museum. Royds was to take a party and return before Armitage was scheduled to leave.

Choosing Arthur Blissett and Frank Plumley, Royds set off the day after Scott left for the south. Armitage assigned William Macfarlane, David Allan, and James Dell with a second sledge and tent to help them outward for thirty-six hours and then to turn back.

Five days later the party found an egg, thanks to Blissett's sharp eye spotting "a round thing" half buried in the snow just as they were about to abandon the search. The egg was 4 inches long by 3 inches across and cracked, and it traveled safely back in one of Royds's fur mitts slung around his neck.[55] Wilson, already far on the road to the south, would not see the historic find or hear that they had found no trace of chicks for another two months.

Before Scott had set out he had discussed the final plan with Armitage and so only had to spell out the general requirements in Sledging Order No. 6 on October 31:[56]

> I leave here tomorrow for the South under arrangements . . . only subject to alteration with the possibility of our finding land to the southward before the return [turning back] of the relief [support] parties. I shall of course communicate with you by those parties. I attach hereto a programme of the dates at which the various sledging parties may be expected to start from and return to the ship. [This, too, has not survived.] With regard to the Western Exploration I leave the details unreservedly in your hands. I fully approve of your plans and of the men you propose to select and shall expect you to requisition such aid as you require for extending your trip.
>
> Lieut. Barne when recruited from his present journey will take to the depot a small stock of provisions for my own party and then proceed to explore to the westward. I wish him to confine himself as far as possible to the Barrier surface with the main object of outlining the lands which we now suppose to be the termination of Victoria Land or of observing any that may be beyond it. He is to be instructed to return to the ship not later than Jan[uar]y 30th 1903.
>
> In view of possible sickness I wish Dr. Koettlitz to be at the ship on the following dates:

From Nov. 18th till the return of the 1st Relief Party

—— Dec. 10th————————— 2nd————

—— Jan. 18th————————— Western Party

. . . [There followed instructions for Royds about various scientific explorations in the area and the need for a standby search party.] . . . In the event of my not returning before the date at which there is any possibility of the ship being again frozen in, you should I think take the ship back to New Zealand, provisioning to suit, and leaving if you think fit a search party which could be recovered in the following season.

The date of arrival of the relief ship is so problematic that it is of little use to make plans concerning her. I do not anticipate [its arrival] before the end of January, and by the time the stores are transferred I shall hope to have returned. The principal stores we shall require are, as you know, as much coal and oil as she can spare and bottled fruit.

Should these be transferred before the end of January, you will [be free] to carry out the programme of further exploration we have discussed. . . . [If not] I should wish Mr. Bernacchi to be sent in her to take pendulum and magnetic observations at C. Adare . . . during the summer the principal task will be to free the boats. . . . I think it will be much assisted if earth or other dark substance is placed round the gunwhales where exposed to the sun's rays.

I attach a list of provision stores which will be brought off from the hut and [Ford] has full instructions as to the stowage . . . but I do not wish [them] touched until . . . it is certain it will not be necessary to again land them. Should the bay ice show signs of breaking away the officer in command will of course use his discretion in this matter. The magnetic huts will be left till the last moment.

The Southern Support Parties had set out the day before under Barne, with Feather, Dailey, and nine men, pulling five sledges in train with 650 pounds of supplies for Scott aboard.* Dailey's party was to turn back five days south of the depot.[57] From there, Barne's was to carry on south for another ten days.

The weather on November 1 bordered on the impossible for sledging, and Scott put his own start back a day. Amid cheers from those staying behind and with the dogs pulling as never before, according to Scott, the five-sledge train went so fast they had two men ride on the sledges for the first 2 miles. Even then, as yet in finnesko, he and the others had to run to keep up.

By that evening they had caught up with the support party, 14 miles off the northern end of White Island, only to find that the foot

---

* See Appendix 5 for the members of each party.

THE SOUTHERN SUPPORT PARTY PREPARING TO LEAVE, OCTOBER 31, 1902. The roofs of the shore huts and the cairn on Hut Point can be seen beyond them. The five sledges, which Barne, Dailey, and ten men were to pull, comprised three 9-footers, an 11-footer, and a 7-footer. Courtesy, the Royal Society.

party was scarcely making a mile an hour, slithering on the icy surface in their finnesko. They needed boots, but those were too cold to walk in. Their skis, until then carried on the dog sledges, were tried in vain. No one in Norway had advised of the need for skins on the underside of the skis for such work, because Nansen had not used them on his first crossing of Greenland. When the surface was unsuitable for skis, Nansen had pulled on foot. Curiously, for the next day and a half Scott and his two companions continued to walk and occasionally run, even when the surface was suitable for skis. After that, Scott and Wilson tried their skis and found them a great relief.

For four days the two parties made more or less equal progress, averaging about 11 miles a day after 250 pounds had been transferred to the dog sledges. A blizzard then blew up in the night, and they could only travel for four hours over the next three days. That brought them within striking distance of the depot. Barne caught up only by marching all night after the wind died down. Waking to a sunny, calm day on November 10, Scott's party ran the last 10 miles to the depot

THE SOUTHERN PARTY DOGS AND SLEDGES LINED UP FOR THE START ON NOVEMBER 2, 1902. Taken just after Skelton had photographed Scott and his two companions in front of the leading sledge, where two other men are being photographed. The dogs successfully pulled the initial load of 1,700 pounds, including the four 9-foot sledges and the 7-footer carrying the cooker and instruments, and continued to do so until an 11-foot sledge was transferred from the support party when Barne turned back in 79°12S. The sledgemeter, at first attached to that party's 7-foot sledge, was also transferred when Scott's party caught up with them. Courtesy, the Royal Society.

and settled down to replenish and repack the sledges. It had taken the dogs less than five-and-a-half days to cover the 67 miles, at first with 1,700 pounds gross load and then with 1,950 pounds, or 108 pounds per dog discounting Blanco, which had never pulled. Barne's team did not appear until 5 P.M. the next day, by which time they were already six days behind schedule.

Ominously, the first shadow over their prospects had already appeared. Wilson had harbored doubts about Shackleton back in July, but he did not spot the potential weak point in his friend's condition and did not know of the all-night bout of coughing Shackleton had suffered on October 9. Shackleton had said nothing about it after quieting it several times with a permanganate gargle.[58] Now, whereas Wilson was fully recovered from an acute cold developed the third day out, Shackleton had started a hacking cough two days later and continued coughing a great deal when the blizzard kept them in their tent on October 7.[59]

The dogs had done much better than the men, so another 150 pounds was transferred from Barne's sledges to equalize the speed. That meant the dogs were now pulling 2,100 pounds. Traveling together, the two parties advanced 10 miles to reach 78°55S, with all of the men happy to have beaten Borchgrevink's farthest south.

Fatefully, the dogs' fine performance swayed Scott into believing that even with a sixth sledge added to the train they could pull as fast as the men, given that he and the other two would lend a hand. The support party still carried 4 weeks' rations and fuel for them, amounting to 230 pounds. With an extra 11-foot sledge and canvas tank container for the food, the total load for the dogs to pull would be over a ton.*

Influenced, too, by the view of the apparent end of Victoria Land and the prospect of what might be discovered on the far side of it, Scott decided to send Barne back after two days to allow him an earlier start on his journey in that direction. At midnight he got into his sleeping bag to write a note for Dailey to take back to Armitage:[60]

Lat. 78°54S; Long. 168°30E; Midnight November 12

My dear Armitage,

   We have had a heavy and annoying time so far, from the frequency of blizzards; but I hope that is over now as we seem to have left it behind with the land. The work has been very trying for the men, but they leave us in splendid health and spirits. The dogs, I find today, will drag 2,100 pounds; they have brought that amount ten miles. This modifies my plan; I shall send Barne back in two days, going on from that date with twelve weeks' provisions, plus 70 pounds of seal for our party, and about forty days' food for the dogs. If conditions hold we ought to do well. The dogs are

---

* Nine days after Barne turned back, Wilson's diary refers to six sledges (WD: 11.24.02). The gross load would have been 2,300 pounds, or 121 pounds per dog (not 150 as stated in Huntford [1985 #2: p. 93]), compared with the nearly 150 pounds per dog Swedish explorer Otto Nordenskjöld had asked of his five-dog team when he had set out on his Southern journey from Snow Hill Island in October. The following spring, on his journey through Prince Gustav Channel with Johansen, his six dogs were each pulling 128 pounds, and as on the other journey, Nordenskjöld and his companion were walking on foot, not on skis (Nordenskjöld 1905: p. 297). By comparison, Nansen, setting out from the *Fram* for his attempt on the North Pole, took twenty-eight dogs for a gross load of 2,100 pounds, or 75 pounds per dog (Nansen 1898, vol. 1: p. 381). In 1911 Amundsen asked his dogs to pull only 64 pounds each (Bernacchi 1938: p. 67).

dragging splendidly. We see nothing yet but a vast white plain to the south, though the weather is quite clear. Barne has done splendidly, and I want him given all the aid possible in his south-west trip, which I think should prove most important, as it seems about certain the land must trend north round from the farthest point we see.

He will be able to leave some of his provisions at the depot, which is very easy to find, and, starting again from the ship earlier than was expected, will be able to make a more extended journey. He has worked his men very well and looked after them thoroughly.

The men are all very pleased at being "Farthest South" . . . there is certainly a very extraordinary surface here which requires special arrangement for footgear.

I don't think skis would do for men dragging heavy weights, though they would be very good when the weights come down say to 120 or 130 pounds; but even of this I am not sure, as in places the surface of the sastrugi is quite hard and polished, and one can only get a grip with a ski boot by digging in the heel.

Will send you another note by Barne—for the present "au revoir." Remember me to all.

Yours ever,

R. F. Scott

P.S.: Should like Barne to have Mr. Dailey's party of six kept intact.

Scott's decision that night would have a momentous effect on his party's fortunes. It would not only shape the third season, which none of them yet knew lay ahead, but its consequences would dictate the British effort in the region over the next decade. Although fully justified by the dogs' splendid performance so far and the tempting prize to the west, Barne's early return removed the very support that would have enabled Scott to see the truly continental scale of the land that lay astride the direct route to the Pole—and might have brought about the discovery of the gateway in it that later won Shackleton such fame.[61] None of this was suspected by the three in Scott's tent then or three days later, when they looked at the land that seemed to end west of them and saw the shimmering image of Barne's party dwindle and finally vanish behind them, leaving them alone with their eighteen dogs[62] and six sledges in the vastness of that empty white wilderness.

Armitage learned of the changed plan only when Dailey and his men arrived back on the 21st, two days behind schedule, having run out of food after being held up by a blizzard. The night before they arrived, he had already had a search party standing by. Reading Scott's letter he saw that Barne should be arriving on November 23, which he did, bringing with him a second letter written on the 14th. The letter reported a strong indication that Armitage would find himself descending to barrier ice on the far side of the western mountains:[63]

> 79°12S 168°15E
>
> My dear Armitage,
>
> Barne leaves us tomorrow, so I send you this last line. We are doing pretty well with our heavy loads; yesterday about eight miles—stopped by snowstorm; today ten at a push. . . . The land certainly trains west-south-west from the Bluff, ending in a cape from which, I think, there is little doubt it turns north again; but there is no high land behind this coastline, and the western hills form a very distinct ridge with an obvious descent on the opposite side.
>
> Whether you will come to barrier level again one cannot say at this distance; but I certainly think it looks as though Victoria Land was very narrow at this end. Barne will tell you about it.

Armitage had decided even before Barne's return that he wanted Horace Buckridge from Barne's party in place of a second man from Dailey's for the western teams, putting their start back to November 29. But by the time all was ready for his own great effort, he had come to the surprising conclusion that Barne could not start before Koettlitz returned with the Western Support Party:[64]

> Winter Quarters SS *Discovery*
>
> 27.11.02
>
> Dear Capt. Scott,
>
> Many thanks for your letters, which I received by Mr. Dailey and "Barne." . . . I had everything ready to start away for Mr. Dailey's relief on the 22nd.
>
> It was very agreeable news that you were making such good progress, and I shall not be at all surprised to hear that you have reached 85°S—or even more. [He continues about work on freeing the boats].
>
> Of course our chief work has been the preparation of our sledge equipment. I had intended departing on the 24th, but as our outfit could not be complete until the return of the depot party I had to postpone it.
>
> We start—weather permitting—on the morning of the 29th . . . with 10 sledges and about 4,000 lbs weight. . . .
>
> I have been struck by the large amount of work to be done by "Royds," with very few hands, in order to prepare the ship for sea, and have gone over it carefully with him.
>
> *There is not sufficient equipment for "Barne" to leave the ship until "Koettlitz" returns.*
>
> *There is only one sledge (besides the big one) left; one primus; and no food bags.*

There are only 9 hands and the Bo'sun remaining, besides 3 Engine Room hands, so that it is imperative that no more leave the ship at present, in case "Koettlitz" requires relief [my italics].

Skelton has made special spirit lamps [cookers] for a relief party. . . . "Barne" should be able to leave here by the 20th December with 5 men, which will leave either 7 (or if he takes a stoker 8) men and Mr. Feather: 2 of whom will be on night duty. The Engine-room staff will have their hands full preparing the machinery for sea.

I have left "Royds" instructions never to be without 6 working hands, except he has to relieve a sledge party. I am sure you will agree that number of men is none too many.

"Barne" will thus be able to be away for six weeks at least, and leave 2 sledges and 2 primus lamps [cookers] for Dr. Koettlitz and . . . relief parties. . . .

The Sports [on November 8 in honor of the king's birthday] were a great success, and have brought the men more together. For instance "Cross" and "Evans" are now great chums.

We continued them the following Saturday as well as an informal concert for all hands in the Ward-room—three Saturdays in succession.

"Ford" has, as usual, done his utmost to promote everything I have wished. The Cook has behaved himself, and I have told him today to continue his "late" record. [Unfortunately, it turned out that the "late record" had included cooking Armitage's party's sledging seal ration in rancid fat.]

I shall send you another few lines by "Koettlitz." Kindest regards to "Billy" and "Shackleton." If you get as far as all the Ship's Company most heartily desire you to do, you will indeed have done well, and my men, I am convinced, will struggle their utmost with their loads.

Yours obediently and most sincerely,

Albert B. Armitage

The final plan in mid-October, based on Koettlitz's return with the Western Support Party on December 10, in time for Barne's return, had foreseen the Southwest Party getting away about December 18. Scott had allowed for a search party and obviously discussed the selection of men for the various parties with Armitage, as the last sledging order testifies.

For the period November 24 to December 10, when Koettlitz's Western Support Party was to have been away while Barne's party was still on its way back from the south, the final plan had foreseen as adequate a deck complement at the ship of only five hands under Quartermaster Thomas Kennar, with five reserves. On Koettlitz's return two more seamen would be added, with two more (Whitfield and Hubert) joining the reserves (see Appendix 6).

As Scott would have seen it from the camp where Dailey's party turned back, if during that period Barne and five men were absent going southwest instead of still on the southern route, the agreed manning of the ship would not have been altered. Equally, two days later, when Barne started back, there was nothing to suggest the Western Parties' start (dependent on the sledges and two men from Dailey's party) or Koettlitz's return would be delayed. Even if they were, there was no likelihood of the ice freeing the ship that early.

There is no basis for Armitage's implied assertion that only one sledge was available for Barne before Koettlitz returned. The arithmetic of sledge availability after Barne's return was extremely simple and unlikely to have confused Scott. Apart from the big 3-foot-wide 12-footer, there were nineteen sledges.* Of these ten had gone south, leaving nine at the ship. With the Southern Support Parties bringing four back and the Western Parties needing ten, not one but three would remain at the ship. There was nothing on that score to stop Barne and five men from starting off with two of those sledges for the southwest. That would have left one at the ship for an emergency search party.[65] And with Koettlitz starting after Dailey's return and before Barne's return from the south, that is clearly what the October plan envisaged. There is no evidence that either Armitage or Royds had objected to that plan—and Royds was never slow to criticize Scott in his private diary.

Likewise, it is hardly conceivable that the October plan could have condemned either Barne's or Koettlitz's parties to travel without a primus stove or food bags or that the search party's need for them had been overlooked. In this respect there is more than a hint that the original allocations to the Western Parties had been tampered with. The change of plan did involve Barne's party being away for a week (December 11–17) when the men would otherwise have been at the ship. For a two-tent party that involved two more food bags, hardly something that could not be improvised. The inference must be that Armitage had commandeered more than originally planned for the Western journey, which, it must be remembered, Scott had given him authority to do, but in complying Armitage can hardly have been said to have given Barne "all the aid possible" as Scott desired.

---

* Scott (1905 vol. 1: p. 423) says there were twenty sledges: two @ 12 feet, six @ 11 feet, nine @ 9 feet, and three @ 7 feet. Subsequent sledge deployment makes it certain none was left at the depot by Barne or Dailey, so Armitage's statement that only one was left is inexplicable.

Nevertheless, the fact was that the decision to undertake two southern sledge journeys had long since involved stretching the expedition's manpower to the limit. With the achievement of Scott's main goal already prejudiced by Barne's early return, Armitage's intervention, which put Barne's party out of action for three weeks, would deny Scott the other great prize his first campaign could have yielded. That was not the discovery of a new island almost the size of Greenland, which the Antarctic's shimmering mirages had held before him for the first 28 miles south of the depot, but the proof of the continuity, and thus continental scale, of the land to the west and south of the Great Ice Barrier they were traveling over. For a marginal gain in readying the ship for a voyage that was not to be, one of the principal aims of the entire expedition was doomed to frustration.

For the three men alone in the south, the defeat of their main aim was already a depressing probability. Their confidence had begun to dwindle almost from the moment Barne disappeared below the northern horizon on November 15, as the surface softened and ground their progress to a crawl.

14

BLIGHTING OF THE SOUTHERN DREAM
Scott's Journey Toward the Pole

For Scott that morning, the great moment had come. Armitage would discover the west coast of Victoria Land* and make the observations that would position the magnetic pole, even if he could not get close to it. Barne would bring back a picture of its southern coast. And the three of them—Scott, with Wilson and Shackleton—that day farther south than any mortal before them, had it in their hand to answer the great question: Was there more land toward the Pole, or did the huge ice sheet just go on endlessly toward the far side of the Antarctic Circle? For all they knew, the *Gauss* might even now be in sight of its other face, far to the south of the Indian Ocean, waiting for the ice to set the ship free to follow it westward.

For the next two weeks Scott and his companions were the only men on the British expedition actually making progress toward the unknown. Before long, however, they became unable to advance the 10 miles a day the dogs had achieved, for they were in softer snow than any yet encountered. With the sledges again on wooden underrunners they seemed twice as hard to drag, so after a mile they removed them. That was a decided advantage, according to Scott, yet the pulling was still hard for the dogs.[1] By 5 P.M. they had advanced only 2½ miles, and the dogs were so obviously played out that the men decided to camp.

---

* For simplicity the modern name is used from here on in place of Ross's "South Victoria Land," still used at the time of the expedition.

Despite the sticky surface Scott could not entirely account for the slow speed. Only about 150 pounds had been added to the total load. The trouble was undoubtedly aggravated by the dogs sensing that the men who had fed and exercised them throughout the winter were nowhere in sight, and they had to work for three comparative strangers. Wilson had to admit that the day's progress was not promising. But at least the weather was calm and clear so they could dry out their sleeping bags that evening.

To their dismay, the dogs could not even move the six-sledge train in the morning, and the only option was to relay them forward three at a time. Even if they had to traverse three times the distance for every mile advanced, the overall speed had to be faster than yesterday's dismal rate. And yet after they had traveled 5 miles with the first three sledges it was apparent that they were going to be able to achieve no more in a reasonable day's work—a nine-hour day, with the only rest at the lunch break.

When they brought the second three sledges up, a fight broke out among the dogs. Shackleton attributed it to hunger because they were now "on a strict allowance of fish [Norwegian torsk, or dried codfish], which is meagre [compared] to their unlimited supply of seal meat during the winter."[2] So there was no question that the dogs' diet was inadequate. Stoked up with the copious vitamins of the raw seal meat and now, for only two weeks so far, on the sledging ration that had served Nansen's dogs well enough over the Siberian wastes in 1893, Shackleton felt the dogs ought to have done better.[*]

At first they could only ascribe the slow pace to the surface, now covered with half an inch of gritty snow crystals that became sticky as the sun warmed them. After two days advancing in a blank whiteness through frozen showers that constantly fed the thick surface coating of loose ice crystals, the sledgemeter had added only 11 miles to the total traveled. It counted in fathoms, so they had to divide the figure by 1,025 to work out the geographical miles covered.[3] Wilson prayed for a wind to sweep the crystals away: "This is wearing us out and the dogs."[4]

---

[*] Here was the clue to why the seal meat had run out four weeks before seals reappeared. The dogs had not been fed on biscuit alone, as claimed by Huntford (1979: p. 169; 1985 #2: p. 81). Beyond reasonable doubt Scott's statement (1905, vol. 2: p. 29) that he had been persuaded to take the dried fish "by one who had had great experience in dog-driving" refers to advice from Nansen, whom he did not wish publicly to blame.

Starting late on November 20 to give the dogs an easier day, they had their first reward as the sky cleared in the afternoon and revealed "new land to the westward."[5] It was a third apparent island, and there were now "three distinct gaps."[6]

With only 3⅓ miles to the good that day, they had reached about 79°42S. For both Shackleton and Wilson the dream of solving the great southern mystery had already degenerated into a round of ceaseless grinding work with little hope of reaching "the high southern latitude we first hoped to do on leaving the ship."[7] This bore out Wilson's belief that the journey would turn out to be an endless trudge over a featureless ice plain. And although they could now see the new "island" of land a little south of due west, looking straight ahead it still seemed as though he might be right.

In the morning the team woke to the clearest day yet, and the situation changed as they made the first relay. More land appeared progressively farther ahead on their southwest flank. For more than five days they had advanced at an exasperatingly slow pace compared with the dogs' achievement before parting from Barne. Now at last there was an opportunity for Scott to alter his plan. If he reverted to the original plan for a second depot, they could leave all of the food for the return journey—perhaps as much as half the load. Furthermore, now that there was land they could reach without too much of a diversion, he could adopt the more cautious plan and set up the second depot on solid land rather than far out on the barrier. That would avoid any risk of the disaster Peary had so narrowly escaped in Greenland in 1895.[8] Over by the land they might also find a packed snow surface, hardened by winds from the land that had obviously carved the *sastrugi* running from that direction. They changed course to SSW.

By now, although the sledges rode on the surface, the three men were sinking in as much as 16 inches as they crossed hollows filled with the sticky crystals. It was no wonder they were having to drive the dogs and getting little response—it was "the most exasperating work," as Wilson put it.[9] But whereas they had felt that the surface was the only plausible cause of the dogs' poor performance, that day they also realized that the dried codfish was not agreeing with the animals on whom the whole plan depended.[10]

As though in answer to their prayer a north breeze sprang up the next morning, November 22. The breeze cleared some of the snow and allowed them to use the sails for the first time, although this barely improved the distance covered. More and more land appeared to the SSW, and by the afternoon it was visible over the horizon straight ahead, raising Wilson's hopes and interest. Now he would have something positive to sketch.

They still had not enjoyed the satisfaction of feeling they had discovered anything like a continent. This latest land was yet another island—all along the horizon the land was divided by "long gaps in between." [11]

Twice they tried to get the dogs to pull the sledges in one train, but to no avail. After ten days, driving them had "become a perfectly beastly business," as Wilson described it, undoubtedly reflecting the feelings of everyone. [12] He had started using his skis on November 23 and found them a relief to his aching leg muscles.

The dogs must have done somewhat better that day, for the mileage scarcely dropped when they adopted the new tactic of having one man stay to put up the tent and get lunch ready while the others went back for the other three sledges, one on skis driving the dogs, and the other riding on the sledge from which they had unloaded the camping gear. The same method was adopted for a second advance in the afternoon.

For the first move of the relay, one man would be ahead of the dogs, hitched to the main trace. He would pull like mad and yell out anything that would encourage the dogs to follow him. Another would pull from one side of the train, and the third would ski beside the leading sledge, driving the dogs on with threats and, much as it went against the grain, copious use of the whip on the laggards.*

Joe, Bernacchi's old *Southern Cross* dog, was already so worn out that he was let loose in the hope that he would recover. The weight was dropping by about 40 pounds a day (the dogs ate 20 pounds of the dried fish daily), and with the total down to about 1,900 pounds the reduction to seventeen dogs made little difference.

At last, the next day, November 25, steering by compass all day without seeing any land, they almost reached the 80th parallel, camp-

---

* The impression created by modern authors (Thomson 1977: pp. 66–67: "Scott had sought out Nansen and then rejected his experience," and Huntford 1979: p. 169: "They were all poor drivers relying, in the last resort, on brute force . . . the dog cannot be driven like a horse") is one of cruelty unique to the inexperienced Britons. Nansen's words paint a different picture (1898, vol. 2: p. 11): "Then came Johansen with the other two sledges, always shouting . . . always beating them and himself hauling. . . . It makes me shudder even now when I think of how we beat them mercilessly." He, like Scott, had been forced to take Ostiak West Siberian dogs instead of the superior East Siberian animals he had hoped Trontheim would procure for him.

ing 1½ miles short of it. The dogs, however, were plainly more exhausted than ever, and a blizzard the following day provided the day's break they needed.

The men were as yet experiencing no ill effects, and they regarded their frugal diet as more than ample. Breakfast was a large cup of chopped-up bacon fried with pounded biscuit, two or three biscuits, and two large mugs of tea. Lunch was minimal—a biscuit and two cups of hot chocolate. Supper was two large cups of soup, boiled with pemmican, pea meal and bacon powder ("red ration"), pounded-up biscuit, and powdered cheese, followed by hot cocoa with "plasmon," a hydrolyzed protein additive. In just a few days, though, they experienced burgeoning appetites bordering on outright pangs of hunger as mealtime approached.

Scott calculated correctly that laboring on with the whole load to a landfall straight ahead would gain little net advantage. If they headed for the nearest land, they would probably be rid of the food for the return journey somewhat sooner. So they started off on the 27th due SW, toward the land on the south side of the fourth gap in the line of apparent islands showing above the horizon.

For the first mile they tried the single-train haul, but the dogs required so much beating that they reverted to a relay. After covering 3 more miles in as many hours, Wilson made the lunch camp while the others went back. That gave him the chance to sketch the new land. It cost Wilson the first touch of snow blindness, a trial that afflicted them all so frequently during the coming ordeal.

By the end of that day, ever ready to find some way to coax the dogs back to their earlier level of performance, the men had convinced themselves that the sun was too hot for the dogs with their thick coats. So they changed to night marches, and at first the dogs seemed to pull better. Lunch was now in the evening, and supper was at 3 A.M. But they immediately paid a price. Scott and Wilson, relaying the second load while Shackleton stayed at the camp to make supper, found it difficult to follow the tracks in the poor light. A breeze sprang up and covered them with drift, and the two men lost the track altogether.

After two nights the land was again visible and appeared encouragingly closer, but they rarely gained much more than 4 miles a night. On November 29 they began adding a small slice of dried seal meat to their lunch menu to help appease their growing appetites.[13] They were strongly aware of the exasperating grind they must endure before making any acceptable progress southward. At 4 miles per night they estimated it would take ten more nights to reach the land.

Nevertheless, a worthwhile discovery was still within their grasp, even though they would only be able to travel south for eighteen days.[14] The dog food would run out in sixteen days. If they cut down on food before the depot, they could extend that figure by three days. At 10 miles a day—surely possible with the lesser load and no relaying—they would reach 84°S. Although it was not the impressive-sounding 85° they had hoped for, they should be able to see at least that far and possibly beyond. That would be halfway into the magic circle that remained blank on everyone's maps and would allow them to establish whether land continued that far and, if so, whether it was continuous or split into separate islands.

In reality, with a further night stuck in the tent during a blizzard and several at an even slower rate of advance, it took them thirteen nights of hard labor to reach the final depot position and then another, the night of December 14, in a vain attempt to get onto the land.

They had suffered another blow on December 5, finding they had finished a can of kerosene three days too soon. That was equivalent to being as much as fifteen days short on the round-trip. They stopped heating anything for lunch, which did not help their already ravenous appetites, and Wilson endured nightmares centered around gargantuan feasts in which the food turned to ashes on his plate or waiters refused to respond when summoned.

Rheumatic pains in Wilson's feet accurately forecast the blizzard that blew up the next day (the 6th). They found one of the dogs mightily swollen and asleep across the mouth of the bag of seal meat. It had devoured a good weeks' allowance for the three of them.

After that, things went from bad to worse. Several of the other dogs began to exhibit symptoms of dysentery. For the first time Wilson began positively to suspect the dried fish, as the 4 miles gained on the 7th and 8th decreased to 2 miles the following night. Scott and Wilson had gone back for the second train and, pulling themselves for all they were worth, had carried food in front of the dogs to get them to move the 500-pound load. It took three hours to cover the 2 miles. The first dog, Snatcher, died the next day. As soon as he was fed to the others, the mileage improved somewhat.

By December 13, however, Shackleton was describing the night's run as "our worst day so far; very heavy soft snow—total distance less than 2 miles; the dogs not pulling any better. We must plant a depot tomorrow in any case. We cannot go on any more like this . . . we hope to struggle on for 3 weeks before turning back."[15] They had tried pulling on skis, but the snow had balled up on the undersides and made them unmanageably heavy. Each ski weighed about 5 pounds as it was and would have been unsteerable with ice lumps unevenly distributed along it.[16]

Peary's experience in 1895 must have weighed heavily on Scott's mind. Halted at last about 10 miles off the cape they had struggled so long to reach, he evidently felt the depot would be easier to find if they placed it on the land.[17] In the event, half a mile ahead lay huge jumbles of ice in a chasm 60 feet deep that put an end to the attempt to reach the shore.

After securing the three-week supply of food they were leaving at the depot,[18] Shackleton photographed the chasms late on the 14th. They were under way again at about 11 P.M., heading toward a double rainbow around the sun where it shone through the driving showers of tiny hexagonal ice crystals. After 300 miles of relay work that had gotten them barely 1½° southward to about 80°29S, Scott found it an inexpressible relief not to have to traverse every mile three times over.[19]

Even now, with only four sledges—one 7-footer, two 9-footers, and one 11-footer—and sixteen dogs (Joe was back in harness again), they had to pull themselves—sometimes on skis, sometimes more effectively in finesko when the surface was too sticky and balled up on the skis. They fed the nine best animals (which they still hoped to bring back) on dog flesh and they seemed to improve, but the others grew visibly weaker each day on the dried fish. Once more the surface had the type of crust that hurt their paws as they broke through it, so the first full night they gained only 7 miles. The weakest dog, Vic, was killed after that run and added to the stock in the dogs' canvas food tank.

Because of the shortage of kerosene, the one hot meal was supper, with lunch a hurried cold snack, sometimes only ten minutes, sometimes longer to give the dogs a rest. Yet apart from bouts of snow blindness and the ever-increasing hunger, Wilson still declared them all very fit at that stage.

The mist was so heavy that after two nights they realized their only chance to survey and sketch was to travel during the day, but the daytime temperature (about 27°F) made the surface so heavy that any idea of gaining 10 miles a day vanished from their hopes. As they would find out too late, the silver-clad runners were totally unsuited to any surface temperature warmer than about 16°F. They learned that fact on December 18.

The next day the dogs were in such a pathetic state that the men abandoned the idea of bringing any of them back to the ship. On Sunday the 21st, down to thirteen dogs, they barely advanced 4 miles. In desperation they uncoupled the large sledge with the dog food to see if it would be better to do without the dogs. Pulling on skis, they could hardly move the other three, which weighed about 500 pounds, and in finesko they managed less than a mile an hour.

During the previous two days the main mountain range unrolling on their right had disappeared behind ice-clad foothills (today called the Darley Hills on USGS maps), but that morning a further group of 9,000-foot summits had appeared beyond the foothills, the first of which was the most perfectly formed pyramid seen so far. From that day on the peak became Pyramid Mountain. At the lunch camp Wilson sketched the whole panorama.[20] After the evening meal he made a larger sketch of the mountain with the two table mountains to the south of it. The orientation of the picture shows they were in about 81°22S.[21]

That evening Wilson also told Scott that during the usual Sunday morning medical inspection he had found that Shackleton's gums appeared inflamed, thus raising the specter of scurvy. They kept it to themselves but stepped up the seal meat and cut out the bacon because Wilson believed tainted meat caused scurvy.

As the temperature dropped to −13°F, the distance gained increased to 8 miles, although the surface remained so soft they could push an ice ax down into it with just one finger. Sights at the December 23 evening camp put them at 81°33½S 163°23E.[22] Scott took those sights first thing the next morning, having found that if left out overnight the theodolite's tripod feet grew lumps of ice that stopped them from sinking into the surface. The mileage recorded by the sledgemeter put them 5½ miles further north (58 miles from the depot), and the comparison supported Shackleton's earlier suspicion that the sledgemeter readings had been low.[23] As they learned later, however, the mileage recorded from that camp to their penultimate camp on the way south entirely supported the position indicated by the sledgemeter.

While Scott worked out their position that morning, the others divided the canvas food tank, now half empty, to make a separate one for the dogs' food. That enabled them to abandon the 11-foot sledge, but the surface remained so soft that they still managed only 8 miles that day.

Christmas Day began with the sun shining through their green tent under a cloudless sky. After a generous breakfast of seal liver and biscuit crumbs fried in bacon and pemmican fat, followed by biscuit and blackberry jam (from the one tin they had), they photographed themselves with the distant coast glistening behind them.[24]

The previous evening they had reached a better surface and now found they could pull the whole load easily by themselves. With much relief they let the dogs lope along on slack traces all day. This seemed an encouraging reward for having dropped the large sledge. Even though they knew they were helped by the good surface that day (a curious bonus given that the temperature was back up to 32°F), it was a relief to know they could pull the sledges by themselves, as by then the dogs were practically useless.[25]

They allowed themselves a double serving of hot chocolate and plasmon for lunch, and Wilson then sketched the 2,000-foot black-and-red cliffs (just south of Cape Laird).[26] By that evening, with 10 miles gained in seven hours of pulling, they felt their supper well earned. Triple rations and a small hot plum pudding with a sprig of artificial holly, long secreted by Shackleton, left them all with a sense of well-being at the end of the day, marred only by the realization that they would have to turn on December 28. That had become imperative as "the Captain and I," Shackleton wrote, "have slight signs of scurvy. It will not be safe to go on."[27]

Now, though, as they basked in the unusual pleasure of feeling replete after a meal, the conversation for once was not about food. As they looked across at the pyramidal peak they had watched grow larger for several days, which was now directly west of them, they had to decide its name there and then. So Christmas Height it became, later renamed Christmas Mountain (81°54S).[28]

The only other shadow that evening was the state of Wilson's left eye, which was so uncomfortable the next day that he had to sketch the mountain using just one eye.* After 5 miles on the march with the eye blindfolded, it became so painful that they had to camp for lunch. Cocaine failed to relieve the intense pain, so Wilson injected himself with morphine and slept soundly, waking up practically well on December 27.

Wilson was so afraid of triggering the blindness again that he went totally blindfolded all that day, pulling on skis. He did not see the next outcrop of "wonderful red cliffs over 2,500 feet sheer" (81°57S), which amazed Shackleton as they advanced about 15 miles from the

---

* The orientation of the sketch on p. 25 in the June 1903 *South Polar Times* shows their camp was in about 81°48S.

shore.[29] Nor could he see the new mountain the others told him had risen over the far horizon by that evening. Shackleton was sure this was the most southerly point they would see and believed it would be named Mount Longstaff.

That day, too, Wilson missed the grandest sight they had seen so far as their 6-mile advance rolled back the land on the starboard bow to reveal a range of mountains that by evening had risen to a twin-peaked giant that had to be 14,000 feet high. It was certainly higher than anything they had seen since Mount Sabine. The afternoon march was cut short at 5 P.M. so the scene could be recorded with the camera and, if possible, sketched by Wilson before the sun spoiled the lighting. That way they would have a faithful record if the photograph failed. They had covered about 6 miles, and the photograph shows they could see as far along the new range as a cape on the south shore of what must be a huge inlet.[30]

The cape appeared to be (and in fact is) north of the great mountain and gave Scott the impression that the inlet turned north around the corner out of their sight. Despite the fact that he was sketching with one eye still blindfolded, Wilson's panorama accords remarkably with the photograph and shows far more distinctly the distant Mount Longstaff far down the coast to the south. The modern map shows their camp must have been in about 82°05½S 165E and, as Scott estimated, about 10 miles from the shore.[31]

They could see that only a few miles more would enable them to see into the inlet and discover whether it was just that or a strait dividing the new land from the coast, along which they had now sledged for slightly over 95 miles. But another dog had collapsed on the march, and at the speed they were managing it would be almost midnight before they could get far enough past the cape to see whether the inlet or strait really turned north. By that time the light might be too poor to see to the real horizon. Scott opted for a brief dash on skis the next day.

But December 29 dawned with drift higher than their heads, blowing hard from the south beneath a tantalizingly clear blue sky. These conditions destroyed any chance of seeing their camp if they left it, to say nothing of masking crevasses, which were more than likely in the region of the cape they would pass to achieve their aim. They could only sit out the blizzard and hope. By late that evening it had ceased, but the huge mountain cast the midnight sun's shadow where they least needed it, making the light unfavorable for credible observation. It would be better to make the dash in the morning.

FARTHEST SOUTH. *Above:* Shackleton's photos of the view from the December 28, 1902, evening camp. Wilson is standing by the sledges and Scott near the tent about 10 miles from Cape Wilson, beyond which can be seen the distant bluff, today named Inaccessible Cliffs, on the southern side of the "strait" that later proved to be a glacier. They could see as far south as the highest of the Longstaff Peaks at 82°56S. Faintly visible, the twin peaks appeared to be a single mountain, which they named after the expedition secretary. Invisible at the far left of this reproduction, it was barely discernible in the print that appeared in *The Voyage of the Discovery.* Reproduced from Captain Scott's *The Voyage of the Discovery. Facing page:* Traced excerpt from the modern U.S. Geological Survey Map of the area. In the right-hand photo the alignment of Cape Wilson and the distant bluff (indicated on the map excerpt) fixes the December 28 camp at about 82°05½S. The advance from there was little more than 5½ miles to their farthest south, which must therefore have been about 82°11S. In a cruel twist of fortune, the mist did not thin enough to reveal only 12 miles beyond Inaccessible Cliffs the Kontiki Nunatak with its plunging icefall, which would have revealed the continuity of the land.

As though to emphasize the capricious character of the Antarctic weather, everything was shrouded in fog when they woke. Again the ski run was out of the question, and that left only one option. They must pack up the camp and press on cautiously in the hope the weather would clear. They started off to the southwest, but pressure ridges soon forced them eastward again, and after a little over 4 miles by the sledgemeter they knew that when the weather cleared they should be able to see well beyond the ground that had masked their view farther westward. So they pitched the tent and lunched in hopes of a clearance.

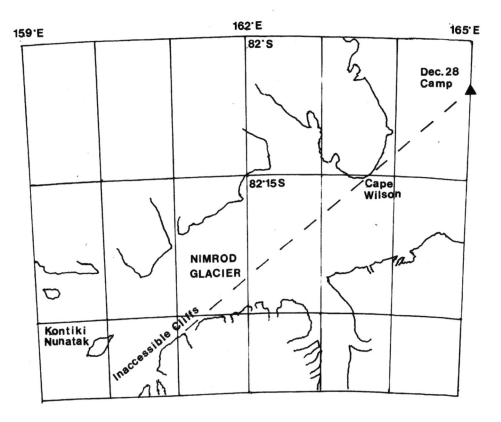

With no sign of a clearance and obviously still believing they stood a better chance of seeing up the inlet with every mile gained, Scott skied southwest into the mist with Wilson (whose eyes had recovered). Wilson was guaranteed to record what they could see if the fog cleared, for his memory was exceptional. But after a mile or so the risk of losing their tracks if the wind got up again outweighed everything else, and the two men turned back.

On the last day of the year the clouds promisingly cleared from the mountains but obstinately refused to lift from the horizon they so desperately wanted to see far to the west. Dallying over the repacking in the hope that the weather would clear, they could see that the far side of the cape west of them (later named after Wilson) did not continue west, strengthening Scott's conviction that its coast turned north. Beyond that and the distant cape on the south side of the strait they could see nothing for sure. Wilson thought there was "apparently a blue horizon line [and that] there was no land blocking the strait. So we must suppose this southernmost high land of 13,000 feet to be insular perhaps."[32]

For all their effort, the question of whether the land they had discovered was a continuous extension on a scale justifying the term *continental* eluded them to the last, most cruelly at this farthest south where the sight of inland ice could have confirmed it and compensated them for the bitter disappointment of having their original hopes dashed. Scott's sights suggested they had reached 82°17S, but the photo of the second-to-last camp and the now known position of the cape west of them make it unlikely that the final camp was much beyond 82°10S or that the last ski run exceeded 82°12S.[33]

Yet dissatisfied as they were with the latitude, they knew they had pushed mankind's knowledge to the 83rd parallel, because from their camp on the 28th the Antarctic's propensity for mirages had shown them two more mountains beyond Mount Longstaff. One of them was almost certainly the peak today named Mount Rifenberg, the other possibly the 9,700-foot Mount Tripp beyond it in 83°17½S.

They would have to start back in the morning because Scott was not going to risk running out of food. The day before he had lost a day of the five days' safety stock. They had cut into the return journey food with the extras they ate on Christmas Day, and the supper they had eaten the night of the 15th–16th was, strictly speaking, extra to the fourteen days of traveling that had brought them to this southernmost camp.[34]

Heading directly north, they found themselves crossing huge snow-bridged crevasses as they closed the cape with the aim of obtaining some rock specimens and finding out if there was a tide crack that would show whether the barrier was still a floating ice mass this far south of its northern face. The most promising land to head for was the nearest of the promontories that jutted out from the snowclad land.[35]

They all set off on skis, with the sun still high in the northern sky. After about 4 miles they faced a chaotic valley a mile wide, its far side about a mile from the cliff they were aiming for and at the foot of a gentle snow slope. Leaving their skis and roping themselves together, they got most of the way across, only to see that the slope ended in a trench with a 40-foot vertical ice face.[36] It was impossible to attempt it without crampons.

Until they saw the great cliffs on December 27, they had believed the land was volcanic,[37] but two days later, recalling the total absence of volcanoes, they had concluded it must be granitic.[38] Now their last chance to prove that was denied them, for they knew they could not afford the time to circumvent the chasm between the second depot and the shore. The geology of the land they had discovered would have to remain a guess. It was sad to have labored this far and be unable to take back the answer to that basic question, which by itself might have solved the problem of the existence of an Antarctic continent. Scott could only hope they might be able at least to clarify the continuity of the land by linking their observations with those of the other wing of the Southern campaign, led by Michael Barne.[39]

More exhausted than Scott thought they should have been as they waited for their food to cook that evening, Shackleton upset the "hoosh"* and was greeted with a chilling silence, for they had decided to go on short rations, having consumed the next day's lunch before they started back. That meant they already regarded themselves as two days short for the return to the depot, for Scott rightly would not cut further into the emergency ration, now down to four days' food, their only defense against bad weather.[†]

As they sat in their tent for that meager New Year's Eve meal, Barne and his five companions were eating their evening meal at the Bluff Depot. Having just offloaded a week's rations for themselves and the Southern Party, they were on the threshold of the journey that might resolve the enigma of the islands.

Simultaneously, 120 miles northwest of the Bluff Depot, the first goal was in sight for Armitage and the eleven men of the Main Western Party. As far as they could see, they were camped beyond the last outcrop of rock and had only one more icefall to climb to the summit of Victoria Land.

Yet as Scott and his companions began their retreat on New Year's Day, with just ten emaciated dogs left and the prospect of soon having none, Armitage's party, marooned by a blizzard the entire day, had also shot their bolt. Their dwindling provisions would force them to turn back in seven days. If the ice cap dipped away beyond the summit,

---

* A boiled stew made with pemmican and the other ration components.

[†] At 6 P.M. on January 12 Scott recorded in his sledging journal (SPRI 1464/3: 1.12.03) that they still had "5 days' provisions." After 6 miles next day they reached the depot. Suggestions that they had no reserves (as in Huntford 1979: p. 174; 1985 #2: p. 107) are clearly without foundation. Whether the four days' reserve they had aboard when they reached the depot was adequate is a matter of opinion, but an allowance of four days for blizzard or fog holdups in a fourteen-day return over known ground can hardly be described as unduly risking his companions' lives.

as it would if Victoria Land had a west coast as Scott believed, the climb back to the summit would mean an even earlier start to their return.

In fact, fate had already decreed their retreat in even less time because the next morning one of the party collapsed into semiconsciousness, felled by what a doctor would quickly have diagnosed as a heart attack. For the second time in seventy-two hours, the chance to prove the continental extent of the land stretching south was thwarted.

15

THE RAMPARTS OF VICTORIA LAND
Armitage's Historic Ascent

Armitage's four teams had started beneath a cloudless sky on November 29.[1] The ten sledges had been lined up on the sea ice for a 10:45 A.M. start, the total load amounting to more than 2 tons (4,734 pounds) for the twenty-one men to pull. Just the food carried on the Main Western Party's sledges weighed over 1,300 pounds; they also carried 18 gallons of kerosene. The sledging ration amounted to a fraction less than 2½ pounds per man per day, including a pound of ship's biscuit, and they also carried 112 pounds of seal meat cooked in fat and dried in the oven until about 60 percent of its deadweight was evaporated, along, alas, with most of the vitamins.

Except for Koettlitz's pair, all the sledges had runners clad with German Silver, protected by wooden underrunners for the run across the sea ice. The sledges, arranged in trains, were divided among four teams:

Main Western Party		Western Support Party	
A Team	*B Team*	*C Team*	*D Team*
Armitage	Allan	Koettlitz	Ferrar
Skelton	Macfarlane	Croucher	Pilbeam
Scott (RM)	Handsley	Clarke	Dell
Evans	Duncan	Dellbridge	Hubert
Quartley	Wild	Whitfield	
Buckridge	Walker		
	Sledges		
12-foot +11-foot +7-foot	3 11-foot	2 9-foot	2 9-foot

LOOKING SOUTH OVER FERRAR GLACIER. A 1970 U.S. Geological Survey aerial photo. Blue Glacier, which Armitage's party used to reach and return from the main glacier, can be seen at left of
the picture beyond the mouth of Ferrar Glacier. Arrows indicate the route the party followed. A
triangle indicates the position of Separation Camp where they left a depot behind the saddle. The
three great Cathedral Rocks buttresses at the north end of the Royal Society Range are on Ferrar
Glacier's south bank, at right of the picture. The narrower of the two glaciers to their left is
Descent Glacier. In Scott's day the 5-mile-wide Ferrar Glacier still extended beyond the hanging
Herbertson Glacier at left edge of the picture. Mount Discovery, with Minna Bluff curving away
beyond it, is at top left corner.

Party members are listed by three-man tent, with Hubert in Dellbridge's
tent.[2]

   Having been defeated by the Ferrar Glacier's fissured face in September, Armitage was aiming to get on to it over what he judged to be
a pass on to its south side, 20 miles from the point he had reached
with Walker. To do so involved ascending the Blue Glacier, so dubbed on
account of the intense color of its ice, and passing across a stretch beyond
its summit that, although invisible, was unlikely to be very steep.

   At first they were aided by the sails, but as soon as the wind dropped
they found the silver-clad runners ran more easily than the wooden

underrunners on the sea ice. Removing them, they got the ten sledges 8 miles across to the fixed ice, which formed the eroded snout of the glacier coming from east of Mount Discovery (now named after Koettlitz). They had no more help from the wind for the two further days they took to reach the Eskers, 34 miles from the ship. On the way, Armitage and Skelton took the first of the planned series of magnetic observations.

With the Main Western Party provisioned for only eight weeks, plus a week's food and kerosene at the Bluff if they returned that way, reaching the magnetic pole was hardly possible unless Victoria Land proved very narrow, with a smooth barrier surface running north at its farther shore. So the magnetic observations became the more vital goal. Like the theodolite, the necessary instruments were carried on the 7-foot sledge so Armitage and Skelton could detach it and then catch the main party, which they did just as the others reached the Eskers campsite.

Killing two seals and adding the liver to their rations, they depoted the rest of the meat in case they returned that way. With steady work up the gully the next day the entire party was on the Blue Glacier by the evening, a good 600 feet above sea level. With the gradient now rather steeper than 3°, alternating snow-covered and slippery ice, all the sledges except the two lightest had to be relayed up singly, with much time lost alternately putting on crampons and skis, so thirty-six hours later they were only another 600 feet up. Here at last the surface leveled out, and they could see that a 10-mile névé slope began some way above them, rising gently toward the point now due west of them where Armitage suspected the pass lay.

The névé flattened out on Sunday, December 7, after five days of ascending, and it felt as though they were on a down gradient. Despite that, they still had to relay the sledges. They camped that night less than 5 miles from their goal, but the saddle was still masked from them by a snow-covered hill hardly 2 miles ahead. Above it appeared the summit of Cathedral Rocks, the triple-peaked cliffs towering over 4,000 feet above Ferrar Glacier, which Armitage had seen from New Harbour.

Skiing on ahead, Armitage climbed to the top, finding the hill was really a moraine heap with granite rubble exposed on its sunnier northern side. From there he could see the best route was over the snow-covered moraine, about 200 feet high, which stretched south from it. By 7 P.M. they were camped on the far side about a mile from the saddle, to which they now had to climb. In the morning Armitage climbed up the shoulder at its northeast end, arriving at a ledge leading around to its north side. He was followed by Koettlitz and Ferrar, and while Ferrar went on 400 feet to the summit, Koettlitz anchored Armitage with a rope so he could look over the edge. Armitage could not see the bottom end of the glacier they would have to descend, but what he saw of the upper reaches was daunting—so much so that when he described them, Koettlitz thought it would be mad to try to get the loaded sledges down that way.[3]

Armitage had not liked the look of the main glacier surface either. Everything appeared to be bare ice riddled with crevasses. They would have to try to get straight through the mountains. Returning to camp, he set the men to offloading the week's rations the Support Party carried. In the afternoon they moved his party's tents to the foot of the slope bounding the southwest side, and somewhat below the crest, of the saddle.

When the camp was set up, Skelton led all the men up to the northern end of the saddle to see the stupendous scene that lay to the west. Skelton recorded it in four panoramic shots,[4] and the men carried the half-plate camera and tripod, weighing 30 pounds, back to the camp, where he exchanged it for Bernacchi's lighter quarter-plate camera, which Koettlitz had been using to take color photos on Blue Glacier.[5] After exchanging a pair of 11-foot sledges for two of the support party's 9-footers and repacking everything, the twenty-one men squeezed into the four tents for the evening meal before the twelve men of the Main Western Party cheered Koettlitz's party off on their way back to the depot camp.

To have felt able to attempt the mountain route, Armitage must have believed the seemingly level snow skyline, visible here and there across the two impassable north-south mountain chains, was the inland ice and that it could be attained by way of a practical slope at the head of the valley in front of the nearer chain. To someone more experienced in Alpine work, to embark on such a route without a lightweight reconnaissance to ascertain what the intervening ground looked like would have been an unjustified gamble with time. Instead, perhaps deceived by the rounded appearance of the intervening ridge at the northern end, Armitage determined to set off in the morning and get all the sledges up it.

The attempt would cost them five precious days and prove impossible. Two days were spent getting the six sledges up the first slope by block and tackle—a rise of perhaps 800 feet in half a mile. By that time the unbushed blocks had worn out, and Duncan had to line them

THE IMPASSABLE MOUNTAIN BARRIER. The view southwest toward the Pimple (center-left peak), which confronted Armitage as he first attempted the mountain route to avoid the perilous Descent Glacier route to Ferrar Glacier. Courtesy, the Royal Society.

with German Silver. That did not lose them time, however, for mist rolled in and stopped them anyway. Eventually it cleared enough to see the way to the ridge, almost as high again above them and about a mile away.

This time Armitage decided to set off to examine the ridge with Wild and Gilbert Scott, only to find the crest was rocky and impassable for sledges. What they saw from that point ruled out further attempts to advance in that direction. They would have to wait for a clear day and go back up to make a survey, photograph the scene, and have Quartley make a sketch in case the photos failed. It was to be an exasperating wait, for that evening a blizzard swept over them, engulfing them all the next day and leaving them marooned in thick fog the day after that.

To Armitage's relief, they woke to a brilliantly clear day on December 15. Leaving the others to start lowering the sledges back down the almost 40° slope, he, Wild, and Scott surveyed, photographed, and

THE VIEW OVER FERRAR GLACIER FROM HIGHEST POINT REACHED. Better than any other picture, this view, looking past the first buttress of Cathedral Rocks from the 4,400-foot ridge they scaled, conveys the menace of the awesome descent they faced. When they started from the summit of Descent Glacier, its lower reaches were again immersed in the fog that nightly blanketed the main glacier. Courtesy, the Royal Society.

sketched the awe-inspiring panorama, now thickly clad in snow, even bringing back some lichen and rock specimens. After lunch Armitage took all the men up to the ridge to marvel at the breathtaking scene. By mid-evening they were once more established at the camp where they had parted from the Support Party.

Skelton, who had seen that the crevassed state of the surface beyond the ridge was hopeless even if they could have gotten down the other side of it, began to think they would have to go back down the Blue Glacier and try again from New Harbour. But he evidently persuaded Armitage that they could save three days if they could somehow get down the frightening glacier, something they had dismissed as impossible five days ago.[6]

For supper they tried the seal liver brought from the ship, and it made all the men sick. Three days later they realized the cook had lied, telling them that all the meat was liver when three quarters of it was full of nauseating blubber.[7]

The 16th dawned fine and clear for their attempt of the descent. Leaving Allan and the others to pack up camp, Armitage set off with Skelton, Evans, Wild, and an empty 9-foot sledge, taking 100 yards of rope. The first slope stretched down 400 yards to a small shelf. After that it disappeared into the billowy fog that rolled up the main glacier each night, usually clearing by about 10 o'clock. Viewed from close quarters rather than from the ledge several hundred feet higher, Armitage could see that the gradient was seldom less than 27° (30 percent). Never short of courage, he got the others to lower him down 100 yards at a time and then to follow on their crampons. After two pitches Armitage led the way on foot down to cloud level, the others bringing the sledge down to him.

They had proved it was possible to get a load down the worst slope, and they started the climb back. Before the four men were halfway up, the clouds dispersed to reveal the rest of the descent at decreasing gradients, interspersed with shelves. One looked promising as a campsite, for it would be impossible to get everything down in a day.

With Skelton going on ahead to tell the others where the surface was negotiable, the other three arrived back at 3 P.M. Less than an hour later the whole party was on the way to the daunting feat that would bring them to the highway to their goal.

Reaching the lip of the saddle, they lashed the sledges together in pairs, and Armitage, Skelton, Allan, and Macfarlane led off gingerly with the 11-foot–7-foot pair, Armitage probing ahead with his ice ax. Some strapping soon broke, and the unwieldy load began to take charge. The trailing strap tripped Armitage head over heels and sent Allan flying into him, so Skelton and Macfarlane found themselves struggling alone to stop the sledges. Amazingly, after about 50 yards they brought the slithering mass to a halt, and they traversed the rest of the slope in safety.

Signaled to start their larger 12-foot–9-foot pair, Evans and Quartley—the two strongest men, paired with Scott and Buckridge—began cautiously, only to become overconfident and temporarily lose control, narrowly avoiding a serious accident. Afterward, Duncan, Wild, Handsley, and Walker brought their 11-foot–9-foot pair down without incident, following the tracks made by the others.

The next slope descended almost 300 feet at around 16° (18 percent) to a 100-yard-long gentle névé slope, followed by a 12° (13

DESCENT GLACIER. The glacier is 3 miles long from the saddle to its junction with Ferrar Glacier and half a mile wide at its narrowest. This dramatic aerial photo, looking south, well shows the three main steps down which the pioneer Western Party manhandled their heavily laden sledges. The daunting upper step, 400 yards long, had pitches at 45° and a slope seldom less than 40°. Beyond it can be seen the ridge Armitage first led the party up, only to find its western face impassable—an attempt involving hauling the sledges up by block and tackle, which cost them five vital days. Separation Camp and the depot they left were in a valley behind the saddle. Photographed by John M. Alexander, operations manager at the New Zealand Scott Base in 1990–1991. Courtesy, the then New Zealand DSIR Antarctic Division (now Antarctica New Zealand).

percent) section about a third of a mile long that led to the next ledge. This they reached safely after almost three hours' nerve-racking work because the mist rose and enveloped them at 7 P.M. They had brought the loads down 1,300 feet, traveled about a mile, and were more than a third of the way to the bottom. The worst was over.

Fearing crevasses at the junction with the main glacier, Armitage went ahead on skis in the morning while Skelton led the teams down for 1¾ miles over gradients diminishing from 5½° (6 percent) to 3° (3 percent) and arrived at the bottom by lunchtime. Mist later rolled up from the sea and prevented further progress, but the chance to overhaul the sledges was welcome, and they congratulated themselves on having conquered the first great obstacle in a day and a half.[8]

With nineteen days gone and only five weeks' rations left, ideas of returning around the Bluff or reaching the magnetic pole had clearly been abandoned, for Armitage decided to make another depot below a prominent mark they could all see on the first buttress of the Cathedral Rocks, which towered ever higher above him as he went ahead on skis for 1½ miles to its foot, probing all the way with his ax. The others followed, relaying the sledges over 3-inch-thick snow that made Armitage distrustful of hidden crevasses.

By the time they lunched abeam of the cliff, he had found only three crevasses. All were bridged over with 3-foot-thick consolidated snow, which carried them and the sledges quite safely. Dumping a week's food, somewhat more oil, and most of the lard for frying the seal, they lightened the load by 350 pounds. Pushing on that afternoon, they found themselves already 500 feet higher than the junction with Descent Glacier, although not yet beyond the first of the three buttresses that they could now see extended for almost 10 miles.

The blizzard that trapped them in the attempt to get into the mountains had alleviated some of the terrors of Descent Glacier, as they dubbed it, but here the resulting mantle of sticky snow made the dragging heavier than any so far. Pausing to set out a line of bamboos to measure glacier movement, they had advanced only another half mile in a little over an hour. Fog then engulfed them for five hours. When it lifted, it took them two hours to advance another half mile, at which point heavy snow blotted out the scene. And there it held them for two nights and a day, with the snow almost falling as sleet. They had been reasonably lucky with the weather to that point, but it was now making serious inroads into their time.

Off again on December 21, relaying three sledges at a time through thicker than ever snow, they had just passed the second buttress when the weather once more forced a halt. They were at the foot of the first step in the glacier, 500 feet high and fearfully crevassed. The next day they had even less luck with the weather and had ascended only a hundred feet up the fall when a furious blizzard swept down on them, with the wind not dropping until the following afternoon. By that time every vestige of snow had been cleared off the ice, and at least they could see the crevasses clearly.

With little of the day left, Armitage set off with Evans and Gilbert Scott to see what lay beyond the top. They found themselves on a

LOOKING UP FERRAR GLACIER TOWARD KNOBHEAD MOUNTAIN FROM ABOVE NEW HARBOUR. On September 19, 1902, when they looked up the glacier from 500 feet above its moraine, about 5 miles downstream from the 3,000-foot shoulder at left of this picture, Armitage's party could not see the first two clefts in the valley wall beyond it. Deterred by the chaotic maze of 60-foot-deep canyons in the ice confronting them, Armitage must have remembered seeing the clefts in the valley wall from the ship the previous February, for he correctly guessed the main glacier could be reached through one of them. He later achieved that by way of the incredibly steep Descent Glacier in the second cleft. Aerial photo taken in February 1957; courtesy, W/Cdr J. R. Claydon, RNZAF (retired).

level plateau with a huge arm of the glacier descending from the south and the much broader main stream apparently coming from the north-west, as Armitage had seen from New Harbour. For all the apparent flatness of the south arm, Armitage decided on the northern route. By lunchtime they were up and over the brow, all pulling with crampons on their boots. Wild, however, was hobbling, for he had lost one crampon on the first pitch up the fall.

To get onto the northwest arm another 500-foot icefall lay ahead, and that was impossible to ascend with just one crampon. Despite having to carry Wild on a sledge most of the afternoon, they were over the top and 230 feet down the other side before evening, finding it was really a ridge dividing the glacier to the southwest and the one they had chosen to go up. The latter seemed to stagnate here in the wide basin they camped on, although they could not see whether it overflowed to the northeast.

Encouragingly, the view from the ridge had shown them they were on the right track, for what looked like inland ice showed clearly 35 miles ahead over the next icefall, which was seemingly no worse than any they had climbed so far (see Upper Taylor Glacier on back endpaper). Well content with their progress that Christmas Eve, they were less so when the wind got up to a full westerly gale, bringing a freezing fog down to immerse them as they enjoyed their Christmas dinner of welsh rarebit and bacon on biscuit.

The weather relented the next day. After Skelton had photographed the camp, they hauled the six sledges up the 500-foot step, camping at 6 P.M. in bright sun just beyond its summit. Skelton's black-and-white photos can hardly convey the spectacle that met their eyes the following morning. The view rivaled the Grand Canyon in its most gorgeous sunset raiment. The southern wall of the valley, illuminated by the early morning sun, gleamed above the snowy white glacier. Stratified in bands of terra-cotta, red, yellow, brown, and stone, the rocks spelled out the forging of the mountains cosmic eons before they had reached there to plant the first footsteps of man on the glacier.

It looked as though they would be on the summit the next day, for nothing could be seen beyond the next big step, 10 miles or so ahead of them. But that was illusory. They took a day to reach the fall

THE MAKING OF A CONTINENT REVEALED. On the upper reach of the great western glacier (later renamed Upper Taylor Glacier) before the final staircase to the summit plateau, looking back from opposite Finger Mountain toward the stupendous southern wall extending past Beacon Heights to New Mountain, 10 miles distant. Part of the 500-foot Upper Finger Mountain icefall appears at right edge of the picture. The broad dark stratum in the thousand-foot cliffs was the result of the catastrophic Jurassic-era magma outflows circa 185 million years ago known as the Ferrar Intrusion, today believed to have triggered the breakaway of the Antarctic from the Gondwana supercontinent (see Appendix 10). Courtesy, the Royal Society.

and a day to climb it, only to find there was another horizon at least 15 miles on atop an icefall larger than any they had surmounted so far. They reached its summit two days later (Sunday, December 28), once again to find more icefalls ahead of them.

Unfortunately, there was only enough food for sixteen more days[9] before they had to be back at the Cathedral Rocks Depot. Allowing five for the descent from this camp, that left eleven days for further travel out and back. So they could only go on for six more days. Even worse, for the first time Armitage felt concern about the party's health: "It appears that some of our party are weakening rather, although in good spirits."[10] Another day was lost when blizzard conditions greeted them the next morning and continued unabated until evening.

After dragging 13 more miles into a sharp westerly wind that grew steadily colder, they drew nearer the real summit, finishing the year another 2,000 feet higher. On their left at last appeared what looked like the last visible land. Consisting of dark columnar basalt—formed similarly to the Giant's Causeway at Portrush in Northern Ireland— the nunatak stood 500 feet above the ice, a mass of hexagonal columns each about 12 feet in diameter, seemingly the last outpost of the mountains they had found the way through.

As they covered the first 2 miles on December 31, Skelton took a small party to depot a 9-foot sledge with a week's provisions and all the wooden runners at the foot of the nunatak. That left Armitage's team to pull the 12-foot, 9-foot, and 7-foot sledges and Allan's the two 11-foot ones as they scaled the second, much stiffer rise. There they encountered the largest crevasse yet, fully 30 feet wide.

Armitage led the way across the snow bridge on all fours, and when several men had followed him they hauled the sledges over, one at a time, anchoring from both sides once the first was across. It was slow and chilling work and provoked the first case of frostbite. Buckridge, the unhappy victim, was also in acute pain from snowblindness. He had left off his goggles for fear of stumbling into another crevasse, having dropped into one on the previous icefall. Camping clear of the icefall, they were almost 7,000 feet up, with no sign of further land west of them.

Scudding drift, driven by force 7 to 9 winds directly from the west on New Year's Day, 1903, robbed them of a further day, and conditions were little better for half of the next. Starting off in mid-afternoon, they had only gone 2 miles when Macfarlane collapsed with pains under the heart, unable to breathe or move. Armitage quickly erected a tent, and they revived him with a strong cup of tea.

Everyone in Allan's team began to declare that they had felt similar symptoms. The similarity to mountain sickness clearly misled Armitage as to the nature of Macfarlane's undoubted heart attack, although he had few illusions about the serious situation that faced him.

Notionally, two and a half days remained in which to get as far beyond the horizon ahead as they could before turning back. Allan's entire team would have to be left where it was, and he left the 9-foot sledge with them, loading minimal supplies plus a safety margin on the 12-foot sledge with the 7-foot instrument sledge hitched on behind.[11] Waiting until Macfarlane seemed to recover, Armitage and his team set off for the unknown another 700 feet above them, promising to be back inside five days.

After a mile they came to what proved indeed to be the last of the icefalls, much cut up by well-bridged crevasses. By 8 P.M. they were across the last of them and camped on a plain that rose gently in all directions west of them. There was no sign of a descent to suggest they were within striking distance of the other side of Victoria Land. If Scott's impression from south of the Bluff was correct, the narrowest part would be at the southern end of the Royal Society Range, and when they reached the summit it was no doubt that obvious conclusion that prompted Armitage to head southwest.

On Saturday they had gone several miles when they found the shovel had dropped off the sledge, and two hours were lost while Armitage and Gilbert Scott skied back to find it, a mile from their overnight camp. So by lunchtime on January 4 they had gained only another 8 miles. At that point, haunted by the memory of Macfarlane's ashen face, Armitage decided a rapid ski excursion was the most they dared to undertake.

First, though, the magnetic observations must be made, and those were completed that afternoon. Armitage found that the dip angle was the same as those at the other "stations" on the glacier. That observation later helped establish the position of the magnetic pole.

With thick clouds about the next morning, they did not risk leaving the camp on skis until after midday, with biscuits, cheese, and chocolate in their pockets and carrying the theodolite and tripod, for a seven-hour round-trip. After 7 miles they stopped, with the ice plain still undulating all around from south through west to north, the horizon marginally below the horizontal only to the northwest as Armitage slowly swung the theodolite around.[12]

To the southeast two mountains (later named after Lashly) stood out in front of the land, and further south they saw a more isolated one, obviously beyond the horizon. It was almost certainly the 8,300-foot peak north of which first Sir Edmund Hillary and then Sir Vivian Fuchs passed fifty-six years later on the 1955–1958 Commonwealth Trans-Antarctic expedition. Thanks to little wind and good visibility, it was easy for Armitage to follow his own tracks back to the camp.

The 8-mile return to Allan's camp went quickly enough with the aid of the sail until they came to the 500-foot icefall. Safely down, Armitage warned Scott not to celebrate his birthday by falling into a crevasse, for some were visible beyond the icefall. At that moment Armitage was looking at what proved to be Allan, Wild, and Walker approaching when, with a sudden jerk that knocked all the breath out of his lungs, he found himself on the end of his trace, 27 feet down a fathomless crevasse that narrowed above his head. For some extremely alarming minutes it almost looked as though they would be unable to get him up. Eventually they did with the aid of a line he maneuvered around his chest. It was the narrowest shave of the entire journey.

Allan told him everyone was now fit except Macfarlane, who still felt giddy and even faint if he walked a few paces. Armitage realized they would have to carry him. What he thought of the task of getting him up Descent Pass can only be imagined.

Packing up the next morning, January 7, it was soon obvious that they could do without the 9-foot sledge, so it was abandoned. All the men asked if they could be photographed, and Skelton obliged. Then, with the tents aboard and Macfarlane strapped on top of one of Allan's sledges, they were on their way down, happy at least that they had all reached the summit even if six of them had been stopped short prior to the last step.

Pausing only to pick up the depoted food and wooden underrunners from the nunatak after 3 miles and to get sandstone specimens from the Finger Mountain cliffs, under which they camped the second night (the 8th), they safely reached the Cathedral Rocks Depot early on the fifth day (January 11), with plenty of food.

Continuing their way through swift-flowing streams of water pouring down Ferrar Glacier, the 40°F high-summer temperature had them all perspiring after the chilling winds of the summit. Armitage took his last magnetic observations beside a lake half a mile long on the way to the lunch break at the foot of Descent Glacier.

Tackling the first relatively easy stage of the ascent knee-deep in snow, they reached the foot of the terrifyingly steep sections by evening.

They had pulled the sledges in pairs while Macfarlane walked up slowly, looking ever more ill.*

They had climbed on only half a mile up the 16° (18 percent) part the next morning when thick snowfall marooned them, and they had to cut a platform for the tents. Macfarlane was in even worse shape. "Poor chap, he looks bad," Armitage was moved to record that evening, still not understanding the cardiac threat that hung over the quartermaster as they faced pitches that steepened to 45°. "I am exceedingly sorry for him, as he is an exceedingly nice-mannered man."[13]

Up those final slopes, which would tax many seasoned ice climbers, they relayed the sledges one at a time, by block and tackle as soon as the angle steepened, with Macfarlane following a few steps at a time. By the time they reached the last 400-yard icefall, 45° at its steepest, the pins were falling out of the blocks, and the sheaves had to be nailed in place, making the pulling harder still from the friction of the rope sliding over wood. Finally, after eight hours of continuous toil, the whole party was safely over the saddle and camped at the depot beyond it, thankful the worst ordeal was over. The rest would be easy.

The fact that Macfarlane survived this climb is scarcely less amazing than his apparent recovery as they prepared breakfast and loaded the provisions in the morning (January 15). But that seeming recovery was to be short-lived.

Understandably, they did not start until after midday, leaving Macfarlane to follow on skis at his own pace. They first made the ascent out of the valley and were just heading downhill again across the névé when Armitage looked back and saw Macfarlane lying motionless in the snow. It turned out he had fainted twice. Two of the men towed him up to the sledges, after which he was carried on them.[14]

The descent of Blue Glacier was not without alarms either, for at one time Skelton, Evans, and Scott were simultaneously hanging in three separate crevasses, despite Armitage sounding ahead of them. Skelton had been surprised at the absence of crevasses on the way up, but at that point the summer sun had not had time to weaken the snow bridges. It was not a case of glacier movement, for the flags Ferrar had planted during the spring reconnaissance were still in the same place.[15]

---

* Eight years later, on February 11, 1911, Evans stood at the same point with Frank Debenham (on Scott's last expedition) and declared it impossible for Debenham's four-man party to get their two sledges up what he described as "the least impossible part of it" (Scott et al. [1913], vol. 2: p. 200).

In three days they were down at the Eskers, feasting on two seals Walker had killed as soon as they arrived; the livers, hearts, and most tender cuts were quickly divided up among the four tents. "Not a diner in London, Paris, or New York enjoyed his meal that night as we did ours," Armitage recalled vividly in his book eighteen months later.[16]

Skelton thought Macfarlane ought to be taken on ahead, but for all his sympathy Armitage thought it was unnecessary.[17] To compound matters, when they reached the ship at 7:30 P.M. on January 19, Koettlitz was not there. Either Armitage had not relayed Scott's instruction properly, or Koettlitz had ignored the order to stay at the ship until Armitage returned and had left on the 14th with Ferrar to try to get geological specimens from Minna Bluff.

So with no one qualified to examine Macfarlane when they got there, with the sick man following on skis under his own power,[18] the heart attack that might so easily have cost him his life went unrecognized, dismissed as something "he was more alarmed about himself than others were for him," as Scott wrote in his book, having found Macfarlane recovered and heard the story from Armitage.[19] That was hardly a fitting tribute to one of the leading spirits of the journey from whom even during the most difficult times, getting the loads up the icefalls or dragging himself up the top pitch of Descent Glacier, never a word of complaint had been heard, in contrast to one or two others in the party.[20]

When Macfarlane was finally examined by Koettlitz, it was recommended that he return home in the *Morning* solely because he had not withstood the rigors of the first winter as well as others.[21] As a result, despite a mitigating recommendation from Scott, which the Admiralty "noted in his favour,"[22] Macfarlane was only awarded a bronze Polar Medal after the expedition returned.

Macfarlane's misfortune, just as they had almost gained the summit beyond the last signs of land, was far from the main limitation of Armitage's achievement. The mountain route, with five days lost on an abortive excursion and seven more lost for want of visibility, had been the main limitation.

Yet as they got back to the ship that evening, if they felt disappointed at not having seen its farthest shore, nothing could detract from their satisfaction at having broken through the ramparts of Victoria Land. And rightly so, for just reaching the summit plateau was a remarkable achievement with the weight and crudity of the gear available, the more so given the fact that the men of the party had spent their lives at sea level and were denied any chance of altitude acclimatization by the shortness of the season.

Given the direction Armitage had chosen to take on the summit plateau, had the best part of the lost days been restored and Macfarlane's crisis not occurred, they would almost certainly have demonstrated that there was no indication of a falling away of the ice cap in the direction in which Scott expected a west coast of Victoria Land existed. In turn, that would have established a likely continuity of the coastline southward to the mouth of Byrd Glacier. There, even as the returning party reached the top of Descent Pass on January 14, 1903, the two southern parties were camped either side of what Scott could still only assume was an inlet, which he had discovered on his way south.

The reward of seeing land or the summit plateau at its western extremity, which would have decisively proved the continental dimensions of the land they had discovered, had only that day been denied to Barne by bad weather and, above all, by ill-fated coincidence, to Scott because of Shackleton's rapidly worsening condition.

16

THE RELUCTANT CONTINENT
The Glacier That Kept Its Secret

The journeys that brought the two southern parties close to each other on January 14 could hardly have been less alike. Scott's was dominated by the menacing fear of scurvy and by failing to find the depot before their food ran out. Barne, in contrast, had five fit companions averaging 11 miles a day, enlivened by the discovery of ever-more land as the "islands" that shaped the Southern campaign became a whole new coast.[1]

Having pulled 190 pounds per man to the Bluff, Barne's party had started west-southwest on New Year's Day pulling 140 pounds each. Of that, 62 pounds was accounted for by the fixed weight of the two sledges—an 11-footer and a 7-footer—two three-man sleeping bags, tents, and other gear, not counting their skis. The rest of the weight represented about four weeks' rations (with two and a half boxes—about 86 pounds—of navy biscuits for an emergency) for the twenty-four days they had left for exploration, for they had to return to the depot by January 24 if they were to get back to the ship by the end of the month. Barne reckoned on fourteen days outward bound to discover what lay beyond the two visible islands they had all, except Plumley, seen on their way south with Scott in November.

Aided by sails catching the ENE wind, they started at 10 A.M. on that brilliantly clear day. Within two hours the two islands had joined into one.

Scott had at first believed the end of Victoria Land was the cape bounding the northernmost gap Barne could see as he sketched the scene west of him on New Year's Eve (see illustration in Chapter 13). Barne set his course for the extreme southerly point of land visible from the depot, so Scott's final instruction must have been based on the premise that the truth about the northern gap would become clear as the party moved southwest. If it was not a strait, no time or mileage would have been wasted, and if it was, they could alter course for it.[2]

As Scott's party had long since been, they were suffering painfully from split lips. Smythe felt as though his mouth had been cut on each side to make it wider.

Pulling all the following day against a stiff breeze that kept the land ahead obscured, they had steered by prismatic compass—a slow business waiting for the heavy disc to settle, then shouting to the men to correct the course and skiing to catch up and get into the traces again. They woke on January 3 to find a third island had appeared above the horizon. The afternoon's advance, in temperatures almost too warm for such work, gradually revealed that the island was part of the new land. As they camped that evening, the six men—five from the navy and one (Isaac Weller) from the merchant fleet—knew they had discovered a whole new coast.

That coast was still apparently separate from the western mountains, now almost north of them, but by lunchtime on the 5th they could see that even that gap was closing—although their new, more southerly course never allowed them to see far enough into the gap to learn whether it was a strait, an inlet, or a glacier. Just before they camped that evening, however, Barne's hopes of discovering the real end of Victoria Land were dashed, for on the horizon appeared "an indistinct white mass" to the south of the new cape.[3]

That mass was gone the next morning as they set off over stickier snow than any so far, the first truly heavy surface since leaving the depot. During the lunch break the sledges sank a foot and could not be moved, tug as they might. For the first time they were facing the sort of surface conditions Scott had encountered, but instead of having to relay they found they could get on fairly well after unpacking the sledges, removing the lumps of frozen snow from the framework and runners, and restowing them.

Sweating profusely from the work of hauling over such a surface all that day and the next morning, they could again see the new land when the mist cleared from the horizon at lunchtime on January 7. Altering course for the farthest point visible to the south, they hauled toward it that afternoon and all the next day, once more steering by compass in fog during the morning.

The wind that cleared the fog enabled them to use the sails again, and soon they could see that their newest discovery (which Scott's party had seen well ahead of them) formed the south side of what was apparently another large strait running westward and that the new land south of it trended somewhat east of south as it shrank toward the southern horizon. Realizing that in that direction it would become visible to Scott's party, Barne knew he had to get into a position to see into the strait. Accordingly, he set course on the 9th for the cape on the north side of it. This would be the last day of serious progress. They had averaged close to 11 miles a day for nine days, and the prize of getting into the strait before the 14th to chart its direction and coasts seemed well within their grasp.

The Antarctic weather had other ideas. The wind had been freshening all afternoon, blowing ever-thicker drifts from the southwest, and although they had a clear sky on the morning of the 10th, that afternoon they were groping against a blizzard until the force of the wind almost stopped them. The chart Barne drew in his report after their return suggests they made about 6 miles that day on a course of S31°W True before the snow had blotted out the land at the cape. At that point Barne had the impression they were close enough to risk blundering into crevasses where the barrier bore against the land.

That same blizzard, which pinned them in their tent all the next day (the 11th), had also overtaken the struggling southern party, now with their three remaining dogs trailing behind the sledges and without the sledgemeter, which had collapsed on the 9th. Clear of crevasses, Scott and his companions used the sail and covered about 22 miles in two days, traveling blind in the drift for most of that time.

Just as the fog that followed the blizzard on December 29 had denied Scott's party the view that would have shown that the strait they had reached was actually a glacier, the same phenomenon now denied Barne the vital view into this gap that could have established the continuity of the coast. With just three days left, Barne could wait no longer. They started off on the 12th on foot because the sticky snow made their skis unmanageable. Williamson and then Barne and Smythe soon dropped into crevasses, and they had to retreat and work away eastward. By the end of the 13th, still in thick fog, they had reached a point 7 miles east and perhaps a mile south of their blizzard camp.

About 36 miles south of them as they camped that evening, Scott and Wilson, exhibiting ominous scurvy symptoms, had at last found the depot they had so feared missing, dragging the sledges up to it with their companion racked by coughing and breathlessness. Scott had been getting a fix on the sun's altitude through a thin patch in the fog and, lowering the theodolite telescope, had accidentally caught sight of the depot less than 2 miles away. Such was their condition that they had taken two hours to reach it, for the blizzard had also caused Shackleton's condition to take an alarming turn for the worse. The previous day Wilson had remarked for the first time about his increasing breathlessness and coughing.

They reorganized the loads, stripping the metal cladding off the runners after an experiment had showed a given load was easier to pull without it. They started off after lunch on January 14, pulling a total of 525 pounds. Shackleton suffered his severest bout of coughing so far, which continued without respite until they had to give up after he started coughing up blood. That evening Wilson told Scott he feared a complete breakdown.

Shackleton wrote of his trouble for the first time: "During a halt my cough which had been troubling me for some days became more severe and haemorrhage started; so I was not allowed to do any more camp work or pull, only doing little jobs such as cooking; it is most annoying. The other poor fellows now have 270 lbs [each] to pull while I am only allowed to walk along. They are awfully good to me."[4]

It was pointless to keep the dogs now and foolhardy to drag the 25 pounds of fish they were carrying. They had found that some of the depoted fish were green. Wilson dispatched the two dogs in the morning and dumped the food and carcasses because Shackleton felt it would be "madness" for them to try eating the flesh.[5] It was not squeamishness that prevented them from benefiting from its life-saving vitamins that day but Wilson's adherence to Koettlitz's belief that tainted meat caused scurvy.

The previous morning Barne and his tentmates Smythe and Plumley, with Williamson, Crean, and Weller in the second tent, still all perfectly fit except for their cracked and blistered noses and lips, had awakened to find the weather as thick as ever. It was their last day, so Barne had determined that if the conditions persisted they could most constructively retreat westward to their old track so that if the fog cleared enough to see the nearer coast, the bearings of its principal features could be taken. It looked entirely unlikely that the weather would clear enough to allow them to see far into the gap. And so it proved on the morning of the 15th—had Barne stayed put, he would have been unable to see to the western horizon, for on reaching their old track he could not even see the south shore.

After taking what bearings he could, he turned the sledges for the northeast, and, ironically, within a quarter hour the mist ahead of them thinned enough to allow them to see Mount Discovery jutting above the horizon. Later Barne spotted a black mark south of them, immediately thinking it might be the southern party, but it turned out to be the biscuit box they had jettisoned on the 10th. On a journey free of crises and pulling about 100 pounds per man at the start, they reached the Bluff Depot in the same time it had taken them to reach that point on the outward journey.

Forty or so miles away, a little east of south from them, Scott and Wilson faced the task of pulling nearly 500 pounds to the same destination. They were too far south for even an encouraging glimpse of the familiar mountain near their goal, and the prospect before the two men was stark in the extreme. If their companion became so ill that he was unable to walk, they would be doomed to relaying the sledges one at a time.

With about 125 miles to the Bluff, Scott doubted if he and Wilson were up to covering the distance involved in the time available. They had left the Southern Depot with 208 pounds of food, enough for twenty-one days at most under such a back-breaking strain. They would have to walk 375 miles, or nearly 18 miles a day, two thirds of that hauling the sledges one at a time, each with a laden weight of 330 pounds, decreasing to 230 pounds at the end. The trip would be out of the question if they encountered some of the surfaces they had faced on the way south. Scott could think of "absolutely no workable scheme."[6] On Wilson's advice he increased the seal meat ration to five pieces at breakfast and again at lunch, still cutting out the bacon.

The fact that their troubles were primarily caused by scurvy was quickly demonstrated, for after two days Scott viewed the situation in a brighter light. The diet "was acting like magic and the scorbutic symptoms [were] rapidly disappearing—both Wilson and I have clean gums, and my leg today is vastly improved. Shackleton's signs have not disappeared so completely, but he is certainly improving."[7]

The next evening he wrote: "Shackleton though still in a disturbing condition is undoubtedly very much better . . . it is easy to see Wilson is much relieved. We cannot of course talk the matter out as the patient is always within earshot . . . [but] today there has been no gasping for breath and no spitting up of blood and this evening he is . . . altogether brighter in spirits. He is very obedient to directions which interdict all exhausting work in camp and all pulling except when the sledges are going steadily."

It was obviously hard to stop such a man from trying to do his part, so without telling him, they must have decided to allow him to hitch on to the sledges the next day (January 17) once they had them going. "Better today," Shackleton wrote in his journal that night, "so hope to be in full swing of work tomorrow. They won't allow me to do anything yet because of the haemorrhage. I do wish the other chaps hadn't so much work."[8]

But he soon paid a price for that slight relaxing of the ban. January 18 was so gray-white and blank that they decided to sledge in the evening when the declining sun might cast enough light through the mist to enable them to see the ridges in the surface and avoid stumbling. Shackleton brought them to a halt after three hours, stopped in his tracks by a sharp pain in his chest. That night Scott recorded their "disappointment not to be able to go on and still more as it puts the old serious aspect of Shackleton's case again before us. It is no use being down about it, we must evidently be prepared to carry him."[9]

Mercifully, the attack was brief, but its cardiac undertone was the harbinger of a distant fate. Wilson wrote the next evening: "Shackle very much better, but allowed to do nothing but just walk along. We cannot carry him. The moment he attempts a job he gets breathless and coughs. The Captain and I can quite well manage everything alone and the surface happily is excellent, so that the sledges run easily."[10]

At first they did stop him from doing any pulling, but in an indomitable display of mind over matter he was back in harness again by January 21, albeit at the rear and only after the sledges were under way. Soon, happily, the wind got up, and they could let the sail do the pulling. After a while the sledges began running away, and they made him sit on the rear one and use his ski pole as a brake, but that wasn't very effective so he skied along behind at his own pace.*

After another day with the sledges driven by a stiff breeze and Shackleton following behind, he was improved enough to go half a mile ahead of them on skis to set the course. The breeze lasted two more days and drove the sledges at a pace that left Scott and Wilson free to talk, as they guided the sledges at much the same speed

---

* Scott's description of the day's progress in *The Voyage of the "Discovery"* (1905, vol. 2: p. 112) is open to criticism for his omission of the reason they put Shackleton on the rear sledge, which suggests it was because of his condition that day, as rightly inferred by Huntford (1979: p. 190; 1985, #2: p. 113). However, there is no hint of resentment in Shackleton's letter to Scott after he had read the book "with great interest. It is beautifully got up and splendidly written" (SPRI 1453/171/2).

Shackleton was capable of. The relief must have been enormous after the days when they could not speak their mind in the face of his alarming condition because he might hear.

After that the weather cleared, but the wind turned against them, so Shackleton would go ahead while they packed up and gradually caught him. On Wilson's orders[11] that was how he went on until they reached the Bluff Depot on the 28th with a third of their three weeks' food in hand*—utterly famished because they had not dared increase their allowance in case the weather marooned them. A letter from Barne told them his party had gotten there four days before.

The first piece of good news had been finding Barne's homeward tracks on the 26th, which told them, much to Scott's relief, that all six men were pulling on skis. That meant Barne had no invalids on his hands. Now, two days later, after gorging themselves three times over— Scott and Wilson endured agonies of indigestion from eating too quickly—they read the other letters left for them. Most were dated New Year's Day and had been dropped there on January 8 by Dailey who, with Ford and Whitfield, had brought out and depoted a week's supplies for Armitage's party.

There was also the not-so-good news that Armitage had been foiled in his attempt to reach the main (Ferrar) glacier. He had been forced to head into the mountains rather than risk a 2,000-foot descent, which Koettlitz, who had brought the support party back safely, had regarded as folly to attempt.

On the other hand, the news that Barne had been able to see the cape south of which Scott had made his depot and discovered a continuous coast north from there to the northernmost gap they had all seen from the Bluff told Scott that one of the aims of his Southern campaign had succeeded. However, neither party had been able to see into the strait they had stood on either side of on December 13. Barne's party had enjoyed only three sunny days with good views of the land.[12] On the first of these (the 20th), they were already too far off and north of its entrance to see into the strait properly. As plans stood then, it had been the last chance to do so.

The weather was foggy again, and Shackleton, who hadn't written of his troubles for ten days, was forced to admit, "I am feeling worse today; have not done any pulling and am not allowed even to cook

---

* Clearly, there are no grounds for the assertion by Huntford (1985, #1: p. 174) that their food was all but exhausted.

now. Kneeling down to get in or out of the tent I find the hardest thing to do."[13] When they woke the next day (January 29) to a howling blizzard, he had relapsed into such a condition that Scott wanted to press on, blizzard or not, to get him back to the ship. But Wilson advised against it—"Shackleton [is] again utterly knocked up with cough and breathlessness, quite unfit to move out of the tent," he wrote, repeating the words "quite unfit to move" a line or two later.[14]

This turned out to be their last bad weather, and they were up very early with one objective: "to get Shackleton back to the ship before we get caught in another blizzard."[15] "Going ahead of the others, as I cannot go very fast now," wrote Shackleton after that first day on the move again.[16]* That day and the next three, all brilliantly clear, brought them north of White Island, truly at last on the final leg of their three-month 600-mile journey. Before lunch on February 3 they had reached the edge of the barrier ice and were met by Bernacchi and Skelton with the great news that the relief ship had arrived with fresh food and supplies. Every report they heard seemed to be good except for the surprising fact that the bay ice was still solid for 8 miles north of *Discovery*.

That hardly seemed to matter as the others met them, first Sub-Lt. George Mulock from the *Morning*, a young surveyor seconded from the navy by the Hydrographer, and then Royds and Koettlitz and a host of others. Skelton and Bernacchi pulled the sledges around Cape Armitage to reveal the *Discovery* decorated from stem to stern with welcoming flags and the rest of the crew in the rigging poised to cheer their arrival.

Reginald Ford was ready to photograph the actual arrival. Scott was walking beside Skelton and Bernacchi, who had pulled the sledges all the way to the ship, and Wilson followed beside the rear sledge. Shackleton was with Koettlitz, Royds, and Mulock, a long way behind and just visible in Ford's first photo but not in the second, which appeared later in Scott's *The Voyage of the* Discovery. In that account Scott refrained from explaining who was pulling the sledges. Since he is clearly the figure walking without harness on the left, the ordinary reader would understandably be left with the impression that Wilson and Shackleton were pulling the sledges.

---

* Scott has it that Shackleton was sent off first but, once he and Wilson had caught up, rode on the sail-driven sledge the rest of the morning. Wilson's diary, not written until February 23, has it that Shackleton, "still very seedy, went his own pace on ski" (WD: 1.30.03).

All three men were sick, for the seal meat, at first so effective in countering scurvy, must have deteriorated in the unexpectedly high temperatures on the sunny days preceding and following the blizzard at the Bluff. Shackleton, with his irrepressible determination, insisted on trying to walk about the deck but was driven back to his cabin time and again by bouts of breathless coughing. Wilson, whose legs were painfully stiff, wisely kept to his bed for the first two weeks and could not bring himself to write in his diary for nearly three.

Although he was the least affected of the three, Scott's legs were nevertheless very swollen, and his gums were thoroughly uncomfortable. Above all, he succumbed to "an extraordinary feeling of lassitude . . . not physical only; to write or even to think had become wholly distasteful, and sometimes quite impossible."[17] It took many weeks before he felt his usual self once more. When it became apparent by February 19 that the ice might not break out and that, even if it did, the *Morning* would have to leave before *Discovery*, he was forced to write his report[18] for the presidents of the two societies long before he was in a fit state to do justice to, let alone express enthusiastically, the achievements of his Southern campaign.

Despite that, the 1,200-word account of his three-month saga was a model of clarity, if understandably lengthened by the story of the dogs' demise and Shackleton's illness. On the latter he allowed no hint of criticism or blame to creep into the report. For that matter, Shackleton's journal never revealed the slightest suggestion of resentment, rather only gratitude for the others' treatment of him.*

Scott hardly felt up to digesting everything in the 27-page report Barne had written for him two days before the southern party returned,[19]

---

* Scott's alleged resentment of Shackleton for his breakdown was surely exposed as a subsequent invention by Scott's call to him that night in the next cabin (lent by Bernacchi so Shackleton could be nearer the stove): "I say Shackles, how would you fancy some sardines on toast?"—hardly the words of a man embittered by his companion's performance (Doorly 1916: p. 110). Shackleton's own diary phrase "but it was a good time" (Huntford 1985, #2: p. 113) that day likewise scarcely suggests he construed orders as an attempt to humiliate him, as asserted by Huntford (1979: p. 175; 1985, #2: p. 110) on the basis of a letter from Wilson's biographer Edward Seaver. Bernacchi's February 28 diary entry (nine days after Koettlitz recommended Shackleton be sent home), referring to "some personal feeling" (SPRI 353/3/3: 2.28.03) evident between Scott and Shackleton (the latter probably did allow some resentment over Scott's decision to show at that stage), has been unjustifiably advanced (Huntford 1985, #2: p. 114) as evidence of friction on the Southern journey that is in no way supported by Shackleton's journal entries.

WILSON'S SKETCH OF THE MOUTH OF BYRD GLACIER. Drawn on January 20, 1903, about 35 miles from the coast on the return leg of the Southern journey; Wilson copied it for the *South Polar Times* in June 1903 to illustrate Scott's article on the journey. The sketch clearly shows how it appeared to be a strait with no land beyond it, as it did to Barne and his companions when they reached a point 20 miles nearer its entrance on their first sledge journey to the southwest. Reproduced from the *South Polar Times*, published in 1908 by Smith, Elder.

let alone to grasping the detail from listening to him. So all he could do was ask Barne to write a summary, and the resulting 200-word text was appended to his own report. To think through the true signifi-cance of his twin-thrust Southern campaign was clearly beyond Scott at that stage, but he understood the stature of Armitage's achievement in breaking through the mountains to discover the summit plateau of Victoria Land, and he devoted the concluding part of the report to it, quoting liberally from Armitage.

For all the disappointment of the lesser record on his own jour-ney, the fact was that the nine men of Scott's Southern campaign had unveiled the backbone range of a vast continent flanking Ross's ice barrier. In largely defining 375 statute miles of coastline bounding the barrier, they revealed something of its enormous extent and of the great ice streams that fed into it.

Scott was not yet prepared to claim the discovery of a continent, for although Barne had eliminated two of the apparent gaps or straits and significantly narrowed another, the weather had prevented Scott from getting a proper view into the southernmost one he had discov-ered. The aftermath of the blizzard that nearly had fatal consequences for his party stopped Scott and Barne from seeing into the gap that separated them. Viewing Byrd Glacier (as it is now named) on January 20, 1903, from much farther away than Barne had approached it and too late to see squarely into it, Scott was in no position to dispute Barne's summary, in which he referred to the two straits (the one in 80°S and the northern one in 79°S) "beyond which (to westward) was an apparently flat horizon."[20]

Shackleton's first crisis had denied Scott a second chance for a landing that would have proved that the rocks were continental. That, combined with Barne's discovery of the extinct volcanoes near the coast north of the strait (Byrd Glacier), persuaded Scott that the most southerly land too was "undoubtedly volcanic."[21] That belief, in turn, robbed him of his first confidence that the spurs they had so nearly reached in 82°S were formed of continental-type rocks.[22] Even so, that proof would have been unnecessary if the "gaps" had been seen to be glaciers (e.g., those now named Mulock, Byrd, and Nimrod). Had Barne's course been a mere 15 miles more westerly, which it would have been had he first made for the northern gap, he would have seen that it was indeed a glacier (e.g., Mulock Glacier). Had the weather cleared on the two vital days, December 30 and January 14, the two other "straits" would have been seen to be glaciers too. By those narrowest of margins the reluctant continent had hidden its identity and denied Scott the just reward for his superb effort—the proof that the coast was continuous and continental and not a chain of islands.

Scott was not alone in believing that Armitage, once over the mountains of the land Ross had christened South Victoria Land, would reach its western shore. Even though Armitage had not reached that shore, however, there could be no doubt about the success of his ascent of the western glacier—a "very fine journey," Scott called it in his report,[23] and a "great credit" to Armitage. His party had broken through the mountain chain to discover an immense summit plateau at nearly 9,000 feet altitude, dipping slightly to the west, Armitage thought, as though to confirm the impression that the ice-clad land might dip down to a western shore. The ramparts had at least been breached in one place.

Like the great Southern effort, that journey had seriously impaired the health of another member of the expedition, William Macfarlane, if not with such dramatic consequences as Shackleton's breakdown had threatened. With these cases in mind, and realizing that the slow break out of the ice raised the possibility of another season in the Antarctic, Scott had written to Koettlitz four days before he wrote his report, asking if the health of any individuals would be seriously risked if they remained in the ship, emphasizing the duties of officers as leaders of sledge parties in the event of their enforced stay for another year.

Koettlitz listed four men, including Shackleton. He had indeed "recovered," but, added Koettlitz, "referring to your memorandum as to the duties of executive officers, I cannot say that he would be fit to undergo hardships and exposure in this climate."[24] As much as it upset Shackleton, Wilson agreed, writing, "It is certainly wiser for him

OFFICERS OF RELIEF SHIP MORNING AT LYTTELTON, NEW ZEALAND. *Left to right* in front: 3rd Officer Gerald Doorly, 2nd Officer Lt. Teddy Evans, Ch. Engr. Frederick Morrison, 1st Officer Rupert England, Capt. William Colbeck, 4th Officer S/Lt. George Mulock, Surgeon George Morrison; seated behind: Midshipmen Maitland Somerville and Arthur Pepper. Courtesy, the Canterbury Museum, Christchurch, New Zealand.

to go home" when he felt well enough to resume his diary entries on February 23.[25]

It was different with Hodgson, as he would not have to lead sledge parties. He was allowed to stay on, but in Shackleton's case Scott had no option: "[As] much as I regret parting with him, I do not think the health of an executive officer should be open to any doubt," he wrote in his report.[26]

With only a handful of six-month-old puppies that might prove useful next season if fed on seal meat, no reasonable critic can doubt Scott's need for potential leaders of sledge parties to exhibit robust and unquestionable health. They might have to cover greater distances to settle the questions still so tantalizingly unanswered in conditions similar to those that had affected Shackleton so disastrously. And Scott had the twenty-one-year-old naval survey officer from the *Morning* as an immediate replacement.

Another farthest-south effort was out of the question, but the chimerical western shore of Victoria Land still beckoned, as did the potential for reaching the magnetic pole. Armitage and Skelton had opened the way to these great prizes by breaching the majestic ramparts toward which they had so often looked during those last twelve months.

Scott would study the Western journey story over and over in the coming months. If only the Antarctic would allow him a second chance by trapping the *Discovery* in the ice, which even then still stretched flat and white for 5 miles north of Hut Point.

In a few days the *Morning* would have to be sent back to avoid being trapped by the pack. Then everything would hang in the balance. If the ice broke away before the pack sealed the sound altogether, they would have to obey the instructions and return with the hope that Markham could raise the money for a further season. If the ice released the ship too late to get out of the sound—and Scott knew that was unlikely if the distant pack continued to damp the swell—or never broke away at all, he would have a chance to achieve the twin goals in the West that would compensate for the frustration of everyone's hopes in the far south.

In less than three weeks the question was settled. The ice had broken back another 1½ miles, but there it stopped. They would have to winter there. Nature had granted Scott the second chance he hoped for. It was the start of a season of suspense.

PART 3

REPULSED BUT NOT DEFEATED
Prisoners of Ice and Money

17

HOSTAGES IN A FROZEN TRAP
The Fate of the German Expedition

Scott now enjoyed the certainty of a second chance, but Drygalski (and even more so the Scottish and Swedish expeditions), on the fringe of the elusive continent that day, had no such assurance. To be sure Drygalski, who had spent the last twelve months captive in the ice, was at last free and facing an open highway to the south. But his decision on March 18, 1903, to seize that chance was at best a measure of desperation, considering the experiences his thirty-two-man party had just survived.[1]

They had sailed from Cape Town on December 7, 1901, after failing to find the source of a leak that had threatened work in the engine room before they even arrived at the Cape. Already far behind schedule, they had taken twenty-four days (against the British ship's fifteen) to reach the Kerguelen Islands, where their magnetic base was being set up by a party taken there from Sydney. The freighter that took the group there had also brought the timber for the huts and the by then fifty-strong Kamchatka dog force, along with the equally vital 370 tons of the best New Zealand coal, donated by the British Admiralty in generous contrast to its grudging treatment of the British expedition.

Hindered by the inability of the Swiss naphtha-fired launches to cope with the wind when ferrying coal and stores to and fro, a whole month was gone before the *Gauss* could sail on January 31—so heavily laden that it had less than 8 feet of freeboard, even less than *Discovery* had when it had steamed out of Port Chalmers a month before.

Although fully 200 miles further south than the New Zealand port, any real advantage for the *Gauss* was canceled out by a decree from Berlin that 148 tons of coal must be reserved for the voyage northward and the daily toll of a ton for the pumps to keep the water level down. Nor was the situation helped when mountainous westerly seas swept overboard the 14 tons stored on deck. Even if they relied on their 40 tons of anthracite intended for heating, Drygalski reckoned there would be little left for steaming in the second and main season.

Already at Cape Town they had needed to replace large quantities of crockery and laboratory apparatus broken in the heavy rolling on the stormy last leg of the Atlantic voyage.[2] Now, headed southeast for Heard Island, the ship rolled so freely that more glass and photographic plates were lost. Even when the wind dropped a week later, the deck hands were working up to their knees in water as they sighted the first icebergs.

Drygalski's objective was the so-called Termination Land, the westernmost of Wilkes's sightings in 64°S 97½E, over 800 miles from Heard Island. If it existed, the question was whether land extended from there to Kemp Land in 66°S 60E or, as Neumayer believed, a sea ran south between the two sightings to join up with the Weddell Sea.

They were a few miles short of their goal early on February 14 when they met the pack, with no sign of land and the sea still more than 1,600 fathoms deep. Turning west, they had searched in vain for a way south until the wind veered into the east on the 18th, opening a wide lead south almost exactly on the 90°E meridian. They were soon across the 65th parallel. Emperor penguins appeared as men came on deck next morning, and they knew they might be fairly close to land.

The trouble was that snow obscured almost everything, as it did at that same moment for Shackleton and his two companions on their way to White Island. At least their ship was safely anchored in the bay, which no iceberg had entered since their arrival eleven days before. For the Germans, with no safe haven in sight, three more hours' steaming brought their ship into open water. Their hopes had risen as, with ice from the rigging raining on the deck, the watch manned the lifts and loosed the sails. Drygalski had opted for a southeast course, and they reaped their first reward at 2 A.M. on February 21 when Capt. Hans Ruser saw continuous ice-clad land fringed with a belt of icebergs.

With no remotely feasible landing place, they still questioned whether it was just a very long iceberg. Retreating from just south of the Antarctic Circle, Ruser made a steady westward run so Bidlingmaier could settle that question with a series of magnetic observations. Undoubted signs of coastal hills under the icecap had just appeared when a new pack of bergs forced them away to the northwest, eventually to be hemmed in by other icebergs as dusk fell at about 9 P.M. Menacingly, the approach of those to the east threatened to crush them against stationary ones to the west. As the wind rose to a full-scale blizzard, the by then invisible ice closed in as Drygalski went below to snatch some sleep.

When he came on deck again as February 22 dawned, the ship was held fast with the helmsman, chilled to the bone, turning the wheel more to keep the rudder free than in hopes of altering the ship's bearing. Their fate had been sealed in those two hours.

When they next saw the horizon four days later, open water was a long way off. The ship was still afloat, as the water gushing in somewhere under the propeller shaft proved. After four more anxious days the last line of escape was closed at midnight on March 2 by a line of icebergs that at first looked as though they would crush the ship but then stopped a mile off, closing a lead about half that distance to the east.

Consoling themselves that they should be able to reach the shore and that there would be an advantage in taking magnetic observations from firm ice that far from it, they set up the instruments in an icehouse out on the floe. Much else from the crowded ship was put out on the ice, including provisions and parts of the windmill generator.

As had happened with the boats Scott put out on the ice to get the snow canopy in place, blizzards buried everything, sinking the floe enough for the water to get in and spoil much of the food. Some caches, including the windmill parts, were poorly marked and soon were irretrievably lost. With less serious consequences, the weight of the magnetic icehouse sank the floe so that Bidlingmaier had to work ankle-deep in salt water that would not freeze in the 23°F temperature he had to maintain for the instruments to work properly.

The ship was still not tightly frozen in, so the coal supply continued to shrink by a ton a day, working the pumps and cutting into the 155 tons they had over and above the safety stock. Unless the ship soon froze solidly in, there would be little coal for exploration when they escaped in the spring. Hostages to the caprice of nature's stormiest domain, their predicament had virtually condemned them to a winter sledging campaign if they were to make any further discoveries.

So it was that as soon as the magnetic house was complete, the first sledge party got away on March 18. Enjoying calm weather the three men—Emil Philippi, the geologist, with Second Officer Richard Vahsel as navigator and the Norwegian seaman Daniel Johanssen in charge of the dogs—set foot on the coast on March 21 after a 45-mile journey over relatively smooth ice with a covering of crisp powdery snow. Traveling on foot, with nine dogs pulling each of the two sledges with ten days' supplies, they had sighted what they first thought to be a large iceberg after the second day and gone on to discover that it was a sizable mountain, which they soon named Gaussberg.

Eager to see what lay beyond, Philippi and Vahsel had scaled the 1,100-foot peak the evening they arrived, the first men to look out over the endless white slopes that climbed away southward to merge with the hazy sky. Away from the mountain not a single outcrop of rock could be seen.

They had made the return journey to the ship in three days actual traveling time but did not arrive back until the 26th, after being pinned in their ridge tent by a two-day blizzard. The storm would hardly have worried them, for they had killed a seal on the way out—much to the delight of the dogs, who sledged on rations of stockfish and, unlike their counterparts on the British expedition, Spratts dog biscuits.

While they were away, the chief engineer had made a hand winch for the balloon, as the coal shortage forbade use of its steam winch. Drygalski made the first ascent, going twice as high as the British balloon, but he could see little more of the coast than the two men who had stood on the Gaussberg.

Although the men were encouraged by the realization that there would be enough light for sledging for perhaps seven more weeks, the 1½ miles of rough ice south of the ship had demonstrated the fragility of the sledges. Like Scott, they had been purchased in Norway to Nansen's design. Their apparent fragility undoubtedly played a part in Drygalski's decision not to attempt travel along the coastal ice foot.

As for the inland ice, the crevasses all around the Gaussberg and the lack of any obvious way to it elsewhere discouraged attempts in that direction. Drygalski resigned himself to achieving magnetic observations ashore and making a triangulation survey that could also measure the movement of the ice cap around the mountain if they made an early spring visit.

It would be a long process, so a four-sledge party with twenty-eight dogs had left on April 4 to build an icehouse to live in on the ice foot and to set up a depot of food. Again blessed with little interference from the weather, they had reached the mountain in three days, completed the construction in six days, and returned on the 16th.

By that time the leak had been virtually stopped. Suspicion had always fallen on the rudder and screw wells. One of the crew was a trained diver with a proper diving suit, and he caulked the seams in the wells. They then tipped in wood shavings, which stemmed the last trickles. After that, the bilge water rose just 14 inches instead of 7 feet in twenty-four hours. Hand pumping took care of the leak after that.

A week later Drygalski's party was ready. They started on April 22 with 400 pounds on each of four sledges divided among twenty-eight dogs. The journey to the icehouse depot still only took four days of actual traveling, despite their having to manhandle the sledges over tilted floes on the last stage. Everyone was on foot using komager with undersoles and crampons except Paul Bjorvik, a Norwegian, who was on skis. On the 24th they had all been able to ride on the sledges because the dogs pulled too fast as soon as they spotted the mountain.

Stopped by a two-day blizzard en route, they arrived on April 28 to find the roof had blown off the icehouse. That restored, Drygalski left the others to get on with the scientific work and on the 30th set off with Gazert, the doctor, and the Norwegian to start the survey on the 30th. Held in their tent for four days by force 10 winds, they completed that work by May 9, returning to find the others back in the tent with the icehouse evacuated and everything flooded 6 inches deep by a spring tide.

This time the storm had landed them in trouble. The dogs had been turned loose to feed on petrels, but those had vanished with the onset of the wind, and only one day's fish ration remained. The dogs finished that after the first day's run on the 10th when a blizzard locked them in their tent all the next day. The men lived on rice so they could give the last of their pemmican to the dogs, and the rest of the journey had turned into a nightmare.

Twice more they ran out of food and were saved only by stumbling on seals in the blinding drift. They were haunted by the prospect of missing the ship and blundering into the unknown until the morning of May 15, when Johanssen recognized an iceberg 10 miles south of the *Gauss*. They hurried on and were greeted with relief onboard, where many had been convinced they could not have survived the storm. Luck alone had saved them, for no sooner were they aboard than another storm engulfed the whole area. It was a salutary lesson for planning future journeys.

Apart from winds that were difficult to stand up in, the worst feature of the winter was the sheer volume of snow. The ship and its surroundings were already scarcely recognizable. The scientific work became so arduous that the weather observations had to be transferred to the ship's officers, so the work ended up being arranged much as it was at Hut Point and, likewise, without loss of quality.

The one benefit of the snow was that it insulated the ship. The much vaunted steam heating was never turned on—a decision determined more by the coal shortage than by acceptance of the cabin temperatures, which hovered around freezing with the doors shut thanks to warmth from the anthracite stoves in the crew quarters, drying rooms, and boilers. Drygalski did not have to sit with his feet in a box of hay as Scott did. He found conditions tolerable enough to work at his desk with sennegrass inside his komager (Laplanders' reindeer-skin boots).

With a small head of steam on one boiler, they enjoyed good electric light until the end of May, when the coal situation dictated use of the windmill. Failing to find vital parts under the snowdrifts, they sacrificed the plates that protected the bows from the anchors to get the windmill going. The resulting light varied unpredictably because the regulator failed to control the voltage, as also happened aboard *Discovery*. After a few days a storm sheared off half of the holding-down bolts, and they switched to kerosene lamps but had to abandon them in late August in favor of blubber lamps.

There were some fine days, and on one a sledge party, sent to explore their surroundings, came back with the unwelcome news that there were stranded icebergs to the west, running over 12 miles north of their position. That meant the entire field might never release them as the wind piled on more ice from the east. Drygalski's thoughts turned to De Gerlache's story and how he had used saws and dark material to hasten melting. So Albert Stehr, the chief engineer, was asked to fabricate saws, and, amid much skepticism, he ordered all dark-colored waste to be saved.

Since March, Drygalski had also been occupied with the question of what, other than the inland ice movement survey, could be done with the short season before escape would be feasible. Proposals for a journey toward the magnetic pole were impractical without a shore base, and as he later revealed, he was at odds with most of Neumayer's preferences. He favored disproving the seaway to the Weddell Sea by joining his new discovery with Kemp Land 800 miles to the west, even if that left a huge gap in the magnetic map.

Preparations had gotten under way in June for a six-week journey over the sea ice to the southeast to learn more about the land first seen about 55 miles east of the Gaussberg. However, they had embarked on the ice movement project at the mountain, so self-imposed manpower limitations meant the Eastern journey could not be tackled at the same time and would have to start in the dead of winter, at the end of July.

The problem was Drygalski's (or was it the captain's?) cautious manning of the ship. With a rig requiring fewer deckhands than *Discovery*, they had decided to leave six more men aboard than Scott eventually left aboard his ship in case the ice carried it away. Except for that concern and too few dogs, there would have been enough men to mount both journeys simultaneously.

Eventually, the weather ruled out any such early start, and when Ruser discovered open water 3 miles east of them after the wind had veered to the west, Drygalski's prediction of an end of November earliest breakout appeared extremely optimistic. His own start was brought forward to September 16, and the Eastern Party plan was dropped. A north-south crack had also opened 600 yards west of the ship, posing a distinct threat that the huge floe would break away, carrying the ship with it and leaving the sledge party marooned, so fifty cases of provisions were sledged out to a berg beyond the crack.

When the time came for Drygalski to start for the mountain, this time with 700 pounds on each of the four sledges including a magnetic hut for Bidlingmaier, he found that the twenty-eight dogs, fed on penguin meat during the winter, could not move the sledges more than 2 miles per hour. The men were held in their tent by a storm that lasted five and a half days—the worst Drygalski had experienced—and ten days were gone when they completed the last stretch on September 25, only to find the icehouse in which they were to live totally destroyed.

The group lived in two tents, with the cooking done in the smaller one, and Drygalski completed the summit survey by October 6. Much work had to be redone in searingly cold conditions, because markers had blown away or were obscured by intervening snowdrifts. After a final excursion on foot along the top of the ice cliffs west of the mountain, they left a note in a bottle claiming the land for the kaiser and started back on the 9th. By then the sledge runners were shod with tin, because the German Silver cladding had completely broken up. As Armitage would learn, the Germans' wooden underrunners dragged heavily over the very surfaces where they were supposed to protect the metal.

Back at the ship on October 14, they found the sawing operations as exasperating as they would prove for the British, for the ice was 20 feet thick. The crew did succeed, though, in freeing the rudder and screw.

Some days later Drygalski found the pack once again solid to the eastern horizon. Putting the deadline for the last of the sledging back to the end of November, he thought it safe to dispatch Philippi with three others and eighteen dogs to search icebergs west of their previous routes for fresh evidence of continental debris—Philippi had found granite rocks on the Gaussberg that he believed could have been carried there only from continental land when the ice had been thick enough to cover the mountain.

Pushing into the unknown about 16 miles south of the ship, the group soon faced a continuous north-south ice cliff that seemed to continue as far as both horizons. Following it southward, they arrived at the coast about 9 miles west of Mount Gaussberg. Tracing the coast to the mountain, they cut across diagonally to follow the cliff northward until they were 27 miles due west of the ship. They were running out of time at that point and were forced to start back without seeing the seaward end, which lay barely 2 miles further north, hidden in the mist.

Back aboard on November 5, the discoverers of the third known Antarctic ice shelf presented Drygalski with fresh questions. By the 24th, Ruser had found the low northern edge of the shelf and had taken soundings that suggested it must be afloat, and Bidlingmaier had extended his magnetic observations westward.

Drygalski risked a final dash to examine the shelf's surface about 65 feet above sea level on December 3. A last 340-fathom sounding more or less proved it was not aground, and Drygalski believed the shelf's surface suggested it had been built by accumulating icebergs driven onto it from the east rather than by inland ice. The West Ice Shelf, as he named it, still exists today.

When the men returned to the ship on December 4, 4 miles of ice lay between them and open water to the east. The crack west of the ship was now 5 feet wide and growing by about 8 inches a day. It pointed to escape in that direction, and the crew had been spreading the waste they had collected along a line running past the astronomical hut to the crack. Dynamiting was tried without success at the western end of the crack, so they could only wait for the slow melting action to cut through the ice, now 20 feet thick.

Twelve days into 1903 the resulting trench was 6 or 7 feet deep, and the crew started to dig and blast through the remainder. They had just realized that the task would take them at least five months when a two-day blizzard undid all their work.

Things looked so bad that Drygalski thought they might be trapped for a second winter and began to consider leading a party over the 450 miles to Knox Land the following spring to rendezvous with the relief ship. But then some of the icebergs astern began moving away, and digging was started again on the port side. In the wake of the diggers, the 20-foot saws fabricated by Stehr were brought into action on January 29.

Two days later the sea was as close to the east as the crack was to the west, and in two more days nature had almost finished what they had scarcely begun to achieve. The entire floe, 2 miles long from north to south and three-quarters of a mile wide, broke away from the western crack on February 2. The floe—agonizingly—drifted back and forth for days until a sharp shock on the 8th brought everyone racing on deck to find the ship afloat in a steadily widening lake.

Amid a rising gale, they hardly had time to get the instruments and dogs onboard before the angry sea split the floe apart along the line of the western trench. Still blocked close to the ship, even that stretch opened two hours later, and the *Gauss* steamed slowly through it and turned north toward freedom. Clear of the northern extremity of the ice shelf by 10 P.M., they were at last beyond the clutches of the trap that might have marooned the ship for good. So there was relief rather than alarm when dense pack surrounded the ship that night.

Five weeks of exasperatingly slow westward travel followed, mostly carried by the pack. The ship always had to maintain a full head of steam and constantly exploit leads. They had been in sight of the ice shelf for at least 100 miles before larger lanes opened to the northwest.

Just 450 miles west of them when they first escaped lay the 78°E meridian on which Nares had crossed the Circle in HMS *Challenger* in 1874 with nothing but a few icebergs in the open waters ahead. As much as Drygalski disbelieved Neumayer's theories, he could not absolutely rule them out, still less resist the prospect of being carried off to unknown coasts by the pack. In Berlin he had successfully insisted that the relief ship plan should not inhibit his movements, so from the moment of their escape he had determined to make another push to the south, even if it meant they might be trapped for another winter.

When they finally emerged from the pack on March 15, still 3° east of Nares's track, only 76 tons of coal remained over the mandatory safety stock. As 53 tons had sufficed to get them through the winter,[3] Drygalski adopted the rashly optimistic view that there was no risk on that score. Drygalski's plan met considerable opposition from others who preferred to carry on work in Australia and from some crew members as well. Nonetheless, he headed the *Gauss* at first west and then south on March 18, setting sail for the first time.

However, late March was a very different season from the mid-February of Nares's farthest south. With coal rapidly diminishing because the ship wouldn't steer closer than 7 points off the wind with square sails set or 4 points with staysails, they twice reached what looked like secure berths in which to winter among stationary floes, only to be faced with the imminent disaster of being crushed against icebergs.

With 65 of the 76 tons of coal used up after they escaped from the second trap on April 8 in about 65½°S, Drygalski's second chance was lost before it had started, as he reluctantly gave the order to retreat northward. Clear of the pack the following morning, he faced some disorder among the crew as they returned to routine seagoing work, with the atmosphere not helped when he ordered many dogs that had become personal pets to be shot to reduce the constant cleaning up on deck. The thirty best dogs were kept for zoos in Germany. Discipline was restored in time for the onslaught of the southern ocean, which first swept their remaining timber overboard and then, just south of the Kerguelens, broached the ship to, fortunately without injury or loss of life.

Sailing past the islands, a five-week voyage punctuated by oceanography and visits to St. Paul and New Amsterdam Islands in the Indian Ocean brought them to Durban by the end of May. Short of coal and drinking water, they arrived to find the town in the grip of a plague. Forced to steam south in the teeth of winter gales, it took them nine days to reach the British naval base at Simonstown, where they learned that tragedy had struck their comrades at the Kerguelen base.[4]

Drygalski, undaunted by being repulsed by the ice, had hoped for permission to try again in the spring, for he knew they had not resolved the geographical problem he had set out to answer because they had obtained no proof that the land was continuous westward to Kemp Land. But they had barely dropped anchor on June 9 when the official welcome from Berlin instructed them to return to Germany because expedition funds were exhausted. They all knew the scientific work had been exhaustive—the results would fill twenty large volumes and take Drygalski most of his life to complete—but he would have to be content with his two discoveries. There would be no second chance.

18

WINTER 1903–SEASON OF SUSPENSE
The Making of Scott's Second Chance

A world away from the men facing another winter in the far south, although not distant in spirit, the man in Europe for whom suspense was most acute was seventy-three-year-old Sir Clements Markham. His persistent advocacy of the campaign inevitably led to a sense of personal responsibility for the safety of the men he had dispatched into the unknown. From the start, he had been determined to provide against the very traps the Antarctic had sprung.

Almost single-handedly, he had raised the money to send out the ship that now brought back to New Zealand the first news of any of the expeditions. The purpose of the *Morning's* voyage had been to provide succor for Scott and his companions if the *Discovery* sank or became trapped in the ice.

In the desperate struggle to gain agreement on the original instructions to Scott, however, no plan was defined as to what should be done if Scott's ship were merely trapped in an iced-up harbor. The situation obviously opened the door to another season of exploration.

In May 1902, when the instructions to Colbeck had to be drawn up, Markham, the only British prime mover seriously devoted to exploration in the Antarctic, had been probing the possibility of Scott staying another year regardless of the circumstances. No doubt impelled by the Royal Geographical Society's (RGS) financial position, Maj. Leonard Darwin, one of Markham's allies in the battle over the expedition leadership, was opposed to extending the expedition. Hastening to preempt any extension, he suggested in a note marked "secret" that the Royal Society should propose that fresh instructions be sent to Scott.[1] Sir William Huggins, president of the Royal Society and one of Markham's erstwhile allies, rejected the proposal: "We have no right to assume that Markham would give any instruction contrary to those of the Joint Committee."[2]

Despite that, Darwin must have carried the day, because on June 16, 1902, instructions to both Colbeck and Scott were approved by the RGS Council. Clause 11 in the instructions to Scott stated: "As at present informed, we are of the opinion that a third season is not feasible from a financial point of view. But matters may have a different aspect in April 1903."[3]

Whether Markham raised the question or not (the minutes do not record the discussion), there was no mention of action in the event of the *Discovery* being unable to get out of the ice. But a week later, with Colbeck sitting between him and Sir William at a farewell dinner for the *Morning* officers, when the Royal Society president told Markham that that society's council had also approved the letter, Markham did not mention the subject, although by his own admission the loss of Franklin and his men in the Arctic had stamped it on his every thought of the coming voyage.

If that was the first noticeable effect of the years of strain on Markham's mental abilities, their impact on the aging man's judgment was demonstrated when, without notice to Sir William, he had an additional sentence inserted in the letter to assure Scott that the *Morning* would be returned the following season should he be unable to extricate the *Discovery*. His suspicions aroused, Sir William quickly noticed the addition "to the effect that a ship would be sent the following season to take back Scott if," as he wrote to the treasurer, underlining words for emphasis: "it is impossible for him to return to Lyttelton next spring." "Now this," he continued, "clearly gives Scott permission to stay another year, if he can say it was impossible for him to return next spring. . . . Of course if it were really impossible for Scott to return, there would be no other course open. But we do not know what private instructions Scott may have received."[4]

Huggins insisted that the reference to the addition to the letter be removed. From then on, the seeds of distrust sown in the mind of Markham's most valuable ally were to grow into the conviction that there was a conspiracy between Markham and Scott, where none in fact existed.

Seven months later, when a letter arrived from Baron Richthofen about plans for a relief ship in case the German ship did not return as planned, the subject was again brought to the fore in Markham's mind as he contemplated the letter to Scott he was about to draft for approval by the RGS Council on February 23, 1903. Writing to the expedition treasurer to alert him to action and to the potential costs if both British ships did not return as intended, he explained that there would be an extra year's pay for both ships' complements, amounting to £7,770. Even if the *Morning* crew was discharged for the winter season, the total cost would be at least £10,000, and only £3,858 remained. Asserting that the only option was to appeal to the government for the extra £6,000, he clearly felt such an appeal would succeed: "A refusal would be unprecedented. Former Governments have invariably complied with appeals of the kind. In this case, though the 4 naval officers volunteered of their own accord, the 28 seamen and marines were invited by the authorities to volunteer. The Government is undoubtedly responsible for their safety."[5]

At the same time, if both ships returned as planned Markham was still keen to grant Scott "a third navigable season," and, knowing the government would not sanction more money, he added that he was prepared to try to raise the extra money: "The two ships [would be] ordered to return home, it being assumed that the balance of £3,858 will be sufficient for expenses. Scott may be very anxious for a third navigable season to settle the Wilkes Land question [westward from Cape Adare]. If so I should be willing to make an effort to raise £6,000 more while the ships are refitting at Lyttelton, which I think will be sufficient if the *Morning* is sent home at once. I have offers from Dundee to buy her."

Five days later he included the figures in a letter to Scott.[6] Wages would amount to £4,854, 18 months' expenses to £3,000, the *Morning* voyage home to £1,500, less balance of £3,858, leaving £5,500 to raise. Markham added that the owners of a ship lost in the Davis Strait had asked whether the *Morning* would be for sale: "We might raise £5,000 on her perhaps."[7] Clearly, no approach to the government would be needed in that case.

The long-awaited news arrived on Wednesday, March 25, in two cables telling of the arrival of the *Morning* without Scott. Markham's suspense regarding the immediate safety of the men was calmed by the first cable saying that the *Discovery* had "revictualled from the *Morning* and the explorers are now in a position to spend a comfortable winter."[8] The cable failed to say whether they would have to do so, but in the second cable Colbeck, after telling of his discovery of two islands and the subsequent search for the *Discovery*, spoke of his conviction that Scott would not escape from the ice that season.[9]* Markham sent copies of the cables to Kempe and Sir William, inexplicably more than doubling the estimate of what had to be raised and speaking of £15,000 being needed.[10]

Despite the Treasury decision that the trustees of the British Museum would bear the cost of publication of the scientific reports (originally to be met by the Royal Society), Sir William's suspicions were once again aroused by the threat of demands on his society's resources. "Were not our instructions to Scott clear and definite that he was not to remain a second year, unless unable to extricate himself from the ice?"[11] he asserted, with some justification, to the treasurer, remembering clause 7 in the letter taken out by Colbeck:[12]

> You will then be in command of the two ships, and you are to take what you require from the *Morning*, and extricate yourself from your winter quarters with as little loss of time as possible. You are then to do as much exploring and scientific work as the time will admit with the two ships, during the navigable season of 1903. The direction you will take, and the methods you may adopt in performing this service, are left entirely to your discretion. You will return to Lyttelton in March or April 1903.

Huggins added, "I suspected all along that Scott had secret instructions from Markham to remain a second year, notwithstanding official instructions to the contrary" and asked, "Is the Royal Society jointly responsible with the Royal Geographical Society for the additional £15,000?"[13]

A further cable from Colbeck that arrived on Saturday, March 28, revealed that the suspicion was groundless, reporting that Scott was "desirous of reaching Lyttelton this season."[14] Huggins saw that cable, but the damage had been done. The loss of Sir William's trust would cost Markham dearly before the summer was half over.

Having reduced the estimate first to £12,000[15] and then to £8,000 when Kempe came to Eccleston Square to discuss the problem the day Colbeck's cable arrived,[16] Markham's lately relieved suspense was replaced by a new fear. The cable indicated that part of the supplies had gone bad and that, as a result, the party was experiencing some

---

* As Doorly (1916: p. 59) relates, Colbeck had at first named the main island after Markham, but Huntford (1979: p. 193) implies that by not mentioning that fact, Scott (1905, vol. 2: p. 158) was trying to enhance his image as a spontaneously respected leader. The facts outlined in note 9 provide no evidence that Scott was ever aware that Colbeck had proposed naming the island after Markham.

privation. Colbeck explained in his March 28 cable that the bulk of the tinned food had been condemned and that, with supplies brought south by the *Morning* at the end of January, Scott had only enough for twelve months. If there was logic in his conclusion that the extra money would have to come from the government, the wild fluctuation of Markham's estimates was perhaps another indication of the faltering judgment that now imagined a threat of starvation where none existed.

Although Markham could not know the actual amounts Scott was laying in for the winter, he seemed to have forgotten the bountiful supply of seals and penguins Colbeck had observed during the *Southern Cross* expedition, as well as the fact that Scott had introduced his men to penguin meat on the voyage to New Zealand. Even with the ice edge at least 3½ miles from the ship, Scott had amassed enough seals and skuas to provide fresh meat daily through the second winter and well beyond with the aid of the mutton brought from New Zealand by the *Morning*.[17]

Markham convinced the RGS Council to approve a joint appeal to the Treasury. On April 2 he wrote to Huggins: "I am in great anxiety about the funds, and trust that the RS Council will agree to our proposal on the 23rd. Time is of the utmost moment if the Government refuses help . . . the *Discovery* only has a year's provisions; and a terrible disaster might be the consequence of relief not being sent."[18]

The move to obtain separate approval by the councils and the upward revision once again of his estimate, this time accidentally quoted as £20,000 when he meant £12,000,[19] led to the very delay he sought to avoid. Colbeck's second cable had advised that Scott's report should arrive by May 16, and the Royal Society Council, faced with the huge new estimate, seized on this to delay action until it arrived.

Unfortunately, Markham reacted by writing to another Royal Society officer, Dr. Larmor, who with the best of intentions sought the advice of the Assistant Hydrographer and thus placed the initiative in the hands of Markham's old adversaries, Capt. Thomas Tizard and Adm. Sir William Wharton. Hearing nothing for a week, Markham sent the revised (£12,000) estimate to the Chancellor of the Exchequer's private secretary and a copy to the Treasury. Before a reply came, the two societies' officers met with their draft letters, the Royal Society one now largely dictated by the Hydrographer who insisted that a second ship be inserted into the plan with a consequent further increase in the estimate.[20]

Hearing that the Treasury would refuse his request, Markham set moves in train to have a question asked in the House of Commons, with a view to forcing the issue of government aid. Meanwhile, he signed the joint letter to avoid further delay, albeit "under protest," as he put it to Kempe, for "that second ship is a source of the greatest anxiety to me; such a suggestion may just tip the scales against us."[21] It not only did that, but having been presented with the even higher estimate, Balfour found himself cornered in the House of Commons on May 26, 1903, with an open attempt to force his hand. The answer he gave, inevitably noncommittal but apparently favorable toward a grant, was accompanied by sharp criticism of the two societies.

By alienating the man about to become prime minister, Markham's impetuous move had forged an alliance between the Admiralty and the Treasury that would wrest from his control not only the relief expedition but effectively all chance of exploiting the release of the *Discovery* should it eventually happen. An ill-informed editorial in Alfred Harmsworth's *Daily Mail* on May 20 and a frantic cable from Colbeck asking for further funds did nothing to ease the suspense before the Treasury decision arrived. It came first in a telegram on June 20 from the Hydrographer to Shackleton, who had returned on the 12th, saying that the Admiralty would undertake the rescue and seeking to consult him—a request Shackleton declined.

Two days later a letter arrived that must have been a bitter blow to Markham. The government would take responsibility for the relief effort "on condition the *Morning*, now in New Zealand, is handed over absolutely and at once to the Board of Admiralty who will control the relief operations on behalf of the Government."[22]

The depth of animosity toward Markham in the Hydrographer's Department had been revealed the day before in a letter from Captain Tizard to Kempe: "If the *Morning* is the private property of Sir Clements Markham, it seems clear that no contribution for repairs to her should be made from funds collected for the despatch of the *Discovery*. If funds are devoted . . . for executing repairs to the *Morning*, it should be made clear that the *Morning*, equally with the *Discovery*, must be considered as the property of the two Societies."[23] Tizard well knew that although registered in Markham's name, the *Morning* really belonged to the RGS.

There was one consolation for the man without whom there would have been no news of Scott's immediate predicament. The Treasury letter contained a fitting rebuttal of the attack in Harmsworth's paper, concluding with the words:[24]

> Their Lordships desire me to add that They are far from desiring herein to reflect in any way on the conduct of the financial arrangements of the original Expedition by the two Societies, and they trust that the Finance

Committee will continue to administer the remaining funds (which their Lordships understand to be adequate) for the purpose of the *Discovery*, as distinguished from the relief expedition of which, subject to investigation, They are ready to assume the whole responsibility and expense as from the date of this letter.

Four days later Markham consented to transfer control of the ship "for the purposes of the relief"[25] and left for Norway on June 27. A week later the real bombshell arrived in a letter from Cyril Longhurst telling that the RGS Council had agreed to a Treasury demand to cede ownership of the *Morning* to the Department of Transport; otherwise, as Markham put it in his diary, "the explorers would be left to their fate."[26]

For those explorers the first priority since the arrival of the *Morning* had been to build up stocks of seal meat in case the ice in the harbor did not break out. Wilson recorded, when he felt well enough to resume his diary on February 24, that the target was 200 seals. Such a large stock was undoubtedly required because the *Morning* had arrived with far less mutton than its ice room could have contained. Installed in response to Scott's remarks about the lack of one in the *Discovery*, it could have held 100 carcasses,[27] but nothing like that number could have been brought south, for by March 11 there were only 20 left.[28]

They had only a handful of dogs, and the party remaining was smaller, too, for besides Macfarlane, Brett the cook, and Hare (there had never been any question of him remaining more than a year if either ship could get him back), six others had responded when Scott put up a notice on February 19 requesting that "all those who do not wish to chance the possibility of another winter" send in their names.[29] Two naval men, William Page and William Peters;[30] three merchant servicemen (William Hubert, James Duncan, and John D. Walker); and the civilian laboratory assistant Horace Buckridge volunteered, leaving a total complement of thirty-seven men to stay with the *Discovery*.*

This made a marked difference in the harmony on the mess deck, in contrast with the rows Hare had recorded as the first winter had set in. "There has scarcely been a friction," Scott later wrote in his journal. "Since their departure stories of various sorts have come to light [that] all go to prove that it is hopeless to expect the Scotch whaling element [rather a misnomer, because only Walker had whaling experience] can pull together with the naval people."[31] Ferrar also described

---

* See Appendix 2.

the better atmosphere as "probably due to the absence of the merchant seamen."[32]

The *Morning* finally left on Monday, March 2, and five days later everyone was still hoping to get out although, as they could see from the heights, the pack still lay firmly across the entrance to the sound. Wilson echoed every man's hopes in his diary on the 7th:[33]

> If we could only get out of this strait, it would be an excellent thing for all of us even if we get stuck fast in the pack . . . for one thing we should be free for a season's navigation in January instead of waiting stuck here until the middle of February. . . . However it would be just as well to get up to New Zealand for the winter, and come down . . . for a summer's work, and then home. At present it looks as though we shall have to remain here, as there is still a good 3½ miles of unbroken floe between us and open water and a heavy mass of pack ice across the mouth of the strait which prevents any swell from the Ross Sea coming in to break up this floe.

As the *Morning* steamed away, it was waved off by a line of men at the ice edge. If Scott was publicly hoping the *Discovery* would be able to follow, as Colbeck's March 25 cable from New Zealand made clear, he was at the same time already aware of the dangers the Hut Point base posed to the ship's ultimate escape. Both for that reason and for the assault on Victoria Land, a new anchorage would be better, as Colbeck's March 28 cable would reveal: "Present position unsuited for more extended operations; will seek new quarters and continue work if ice breaks up too late for return north."[34]

Scott probably had Granite Harbour in mind, for he referred to it as excellent in the cable, and it had at least been free of ice when they discovered it in January 1902, even if it had taken twenty-three hours to push in through the pack. By contrast, New Harbour had been blocked by pack 12 feet thick.

But by March 13 any hope of improving their position was gone— "I have abandoned all hope of the ice going out," Scott wrote that evening.[35] It was colder than the previous March, too, which further reduced the chance of the ice going out. So the next day he gave orders to prepare the ship for wintering, and the men started to dismantle the engines, so carefully readied for the voyage that was not to be.

The one thing in short supply was kerosene, much to Wilson's regret, for he could not spend the amount of time in his cabin needed to work up watercolors and make fair copies in ink of the sketches he had made at such cost to his eyes on the gruelling Southern journey. They were each allowed one candle a week to light their cabins for getting up and going to bed, and the absence of lamps vastly increased the condensation—twice a day Ferrar had to mop up water dripping from the ceiling in his cabin.[36]

There were still nine hours of daylight, but otherwise the only lighting in the evenings, when Wilson did much of his work, was a single Hitchcock lamp over the wardroom table. However, relief came soon, for Skelton was working on setting up acetylene lighting, and by the week of April 12 Wilson was singing its praises.

So it made little difference when the awning went up on April 21. Only one boat was put out, on the land ice this time, and the others were stowed aboard clear of the awning. Two days later, as the sun dipped below the northern horizon to disappear for 123 days, there were still eight hours of daylight and plenty of scope for exercise. Wilson's legs were fully recovered, and he could take part in the games of hockey played in the afternoons.

By late June Scott began to talk of his plans for the new season's sledging. He was in almost the same predicament as Drygalski had been once the *Gauss* was trapped in the pack. Scott knew there was not enough money left to pay another year's salaries and wages if *Discovery* could not be extricated from the ice-locked bay. Since the departure of the *Morning* he had spent many hours considering whether this had been a normal and not exceptional state of affairs in McMurdo Sound, and he concluded it had been an abnormal season.

If the earliest date he could hope for the breakout was mid-December and, like Drygalski, he intended to improve the chances that they could get out then by cutting and blasting, that gave him only four weeks more than the German had allowed for further exploration. They were much further south than the Germans, and the real sledging weather only came in October, so they would have to lay depots in September. Then, with luck, just ten weeks would remain to solve the riddles so frustratingly unanswered after the previous campaign.

The day after the Midwinter celebration—Ferrar's diary almost exuded italic letters as he wrote of "real" turtle soup and "real" roast beef—Wilson knew there would be "at least three attacks on the western and south-western lands by three parties . . . each six to eight weeks."[37] A couple of days later Scott asked Ferrar where he wanted to pursue his geological exploration, and he immediately chose the land at the top of the big western glacier Armitage's party had ascended. At that time Scott was considering naming it the "Teall Ice Stream" after the director of the British Geological Survey.[38] With virtually no dogs and his confidence in them shaken, the need to haul seal meat for them, and the expenditure of fuel to defrost that meat if conditions were as cold as those encountered the previous spring, it was hardly surprising that Scott opted for manhauling.

On July 1 Wilson went for a moonlight ski run with Royds and learned that the details of the plan were nearly settled. After the necessary depot-laying journeys, Scott would lead the main summit three-sledge party with Skelton and seven men, accompanied as far as the top of the glacier by Ferrar and two others. Barne, with George Mulock from the Morning and seven other men, would make the second attempt to get into the strait that had eluded his and Scott's parties the previous season, with Mulock surveying the coast as they went. Wilson with two men would make three trips to study the Cape Crozier penguin rookery, and Koettlitz would also make at least one journey.[39]

Just those parties accounted for twenty-four of the thirty-seven men at Hut Point. With three not fit for sledging—Ford, Hodgson, and Dell, whose arm had been poisoned and operated on to remove a gland—three more tied down recommissioning the engines, and either Royds or Armitage in charge at the ship, there was a margin of only six men for any other sledging, as well as for the other work needed to get the ship ready for sea.

Armitage wanted to get further south on the barrier, but with such a narrow reserve of manpower and the surface conditions they had encountered, Wilson agreed with Scott's rejection of the plan. Certainly, the reserve men did not run to both another Southern attempt and what would amount to a third depot party, even assuming Scott would have been prepared to let Armitage risk one in midbarrier, which was hardly likely after Peary's experience had been so nearly repeated on his own journey—unless the Western objectives were abandoned.[40]

Furthermore, the surviving complement of sledges made the rejection of Armitage's proposal inevitable. Leaving aside the "elephant" and the two 7-foot sledges for the ship's local needs, just eleven sledges were usable for extended journeys. Scott, Ferrar, and Barne needed a total of seven, and Wilson's Crozier journeys, vital to the study of the newly discovered Emperor rookery, and the "relief," or rescue party, sledge locked up another two. That left just two sledges for any other major thrust. Those two were needed for Barne's Support Party and wouldn't be available until after their planned November 7 return, leaving five weeks for any journey if the party was to be back at the ship by mid-December like the others.

In the end, a third party was squeezed out of the meager force left at the ship. As Scott acknowledged in his book,[41] the plan was instigated by Bernacchi, who pointed out that they had been assuming the barrier was flat to the east of them because it had appeared that way on their voyage along it and from the heights above Cape Crozier, but none of that constituted proof. So a third party, for which there were too few men to lay out a depot in September, would explore to the southeast. They might just have the luck to sight new land in that direction.

Bernacchi would go along because along with Scott's own traverse westward on the summit, the two parties could plot out the magnetic forces and achieve a location of the South Magnetic Pole even if Scott didn't reach it. For all practical purposes it would be as effective as if he had and for navigational ends even better, as a large area of the magnetic map could be constructed and thereby confirm or correct Armitage's observations at sea.

Royds was chosen to lead that third thrust, which probably had a dual origin. First, Scott's choice created a fair sharing of the chances for a major discovery among the executive officers of the expedition. Armitage, however, viewed the decision as reflecting something else, a point that rankled him for most of his life. In his autobiography, published more than twenty years later, he claimed the decision broke an unwritten agreement with Scott that he was to be given a free hand with the sledging.[42]

Almost certainly, however, Scott had also been influenced by Skelton, with whom he had particular ties as a fellow officer from the *Majestic*. Skelton believed Armitage's handling of the Ferrar Glacier ascent had been somewhat less than an unqualified success in terms of leadership as well as speed, and with the short season Scott was planning for, speed must have loomed large in his priorities. Not only had Skelton disagreed with the attempt at the mountain route but at the head of Blue Glacier he had felt impelled to record in his journal, "Some of the men complained to Armitage about the slow step—he took it rather badly at first, as he often does when he is not agreed with . . . but he saw the sense of the remarks . . . and asked me to set the step."[43] Armitage's attitude toward the young Ferrar had also irritated Skelton: "Armitage talks to him in a most absurd way, a sort of bullying or ridiculing tone, in front of the men—very bad form I think and as I told Koettlitz—I wouldn't stand for it—but then he knows better than to speak like that to anyone who knows the ropes."[44]

Matters had evidently come to a head between Skelton and Armitage on December 30, as they had begun to run out of time approaching the head of the glacier. Skelton had found holes in the cooker, which had been strapped down hard onto the primus box lid from which nailheads were protruding. In his diary Skelton wrote that Armitage had complained about him "wasting time outside tinkering with the cooker—that was a little too thick considering that the thing would be entirely useless if I were not here—it is the second time I have mended it—besides the job took considerably under 10 minutes. . . . I promptly started at him again . . . as usual with baiters they can't stand being baited, and he got angry and talked of my being sent back. . . . I really think a man has no right to take advantage of a temporary position of command to say things he did to me."[45]

If such remarks suggested jealousy or disloyalty in Skelton, any such motive was to be discounted by his reaction to grumbling about Armitage among the other men in the group. Some of the men were, he felt, "positively objectionable, always making remarks about the leading . . . there is a lack of loyalty to the leader in them."[46] With even a hint of criticism of Armitage's leadership by Skelton, the men's grumbles could also be taken as justifiable. In that situation, Scott's choice of Royds for the other major journey was no more surprising than his determination to lead the summit party himself.

Everything was ready by the end of August. But Scott knew his chances of success depended on being able to avoid the Blue Glacier route and get directly onto the great western glacier from the sea ice in New Harbour. He could not tell whether that would be feasible until the depot journey planned for September. The second winter had indeed become a season of suspense.

PART 4

FRUSTRATION RICHLY REDEEMED
Scott's Second Campaign

19

SLINGS AND ARROWS OF MISFORTUNE
The Thwarting of Scott's Start for the West

To Scott, with inadequate time and resources for a push beyond his own farthest south, the most dramatic discovery within his grasp was not just what lay beyond Armitage's farthest west but the existence of a western shore of Victoria Land, so strongly hinted at by the descending summit surface Armitage had seen to the west of his farthest advance.* Taken with the southern limit of Victoria Land suggested by the apparent strait Barne was being sent to explore and the theories advocated by Murray and Neumayer, which the *Gauss* had been sent to test, it was not illogical to conclude there might be another sea between Wilkes's Cape Hudson in 153°45E and Ross's Cape North in 165°20E.

If that were so, speed was vital, for there would be a glacier to descend and get back up even if the time remaining did not allow a journey northward to the magnetic pole. Scott's six-man Western Party—with Skelton, Feather, Lashly, Evans, and Handsley—would tackle

---

* First gleaned from the Germans' ideas during his Berlin visit, then strongly reinforced by what he had seen during the first stages south from the Bluff, Scott's belief that there was a western coast of Victoria Land persisted to the end, for in a letter written on the voyage back to New Zealand he described how he had "failed to get across S. Victoria Land" (Lot 250 Sotheby 12.18.89 sale; 2.27.04 letter to Mrs. Noble-Wilson). It has now been established that Victoria Land and the Cook Mountains form a peninsula beneath the ice sheet, its western "coast" (i.e., at sea level) bordering the Wilkes Sub-Glacial Basin lying in 143E (GJ Nov. 1987, 153/3: p. 365).

the attempt to force a direct route from New Harbour and place a depot by Cathedral Rocks.[1] At the last minute Feather was put on the sick list, so Dailey replaced him, joining Skelton in Scott's tent with the others in the second tent.[2]

Royds's Crozier Rookery Party got away first on September 7, with Scott starting westward two mornings later. His two sledges in train were helped by the prevailing easterly wind filling the sail, to the extent that only four men had to pull on skis to keep them moving along smoothly, despite the 430 pounds of provisions for the depot.[3] Traveling by way of the Eskers and pinned down by a blizzard for most of the third day, they camped for lunch at Butter Point on the 13th and began the haul along the south shore of New Harbour.

The next morning the surface of two-year-old ice forced them to pull on foot rather than skis, with the imposing 30-mile view up to Knobhead Mountain ahead of them. "Tomorrow with luck [we] should be able to decide whether this route to the inland ice is practicable," Skelton wrote that evening as the thermometer dropped to –49F.[4]

Already past moraine heaps over 20 feet high, they started up the frozen water course between the land and the glacier snout that had presented such an awesome sight to Armitage and Walker: "The ice is in enormous mounds . . . some of the boulders were suspended on tops of the columns just like tables."[5] Reaching the point where the glacier ice met the land, they halted for the lunch camp on the 15th, after which Scott sent Dailey, Lashly, and Handsley up the hillside for a better view while he plunged into the towering maze with Skelton and Evans.

After about a mile Scott's party found what they were looking for, as they came to a point where the bed of the chasm rose gradually toward the surface of the glacier. The surface was broken enough that the sledges had to be carried some of the time, but Skelton nevertheless thought it would only take a morning to get up it. Evans reckoned it would take a day.

Following their tracks back through the maze, they were greeted at the camp by Dailey with news of an even better passage starting nearer the camp. Setting off straightaway it was[6]

> just like a race—the turnings sometimes lead east, sometimes west, north or south, in fact in every direction; but we kept steadily on, one sledge at a time, and all the time making progress towards the smooth part. We had to do short stages as the ice masses were so confused and high, and the turnings so frequent, that one might easily lose a sledge [e.g., in front]

if we hadn't a track to go by. Occasionally it was advisable to have an outlook from the top of one of the ice heaps to choose the best channel . . . made [a] good 7 miles.

With half a mile's relaying the next morning and a final pull up with both sledges together, they emerged on the glacier surface beside what Skelton took for the medial moraine trench, as much as 80 feet deep and 100 yards wide. Reaching smooth going by lunchtime, they went on to camp off the Overflow Glacier after making 8½ miles that day.[7]

Establishing the depot alongside a huge quartzite boulder in the moraine opposite the central buttress of Cathedral Rocks by lunchtime on September 17, they turned for home. They had cached three weeks' provisions for six men and four gallons of oil, along with crampons, alpine rope, blocks, and the repair kit. The party had achieved the 66-mile journey in six days less than the Descent Pass route had taken, despite a day lost in a blizzard. The other great gain was the state of the surface. Armitage's party could barely stand on the hard, glassy ice; this time they could pull without using crampons.

From that night's camp just downstream from Overflow Glacier, Scott at first headed for the north side of the valley where he believed they might find an easier way onto the glacier on the main journey. Eventually, one of the melt trenches prevented progress toward the other bank. Scott climbed a huge ice block to find they were only 300 yards from the sea ice. They emerged from the 30-foot face of the glacier to find they were still too far from the north bank to see if he was right in believing there was an easier way up from the sea ice there.

The afternoon's run brought them back to Butter Point, and they covered the remaining 45 miles in two days, reaching the ship in the dark, half an hour before midnight on the 20th. Scott turned in knowing he had opened the vital door to the rapid ascent of the glacier, so essential to his chances on the summit.

The other parties were safely back. Barne's group had returned earlier that day after laying a depot southeast of White Island in temperatures that had dropped to a dangerous -67°F at night. Even the spirit thermometer split its liquid column. As spirit does not freeze above -80°F, they were right in believing it had been even colder the following night.[8]

Despite that, Joyce had been the only near casualty, with all of his face and then a foot frostbitten. Barne and Mulock had taken turns holding his foot against their chests inside their vests, and that had saved it. The description of the ordeal elevated Barne even further in

Scott's esteem—"his pluck and stamina are unfathomable," Scott wrote, wincing at the thought of the men undoing their clothes in such temperatures.[9]

Royds's party, having left on September 7 to observe the hatching of the Emperor chicks, had reached the rookery a week later, five weeks earlier than when the chicks had been found the previous October. To Wilson's total surprise, they found at least a hundred as old as the ones Royds and Skelton had brought back when they discovered the rookery. It was obvious that the chicks must have been born in the dead of winter.

There had been no sign of live eggs, only frozen ones, of which Wilson, Royds, and Cross collected eight unbroken specimens along with two live chicks. Whitfield, Williamson, and Blissett had made an 8-mile round-trip from their camp to collect two dead Adélie penguins for Wilson's collection. With temperatures only a few degrees warmer than those Barne had experienced, they got back to the ship in four days with the eggs intact and the chicks still alive in spite of more than one capsize of the 11-foot sledge.[10]

The plan for the main journeys allowed ten weeks for Barne's and one week less for Scott's, with both parties to return by December 15.[11] Barne got away on October 6, and the western teams lined up their four 11-foot sledges for the start six days later. The six men in each team harnessed themselves to two sledges in train. Scott's men, with Feather replacing Dailey in his tent, were pulling 205 pounds per man. The three-man support party led by Dailey formed half of Ferrar's party, each pulling 170 pounds. Aided by a force 6 following wind, they completed 13 miles that day and cached 6 pounds of butter and a gallon of oil at Butter Point at lunch on the third day.

In the harbor mouth where the wind fell away, the going became softer, and the drag quickly took a toll on Dailey's trio. The carpenter's hip became so painful that Scott decided to camp in midafternoon after only 9 miles' progress—half what they had managed the day before when able to use the sail. To make matters worse—although he made light of it at the time—Plumley cut the tip off his left thumb while chopping a block of pemmican, and Williamson was already complaining of sore feet.

However, as Scott had guessed, the way onto the glacier near its north side proved far easier when they tackled it on the 15th. By lunchtime they were already opposite the "cascade,"[12] as Skelton called Overflow Glacier, and they completed 11 miles for the day according to Scott's estimate, for the surviving sledgemeter had been allocated to Royds for the Southeast Barrier journey. Scott counted on his watch at noon and other sun transit times to gauge their progress westward on the summit, using navigational tables packed in the instrument box.

After they picked up the first depot, two 12-mile days brought them to just below the Knobhead Mountain moraine. Having achieved a satisfactory average of 15 miles a day, they were within 5 miles of the point planned for the B Depot, beneath New Mountain. However, to Scott's dismay the runners on three of the sledges were so damaged that when they were unpacked at the depot on the 18th it was obvious that the summit journey was out of the question.* Thus on October 20, as Barne repacked his sledges at the Bluff Depot on his way southward, Scott's party was back opposite Descent Glacier, having left the "good" 11-foot sledge at the depot and set off for the ship with just three and a half days' rations.

They set up a small depot for the skis and crampons at the end of the glacier and reached the ship on the 21st. The sledges were in such a state that it was easier for Dailey to narrow the 12-foot "elephant" than to repair any of the others for the summit party. For Ferrar's geological party he made a 7-foot sledge from the wreckage of the others. He also had to make a pair of silver-clad underrunners for the big sledge.[13]

As the six men of the summit party put on their harness for a fresh start the following Monday, October 26, Kennar and Weller were assigned to Ferrar. With little more than half the previous load per man, they covered 45 miles in the first two days, despite the soft surface they encountered in New Harbour—a good start to recovering some of the two weeks lost.

Reaching the depot at the glacier face early on the 28th, they picked up the skis and crampons and, despite fresh trouble with the runners, were almost as far as the Knobhead moraine the next evening—in two days less than it had taken on the abortive attempt. On the 30th violent gusts of wind swept down on them without warning, and they had a hectic chase to recover clothes put out to dry. Thanks to the improved crampons Skelton had made up during the winter, which allowed them to move more quickly, they rescued all but a few items

---

* The cladding was already splitting before they got onto the glacier (SPRI 342/2/6: 11.2.03). This was more a case of inexperience than poor maintenance (as alleged in Huntford 1979: p. 181) because Duncan, who had experience applying the cladding at the temperatures advised by Nansen, had gone back in the *Morning*.

and, buffeted by gusts they could barely stand up in, set about moving the camp a mile closer to the south bank of the glacier.

Relatively sheltered from the wind sweeping down the west side of the mountain, they saw the two days they had gained slip away before the wind subsided enough for them to advance safely over the 5 miles to the depot on November 1. The depot lay beyond the tributary glacier known to this day as Windy Gully, down which furious winds continued to funnel and batter them with force 9 gusts.[14]

Once there, they found what Skelton described as "one of the worst losses we could have had."[15] On the depot trip they had failed to fasten properly the lid of the instrument box, and winds blasting down the upper glacier had ripped it open. The *Hints to Travellers* volume was gone. Published by the RGS for explorers, it contained the data needed to work out latitude and, above all, longitude from sun sights. As Mulock would for Barne's party, Scott was relying on the tables to calculate how far they had traveled.

The attempt could have been ended then and there, but Scott realized there should be a way to work out the sun's noon altitude, which would allow him to use the sun compass to keep tabs on their latitude and hold them on a due west course (east on the way back), both so vital to their return to the top of the right glacier.[16] Apart from the capacity to balance risk with caution that had brought Scott through on the Southern journey, the daring that persuaded him to ask his companions to go on was bolstered by his belief that they would soon come to the western shore of Victoria Land, a prospect that would put a more finite limit on the journey. Scott was confident that his watch, set by the time at the known longitude of the ship, would give the longitude of that coast from the sun's noon azimuth.

The others all agreed to go on, almost certainly in part because they were unwilling to be seen as fainthearted. It is inconceivable that Scott did not explain at least some of his grounds for confidence. Skelton, however, was not convinced, as shown by his journal remark "now we shall never know exactly where we are."[17]

They left a week's provisions for their own return, as well as half the remaining six weeks' rations for Ferrar's party, so the total load, according to Lashly, now amounted to 230 pounds per man. With perhaps 600 pounds fixed weight, the consumables must have weighed 780 pounds, of which 550 pounds represented a day less than seven weeks' standard sledging rations. These were supplemented by seal meat, as is also clear from Lashly's diary.[18]

The load immediately took its toll on the sledge runner cladding, with both runners on the 12-footer and one on the 11-footer "going badly" that afternoon, forcing them to camp early beneath the Lower Finger Mountain icefall. The next day Skelton and Lashly finished patching up the cladding, and they found the ascent of the lower fall relatively easy beneath a brilliant sun that lit up the valley in unusually calm conditions. Although the snow-covered surface mid-glacier made the going stickier, it saved further damage to the runners.

The lull did not last long. Making for the north side of the glacier, they drew out of the lee of the upper falls to find themselves on hard ice with a wind springing up. They were compelled to camp after only 8 miles as the gusts reached force 10. All of the men were rapidly assailed by frostbite as the temperature fell to -9°F. Struggling on after finding it impossible to pitch the tents on the windswept ice, they eventually found some packed snow in the moraine stretching downstream from Northwest Mountain, and in an hour's freezing work they succeeded in pitching the tents.[19]

They had bypassed the Upper Finger Mountain icefall but at a price, for the wind was unabated in the morning. Progressing slowly in the flying drift, they somehow got past Northwest Mountain but were forced to enter the horseshoe-shaped bay beyond it. There they found enough shelter to repair Ferrar's sledge, which was giving them trouble for the second time.

It was clearly better to strike directly across to the south side of the glacier, where Armitage had not experienced such winds. Scott's conclusion was almost miraculously borne out as they walked into a dead calm after the lunch camp in the middle of the glacier. He was tempted to turn west again, but crevasses soon showed there was nothing but danger ahead, and they resumed the crossing and camped on the moraine west of Finger Mountain. Although heartened by a beautifully calm evening, the sledge runners were in such a state that Scott began to doubt if they could survive the last stage of the glacier.

The group arrived at Depot Nunatak the next morning (November 4). The view to the west was dominated by the crest of the next major icefall 700 feet higher and 4 miles ahead. Scott reckoned there would be a sheltered place at its foot for their next camp. To reach it they had to surmount a steep 200-foot slope over a mile from them and then cross a long snowfield to the foot of the main 500-foot cascade.

Surmounting the slope was one of the hardest struggles of the outward journey. Halfway up the slope a fresh gale burst over its brow, and when at last they reached the top, in plunging temperatures, they found another bare field of ice on which it was impossible to pitch the tents. With all of them suffering from frostbite, shelter had become imperative.

In the whirling drift they dared not leave the sledges to search for a patch of snow, so for a solid tortuous hour they dragged them this way and that until, at 2:30 P.M., they found some hard frozen snow the winds had been unable to move. With his typical laconic understatement, Lashly described the next hour as "rather a rough time."[20]

With another half-day lost, frustration clearly got the better of Scott as they struggled to set up the camp, and Skelton betrayed some irritation in his journal that evening. "The skipper gets very impatient under these delays and says rather hasty and unkind things sometimes but," he hastened to qualify, "I don't think he means anything at all, and certainly the weather we are having is enough to try the patience of Job."[21]

The hasty criticism that touched a raw nerve for Skelton that day was obviously addressed to him and possibly to Scott's other tentmate, the bosun, for there is no reference to it in Lashly's diary (and he was not averse to recording Scott's impatience on another occasion). Similarly, in a letter home after his return to the ship, Ferrar did not mention the outburst: "We have all been much better this last winter. We all know each other much better and it is entirely due to the Captain for his friendliness and the example he sets of how to pull together."[22] No man who had other than a high regard for the man and his leadership would have volunteered such a statement in a private letter if Scott had been prone to treat subordinates unfairly.

There was every reason to fear the weather, because they were there two months earlier than Armitage had been. Its collapse that day trapped them in the tents for the next six days, during half of which thick snow was combined with winds of force 8 or more.

When they could at last see to move on November 11, it was impossible to recover the time lost by going on after the November 30 turning-back date laid down in the revised plan.[23] Provisions for thirty-five and a half days remained on the sledges as they packed up that morning. That meant a return to New Mountain Depot by December 16 at the latest, and even that date allowed for no safety margin.

The question Scott now had to face was whether they could go on even until the November 30 date. To keep to that date would mean traveling twenty days outward from the blizzard camp. Subtracting two and a half days to get from that camp to the depot, they would

have provisions for only thirteen days for the return. That was dangerously little time to allow, despite the load being reduced by that time.
Unless Scott could get some noon sun sights to calculate their position, the trip could be doubly perilous without the navigation tables.

Caution must have told Scott that five days ought to be subtracted as a reserve. With a two-day climb to the summit and a day for
the descent over the two icefalls above them—one 3 miles ahead, the
final one beyond that—that would leave just fourteen or perhaps fifteen days outward on the summit proper. Gone was the hope of achieving the sort of mileage Scott had hoped for. No wonder he later called
it Desolation Camp.

Because the navigation tables had been lost and the Barrow Dip
Circle (which would tell them when they had reached the magnetic
pole by pointing straight down) had been reserved for Bernacchi's use
on Royds's Barrier journey, heading for the magnetic pole was not a
safe option. Although magnetic variation change when traveling west
would provide vital data to fix the pole's position, the distance Scott
could achieve might barely allow him to reach the western shore of
Victoria Land—the prize he believed would compensate for the blight-
ing of his Southern dream.

The blizzard had also cost Ferrar his chance to reach the summit,
which lay over a thousand feet above. He would have to head back to
Depot Nunatak with his remaining ten days' rations and try to examine the rocks of the western mountains in that time.

Scott had asked him to leave the camera at the depot, along with
the cladding Skelton and Lashly had stripped off the runners.[24] The
half-plate camera weighed 30 pounds, and every pound saved would
help the summit party. Even if they kept going until November 30, in
the distance they could achieve there might be nothing to photograph.

The last steps to the head of the glacier were far from straightforward. By the time they camped for lunch on top of the first icefall,
Scott could hardly believe they had escaped an accident. The air had
been "thick as a hedge" when they started, and within 100 yards they
"as nearly as possible walked into an enormous chasm."[25] Camping
about 3 miles south and somewhat east of Allan's camp, they found
an easier climb up the final icefall than the one the day before, arriving
safely on the summit on November 12. As Scott looked out over the
summit, half a day had already been lost from the two weeks he could
count on as a completely safe time limit for their westward journey.

A hundred and fifty miles to the south, Barne was almost at his
goal, despite being the victim of bad weather that had robbed him of

four days' support from Dellbridge's party. He was among the first mounds signaling the turbulence ahead that had forced him eastward as his time ran out on the first attempt, and he had only enough rations for a further week's advance. That would surely be enough, he believed, to get into the mouth of the strait and obtain rocks from its northern shore. Even if he could not see what lay to the west in the strait, rock specimens should be enough to determine whether the land was continental.

20

THE EPHEMERAL HORIZON
Barne and the Key to the Great Enigma

When first announced, the purpose of Barne's journey was to explore the nearest of the apparent gaps in the coastline (today named Mulock Glacier), and only if it was inaccessible or easily observable would he move on to the southerly one both he and Scott had seen. But in the end Scott decided Barne should head straight for the southern gap in 80°20S, to try to land on the coast, and bring back rock specimens for Ferrar.[1]

The original plan had envisaged the party following the coast from the northern gap Scott and Barne had at first taken to be the end of Victoria Land down to the "more interesting" one, as Scott termed the southern gap.[2] That involved a journey of over 230 miles outward and a round-trip of 420 miles, not counting the effort required to get into either inlet or to land and climb high enough to see whether they were straits or glaciers.

Barne had many other questions to answer about the form of crevassing and ice disturbance, all devoted to establishing whether the barrier was afloat, whereas Mulock was to survey the entire coastline by angles from known positions. So it was hardly surprising that on reading the report of Barne's first journey, Scott had second thoughts about what could be accomplished in ten weeks and ultimately changed the orders and told Barne to head straight for the southern gap.[3]

Starting on October 6 and held up by bad weather for one day only, the party took a week to reach the depot beyond White Island and then—sometimes on skis, sometimes on foot—another week to

reach the Minna Bluff Depot, proof enough of the wisdom of shorten-
ing their journey. To their surprise the depot was out of its original
alignment. Barne and Wild paced 450 steps to the original sight line
as they grasped the significance—the barrier was not a stationary ice
shelf but was moving toward the sea. On the way back they would
measure the change accurately, but in the meantime a bearing to Mount
Discovery would suffice to tell each party where to find the depot.

After caching the week's stores for their party (the same amount
already there would get second engineer Dellbridge's party back to the
ship) and repacking the sledges, Barne made a sketch of the Bluff and
leading marks for Dellbridge, showing him how to use the sun compass while Mulock took the sights to fix the new position of the depot. They traveled two more hours before camping at 6 o'clock.

Barne was under strict instructions not to overstretch the men,
and he settled on a daily start around 9:30 A.M., with no more than
eight hours on the move before making camp at around 6:30 for the
evening meal. Traveling without a sledgemeter, they relied on Mulock's
noon sights to measure their advance, which was usually possible even
when drift was blowing well above their heads, for the sun could be
mistily sighted in such conditions. Progress the day after they left the
depot was encouraging, for a following wind enabled them to use the
sail, but it was the only time they had that good fortune on the entire
outward journey. From then on they were generally sledging into a
head wind. For Dellbridge's party, scheduled to accompany them for
a week, it was the only relief from the extra drag of the 12-foot sledge
they were pulling in tandem with a 9-foot one.[4]

On the following two days, with virtually no wind to help them,
the slow pace they could hope to achieve was revealed. More than
sixteen hours' heaving on the traces advanced them only 12 miles by
the evening camp on the 23rd, when a blizzard started.[5] They were
weatherbound in their tents for four days in zero visibility. A force 6
head wind raged for the first day, and wet snow fell when it dropped
to force 4, making it doubtful whether Dellbridge could even move
his sledges. The lost time and help that would cost Barne could not
be recovered. In those four days the Support Party should have carried
supplies a further 25 miles, a quarter of the distance to their goal.

When they dug the sledges out on the 28th, time had run out for
the Support Party, which had a week's food and kerosene left for the
haul back to the depot. Although the southwest drift was still blowing above their heads, it would at least allow them to use the sail.
They were tentbound for five out of the eleven days it took for them

to reach the ship with three days' supplies in hand, a none too generous margin.[6]

Still hesitant about subjecting his men to the force 4 drift that would blow in their faces, Barne delayed the start until after lunch. Pulling off into the drift with six weeks' supplies and steering by compass, they enjoyed only one fine day (the 29th) out of the next fifteen.

Pulling the three sledges in train—their kit on the 11-foot one, the food tank on the 9-foot one, and biscuit boxes and theodolite on the 7-footer—they covered 73 miles over nine and a half days, stopping only when outright blizzards, driven by force 5 or 6 winds, struck. Often trying to pull the sledges on skis, they were defeated again and again by sticky snow or glassy ice that demanded crampons

By November 7 they could make out the top of the cape (Cape A), off of which Scott had established his depot, and to the north of the strait they could see dark volcanic craters. The next day they began to cross undulations arcing outward around the mouth of the strait and running across their line of travel. These undulations were around 300 yards apart, and the summits were crowned by transverse crevassed mounds 5 feet high. They soon came upon an 18-inch-wide crevasse between two of the mounds.

On the 13th the risk was great enough that the six men roped up. The next day they changed into ski boots at the lunch camp after pulling on skis in the morning. By then they were traveling between rather than across the undulations, which now ran parallel to the hugely disturbed ice, about 2 miles away on their right, that extended toward them from the northern flank of the strait.

They still had twenty-four days' rations, and the prospect of improving weather meant that with the wind behind them, half of the remaining provisions should be more than adequate for the return to the Bluff. Barne could therefore afford a week for the advance into the 15-mile-wide strait and the attempt to obtain rocks from its coast for Ferrar.

During four days of sledging steadily upward from barrier level among ever larger corrugations, often with vertical windward faces overhanging pits as much as 60 feet deep, the six men dragged and manhandled the three sledges 25 miles to arrive "abreast of Cape A" on the 17th.[7] There in the entrance to the enormous channel, Barne climbed up one of the higher ridges to see the sides of the strait ending in "two large bluffs" and beyond them "a thin blue line stretching across the horizon, which I think is the inland ice."[8]

The horizon was clear enough for Mulock to measure its elevation with the theodolite, despite the fact that the sun was almost against them, for it was 6:45 P.M. Although he could register only ¹⁄₃₀th of a degree elevation and the general level of ice ceased to rise ahead, the two men saw enough to convince them that the great ice river (now called Byrd Glacier) they stood on was no channel to another frozen sea.*

Still more than 4 miles from the nearest exposed rock on the north side of the glacier, Barne determined to move further upstream and then cut in to the foot of the nearest cliff to fulfill his other assignment. But before the night was out they were engulfed in a blizzard that pinned them in the tents for thirty-six hours. When it ceased on November 19, they were able to get 2 or 3 miles further along the line of ridges, reaching their farthest west that evening.

On November 20, with visibility further improved, Barne took photos and sketched the land in case the photos failed (which they did), and Mulock took sights and angles. They were perhaps 2 miles from the shore, and at 2:45 P.M. they started to work toward the nearest cliff. After a mile the snowcapped ridges gave way to ones with sharp ice crests that threatened to destroy the runner cladding. There was no choice but to retreat and try to gain the coast from the barrier.

With four days left before he must start for home, Barne also hoped to collect rocks from the southern cape (later Cape Murray) of what he called "b range" (now the Conway Range) about 30 miles up the coast. However, he had not considered the difficulty of getting through the disturbed ice at the edge of the glacier tongue. Barely through it two days later, he pitched camp and made an attempt to reach what he described as a "tumulus"⁹ in the barrier surface, which appeared to be separated from main range snow slopes or piedmont. After covering 3 miles with Crean and Joyce over a chaotic jumble of ice, the men climbed a particularly high ridge to gain a better view. They found themselves atop an 80-foot ice cliff looking down at the low ice foot where the tumulus met the barrier surface less than a quarter mile ahead.¹⁰

Still hoping to reach the distant cape to the north and not having had supper, Barne turned back, reaching the camp at 9:35 P.M. after passing many large blocks of granite. The pink-and-gray specimens he brought back constituted the proof of the continental nature of the

---

* The edge of the inland summit lay 130 miles ahead of them, so it is doubtful that they actually saw it, but they were in fact standing on the glacier carrying the largest flow of ice through the transcontinental mountains, larger even than the great Beardmore Glacier Shackleton would discover five years later.

CLIFFS ON THE NORTH BANK OF BYRD GLACIER. Closely approached by Lt. Michael Barne's Sledge Party in November 1903. The six men narrowly failed to reach the long cliff (center-right beneath the eastern peaks of the Britannia Range) on November 20, when sharp ice ridges threatened to destroy their sledge runners a mile from their goal. The Horney Bluff cliffs are at left, and to the east of them can be seen the cliff labeled B on Barne's sketch map (overleaf). Some of the 60-foot rifts described in his report to Scott can be seen in the foreground of the photo, taken in December 1998 from about 500 feet altitude at 80°14S, 161°09E. Photographed for the author by New Zealand mountaineer Peter Braddock, who for many years has worked in support of American scientific research in the Antarctic.

land that Scott had failed to obtain at his farthest south. Barne would receive too little recognition for that discovery.

It had taken two days to bypass the disturbance, and after a 6-mile run on the barrier surface on the 25th they were still 15 miles from the cape and a little more than that east of the dark volcanic foothills, later dubbed the Goorkha Craters. The weather was perfect, with the thermometer at a mere 23°F, so Barne sensed it would be his only chance to record the scene. He sketched what was perhaps his finest contribution to the discovery of the coast named after him. The panorama he drew that night as the sun dipped toward the southern horizon was over 16 feet long, extending from the southern cape of the great glacier all the way to Mount Discovery.[11]

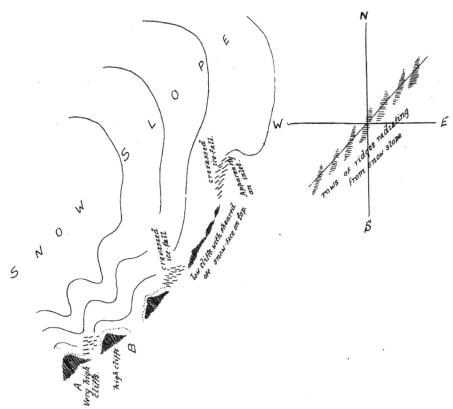

LT. BARNE'S SKETCH MAP OF CAPE KERR AND NORTH BANK OF BYRD GLACIER. The map was included in his report to Scott, on the page facing his account of progress on November 15 and 16, 1903. The "very high cliffs" (A) are today named Horney Bluff. On November 19 the party camped opposite and about 2 miles from the unlabeled cliff west of the "crevassed ice-fall." They set off the next day on the abortive attempt to obtain rock specimens from that cliff, pictured in the preceding plate. Courtesy, the Scott Polar Research Institute.

Barne knew their time was up when they awoke on November 26 beneath an overcast sky with freshening wind. They would have to average 8 miles a day if they kept to a direct course. For all Mulock's training, that was not easily accomplished in sunless conditions with poor visibility. In four days' going they had only a brief glimpse of patches of rock abreast of them on the 28th and the odd sight of the sun to set their course late the next afternoon.

Not surprisingly, when they awoke on the 30th with only the lower levels of the coast visible, Barne could see they were well to the west of the direct course and even west of his route the year before. He could not tell how far west they had veered in the fog of drift and then thick snow.[12] What that meant as they camped that evening with the temperature falling from a comfortable 32° to 19°F, fully 16° warmer than Scott was experiencing on the summit, was that they had at least 50 miles to cover in the five days for which they had kerosene. On the bright side, they had traveled somewhat more than that over the last four and a half days, with the sail helping them avoid more than eight hours' sledging per day. In spite of two days of blizzard conditions, they had been held in the tents only one morning.

As it turned out, the sail took the brunt of the load, and with the sledge overtaking the men pulling on skis they were in sight of their goal by the evening meal on December 5, with enough kerosene left to last until lunch the next day. Reaching the depot turned out to be somewhat difficult. The depot flag was briefly visible when they got up, but even though Barne took its bearing they missed it and realized they were well past it when they halted for lunch.

Fortunately, the summit of Mount Discovery was visible above the flying drift, and they were able to sledge back until it was on the bearing Barne had given Dellbridge. That evening he and Mulock measured the distance the depot had moved in the year since his first journey, finding it was 608 yards from its old alignment and thus for the first time establishing the rate at which the barrier ice was moving toward the sea.

December 7 was spent carrying out Barne's final assignment, which was to obtain rocks from the Bluff for Ferrar. Camping 2 miles from the coast, he and Mulock succeeded in getting ashore below the easternmost peak, where they found yellow lichen growing on the rocks. Forced to sledge about 4 miles outward to get around an 80-foot chasm on the 8th, they were back at the ship after six days, arriving the afternoon of December 13.

To Wilson, who had returned the previous night from a seventeen-day journey up Koettlitz Glacier with Armitage and William Heald, Barne "looked a perfect wreck [with] signs of scurvy about him," but "Mulock was as fit as possible."[13] There was suspicion that Barne had looked after the others at the expense of himself. He later admitted to having held back some seal meat for emergencies, and that was probably from his own ration, with the inevitable consequence.[14] In spite of the relatively warm temperatures on the way back, "their faces were a sight to see, all scabs, sores and swollen."[15]

Barne must have been too modest that evening, for Wilson was left with the impression that "they had not got into the strait they were to have explored,"[16] and Armitage understood he had only been about 10 miles beyond his previous farthest.[17] Ferrar believed the journey had been "little better than last year."[18]

However, as Barne soon wrote in his report to Scott, on November 21, working back out of the strait, they had passed over a ridge "connecting the ends of the snow slopes on the N & S sides of it"[19] (namely, "a" range slope and Cape A slope, later Capes Kerr and Selborne). The camp on the 19th must therefore have been well inside the "strait" and over 26 miles further than Barne's first attempt.[20]

21

THE ORIGIN OF ANTARCTICA
Ferrar and the Continent's Hidden Sensation

Armitage had told Scott that accessible sandstone of the type that could contain fossils was found on the flanks of Finger Mountain at the head of the upper section (now known as Upper Taylor Glacier) of the great western glacier he had scaled, which was why Scott had taken Ferrar's party with him all the way to Desolation Camp. The easiest access seemed to be on the western face of Finger Mountain, flanking the tributary glacier flowing in from the southwest between it and Depot Nunatak. So the young geologist headed for that point two hours after Scott's party had left the camp on November 11, 1903.

Feeling their way through the drift, the group had only one scare when the rather battered sledge dropped a runner over the edge of a crevasse and partly capsized just in sight of the nunatak. After three hours on the move, another hour's work brought them around to the sheltered eastern face of the 500-foot nunatak. There beneath its sheer wall they pitched their camp, safe from the drift that still hid the surface of the main glacier and its tributary between them and their goal.

Waking to bright sun on November 12, Ferrar set off with Kennar and Weller across the South West Glacier (unnamed on today's maps), ascending it for 3 miles to the foot of a 500-foot sandstone face showing below the same sort of columnar dolerite that formed the nunatak.[1] Climbing about 300 feet to reach some dark bands, Ferrar found, with what he afterward wrote of as mounting "delight," some fossilized "plant remains."[2] They were badly charred, which defeated attempts to identify them, but to the young geologist, unaware of any similar find on Antarctic land, it must have been a fantastically exciting moment as he grasped their significance. The fossils meant there must have been a warmer, even tropical climate in the Antarctic in the distant past![3]

As yet, the world knew nothing of Gunnar Andersson's find of Jurassic plant fossils, then believed to be 130 million years old, on the Antarctic Peninsula the previous January. Even if anyone did, no one had yet proved that the peninsula was part of the mainland.[4]

Camping at the northwest corner of the mountain, Ferrar made another search with Weller on November 13 but could not extract a worthwhile specimen from a thin dark band with his hammer. So the three men pulled their increasingly rickety sledge back across the main glacier to the spot at which the entire party had camped on November 2. As promising as the mountain's huge sandstone cliff had looked, once they got close to it they could see no sign of vegetable remains.[5]

They spent three days combing the outcrops below the knucklelike "Inland Forts." On November 16 an 800-foot climb up the "West Groin" (on the eastern side of the cirque, today known as Mudrey Cirque, between Northwest Mountain and Hess Mesa) yielded only some specimens of "doubtful" organic matter.[6] After another day spent surveying, they crossed back to the moraine half a mile downstream from Finger Mountain.

From there, on the morning of the 19th the three men succeeded in reaching the point where the valley glacier behind the mountain (today's Turnabout Glacier) falls into a southern valley 6 miles long (today's Beacon Valley) into which the main glacier overflows.[7] Weller was complaining of sore feet, so Ferrar and Kennar left him in the camp and climbed about 4 miles up the boomerang-shaped Turnabout Valley until they could see its head. Once again there was no sign of fossilized plant matter.

Their salt was gone, and they were short of oil, biscuits, sugar, and oatmeal, but Ferrar decided they could afford another day to explore the two valleys before moving on to New Mountain Depot. He was disappointed, as he made excursions into both valleys without finding anything. However, the strenuous two days had at least given the three men a break from the hours of dragging the sledge over a route they had previously covered, an increasingly hard task as the cladding on the runners broke up and the load of rock specimens grew.

Kennar awoke almost totally snowblind on the 21st, so Ferrar led the three-hour haul to the depot, where they replenished their food

HARTLEY FERRAR'S PANORAMA OF NORTH BANK OF UPPER TAYLOR GLACIER. Drawn in pencil in his sledging journal at 9 A.M. November 13, 1903, before crossing the glacier to camp on the moraine at the entrance to Mudrey Cirque, the site of Scott's November 2 camp. The sketch clearly identifies the true position of Beehive Mountain as in 77°35S 160°24½E. On the U.S. Geological Survey Map it is shown appended to Northwest Mountain. X marks the position, 1,000 feet up West Groin, where Ferrar collected the specimen containing the vital *Glossopteris* leaf fossil fragments that remained hidden for twenty-five years until it was split open on the initiative of Dr. W. N. Edwards. ▲ marks the position of the November 3 lunch camp where Ferrar's sledge runner cladding was repaired on the way to what became Desolation Camp. Names and geological features Ferrar inscribed on his sketch are printed in quotes. Underlined names appear in Chart 8. Courtesy, the Scott Polar Research Institute. Below: THE FOSSILIZED *GLOSSOPTERIS INDICA* V. SCHIMPER LEAF FRAGMENTS revealed at the Natural History Museum in London in 1928. Courtesy, Cambridge University Press, pp. 324–325 in vol. 65 of *Geological Magazine*.

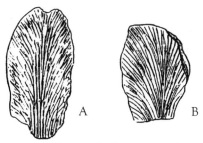

Glossopteris indica Sch., from Ferrar Glacier. A. Fragment with anastomosing venation clearly shown at one point on the right-hand side. x2. V. 20445   B. Smaller fragment, anastomoses not clearly seen. x2. V.20447

Glossopteris indica Sch. Ferrar Glacier. Incomplete leaf with nearly parallel veins and with apparently few anastomoses. Natural size. V.20446

and oil. Another three-hour stint brought them to the campsite at Knobhead Moraine. There Kennar and Weller, now suffering from backaches, were able to rest for two days while Ferrar climbed 800 feet up the mountain, finding firm evidence that the ice level had once been at least as high as, and probably higher than, that.[8] In search of water to fill the cooker and thus save the fuel needed to melt ice, he cut steps down into the huge *bergschrund* (channel) separating the glacier from the mountain but found only enough water for a drink.

Wearing ski boots for the first time after lunch—the temperature had risen to 18°F, and he hardly needed gloves—Ferrar went to collect samples from the Solitary Rocks.* The second morning the mist came up the main valley to the base of the mountain but cleared after lunch, allowing him to work around to the south side of the mountain. There were two more places he wanted to search from that camp.

Mist again stopped him in the morning, but he completed his search of the south side of the mountain that day. On the 24th, leaving the other two men to shorten the traces for the next stage of the journey, he walked to the most westerly point of the Kukri Hills. Ferrar was the first to see into the lower part of Taylor Glacier, and he was as yet unaware of what he would discover less than a week hence; he thus assumed the ice in it flowed into McMurdo Sound in the same way the main (Ferrar) glacier does.

The others had packed the sledge by the time he returned for lunch, after which they headed back down their outward track to camp more than halfway to where the flags had been set out on October 16 to measure the glacier movement. They were disturbed by continuous cracking of the ice during the night. Weller's feet were so sore that despite rubbing them with embrocation he couldn't sleep for more than five hours.

Collecting specimens from the southern side the next morning, Ferrar spotted a white-edged black lichen growing but could find no trace of fossilized matter. Pushing on in the afternoon, they camped at the line of flags set out between Sentinel Peak and the center buttress of the Cathedral Rocks. Using the sextant on its side and reference

---

* Not until Scott's second expedition was the more northerly summit of what they had seen as a twin-peaked island in the middle of the glacier found to be connected to its north shore. The southern peak was then recognized as a separate island and renamed Cavendish Rocks, and it was undoubtedly to that island's nearest point that Ferrar crossed from the Knobhead Mountain Moraine.

points arranged with Scott to measure the movement of the flags, Ferrar calculated the first two had moved over 50 feet and another nearly 80 feet, but he suspected something was wrong with the calculation, as the movement of flags he had left on Blue Glacier would demonstrate.[9]

After a heavy pull over 4 inches of snow on the 27th, the three men were once more in a relative land of plenty, picking up their share of the depot and "leaving the lion's share for the Captain."[10] After they had stripped the German Silver off the runners, the sledge ran much better as they went on to lunch opposite a black mark on the hill beyond Descent Glacier. They collected specimens after lunch and crossed the glacier once more to camp near the left side, directly opposite Overflow Glacier. The next morning Ferrar climbed 700 feet in thick snow, getting his feet soaked as the temperature climbed to 28°F.

Reaching the ski depot below the glacier face at noon on the 29th, they headed north across New Harbour for the presumed outlet of Taylor Glacier, regarded at that time as a northern branch of Ferrar Glacier. Camped at the foot of the next valley that night, Ferrar recognized the Beacon Peaks beyond New Mountain Depot, jutting above the Kukri Hills skyline. It had to be the valley he had looked into five days before—only the ice stream was not there!

From their camp to a glacier spilling across the valley from its north side lay about 2 miles of bare stony ground between bare hillsides, which continued beyond the glacier (now known as Commonwealth Glacier). They had steered for it when they sledged directly across the sound from the ship to New Harbour with the main party. Viewed from their camp near the shore, the glacier hid the floor of the valley beyond. Certainly, no ice was pushing past its snout. Only the valley's snowclad northern flank was visible in the distance, arcing around toward the invisible Knobhead Mountain, now hidden behind the Kukri Hills.

On the last day of the month, as Scott started his last outward march on the summit, Ferrar set off for the glacier's 50-foot face, meaning to get past it. No sooner had he reached it than the whole scene was blotted out by snow, so he never got to see the startling surprise that lay behind it. A few days later, the valley would reveal its secret to Scott.

Setting off in thick drift, they could just see the Knobhead Mountain peak from their lunch camp, traveling blind until, with Butter Point just visible but no sign of the depot, they were forced to camp. Later, the wind slackened, and they found they were less than a hundred yards from their goal. They took their share from the depot but were disappointed at finding no seals when an Adélie penguin "walked almost straight into the pot" just in time for their supper.[11]

Heavy snow was falling as they traveled on the fast ice, coming upon a seal that assured them of an adequate supplement to the pemmican diet for the rest of the journey. They were camped on solid debris at the Eskers. The sun came out and allowed them to dry their clothes and kit, but one discomfort was replaced with a worse one for Ferrar, by then snowblind, could scarcely see 2 yards ahead. A good night's sleep improved matters, and the next morning he was able to sketch. More than three hours' pulling brought them to the point where the climb up to Blue Glacier had started the year before. Reaching the surviving flag half a mile out on the glacier—the others had blown away[12]—Ferrar found it had moved about 4 feet in the year and a day since he planted it on December 3, 1902.

With Ferrar's snowblindness becoming worse, the other two led the way down with the sledge while he reflected on what he could best do with the day they had gained. But after dosing his eyes with zinc sulphate that evening he had to stay in the tent, losing all of the next day before he felt up to exploring 2 miles along the glacier face on the 6th to see what had changed since he last saw it.

Setting off for the ship on December 10, the scheduled first of three days allowed for the return, the three men found they had traveled half the 30 miles by lunchtime and got back to the ship at 10 o'clock that evening after the third-longest day's march achieved on the expedition, despite the weight of specimens on their sledge. Not surprisingly, although he had eaten seal meat for the last week, Ferrar found he had lost 2 stones (12 kgs) in weight, but he put half of it back on over the next three days.

The weather had robbed him of one great prize—the actual sighting of the first dry valley to be discovered in the Antarctic. Had it allowed him another fine day at the "valley of the glacier that didn't arrive," the discovery of its secret would have been his rather than Scott's. As it was, he could only assume that the valley might have petered out behind the glacier that blocked his view.

Ferrar also did not realize the ultimate significance of the fossilized vegetable matter he had brought back. If he was aware of having made a startling find, he hardly shows it in his letters home and only hints at it in his report to Scott—"best find I have had down here" was all he accorded it.[13] Wilson makes it clear that the others, who heard his story before Scott's return, understood that his "great find of fossil plants in some coal shale beds" meant "the South Pole has at one time had an abundant vegetation."[14]

Captain Larsen's little publicized find of petrified wood eleven years earlier had already convinced some scientists of a warmer Antarctic climate in Miocene times (12–15 million years ago). Even if the recently graduated geologist was aware of that discovery, it had taken place on the other side of the Antarctic and on an island.[15]

Here were plant fossils from the mainland. On the return to New Zealand a fellow of the Royal Society, interviewed by the local press, assessed the fossils as "the most sensational discovery" made on the Western journeys.[16]

Formal examination by a leading paleobotanist, Dr. W. N. Edwards, dubbed some of the specimens unpromising material that did not "permit of any opinion as to [their] botanical nature [or] . . . geological age."[17] Later, however, they would yield an infinitely more spectacular message.

In 1928, when Dr. Edwards was rearranging the collections at the Natural History Museum, he examined a rather large example of hard shale with dark bands, which Ferrar had found. Surface impressions were unrecognizable, but he reckoned that if broken up the sample might show something of value. Little would be lost if it didn't, so he had it split open.

To his delight, there were undoubted fragments of the leaf *Glossopteris indica*. Ferrar's find 800 feet up the West Groin[18] was after all the first physically recovered Antarctic evidence of the unknown continent's place in the great southern supercontinent of Gondwana, 300 million years ago.[19]

None of the men who heard young Hartley Ferrar's story aboard *Discovery* could foresee the tragic circumstances in which the next example would be found with the bodies of Scott and his companions a decade later.

22

THE RIDDLE OF THE BARRIER
Royds's Quest for the Eastern Shore

Finding out more about Ross's still mysterious Great Barrier was one of the scientists' key goals for the expedition. Ferrar arrived back to find that Royds had the answer to one of the great questions about it.

From the Southern journey all Scott could say of the barrier's extent to the southeast was that down to almost 83°S his eastward horizon had been at about the 175°E meridian, and no mountain peaks had appeared above it. That was scarcely a quarter of the way to the meridian of King Edward VII Land. From his farthest south he had seen that the mountains on its western shore gradually trended southeastward, and there was at least a suspicion they might curve around and end up at the newly discovered land he had named after the king.[1]

When Scott had worked out the manpower, sledges, and cookers needed for the Western journey and Barne's to the southwest, just enough of each remained for an officer, with a scientist and four men, to take two sledges and be away for thirty-six days starting November 10.[2] As the only officer who had not led a sledge party with the prospect of a major discovery, Royds was the natural choice to lead it. His initial southwest reconnaissance and the four Cape Crozier journeys he had led constituted a more than adequate apprenticeship.

If the party could make 10 miles a day for twenty days outward,[3] they could push the frontier of knowledge about the barrier's extent beyond the 175°W meridian. They should be able to see any mountain peaks high enough to appear above the eastern horizon down to about 82°S and further if any 15,000-foot giants showed their heads. The prize would be the first clue about the size of the great ice mass that was one of the wonders of the world.

Another of the expedition's aims was to construct the Southern Hemisphere Magnetic Map, so urgently needed in the days of compass navigation that still relied on Ross's data, now sixty years old. Bernacchi would be able to make magnetic observations far from the influence of the volcanic coast. Such observations could be achieved more accurately than aboard ship, although the sensitivity of the Barrow Dip Circle in measuring dip and magnetic force would demand an hour or more inside one of the tents at the end of a day's march if there was any wind, delaying supper for Bernacchi and his tentmates.

With Bernacchi and Gilbert Scott as tentmates, Royds's team started out with the leading sledge on November 10. Cross, Plumley, and Clarke, the cook, followed with the other. Royds had intended to take Whitfield, but his leg had not recovered from a strain suffered during Wilson's final Cape Crozier journey, so Plumley took his place.

Despite the load, which amounted to 173 pounds per man including the sledges, the rations carried amounted to only 2 pounds per man-day, plus 3 ounces of dehydrated seal meat. They had the last of the Nansen cookers (any search party would have to improvise one), and it sprang a leak the first day out. Plumley managed to seal it with beeswax. The three-man sleeping bags were molting hairs over everything in the tent. The sledging equipment was "nearly played out," as Royds put it in his sledging diary that first evening. He recorded a first day's march of barely more than 6 miles. "Looks rather bad for our proposed 10 miles per day," Bernacchi remarked when the sledgemeter read no more for the next day's advance.[4]

At least nine hours' hard pulling each day was needed to edge up the speed. Faced with varying surfaces, initially they had to surmount sastrugi, cut by the predominantly southwest wind directly athwart their line of advance. Stretches suitable for skis were often followed by glassy ice patches, so pulling on foot was the only practical method. By the fourth day out they were encountering patches of thick snow into which they would sink as much as 9 inches. That afternoon the sky began to brighten, and the drift ceased after blowing for nearly two days.

Two bright windless days saw their daily advance rise encouragingly to over 12 miles, only to fall somewhat as the southwest wind set in. It blew, with only two days' remission, for the rest of their outward journey. With only 55½ miles recorded after the first week, they managed to get the daily average up to 8.7 miles by the 22nd, when the noon sights had placed them 4 miles south of the 79th parallel in 173°10½E.

They had first tried skis the day before but found progress with them slower than on foot. Now on the 23rd, as the weather turned against them, they found a surface that suited them, pulling on skis through drift and snow that day and all the next. The wind was always directly on the beam and was never strong enough to justify trying the sail. "This weather is perfectly sickening," Royds wrote in his diary that evening. "There were we expecting a summer trip, and except for one day we have had to wear our burberrys . . . and one can never sleep comfortably with head out of the bag."[5] They had to keep their windproof clothes on all night.

Things would get worse, for fine snow all day on the 24th pulled down their speed, and the surface the next day slowed them further. The snow thickened after the lunch camp on Thursday the 26th, and their mileage that day was barely more than 6½ miles after more than nine hours' work. Royds realized they could achieve 160 miles only if he took Cross and Scott for a lightweight dash on Sunday. They could start back no later than Monday the 30th, and even that would demand 10 miles a day if they were to reach the ship by the 15th. Any holdups would mean cutting down on food.[6]

The food already seemed thoroughly inadequate for the energy they were expending, and the biscuits had to be carefully counted out. Breakfast was a pannikin of pemmican boiled with a few spoons of Red Ration (dried bacon powder and pea flour), some oatmeal, and pea soup. Three-quarters of a ship's biscuit completed the meal before the morning's pulling. Lunch was a meager one-and-a-half biscuits and a small piece of Dutch cheese, backed up by tea with seven lumps of sugar and some plasmon mixed in. Supper was a pannikin and a quarter of pemmican boiled with the day's ration of seal meat and a few spoons of oatmeal, supplemented with another three-quarters of a biscuit and a pan of cocoa or chocolate to drink. To Bernacchi, who thought Koettlitz had not approved so small a daily allowance, it appeared "quite unwise coming away with an inadequate food supply . . . our appetites are absolutely insatiable."[7]

The next day they were pulling on skis, on which the snow continually clogged, when a head wind was added to their woes. "No horizon . . . only able to steer by wind and snow driving in our faces,"[8] Royds wrote that evening. Conditions had gotten worse in the afternoon, forcing him to decide they would have to settle for what they could achieve by noon the next day before starting back on Sunday.

The snow, which continued all night, made him abandon the three-man dash. By lunch they had advanced another 3½ miles to their farthest point, which Bernacchi recorded as 79°35S 175°55½E. They were 155 miles out.

That afternoon they dug a trench 7 feet deep, 9 feet long, and 4 feet wide to record the stratification of alternating soft snow and loose crystals, one of the nine objectives of the scientific program Bernacchi noted in his journal.[9] He made the final magnetic observation with the Barrow Dip Circle, the ninth of a line that "prolonged northwest will almost cut the calculated position of the magnetic pole, [which] ought to prove of value in locating it more accurately."[10]

Every third night on the march, Royds and Gilbert Scott had waited outside their tent after the gruelling day's work while Bernacchi worked for an hour or more measuring the magnetic dip and force with the Barrow Dip Circle. Only twice could he use the delicate instrument outside in the windless conditions it demanded. Armitage had used it during the ascent of the western glacier the year before, and his observations also played a part in locating the magnetic pole, but that had been among massive mountains with unknown residual magnetism. It was believed that Bernacchi's readings, taken progressively farther from such influences, would be more accurate.

Royds's ten observations of compass variation on the outward journey added to the data so crucial to the construction of this part of the magnetic map of the Southern Hemisphere. Like his other sights for position, their location was subject to the vagaries of artificial horizon sextant observations in high southern latitudes.

They saw no vestige of land in the direction in which they had been hoping to find it. Conditions had obscured the Bluff and Mount Discovery behind them for the past week, but they were not quite alone for far away, low over the northern horizon, a snow petrel was flying.

When unable to use skis, they sank up to a foot through the thin crust. It had borne the weight of the sledges without breaking, except when huge sheets of the crust had sunk several inches with them and the sledges on it, just as Scott and Barne had experienced on their journeys.

The wind obligingly veered to the south as the barometer rose that afternoon, holding between force 1 and 2 as they started back on Sunday, November 29, with the two sledges in train. They tried the sail on the leading 11-foot one for the first time. The sun shone in their faces instead of behind them, and the surface was perfect for skis, although the sledges did not run easily. That difficulty was encouragingly overcome the next morning, as the wind veered SSE and the sail took the whole load so that for the first time they could ski alongside without pulling. That situation lasted until December 1, the queen's birthday and also Clarke's 26th birthday. In spite of snow falling steadily, their mileage that day rose to 13½ miles.

On the 3rd, with the wind back in the southwest and up to force 4, Bernacchi complained in his journal that "taking sights with sextant and artificial mercury horizon is miserable in this weather."[11] That day the Ross Island peaks and the Bluff reappeared.

They were able to use the sail again for three hours on the 5th and all day on the 6th, and they covered 29 miles in those two days despite encountering 2-foot-high *sastrugi*. They slept for the first time without their outer windclothes and with the sleeping bag flaps open.

So far they had done much better on the return journey, covering 100 miles in eight days compared with only 61 miles the last eight days of the outward journey. They were about 21 miles from White Island. Royds wanted to stay there to conduct more research on temperatures and snow composition below the barrier surface, planning to send Bernacchi back with the other sledge and return himself by the 15th.

But after 14 miles on the 7th, Royds found a kerosene can that was almost empty. The culprit was a small rust hole, and it left only enough fuel for three days, so they had to head straight back to the ship, 39 miles away. That evening they ate well for the first time on the journey, as a full week's rations remained. Fortified with their fulsome dinner, they dug another 7-foot trench to record the stratification again.

With enough food in hand to spend some time measuring temperatures at various depths, Royds set about doing so, lowering the sling thermometer into undercut crevasses to progressive depths, giving them time to register, and then hauling them up as fast as possible to read them before the column changed. After falling steadily down to 10 fathoms below the surface, after a further 4, to everyone's surprise, the temperature had risen by 6°F, registering +5°F! This was the vital clue Scott was seeking to establish the fact that the barrier was afloat.

They repeated the exercise with similar results in another crevasse the next day. Feeding "like fighting cocks,"[12] as Royds expressed it in his diary, they reached the depot off the northern end of White Island at 9 A.M. on the 10th and arrived at the ship at 12:30 P.M., where they were met by Koettlitz.

As disappointing as it had been to see nothing of the eastern shore, they had pushed the boundary of knowledge about the barrier's interior beyond the 180° meridian, about twice as far as Scott had been able to see in that direction before he turned westward at the 80th parallel. And they had proved that the barrier was afloat. Royds and Bernacchi could feel well pleased.

23

THE CAPE CROZIER MYSTERY
Wilson and the Emperors' Secret

Fourteen men were at the ship when Royds's party returned. Ford, who had been cooking for all of them, was glad to have Clarke take over. The indefatigable Wilson was away with Armitage and Heald on his fourth journey of the season, once more fulfilling his additional role as artist backup to the camera when new territory was explored. For him, the short season had been dominated by the mesmeric lure of the unknown life cycle of the Emperor penguin, which the rookery discovered by Skelton, Wild, and Quartley a year ago offered the first chance to reveal.

While Wilson was away on the Southern journey, Royds had led his third Cape Crozier Party in November 1902 to try to get an Emperor's egg and a newly hatched chick. To Wilson's surprise, Royds told him the chicks were all gone when the party arrived there on November 8. Only Blissett's now-famous egg had been brought back for him to study.

Wilson thought it was impossible that the chicks had developed their feathers in the three weeks since Skelton had photographed them on October 18. King penguin chicks took ten weeks to grow theirs, and he couldn't believe the Emperors had taken their chicks out to sea on floes that broke away.

So they had to schedule a fourth Crozier journey, on which he could accompany Royds, at the very beginning of the second season and another a month later to see if any of the chicks had shed their down by October. The team chosen this time included Wilson's now fully trained assistant, Jacob Cross, along with Williamson, Blissett, and the leading stoker, Thomas Whitfield. They would start on September 7.

Wilson's preparations were lengthened because he had been using someone else's skis the whole winter, his own having been jettisoned with Scott's on the Southern journey to save weight. He had to find a new pair that suited him from the remaining twenty-odd pairs, mostly damaged, and fit each pair with straps before testing them. Still more time was needed to prepare clothing and equipment—patching the burberry overalls, making a sleeping jacket and foot bags from the same material, and fitting new wolfskin gloves with felt lining. His finnesko had to be entirely resewn, as the stitching was rotting.[1]

Wilson had been suffering from rheumatism again for the past two weeks after being free of it all winter. Apart from that, he was in fine form, doubtless because of the diet, which still included seal as well as mutton and beef brought by the *Morning*. Only on Thursdays, dubbed "Scurvy Day," had they eaten tinned food for the main meal to give the cook a break. Mutton was the main dish every Sunday, with beef another day, although by the end of August Wilson believed both were "tainted"—in modern parlance, well past their use-by date. For the other four main meals they enjoyed half a skua each on Tuesdays and three seal recipes—stuffed heart, steak and kidney pie, and steak and onions—"fresh, palatable, and well cooked." For breakfast they had seal liver twice a week and seal stew or curry the other five days. He still found the potatoes "eatable," but the other fresh vegetables, long-since frozen, were "a hopeless failure." They drank lime juice every day and in the wardroom claret once or twice a week.[2]

The weather hardly blessed the 11 o'clock start on September 7. After rounding Cape Armitage, a strong southeasterly blew drift from the right as they hauled the two sledges in tandem with unclad runners eastward onto the barrier.

The sun had shown above the horizon again only on August 23, and the short days dictated the 5 P.M. camping time. By that time they had covered 6 miles and reached a "perfect" surface, well away from the soft snow that accumulated near the shore of the peninsula.[3]

Cooking by candlelight in their tents—Wilson was in Royds's along with Williamson—they were in their sleeping bag as early as 8 P.M. There was little point in turning out of it until 6:30 A.M., as they were not ready to risk capsizes and possible injury, threatened by sastrugi in the dark. Experiencing a three-man reindeer skin bag for the first time, Wilson thought there could be "nothing more uncomfortable," as his diary entry made clear. To leave the bag flap open let in cold air that cut like a knife, and no one could move without waking the others.

Getting away at 9 A.M. each day, they would march for four hours with a few minutes' rest every forty-five minutes, then put up a tent to have tea, cheese, and a ship's biscuit. For the afternoon stage they sledged for three hours, with rests at the same intervals. With temperatures falling to -42°F on the 10th, they reached the first of the pressure waves in the barrier. These curved around and squeezed past the eastern end of the island, ending in a jumbled chaos at the Cape. At first the waves were about 600 yards apart and up to 15 feet high, with their crests cut across by crevasses. Traveling parallel to and then across them on the 10th, they camped on the névé slope of the second spur on the southeastern side of Mount Terror, 29 miles from their first camp.

The fog that night failed to lift in the morning, but groping their way down to the barrier surface again, they managed to advance about 4 miles over worsening sastrugi. The sledges capsized frequently, so they got into the sleeping bags after lunch and waited in vain for a clearance. Next morning the fog thinned enough to reveal the 1,000-foot cone Royds had named "the Knoll." It stood right above the eastern point of the Cape 6 miles ahead of them.[4]

Advancing along the lower névé slopes above the quarter-mile-wide tide crack from 20 to 50 feet deep between the land ice and the barrier, they reached their prospective final campsite by lunchtime. The camp was on a small windswept plain a mile short of the cape, its cliffs beginning less than half a mile from them. Royds had told Wilson there had been a snowdrift at that point that led easily down to the rookery. With all six roped together, they soon found their way blocked by a huge chasm in a large fall of ice. Working back gingerly so as not to provoke another fall of the ice that hung already half detached above them, they could see that it would take several hours to reach the rookery through the chaotic pressure ridges.

At last, the next day, Sunday the 13th, Wilson had his first close-up sight of the birds whose mystifying birth he would never see but would accurately predict. Royds sent Blissett off with Whitfield and Williamson to obtain two or three dead Adélies for Wilson's collection from the now deserted mail post rookery. Leading Wilson and Cross on a two-hour ice climb through the pressure ridges, Royds and his companions reached the bay where the birds congregated. Almost filled with sea ice and, in 1903, 5 miles long by almost 3 miles deep at the cape, the bay was formed where the line of the barrier cliff retreated southward as it neared the cape.

The three men emerged at the site where the birds had stood massed together on Royds's first visit, but now they saw only deserted eggs lying about, just clear of what had obviously been a massive fall of the barrier face. There were five or six perfect eggs, but many of the broken ones were well incubated, showing that the fall had scared the birds off. The fall had buried many alive shortly before the chicks were due to hatch. Wilson hoped to find out when that had been.

They soon found the new rookery to the east in an inlet in the barrier face. Close to a thousand Emperors stood under the ice cliff, with other isolated groups farther out toward some open water leads. Two or three columns of birds, clearly full of food after an excursion to the sea, were approaching, but to their surprise, when the leaders reached the main group they made no move to feed the others or their chicks.

To Wilson's greater surprise as he endured some vicious pecks while inspecting the offspring, the chicks appeared to be just as large as those Skelton had photographed on October 18 the year before. There was little time to study them further, for the light soon became poor and the fog thickened rapidly as they started back. Royds led with the ice ax, Wilson following with a satchel containing eight precious unbroken eggs and a cumbersome load of fifteen frozen chicks inside his blouse. Cross came behind with the ski pole, a bag of cracked eggs, and two live chicks inside his blouse.

The three men were saved from what could have turned into a nightmare journey by finding a shortcut into a drifted-up valley that led them back to the camp after an hour's cautious going. To their dismay, there was no sign of the others. Royds and Wilson set off immediately on a search, fortunately meeting the party after 2 or 3 miles, with everyone suffering from sore feet and Blissett's face badly frostbitten.

The journey back to Hut Point was the coldest of the expedition and colder than any polar journey they knew of, with nighttime temperatures down to −76°F. The kerosene poured slowly, like condensed milk. Nevertheless, Wilson found his clothing was excellent, although he felt cold all day except in his hands and feet.

The burberry outers froze rapidly in the mornings. No one could hear another speak on the march, even on windless days, such was the crackling that sounded like the continuous clash of tin armor. In the sleeping bag, each man wore an extra jacket under his burberry top but changed into a single pair of socks inside thigh-length sheepskin leggings, which had to be thawed out in the tent before they could get them on.

With the eggs packed in paper in a biscuit box, they nursed the leading sledge through the pressure ridges and sastrugi on the 14th. All of them were on foot, with one man beside each sledge to steady it. Three more days' pulling on skis over what Wilson described as an excellent surface brought them back to the ship for tea on the 17th. Cross fed his chicks nightly on chewed-up seal meat.

Wilson took the eggs and dead chicks to the main hut, the best frozen storage for them and other specimens. In his cabin he could not resist opening the three eggs before lunch, filling the wardroom with nauseous gas right before the midday meal. Two of the eggs revealed dead chicks instead of embryos. That afternoon he started the brilliant series of sketches of the handsome birds and their rookery that would grace the next issue of the *South Polar Times* and continue to fascinate nature lovers for all time.

The live chicks, one weighing almost 1½ pounds, were kept on the upper deck for a week after they returned, but it proved too cold for them and Wilson then looked after them in his cabin, feeding them every four hours. The weaker one died two days later, but by October 4 the survivor had almost doubled its weight, although it lived little more than another month.

Seals had surfaced again to replenish their fresh meat diet, and Wilson found no signs of scurvy among the crew on the 5th. Barne's and Dellbridge's parties set out for the southwest the next day.

Wilson's days of work on the eggs and dead chicks were punctuated by an impromptu concert for everyone in the wardroom one evening and a hilarious episode involving Weller's fish. Isaac Weller, out with a harpoon a few hundred yards from the ship, saw both a seal and a large fish's head appear. Striking out at the fish, he had to struggle for quite a time before he could lash the line to another harpoon. He returned with others to haul it out, only to have not the fish but a large seal nearly 9 feet long emerge. Weller's fish tale was soon the tallest story of the year, but as Wilson was cutting up the seal, Skelton began clearing ice out of the hole and, after a few moments, pulled out an immense headless fish almost 4 feet long. Weller enjoyed the last laugh and undoubtedly the largest helping from the 39-pound corpse whose fine white flesh made a splendid feast for everyone.[5]

The second Crozier journey had been scheduled to begin on October 12, the day of Scott's abortive start for the west. This time

Wilson was the leader, with Cross and Whitfield pulling an 11-foot sledge. Leaving at noon after the Western Party got away, the trio once more rounded Cape Armitage and headed southeast to get away from the shore, camping for lunch on the barrier ice edge. On skis until then, they soon met alternating stretches of soft snow on which they couldn't budge the sledge and hard ice on which it was impossible to keep on their feet. They had to use crampons the rest of the day. Turning northeast in the morning, their luck was out, as surface conditions stayed the same for a day and a half until snow squalls blew up from the southwest.

An improvised sail didn't help, and on the 15th, even with the beefy Cross and herculean Whitfield on the traces, the only way to advance was to relay half the load at a time. It took them two full days of that laborious process to reach the Mount Terror névé. Relief came after lunch on the 17th as they moved up the southeast coast of the island. The surface was hard, with sastrugi they could dodge, and a good southerly breeze filled the sail, which brought them to camp off a blue icefall.

Starting at 5 A.M. the next day, they arrived within a quarter mile of their old camp by 3 P.M. and immediately roped up to try to get down to the rookery that day. They had daylight far into the evening, which allowed them to achieve their goal, as the sun dipped only briefly below the southern horizon at midnight. The chasm below the cliff still blocked their way, but an hour sufficed to get down between the 60-foot ridges.

The Emperors were still there, and little seemed different except that the chicks were larger, but they were still fluffy with down and far from ready to take to the sea. And they found many more dead chicks. It would be a long wait to see any go out to sea. This time the seals were there, too, and they had killed a second one for its blubber to use for cooking. Wilson was tempted to extend the trip "to a month," as the blubber would fuel an improvised stove for a week.[6]

Carrying out their other assignment on the 19th, they delivered Scott's report of their progress and his second-season plan for Colbeck to pick up at the Adélie rookery mailpost if ice blocked his entry into the sound. Finding about twenty penguins busy building nests, they guessed they could enjoy the luxury of penguin eggs if they went back a week later.

Two days later Wilson saw the first signs of what he had predicted: the Emperors were filing out onto the new sea ice. After a day marooned in the tent by a blizzard, he went to the cliff top on the

23rd and saw as many as 300 waiting at the ice edge. Large sheets of ice were breaking away nearby and drifting out to sea. He believed the Emperors were hoping their bit of ice would break out and carry them north to warmer feeding grounds. But they did not have their chicks, for the other mature birds filing out toward them were walking too quickly to be carrying the young between their legs.

Wilson believed the Emperors knew the threatening sky to the south portended another warm blizzard. If so, they were right, for blinding snow and furious winds made movement impossible in that terrain for six of the next ten days and barely safe on two others.

The lure of penguin eggs for breakfast made them sacrifice one of the three good days they experienced for what proved an abortive second trip to the rookery. The birds were there in the thousands, but they could not find even one egg. On the return, Whitfield sprained a knee struggling with a 10-pound live and flapping penguin. On the 25th and 28th, Wilson was able to look down from the top of the cliff to see a repetition of the migration to the ice edge, but they could not reach the rookery again until November 2.

The sight that greeted them was radically changed. Only 400 birds remained, the same number as the day Skelton had first photographed them, and, just as on Skelton's visit, there appeared to be 30 live chicks. Wilson counted 24 of them and 63 dead chicks, so he reckoned that 100 would be dead by the end of the month out of a total of 130 that had hatched. Only the birds not rearing young were leaving, and Wilson later concluded that the real reason they had all left the previous November was not because the chicks had been carried to the ice edge before their feathers developed, as he first believed, but that the chicks grew them in just four months, compared to ten months in the case of the King penguin.[7]

What surprised him was the phenomenal mortality rate. This year 77 percent had died before they had shed their down, and the adults clustered under the barrier face were those looking after the survivors and others still nursing dead chicks. Second only to the breeding instinct was clearly the desire to rear a chick—which was so strong, regardless of the bird's sex, that even a lump of ice would do in extremity.

Back with two live chicks, Wilson knew that had been his last chance to observe the birds, for only a gallon of fuel was left for the return journey, which could take a week. With Whitfield's leg getting worse, there was no question of returning by way of the island's south coast to see whether there was a continuous tide crack, which would determine whether the barrier was afloat there.

With better weather they made the 50-mile return journey in three and a half days, much of it on skis. They were four days overdue, and Royds was ready to start out with a search party. One of the chicks, to which Cross had given up his sleeping jacket for warmth, did not survive a capsize, and the other died the night after they got back.

Undaunted by feet rubbed raw by the ski straps, Wilson asked Armitage to sanction a further trip to the south coast of the island and set out again on the 16th with Hodgson and Croucher on what, before starting, he described as a "picnic trip."[8] They had better weather, and they worked around the coast from Cape Armitage to their goal. They reached one rock exposure at the northern end of the peninsula but were repulsed by conditions at the next, the first of only four visible above the south coast of the island. They moved on to camp on the 18th, 2½ miles out from the highest cliff. As he had done at Cape Crozier, Wilson wanted to get rock samples for Ferrar's collection while carrying out the main aim of the journey.

As they were packing up the gear the next morning, a huge roar announced a vast avalanche pouring down the cliff. It was obviously going to be risky to get close enough to see the tide crack, let alone to reach the cliff, so they left the sledge and, roping together, skied in to the foot of the avalanche debris. Wilson and Hodgson then set off for the cliff face, leaving Croucher with instructions to bring the shovel and dig them out if he saw they were buried!

Finding the tide crack *was* there—it was from 2 to 5 feet across, its depth a bottomless abyss—the two men got across it and returned with their rock samples, relieved that more of the ice cliff poised on the edge of the 300-foot cliff had not fallen on them. They spent the afternoon sledging eastward along the coast for three hours, and from their camp Wilson sketched the entire glaciated face of the island the next morning. Here at the southeast corner of the island there was no tide crack, just as Royds had noticed the year before, but Wilson saw that was the case because the great pressure ridges rode over it, masking the rise and fall of the barrier with a chaos of broken ice. The tide crack they found below the cliff was evidence enough that the barrier was floating there.[9]

They set off on the return journey after lunch, with the view toward their destination bathed in sunshine worthy of a high summer's day. They followed one of the pressure ridges around as it swung gradually westward and petered out south of the island.

Reaching the ship on November 22, Wilson could be pleased with the results he could report on Scott's return. He believed he had solved the Emperors' secret: an utterly surprising early July start of incubation and, given the chicks' absence the previous November, an amazingly rapid four-month rearing of the chicks. Violent competition frequently took place for a dwindling number of surviving chicks, but Wilson had established that there was a communal sharing of that instinctive process. Even in those arduous conditions, all of the birds, male as well as female and regardless of parentage, took their turn.[10]

Wilson was remarkably close to the truth about the timing of the chicks' birth. On September 13 he had seen returning females that had gone north to feed at sea after laying their eggs in late May or early June. They were coming back to take over the rearing of the chicks (and not necessarily their own). The chicks would have hatched after seven or eight weeks and would be ready to swim by midsummer.[11]

But the zoologist's prize of an unbroken and unfrozen egg with a live embryo had eluded him. For that and the realization of just how early the eggs were laid,* he would have to wait eight years until the chance came to set out in moonlight on what would be dubbed the "worst journey in the world." By that time, as Wilson explained to Apsley Cherry-Garrard, who, with Henry Bowers, shared that excruciating ordeal with him, he believed the embryos they sought would show the Emperor penguin was the missing link between birds and the Jurassic *Archaeopteryx* from which birds were then believed to be descended.[12]

---

* At the 1905 Fourth International Ornithological Congress in London (Proceedings: p. 232) he said the incubation "must occupy about 7 weeks and . . . commence very early in July," but in his diary entry for the day (June 27) he set out on the 1911 winter journey he wrote, "The Emperor Penguins at Cape Crozier laid their eggs, as far as we could judge from what we found in the *Discovery* days, in June." After the winter journey, writing to Sir Archibald Geikie on October 31, he said they had found the eggs were laid "before mid-winter's day" (GJ29/6 June 1912: p. 582).

24

IN SEARCH OF A PHANTOM COAST
Scott's Record Journey on the Summit

As Wilson's party raced to catch breakfast at the ship on November 22, a despondent Skelton was leading his sledge on the last outward march he would make with Scott. That morning, Scott had announced his decision to send Skelton back with Feather and Handsley.

Once the six men had gotten their sledges up the final icefall on November 12, they soon faced "enormous"[1] *sastrugi* diagonally across their path and two days' further steady climbing through incessant drift. Skelton rated it an outright blizzard the first day, and the wind worsened to force 6 on the 14th, although it was less trying, having backed into the south. That was some compensation for the soft crusty snow with small *sastrugi*, which as the thermometer fell first to 7°F and then -24°F on the 16th became ever more gritty and resistant to the wooden sledge runners.

The clouds had cleared on the 14th, and that had allowed Scott to establish their latitude from the bearings of known peaks before they pushed into the unknown. Two evenings later it was clear they were advancing at less than 1 mile an hour; at seven or so hours a day that did not amount to much. So they decided to try pulling the sledges separately with Skelton, Lashly, and Handsley taking the longer one.

That resulted in a slight improvement on the 16th, when they gained 9½ miles in eight hours. With snow falling throughout the following day, the inherent drawback of the 12-foot sledge—so prone to disproportionate drag—was all too apparent, as it had recently been for Dellbridge's party on the barrier. By the end of the morning's march, Skelton's team was three-quarters of an hour behind Scott's.

The story now becomes confused by Skelton's journal entry for that day:[2]

> [After lunch] the Captain said that something must be done to prevent separating, or else we must make two complete units, or rather I believe I made the latter suggestion, which he readily accepted. I told him I thought the strain rather too much and might damage some of us, but he said the Boatswain and Evans both wished to go on as at present, so I said I was willing to abide by his decision and if we couldn't keep up, work longer hours and so arrive in the same camp every night. So it was arranged that Evans and myself should change tents.

There is no evidence that Skelton moved into Scott's tent. Scott's hopes were so threatened by the slow pace of the 12-foot sledge that at one stage, in what must have been an argument, it is clear that Scott agreed to the two parties traveling separately. Equally clear is that when there was a question of separating, he wanted Skelton with him.

However, putting the bosun, let alone Evans, a petty officer second class, in charge of a party alone on that featureless wilderness would have been a negation of Scott's responsibility for the men's safety. That realization must have caused him to revert to his first concern to keep the parties together, which provoked Skelton's warning that the pace Scott was setting might endanger their health. The warning was well borne out as events unfolded.

Skelton must have argued vigorously, for Scott evidently had to call on Feather and Evans for support. It is hardly surprising that they preferred to carry on with the captain's 11-foot sledge.

But Skelton subverted his compromise that very afternoon, for having placed Handsley in the lead position, he allowed his team to keep up with Scott's sledge, "back-breaking work"[3] as it was. The penalty was soon clear.

They encountered larger *sastrugi* again on the 19th. Clearer conditions enabled Scott to establish that they were about due south of the magnetic pole (e.g., ± 157°E). The land reappeared behind them, refracted above the horizon, but fresh snow in the afternoon made the pulling so hard that Skelton feared "something might snap."[4]

That evening Handsley, who had complained of a sore throat the night before, asked Scott if there was anything in the medical chest for it. Not surprisingly in that germ-free environment, there was not. It came out then that he had completely lost his voice at breakfast that morning and had been "suffering from his chest" for some days.[5]

For Scott, the specter of the Southern journey crisis must have returned, only this time it looked as though he might have an invalid on his hands even before he had reached his goal. Whatever Barne might discover, Scott must have seen the prize, which would more than justify his second season, slipping from his grasp. It was no wonder that even when the inevitable crisis broke the next day, he was reluctant to make the only logical decision and send Skelton back with Handsley and Feather, whose back he knew was giving the bosun much pain.

It snowed all night, with the inevitable effect on the surface. After nearly two hours' struggle over the first excruciating mile on November 20 Handsley collapsed, unable to breathe. As with Macfarlane, the trouble was a form of mountain sickness but without the dire cardiac result his tentmate on Armitage's ascent had suffered.* For Scott, the affinity with Shackleton's case was inescapable.

They camped for lunch, and revived with some brandy, Handsley insisted he could go on. Scott, who had faced a forthright protest from Skelton, felt compelled to adopt relaying, a bitter pill after the crippling blow it had dealt his hopes in the south. That evening Skelton groped to express simultaneously his disagreement with the pace Scott was setting and his understanding of the dilemma Scott faced: "The whole question arises from the Skipper's impatience and hatred of relay work which he got on his southern journey." He already half expected to be sent back with the ailing men.[6]

The relaying was repeated in the morning, and after lunch, with a better surface and Handsley feeling better, they were able to resume separate working of the two sledges. They were only 4 or 5 miles to the good that evening (Skelton estimated 6), so the choice was clear—risk more delay from relaying when the surface deteriorated, as it surely would, or push on with the two fittest men and send the others back in Skelton's charge.

Calling him and Lashly into his tent after lunch on the 22nd, Scott told them of his decision to send the two men back with Skelton, "as he was anxious about Handsley . . . [and] of course [Skelton as an officer] must go back in charge of the party."[7] He had chosen Evans and Lashly as "apparently the fittest," because the bosun was suffering from back trouble. Inevitably, Skelton found the order to retreat hard

---

* Like Macfarlane, Handsley had been no higher than Allan's Camp (6,500 feet) on Armitage's ascent. Now he was undertaking far harder work at over ± 8,500 feet. For men who had spent their lives at sea level with little chance to accustom themselves to altitude, it was fortunate the trouble did not strike more of the party.

to take after coming all that way: "I said I hoped we hadn't delayed him at all and that it was hard lines to come up here a second time and not get farthest west, to which he answered that it was hard lines, that he was very sorry to part company, but that he was anxious about Handsley having already had experience of a chest breakdown last year, so that something must be done. . . . After lunch he wrote out my orders which clear up everything."[8]

For Skelton, it was the culmination of a ten-day struggle to move the 12-foot sledge as fast as Scott, with Feather and Evans, was pulling the 11-footer. At that altitude it was a very different ordeal to the work on the Ferrar and Upper Taylor Glaciers.

The three men helped haul Scott's sledge onward for two hours and then turned back to retrace their tracks to the lonely tent. They faced a journey of 73 miles back to the glacier.[9] It was no mean responsibility for Skelton, whose only directional aid was a compass usable only over the first half of the route. Because his course lay astride the 180° magnetic meridian, the needle pointed roughly to the South Pole, and to stay on course he simply had to steer due west.

They were fifteen and a half days' actual sledging out from New Mountain Depot, so with twenty-four days' rations they had a reasonable safety margin but not enough to transfer any to Scott, given the difficulty of finding the glacier combined with the ailing men's condition. If Scott's statement that "nearly five weeks' rations"[10] were left after the evening meal on November 13 meant they had enough for thirty-three days, then his party likewise had twenty-four days' rations left that evening (the 22nd).* Going on to the end of the month would leave them with sixteen days' food for the return, as against twenty-three days outward, excluding holdups.

With no margin for such delays, Scott was tempting fate, and Lashly's diary reference that night to "going on for a few more days"[11] strongly suggests Scott may have intended to turn back sooner than the end of the month. However, Scott had picked the two men best suited mentally and physically for the final dash they now set out on. Like himself, both were in peak condition, so their speed not only nearly doubled but they increased their time on the move to nine

---

* See Appendix 7. This figure equates well with his December 2 ("more than 14 days") and December 9, 1903 ("a week's" food), references to remaining rations. The whereabouts of Scott's sledge journal written on this journey is unknown, so these and other quotations attributed to Scott are taken from his account in *The Voyage of the "Discovery,"* vol. 2.

hours per day, bringing their daily average to 16 miles. If they could achieve that rate with the wind against them, then with the wind behind them and a diminishing sledge load, the final decision to count on two-thirds of the outward time to get them back must have looked less risky.*

With long spells either side of their only break for lunch and particularly with earlier starts, the head wind ensured painful frost-bites. At their worst on the 26th, Scott wrote: "The wind is the plague of our lives . . . it has cut us to pieces. . . . We suffer most during the first half hour of the morning march. . . . There is a good deal of pain, also in the tent at night . . . laughing is a really painful process."[12]

At least they had clear skies as they advanced across the undulating plain. The east-facing slopes climbing to each new skyline were smooth and glazed. The west-facing slopes were deeply carved, with higher *sastrugi* than any yet encountered. The ridges led to frequent capsizes, with inevitable loss of kerosene through the less than airtight seals. A night blizzard on the 26th left a heavy surface on the 27th. An overcast sky as they awoke on the 28th threatened to deny them the sights that were the best means of keeping them on a westward course.

But matters improved to allow them thirty-six hours of faster travel until, camping for lunch on the last day of November after several capsizes on a downward slope, Scott realized that the next horizon must be their last. For the first time, that night Scott betrayed the hope that animated his Western journey as he wrote of his thoughts on the long ascent that followed: "Perhaps there would be a gradual slope downwards, perhaps more mountains to indicate a western coast for Victoria Land. Greenland I remembered would have been crossed in many places by such a track as we have made. I thought, what a splendid thing it would be to find a coast in this way."[13]

The depth of Scott's disappointment after they reached the top, only to find an unchanging vastness stretching away without a single feature, stares from the pages of his book like an omen of his destiny: "Here then tonight we have reached the end of our tether, and all we have done is to show the immensity of this vast plain . . . beyond that horizon are hundreds and even thousands of miles [with] nothing but this terrible limitless expanse of snow. . . . Could anything be more terrible than this silent wind-swept immensity?"[14]

---

* But in light of the fact that those amounts allowed no margin for holdups, Huntford's assertion (1979: p. 183) that Scott overran his supplies on this journey appears justified.

Scott never allowed his disappointment to show in the tent, and such thoughts never clouded the spirit of his companions: "Few of our camping hours go by without a laugh from Evans and a song from Lashly."[15] And they were certainly not despondent that night, for they knew they had, after all, gone as far across the ice sheet as Nansen had in Greenland.

However, for Scott that realization could not hide the uncomfortable fact that even if he reasonably believed they could get back to the depot in seven and a half days less than the time on the move outward and had food left to accomplish that, the kerosene was two days short. Curiously, journal references to remaining quantities were hedged about with words such as "perhaps" (Scott, December 2) and "about" (Lashly, November 30).

By some malign coincidence, that day Barne and his five companions were also about two days short on their kerosene allowance on their return toward the Bluff.

Skelton's supplies were in better shape—"no particular point in hurrying,"[16] he had written two days before, on the 28th, after covering 31 miles in four days and then being laid up on the 27th while an ESE blizzard howled about the tent. When it slacked off the three men made only 3 miles that day, managing with difficulty to keep to the track in thick snow as the wind went back to the SSW.[17] The cairns they had built to mark each camp helped them to spot the camps.*

For Scott, still outward-bound 100 miles west of them on the 27th, the day had brought only a heavily overcast sky and the usual head wind, which wrought havoc with his party's faces. However, the blizzard that hit Skelton's party moved westward, rapidly obliterating the outward track. Once Scott had begun the return, the surest guide to navigating back to the right glacier was present only for three days. Early on December 4 the track's faint remains disappeared.

By December 6 the effect of the capsizes on their kerosene stock forced Scott to increase their marches to nine and a half hours daily. The surface then improved, and they got on well enough to contemplate increasing their rations as they ate breakfast on the 9th.

Less than an hour's march ahead, however, they got onto crystalline snow. That was the beginning of five days Scott would never forget.

---

* Skelton refers to cairns at three of the outward camps (SPRI 342/2/6: 11.24.03, 11.28.03, 11.29.03), and there is no reason to suppose that Scott and his companions did not build cairns at all their outward camps.

On skis, they could not move the sledge and barely achieved a mile an hour for the rest of that day. That night they had a week's provisions and only a few days' (as Scott put it) kerosene for their stove (probably about a four-day supply). Scott told his companions they would have to march yet another hour every day, fry their breakfast instead of making the usual *hoosh,* and make do with cold lunches to eke out the kerosene.

After parting from the others on the outward march, they had averaged 16 miles a day, but now, with perhaps only 50 pounds of rations left, they were making barely 11 miles daily. For the last four days Scott had firmly resisted reducing rations, as the deficit of calories had manifested itself in increasing pangs of hunger—although, probably because of the seal meat, not to the extent experienced on the Southern journey.[18]

The almost certainly fatal prospect of reducing rations was eliminated the next day, December 10, when Evans spotted distant peaks appearing over the horizon. But they were far from recognizable, and Scott could not tell where they were. The nearly continuous cloud cover had impaired the chart he had worked out to help keep them to the right latitude, and the only guide to their progress had been the compass variation from true north on the occasional glimpse of the sun at noon: "I have been struggling with my sights and deviations table but although I believe we cannot be far off the glacier the sense of uncertainty is oppressive. We are really travelling by rule of thumb, and one cannot help all sorts of doubts creeping in when the consequences are so serious."[19]

Whether that was a verbatim copy of his journal or, as he said they frequently were,* the words in his book quoted here are an expanded version of the brief penciled records, there is no more honest exposure of the anguish of personal responsibility for other men's lives than Scott's account of the following days on the desolate summit, which for all the encouragement of the peaks ahead was featureless now that they had lost their outward track. Haunting Scott for the next three and a half interminable days was the fear that they might arrive at the wrong glacier and see no recognizable clue as to which way

---

* Scott could have stated more clearly his intention to expand his "laconic" sledging journal entries than he did on p. 519 in vol. 1 of *The Voyage of the "Discovery,"* but the reader cannot have failed to grasp that transcripts in the book subsequent to September 17, 1902, would not be literal. Charges of dishonesty and "falsification" in the book (Huntford 1979: pp. 188–191) cannot be sustained.

to turn to find the one with their depot in it. Even if he had gotten the landfall right, there was still the upper icefall ahead. All day on the 13th the drift was thick, and "for aught we knew we might have been walking over the edge of a precipice at any moment. Tonight it is as thick as ever; it is positively sickening, but good weather or bad we must go on now."[20]

That evening the anxiety that had accompanied Scott every waking moment of thirteen days of unparalleled physical toil reached its agonizing climax. The two-day deficit of kerosene was not disastrous if the weather held, for they would have the wind behind them. But any possible advantage was negated by a sky so overcast that they could not see the *sastrugi* properly. The resulting capsizes and falls forced them to camp early for fear of injury, canceling out the help of the sail.

The change in their fortunes over the next twenty-four hours seemed almost as miraculous as their survival by the narrowest of margins twice within a few hours. Early on the 14th they were in sight of hummocks of chaotic ice and among the first signs of crevassing. This must be the top of a glacier, but they still could not recognize where they were. And the drift was starting again. Scott faced a perilous dilemma. To go forward would be very dangerous, but if they stopped they might be marooned in a new blizzard, and that would be the end of them. They all agreed to risk going on.

It turned out they were on the top of an icefall, with the ice at first smoothing out and then becoming steeper. With the two men holding the sledge back, Scott led off. Within minutes Lashly slipped, and the sledge took control, knocking Evans off his feet. In a second men and sledge overtook Scott, dragging him in their wake. For several more seconds that unrolled like a nightmare, the tangled group slid and then bounded to the foot of the cascade. They clambered painfully to their feet, at first marveling at their escape and then overwhelmed with relief at recognizing familiar landmarks in the valley they had left thirty-one days before!

Pausing only for hot cocoa on the way to the first cascade above the old Desolation campsite, they were no sooner safely down a particularly rough part than Scott and Evans found themselves hanging by their harness in a bottomless crevasse. After endless minutes, Lashly saved their lives and his own by hanging onto the sledge, which would surely have followed them down if not for his efforts.

After an excruciating climb up the rope with frozen hands, Scott at last grasped the sledge and heaved himself over the edge to the fervent relief of the imperturbable chief stoker, whose quiet "Thank God!" alone betrayed the strain he had been under. Together they got Evans out after he had hung in the abyss for another five minutes while Scott recovered.

They reached the Nunatak Depot in thirty minutes. Although Scott felt it was impossible to put into words the anxiety he had felt for their safety, something he wrote a year later poignantly revealed the effect on their morale of the sudden reversal in their fortunes:[21]

> All Nature seemed to say that our long fight was over, and that at length we had reached a haven of rest. And it has been a fight indeed; it is only now that I realise what discomforts we have endured and what a burden of anxiety we have borne during the past month. The relief of being freed from such conditions is beyond the power of my pen to describe, but perhaps what brought it home to us most completely was the fact that the worst of our troubles came at the end, and that in the brief space of half an hour we passed from abject discomfort to rest and peace.

That relief was further enhanced by the note telling of Skelton's safe arrival at the depot on December 4. His group had comparatively light following winds for the first four days but then had to pull through another five of blizzard conditions before the sky cleared on December 2 to reveal the mountains ahead of them. Their 7-mile daily average over the 86 miles had been remarkable given the condition of Feather and Handsley. Scott's average over his 163 miles, working longer hours, had been a little over 11½ miles daily.

Much to his additional relief, Scott found the 9-foot sledge brought to the depot by Skelton from Allan's Camp, where it had been left by Armitage the year before. Handsley had spotted it on the evening of the 3rd, and by diverting to fetch it they had avoided the worst of the upper icefall. They got back to the old track as they negotiated the one above Desolation Camp. Although he experienced little trouble with crevasses, Skelton had nevertheless seen "what a lot of luck" they had in ascending it.[22]

By the time Skelton had reached the safety of Depot Nunatak at 2 A.M., they had been on the move for thirteen hours and covered 22 miles. The force 7 following wind had been too strong for the sail, and they had soon lost the track and strayed to the north.

Skelton and the bosun were both snowblind by that time, and with the drift blasting down the glacier for the next three days, they had stayed put. That meant Skelton could only leave enough pemmican, biscuit, cocoa, and sugar for one meal for Scott's party. More important, he was able to leave "a small amount" of kerosene.[23]

Scott had arrived one meal short of what they needed to reach the New Mountain Depot, which is clear from his remark that the food they found was "enough to carry us to the main depot."[24] Curiously, he didn't mention the kerosene, implying that the saving the cold meals had achieved had gotten them through with just enough.

Even with the undamaged 9-foot sledge, Scott wanted to save the battered 11-foot one, which Lashly and Evans rearmed with silver cladding the next morning.[25] With most of the load on the smaller sledge as they started off, they reached the main depot the next day, December 16, going on to camp at Knobhead Moraine with all worries over food and kerosene set at rest.

Another reassuring note told them Skelton had stayed there all of December 9. He had picked up the heavy half-plate camera and taken some of his most impressive photos of the glacier's surroundings over the following days—Ferrar used Skelton's photo of the Inland Forts taken from the middle of the glacier to illustrate his report on the geological work in Scott's book. From this camp Skelton had taken the camera into the Knobhead Mountain *bergschrund* and 4 miles across the glacier to within a mile of where the three of them could have seen what Ferrar had of the northern arm and realized it was not a "fjord," as he called it, but a valley leading to the sea.[26]

The day Scott reached the depot, Skelton got the two invalids safely back to the ship. Handsley had again lost his voice, and the bosun had suffered severely from diarrhea at Cathedral Rocks. Skelton had dosed him with "lead and opium," to good effect, but he hadn't been able to pull for two days.[27] According to Wilson, his back was no better when they reached the ship.[28]

Scott's recuperative powers must have been of a high order, for no sooner had they eaten their fill at New Mountain Depot than he recognized that with 8 days' rations left and the prospect of seals at Butter Point, he had a not-to-be-missed chance to explore the north fjord. On the evening of December 17 the men, with one of their sledges and their tent, camped at the northern glacier's edge, nearly 5 miles below the turn everyone had seen from Knobhead Moraine. They had reached a point some way down the steeper part of the glacier, where the surface had become too dangerous for the runner cladding.

Ahead of them the ice disappeared where it plunged at an even steeper angle, and the valley beyond looked as though it was entirely blocked by a great shoulder projecting from the Kukri Hills. Abandoning the sledge the next day, they soon stumbled on the surprise that lay beyond.

Taking one of a maze of melt channels almost as daunting as those they had overcome to get onto the main glacier, they suddenly found themselves standing 20 feet up the glacier's terminal ice cliff and looking down at a lake. Beyond that was the narrowest of defiles, which proved to be only 17 feet wide as they passed through it between rock cliffs several times that in height.[29]

Once through the defile, they looked down past more small lakes along another bare valley to the next buttress, which again seemed to be blocking the valley. Jutting from the mountain, today named Nussbaum Riegel, on the south side of the valley, that buttress stood about 11 miles from where Ferrar had reached the Commonwealth Glacier face. Gaining its flank, they could see that the lakes they had passed were brief oases in a truly "dry" valley from which the ice had long since retreated except for the glaciers hanging down its walls. This was the first of many ice-free areas discovered subsequently on the otherwise ice-clad continent.

Back at the camp after fourteen hours on the move, they pulled the sledge back up to the moraine on the 19th and reached Cathedral Rocks Depot on the 20th. The three men were then greeted by the sight they least wanted to see: McMurdo Sound was still full of ice as far north as Cape Royds! Would they be trapped for another winter? Without the means to exploit the following season, that would be a total frustration for everyone except the scientists.

Happily, Skelton had found a seal and left some of it at the point. The weather was obliging, so instead of cutting straight across the sound Scott felt able to make a leisurely return by way of the Eskers, which he had never seen at close quarters. Late on Christmas Eve the comforting sight of *Discovery*'s masts rose into view, and an hour later they were aboard and being greeted by Koettlitz, Ford, Quartley (who had injured himself on the last stage of Barne's return), and Handsley, now almost recovered.

Ford had prepared Christmas delicacies, and the emaciated sledgers gained weight almost visibly from one meal to the next. Scott did not betray how much weight he had lost, but he suffered agonies of indigestion as that process was rapidly reversed.

Once sufficiently recovered, Scott set about calculating his positions on the twenty-one occasions when he had been able to establish compass variation from true north. Limited to the single question of how far they had penetrated the inland ice sheet, the resulting 146°33E (later corrected to 147°E on Mulock's chart) put them more than 160 miles beyond Desolation Camp when they turned back. Except for the shortage of 11-foot sledges, which condemned him to use the narrowed 12-foot sledge after the others had been damaged (and the failure to shorten it, knowing the reputation for dragging the other 12-foot sledge had), Scott would undoubtedly have penetrated the inland summit still further.

Although Scott had been robbed of the spectacular discovery he had hoped for, the sheer distance covered—nearly 600 miles (700 statute) measured on modern maps—was a matter of understandable pride. Scott could not help reflecting that he, Lashly, and Evans had traveled more than 1,000 statute miles (actually 950) since they set off on September 9. That was a sledging feat to rank with the Arctic exploits of McClintock half a century before, which Nansen so admired.[30]

25

ESCAPE TO INTERNATIONAL ACCLAIM
Scott's Just Reward

Scott had returned to find that there was a daily supplies service to the sawing camp run by James Dell, who had been put in charge of the puppies after the operation on his poisoned arm and had trained the four survivors of the first litters to become a thoroughly effective sledge team. So it was Dell who carried Armitage's first report to Scott in which, as he later admitted, he had misled Scott by being "somewhat too optimistic" about the progress of the sawing.[1]

Although Bernacchi, who arrived to rate Scott's watch, gave him a less rosy account of the proceedings, Scott did not immediately call off the work on Christmas Eve. Eventually, traveling out to the camp with Lashly and Evans on December 31, 1903, he declared a New Year's Day holiday and invited Wilson to move into the tent Dell had brought out on the sledge for him. The 50-foot-long tent, made from the awning, was already so crowded that some were using their sledging tents outside it.

Wilson found Scott anything but recovered and still "feeling the effects of his journey pretty badly—he has very bad indigestion—and wants to get away from the ship and everyone and rest a bit."[2] Despite that, Scott set off with Wilson and Royds to measure the distance to the ice edge (8½ miles by the sledgemeter). The next morning Scott watched the work for thirty minutes and was quickly convinced that the project was futile, even if the ice did break back to the islands. At most, they might be able to blast some of the ice around the ship.

Having returned to the ship on November 22, Wilson had barely four days to recover before leaving again on November 26 with Armitage and Heald for the big glacier between Mount Discovery and the western mountains. Armitage had organized the journey on his own initiative, realizing it was the one sector they had never explored or surveyed. In spite of his advice a year before, Koettlitz had evidently agreed to go with Armitage, but he had injured a leg on the trip with Wilson, and William Heald was chosen instead.

Crossing over to Blue Glacier, the three men followed the coast southward for four days through chaotic ice until they ran onto frozen thaw water that formed a rubbly road along the shore to the foot of the glacier's main sweep, which could be seen clearly from the ship. On December 6 they camped about 20 miles down the coast from Blue Glacier. From there, on December 7, just west of the 164E meridian, they climbed about 2,600 feet with the camera to look out over an enormous 15-mile-wide frozen amphitheater tumbling from the skyline. Dominated by the rounded snowcapped mountain later named after the *Morning* (which they knew as Discovery Saddle, as Barne's panorama of the coast beyond it showed), the main glacier, later named after Koettlitz, swept down from the southwest. Wilson's dramatic words in his diary did more justice to the majestic scene before them than to the accuracy with which he described the position of the red cone they could see from Hut Point on the glacier's western edge: "In its centre [is] the red Pyramid we see from our winter quarters, with a deep thawpit round the upper side. This pyramid is quite detached and below it the glacier is parted by a similar mass of red rock, ridge shaped, and a small arm of the ice sheet comes down steeply to spread out in a fan shape to the northwest in a blind valley . . . joining up again with the main ice flow in a terribly weatherworn condition. This part it is we are camped by."[3]

From their position they could see that Brown Island was not really an island but was joined to Mount Discovery. The ridge-shaped rock, which clearly *was* an island, was later named Heald Island after the man who helped Armitage take photographs that day. Camping in the first bay south of Blue Glacier on December 9, Wilson made a last climb into the foothills the next day, this time reaching 3,000 feet to sketch the scene around him, while Armitage and Heald worked at the last photographs and bearings before returning to the ship at midnight on December 12.[4]

As it turned out, Scott scarcely got the chance for the rest he craved. He got away with Wilson the afternoon of January 3, 1904, and the two men camped that night near the cape (now Cape Evans) immediately north of the islands named after Dellbridge. They went on slowly the following day to camp above the beach between Flagstaff Point and Derrick Point where Shackleton later landed to set up his base on February 8, 1908, at the cape Markham had named after Royds. From there they could watch for the arrival of the *Morning*.

In those leisurely hours Scott must have had the chance to reflect on what he had achieved. Even if he was doubtful about the "thin blue line" of the inland ice Barne and Mulock had set their theodolite on, as he pieced together the results of his second campaign he must have realized that the evidence the expedition had gathered for the existence of a vast southern continent was almost overwhelming. For all the disappointments, he had almost certainly answered that and the two other great questions he had been sent south to resolve.

There *was* an Antarctic Continent—he believed the great mountain chain went right onto the Antarctic Peninsula[5]—and he had been far onto its summit. Ferrar had unraveled the first of its geological secrets.

The Great Ice Barrier was moving. Its flatness and features, such as the warmer temperature in the depths of crevasses as one moved away from the land, showed it was afloat, as did the tide cracks at Ross Island.

His own and Bernacchi's and Mulock's observations on their journeys would locate the magnetic pole almost as well as if they had actually been to it, certainly well enough to build the magnetic map of the Southern Hemisphere that had been one of the prime aims of the great European assault, of which his expedition had been part. Their endeavors had surely reaped a rich harvest.

The only cloud on the horizon was the sheet of ice stretching 18 miles back to the ship, which threatened to trap them for another year. They had no fears for their safety, but they had too few resources, especially sledges, for any journey capable of extending their discoveries.

They would not starve, and the scientists would be glad for further chances. Ferrar might come up with even more dramatic fossils. For Scott, though, the one major discovery within reach was finding the truth about Wilkes's "landfalls" east of d'Urville's Côte Clairie, a subject of controversy ever since Ross had sailed south of Wilkes's Ringgold's Knoll and revived when Borchgrevink claimed to have done likewise. For that discovery, however, Scott needed his ship and enough coal to force a way in the ice.

THE 290-TON RELIEF SHIP *MORNING* AT THE ICE FRONT IN MCMURDO SOUND. Photo taken by ship's Master Lieut. William Colbeck RNR, on January 25, 1904, 7 miles from the *Discovery*, trapped at Hut Point. At the foot of Mount Erebus in the background is Cape Evans, with the dark outline of Inaccessible Island between there a0nd the ship. The picture clearly shows the open bridge structure and barque rigging, lacking the yard for a royal sail on the foremast. © P. A. Theelke.

He did not doubt that Markham would send the *Morning* south with the coal he needed, and indeed, the next morning he looked up and saw the familiar ship not 3 miles from them. But even as he felt relief at the ship's arrival, he knew the ice might yet deny him the ship so vital to that third chance. He would have to wait for nature's decision.

No one in McMurdo Sound that day would have guessed that Scott would soon see a second ship steam into view. When the moment of astonishment had passed for him and Wilson, their thoughts were on mail from home and the hard fact of 18 miles of ice between them and their escape.

Racing back to the sawing camp, Scott sent the three men looking after the camp to summon a sledge party for the mails and then skied north toward the ships. Four men came out on skis from the larger ship and, in thick Dundee accents, explained they were from the *Terra Nova*. In a few minutes the two weatherbeaten men were aboard the *Morning* being greeted by Colbeck and his officers.

"Ah! What it was to be given a bundle of mail!"[6] Wilson exclaimed in his diary. It took him more than two days to read through a year's worth of letters, above all those from his wife, Oriana.

The first letter Colbeck handed Scott, however, brought a very different message. It was an official instruction from the Admiralty to abandon his ship and return in the *Terra Nova* if the *Discovery* could not be released. Not one of Scott's men would have considered abandoning the ship, least of all Scott, for whom the exploration westward from Ross's Cape North to Adélie Land still held the lure of discovering a west coast of Victoria Land.

With ice conditions possibly forcing the relief ships to leave as early as mid-February, just six weeks away, packing the natural history and geological collections for transfer to the *Terra Nova* would have to start straightaway. For two days Scott could not bring himself to write the orders. When he did, the work only seemed to emphasize to everyone the rather bitter prospect of returning like refugees crammed into a whaler instead of under the proud flags of their own ship.

For ten days the unbroken ice continued to spell out the uncomfortable message without a sign of the seaward edge breaking back. The pack reappeared across the mouth of the sound long before it should have, meaning they would once more be without the swell needed to break up the ice in the harbor.

Then, for no apparent reason, the ice began to yield to the combined onslaughts of Royds's blasting parties and ramming by the *Terra Nova*. For two weeks the ships advanced with frustrating slowness until January 28, when the men sawing and blasting around the *Discovery* woke to find the ship and ice rising and falling 18 inches on the swell they had all been waiting for. It continued for four days, during which the other ships gained another 10 miles and reached the glacier tongue, their hulls easily visible from the flagstaff on Hut Point.

By that time just about everything including the piano and harmonium* was aboard the *Terra Nova*. Despite the open pool off Hut Point, spirits fell again, hardly helped by the bleak look of the living quarters. The death of Quartley's cat Blackwall, killed by the dogs the next day, seemed yet another ill omen. A week later, pushing

---

* Presented by the people of Lyttelton and now at Discovery Point, Dundee.

the date as far back as he dared, Scott settled on March 3 as the day for abandoning ship, with the *Morning* leaving a week earlier.

Then, as unpredictably as it had gone, the swell returned on February 11, and for four days McKay led the way with the *Terra Nova*, alternately backing and ramming its way into the deepening cracks to break through amid frantic cheering into the Hut Point pool, which now extended to within a ship's length of the beleaguered *Discovery*. Festivities went on far into the night, and Scott's diary betrayed his sudden relief: "It seems unnecessary to describe all that has followed: how everyone has been dashing about madly from ship to ship, how everyone shook everyone else by the hand, how our small bay has become a scene of wild revelry, and how some have now reached that state which places them in doubt as to which ship they really belong to. Much can be excused on such a night."[7]

The rapid change of fortunes had caught everyone by surprise, most of all in the engine room. There was more to do than time to do it before the ice around them broke out, as it would assuredly do given a little help from guncotton. After a second winter's accretions, the ice was 12 feet thick at the seaward edge and 17 feet thick around the stern.

Putting the other crews to filling the boilers, Scott exploded a quadruple charge 15 feet ahead of the bow the following night, cracking the ice in all directions, while everyone worked through the night to get the rigging ready. Satisfied with the result of the explosion, he turned in, waking a few hours later to find a foot-wide crack in the ice at the stern—the ideal chance to shatter its grip on the ship. A large charge was exploded in the crack at noon on February 16, and the *Discovery* floated free, wildly cheered by the crews of all three ships. The wind was coming through the Gap from the usual southeasterly quarter, and as the stern swung almost 180° westward, *Discovery*'s starboard anchor was hurriedly raised to avoid the two cables becoming crossed.

The priority then was to get the extra coal aboard. By 2 P.M. the *Terra Nova* was warped alongside. Later, while the Dundee men carried on with the coaling, Scott took the entire company ashore for a short dedication of the cross in memory of George Vince they had put up on the point the day before.[8] That was the only shadow on an otherwise carefree day, and it failed to dampen spirits that evening as they entertained McKay along with most of the *Terra Nova* crew.

The first act of the drama to come began as the wardroom meal ended. The *Terra Nova* broke its forward warps in the rising sea as the gale increased to force 9 by 11:30 P.M.[9]

FREE AT LAST! *Discovery* swinging around on the port anchor after the ice broke away. The *Morning* is beyond the floe, against the backdrop of Observation Hill. *Discovery*'s starboard anchor has been hoist to the forecastle deck to avoid tangling with the port anchor's chain as the wind blowing through the gap swung the ship around. Courtesy, the Royal Society.

Summoning his men, McKay was over the side in a flash, casting off under full steam. The wind had backed westerly and brought slushy ice into the bay, threatening to drive the nearby *Morning* onto the shore of Observation Hill. After vainly trying to escape into the sound, Rupert England barely worked it south until clear of Cape Armitage.[10] The rising gale then veered south, bringing a furious blizzard in which both the *Morning* and *Discovery* faced the most dreaded situation in the days of sail—being trapped against a lee shore, one with inadequate power and the other with none at all.

Determined to complete the coaling in the safer shelter of the glacier tongue, Scott nevertheless knew that to call for steam prematurely would court unreliability in the engine. That could be potentially fatal on the route he intended to follow. Leaving it to the officer of the watch to let the second anchor go if the ship dragged toward the lee shore, Scott went below.

TERRA NOVA AFTER TYING UP ALONGSIDE DISCOVERY. Colbeck's photo taken on February 16, 1904, some time before Scott led a party ashore to dedicate the Memorial Cross for George Vince on Hut Point. Courtesy, P. A. Theelke. The starboard anchor shank can be seen catted (hanging vertically beneath the bow), showing it was subsequently hoist out again. However, the southwest gale, which sprang up shortly before midnight, forced the *Terra Nova* to cast off and once more swung the stern around to the east. With the wind liable to such extreme changes, the single anchor remained the only option. When the storm rose to hurricane force the next day, it failed to hold the ship, which with watering incomplete and steam not yet available was driven shoreward until the stern struck the ice front. Scott's decision to run for the open sound as soon as the first engine could run saved the ship from a worse fate on that lee shore than the grounding that awaited them at the hands of the current running past Hut Point. The memorial cross, erected the day before, is almost invisible. © P. A. Theelke.

Waking on the 17th, he found the wind had dropped at 6 A.M. Calling for steam as soon as possible, he saw the *Morning* reappear. England had struggled all night to avoid being wrecked on the point of Cape Armitage. Doorly came over to pick up a relieved Colbeck, who had spent a sleepless night well aware of the ordeal his men must have faced. The *Terra Nova* was invisible somewhere to the south, having steamed full ahead for hours.

Colbeck had barely reached his ship when the gale was on them again "fiercer than ever," which meant it could hardly have been less than force 10. At about 11:30 A.M., stern onto the lee shore, *Discovery*'s anchor began to drag just as Skelton reached the bridge to promise steam in thirty minutes, albeit on one boiler only because they had not taken on enough water for two.[11]

The anchorage had been chosen as a secure defense against pack sweeping into the sound from the north—it was as safe a place as any to allow the ship to be frozen in. The bottom was not the best holding ground for a ship at anchor, even though it had held the port anchor during the night's gale, but Scott reckoned that steam would be ready before the anchor had dragged the 150 yards that separated the stern from the shore.

For twenty-five increasingly fraught minutes, the wind increased and the distance to the 20-foot ice foot shrank until, too late to bring the second anchor to bear, the stern hit the ice with a shuddering blow. Five minutes later, after a second shock had shaken the ship from stem to stern, Skelton announced steam on one boiler just as the bow was falling off to starboard and threatening to lay the ship beam-on against the ice wall. If Scott, handling the ship for the first time in two years, could be accused of failing to gain time by letting the starboard anchor go, his decision to run for the open sound on one boiler almost certainly saved his ship from total destruction on that shore.[12]

The log, written up by Mulock after they had escaped that fate, shows that five minutes after midday the ship began to make headway toward the anchor with, as Scott later put it, "the engines [he meant engine] going ahead and the windlass heaving in."[13] Once there, after twenty anxious minutes the anchor was weighed, but the ship could make no further progress against the wind. Scott gave the order to put the helm over and make for the open water beyond the point, a run of little more than a quarter of a mile, with the squally wind almost at violent storm strength on the port bow.[14]

It took almost ten minutes to reach the point, but then, as the bow breasted the shoal, a strong current—unseen until then in the flying drift—swung the ship around.[15] In an instant, wind and sea had combined to drive the ship aground on the shoal.

The leadsman found 3 feet more water under the bowsprit than under the stern, and the ship was aground amidships.[16] So with the elements still tending to drive the ship forward, it seemed logical to try to force it over the shoal, but as soon as they moved forward the condenser inlets promptly choked, the engines stopped, and the stern slewed around until the bowsprit almost touched the rocks of Hut Point.[17]

That close to disaster, the ship lay with its starboard quarter to the wind, listed heavily to port, as the storm rose to hurricane force. For an hour and a half, with the sea breaking over the deck, it seemed, as Scott put it, that they had rescued their ship only to be dashed to pieces beneath the cross they had just erected. High above them, it loomed darkly through the spray left by each new wave.

For all the imminent danger, Scott found that Skelton and Feather, among others, had, like himself, turned their minds to how to lighten the ship and what else could be done to get it off. When the wind moderated at last after more than six hours of furious noise as the ship crashed up and down on the shoal, it veered north by west around 7 P.M. Dinner was promptly served by the imperturbable Gilbert Scott as though nothing had happened.

Halfway through the meal, Mulock reported the ship was moving astern. Scott was on the bridge in record time and found the current flowing southward as fast as it had flowed northward when it thrust the ship aground. The ship was indeed moving astern by several inches as each wave lifted it. Skelton soon announced that the inlets were free again. Summoning all hands to sally the ship,* Scott rang for full astern and *Discovery* grated off the shingle bank, little the worse except for the loss of several pieces of false keel and some of the deck lights cracked.

It seemed a miraculous escape as they ran southward to join the *Terra Nova*, struggling with its bow to the ice edge at the head of the sound. Powerless to help, McKay and his crew had glimpsed the other ship's fate between the squalls that heralded the worst of the storm, which, according to the *Terra Nova* log, had risen to continuous hurricane strength by 4 P.M.

Much concerned about the fate of the missing *Morning*, the two ships resumed watering and coaling at the north side of the glacier tongue the next morning. To their relief, Colbeck's ship reappeared. They had escaped to the middle of the sound during the lull the previous morning, but the storm had carried the ship 40 miles up the sound where it had continued to blow all night as though determined to keep them in its grip.

The coast Scott now hoped to explore would probably be as ice-infested as Wilkes and d'Urville had found it on their voyages. Before the storm Scott had learned to his dismay that after the long struggle to break through the ice to Hut Point, the two ships were far

---

* The nautical term for rolling the ship by all hands running from side to side.

short of the amount of coal he needed. Apart from the 17 tons of provisions to be transferred, McKay could spare just 55 tons of coal.[18] That brought the total in the bunkers to only 90 tons; Scott wanted 200 tons.[19]

In the long struggle up the sound, the *Terra Nova* had burned more coal than anyone expected. Colbeck, who took over command after joining the other ship at Hobart, could only guess at the amount of coal Scott would have left. Believing the 100 tons McKay estimated they could spare would be enough and worried about his own ship's ability to keep up with the *Terra Nova*, Colbeck had opted to set off from Hobart with 250 tons instead of the 300 the *Morning* could carry.[20]

Now, with only 25 tons more than the minimum for ballast and emergencies, if he sailed straight home the surplus was insufficient to allow him to accompany Scott for any distance. Colbeck did what he could to help, giving the 25 tons to Scott. That brought the total in *Discovery*'s bunkers up to 115 tons, of which 50 had to be kept for the return to New Zealand. That left enough for a mere eleven days' steaming if there was any ice to push through, and even if there was none they would be working against the prevailing winds.[21]

With the *Morning* warped alongside *Discovery* on the south side of the glacier tongue, the last bag was safely down the canvas chutes through the wardroom by 6 A.M. on February 19. Watering the ship then began, but tubes fractured in the melter, and the watering was not completed when another southerly gale sprang up. *Discovery* had to cast off, once more without full tanks although at least able to maintain full pressure on both boilers.

The three ships steamed up the coast south of the Drygalski Ice Tongue, with Mulock carrying out the first-ever running survey of the tongue. Wilson sketched all day until they rounded the snout of the tongue on the evening of the 20th, when Scott made straight for Cape Washington. He planned to complete the watering in Wood Bay just beyond the cape. There the *Morning* left them to sail directly to the Auckland Islands rendezvous, where the ships were to meet before the final leg to New Zealand.

The part of the bay where the *Discovery* could have tied up to the shore was filled with pack ice, so they had to make do with a large floe floating in a strip of water along the south side of the bay. The crew completed the watering just before the floe was broken up by the swell. That stopped Armitage in the middle of swinging the ship, so the vital validation of the magnetic bearings, upon which the positions fixed by running survey depended, had to be abandoned. Pack threatened to trap the ships in the bay, so Armitage's magnetic observations—closer to the magnetic pole than any achieved before—were also cut short.

As the two ships moved northward, Skelton needed only two or three days' work to complete the engine room overhaul, so vital for the push to the west. But within hours the work was brought to a standstill as water rose over the stokehold floor, forcing Lashly to dowse the fires. None of the pumps would work, and the problem was not overcome until someone found the inlets were choked with coal dust. Once the water was lowered to bilge level, the leaks resumed their former insignificant scale, and they never learned why more water had come in at that stage.

They were free at last for the final effort. All seemed to go well until Dailey, the carpenter, noticed the rudder was moving less than the tiller. His inspection, slung out over the stern in calm conditions as they passed through the Possession Islands, revealed that the rudder head was splintered through and was held to the rudder only by its own weight. No one was ever sure how it had happened. The ice foot at Hut Point was too vertical for the rudder to have been harmed when the overhanging stern struck it, but the damage was almost certainly done when the rudder struck an underwater projection as Armitage was moving the ship from one side of the glacier tongue to the other during coaling.[22]

The shipping of the spare rudder, only half the size of the broken one, spelled the end of the ship's maneuverability under sail, so vital for eking out the paltry amount of coal the *Discovery* now had. The replacement was done in the shelter of Robertson Bay, which allowed Skelton to finish the overhaul work in the engine room. When they stood out westward at 10:15 A.M. on February 25, Scott at least had confidence in the little steaming capacity the bunkers would provide.

Within 45 miles his hopes were dashed by a fleet of icebergs and growlers on the move in jostling pack. It would be fatal to be caught there after dark, and there were now four hours of darkness each night. Just 80 tons of coal remained, which meant they had only 30 tons for breaking through the pack. That amount was just enough for 6 days' steaming, and it would barely start them on the thousand-mile stretch to Adélie Land unless they could keep in open water.

They were forced to follow the edge of the pack northward. A westerly blizzard then drove it and them to the east until, at noon on the 27th, they were back beyond the point they had started from.

That same day the French expedition, aboard the *Français*, also had to turn back from unbreachable ice fronting the coast of Alexander Land, which their leader, Jean Charcot, had hoped to reach. In that season of reluctant ice, only the Scottish expedition advanced southward, as the *Scotia* crossed the Circle in the Weddell Sea that day.

Running north as a southeast blizzard replaced the westerly one, Scott lost sight of the *Terra Nova* and would not see it again until the *Discovery* reached the rendezvous site. Forced to use sail alone to conserve his meager six days' coal, and beset by fog with bergs looming out of blinding snow showers, Scott was faced with the real shortcomings of the small rudder under sail. A few days later that experience prompted him to write, "The *Discovery* is an impossible sailer and now that we have had to fall back on the spare rudder we can scarcely get on without steam."[23] Later, in his report to the societies' presidents, Scott qualified his criticism, adding that "under steam and sail she behaves excellently well for a ship of her class."[24]

Matters were made worse by the reduced crew. With only ten seamen on board, alternating deck watches of five men were too small for emergencies, such as avoiding collisions with bergs looming out of the mist. The rudder would not help, and the only resort would be having all hands on deck to throw several sails flat aback.[25*]

After a vain attempt to go about under sail to search for the *Terra Nova* on the 29th, the pack edge at last turned west in about 67½°S. Fully 150 miles from the coast he hoped to follow, Scott vainly searched for a way south, heaving to in the darkness each night as he sailed westward for 500 miles.

Passing through the Balleny Islands on March 2, sixty-three years to the day after Ross, he recognized that Ross's "Russell Islands" were none other than the peaks of Sturge Island, the largest and southernmost island of the group. Approaching from the southeast in 1832 and hampered by poor visibility, Ross had sighted the peaks of the island from a great distance and taken them for a new group.[26] Scott had been lucky enough to arrive close to Sturge Island in good conditions.

In contrast to Borchgrevink's turn away eastward on the 66th parallel north of the Balleny Islands, Scott really did pass south of the claimed positions of "Ringgold's Knoll" and "Eld's Peak," Wilkes's easternmost 1840 sightings. When Scott was forced to turn for home

---

* This involved swinging more than one of the main-mast yards through as much as 90°, its wire rope stays being strong enough to stand the shock reversal of strain.

on March 4 with little more than 50 tons of coal left, the *Discovery* was in 67°23S 155½E and nearer than Wilkes's ship, the USS *Peacock*, to the claimed position of Cape Hudson, with a perfectly clear horizon and no sign of the cape. Characteristically, Scott was reluctant to discredit Wilkes, feeling he had merely revived the controversy rather than resolved it, as he wrote to Professor Gregory the next day.[27]

Six days earlier he had again written of his belief in a west coast of Victoria Land,* although now he must have seen it as bordering a sea extending to Adélie Land with a southern shore somewhere north of his summit sledging track. Sailing south of Wilkes's sightings seemed to have reinforced that impression, for after turning north Scott concluded there was "no case for any land eastward of Adélie Land."[28]

For the second time, *Discovery* sailed northeast through the southern ocean, this time at the stormiest season of the year and with less than 10 tons of ballasting coal by the time they entered Ross Harbour in the Auckland Islands. Inevitably, the ship behaved like a cork as they pitched northward, with the wind more often than not off the port bow and always at gale force until March 15, the day they reached the rendezvous.

Constantly close-hauled under sail and steam, they were spared the worst of the rolling associated with calms, but it was the nastiest spell of seasickness any of the crew could remember. It was hard work holding the course, for with the small rudder the ship fell away 3 to 4 points compared with the 1¼-point leeway usual with the proper one.

The luxury of seeing green vegetation around the shores of the sheltered harbor was tempered by the realization that they had too little coal to reach New Zealand and a nagging anxiety that the other ships might have none left to spare. Happily, though, the *Terra Nova* arrived on the 19th with enough coal, despite having had great difficulty reaching the islands, largely because Captain McKay had not brought the ship westward with the *Discovery* and so had to beat more against the prevailing wind.

When the *Morning* arrived the following day, the exhausted state of its crew testified to the grim experience of several times having had to fight mountainous seas with the engines out of action. On February 26, as Scott was being pushed eastward away from his goal, Colbeck's ship had been overtaken by a storm in 64°S that swept the whaler overboard and so severely damaged the bridge that Doorly,

---

* See footnote on page 257, Chapter 19.

who was on watch, thought for one terrifying moment that the whole structure would follow the whaler with him on it.[29]

The sheltered harbor had given little hint of the gales on the other side of the island that had prevented Colbeck from getting in since arriving on the 17th. He had been within 80 miles of New Zealand on the 15th but, not wanting to arrive there before Scott, had beaten back across the gales to meet the others at the rendezvous.

One man was so seriously ill that the *Morning*'s surgeon had to consult Koettltiz and Wilson about his condition. There was no question of going on until they had all recovered their strength, and then they would face the lengthy job of loading ton after ton of stone aboard until the *Morning* had a safe weight of ballast. That job and the transfer of coal to *Discovery* were accomplished by the 28th.

Sailing the next day, the three ships steamed into the harbor at Lyttelton at noon on Good Friday, April 1, 1904, greeted by excited crowds as they passed the packed jetties. "Full and most glorious news . . . the second sledging season [was] as important and successful as the first"[30] was the excited entry in Markham's diary after the first official cables had reached him the following day. The seventy-four-year-old man, for whom the outcome of the expedition meant so much, had been struck down in mid-February with chest pains that could only be quelled by morphia injections. He was barely on his feet when he faced mounting anxiety over the lack of news from New Zealand, for it was more than three months since the relief ships had sailed from Hobart.

Suddenly, everything had come right. Two days later Markham had the satisfaction of seeing the *Terra Nova*'s voyage branded a waste of public money in Scott's first cable to the press. The money spent getting the ship to Hobart—cruisers had towed the ship through the Mediterranean and on into the Indian Ocean—would have more than covered two trips by the *Morning* had the ice not released the *Discovery*. Although Colbeck alone could not have brought enough coal for the western coastal exploration, even in two voyages, the money spent by the Admiralty had not succeeded in doing that either. Having already laid on the finance for the work in New Zealand and the voyage home, the father of the expedition would at least have breathing space before organizing the sort of reception he felt Scott and his companions deserved.

They were already reveling in their reception by the New Zealanders. Feted and entertained in a veritable Land of Eden, Wilson and his wife at last enjoyed the second honeymoon they had waited for so long. Teddy Evans and Isaac Weller both married New Zealand women, and other romances bloomed—not least with the country, where the warmth of welcome was matched by Mediterranean autumn days and the frosty nights seemed almost mellow to men who had lived in the cold for so long.

But it was not all a holiday. Scott assured Markham that he would exercise the utmost economy, so much of the work to put the ship in good order for the voyage home had to be done by the crew. The collections had to be prepared for handing over for study by the leading authorities in each discipline immediately on arrival in England. All the magnetic records had to be correlated with observations at the Christchurch base observatory. The *Discovery* did not finally sail until June 8.

Meanwhile in London, Markham was seriously ill. He still hoped to raise £15,000 by selling the *Discovery* and thereby restore the society's depleted capital. Although disappointed when an early inquiry by a potential buyer came to nothing, on May 26 a copy of the king's telegram to Scott assured him that royal approval would underpin the reception he planned for the explorers' return.

Markham had gotten the RGS Council to approve the award of a gold medal to Scott and silver replicas to those who had served two years, along with the invalided Shackleton, but the medals still had to be designed.[31] With £160 voted for the medals, Markham engaged artist Gilbert Bayes to prepare designs. He had chosen the design for the medals and was already organizing receptions at Portsmouth and London before the *Discovery* reached the Azores on August 31.

A grand luncheon was to be given by the two societies for the entire company. Markham became aware that the invitations in his and Sir William Huggins's names had gone out too late to ensure acceptance by some of the people Markham wanted to hear of the triumph of the expedition.

The reception and luncheon were to be held in a specially decorated warehouse beside the berth Markham had reserved for *Discovery* in the East India Dock. The ship would be thrown open for the guests' inspection.

On September 8 the Markhams were in Portsmouth. He discussed the civic banquet being arranged in the town hall there with the mayor while his wife was a guest at the commander in chief's home. With hordes of pressmen already in evidence, the affair became more than just a naval occasion.

Discovery was sighted at 8 A.M. on Saturday, September 10, coming from the east of the Isle of Wight. Markham was first aboard from the launch carrying the officer who would take over the instruments from Armitage. The work went on all day, with crowds thronging the shore and straining to catch a glimpse of the slightest movement aboard. By 5:30 P.M. the work was finished, and pausing off Spithead for a pinnace bringing out Scott's mother and other officers' relatives, *Discovery* steamed through the entrance, cheered from every warship, gantry, and vantage point, to tie up in the harbor.

Pursued by journalists, Scott was escorted to the commander in chief's house, where he learned he had been promoted to captain. Acclaim followed thick and fast from a public and press eager to forget the setbacks suffered in the recent Boer War.

A royal household aide-de-camp came aboard the next morning, bearing a message of congratulation from the king, and on the Monday, before the dock gates were thrown open for the public to view the ship, the *Times* carried the Admiralty's announcement of Scott's promotion and the king's approval of a new medal for polar service to be awarded to the entire ship's company. Whatever antipathy persisted in the Hydrographer's Department, Adm. Lord Walter Kerr had no such reservations, having initiated the question of such an award the first working day after the news of the ship's return reached England. Within two months he had won agreement from the First Lord (the Earl of Selborne), and the king's approval had followed at the end of July, but as with all expenditures outside the realm of defense, the awards required Treasury approval.[32]

It was hardly surprising that the cost of the formal welcome at the home of the navy had been shunted onto civic funds, so the highlight had become the banquet in the Town Hall on Tuesday evening, September 13. Scott sat on the mayor's right. Prime Minister Balfour had been quick to join the tide of royal approval, sending the Civil Lord of the Admiralty from the House of Commons to proclaim the navy's welcome. In his first public speech Scott said that with all but seven aboard being naval men, they felt it was like coming home.

The plan had been to reach London early on Thursday, but even this far from the Antarctic nature was to have the last say. With everything ready for the departure after Markham joined in a group photo on deck, an autumn gale held them in harbor for the rest of Wednesday, September 14. By 1 A.M. it had eased enough to get the ship safely out of the harbor.

Carried up the Channel under full sail, they tied up in London at 5 P.M., where they were met by many relatives and by Shackleton, whose letter of welcome to Scott had given no hint of animosity:[33]

MARKHAM, SCOTT, AND WILSON WITH MOST OF THE SHIP'S COMPANY ABOARD *DISCOVERY*, SEPTEMBER 14, 1904. Photographed the morning after the mayor's banquet. *Left to right*, at back: Quartley, Crean, Joyce, G. Scott, Handsley (behind Allen), Williamson, Clark; 4th row: Pilbeam, Weller, Heald, Allen, Kennar, Plumley, Lashly; 3rd row: Cross, Ford, Lt. Barne, S/Lt. Mulock, Feather, Dellbridge, Dailey, Smythe; seated: Lt. Royds, Sir Clements Markham, Cdr. Scott, Lt. Armitage, Lt. Skelton, Wilson; front row: Croucher, Wild, Evans, Dell. (Of those who served through two seasons, only Cpl. Blissett and Ldg. Stoker Whitfield were absent.) Courtesy, the Canterbury Museum, Christchurch, New Zealand.

My dear Captain Scott,

Just a line to welcome you safely back again after your long anxious time. I had hoped to have had a line from you but I expect you have been very busy all the time. I am so glad that the whole show has been such a complete success, and [that] you will now for a time be able to enjoy a rest from your work.

As you know no doubt, I am married and settled down as Secretary to the RSGS, the pay is only £200 a year, but it is better than going to sea; . . . I had thought of trying to go on another expedition sometime but have given up the idea now as there seems to be no money about, and besides I am settled now and have to make money. It would only break up my life if I could stand it which Wilson says I could not. I do hope to see you do the NW Passage some time. I should think you could easily get an expedition if you wanted to. . . .

I will be writing to you officially in a few days that the council of the RSGS has voted you the Livingstone Gold Medal, and I hope you will be able to open our session up here in November and receive the medal. We are going to have Sir C. M[arkham] up and make it a fine affair. You will have a most enthusiastic welcome for all of Scotland takes an interest in the Expedition. . . .

Yours very sincerely

E. H. Shackleton

With much to discuss with Scott about the societies' reception the next day, Markham arranged to dine aboard, and Shackleton was invited to join the two men for what Markham described as a "very jolly evening."[34]

As the principal guests were shown around the ship on the morning of September 16, the most tangible seal of royal approval yet arrived: an invitation to Scott to stay at Balmoral, the royal residence in the Scottish highlands. Then, with crowds gathering outside the dock gates in ever increasing numbers, the entire company, including Shackleton, marched to the luncheon to find themselves seated in what amounted to a vast marquee, in company with admirals in gold lace and welcomed by a sheriff in full regalia speaking for the city of London. Among the guests was William Bruce, who had returned that July in the *Scotia* after discovering the eastern shore of the Weddell Sea, which had effectively solved the riddle Drygalski had been sent to answer.

Markham's announcement of the royal invitation was followed by a message from the First Lord of the Admiralty that could hardly have been a more direct reversal of their attitude the year before: "Will you tell Captain Scott and his officers and men the satisfaction of the Board of Admiralty at the manner in which they have so thoroughly upheld the traditions of the Navy, and with what pleasure they greet them on their return to England."[35] In the wake of royal endorsement, even the Hydrographer Admiral Wharton had come with Capt. Mostyn Field, one of Scott's fiercest denigrators in the row over his appointment, to signify the department's conversion.

Both Markham and Scott went out of their way to praise the crew's role in the achievements.

The ship was opened to the public in the afternoon, and that evening Scott faced an audience of 280 at a dinner for the officers and scientists and their relatives at the Criterion Restaurant. Bruce was again among the guests. In a speech that anticipated some of the finest narrative in *The Voyage of the "Discovery,"* Scott accorded the scientific work pride of place—"Mr. Hodgson staggering in with his arms full of frozen specimens," Mr. Royds changing the weather records "with frozen fingers"—leaving his audience with no doubts about the contributions of the second year. He took the opportunity to praise the achievements of the Scottish expedition as precisely what everyone would have "most wished to see done."[36] Responding to the toasts, Armitage spoke particularly of Scott as a comrade as well as a commander for whom they all "felt they could do anything at any sacrifice."[37]

With Scott leaving for Balmoral on the 26th and taking photos and some of Wilson's watercolors, it became urgent to name as many as possible of the peaks and glaciers they had illustrated. Starting the work with Scott on Sunday, September 18, Markham finished the job with him and Mulock on Wednesday.

At Balmoral Scott found the atmosphere much more relaxed than he had feared—"I never had to wear knee breeches or a frock coat," he assured his mother afterward.[38] He arrived on Tuesday, and the king personally gave him the Commander's neck badge of the Royal Victorian Order before dinner, at which he sat at the king's table with, among others, the Princess of Wales, the future Queen Mary, and the prime minister.

Scott spent Wednesday preparing his lecture. He was again at the king's table for dinner. His talk went very well. It lasted nearly two hours, almost twice as long as he intended, because the king kept asking questions. The speech received flattering compliments from everyone, although Balfour's seemed more self-congratulatory when, as Scott wrote to his mother, he said "he regarded himself as the Father of the Expedition!!!!"[39]

Knowing Scott wished to send a telegram to the men being paid off on Friday, the king sent one as well for Royds to read at the ceremony attended by Markham. Scott had not forgotten the men in his report to the Admiralty either. Lashly's acting promotion to chief stoker was made substantive and backdated to June 1902; Edgar Evans was promoted from petty officer second class to PO first cass. In the biggest step-up of all, Able Seaman Thomas Crean was promoted to PO first class, with his promotion, like Scott's, dating from the day they reached Portsmouth.[40]

Markham had rented Albert Hall for November 7 and was now at work on what was to be the climax of the national acclaim: a public lecture with slides and the presentation of the RGS medals before an audience of 7,000. On top of that, the *Morning* arrived at Plymouth on October 8, and Markham was immediately involved in the mayoral reception at Hull, hurriedly arranged for the 26th. He and Scott attended, and Shackleton came down from Edinburgh for the evening.

The great evening in London arrived with just one detail not as Markham had wished. The plaster casts of the approved design had been received so late that when Allan Wyon's quote for the medals was received on October 17, it was already far too late to have even one medal ready for November 7. The society had to settle for a single dummy medal to present to Scott that night.[41]

After a dinner at the South Kensington Hotel for the American ambassador, they went to Albert Hall, where Scott and the officers, again including Shackleton, presented Markham with a model of a silver sledge before going onstage for Scott's lecture.* With the sledge flags arranged either side of the organ, they were joined onstage by the RGS Council and fourteen of the twenty-six crew members who were to receive medals, as well as Colbeck and the officers of the *Morning*.[42]

Scott's lecture, which lasted about ninety minutes and was accompanied by 150 slides, was punctuated with bursts of clapping as the more thrilling incidents were related. After he sat down to thunderous applause, Markham presented Scott with the dummy that the audience assumed was the real gold medal. He then introduced the American ambassador who had come to present the Kane Gold Medal, instituted by the Philadelphia Geographical Society in honor of the American Dr. Elisha Kent Kane, who had mounted two hazardous expeditions in search of Franklin. The ambassador's tribute to Scott included a ringing exhortation that the government of Britain and Markham's successors at the RGS pointedly ignored:[43]

> The magnificent tribute which the audience paid to Captain Scott tonight, in recognition of the hardships and perils that he has encountered and [his] great achievements could hardly be complete, I think, without a single word of sympathy from the other side of the Atlantic . . . for years and generations . . . the government and people alike [of my country] have been interested in [polar exploration] and if you will only let Captain Scott continue his great work and complete the map of the world by planting the Union Jack upon the South Pole, and let our Peary . . . plant the Stars and Stripes upon the North Pole, why then you will make the

---

* The silver sledge model is now in the National Maritime Museum at Greenwich.

two ends of this great world meet, and leave the globe . . . in the warm and fraternal embrace of the Anglo-Saxon race.

Scott's diffident speech of thanks was followed by praise from Markham for the part played by the *Morning*, its officers, and its crew, who had "done honour to the mercantile marine."[44] Presenting Captain Colbeck with a magnificent punchbowl from the Council, he explained that it was intended to represent the voyage of the *Morning*— standing over a foot high, it had the track of only the first voyage engraved on the globe that formed the cup and its lid. Colbeck's discovery was represented by the handle, which was a model of Scott Island, and three of the four kinds of truly Antarctic seals formed the base. It was a fitting tribute to Colbeck's masterly seamanship.

Scott, a torpedo lieutenant in 1899 who was now a national figure and who had certainly justified Markham's confidence in his ability, had received the congratulations of Nansen, the man whose achievements he had sought above all to emulate. Nansen had written on September 29 from his remote hideaway in the Norwegian mountains, where the news had just reached him: "I congratulate you upon your successful expedition and your great results."[45]

Scott's pay was now £410 per year, and he promptly raised his widowed mother's allowance to £200 per year, at last assuring her of the comfort he had yearned to see her enjoy. Appointed to an Admiralty job and granted half-pay leave to write the story of the expedition, he had been able to move her and his sisters to a rented house in Chelsea, more in keeping with his new status.

He may have dreamed of that status and public acclaim, but he could hardly have believed both had been realized as he listened to the dizzying series of tributes that crowned the exploits of his expedition as its story emerged.[46] In their wake, memories of the bitter disappointments at the extremes of his greatest efforts must have been placed in perspective, as the slides and maps he brought home documented the extent of his achievement.

Silver Punchbowl Presented to Lieut. William Colbeck RNR at Albert Hall, November 7, 1904. Standing about 14 inches high, the bowl is in the form of a globe engraved with a map of the world showing the track of the *Morning* on its first voyage to McMurdo Sound from New Zealand and supported by Weddell, Ross, and crabreater seals, three of the four types of seal found south of the Circle. The top half of the globe serves as the lid, with its handle topped by a model of Scott Island and Haggitt's Pillar, discovered by Colbeck on Christmas Day 1902. Engraved around its rim are the words "Bread to the full we bring you in the Morning," a reference to Moses's promise of Manna from Heaven in the book of Exodus (Ch. 16, v. 8). The inscription around the handle reads "Joy cometh in the Morning," from verse 5 of Psalm 30, which according to Gerald Doorly in *The Voyages of the Morning* (p. 105) Scott had delightedly exclaimed as he first looked through the mail in the wardroom aboard *Discovery* on February 3, 1903, the day of his return from the Southern journey. Courtesy, the late Captain William R. Colbeck, OBE (currently on display at Discovery Point, Dundee, Scotland).

CAPTAIN SCOTT'S ORDERS AND SOME OF THE GOLD MEDALS AWARDED FOR THE NATIONAL ANTARCTIC EXPEDITION, 1901–1904. *Above:* The commander's neck badge of the Royal Victorian Order, presented by the king at Balmoral, and the Polar Medal, which he received from the king at Buckingham Palace, shown with the officer's badge of the French Légion d'Honneur awarded in 1906. *Opposite:* Some of the ten gold medals awarded by leading geographical societies. Shown here are the Patron's Medal and Special Gold Medal awarded by the Royal Geographical Society of London (reverse of the latter medal is shown beside the obverse), together with the Kane Gold Medal of the Philadelphia Geographical Society and, below that, the Vega Gold Medal of the Swedish Geographical Society. Following the king's approval Scott received the Patron's Gold Medal at the London society's annual general meeting and later, before 7,000 people at Albert Hall in London on November 7, 1904, was presented with the Special Gold Medal and the Kane Gold Medal. The latter, presented by the U.S. ambassador, was America's most immediate recognition of the expedition's achievements, later followed by the Geographical Society of New York's Cullum Gold Medal and, among others, the Royal Scottish Geographical Society's Livingstone Gold Medal and the Berlin Geographical Society's Gustav Nachtigal Gold Medal. The CVO and gold medals photographed by kind permission of the late Sir Peter Scott CH, CBE, DSC, FRS. The Polar Medal and Officer's Badge of the *Légion d'Honneur* photographed and reproduced courtesy of the Canterbury Museum, Christchurch, New Zealand, to which they were presented by Sir Peter in recognition of that city's support of his father's expeditions.

EPILOGUE

THE LURE OF THE POLE
The Expedition's Fateful Legacy

For each of the seven men who had died in the Antarctic by 1904,[1] at least one more had come back with an irresistible urge to know what lay beyond the farthest south they had seen. For the author of *The Voyage of the* Discovery, Scott's account of the British expedition, the financial realities tying him to a naval career seemed to offer him no chance to assuage his ambition to reach the Pole.

The year after the expedition's return was almost entirely taken up with writing the book. At first writing at Markham's house to escape mounting social pressures at home, Scott had finally retreated to various country hotels to get the peace and quiet he needed for the task. The result was a tour de force.

The book's phenomenal success following its publication in October 1905 eased Scott's financial constraints, but it also lit the long fuse of international rivalry. In England, the two men the book most immediately inspired were Ernest Shackleton and Michael Barne. Before the month was out, Barne visited Markham to propose an expedition to the Weddell Sea coast of Graham Land that had repulsed Nordenskjöld's efforts to reach it beyond the Antarctic Circle. Scott quickly encouraged the scheme.[2]

Shackleton, who read the book in less than ten days, wrote to Scott on October 20, 1905, without a hint of the resentment later supposed to have inspired his determination to go south again: "My dear Captain Scott, Many thanks for your book which I have read with great interest. It is beautifully got up and splendidly written, though of course my opinion is only following out the general impression. Yours very sincerely, E. H. Shackleton."[3]

Adopted as candidate by the Dundee Unionist Party at the beginning of 1905, Shackleton had been out of a job since resigning from the Royal Scottish Geographical Society in July. With no election declared and his first attempt to raise money for an expedition rebuffed early that year, it took little effort to enroll his interest in Barne's scheme. Two weeks after Barne first outlined it to Markham, Shackleton joined him and Cyril Longhurst at Eccleston Square for a full review of the plan.[4]

As a result of that meeting, Barne left for Norway to cost out supplies and equipment. By the time he returned on December 5, the government had resigned, and within six weeks not only had Shackleton been defeated at the polls but implicit royal support for the new expedition had been rebuffed at the Admiralty.[5] Then, on January 18, 1906, the RGS Council refused its support.

To Shackleton and no doubt Barne, the contrast with the scene at the palace exactly a month before must have been depressing. With Scott and seven other *Discovery* comrades, they had knelt to kiss the king's hand after he had pinned the new Polar Medal to their tunics.[6]

Shackleton, who might well have joined Barne's expedition, now had no alternative but to take the job offered by William Beardmore, the Glasgow magnate, held open for him since his formal resignation as secretary of the RSGS the previous July. Happy about the birth of his daughter two days before Christmas, he seemed to give up his *Discovery* expedition contacts and did not even visit Markham when he was in London.

As for Scott, lionized by society in the wake of the instant success of his book—even Gregory was fulsome in his praise for it, although still critical of the decision to winter the ship[7]—the security of his prospects in a navy now dominated by Admiral Fisher lay in *not* returning to the Antarctic. Yet within six months he had raised the question of a new expedition with Markham, and although advised against it in the interests of his naval career,[8] the last week of September 1906 he wrote to Barne asking him to go as his first lieutenant. By coincidence, Scott's letter crossed one from Barne urging Scott to mount a new expedition.[9] Barne, who had tried and failed once more to raise funds, quickly accepted Scott's offer and was happy to go on to half pay, but he could not get his release until the following March.[10]

Scott's resolve to go south again was cemented when Markham came to Gibraltar as the guest of the admiral commanding the Atlantic fleet, and Scott accompanied him on a brief visit to Majorca.[11] The road to the Pole was to be conquered with motorized sledges, and they would need to be developed from scratch. Scott would not be free until he had served a year in command at sea. That meant he could not opt to go on half pay before August 1907. So Barne would have to find someone to design and build a prototype sledge for testing in Arctic conditions. In the meantime, before Christmas 1906 Scott let the RGS secretary, Scott-Keltie, and president, Sir George Goldie, know in confidence of his intentions.[12] Shortly afterward, he asked Mulock if he would join the expedition.

Never dreaming that Shackleton was also contemplating another expedition after what he had written in his letter to Portsmouth, Scott did not think of writing to him. His isolation in civilian life had sown the seeds of conflict athwart Scott's road to the Pole as surely as the events of February 1907 would germinate them. On Boxing Day Shackleton wrote to Mill: "I see nothing of the old *Discovery* people at all. We are all scattered and the fickle public are tired of the polar work at present. What I would not give to be out there again doing the job, and this time really on the road to the Pole!"[13]

Beardmore admired Shackleton for what he had done for the RSGS. Shackleton's yearning to try for the Pole beyond the mountains he had photographed from their farthest south three years before was ripe for the slightest pretext to ask his employer to back an expedition for that purpose. The pretext arose before the first month of the new year was out. In late January 1907 Shackleton learned of an attempt to reach the Pole with motorized sledges from McMurdo Sound being planned by Henryk Arctowski of De Gerlache's Belgian expedition. It took Shackleton three weeks to muster courage to put his idea to Beardmore.[14] As he guessed, the spur of the continental challenge to British aspirations did the trick. "I at last took my courage in both hands and asked him straight out, and he came up splendidly," Shackleton wrote to Mulock a month later, unaware that Mulock also knew of Scott's intentions.[15]

Shackleton met with Beardmore on Sunday, February 10, and he knew Arctowski was going to be at Amundsen's Northwest Passage lecture at the RGS the following day. Hastening to London to assure himself of RGS moral support, he first tried to see Markham, but as fate would have it the man who above all would have told him of Scott's plans was on holiday in Majorca.[16]

Going to the RGS he went straight to the secretary's room, where Arctowski had just assured Keltie he was far from having the funds to mount his expedition but still hoped to sail in October 1908.[17] Keltie accordingly told Shackleton he had nothing to fear. Goldie gave Shackleton the assurance he sought, but imagining themselves bound to the strictest confidence, neither man breathed a word of Scott's intentions. Thus, for the second time that day, the vital information that would have put the two men in touch and thus left the field clear for Scott was denied to the man who would have been the first to do so.

Later that afternoon Arctowski told Shackleton about his plans, including the ordering of a ship from Dundee, and said he would probably announce the plans at the dinner that evening.[18] Shackleton thus was forced to announce his own plans at the dinner to forestall the Belgian. Having done so, he would have to release the news to the press, so he contacted the *Times* that night.

The sensational announcement reached Scott a week later in the wake of an unnerving accident on night maneuvers in which the battleship ahead of his failed to give the signal that would have avoided a collision. The two letters he wrote to Shackleton on February 18, 1907, from HMS *Albemarle* were mild considering his ambitions would be ruined if Shackleton forestalled him:[19]

> My dear Shackleton, I see by the Times of Feb. 12th that you are organising an expedition to go on our old tracks and this is the first I have heard of it. The situation is awkward for me as I have already announced my intention to try again in the old place, and have been in treaty concerning the matter. As a matter of fact I have always intended to try again but as I am dependent on the Navy I was forced to reinstate myself and get some experience before I again asked for leave, meanwhile I thought it best to keep my plans dark—but I have already commenced fresh preparations and Michael Barne is in London seeing to things in preparation for August when I shall be free to begin work myself. You see therefore that your announcement cuts right across my plans and to an extent which it would not have done two months ago when I first intimated them to the Geographical Society and others.
>
> I needn't tell you that I don't wish to hurt you and your plans but in one way I feel I have a sort of right to my own field of work in the same way as Peary claimed Smith's Sound and many African travellers their particular locality. I am sure you will agree with me in this and I am equally sure that only your entire ignorance of my plan could have made you settle on the *Discovery* route without a word to me. . . . I was going to delay my attempt [until] later as I don't want to take anything that is not well tested.

Finishing with kind regards to Mrs. Shackleton, Scott added a postscript: "I feel sure with a little discussion we can work in accord rather than in opposition. I don't believe the foreigners will do anything much. The whole area is ours to attack."

Later that day Scott wrote the second letter, clearly feeling he owed Shackleton more explanation (the letter is undated, but Shackleton's reply makes it clear it was mailed the same day):[20]

> I ought perhaps to explain to you what has been my attitude with regard to the South a little more carefully as I wrote in some haste. I have never abandoned the wish or intention of getting up another expedition but I have had to be guided by certain circumstances which did not allow me to be a free agent. You know that I support my mother and family, it is therefore essential for me to have an assured income. Now if I had taken steps immediately after our return I should have had to practically chuck the Navy, my only source of assured income. I therefore decided to be very quiet about the matter, to go back to my profession and accept appointments which would give me the chance of getting quite up to date in Naval matters.

Explaining that in August he could apply to go on half pay, having gained the year's experience at sea with the fleet necessary to his future prospects, Scott went on to say that perhaps he had been wrong to keep his intentions quiet, having feared Admiralty reaction. He had already received several offers of support, but he had also feared "press criticism" if plans were announced before adequate finance was assured.

Again asserting his right to continue exploration from the old winter quarters, Scott went on: "I don't want to be selfish at anyone's expense and least of all at that of one of my own people, but still I think anyone who has had to do with exploration will regard this region primarily as mine,"[21] arguing that, as everyone he had met abroad in October 1900 had conceded, the area belonged to the English "on account of Ross" and that surely the same principle should apply among the English. Like Peary, the French explorer Charcot, already planning a new expedition after his tantalizing discoveries on the 1903–1905 voyage of the *Français*, also subscribed to that view.

Telling Shackleton that having recruited Barne he had revealed his intentions to Goldie, Keltie, "and several others" in December, Scott continued:[22]

> The reason I did not write to you was because it never entered my head that you had a wish to go on. I have imagined you as very busy with various business schemes and surrounded with increasing home ties, otherwise you may be sure I would have written to you; I had naturally no object in keeping any of our old company in the dark, [for] you know well how attached I am to all and how gladly I would take anyone who cared to come again.

I think therefore you will now see how and why I was surprised to hear first of your scheme through the medium of a newspaper, besides being a good deal hurt that in any case you shouldn't have said a word to me. I find you directly cutting across my plans . . . but feel sure that you knew nothing of them.*

At this point the tone of the letter hardened, and the intensity of Scott's ambition to complete the goal that had eluded him burned in the words as he continued:[23]

The question now is what you intend to do? On the one hand I do not wish to stand in the way of any legitimate scheme of yours—on the other it must be clear to you now that you have placed yourself directly in the way of my life's work—a thing for which I have sacrificed much and worked with steady purpose. Two expeditions cannot go to the same spot either together or within the compass of several years. If you go to McMurdo Sound you go to winter quarters which are clearly mine, and I must either abandon my plans or go elsewhere. Let me know plainly how you look at this matter. I do not like to remind you that it was I who took you to the South or of the loyalty with which we all stuck to one another or of incidents of one [journey] or of my readiness to do you justice on our return . . . at least they must command a full explanation and deference to each other's plans.

Then more calmly, explaining that the fleet would be in home waters in late April, which would allow them to meet, he went on:[24]

I do not know how far you have gone but I should be glad to know as I think at present that there are quite a number of ways in which a compromise could be arrived at and I feel sure that you will be anxious to clear this rock ahead. . . . I want to benefit by every atom of experience we gained, to go slowly and deliberately to work to ensure the perfection of detail and finally to do something that is worthy of our Country. My dear fellow it would be a thousand pities to rush this effort that should crown the Discovery work—we can well afford to wait and none of us are clamouring for sensation.

I am writing these main facts to Wilson—he is a person I think who commands our respect and who could not be otherwise than straight. I shall ask his advice and ask him to communicate with you. . . . I feel we must not make a fiasco . . . there should be heads together for . . . the

---

* Given Shackleton's breakdown on the Southern journey, the implication that Scott would have been ready to ask him to join can only have been the product of a theoretical confidence in the tractors he hoped to develop, for one can hardly imagine him inviting Shackleton to be part of the Pole Party. Scott's critics have doubtless viewed this passage as disingenuous.

worst thing possible would be a half success as it must put the clock back for half a century.

Well goodbye for the present, the subject is very close to my heart so please write openly and freely.

The letters took a week to reach Shackleton, who the day after Scott wrote had been astounded to learn of Scott's intention to mount another expedition. He had already written to Wilson, Barne, and Mulock asking them to join his, and Mulock's reply, which reached him on the 19th, contained the totally unexpected news that he had agreed to join Scott's expedition.[25]

For more than fifteen anguished days, Scott waited for Shackleton's reply. Writing first on February 27, explaining developments up to the press announcement, Shackleton dated the letter the 28th and sent it to Wilson to forward if he approved. Promising to consult with Wilson and Barne, he ended with an assurance of his willingness to cooperate within limits: "You may rest assured that everything you write will have the fullest consideration . . . naturally I would like to fall in with your views as far as possible without creating a position that would be untenable to myself in view of the arrangements already made."[26]

Shackleton's anguish was if anything greater than Scott's, as Keltie sensed when, after four sleepless nights, Shackleton sought his advice on Thursday, March 1.[27] By that stage he was even thinking of attacking the Pole from the Weddell Sea, for Wilson had written the day before: "Now Shackles, I think your position is quite clear and no one can say you have not behaved as straight as daylight about it, but I think you ought to offer to retire from McMurdo Sound as a base. . . . It is no small matter in my mind to say so to you—because it largely diminishes your prospects of a big or the biggest success. But I do wholly agree with the right lying with Scott to use that base before anyone else."[28] Saying he was sure Arctowski would alter his plan when he knew Scott's intentions, Wilson went on:[29]

> I think that if you go to McMurdo Sound and even reach the Pole the gilt will be off the gingerbread because of the insinuation that will almost certainly appear in the minds of a good many, that you forestalled Scott who had a prior claim to the use of the base.
>
> Now my boy, a friend is worse than an enemy if he doesn't tell you what he thinks—and that is really what I think . . . [and] having upheld your position to Scott, I want to see you follow it up by the very best possible [action].
>
> One's motives are always mixed, but I think that the tarnished honour of getting the Pole even, as things have turned out, will be worth infinitely less than the honour of dealing generously with Scott. One never loses by

being quixotic, if this really appears to you quixotic. I have written in great haste, but I hope I have shown you my mind as a friend of yours and Scott's. Yours ever, "Bill."

That letter must have added to Shackleton's mental torture as he went to see Keltie. The interview unquestionably caused him to determine to give way, a decision that earned him scant applause from some of the supporters he went to see before discussing the alternatives with Wilson in Cheltenham on Sunday, March 4. From there he sent the painful telegram to Scott: "Will meet your wishes regarding base. Please keep absolutely private at present as certain supporters must be brought round to the new position. Please await second letter. Shackleton."[30]

That letter, written on the 7th,[31] made it clear that had he heard a word of Scott's intentions, he would have written to advise him of the need to announce them before the Belgians announced their own plans, explaining that he still doubted whether they would defer to the British claim to the area, even though it had been negotiated with the Germans in the wake of the 1895 International Geographical Congress.

They could decide in due course the best method and timing of the announcement of the change in his plans. Agreeing that Scott was right in believing he would do anything in his power to clear "the rock ahead," he felt it necessary to explain once more:[32]

> I was quite of the opinion that you had given up all idea of ever going south again because of your position in the Service, which you said down south would preclude you from continuing this work, and even in your book you say that the pages are written for those who come after you. It is the last thing in the world for me to ever wish to forestall or cut across anybody's plans as long as they are British, but you will realise the urgency of the matter to my mind in view of what you now know the Belgians proposed doing, though, of course, they have not made a public declaration to the effect that they were going to our quarters. . . . I would like to know when you propose to start, and hope, when you do, that you will have as successful a trip as the Discovery had.

Scott quickly apologized for the suspicions that had haunted him, as they had Wilson for a time, writing on March 12:[33]

> I write not only to acknowledge your telegram and the letter which followed it. I realise that you have been placed in a difficult position and therefore I should like to have time for thought before replying to your questions or making suggestions. I need not wait however to clear up one misconception which has given me a good deal of trouble—until you wrote I could hold no other opinion but that you had known of my plan before you published your scheme and had rushed it to be first in the

field. I am sorry to have done you this injustice and I think it right to tell you how it came about.

In January I had several talks to Keltie about my purpose and at our last meeting I explained to him my position and my desire to work quietly on for the present till I was free to devote my whole time to the subject. He knew everything except the steps I afterward took to make Barne my agent (so to speak) [and] with a preliminary programme arranged between us I am not sure he did not know about Barne. Anyway he knew my plan perfectly well.

Soon after I had read your statement in the Times I had a long letter from Keltie telling me he had seen you and discussed the whole thing before you published, and giving me to understand you had acted against his advice.

It seemed incredible that during this interview he should have told you nothing of my intentions, but in subsequent letters he acknowledges that this was so.

I therefore have the relief of knowing that you did not intentionally wreck my plans and the thought that you had done so was very distressing to me, for it seemed an action of which an old *Discovery* [shipmate] should have been incapable and one that surprised me beyond measure in you.

I apologise for having thought you guilty of it.

The letter went on to show how Keltie's silence now looked extremely suspicious to Scott, and it was only after posting it that he got Keltie's and Wilson's March 8 letters and learned why Keltie had said nothing.[34] Wilson, too, had come to the same conclusion after Shackleton's visit, finding Keltie's silence "inconceivable," as his March 8 letter shows:[35]

Before all else I want to assure you of two things with regard to Shackleton. First that he came here fully convinced that it was right for him to give up the idea of using McMurdo Sound as his base, and secondly that when he allowed his plans to be published in the papers he had not the ghost of a suspicion that you had any intention of going South again. I cannot help thinking that Keltie made a great mistake in not immediately wiring to Barne at any rate, or in not giving Shackleton some hint which would have saved him from putting himself into such a difficult position. Yet even so, if he had given him such a hint, I believe Shackleton would have announced his plans to cover McMurdo Sound, because he was absolutely convinced in his own mind that the Belgians were on the point of claiming it. Whether rightly or wrongly I cannot say, but in that case he would have at once explained to you that it was done provisionally to assert your right and to avoid premature publicity of your plans. It has really been a very difficult thing for Shackleton to see what was the right thing to do, but that he fully means to do it I am now quite sure.

When I answered your first letter I was not so free from doubt as I am now for I also thought it was inconceivable that Keltie could have allowed him to proceed and publish his plans without giving him a hint of your intentions. But he did not and Shackleton only heard of it accidentally afterward.

Wilson went on to recap events up to Shackleton's visit to Cheltenham and how Shackleton had asked whether he thought an attempt to establish his base in King Edward VII Land would be open to objection. Unfortunately, having told Shackleton that he thought it would not, Wilson opened the door to just such an objection:[36]

> But it now occurs to me that you may have some intentions in that direction yourself and that you might not care to limit yourself at this early stage to McMurdo Sound itself. Altogether I think you will be wise to let him know your views on other possible bases as soon as you can to save further trouble and disappointment, and I shall advise him not to settle anything in a hurry now until he knows more of your views. He thinks of course of Weddell's Sea, and the Magnetic Pole, but everything is uncertain except that he starts this year for somewhere.

Wilson wrote Shackleton the same day reflecting his unfounded suspicion that Scott might object to Shackleton's proposed King Edward VII Land base: "Don't on any account make up your new plans until you know definitely from Scott what limits he puts to his rights."[37] Shackleton, too, could respond angrily under stress, writing on March 11:[38]

> Dear Billy, please excuse typewritten letter but I am very rushed as usual. I have received your letter this morning dated the 8th of March, and note all you say. . . . I do not agree with you, Billy, about holding up my plans until I hear what Scott considers his rights. There is no doubt in my mind that his rights end at the base he asked for, or within reasonable distance of that base. I will not consider that he has any right to King Edward the Seventh's Land, and only regard it as a direct attempt to keep me out of the Ross quarter if he should even propose such a thing. [Scott had not, as he was quick to say in the next paragraph.] I have given way to him in the greatest thing of all and my limit has been reached. Furthermore I wrote to him on the 8th telling him I was going to King Edward the Seventh's Land if I got away on time.

He went on to recap the arguments, the crux of which was, as he reminded Wilson, that Scott had written "I do not think the foreigners will do much. The whole area is ours to attack."[39] He had not said "the whole area is mine to attack."

Shackleton had followed up his March 7 letter to Scott with one from his club in London the next day, telling of his decision to site his base in King Edward VII Land.[40] Scott's reply raised no objection to Shackleton's plan, revealing that he himself had proposed the eastern end of the barrier in his first letter to Wilson, for his real aim all along had been the same as Shackleton's: to push south beyond the farthest point they had reached in 1902. It was the original southern dream—the Pole itself—but this time with motorized sledges. Now, at Wilson's prompting, he suggested in a letter dated March 16 that they agree to operate either side of the 170W meridian, clearly because one of the questions left unanswered had been how far the barrier extended beyond the farthest point reached by Royds:[41]

I have been so much pushed by my work that I have not been able to send a carefully considered reply to your letters during the past week. I will deal now only with that of the 7th and the short note written from your Club on the 8th.

In the first place you know that I am now aware that you fixed on the *Discovery* winter quarters without knowledge of my plans and that since you have learned of them you agree in a very honourable manner to modify your scheme.

I hope you will understand that although I much regret that there was no understanding or communication before you published, I fully realise the difficulties of your position and the sacrifice you are making.

Some days before receiving your note of the 8th I wrote to Wilson concerning a change of your plan to K.E. Land and the Eastern end of the Barrier. I see you have decided on that region and candidly I believe there is very great work to be done there, and as great a prospect of reaching a high latitude as to the Westward. It will be a great work alone to find out what K.E. Land is like and what it is made of. At all events and in any case my heartiest good wishes will go with you and I shall seize the earliest opportunity to give you my views on what you should strive for.

I am not sure that you require such a very good ship for [that] region—we saw some heavy ice but no pack under pressure, also the prevailing wind is off shore. I believe you could certainly land and winter anywhere between the balloon inlet and the ice inlets off the Eastern land.

I suppose you are still intent on getting away this year—1908 is the earliest I can hope for. In any case whether we go the same year or on different ones it is well to definitely agree on a demarcation of our spheres of work. I propose a mutual agreement not to operate beyond the 170 meridian W.

You ask what I intend to do. My plan is to get South beyond our farthest point. Of course with the aid of mechanical propulsion—I foresee great difficulties in obtaining this and until the perfected machine exists it is no use attempting to start—that is my first object. . . . My experience with machines of many kinds makes me very cautious in relying on their excellence and so I look for exhaustive trials with the watchword of "patience"—of course I also want to clear up all the other points we left in doubt—the geology of Victoria Land and its extension beyond Cape North. . . . . Now as regards publication. My position is this: an announcement from me would in my opinion be premature—it was in my mind to make none until I could announce that I had a workable machine that had been thoroughly tested. The position will then be so very much stronger. . . .

There is little doubt now that I shall be in London in May. Half an hour's conversation will do more than many letters. . . . Hoping you will surmount your preparation difficulties.

Shackleton responded immediately to reserve his rights until their meeting after the fleet was back at Chatham, rightly pointing out that the 170W meridian might make "a position untenable to me on my Southward journey," continuing "I am ready to discuss the whole matter but I want you to understand I do not look upon either Wood Bay or the land to the west of Cape North as being within the province of any particular previous expedition."[42]

The two men met on May 17, and although Shackleton conceded the entire Victoria Land coast, including Wood Bay, Scott agreed *the 170W meridian should not impede Shackleton's journey south* [my emphasis] or his exploration of Wilkes's coast beyond the Balleny Islands. Shackleton recorded the agreement in a letter dated that day from his expedition office at No. 9 Regent Street:[43]

My dear Captain Scott,

To make everything clear as regards our arrangements and plans for the two Expeditions to the Ross Quadrant of the Antarctic, I am following your suggestion and writing it down. [Here he reiterated why he had agreed to change his plan.]

I am leaving the McMurdo Sound base to you, and will land either at the place known as Barrier Inlet or at King Edward VII Land whichever is most suitable; if I land at either of these places I will not work to the westward of the 170 meridian W. and shall not make any sledge journey going west of that meridian *unless prevented when going south from keeping to the East of that meridian by the physical features of the country* [my italics]. If I encounter mountains and it is possible to ascend them by the glaciers, I shall do so.

I do not, however, expect, and neither do you, that there will be any land or open sea that will necessitate my going to the west of 170 W.

I propose to make one journey to the South of King Edward VII Land, one journey to the East and one to the Northeast.

He went on to say he would try to leave a note describing what he had achieved at Cape Adare and then explore west of the Balleny

Islands before returning to New Zealand, adding "I shall not touch the coast of Victoria Land at all."[44] If it proved impossible to land east of the demarcation line, he would try to get ashore south of where Drygalski, and before him the Challenger expedition, had been turned back.

Three days later the newspapers signaled that the international challenge was far from dead. Arctowski had withdrawn, but now Cook was said to be starting in July for a base within 750 miles of the Pole, and that could only mean the Ross Sea area. Shackleton found an article in *Harper's Weekly* that actually named Ross Island as the base. He hesitated no longer and announced his change of plan. But although Markham advised Scott that it might be good to announce his intentions, Scott reckoned Cook's threat was of little account and continued to keep his plans from the public and Admiralty ears.[45] Events proved him right, and the American challenge never materialized.

Nature, as the public learned the following March 10, was no respecter of theoretical agreements. On January 26, 1908, Shackleton, aboard the 1866 Dundee-built 300-ton sealer *Nimrod*, had found no haven at the eastern end of the barrier. Dangerous ice blocked the way to King Edward VII Land, and Borchgrevink's Inlet and Balloon Bight had become a single 80-mile-wide bay.[46] Huge amounts of the barrier had broken away. If they set up base there, how much more might fracture into icebergs and carry them away or capsize and destroy them all?

To shift his base to the *Challenger* coast or even the nearer eastern Wilkes sightings or to the sea that might lie beyond them had been impossible because the 500-ton Norwegian sealer *Bjorn* had proved too expensive to buy. After landing the shore party, the *Nimrod*'s coal capacity would barely cover the return voyage to New Zealand. Not to go to McMurdo Sound would have meant returning with nothing, for funds would not stretch to another try a year later. Shackleton had seen no alternative to the agonizing decision to renege on his promise to Scott.

The news reached England as the train carrying Scott's prototype sledge traveled toward Briançon in the French Alps, shipped for trials in Alpine winter conditions the previous afternoon with those built for Barne (at Scott's instigation) and the French explorer Jean Charcot, preparing for his second attempt to get ashore at or beyond Alexander I Land.[47] The trials were not a success for Scott's sledge and even less so for Barne's, built, like Charcot's, at the De Dion Bouton works outside Paris. Although Charcot's performed quite well in the end, Skelton did not think it had much pulling power.[48]

SCOTT'S PROTOTYPE MOTORIZED SLEDGE AT LAUTARET PASS, 1908. Skelton is holding the hammer, with Scott looking on beyond him. Courtesy, the Scott Polar Research Institute.

News of Scott's intentions had leaked out in Paris. A reference to his "next expedition"[49] appeared in the report of the trials in *Le Monde Illustré*, which described the British team as helping Charcot. Scott can hardly have evaded divulging the reason for his visit when he was invited to the Paris Academie des Sciences on his return through Paris.[50]

Even so, Scott still wanted the news kept out of the British press, so when the news from the Antarctic reached him all he could do was wait for a year and see what happened. Shackleton had established his base at Cape Royds on Ross Island, 20 miles north of Hut Point.

The cloud hanging over Scott's plan was alleviated by his conviction that Shackleton could not reach the Pole without the sort of mechanical help Scott was patiently developing. Keltie was sure Shackleton would break down on any long sledge journey, but it remained a cloud that was joined by another before his wedding to Kathleen Bruce on September 2.

The prospect of marriage may have had something to do with his decision not to go on half pay, but the new Fisher "broom" sweeping through the navy probably demanded more than a year's service at sea to avoid damaging his prospects. The demands of service life had grown more intensive following his appointment to command the flagship of the Nore Division, HMS *Bulwark*, just eight days after the meeting with Shackleton on May 17, 1907. The dilemma of future prospects versus the expedition was resolved when Scott was appointed naval assistant at the Admiralty.

He took up his post on March 26, 1909, the day the news of Shackleton's success was being shouted in the streets outside the Scotts' new home at 174 Buckingham Palace Road. A friend visiting the re-united couple at the time recorded that Scott had enthusiastically traced the journey on a map spread over his knees.[51] Interviewed by reporters, his generous reaction reached Shackleton by cable. Even Markham, who received the news two days later, could not suppress his interest, setting out the principal details in his diary without a word of criticism, although skeptical of the latitude: "Shackleton places himself 88°23S in 162°[E] long, but dead reckoning! . . . Away 126 days, he gives himself 1706 statute miles including relays!"[52]

Scott wanted nothing said of the promise that had been doubly broken, for the coast of Victoria Land had been traversed by the Mag-netic Pole Party despite the agreement to leave it to Scott. Although he doubted the latitude, Scott never allowed it to show and was the first to greet Shackleton at Charing Cross Station on June 14. He attended the lunch the Royal Societies' Club gave for the Shackletons the next day and presided at the Savage Club dinner and at the Albert Hall presentation of the RGS Special Gold Medal. Scott's praise did much to win the geographical world's acclaim for the rival whose ex-pedition had received scant official support from the society.

Rumors of an American expedition to the Antarctic then surfaced and had gained the status of "reliable" reports by the time Cook's and Peary's claims to have reached the North Pole hit the headlines the first week of September. Within a week the official announcement of Scott's plans appeared in the *Times* on Monday, September 13, 1909, with an appeal for £40,000. The main object was "to reach the South Pole and to secure for the British Empire the honour of this achieve-ment." It was the only one likely to gain public support. The expedi-tion office at 36 Victoria Street was rented that same day.

The claim had been staked not a day too soon, for on September 15 a Reuter message from Newfoundland gave the "absolutely authen-tic" news that Peary had decided on an expedition to the South Pole.[53] By then German Lt. Wilhelm Filchner had also announced his inten-tion to aim for the Pole from the Ross Sea.

The race for the Pole was on, and Scott had been forced to reveal his intentions before the motorized sledges were perfected. He could well be obliged to leave with their development unfinished, for the

SKELTON'S PROTOTYPE TWIN-TRACKED MOTOR TRACTOR AT 1909 LILLEHAMMER TRIALS IN NORWAY. Scott (*right*) looks on as Skelton supervises operations. Bernard Day, returned from Shackleton's *Nimrod* expedition, is adjusting the track. Courtesy, Messrs. Sotheby and Co.

sailing date could not be delayed beyond the following June. With their reliability far from established in the two test outings so far, Scott decided his chances could not be left to the sledges alone. That decision was all the more justified six months later, when Charcot wrote on the way back from his second expedition, "I have lost all confidence in motors for Polar sledge work."[54] Once again Scott found himself compelled to prepare in less than a year.

Peary's challenge came to nothing. But an unseen adversary had silently changed his goal once the North Pole fell to the American. Amundsen, untied by the demands of a shore job, had been preparing his new expedition ever since he had announced it in November 1907.

His plan had been to complete what Nansen had partly done and not only drift across the Arctic Sea to Alaska but garner in the North

Pole on the way. That, he knew, was vital to financial success—it had probably underlain the new King Haakon's support and gift of over £1,000. The scheme had become possible only when Nansen ceded his right to use the *Fram*, which by then belonged to the state. However, from September onward Amundsen had worked quietly at the additions he would need for the longest sledge journey he would ever undertake—the one to the other Pole.

Within two days of the news of Peary's North Pole claim reaching Norway, Amundsen had ordered fifty Greenland dogs from the inspector of North Greenland in Copenhagen. He soon knew where to take them. He had found the first clue in Scott's February 1905 lecture to the RGS: "I am inclined to place the eastern limit of the floating portion of the barrier near the inlet which we entered in 163°W *as the ice cliff to the east of this has not broken away since Sir James Ross traced it. Mr. Ferrar thought he actually saw . . . a tide crack*" [my italics].[55]

Now, on November 4, 1909, Shackleton's book appeared in Norwegian, and Amundsen read of how at about midnight on February 23, 1908, the *Nimrod* had entered what had been Balloon Bight, only to find it was an open bay full of whales. "Our astonishment was great to see beyond the six or seven miles of flat bay ice. . . . Due south of us and rising to a height of approximately eight hundred feet, were steep and rounded cliffs, and behind them sharp peaks."[56] There was a sketch of the scene by the expedition artist George Marston, which although the peaks he depicted were less than sharp, showed what was unmistakably land beyond the barrier cliffs.[57]

Amundsen must have been aware of the brief statements about Scott's expedition aims appended to the reports of Scott's wedding in the London press that autumn and of the significance of Scott's next tractor trials at Lillehammer, not far from Oslo, in March 1909. For a multitude of reasons ranging from fear of Nansen's retraction of the *Fram* to parliamentary disapproval, Amundsen could say nothing in public. But it was probably the talk of British rights to the Ross Sea area, which had echoed from Shackleton's expedition, that deterred him from telling Scott when the announcement of Scott's expedition appeared in the Norwegian papers on September 18.

Unlike Filchner, who had respected the fledgling territorial rights implicit in the 1895 Geographical Congress Resolutions by publicly opting for the Weddell Sea route, to abandon his new intention in favor of Scott might win Amundsen the acclaim of chivalry, but it would kill his expedition as surely as announcing his intentions. In spite of the support he might lose from the Norwegian parliament

Bay of Whales, January 1908. Marston's sketch that told Amundsen where to establish his base. Reproduced from Shackleton's *The Heart of the Antarctic*.

(over £6,000), there was only one thing to do: set off first and announce the change when no one could do anything about it.

The scene was set for the third great conflict in the struggle for the Poles. The second had already broken out between Peary and Cook over the latter's claim to have reached the North Pole before Peary. Like the first between Scott and Shackleton, silence had sown the seeds of the third. Memories of its bitter harvest would echo down the years, as long as the controversy over the two Americans' claims.

Amundsen's challenge was first revealed in the telegram he sent from Madeira, which Scott received on arrival at Melbourne. It simply said, "Am going south" without a word of Amundsen's intended base. A dramatic meeting in the Bay of Whales followed when the *Terra Nova*, sent east to establish a second base on King Edward VII Land, encountered the *Fram* with Amundsen's hut already erected. Scott refused to be panicked into haste, but the fear that the others might get there first would overhang the British journey as much as the British potential had overhung the Norwegians', for whom the tractors spelled the greatest threat, every mile of their way to the Pole.

Given another year or two for their development and with Skelton in charge of them, the tractors in their final twin-tracked form—forerunners of the tank in World War I and the key to modern polar travel—would almost certainly have proved successful. Scott wrote in his 1911 diary that a "season of experiment with a small workshop at hand" might have been all that stood in the way of success.[58] As it was, the brief third testing at Fefor in Norway, with virtually no running on hard ice, was inadequate to reveal the troubles that would beset them on the expedition. The last tractor would be abandoned east of White Island after a run of 50 miles.

The resulting race first saw the triumph of Scott's arrival at the Pole slighted by the bitter sight of Amundsen's tent and then by the long struggle back, which ended in tragedy for Scott and his companions. All the while, the evidence that would perhaps have avoided the tragedy lay undetected in London among the specimens Hartley Ferrar had brought back.

Unaware, as were the geologists, of the secret (the Glossopteris and other plant fossils) locked in those rocks, Scott and his companions had spent half a day obtaining 35 pounds of fresh specimens* from the head of Beardmore Glacier and dragged them for forty days in the hope that they would reveal the age of the Beacon sandstone and the key to the origin of Antarctica, which they did—in contrast to those brought back by Shackleton, which had not.[59] To those rocks must be ascribed the loss of three lives (although not the deaths of Oates or Evans), for they had increased the average load by a tenth. That would have more than cost them the thirtieth gain (barely 500 yards) in their average daily advance, which would have brought them to the life-saving One Ton Depot *before* the fatal blizzard struck.[60]

The lure of the Pole had exacted its greatest sacrifice just eight short years after the return of the Discovery Expedition, the first to unveil the true nature of the Antarctic Continent since Ptolemy propounded a terra incognita in the second century and Leonardo da Vinci first guessed its outline during Henry VIII's reign. That achievement should more famously accord Scott and his pioneer companions an enduring place in the roll of those honored for discovery.

---

* Contemptuously dismissed by Huntford (1979: p. 556) as "a pathetic little gesture to salvage something from defeat at the Pole," claiming that the specimens meant almost nothing, as Shackleton "had already done most of the work."

APPENDIX 1

INSTRUCTIONS TO THE COMMANDER OF THE NATIONAL ANTARCTIC EXPEDITION AND THE DIRECTOR OF THE SCIENTIFIC STAFF

Note: The instructions to Scott as commander (RGSAA:1/11 in the RGS Antarctic archive), handed to him by Sir Clements on Saturday, August 3, aboard *Discovery* anchored in Stokes Bay off Gosport (before it sailed the following Tuesday), were dated May 20, 1901, and signed by the presidents of the two societies and the three representatives of each who had hammered out the final version of both these and the scientific director's instructions (RGSAA:1/10). A copy of the latter document was attached to Scott's instructions. Scott had long known the content The original version of the scientific director's instructions, signed by the two presidents only, was probably handed to Dr. George Murray when he joined the following day, despite the fact that he had only been granted sufficient leave from the British Museum to allow him to accompany the expedition as far as Melbourne, which meant that the scientific staff would be under Scott's orders after that. The copy in the RGS archives is undated. As it names Louis Bernacchi as the physicist, it must have been printed after he accepted the post on July 27, 1901.

Passages in italics indicate the instructions that can be seen to have decisively shaped Scott's decisions during the course of the expedition. Passages in square brackets have been inserted to provide additional information or to clarify technical expressions.

I: INSTRUCTIONS TO THE COMMANDER

1. The Royal Society and the Royal Geographical Society, with the assistance of His Majesty's Government, have fitted out an expedition for scientific discovery and exploration in the Antarctic Regions, and have entrusted you with the command.

2. The objects of the Expedition are (a) to determine, as far as possible, the nature, condition and extent of that portion of the South

Polar lands which is included in the scope of your Expedition; and (b) to make a magnetic survey in the southern regions to the south of the 40th parallel and to carry on meteorological, oceanographic, geological, biological and physical investigations and researches. Neither of these objects is to be sacrificed to the other.

3. The scientific work of the Executive officers of the ship will be under your immediate control, and will include magnetic and meteorological observations, astronomical observations, surveying and charting, and sounding operations.

4. Associated with you but under your command, there will be a civilian scientific staff, with a Director at their head. A copy of his instructions accompanies these instructions to you.

5. In all questions connected with the scientific conduct of the Expedition you will, as a matter of course, consider the Director as your colleague, and on all these matters you will observe such consideration in respect to his wishes and suggestions as may be consistent with a due regard to the instructions under which you are acting, to the safe navigation of the ship, and to the comfort, health, discipline and efficiency of all under your command. Those healthy relations and unreserved communications should be maintained between you which will tend so materially to the success of an expedition from which so many important results are looked for.

6. As the scientific objects of the Expedition are manifold, some of them will come under the immediate supervision of the Director and his staff; others will depend for their success on the joint co-operation of the naval and civil elements; while some will demand the undivided attention of yourself and your officers. Upon the harmonious working and hearty co-operation of all must depend the result of the Expedition as a whole.

7. The Expedition will be supplied with a complete set of magnetic instruments, both for observations at sea and on shore. Instructions for their use have been drawn up by Captain Creak, R.N. [Director of Compasses in the Royal Navy Hydrographer's Department who was appointed Commander of the Bath later that year], and yourself and three of your officers [Armitage, Royds, and Barne] have gone through a course of instruction at Deptford with Capt. Creak and at Kew Observatory. The magnetic observatory on board the *Discovery* has been carefully constructed with a view to securing it from any proximity to steel or iron, and this has involved considerable expense and some sacrifice in other respects. We, therefore, impress upon you that the greatest importance is attached to the series of magnetic

observations to be taken under your superintendence, and we desire that you will spare no pains to ensure their accuracy and continuity. The base station for your magnetic work will be at Melbourne, or at Christchurch in New Zealand. *A secondary base station is to be established by you, if possible, in Victoria Land.* You should endeavour to carry the magnetic survey from the Cape to your primary base station south of the 40th parallel, and from the same station across the Pacific to the meridian of Greenwich. It is also desired that *you should observe along the tracks of Ross in order to ascertain the magnetic changes that have taken place in the interval between the two voyages.*

8. Geographical discovery and scientific exploration by sea and land should be conducted in two quadrants of the four into which the Antarctic regions are divided for convenience of reference, namely the Victoria and Ross Quadrants. It is desired that the extent of land should be ascertained by following the coast lines, *that the depth and nature of the ice cap should be investigated, as well as the nature of the volcanic region,* of the mountain ranges, *and especially of any fossiliferous rocks.*

9. A German Expedition will start at the same time as the *Discovery,* and it is hoped that there will be cordial co-operation between the two expeditions as regards magnetic and meteorological observations, and in all other matters if opportunities offer for such co-operation. It is understood that the German Expedition will establish an observatory on Kerguelen Island, and will then proceed to explore the Enderby Quadrant, probably shaping a course south between the 70°E and 80°E meridians, with the object of wintering on the *western side of Victoria Land,* whence exploring sledge parties will be sent inland. The Government of the Argentine Republic has undertaken to establish a Magnetic Observatory on Staten Island.

10. You will see that the meteorological observations are regularly taken every two hours and, also, in accordance with a suggestion from the Berlin Committee, every day at Greenwich noon. It is very desirable that *there should, if possible, be a series of meteorological observations south of the 74th parallel.*

11. As regards magnetic work and meteorological observations generally, you will follow the programme arranged between the German and British Committees, with the terms of which you are acquainted.

12. Whenever it is possible, while at sea, deep-sea sounding should be taken with serial temperatures, and samples of sea water at various depths are to be obtained, for physical and chemical analysis. Dredging

operations are to be carried on as frequently as possible, and all opportunities are to be taken for making biological and geological collections.

13. Instructions will be supplied for the various scientific observations; and the officers of the Expedition will be supplied with a Manual, prepared by Dr. George Murray, on similar lines and with the same objects as the Scientific Manuals supplied to the Arctic Expedition of 1875.

14. On leaving this country you are to proceed to Melbourne, *or Lyttelton (Christchurch) New Zealand,* touching at any port or ports on the way that you may consider it necessary or desirable to visit for supplies or repairs. Before leaving your base station you will fill up with live stock, coal and other necessaries; and you will leave the port with three years provisions on board, and fully supplied for wintering and for sledge travelling.

15. *You are to proceed at once to the edge of the pack and to force your vessel through it to the open water to the south.* The pack is supposed to be closer in December than it has been found to be later in the season. But this is believed to depend rather on its position than on the time; and the great difference between a steamer and a sailing vessel perhaps makes up for any difference in the condition of the pack.

16. On reaching the south water you are at liberty to devote to exploration the earlier portion of the navigable season; but *such exploration should, if possible, include an examination of the coast from Cape Johnson [at the northern boundary of Wood Bay in 74°05S] to Cape Crozier, with a view to finding a safe and suitable place for landing* in the event of your deciding that the ship shall not winter in the ice [my emphasis]. *The chief points of geographical interest are as follows:—To explore the Ice Barrier of Sir James Ross to its eastern extremity; to discover the land which was believed by Ross to flank the Barrier to the eastward, or to ascertain that it does not exist; and generally to endeavour to solve the very important physical and geographical questions connected with this remarkable ice formation.*

17. Owing to our very imperfect knowledge of the conditions which prevail in the Antarctic seas, we cannot pronounce definitely whether it will be necessary for the ship to make her way out of the ice before the winter sets in, or whether she should winter in the Antarctic regions. It is for you to decide on this important question after a careful examination of the local conditions.

18. *If you should decide that the ship shall winter in the ice, the following instructions are to be observed:—*

(a) *Your efforts, as regards geographical exploration, should be directed, with the aid of depôts, to three objects, namely, an advance into the western mountains, an advance to the south, and the exploration of the volcanic region.*

(b) The [scientific] Director and his staff shall be allowed all facilities for the prosecution of their researches.

(c) In carrying out (a) and (b) due regard is to be had to the safety and requirements of the Expedition as a whole.

(d) *You have been provided by Sir Leopold McClintock and by Dr. Nansen with complete details respecting sledge work both by men and dogs,* and you have yourself superintended every item of the preparations connected with food, clothing, and equipment. You will be guided by the information and knowledge thus acquired.

(e) Lieut. Armitage RNR, who has been appointed second in command and navigator to the Expedition, has had experience in the work of taking astronomical, magnetic and meteorological observations during three polar winters. He has also acquired experience in sledge travelling, and in the driving and management of dogs. You will no doubt find his knowledge and experience of great use.

(f) Early in 1903 your ship should be free from the ice of winter quarters, and you will devote to further exploration by sea so much of the navigable season as will certainly leave time for the ship to return to, the north of the pack ice. Having recruited at your base station, you will then proceed with your magnetic survey across the Pacific and return to this country.

19. If, on the other hand, you should decide not to winter, you will bear in mind that it is most important to maintain scientific observations on land throughout the winter, and therefore, if you are able, in consultation with the Director, to find a suitable place for a landing party between Cape Johnson and Cape Crozier, and decide that such a party can be landed and left without undue risk, the following instructions will apply:—

(a) You will land a party under the command of such person as you may appoint. Such party shall include the Director, the physicist, and one of the surgeons, and such other persons as you may consider desirable. But no person is to be left without his consent in writing, which you will be careful to obtain and preserve.

(b) You will give every practical assistance in establishing on land this party, which you will supply with all available requisites, including a dwelling hut, an observer's hut, three years' provisions, stores, fuel, sledges and dogs.

(c) No landing party is to be established on any other part of the coast than that between Cape Johnson and Cape Crozier, as it is above all things essential that in the case of accident the approximate position of the party should be known.

(d) Before it is so late as to endanger the freedom of your ship, you will proceed north of the pack and carry out magnetic observations with sounding and dredging over as many degrees of longitude (and as far south) as possible, so long as the season and your coal permit, and then return to your base station, whence you will telegraph your arrival and await further instructions.

20. *You are to do your best to let us have, and to leave where you can, statements of your intentions with regard to the places where you will deposit records, and the course you will adopt,* as well as particulars of your arrangements for the possible need of retreat, so that in case of accident to the ship, or detention, we shall be able to use our best endeavours to carry out your wishes in this respect.

21. In an enterprise of this nature much must be left to the discretion and judgement of the commanding officer, and we fully confide in your combined energy and prudence for the successful issue of a voyage which will command the attention of all persons interested in navigation and science throughout the civilised world. At the same time we desire you constantly to bear in mind our anxiety for the health, comfort and safety of all entrusted to your care.

22. While employed on this service you are to take every opportunity of acquainting us with your progress and your requirements.

23. In the unfortunate event of any fatal accident happening to yourself, or of your inability, from sickness or any other cause, to carry out these instructions, the command of the ship and of the Expedition will devolve on Lieutenant Armitage, who is hereby directed to assume command, and to execute such part of these instructions as have not been already carried out at the time of his assuming command. In the event of a similar accident to Lieutenant Armitage, the command is to devolve on the executive officer next in seniority on the Articles, and so on in succession.

24. All collections, and all logs (except the official log), journals, charts, drawings, photographs, observations, and scientific data will be the joint property of the two Societies, to be disposed of as may be decided by them. Before the final return of the Expedition, you are to demand from the Naval Staff all such data, which are to be sealed up and delivered to the two Presidents, or dealt with as they may direct. The Director of the civilian Scientific Staff will be similarly responsible for the journals, collections, &c., of the officers under his control. You and the other members of the Expedition will not be at liberty without our consent to make any communication to the press on matters relating to the affairs of the Expedition, nor to publish

independent narratives until six months after the official narrative. All communications are to be made to us, addressed to the care of the Secretary of the National Antarctic Expedition, London.

25. The *Discovery* is not one of His Majesty's ships, but is registered under the Merchant Shipping Act, 1894, and is governed by it. Copies of this Act will be supplied to you. You will see that the officers and crew sign the ship's articles as required by the Act. The scientific staff will not sign articles but are to be treated as cabin passengers. You must be careful not to take more than 12 persons as passengers.

26. The vessel has been covered by insurance, and, in the event of her sustaining any damage during the voyage, to recover the claim from the Underwriters, it will be necessary for you to call in the services of Lloyd's agent, or, in his absence, an independent surveyor, at the first port of call, in order that the damage may be surveyed before repairs are effected. His Survey Report, together with the accounts for the repairs and supporting vouchers, should be sent to us by first mail, together with a certified extract from the official log reporting the casualty. In the event of damage occurring after you have left civilised regions, precise particulars should be entered in the log, and the damage should be surveyed as soon as you return to a port where Lloyd's agent, or other surveyor, is available.

27. The *Discovery* is the first ship that has ever been built expressly for scientific purposes in these kingdoms. It is an honour to receive the command of her; but we are impressed with the difficulty of the enterprise which has been entrusted to you, and with the serious character of your responsibilities. The Expedition is an undertaking of national importance; and science cannot fail to benefit from the efforts of those engaged in it. You may rely upon our support on all occasions, and we feel assured that all on board the *Discovery* will do their utmost to further the objects of the Expedition.

II: INSTRUCTIONS TO THE SCIENTIFIC DIRECTOR

1. The Royal Society and the Royal Geographical Society have approved your appointment as Director of the Civilian Scientific Staff of their Antarctic Expedition.

2. A copy of the Instructions to the Commander of the Expedition accompanies these Instructions, which are supplemental to them. You will see from the Instructions to the Commander what the objects of the Expedition are, and your position relatively to him.

3. You will direct the scientific work of the gentlemen who have been appointed to assist you.

4. The names of the gentlemen associated with you are as follows:—(1) Mr. Hodgson (biologist), (2) Mr. Ferrar (geologist), (3) Mr. Bernacchi (physicist). The services of the two medical officers will be at your disposal for scientific work when not engaged on work of their own department, namely Dr. Koettlitz (botanist) and Dr. Wilson (zoologist).

5. You will note that the Commander of the Expedition has been instructed to communicate freely with you on all matters connected with the scientific objects of the Expedition, and, as far as possible, to meet your views and wishes in connection with them. The Societies feel assured that you will co-operate and act in concert with him, with a view, as far as possible, to secure the success of an enterprise which it is hoped will be attended with important results in the various branches of science which it is intended to investigate.

6. All collections, logs, journals, charts, drawings, photographs, observations and scientific data will be the joint property of the two Societies, to be disposed of as may be decided by them. Before the final return of the Expedition, you are to demand from the staff under your control all such data, which are to be sealed up and delivered to the two Presidents, or dealt with as they may direct. On the return of the Expedition, you will be expected to superintend the distribution of specimens to specialists approved of by the two Councils or their representatives, and to edit the resulting reports. You will also be expected to contribute a report on the scientific results of the Expedition for the official narrative. As it may be desirable during the progress of the voyage that some new scientific discovery should be at once made known in the interests of science, you will, in such a case, inform us of it by the earliest opportunity.

7. You and the other members of the Expedition will not be at liberty, without our consent, to make any communication to the Press on matters relating in any way to the affairs of the Expedition, nor to publish independent narratives until six months after the issue of the official narrative. All communications are to be made to us, addressed to the care of the Secretary of the National Antarctic Expedition, London.

8. Should any vacancies in the scientific staff occur after the Expedition has sailed from England, you may, with the concurrence of the Commander, make such arrangements as you think desirable to fill the same, should no one have been appointed from England.

9. You and the members of the scientific staff will be cabin passengers joining the Expedition at your own risk, and neither the owners

nor the Captain are to be responsible for any accident or misfortune which may happen to you. You will obtain from each member a letter to this effect.

APPENDIX 2

THE CREWS OF THE BRITISH AND GERMAN SHIPS

ABBREVIATIONS USED IN ALL CREW LISTS

CPO	chief petty officer (naval warrant officer)
CST	chief stoker
DD	lost his life
DES	deserted
DIS	dismissed
INV	invalided
KP	to Kerguelen shore party
LS	leading seaman
LST	leading stoker
MC	discharged by mutual consent (a euphemism for dismissed)
PO1	petty officer 1st class
PO2	petty officer 2nd class
PR	promoted
RES	discharged "at own request"
RM	returned to Lyttelton in the *Morning*, 1903
SP	to shore party
x	man on previous voyage (or leg of voyage) was replaced by
=	same man as on previous voyage (or leg of voyage)

1: VOYAGE OF THE DISCOVERY TO THE ANTARCTIC AND BACK TO NEW ZEALAND*

Crew	(no. aboard)	London-Cape — Name	(Age)	Cape-Lyttelton	(Age)	To Pt Chalmers	(Age)	To McMurdo Sound	(Age)	Ret'n to NZ
Executive Officers[1]	(4)			4 =		4 =		4 =		4 =
Ch. Engr.	(1)	Skelton		1 =		1 =		1 =		1 =
2nd Engr.	(1)	Dellbridge	(29)	2 =		2 =		2 =		1 =
Donkeyman		*Hubert*	(35)	=		=		=		RM
Stokers	(4)	Lashly[2]	(33)	5 =		5 =		5 =		4 =[9]
		Quartley	(28)	=		=		=		=
		Whitfield	(32)	=		=		=		=
		Page	(25)	+ Plumley	(26)	=		=		RM
Bosun & Deputy	(2)	Feather	(31)	2 =		2 =		2 =		2 =
		Allan[3]	(31)	=		=		=		=
Carpenter & Mate	(2)	Dailey	(28)	2 =		2 =		2 =		1 =
		Duncan	(31)	=		=		=		RM
Sailmaker	(1)	Miller	(36)	1 =		INV		0		0
Stewards	(3)	Ford	(23)	4 =		4 =		4 =		3 =
		Blissett	(23)	=		=		=		=
		Dowsett	(24)	+ Scott[4]	(25)	MC x *Hare*	(21)	=		RM[9]
Cooks (2)		*Roper*	(23)	2 =		MC x *Brett*	(35)	2 =		1 RM
		Clark	(24)	=		=		=		=[9]
Deck Watch	(12)	*Baker*	(25)	12 =		11 DES		10		7*[9]
Seamen		*Bonner*	(23)	=		=		DD x Handsley	(25)	=

Continued on next page

* Merchant Marine and civilian men's names in italics. For first names see crew pictures and Appendix 8, which also gives ratings.

1: *Voyage of the Discovery—continued*

Crew	(no. aboard)	London-Cape Name	(Age)	Cape-Lyttelton	(Age)	To Pt Chalmers	(Age)	To McMurdo Sound	Ret'n to NZ
Seamen (contd.)		Dell	(23)	=		=		=	=
		Heald	(25)	=		=		=	=
		Peters	(22)	=		=		=	RM
		Pilbeam	(23)	=		=		=	=
		Waterman	(21)	INV x Croucher	(20)	=		=	=
		Williamson	(24)	=		=		=	=
		Mardon	(25)	MC x Vince	(22)	=		=	DD
		Masterton	(33)	RES x Sinclair	(31)	=		=	DES[6]
		Walker	(25)	=		=		=	RM
Working Complement:	(33)[5]					35		33	32 24*
Extra Ratings for Shore Party	(5)	Cross	(26)	6=		8=		8=	7
		Macfarlane	(27)	=		=		=	INV+RM
		Smythe	(24)	=		=		=	=
		Evans	(26)	=		=		=	=
		Kennar	(25)	=		=		=	=
				+ Joyce	(26)	+ Crean	(24)		
						+ Weller	(23)		
Commander, Scientists & Laboratory Asst.	(8)	Cdr SCOTT		6=		7=		7=	6=
		6 scientists		4 scientists[7]		5 scientists[8]		=	=
		Clarke	(26)	x Buckridge	(26)	=		=	RM
TOTAL ABOARD:	(46)[8]			47		48		47	37
No. in Crew's Qtrs.	30			33		33		32	22
No. in CPO's Mess	4			4		4		4	4

* Deck watch really fourteen including returning shore party ratings, so effective complement was thirty-one.

NOTES

1. The four officers were Armitage, Royds, Barne, and Shackleton, the last invalided back and replaced by S/Lt. George Mulock in February 1903.

2. William Lashly appears in a photo of the ship's crew before leaving London (X115 in RGS collection) wearing the insignia of a PO1 on his left sleeve, indicating that Scott had appointed him acting chief stoker.

3. David S. Allan was the senior PO1 after Thomas Feather. He, Macfarlane, and Kennar carried out duties of quartermaster, effectively acting as deputy bosun and in charge of the helmsmen in bad weather. Jacob Cross replaced Macfarlane in the second year.

4. Edward Else, steward and purser from the *Windward* on the Jackson-Harmsworth expedition to Franz Josef Land, was to join at Melbourne after accompanying Bernacchi, Weller, the dogs, and stores aboard ss *Cuzco* but resigned at the last moment because of his wife's serious illness. See Chapter 8, note 35 for eventual shipping arrangements.

5. Excluding Else. The intended complement was thirty-four.

6. Sinclair's shipmates believed he held himself responsible for Bonner's death. He was not replaced.

7. The six scientists aboard (including the two surgeons) when *Discovery* sailed from England were Dr. George Murray, Dr. H. R. Mill, Koettlitz, Hodgson, Wilson, and Ferrar. Mill returned from Madeira, Murray returned from South Africa.

8. Bernacchi joined when *Discovery* arrived in New Zealand.

9. For the voyage home to England, the following were signed on on June 8, 1904: three RN able seamen, two RN stokers (raising engine room strength to six, e.g., three on duty, three off), a merchant navy cook's mate, and Clarence Hare, who was reengaged as assistant steward.

Source: Crew Agreements in Public Record Office ref: BT100/145

2: VOYAGES OF THE MORNING

Crew	(no. aboard)*	London to New Zealand	(Age)	New Zealand to McMurdo Sound	(Age)	Hobart-McMurdo Sound & return to New Zealand	(Age)
Master and Executive Officers	(5)	W. COLBECK	(30)	5 =		4 =	
		R.G.A. ENGLAND	(25)	=		=	
		E.R.G.R. EVANS	(21)	=		=	
		J.G.S. DOORLY	(22)	=		=	
		G.F.A. MULOCK[1]	(20)	=		SP	
Chief Engineer	(1)	J. D. MORRISON	(29)	1 =		1 =	
Donkeyman	(1)	H. King	(29)	1 =		1 MC x W. J. Marsh[2]	(21)
Stokers	(3)	F. W. Kemp	(38)	3 =		3 =	
		F. Taylor	(29)	=		MC x D. Nelson	(28)
		J. A. Beer	(26)	=		MC x J. S. Partridge	(19)
Bosun & Mate	(2)	A. B. Cheetham	(34)	2 =		2 =	
		J. T. Good	(33)	=		=	
Carpenter	(1)	W. G. Bilsby	(30)	1 =		1 =	
Sailmaker	(1)	G. W. Rolfe	(37)	1 =		0 MC	
Stewards	(2)	J. Sullivan	(22)	2 =		1 =[3]	
		C. A. Parkins	(23)	MC x J. A. Chester	(26)	=	
Cook	(1)	J. Hancock	(23)	1 =		1 DES x J. H. Maxwell[4]	(44)
Deck Watch	(12)			11		12	
Midshipmen		A. N. Pepper	(18)	=		=	
		F. M. Somerville	(16)	=		=	
Able Seamen		L. Burgess	(33)	=		=	
		F. W. Burton	(30)	=		=	
		A. Casement	(31)	=		=	

	Acting Asst. Steward[5]	Returned to Deck Duties
J. A. Chester (26)		
W. W. Hender (22)		MC x R. A. Beaumont (21)
G.R.W. Leary (34)		=
A. Noyon (26)		MC x H. D. Jarvis (26)
O. Riley (21)		=
J. Wainwright (38)		MC x W. E. Knowles (28)
Ordinary Seaman		
A. Cavelho[6] (20)	MC x J. Paton (34)	=

Working Complement:			
Surgeon (1)	29	28	27
G. A. DAVIDSON (27)		1=	1=
TOTAL ABOARD:	30	29[7]	28

* See Appendix 8 for first names of the twenty-four awarded the Bronze Polar Medal. S/Lt. George Mulock received the Silver Polar Medal.

NOTES

1. Intended as relief in case of shore party officer casualty.
2. Rated assistant engineer.
3. Deserted at Lyttelton, June 7, 1904.
4. Crew Agreement records Hancock as having deserted after the second voyage, but this must be an error as he is not shown as aboard on December 5, 1903, in a listing of next-of-kin prepared by Colbeck for Markham at the start of second voyage (RGS Antarctic Archive:16/3/2), and Markham lists him as having been discharged in April 1903 (RGSAA:16/3/1). Colbeck's list states Maxwell was bound for *Discovery*. Clearly, intention was to exchange him for Clarke, but he was never transferred.
5. Acted as asst. steward from September 9, 1902, to December 6, 1903.
6. Joined at Madeira. Replaced at Lyttelton by Able Seaman James Paton.
7. Less Mulock and plus ten from *Discovery*, total was thirty-eight for return to Lyttelton.

Source: Crew Agreements in Public Record Office: ref. BT100/146

3: VOYAGE OF THE TERRA NOVA

Crew	(no. aboard)*	Portland-Aden	(Age)	Aden-Hobart	(Age)	Hobart-McMurdo Sound & Return to New Zealand	(Age)
Master and Executive	(4)	H. D. McKAY	(47)	4 =		4 =	
Officers		A. P. JACKSON	(32)	=		=	
		A. J. ELMS	(34)	=		=	
		R. DAY	(22)	=		=	
Ch. Engineer	(1)	A. SHARP	(37)	1 =		1 =	
Asst. Engineers	(2)	W. Smith	(23)	2 =		2 =	
		C. McGregor	(43)	=		=	
Stokers	(3)	W. Batchelor	(31)	3 =		3 =	
		J. Fredrick	(25)	=		=	
		D. T. Milne	(28)	=		=	
Bosun	(1)	A. Aiken	(48)	1 =		1 =	
Carpenter and Mate	(2)	A. Smith	(45)	2 =		2 =	
		A. Smith	(21)	=		=[1]	
Sailmaker	(1)	E. Morrison	(33)	1 =		1 =	
Stewards	(2)	R. H. Morgan	(44)	2 =		2 =	
		T. A. Shearer	(25)	=		=	
Cooks	(2)	J. Grant	(44)	2 =		2 =	
		W. Clark	(21)	=		=	
Deck Watch[2]	(14)			20		20	
Able Seamen		T. Burns	(25)	=		=	
		J. Cairns	(28)	=		=	
		T. Cosgrove	(27)	=		=	
		J. Coupar	(38)	=		=	
		W. Craig	(27)	=		=	
		J. R. Dair	(31)	=		=	

J. Grant	(39)	=	
G. Lawrence	(20)	=	
J. Lawson	(42)	=	DIS x T. Spaulding (23)
G. Mitchell	(38)	=	
A. Morrell	(38)	=	
J. Reilly	(23)	=	
C. Stanistreet	(21)	=	
J. Thors	(39)	=	
+J. G. Anderson	(28)	=	
+J. Clark	(35)	=	
+R. Christie	(?)	=[3]	
+D. H. Fredrick	(29)	=	
+A. McNeil	(?)	=	
+M. Strachan	(?)	=	

Working Complement:	32	38	38
Surgeon (1)	W. C. Souter	1=	1=
TOTAL ABOARD:	33	39	39

* For first names of those who received the Bronze Polar Medal, see Appendix 8.

NOTES

1. The forty-five-year-old carpenter was from Peterhead, his twenty-one-year-old namesake was from Dundee.
2. Seventeen signed on at Tayport, but three deserted before sailing; one drowned in his attempt to reach shore.
3. Deserted at Tayport, rejoined at Aden, and then deserted on May 9, 1904, at Lyttelton.

Source: Crew Agreements in Public Record Office: ref: BT100/50

4: OFFICERS AND CREW OF THE GAUSS

Crew	(no. aboard)	Kiel-Cape	(Age)	Cape-Kerguelens & return to Cape Town	(Age)	Kerguelens-Antarctic
Captain & Executive Officers	(6)	Hans RUSER	(38)	=		=
(1st Officer)		Wilhelm LERCHE	(37)	=		=
(2nd Officer)		Richard VAHSEL	(33)	=		=
(3rd Officer)		Ludwig OTT	(25)	=		=
Chief Engineer	(1)	Albert STEHR	(35)	=		=
Asst. Engineers	(2)	Paul Heinacker	(19)	=		=
		Reinhold Mareck	(31)	=		=
Stokers[1]	(2)	Leonhard Muller	(43)	x Emil Berglöf	(22)	=
		(?)				=
1st Bosun and 2nd Bosun	(2)	Josef Müller (24)		x Hans Dahler	(25)	=
		(?)		=		=
Carpenter & 2nd Carpenter	(2)	August Reimers	(25)	=		=
		Willy Heinrich	(23)	=		=
Steward	(1)	August Besenbrock	(19)	=		=
Cook	(1)	Wilhelm Schwarz	(28)	=		=
Deck Watch	(14)			14		13
Able Seamen		Gustav Bähr	(24)	=		=
		Paul Björvik[2]	(44)	=		= (Norwegian)
		Max Fisch	(26)	=		=
		Karl Franz[1]	(24)	=		=

(?)		x Wilhelm Insell	(28)	=	(Swedish)
Daniel Johansen[3]	(28)	=		=	(Norwegian)
Karl Kluck	(32)	=		=	
(?)		x Wilhelm Lysell	(28)	=	(Swedish)
Reinhold Michael[1]	(25)	=		=	
Georg Noack	(24)	=		=	
(?)		x Albert Possin	(22)	=	
Lenart Reuterskjöld	(19)	=		=	(Swedish)
(?)		x Curt Sternblad	(19)	=	(Swedish)
Josef Urbansky	(24)			KP[4]	

Working Complement:	(31)	31		30
Leader and Scientists	(6)	6 =		5 =
Prof. DRYGALSKI				
5 Scientists				4 Scientists
including Dr. Werth				KP[4]
		KP[4]		
TOTAL ABOARD:	(37)	37		35

(?) At Cape Town the second bosun, three seamen, and a stoker were sacked, another seaman discharged at his own request (see Drygalski 1989: p. 87).

NOTES

1. These two seamen helped out in engine room.
2. In charge of dogs.
3. Experienced skier.
4. Transferred to Kerguelen Island party, joining Josef Enzensperger, Dr. Karl Luyken, and seaman Georg Wienke who had landed from the *Tanglin*.

APPENDIX 3

WAS THE *DISCOVERY* OVERMANNED?

In these days of small-party expeditions, made possible by food processing and lightweight equipment not dreamed of in Scott's day, it is too easy to question the level of manning of his first expedition,[1] dictated in part by the diversity of its aims. Once ashore, given the decision to buy only 22 dogs and reserve them for the Southern journey, the expedition was shorthanded.

Whatever its demerits and the feasibility of using dogs on the western glaciers (rejected as impractical 55 years later by Dr. G. W. Marsh on the Commonwealth Trans-Antarctic expedition, who found Ferrar Glacier "virtually impassable for dog teams in its present condition"[2]), that decision makes it hard to believe that more than a Southern journey and none too ambitious explorations toward the magnetic pole could have been attempted had no suitable harbor been found for the ship to winter in the Antarctic. That eventuality would have limited Scott's resources to a shore party comprising himself, Armitage, and one officer; 3 scientists, including Wilson doubling as doctor; and the 8 ratings talked of at the planning stage of ship design, plus a cook and possibly one other.

However, that very eventuality gave rise to the charge of overmanning Scott encountered during his consultations in Norway and Denmark. Given that the potential shore party could hardly have been smaller, the criticism essentially related to the ship's complement, as Scott's journal entry after the meeting in Copenhagen confirms (see Chapter 5).

Except for the manning of the commissariat, that criticism, justified as it was at the time, was ultimately far from merited when the expedition went south. When the ratings included for the shore party are deducted from the eventual total ship's company on sailing from Lyttelton, the intended working complement of 34* compares with those of the *Gauss* (30 ex their Kerguelen base) and the *Morning* (27 discounting S/Lt. Mulock). The excess over the Germans' complement was accounted for by the extra cook and 3 stewards. The *Morning* saved 3 crew in that department and a further 3 in the engine room, and the ship had no carpenter's mate.

All three ships had an intended deck watch of 12, but following the desertion of Able Seaman Sinclair after Bonner's death, the "front line" deck force could have been maintained only with the aid of shore party men. If they had to be left ashore, only 10 seamen would have remained aboard. That total would have required all hands on deck in anything approaching the weather conditions that could prevail in the furious southern ocean. Surprisingly, that total had been all the original Ship Subcommittee had believed necessary.

Markham's first idea had been for a total of 35, made up of 6 officers (including 2 surgeons), 3 scientists, and 26 others.[3] Excluding the scientists and 2 surgeons, that made a working complement or crew of 32, which had effectively been confirmed at the first formal Ship Subcommittee meeting on April 26, 1899. However, "8 other ratings requiring only mess table and hammock accommodation" were added for a purpose unspecified in the minutes.[4]

It is clear they were intended for shore duty "if," in the words of the June 1900 plan, "a landing party is decided on."[5] In the end, only 7 extra men were aboard when *Discovery* sailed from Port Chalmers. But if the intended 8 are subtracted from the ensuing statements about the ship's complement, a clearer picture emerges from the successive proposals to show how the working complement had grown to 41 by the time Scott arrived in Norway.

Starting with the April 1899 crew of 32, the first increase had taken place by the time Markham spoke at the Berlin Congress in autumn of that year. He referred to a total *complement* of 48, including 3 scientists.[6] Deducting the 3 scientists, 2 surgeons, and 8 extra ratings for the work ashore, that meant the crew had grown to 35.

---

* Thirty-four less Baker, whose replacement (Crean) would have to join a shore party if no harbor could be found, making the deck watch 11 for the return voyage in that event.

Gregory's January 1900 letter from Suez[7] pleaded for a whaling captain experienced in ice navigation, which would have matched the Arctic experiences of Markham and his RGS companion on the Executive Committee, Adm. Sir Richard Vesey Hamilton. That probably accounts for the addition of 3 ice quartermasters at the June 8 meeting of the committee. The addition of an engine room artificer and 4 able seamen—the latter possibly to have enough men for "cutting docks" in the fast sea ice to make a harbor, which Markham refers to in his plan prepared at the end of the year—brought the crew up to 41.[8]

That was the number Scott would have talked of to his hosts in Oslo and Copenhagen, although he already knew, *from a previous letter from Markham*, that the ice quartermasters might be cut.[9] Naturally, the total seemed excessive to his Scandinavian listeners.

APPENDIX 4

THE ORIGINAL CABIN OCCUPANTS
ABOARD *DISCOVERY*

The original assignment of wardroom cabins on Scott's famous first voyage appears to have been lost. The cabins were destroyed when the Hudson Bay Company converted the space between bridge and engine room into cargo holds, and the problem of identifying the original occupants is further complicated by the new cabin layout installed in the 1924–1925 rebuild.

There is no problem about Scott's and Armitage's, which were rebuilt in the same positions in the starboard and port corners between wardroom and engine room. But the original and 1925 lower deck arrangement drawings show that the forward portside cabin became the pantry, the pantry in the original arrangement became a laboratory, and two cabins were installed in place of Scott's original day cabin—a situation hardly conducive to matching the original occupants to their cabins.

The problem that hinders an easy solution lies in the fact that Scott's wardroom companions had shown at least one member of their families over the ship and so had little incentive to mention the position of their cabins in diaries written largely for family consumption. Scott, in *The Voyage of the* Discovery, makes no mention of the position of any cabin except Ferrar's,[1] which was not in the wardroom, and the surviving drawings do not name the intended occupants.

Then there is the curious fact that although Scott and nine other officers and scientists were housed in wardroom cabins when the ship sailed from New Zealand, the well-known original lower deck arrangement drawing shows only nine cabins in the wardroom. The possibility that two men shared one of the cabins is ruled out by Bernacchi's positive statement that each officer "had his own sanctum."[2] Scott also emphasizes that point in his book.[3] So where was the tenth cabin?

The fact is that the well-known drawings, of which the originals survive (the Scott Polar Research Institute has blueprints), are those prepared in 1899 and made available to firms tendering for the shipbuilding contract in November of that year. The Ship Subcommittee, responsible for drawing up the inquiry documents, submitted a report to the Executive Committee on October 26, 1899, in which it referred to nine cabins being required for the commander, navigating officer, and seven others.[4] That was the basis for the lower deck arrangement drawing referred to in the specification that accompanied the inquiry. Paragraphs 25 and 26 of the specification required the successful tenderer to submit detailed proposals for approval before starting installation of the cabins and wardroom fittings. Whether the Dundee Shipbuilders Company prepared an arrangement drawing to accompany its proposals is uncertain, and the whereabouts and date of the actual proposals are unknown.

The fact that the proposals and drawing, if one was made, would have included ten cabins in the wardroom is demonstrated by a report of the June 8, 1900 meeting of the Executive Committee in the archives of the Royal Society. The report shows that by that time—almost three months after the keel was laid—the staff was to comprise the commander, three executive officers, engineer, surgeon, second surgeon (and botanist), the head of the civilian scientific staff, and three scientists—a total of eleven, which was the eventual number that sailed for the Antarctic.

The general arrangement drawings of the hull and the crew numbers proposed make it virtually certain that at that stage the eleventh cabin could not have been fitted into the wardroom, hence the eventual position of geologist Ferrar's cabin on the starboard side of the galley compartment, along with the darkroom and physical laboratory. Hence also the certain provision of ten cabins in the wardroom but no hint as to where the tenth was to be. Fortunately, the answer, and the equation of most occupants to their cabins, can be found in chance remarks in their diaries and in Bernacchi's 1938 book.[5]

Bernacchi, the only one who made a decisive statement about the position of his cabin, identifies it as next to Scott's. Wilson, in the September 21, 1901, entry in his diary, confirms his was also on the starboard side, but he never states exactly where. However, Sir Clements

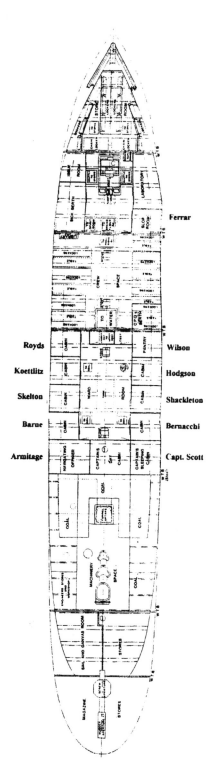

Royds

Koettlitz

Skelton

Barne

Armitage

Ferrar

Wilson

Hodgson

Shackleton

Bernacchi

Capt. Scott

ORIGINAL CABIN OCCUPANTS ABOARD
DISCOVERY, DECEMBER 1901. The 1899
lower deck arrangement drawing,
which formed the basis of the original
tender, marked up to show cabin occupants on the voyage from New
Zealand and during the first year in
the Antarctic. In the as-built layout the
Warrant Officers' Mess was moved to
the port side of the crew's quarters
next to Royds's cabin, and the pantry
was relocated forward of the bulkhead
to make room for Wilson's cabin,
which became the laboratory in the
1924 rebuild. The wardroom entrance
was opposite Royds's cabin door.
Courtesy, the Royal Geographical
Society, from a paper by William E.
Smith CB, read at the April 12, 1905,
meeting of the Institution of Naval
Architects.

Markham comes to the rescue. In his original account of *The Starting of the Antarctic Expedition*,[6] he describes the pianola as "between Hodgson's and Wilson's" cabins, with the piano between Skelton's and Koettlitz's.

So Hodgson's cabin was next to Wilson's on the starboard side, and the clue to which was Hodgson's comes in the October 1, 1901, entry in his diary.[7] Hodgson describes how he had removed the chair from his cabin, not knowing the coal chutes would be put in place that soon, in readiness for recoaling at Cape Town and then found he could not get the chair back into the cabin. At that time Bernacchi's cabin would have been occupied by George Murray, who returned to England from Cape Town. So Hodgson's can only have been the second one along from Bernacchi's.

That seems to place Wilson's between Bernacchi's and Hodgson's. However, in his June 9, 1902, diary entry, Wilson tells how the forward wardroom stove had been lit instead of the after one, complaining that it made his cabin uncomfortably warm as the forward stove was "much nearer" to it. As the drawing shows, the cabin next to Bernacchi's was about halfway between the two stoves, so that one cannot have been Wilson's. That leaves only one position for Wilson's cabin, namely, in the forward starboard corner of the wardroom. In other words, the tenth cabin was Wilson's, and it was in the position originally intended for the pantry. That position is now occupied by part of the laboratory installed in the 1924–1925 rebuild.

The original pantry must have been relocated forward of the bulkhead between the wardroom and crew's quarters. Was the mess deck large enough for that? The answer is yes, for as the 1899 drawing shows, apart from the chief petty officers' mess there were six mess tables with seating, respectively, for 10, 9, 8, 6, 6, and 3. Added to the 3 CPOs then intended, that gave accommodation for 45 crew, the number mentioned in the October 26, 1899, ship subcommittee report just prior to the inquiry. The eventual crew was significantly smaller.

The 1902 midwinter "Christmas" party pictures in Scott's[8] and Bernacchi's[9] books show there were eventually only 4 mess tables, each for 6 men.* But the crew pictures (held by the Royal Geographi-

---

* Picture no. 89 in Album 1 in the Royal Society set identifies Bernacchi's picture as showing two of the starboard messes, so the one in Scott's book is of two on the port side. In both pictures the camera is pointing slightly forward, and men on the forward seating had their backs against the galley compartment bulkhead, on which many pictures were hung.

cal Society) taken by Skelton on September 30, 1902,[10] show 5 messes and a total of 31 men. That number added to the 4 CPOs represents a reduction of 10 from the plan embodied in the 1899 drawing.

Furthermore, a week after the photos were taken (October 7), Wilson refers to 5 men sleeping in the galley. That corresponds to the number in the chief steward's department, so clearly they also ate there. That leaves 26 to eat at the four tables on the mess deck, but if 2 were serving at the party, that discrepancy is accounted for. At normal meals there would have been ample room for them at the end of two tables. So with only two tables either side of the mess deck, there would have been adequate space for the pantry to have been sited forward of the bulkhead, probably still on the starboard side, with the CPO's mess resited on the port side. As another photo shows, that mess became rather large, with the table running fore and aft instead of athwartship.

With Bernacchi, Hodgson, and Wilson in starboard cabins, the one remaining cabin occupant to identify on that side of the wardroom is the man in the cabin next to Bernacchi's. As the 1899 drawing shows, that cabin was the only one to have a beam positioned directly against its after-partition wall, which is precisely how Shackleton's cabin appears in a contemporary picture.[11] If the cabin in that picture had been on the port side, the beam would be against its forward-partition wall, and as the drawing shows, only Armitage's cabin had a beam positioned that way. So Shackleton's cabin must have been between Bernacchi's and Hodgson's on the starboard side.

Regarding the port side cabin occupants, Wilson and Markham once more provide some answers. An entry on August 1, 1902, in Wilson's diary describes how Royds's cabin was "the coldest and dampest of all . . . being next [to] the door and the gangway."[12] So the forward cabin on the port side was Royds's. In 1925 the wardroom pantry was installed in that position.

Markham describes the piano as between Skelton's and Koettlitz's cabins, so theirs must have been on the port side. The question then is, which two of the three cabins between Armitage's and Royds's were occupied by the chief engineer and the surgeon, and which way around? The answers emerge from two sketches reproduced here that appeared in the April and June 1903 issues of the *South Polar Times*.

The first, by Leading Stoker Arthur Quartley, reveals the position of the piano and the two cabins by its inclusion of the stove hearth in its bottom right-hand corner. As this can only be the forward stove, the cabins either side of the piano must have been the two forward

I MUST BE OFF NOW TO LOOK AT THE
THERMOMETER

WHO STOLE OUR CHARLIE'S SARDINES?
BLACKWALL,
AND Meow!! It was not me.
Poplar.

Two Cartoons From *South Polar Times*. Sketches by Arthur Quartley (*left*) and Michael Barne. From *The South Polar Times*, published in 1908 by Smith, Elder.

ones out of the three. This accounts for the absence of any sign of the piano in the midwinter wardroom picture in Bernacchi's book looking diagonally aft toward Armitage's cabin—it was too far forward to get into the picture.

The second sketch, a caricature of Koettlitz illustrating a satirical mock interview with him, clearly shows his cabin was the one forward of the piano and therefore next to Royds's. So Skelton's cabin was immediately aft of the piano, and Barne's was next to Armitage's.

APPENDIX 5

MEMBERS OF EVERY SLEDGE PARTY ON THE *DISCOVERY* EXPEDITION

Duration	Name/Purpose/Dest'n	Sledge Party by Tents Where Known (/.../.../)	Notes & Footnotes (*)
AUTUMN 1902			
Feb. 3–4	Barrier ex Balloon Bight	Armitage, Bernacchi, Cross/ Handsley, Joyce, Crean	1
Feb. 18–22	White Island	Shackleton, Wilson, Ferrar	2
Mar. 4–19	Cape Crozier Attempt	Royds, Koettlitz, Wild / Barne, Skelton, Hare / Quartley, Vince, Weller/ Evans, Plumley, Heald	3 *
Mar. 31–Apr. 4	Southern Depot Attempt	RF Scott, Wilson, Macfarlane/ Dellbridge, Walker, Blisset/ Armitage, Ferrar, Feather/ Allan, Smythe, Williamson	4 †
SPRING 1902			
Sept. 2–5	Dog Trial	RF Scott, Wilson, Shackleton/ Skelton, Ferrar, Feather	5

Continued on next page

Continued on next page

---

* Barne's party turned back with 9 dogs, 2 sledges (11-foot and 7-foot). Royds took on 8 dogs, 1 sledge (7-foot). Wild and Skelton swapped places.

† Scott's and Armitage's parties each had 4 sledges pulled by 9 dogs.

Duration	Name/Purpose/Dest'n	Sledge Party by Tents Where Known (/.../.../)	Notes & Footnotes (*)
SPRING 1902–continued			
Sept. 10-19	SW Recce (Mt. Discovery)	Royds, Koettlitz, Lashly / Evans, Wild, Quartley	6
Sept. 11-26	Western Recce	Armitage, Ferrar, Scott/ Cross, Heald, Walker	7
Sept. 17-19	Southern Recce	RF Scott, Barne, Shackleton	8
Sept. 23-Oct. 2	Brown and Black Islands	Koettlitz, Bernacchi, Dailey	9
Sept. 23-Oct. 4	Bluff Depot (+ 16 dogs)	RFScott, Shackleton, Feather	10
Oct. 4-24	Cape Crozier (message delivered)	Royds, Skelton, Lashly/ Evans, Wild, Quartley	11
SUMMER 1902-1903			
Oct. 30-Nov. 21	Southern Support #1	Dailey, Kennar, Williamson, Pilbeam, Weller, Buckridge	12 *
Oct. 30-Nov. 23	Southern Support #2	Barne, Feather, Smythe, Crean, Handsley, Joyce	12
Nov. 2-Feb. 3	Southern	RF Scott, Wilson, Shackleton	13
Nov. 3-5	Erebus Bay	Koettlitz, Skelton, Hare	14
Nov. 3-20	Cape Crozier Rookery	Royds, Plumley, Blissett	15
Nov. 3-5	Crozier Support	Macfarlane, Allan, Dell (turned back 13½ miles out)	15
Nov. 29-Jan. 18	Main Western	Armitage, Skelton, Scott/ Evans, Quartley, Buckridge/ Allan, Macfarlane, Handsley/ Duncan, Wild, Walker	16
Nov. 29-Dec. 18	Western Support	Koettlitz, Ferrar, Dellbridge, Croucher, Clarke, Dell Pilbeam, Whitfield, Hubert	17
Dec. 12-Jan. 30	Southwest Barrier	Barne, Smythe, Plumley/ Williamson, Crean, Weller	18
Dec. 29-Jan. 8	Brown and Black Islands	Koettlitz, Hodgson, Ferrar	14
Jan. 1-17	Bluff Depot	Dailey, Whitfield, Ford	19
Jan. 14-26	Minna Bluff	Koettlitz, Ferrar	14

Continued on next page

Continued on next page

---

* Armitage (1905 p. 153) mistakenly gives Peters instead of Pilbeam.

Duration	Name/Purpose/Dest'n	Where Known (/.../.../)	Notes & Footnotes (*)
SPRING AND SUMMER 1903			
Sept. 7–17	Cape Crozier Rookery	Royds, Wilson, Williamson/ Cross, Whitfield, Blissett	20
Sept. 9–20	Western Depot	RF Scott, Skelton, Dailey/ Lashly, Evans, Handsley	21
Sep. 13–20	Southwest Depot	Barne, Mulock, Quartley/ Smythe, Crean, Joyce	21
Oct. 6–Dec. 13	Southwest	Barne, Mulock, Quartley/ Smythe, Crean, Joyce	22
Oct. 6–Nov. 7	SW Support	Dellbridge, Pilbeam, Wild/ Allan, Croucher, Heald	22
Oct. 12–21	Western Attempt	RF Scott, Skelton, Feather/ Lashly, Evans, Handsley Ferrar, Kennar, Weller/ Dailey, Williamson, Plumley	14
Oct. 12–Nov. 5	Cape Crozier Rookery	Wilson, Cross, Whitfield	23
Oct. 26–Dec. 10	Western Geology	Ferrar, Kennar, Weller (parted from Western Party Nov. 11)	14
Oct. 26–Dec. 16	Western Support	Skelton, Feather, Handsley (turned Nov. 22)	24
Oct. 26–Dec. 24	Western Summit	RF Scott, Lashly, Evans	14
Nov. 10–Dec. 10	Southeast Barrier	Royds, Bernacchi, Scott/ Cross, Plumley, Clarke	25
Nov. 16–22	Ross Is. South Coast	Wilson, Hodgson, Croucher	23
Nov. 26–Dec. 12	Koettlitz Glacier	Armitage, Wilson, Heald	23

APPENDIX 6

THE MANPOWER CONTROVERSY
AT THE DECISIVE STAGE OF SCOTT'S
1902–1903 SEASON

The following tabulation showing the deployment of the crew, which Armitage ordered on November 27, 1902, illustrates the increment of four men to deck crew strength from then until December 18, the day Koettlitz returned with the Western Support Party.

Deck crew are indicated in bold. Possible reserves for night watch duty, the search party under Carpenter Dailey, and general help to deck watch indicated by italics.

Men ex Southern Support Parties indicated thus: (1) = Returned November 21 with Dailey; (2) = Returned November 23 with Barne

To leave with Armitage			To stay at Ship		
MAIN WESTERN PARTY			**SW PARTY**		
			to stay until Koettlitz's return		
ARMITAGE, SKELTON, plus			BARNE plus		
Allan	QM		**Smythe**	AB*	(2)
Macfarlane	QM		**Crean**	AB	(2)
Evans	PO 2nd Cl.		**Williamson**	AB	
Duncan	Shipwright		**Weller**	AB	
Quartley	Ldg. Stkr.		*Plumley*	Stkr.	
Scott G.	RM (Stwd.)				
Walker	AB				
Wild	AB				
Handsley	AB	(2)			
Buckridge	Lab Asst.	(1)			
WESTERN SUPPORT PARTY			**SHIP PARTY**		
KOETTLITZ, FERRAR, plus			ROYDS plus		
Dellbridge	2nd Engr.		Dailey	Carp.	
Whitfield	Ldg. Stkr.		**Feather**	Bosun	(2)
Hubert	Stkr.		**Kennar**	QM	
Clarke	2nd Cook		**Cross**	PO 1st Cl.	
Pilbeam	Ldg. Seaman	(1)	**Heald**	AB	
Croucher	AB		**Joyce**	AB	(2)
Dell	AB		**Peters**	AB	
			Lashly	Ch. Stkr.	
			Page	Ldg. Stkr.	
			Ford	Ch. Stwd.	
			Brett	Cook	
			Blissett	RM (Stwd.)	
			Hare	Stwd.	

* At first demoted to able seaman after going absent without leave at Christchurch but later reinstated as PO 1st Class on Scott's recommendation following the first season.

APPENDIX 7

FURTHER DETAILS OF SCOTT'S
TWO MAIN SLEDGE JOURNEYS

SOUTHERN JOURNEY, NOVEMBER 2, 1902, TO FEBRUARY 3, 1903

CAMP POSITIONS AND RETURN ROUTE

In plotting the course and camp positions on the first leg of the outward journey, the only positive evidence to work from is the near certain position of the Bluff Depot ("A") and the present position of the chaotic rifts curving southeast from Cape Selborne, the eastern edge of which Wilson describes as about ¾ mile beyond their Depot "B." No evidence suggests that the rifts changed their position to any significant extent in the 60-odd years preceding the survey for the USGS maps used here.

Lieutenant Mulock, both in the South Polar Times[1] and in 1908,[2] showed the latter depot west of the 162°E meridian in 80°27S. That and the courses he charted were undoubtedly calculated from Scott's observations pocket book, which does not appear to have survived. However, transferring those courses and distances (133 geographical miles [g/m]) to modern maps places the depot beyond the rifts and in 80°31S. Plotting Wilson's mileages (138 g/m) on the same courses places the depot in 80°34S, which is beyond and further south than the end of the rifts. To "bring" the depot east of the rifts requires a 2 percent (nonuniform) reduction in Mulock's mileages and a 5 percent decrease in Wilson's. Both are well within credible limits of inaccuracy in the sledgemeter readings Wilson used, and the resulting track equates to a 80°29S latitude for Depot B.

Further evidence supporting that latitude is found in Scott's January 15 statement, as they started north from the depot, that "in the morning . . . we could see the northern side of the high rounded snowcap abreast of which we left our depot," which would have been impossible had they started from farther south.[3] Although he said they could not see any land, Wilson's diary reference that day to "miles of broken, irregular, hummocked up ice" between them and the shore aptly fits the rifts stretching east from Cape Selborne (their Cape 'A'). However, if the rifts were still to their west at the evening camp, they might have started from as far south as 80°32S that day. Another pointer is Scott's December 14 reference to a "conspicuous rocky patch in line with one of three distant peaks."[4] Such a feature exists at 80°37½S 159°23E and would align with Mount Hamilton from a position just east of the rifts in about 80°29S. Taken with Scott's 80°30S midnight sight on December 15, an hour after starting south from the depot, and his *South Polar Times*[5] reference to the depot being in "*about* 80°30S" [my italics], the balance of evidence favors 80°29S, the latitude adopted here.

The key to plotting the final leg of the outward journey is the inescapable evidence of the alignment of Cape Wilson and the Inaccessible Cliffs in the panorama photo taken by Shackleton on the evening of December 28, 1902, which establishes that night's camp as in about 82°05'30"S. When the positions of the December 22 lunch and Christmas evening camps, indicated by the orientation of Wilson's sketches, are found to equate precisely to the sledgemeter mileages Wilson recorded, there can be little doubt about the approximate latitude (82°11S) Scott and Wilson reached on skis on the afternoon of the 30th or about the camp positions from the December 18 evening camp until the New Year's Eve camp.

No mileage was recorded in any of the journals for the 2 P.M.–9 P.M. run on December 18, but plotting the first three camps south from the depot by the sledgemeter mileages produces a distance of over 10.5 miles for the December 18 run. That is consistent with it being their best day's run, as implied by Wilson's diary description of progress, weather, and surface.

However, the noon sight latitudes Wilson records cease to equate properly after the 81°22S sight at the December 22 lunch camp, first overstating the latitude by more than 3' on December 24 and then by 5'30" on the 28th. This is relevant to the problems that arise when trying to place the camps on the return journey after the sledgemeter broke down on January 9. Using the sledgemeter mileages from the New Year's Eve camp (they equate to the orientation of Wilson's January 2 sketch of the "high red cliffs" and the crossing of their old track on the 6th) places the January 9 lunch camp in 81°01S, with Scott's 81°06'30"S sight again 5'30" different. After that, the only clue is the 7 miles between the "80°44S" noon sight on the 11th, which with Wilson's remark "about 10 miles only from Depot B" doesn't add up, and the "80°37S" sight 24 hours later, which, with his estimated 2 miles that afternoon and 6 the next day, suddenly equates precisely with the 80°29S position postulated for the depot.

The frequent lack of any reference to mileage after leaving the depot on January 14 makes it fruitless to try to plot the camps from there to the arrival at the Bluff Depot. Scott's sights on the 19th (79°58S), 20th (79°51S with Mount Discovery just visible above horizon), 22nd (79°34S), 25th (79°13S), and 27th (79°57S), with the orientation of Wilson's January 25 panorama, are the only serious clues to their progress. On Map VI a dotted line indicates the approximate route.

The puzzle remains as to why some of the sights recorded by Wilson and Shackleton fit the course suggested by Wilson's mileages but are so clearly wrong if the depot is no further south than 80°30S, which Shackleton years later confirmed to Frank Worsley.[6]

SUMMARY OF CONDITIONS IN TERMS OF HEADWIND AND SURFACE: BLUFF DEPOT TO FARTHEST SOUTH AND RETURN

	Days on Move	
	Southward (41)	*Return* (27½)
Adverse conditions		
Headwind force 2 or worse		
with heavy surface	2	2
with fair surface	3	1
Heavy-going surface		
without headwind or sail aid	16	5
	21	8
Average conditions including		
sail-aided on heavy surface (1 day		
outward, 2½ on return)	20	6½
Favorable conditions		
Sail-aided on fair surface		6
Good, easy, very fair, or excellent surface		7
	0	13

DEMISE OF THE DOGS

After Blanco was sent back with Barne's party, 18 dogs remained. Bernacchi's *Southern Cross* dog, Joe, was removed from the trace on November 24, and it is not clear when it was again harnessed up, although probably no later than December 8. The first signs of illness occurred when some dogs developed dysentery on December 6. By the 8th Shackleton was writing "dogs weakening rapidly with dysentery and scurvy."[7] The next day the first dog died "of acute peritonitis," as Wilson recorded after he had cut up the carcass to feed to the others.

Six dogs died or were killed and fed to the 9 fittest dogs on the way south, according to the three men's journals: December 9, Snatcher (EAW, RFS); December 16, Vic (RFS); December 19, Wolf (EHS); December 20, Grannie (RFS); December 26, Brownie (EHS); December 28, Stripes (EAW). In the order of the dates on which they died or were so weak that they had to be killed, the 12 dogs that reached the December 30 (2 P.M.) camp in 82°10S were:

Fitzclarence	December 31	Boss	January 7
Spud	January 1	Joe	January 8
Nell	January 3	Birdie	January 10
Gus	January 3	Lewis	January 11
Bismarck	January 4	Jim	January 15
Kid	January 5	Nigger	January 15 (team leader)

Some confusion surrounds the loss of Boss and Kid. EHS says Boss died on the 5th (EAW: no mention), whereas Scott gives the 7th after being carried on sledge on 6th. Kid appears to have dropped in the traces on the 3rd (RFS) and been killed on the 5th (EHS), the day they stopped using the dogs and pulled the two 9-foot sledges by themselves. It took them eight days to reach their depot with only 2 dogs left alive.

WESTERN JOURNEY, OCTOBER 26 TO DECEMBER 24, 1903

SUMMARY CALENDAR OF JOURNEY

(Royds's SE Barrier Party had the surviving sledgemeter. Mileages are Skelton's estimates.)

Oct. 26–Nov. 1	Ship to 5 g/m beyond New Mountain Depot B (87 g/m), losing a day weatherbound at Knobhead Moraine camp.
Nov. 2–Nov. 4	To "Desolation Camp" (1:30 P.M.) (20 g/m).
Nov. 4–Nov. 10	At "Desolation Camp" weatherbound.
Nov. 11–Nov. 12	Ascent to summit. Scott's "We rose nearly 700 feet on the 11th, and over another steep fall . . . on the 12th" equates to

the route indicated.[8] Skelton's "much further NE than previous year" meant NE magnetic (11 g/m).[9]

Nov. 11–Nov. 22 — 66½ g/m to point where Skelton, Feather, and Handsley turn back. Sledges pulled separately from 16th when Skelton and Evans swapped places in tents. Scott, Feather, and Evans pulled the 11-foot sledge in the lead until relaying began on November 20, when Scott wrote that Feather "has been suffering agonies from his back."[10] Normal progress resumed P.M. the next day.

Nov. 23–Nov. 30 — Scott, Lashly, Evans continue to farthest west.

Dec. 1–Dec. 13 — Return to just short of upper icefall in 159°24'30"E.

Dec. 14 — Reached Depot Nunatak, mended damaged 11-foot sledge, picked up 9-foot sledge and two days' rations.

Dec. 15–Dec. 16 — To Knobhead Moraine, eating main meal at New Mountain Depot B.

Dec. 17–Dec. 19 — To defile beyond Mummy Pond in Dry Valley and return.

Dec. 20–Dec. 24 — Return to ship via Butter Point and the Eskers.

SUMMARY OF CONDITIONS IN TERMS OF HEADWIND AND SURFACE

Table 23 in the Scientific Report[11] compiled by the Meteorological Office purports to be a record for Scott's entire journey but was in fact taken from Skelton's report and therefore shows weather and surface conditions on the outward journey up to November 22 and for his party's return journey until arrival at the ship on December 16, 1903. In the following table, conditions after November 22 are therefore approximations deduced from Scott's incomplete published account and occasional remarks in Lashly's diary. In comparing this with the Southern journey, the term *favorable* needs to be qualified by allowing for the 8,000+-foot altitude, to which they had little chance to acclimatize.

JOURNEY FROM AND TO UPPER ICEFALL CAMP

	Days on Move	
	Westward	*Return*
Adverse conditions		
Headwind force 2 or more:		
with heavy surface or high *sastrugi*	6	0
with fair surface	7	0
High *sastrugi* or heavy surface		
with force 1 wind or less hindering		
outward march or helping return	3	5
	16	5

Continued on next page

Journey From and to Upper Icefall Camp–continued

	Days on Move	
	Westward	*Return*
Average conditions		
Sail aided on heavy surface		
with some *sastrugi*	0	7
Favorable conditions		
Fair surface (on return, sail-aided		
on Dec. 8 only)	2	1
TOTAL:	18	13

DID SCOTT CONTINUE BEYOND
THE SAFE POINT OF RETURN?

After the expedition, Scott wrote that the "original" plan was to sledge westward until November 30.[12] That date would have been based on the rations they could take when they set out from New Mountain Depot B on November 1. According to Lashly (diary, November 1), they had 48 days' rations (meaning for the Summit Party). After 30 days westward there would have been 18 days' rations for the return and a safety margin. As noted in Chapter 24, Scott's account effectively establishes they had 16 days' food left after the evening meal on the 30th.[13] That was equal to the actual time it took them to get back to New Mountain Depot. They still had 7 days' food after supper on the 9th, but during the 5 days that brought them to the Nunatak Depot they must have consumed virtually all of it, for Scott wrote of finding a "small quantity" there, "enough to carry us to the depot . . . provided we marched hard."[14]

The evidence on kerosene appears contradictory. Whereas Lashly (November 30) wrote of a 16-day supply remaining (no shortage), two days later Scott spoke of "perhaps 12 days' "[15] in hand, meaning either that they were 2 days short when they started back or that that amount had been lost during capsizes the first 2 days, when visibility was frequently very poor.

Common to both food and fuel is the absence of a safety stock of the kind Scott had insisted on preserving on the last outward leg of the Southern journey. The question remains: Knowing of the unexplained losses on the Southern journey, why did Scott not seize the proffered second chance to bring out more fuel, at least for the Nunatak Depot if not for the Summit Party? If he had insisted on a 5-day safety margin for a 2-week journey back from his farthest south to the second depot on the Southern journey, then a similar precaution was surely essential for the 16-day return from farthest west on the summit. Strictly speaking, the conclusion correctly asserted by Huntford (1979: p. 183) must be that he depleted that margin by going on for 2½ days more than was safe. Many great explorers have taken greater risks.

APPENDIX 8

MEDALS AWARDED FOR THE BRITISH AND GERMAN EXPEDITIONS

THE POLAR MEDAL[1]

Just three days after the return of the expedition to Lyttelton on April 1, 1904, the First Sea Lord, Adm. Lord Walter Kerr, began to investigate whether the expedition would qualify for award of the Arctic Medal, last struck in circular form for the 1875–1876 Arctic expedition during which Markham's cousin had achieved a farthest north at 83°20'30"N beyond Ellesmere Island. By May 26, having established that no medal had been granted for Sir James Ross's 1839–1843 expedition, his colleague Vice Admiral Drury, the Second Sea Lord, proposed that a new Antarctic Medal be instituted. The First Lord of the Admiralty, the Earl of Selborne, quickly approved an approach to King Edward VII, as the monarch's approval was a prerequisite for all new medals bearing the royal effigy.

After consultations with the Deputy Master of the Mint and Prince Louis of Battenberg, Commander in Chief Atlantic Fleet, Treasury approval was obtained, followed by the king's approval for an octagonal medal after the pattern of the original Arctic Medal sanctioned for expeditions up to 1855 but with clasps indicating dates of service in the Arctic or Antarctic. The new medal was announced in the *Times* on September 12, 1904, two days after the *Discovery* returned to Portsmouth, as being awarded to "the crew of the *Discovery*."

But the possibility of also awarding the medal to men serving on the *Morning* had been mentioned in the approach to the Treasury in the context of probable cost involved. Unquestioned then or since, letters were sent to both Scott and Colbeck after their return to England requesting lists of those who served on each ship and asking each to state whom they were not prepared to recommend for the award. In February 1905 news of this plan reached the now retired Hydrographer, Adm. Sir William Wharton, who had chaired the committee that organized the second relief expedition. He and Vice Admiral Aldrich wrote on behalf of the committee to the permanent secretary of the Admiralty, Sir Ivan McGregor, arguing that if the *Morning* was to be included, there was an equal case for the medal being awarded to men of the *Terra Nova.*

Markham and Scott heard this news from Admiral Aldrich, and the two men clearly saw it as watering down the medal's prestige. In a letter bearing a heavy imprint of Markham's dictation, Scott wrote to the Admiralty on February 17, saying that although he could see no good case against inclusion of the *Terra Nova* if the matter were raised in the House of Commons, he agreed with the reference in the *Times* confining it to the men of the *Discovery.* His "private opinion was a different matter. I should be proud to share an award with some who served in the *Morning* and I shall cease to value it when shared with some who were in the *Terra Nova.*"[2]

Reaction at the Admiralty was similar. In a minute to McGregor, the naval branch secretary pointed out that the medal ought to be more highly prized than the RGS medals,* which were only going to those who had served throughout aboard *Discovery* with the exception of Shackleton and Mulock. But, he continued, the October letter to Colbeck "might be held to be an indication of an intention to grant the Medal to some, at any rate, who sailed in the *Morning.*"[3]

The First Lord's reaction was to minute that he had always envisaged the award being given to *Discovery* men only, and the approach to Colbeck without his authority "was most irregular." But the award to *Morning* men had been implied and would have to be honored. He saw no difference in the case of the *Terra Nova* and believed those who returned in the *Morning* should receive it too—"the precedent of the *Pandora* seems to be against us too." But he suggested that only those who served through two Antarctic winters should receive the medal with clasp, as should "those who, like Lieut. Shackleton, were compulsorily invalided."[4]

---

* In certain museum and numismatic circles the Society medals are referred to as medallions. However, the term *medal* is used throughout this book because they are described as medals in the Admiralty correspondence file on the Polar Medal.

Until then, the medal had been approved in silver, but clearly with the original Treasury approval in mind and the prospect of perhaps a hundred medals now required, Rear Admiral Durnford, the Fourth Sea Lord, suggested the medal be in bronze for those who did not serve two winters, except for Shackleton. The following day the Earl of Selborne approved the Bronze Polar Medal. The conditions for that award, justified in this case by the award of the 1876 Arctic Medal to Sir Allen Young's steam yacht *Pandora*, remained widely variable, finally becoming almost impossibly contorted on the last occasion on which they were awarded—in 1942 for the interwar Discovery Investigations whaling research voyages.[5]

The final conditions for silver and bronze medal awards, approved by the king at the end of March 1905, read:

> The Medal in Silver with the clasp inscribed "Antarctic 1902–1904" may be awarded to all those who went out in the "Discovery" and remained throughout the stay of the ship in the Antarctic Regions, from the time of her arrival to the time of her departure, namely 3 Jan 1902 to 5 Mar 1904, or to any member compulsorily invalided after 3 Jan 1902, or to any who joined "Discovery" during her second winter in the Antarctic.
>
> A Bronze Medal of the same design [is] to be awarded to those members of the "Discovery" who did not remain, for causes other than sickness, throughout the stay of the ship in the Antarctic Regions; also to the members of the relief ships "Morning" and "Terra Nova" who served in the Antarctic. The Medal [is] not to be granted to any person whose conduct was unsatisfactory.[6]

THE ROYAL GEOGRAPHICAL SOCIETY MEDALS[7]

On Friday, April 2, 1904, Sir Clements Markham first received news of the return of the *Discovery* and relief ships to Lyttelton. At the Society's Council meeting the following Monday he proposed the award of the Patron's Gold Medal and a Special Gold Medal to Scott after the style of the Special Medal presented in 1896 to Nansen, with silver and bronze replicas to his companion officers and crew aboard the *Fram*. The Special Gold Medal was to be designed by Gilbert Bayes and struck by Allan Wyon, whose father had designed the reverses of the British Gold Sovereign and the Society's Founder's and Patron's Medals, the latter first awarded to Wilkes in 1848. Glazed like the other medals with "lunettes" held by a shrunk-on gold band, the Special Gold Medal was 2¾ inches in diameter, as were its replica silver medals, which were named on the edge. The order finally placed on October 19, 1904, was for the gold medal, thirty-seven silver, and six bronze replica

REVERSE FACES OF THE ROYAL GEOGRAPHICAL SOCIETY'S PATRON'S GOLD MEDAL AND THE POLAR MEDAL WITH THE EXPEDITION MEDAL AND THE TWO VERSIONS OF ITS REVERSE FACE. The engraved reverse (*left*) was awarded by Lt. Armitage to an unknown number of the officers and men he led on the first ascent to the Victoria Land icecap. At right is the die-struck reverse of the medal awarded for sports and other winter competitions. Courtesy, the late Sir Peter Scott CH, CBE, DSC, FRS; the Scott Polar Research Institute; Messrs. Sotheby and Co., and John G. Scott, grandson of Cpl. Gilbert Scott RM.

medals—the last for museums, with one for the Society's collection. All were supplied in cases.

The medals were received from Wyon in mid-February 1905. Markham presented the gold medal to Scott at the February 27 Council dinner following Scott's lecture on the scientific results of the expedition. Markham also presented replica silver medals to Royds, Skelton, Wilson, Bernacchi, Ferrar, and Wild.

THE SMALL EXPEDITION MEDAL

These small 30 mm silver medals were struck before the expedition left England and were in two forms. One type, for Antarctic sports, had a die-struck reverse inscription "Antarctic Sports won by"; the other had a plain reverse for award at the discretion of officers.

The numbers struck and won or awarded are unknown. The *South Polar Times* of April 1903 gives the winners of the 1902 King's Birthday Sports events but only refers to medals won by Wild for draughts and acrostics. The medal illustrated here must have been one of those, as Wild did not figure among the Sports Day winners. By contrast, Bernacchi is given as a member of Koettlitz's team that won the 1-mile sledge dragging race, and his sports medal, in the Canterbury Museum at Christchurch, NZ, is probably for that event. If so, medals would also have been given to Skelton, Ferrar, Dellbridge, and Croucher, the other members of his team. Other winners who would have received medals were Quartley and Hubert (two-man toboggan race), Clarke (putting the weight), Quartley's six-man team (Tug o'War), Ferrar (shooting), Skelton (downhill skiing), and Edgar Evans (ski race on flat). The King's Birthday program records that all the prizes were presented by Gilbert Scott, described in Duncan's diary as presenting the medals after the evening concert.[8] No evidence could be found of other blank-reverse medals, of which the medal to Gilbert Scott appears to be the sole example known.

LIST 1: POLAR MEDALS AWARDED TO MEN OF THE DISCOVERY

A: SILVER MEDALS WITH CLASP ANTARCTIC 1902-04

Name	Rank/Rating In Roll	No. of Clasps (Add'l Dates)	Notes	Other Service Medals	Polar Medal with Others	RGS Medal	Museum/Private Collection?
Scott, Robert Falcon	Commr. RN	2 (1910–13)	(1)	List 2	–	No	F+CNZ
Armitage, Albert Borlase	Lieut. RNR	1	(2)	List 3	Yes	Yes	PC
Royds, Chas Wyatt Rawson	Lieut. RN	1	(2)	List 3	Yes	Yes	PC
Barne, Michael	Lieut. RN	1	(1)	List 3	Yes	Yes	
Shackleton, Ernest Henry	Sub. Lieut. RNR	3 (1907–09) (1914–16)	(1)	List 3	Yes	No	
Mulock, Geo. Fredk Arthur	Lieut. RN	1	(1,4)	GW?	*	*	
Skelton, Reginald William	Engr Lieut RN	1	(1)	List 3	*	*	
Koettlitz, Reginald	Surgeon	1	(3)	–	–	*	
Wilson, Edward Adrian	Surgeon	2 (1910–13)	(1,5)	–	–	Yes	SPRI
Bernacci, Louis Charles	Physicist	1	(1)	List 3	Yes	Yes	CNZ
Hodgson, Thomas Vere	Biologist	1	(1)	–	–	*	
Ferrar, Hartley Travis	Geologist	1	(3)	GW	Yes	Yes	SPRI
Feather, Thomas Alfred	Boatsn PO 1cl	1	(1)	GW3, LSGCE7	Yes	No	PC
Dailey, Frederick E.	Carpr RN	1	(1)	List 3	Yes	Yes	PC
Dellbridge, James H.	ERA 2cl RN	1	(2,6)	List 3	No	No	PC
Ford, Chas Reginald	Dom 1cl RN	1	(3,7)	?	*	*	ANZ
Clarke, Charles	Ship's cook	1	(3)	?	?	?	
Blissett, Arthur Henry	Pte RMLI	1	(3,8)	GW ?	Yes	Yes	CNZ
Scott, Gilbert	Pte RMLI	1	(2,8)	List 3	Yes	Yes	
Allan, David Silver	PO 1cl RN	1	(2,9)	BWM, LSGCE7	Yes	Yes	PC
Cross, Jacob	PO 1cl RN	1	(2)	LSGCE7	*	?	
Smythe, William	PO 1cl RN	1	(9)	No	No	No	RNM

Name	Rank	Expeditions	Ref	Awards			
Evans, Edgar	PO 2cl RN	1	(2,10)	—	—	Yes	PC
Kennar, Thomas	PO 2cl RN	1	(2)	GW?	*	?	
Pilbeam, Arthur	Ldg Smn RN	1	(2)	GW3, LSGCG5	*	?	
Crean, Thomas	AB RN	3 (1910–13) (1914–16)	(2)	List 3	Yes	Yes	DM+PC
Croucher, George Beaver	AB RN	1	(3,11)	GW3, LSGCG5	Yes	Yes	
Dell, James William	AB RN	1	(2)	List 3	Yes	Yes	
Heald, William Lofthouse	AB RN	2 (1910–13)	(2)	GW3	Yes	No	DF
Hansdley, Jesse	AB RN	1	(2,11)	GW3, LSGCE7	No	No	PC
Joyce, Ernest Edward Mills	AB RN	4 (1907–09) (1914–16) (1917)	(3)	List 3	Yes	Yes	SPRI+CNZ
Wild, John R. Frank	AB RN (1912–1914) (1914–1916)	4 (1907–09)	(2)	List 3	No	No	F+PC
Williamson, Thomas Soulsby	AB RN	2 (1910–13)	(2)	GW, LSGC	*	*	
Weller, William Isaac	AB	1	(3,12)	?	?	?	
Lashly, William	Lg Sto 1cl RN	2 (1910–13)	(2)	List 3	Yes	Yes	PC
Quartley, Arthur Lester	Lg Sto 1cl RN	1	(2)	List 3	Yes	Yes	PC
Whitfield, Thomas	Lg Sto 1cl RN	1	(2)	List 3	Yes	Yes	PC
Plumley, Frank	Sto RN	1	(2)	List 3	Yes	Yes	
B: Bronze Medals Without Clasp							
Duncan, James	Carp Mate	—	(3,4)	—	—	—	CDM
Hare, Clarence H.	Domestic	—	(3,4)	GW	Yes	—	
MacFarlane, William	PO 1cl RN	—	(2,4)	GW, LSGCE7	Yes	—	PC
Vince, George Thomas	AB RN	—	(3,13)	QSA (no clasp)	Yes	—	PC
Walker, John D.	AB	—	(3,4)	—	—	—	NMM

* RGS Medal in National Maritime Museum, Greenwich.

NOTES TO LIST 1:
POLAR MEDALS TO MEN OF THE DISCOVERY

1. Polar Medal presented by King Edward VII at Buckingham Palace, December 18, 1905.

2. Polar Medal sent to recipient via ship, unit, or establishment.

3. Polar Medal sent directly to recipient.

4. Naming on edge includes dates 1902–03 after ship's name (probably 1903–04 on Lieutenant Mulock's medal).

5. Also in the SPRI collection with his Polar Medal and RGS 1904 Silver Medal is his RGS 1913 Silver Medal (unnamed as issued) together with the Royal Italian Geographical Society's Silver Memorial Medal with the inscription in raised capital lettering on the reverse reading: Alla memoria / del dottor / E. A. Wilson / compagno / di R. F. Scott / nella gloria / e nel martirio /1913 (oblique strokes indicate division into lines).

6. Roll also states "Second Engr (WO)" under rating.

7. Roll also states "Acting Ship's Steward (WO)" under rating.

8. Roll also states "Wardroom Servant" under rating.

9. Names given in roll as Allen and Smyth but given here as they appear on Allan's and Smythe's Polar and RGS Medals, which were the spellings in Scott's September 22, 1904, listing for the Admiralty.

10. A duplicate Polar Medal was issued to his widow, Lois Evans, on January 20, 1914. In addition to the replacement 1902–04 clasp issued with it, the medal has the "Antarctic 1910–13" clasp presented to her by King George V at Buckingham Palace on July 26, 1913, and was carried to the South Pole by Robert F. Swan on his 1984–1986 "In the Footsteps of Scott" expedition. Evans's bronze 1913 RGS Memorial Medal is in the possession of Robert Swan's family. Evans's original Polar Medal (offered at auction in December 1984 with his RGS 1904 Silver Medal named Edgar Evans, RN) also has the 1910–13 clasp. This clasp was clearly made privately, for it is about a millimeter narrower than the clasps struck at the Mint, which were identical in dimensions to the original 1902–04 clasps. There is little doubt that Evans had sold both these medals before joining Scott's second expedition, as almost certainly happened in the case of Quartley's RGS Silver Medal (now reunited with his medals), which he had at one stage offered to the British Museum for £20.[9] The whereabouts of Evans's Italian 1913 Silver Memorial Medal is unknown. The inscription on its reverse is similar to that on Wilson's but with the second and third lines reading / di / Edgar Evans /.

11. Killed in action in World War I.

12. The medal is undoubtedly named to I. Weller, as the roll gives his first name as Isaac.

13. The naming on Vince's QSA Medal gives his ship as HMS *Beagle*.

LEGEND TO ROLLS OF POLAR MEDALS FOR THE EXPEDITION
(LISTS 1, 4, AND 5)

Ratings

Dom 1cl	Domestic 1st Class
PO 1cl	Petty Officer 1st Class
ERA	Engine Room Artificer
AB	Able Seaman
Pte RMLI	Private, Royal Marine Light Infantry

Other Medals

AGS	Army General Service Medal
BWM	British War Medal
GW	British War and Victory Medals
GW3	1914-1915 Star, British War, and Victory Medals
GW?	Known to have served but medals unknown
LSGC	(E7) or (G5) Naval Long Service Medal (with reign where known)
MSM	Meritorious Service Medal (extant 1919-1928, then merged with British Empire Medal)
MWM	Mercantile Marine War Medal
NGS	Naval General Service Medal
QSA	Queen's South Africa Medal for Boer War
WW2	1939-1945 War Medal

Location

SPRI	Scott Polar Research Institute, Cambridge
ANZ	Auckland Museum, Wellington, New Zealand
CNZ	Canterbury Museum, Christchurch, New Zealand
ONZ	Otago Museum, Dunedin, New Zealand
CDM	City of Dundee Museums, Scotland
DM	Dingle Museum, County Kerry, Eire
GM	Glenbow Museum, Calgary, Alberta, Canada
NMM	National Maritime Museum, Greenwich
RNM	Royal Naval Museum, Portsmouth
PC	Private Collection
DF	Medals known to be divided among relatives
F+	Some of recipient's medals with family

LIST 2: CAPTAIN SCOTT'S MEDALS

A: Awarded for the 1901-1904 National Antarctic Expedition

	Date	Diameter	Notes
Commander Royal Victoria Order (CVO)	(1904)*		
Polar Medal with clasps Antarctic 1902-1904,			
Antarctic 1910-1913	(1904)*		1
Légion d'Honneur (officier) (France)	(1906)*		1
Royal Geographical Society			
Patron's Gold Medal	(1904)*	glazed 54 mm	2
Special Gold Medal	(1904)*	glazed 70 mm	2
Royal Scottish Geographical Society Livingstone Gold Medal	(1904)*	63 mm	3
Philadelphia Geographical Society Elisha Kent Kane Gold Medal	(1904)	41 mm	4
Swedish Geographical Society "Vega" Gold Medal	(1905)*	56 mm	5
Royal Danish Geographical Society Gold Medal	(1906)	43 mm	5
Royal Antwerp Geographical Society Gold Medal	(1906)	60 mm	6
Royal Belgian Geographical Society Silver Medal	(1906)	60 mm	7
American Geographical Society of New York Cullum Gold Medal	(1907)*	70 mm	8
Berlin Geographical Society Gustav Nachtigal Gold Medal	(1908)*	51 mm	9

Captain Scott also received the Gold Medal of the Royal Yacht Club of Belgium (35½ mm diameter) in 1904 and a silver plaque awarded by the 1906 Marseilles Exposition Coloniale Council (71×52 mm rectangular).

B: Awarded for His 1910-1913 British Antarctic Expedition

	Date	Diameter	Notes
Royal Geographical Society Silver Memorial Medal	(1913)*	55 mm	10
Royal Italian Geographical Society King Umberto Gold Medal	(1913)*	55 mm	11
Royal Geographical Society of Vienna Silver Memorial Medal	(1914)	60 mm	
Geographical Society of Chicago Helen Culver Gold Medal	(1914)	63½ mm	

*A lifesize color photo montage of these medals donated by the author can be seen at the Dundee Heritage Trust's Discovery Point Centre beside the *Discovery* berth at Dundee. In addition to the medal faces shown in the illustration of Scott's medals, the picture includes both faces of the RSGS Livingstone Gold Medal and the RGS 1913 Silver Memorial Medal plus the reverse faces of the Swedish and Italian Gold Medals and the obverse of the New York Society's Cullum Gold Medal.

NOTES

1. These medals are displayed in the Canterbury Museum, Christchurch, NZ. The central République Française 1870 plaque is missing from the Légion badge. In the color plate the plaque from another example has been superimposed.

2. Engraved in capitals on the "lunette" retaining band: Commander Robert F. Scott, R.N. 1904.

3. Engraved in capitals on the edge: Captain Robert Falcon Scott R.N. C.V.O. National Antarctic Expedition 1901-04.

4. Engraved in capitals on reverse: Capt. / Robert Falcon Scott R.N. / 1904.

5. Engraved in capitals on the edge: Robert F. Scott 1906.

6. Engraved in capitals on obverse: Au Capitaine / Robert F. Scott CVO RN / 19 Avril 1906.

7. Engraved in capitals on reverse: 24 Avril 1906 / au Capitaine R. F. Scott / Commandant de / l'Expedition Antarctique Anglaise / 1901-1904.

8. Engraved in capitals on the obverse: Awarded to Captain / Robert F. Scott R.N. / for the voyage of the / ship Discovery and / the sledge journey / to Lat. 82°17'S / MCMI-MCMIV.

9. The Berlin Society's title was Institut für Erdkunde (earth sciences). The medal, instituted in honor of the first European to cross the Sahara (in 1824), is engraved in capitals on the edge with the recipient's name, Robert F. Scott at the top of the medal, and the date 1908 at the bottom.

10. Unnamed.

11. The inscription in raised lettering in capitals on the reverse reads: Alla memoria / di / Robert F. Scott R.N. / giunto secondo / alla polo australe / surgella / colla morte / la verita della scoperta 1913 [second to arrive at the Pole sealing with death the truth of the discovery].

LIST 3: KNOWN ORDERS AND SERVICE MEDALS TO OTHER *DISCOVERY* POLAR MEDAL RECIPIENTS

Name	Orders and Service Medals	Notes
ARMITAGE	BWM, MWM, Volunteer Decoration	
ROYDS	KBE, CMG, GW3, Coronation 1911, Foreign: Légion d'Honneur (France), Nile (Egypt), Rising Sun (Japan)	
BARNE	DSO, GW3, WW2, Royal Humane Society Silver (1914)	
SHACKLETON	CVO, OBE, GW	1
SKELTON	KCB, CB, CBE, DSO, GW3 Foreign: Légion d'Honneur (France), St. Stanislas, St. Anne (Russia)	
BERNACCHI	OBE, GW3 Foreign: Légion d'Honneur (France), Navy Cross (USA)	
DAILEY	DSC, GW3 Foreign: St. Anne (Russia)	
DELLBRIDGE	GW3, LSGC	2
G. SCOTT	GW3, LSGC, 1911 Durbar Medal	
CREAN	Albert Medal (land), BWM, MWM	3
DELL	NGS (1915) clasp Persian Gulf 1909-1914, GW3, Defence, LSGC(G5)	
JOYCE	Albert Medal (land), QSA clasp Cape Colony	4
WILD	CBE, GW	5
LASHLY	Albert Medal (land), AGS clasp Somaliland 1908-10, GW, LSGC	
QUARTLEY	GW, MSM, LSGC	
PLUMLEY	QSA (no clasp—stoker HMS *Gibraltar*), GW3, LSGC	

ORDERS AND DECORATIONS
(SEE ALSO MEDAL ABBREVIATIONS IN LEGEND TO LIST 1)

CB	Commander of the Order of the Bath
CBE	Commander of the Order of the British Empire
CMG	Commander of the Order of St. Michael and St. George
CVO	Commander of the Royal Victorian Order
DSC	Distinguished Service Cross
DSO	Distinguished Service Order
KBE	Knight of the Order of the British Empire
KCB	Knight Commander of the Order of the Bath
OBE	Officer of the Order of the British Empire

NOTES

1. All of Shackleton's gold medals were stolen. With the exception of the RGS 1904 Silver Medal, they were awarded for his subsequent expeditions and are too numerous to list here. A lifesize color photo montage of his Polar Medal, British Orders, and miniatures is on display at the Dundee Heritage Trust Discovery Point Centre, and a larger picture including the principal orders he received for his *Nimrod* (British Antarctic) and *Endurance* (Imperial Trans-Antarctic) expeditions is on display in the New Zealand Antarctic Society central office in the Christchurch Arts Centre and occasionally at functions organized by the Antarctic Heritage Trust to which it was presented by the author.

2. Dellbridge's original Polar Medal is in a private collection. A duplicate was issued in 1908 and is assumed to be with his service medals. It is unknown whether his replacement medal was engraved on the edge in the original style or named in impressed letters.

3. Crean received a duplicate Polar Medal with 1902-04 clasp issued to Cdr. Evans at the Expedition Office on July 24, 1913, two days before receiving his 1910-13 clasp from King George V at the palace. That Polar Medal is with his Albert Medal (for saving Cdr. Evans's life in 1912) and other medals in Dingle Library, County Kerry, Ireland. Duplicate medals were named in the style prevailing at the time of issue so that, as in Edgar Evans's case, Crean's duplicate Polar Medal would be named in impressed lettering 174699 T. CREAN, A.B. DISCOVERY. The original medal with 1902-1904 clasp was sold by a dealer in 1974.

4. Joyce received a duplicate Polar Medal with clasps Antarctic 1902-04 and Antarctic 1907-09 issued on December 16, 1920. He had also received the 1914-16 and 1917 clasps and was to receive the Albert Medal for saving the life of Lt. Aeneas Mackintosh when with the Ross Sea Party on Shackleton's Imperial Trans-Atlantic expedition (ITAE), and these clasps were fixed to the duplicate medal, which is with his Albert Medal, RGS 1904 and 1909 medals, and original Queen's South Africa Medal in the SPRI collection. His original Polar Medal, also with four clasps, is in the Canterbury Museum at Christchurch, NZ, along with the duplicate QSA Medal. The 1914-16 and 1917 clasps have numeral 1s with hooked tops, whereas the official clasp dies had 1s with straight tops. Clearly, he had the two clasps made privately.

5. With the exception of his CBE and four-clasp Polar Medal, Wild's medals were offered at auction in 1971. His CBE was awarded in 1924, as were his RGS Patron's Gold Medal and the American Geographical Society of New York Livingstone Gold Medal, all for his long career serving on Antarctic expeditions. The RGS and RSGS 1909 Silver Medals, along with the Royal Belgian Geographical Society Bronze Medal, were for his part in the *Nimrod* expedition, and the lot included his Antarctic Sports Medal illustrated in this appendix.

LIST 4: BRONZE POLAR MEDALS WITHOUT CLASP AWARDED TO MEN OF THE MORNING

Name	Rank/Rating in Roll	Dates on Add'l Clasps	Also received Silver Medal Reign/Clasps	On RNR Payroll	Notes Below	In Museum or Private Collection
Colbeck, William	Lieut. RNR	—	—	RNR	1	—
England, Rupert George	First Officer	1907–09	—	—	2	—
Evans, Edw. Ratcliffe Garth	Lieut. RN	—	Geo5/1910–13	—	3	—
Doorly, James Gerald Stokely	Mid. RNR	—	—	RNR	4	ONZ
Morrison, John Donald	Engineer	—	—	—	—	—
Davidson, George Adam	Surgeon	—	—	—	—	—
Pepper, Arthur Neville	Midshipman	—	—	—	—	—
Somerville, Fredk Louis Maitland	Midshipman	—	—	—	—	—
Marsh, Walter John	2nd Engr.	—	—	—	5	PC
Bilsby, Walter George	Carpenter	1907–09	Geo5/1910–13	RNR	—	—
Cheetham, Alfred	Boatsn	1907–09	1914–16	RNR	—	—
Good, John Thomas	Boatsns Mate	—	—	RNR	—	—
Rolfe, George William	Sailmaker	—	—	RNR	—	—
Beaumont, Robert Arthur	AB	—	—	—	6	CNZ
Burgess, Leonard	AB	—	—	RNR	7	PC
Burton, Francis William	AB	—	—	—	—	—
Casement, Arthur	AB	—	—	RNR	—	—
Chester, James Arthur	AB	—	—	—	8	PC
Hender, W. William	AB	—	—	—	9	—
Leary, Geo. Robert William	AB	—	—	RNR	10	PC
Paton, James	AB	1907–09	Geo5/1910–13	—	11	CNZ
Riley, Owen	AB	—	—	RNR	—	—
Kemp, Fredk William	Fireman	—	—	RNR	—	PC
Nelson, David	Fireman	—	—	—	6	CNZ

NOTES

1. All medals except three bore the dates 1902–04 after the ship's name in the engraved naming on the medal edge. Royal Naval Reserve Officers had the initials RNR included in their medal naming, but crew on the RNR payroll did not.

2. Duplicate medal without clasp issued December 3, 1937, engraved on edge: 1st OFFR. R.G.A. ENGLAND, "MORNING," 1902–04.

3. Promoted commander after serving as second in command on Scott's last expedition for which he received the CB prior to winning the DSO in World War I, when he became known as "Evans of the Broke." He subsequently received many other orders and promotion to KCB after rising to admiral's rank in 1936.

4. 4th officer on first voyage to McMurdo Sound, then replaced S/Lt. Mulock as 3rd officer.

5. No issue date given in roll, but extant in private collection. Edge naming includes dates 1903–4 after ship's name.

6. Edge naming includes dates 1903–4 after ship's name.

7. Also received a Russian lifesaving medal and RNR LSGC medal.

8. Served as 2nd steward on second voyage.

9. Edge naming includes dates 1902–3 after ship's name. Markham[12] recorded that he was the "best and most reliable man on board" and had passed the exam for mate, which he became after leaving the *Morning*.

10. Also received RNR LSGC medal.

11. Paton's silver medal was sent to the Expedition Office on July 26, 1913, after Scott's last expedition but was not in his daughter's possession when she gave his bronze medal to the Canterbury Museum, Christchurch, NZ. By the time the medals with 1914–16 clasps were issued in 1918, Paton had been lost with the *Aurora* in the Pacific, having served on the 1914–1916 and 1917 (relief) voyages in support of Shackleton's ITAE Ross Sea Party, and the Admiralty had no record of his next of kin. Despite the roll stating entitlement to a clasp, only a silver medal was struck, named and fitted with a 1914–16 clasp. That medal was never issued and is now in the RN Museum at Portsmouth. His bronze 1917 clasp, struck in 1921, was also never issued. James Paton is listed in the *Guinness Book of Records* as having the greatest number of Polar Medal awards—five—one more than Wild and Joyce.

LIST 5: BRONZE POLAR MEDALS WITHOUT CLASP
AWARDED TO MEN OF THE *TERRA NOVA*[1]

Name	Rank/Rating In Roll	Notes	Remarks	In Museum or Private Col'n
McKay, Henry	Master			
Jackson, Alfred P.	Chief Mate		received two-clasp Transport Medal	GM
Elms, Arthur James	2nd Mate			
Day, Roderick Wilson	3rd Mate			SPRI
Souter, William Clark	Surgeon			
Sharp, Alexander	Chief Engineer	2		CDM
Smith, William	2nd Engineer	2		
McGregor, Colin	3rd Engineer	2		
Aiken, Alexander	Boatswain	2		
Smith, Alexander	Carpenter		Not issued	
Smith, Alexander	Carp. Mate	2		
Morrison, Edward	Sailmaker	2	Duplicate issued (date not recorded)	
Shearer, Thomas A.	Asst. Steward	2		
Grant, John	Cook	2		
Clark, William Oliver	Asst. Cook			PC
Cairns, James	AB	2		
Clark, James	AB			PC
Christie, Robert	AB		Not issued	
Coupar, James	AB	2	Named to J. Cooper	
Cosgrove, Thomas	AB	2		
Dair, John R.	AB	2		
Lawrence, George	AB	2		
Morrell, Alexander	AB		Died in 1905; medal sent to sister Dec. 1906	
McNeill, Alexander	AB		Named to A. McNeil	
Reilly, James	AB	2		
Spaulding, Tasman	AB		Not issued; named to S. Tasman	Royal Mint
Stanistreet, Cyrus	AB		Named to C. Stannistreet	
Strachan, M.	AB		Not issued	
Frederick, John	Fireman	2		
Milne, David T.	Fireman	2		
Frederick, David Henderson	AB	2	Crew agreement gives rating as Trimmer	

NOTES

1. The edge naming on all medals has the dates 1903–4 after the ship's name.
2. Medal issued to the Lord Provost of Dundee for presentation.

AWARDS FOR THE GERMAN EXPEDITION

On December 30, 1903, Drygalski received the Berlin Geographical Society Gold Medal (1904) and the Prussian Order of the Crown 3rd Class (commander), and Kapitän Ruser and Prof. Ernst Vanhöffen received the 4th Class (officer) of the Order. Two years later Drygalski received the Austrian Order of Franz Josef (commander).

APPENDIX 9

THE METEOROLOGICAL OFFICE BLUNDER

In June 1908 the second volume of the scientific reports was published. It contained sharp criticisms of the meteorological observations. The report was published by the prestigious Royal Society, and the criticisms by the Meteorological Office were potentially damaging to the financial prospects for Scott's second expedition, especially when the *Times Literary Supplement*—albeit alone among the reviews—mirrored the criticisms a month before the first public announcement of the expedition.[1] Not even the award of the German Geographical Society's premier Gold Medal in May—the only expedition leader other than Drygalski to receive it—could compensate. The Berlin society's citation referred to the *Discovery* expedition as the most fruitful of any in its results.[2]

Scott faced the principal charge that in the observation of wind direction on the sledge journeys, magnetic and true bearings had been confused by "untrained" observers. Scott and several of his companions were rightly incensed because the Metereological Office had assumed the southwesterly directions reported on Royds's Southeast Barrier journey were magnetic. The report claimed Royds and others had been uncertain about the records, despite the column heading requiring true wind directions to be entered on the forms.

When Scott inquired into it, Royds pointed out that he had stated that all wind directions had been true, expressing some doubt only about two of the early journeys. Others emphatically denied having been vague on the question.[3] The proof that Royds had reported true wind directions on his Barrier journey lay in his November 26, 1903, diary entry during the outward marches to the southeast, in which he describes the wind as "blowing strong in our faces from the SE,"[4] the wind direction entered on the official form that day.

The report also charged that opportunities for instruction at the Meteorological Office had been neglected, whereas Scott knew that many of the instruments on loan from the Hydrographer had not reached Kew until July 15, 1901. It was hardly feasible to have sent officers for more than cursory training in their use with just sixteen hectic days left before the projected sailing date.[5]

Scott also found that the daily positions given in the meteorological tables for some of the sledge journeys bore little relation to fact. The table for his Western Summit journey cited Skelton's reports after his November 23, 1903, turn-back, making them appear as though they were Scott's observations on his continuing outward journey.[6] Challenged by Scott as to why they had ignored the implicit contradiction of the account in *The Voyage of the* Discovery, the Meteorological Office said it did not regard the book as an "official" document![7]

In the case of the Southeast Barrier journey wind directions, Royds's predominantly (68%) SW winds had been arbitrarily converted to east by north winds, the bearing, assumed to be magnetic, corrected for 145° variation.[8] That easterly direction fitted neatly with the prevailing but unproven belief in meteorological circles that an anticyclone persisted at the South Pole, with winds rotating anticlockwise (as is the case in the Southern Hemisphere) around it. The trouble was, as Scott was quick to recognize, the Meteorological Office had applied the variation backward![9]*

Much of the deficiency in the handling of the instruments criticized in the report—for example, the cards had been placed the wrong way around in the sunshine recorder—sprang from the late delivery of and lack of complete instructions for the instruments, which, in turn, were the direct result of defects and dissensions in the early stages before Gregory's resignation. No reference to that fact had been made in the published criticisms, which consequently seemed to Scott and Bernacchi, among others on the expedition, to be directed against them when they should have been directed at the then Hydrographer,

---

* The unjustified charge was still being repeated seventy-five years later. Huntford (1979: p. 241) paraphrased the report's conclusion as follows: "The elementary error of confusing true and magnetic compass bearings had been made, and the wind observations were largely worthless."

Sir William Wharton, who had died in 1905, and the scientists appointed to the original Meteorological Subcommittee. Its members had only met once, with little or no practical profit to the men who would have to carry out the observations in conditions few in the committee room could have foreseen.[10]

Scott asked Sir Archibald Geikie, the president of the Royal Society, for an "official" inquiry (but not, as he later made clear, a public one) to get the error acknowledged, followed by the issue of an errata slip for Vol. 1 of the Meteorological Report to correct those points found in favor of him and his companions.[11] Geikie had thought he meant a "public" inquiry, but even so refused to support a private one, fearing it would stir up the original dissensions—"a subject best left in deserved oblivion," he wrote, appealing for Scott to take the magnanimous course.[12]

Scott then learned of the presidential address to the Physical Society of London, delivered the previous February by Dr. Charles Chree, the Meteorological Office director. Even though it advocated the very support for future expeditions that the National Antarctic expedition had so signally lacked and that Scott so badly needed for his new one, the speech had been couched in terms that could be taken as a criticism of the naval officers on the expedition. In the middle of a frustrating and protracted attempt to set the record straight while starting to organize an expedition that would depend for support on public and scientific rather than Treasury confidence, it was hardly surprising that Scott took it almost personally. Dr. Chree had begun with some perfectly justifiable remarks:[13]

> When referring to any British national undertaking, such as a war or a scientific expedition, one is expected to apologise for a greater or less amount of preliminary muddle. Perhaps as a variant I may be allowed to say a few words as to what should in my opinion be done when the next National Scientific Expedition is being prepared. . . . All the apparatus for the expedition should be ready and thoroughly tested at least three months before the expedition sets out, and the observers should use this apparatus sufficiently to become entirely at home with it. A programme [for each subject] should be drawn up and the observers practised in its execution. . . . The necessity for a programme would no doubt be lessened if the expedition were under the command of a Physicist of resource and ripe experience.

Moving onto thinner ice and seeming to have forgotten about the *Antarctic Manual*, prepared by the foremost scientists of the day to guide the scientific program, Dr. Chree plunged on toward the boundaries of tact:

But if, as is most likely, it is under the command of someone whose knowledge of physical science is very limited, it is eminently desirable that some authoritative instructions should exist. . . . It might also serve a useful purpose—though in so hurried an era as ours the idea may appear quixotic—if, on the return of the expedition and after a general examination of its results, something equivalent to a scientific court-martial were held by a competent judicial body whose expressions of approval or blame would carry weight. As matters stand, the observer who confines himself to purely scientific work—however efficient—can have no assurance that he will not be entirely overshadowed by the doers of exploits which appeal to the popular imagination.

More than ever, Scott wanted an inquiry to set the record straight. The situation was not helped when the Royal Society Council referred the matter to Admiral Mostyn Field, now Hydrographer, the very man who had so vehemently opposed Scott's appointment. Field conceded the point about the variation mistake, but although he regretted that the Meteorological Office had not consulted Scott before publishing its criticisms, he generally took their side. But he had changed his mind about Scott's ability to lead the expedition: "I have the highest admiration for the way in which Captain Scott conducted the Expedition, and as a leader of men he showed that no officer could be better qualified for carrying out what he undertook. His misfortune lay in the fact that his officers were imperfectly trained in the scientific duties."[14]

Unfortunately, at that stage Scott was so incensed that he offered to bring forward more evidence. That gave Sir Archibald the license he needed to avoid a public row and leave the matter hanging. With the ever rising tempo of preparations, Scott found no more time to marshal the further grounds for the inquiry he had in mind.

A year later, with Scott's new expedition scheduled to leave shortly and the second meteorological volume—containing the first weather mapping of the entire Southern Hemisphere—scheduled for publication at the end of the year, Geikie proposed that a résumé of Scott's objections to the first volume be included in the preface. Scott approved it the day before his expedition sailed and never lived to see it published. The report finally came out in 1913.

APPENDIX 10

GEOLOGICAL TIMETABLE

Based on A *Geologic Timescale 1989* by W. B. Harland, R. L. Armstrong, and others; published by Cambridge University Press 1990, with modifications to event dating suggested by Dr. Margaret A. Bradshaw, who advised most recent radiometric age of 178 million years for Ferrar Intrusion (*overleaf*).

APPROXIMATE DIAGRAM OF GEOLOGICAL PERIODS

Era	Millions of Years Ago (Ma)	Period	Ma	Epoch	Events/Remarks
Cenozoic (Quaternary)	0			Pleistocene	
	1.63		1.63	Pliocene	
		Neogene	12	Miocene	
Cenozoic (Tertiary)	23.3		23.3	Oligocene	
	40	Paleogene		Eocene	
	60			Palaeocene	Higher animals appeared
	65		65		Dinosaur extinction
Mesozoic	145.6	Cretaceous			Modern plants appeared

"Ferrar Intrusion" (178 Ma)
(visible on Finger Mountain cliffs)

Mammals first appeared

Antarctica part of Gondwana
southern supercontinent

Jurassic

208——

Triassic

——246——

Permian

290——

Carboniferous

362.5——

Devonian

408.5——

Silurian

439——

Ordovician

510——

Cambrian

——570——

Paleozoic

Pre-Cambrian

NOTES

LEGEND

ARCHIVAL SOURCES AND SOCIETY JOURNALS

CMA   Canterbury (NZ) Museum Archives

GJ   *Geographical Journal* (Journal of Royal Geographical Society, vol./ issue no. indicated)

PRGS   Proceedings of Royal Geographical Society, London (vol./issue no. indicated)

PRO   Public Record Office, Kew

PRS   Proceedings of Royal Society, London

RGS   Royal Geographical Society, London

RGSAA   Royal Geographical Society Antarctic Archives with file/document number

RSA   Royal Society Archives

SGM   *Scottish Geographical Magazine* (Journal of Royal Scottish Geographical Society)

SPRI   Scott Polar Research Institute Archives, with manuscript reference

SR   Expedition Scientific Report

DIARIES AND OTHER DOCUMENTS REFERRED TO BY ABBREVIATION

DD   Diary of James Duncan, Shipwright

Ellis   Diary of William Lashly, Chief Stoker (extracts edited by Cdr. A. R. Ellis)

FD   Diary of Hartley T. Ferrar (from extracts he compiled and sent home from New Zealand)

FR   H. T. Ferrar's 1.25.04 report to Scott (copy in possession of his family)

MD   Diary of Sir Clements R. Markham

WD   Edward Wilson's 1901–1904 diary (edited by Ann Savours)

Diaries and Journals in SPRI Archives Referred to by Manuscript Number

342/1	R. W. Skelton diary
352/2	R. F. Scott journal, Oct. 10–26, 1900
353/3	L. C. Bernacchi journal
366/6	M. Barne sledging journals
436/2	Geo. Murray diary
575/2	E. H. Shackleton diary
595/1	T. V. Hodgson diary
641	C.W.R. Royds diary
689/13	H. T. Ferrar sledging journal, 1903
753	C. H. Hare diary
774/1	T. S. Williamson diary
972	F. Plumley diary
1254	H. T. Ferrar journal
1264/2	H. T. Ferrar W. Supporting Party sledge journal
1456	E. H. Shackleton journal (Fisher transcript)
1464	R. F. Scott journal

Published Books Referred to by Author's Name and Year of Publication (plus vol. number, where applicable, except for following: SLE = *Scott's Last Expedition*; SPT = *South Polar Times*.

PROLOGUE

1. Neumayer story based on his *Auf zum Südpol* (1901).

2. Markham story based on Markham (1917).

3. Markham's first encounter with the effects of scurvy occurred as the story of its ravages emerged after the expedition returned. The Admiralty committee ascribed it to absence of lime juice in the sledging rations, but Markham disagreed on the grounds that several who remained with the ships and drank ample lime juice also developed severe symptoms. Knowing of its failure in their cases, it is hard to understand how twenty-five years later he allowed the surgeon on the *Discovery* expedition to recommend lime juice instead of lemon juice.

4. GJ 3/1: Jan. 1894, p. 1–41.

5. Bertrand (1971): p. 150.

6. PRGS 21/6: Sept. 1877.

7. Neumayer was appointed a Privy Councillor in the 1890s, at which point he added the titular "von" to his name.

CHAPTER 1

1. GJ 14/2: Aug. 1899, pp. 191–203.

CHAPTER 2

1. RGS: Report of the VIth International Geographical Congress, July 1895.

2. Markham (1986): p. 7.

3. MD: 9.9–10.1896.

4. Drygalski (1989): chapter 1.

5. PRS 1898: pp. 424–451.

6. Credited with being the first to set foot on the unknown continent when landed from a whaling reconnaissance at Cape Adare in January 1895 (unknown at that time was the landing by American sealers near Cape Sterneck in Graham Land in January 1821), Borchgrevink had addressed the 1895 London congress, declaring his belief that a party could winter there. Subsequently, he won the backing of London publisher Sir George Newnes early in 1898 to the tune of £35,000, a sum that would have saved much anguish in the funding of the national expedition and ensured government support at least a year earlier. Aware of De Gerlache's intention to land a wintering party at Cape Adare but assuming that the Belgian expedition was a total loss, the *Southern Cross* expedition had among its aims an approach to the South Magnetic Pole. The coastline proved impenetrable, but the first year-round scientific observations from the Antarctic shore were brought back, and in the second season a short sledge journey was made on Ross's barrier surface near the Bay of Whales to establish a new farthest south record. However, although the existence of McMurdo Sound was not revealed, a landing at Wood Bay on the north flank of Mount Melbourne in 74°S on the coast of Victoria Land, and the deceptive appearance of an easy route to the summit, significantly influenced the planning of the national expedition.

7. Drygalski (1989): chapter 1.

8. MD: 3.21.1899.

9. GJ 14/2: Aug. 1899, p. 200.

10. Ibid., p. 201.

CHAPTER 3

1. RGSAA 5/1/2: 3.29.1899, 5/1/3: 3.30.1899. Dated "29th" and "30th." File sequence indicates written in March 1899.

2. Ibid., 5/1/4: 3.25.1899 (only Sir William's reply in file).

3. Ibid., 5/1/4: 3.25.1899.

4. Ibid., 5/1/6: 4.4.1899.

5. SPRI 342/1/1: undated, p. 1. How right he was to prove is shown by the widespread departure from the types of wood specified in the inquiry for tenders and the varied origins of timber used in the hull. American oak was used for the stem, keel, stern, and rudder posts and Scottish oak for the frames, with some of the beams in Russian oak and others in pitch pine. The outer planking was of Canadian elm below the waterline, with planking above that level and all the inner lining in pitch pine. Even the ice sheathing, which the committee was adamant should be greenheart, was replaced by iron bark forward of the fo'castle break. The upper deck, specified as teak, ended up Riga fir.

6. RGSAA 5/1/12: 4.26.1899, McGregor to C.R.M.

7. Ibid., 5/2/31: 3.7.1900, Smith to Markham.

8. Ibid., 5/2/2: 5.6.1899.

9. GJ 21/1: Jan. 1903; Proc. Berlin Univ. Geogr'l Institute, March 1902: p. 95; SR 1/1: p. 57.

10. RGSAA 5/2/39: 4.12.1905.

11. Ibid. "For 8 days after leaving the Cape, we had annoyingly fine weather and couldn't find any wind at 45°S but it came at last. The shape of the stern is excellent. In the heaviest following seas it rises quietly and naturally, and without

risk of 'pooping' as long as the ship has way on. This is the greatest relief for me . . . our helmsmen have always, or nearly always, dry quarters."

    12. GJ 24/2: Aug. 1904, p. 131. Even the 8,000-ton icebreaker *Yermak,* built by Armstrong Whitworth in Newcastle in 1898 for the Russians, had none, and Vice Admiral Makaroff declared, "I did not dare give the *Yermak* any bilge keel." Later he believed the ship could have benefited from small ones astern, but then his ship had 10,000 HP engines (GJ 15/1: Jan. 1900, p. 45).

    13. MD: 6.5.1901.

    14. SR 1/1: p. 26.

    15. Proc. Berlin Univ. Geog. Institute, March 1902, pp. 96–97.

    16. SPRI 342/4.

    17. Nansen (1898): p. 56.

    18. MD: 10.1.1899, 10.4.1899. It is scarcely credible that he would not have pointed out the construction of the ship, whose oak frames were 10 inches thick by 21 inches wide, separated by gaps of only 12 inches filled with pitch and sawdust, with two layers of outer planking 7 inches thick and the start of the third green-heart 6-inch layer halfway down the walls of the cabins, with pitchpine planking on the inside from 4 to 8 inches thick. That made the cabin walls at least 21 inches thick, the same as *Discovery*'s were to be, except that the frames would be about 10 inches apart. But evidently Nansen did not mention the outer wall insulation that day, for Markham simply noted in his diary that there was more than a foot of felt and other insulating material under the upper deck and over the beams (MD: 9.10.1896).

    19. SPRI: 5.16.1900, letter Drygalski-Markham.

    20. MD: 6.8.1900.

CHAPTER 4

    1. *Nature* 61: 7.12.1899, p. 136. Wilkes also believed d'Urville's Adélie Land (140°E) connected to Sabrina Land (121°E), sighted by Balleny in 1839, the year before Wilkes's sightings on that coast. Ross believed Balleny's sightings were islands. With today's technology we know that although Ross was wrong, his and Neumayer's ideas accidentally equated to what lay beneath the Antarctic ice cap, for Victoria Land does have a west coast, and the land forming Wilkes's coast is almost an island by virtue of two sounds that run almost 700 miles toward the Pole and nearly meet 500 miles inland from the coast, cutting off the land between from the main body of the continent (GJ 153/3: Nov. 1987, p. 365).

    2. Prof. Schuster and Captain Creak were two of the Royal Society's four representatives, and Profs. Drygalski and Eschenhagen were on the German team (*Nature* 61: 1.2.1900, p. 321) The magnetic stations were at Potsdam, Kew, Falmouth (Kentucky, USA), Bombay, Mauritius, Melbourne, Christchurch, NZ, and Staten Island (Markham [1921]: p. 451).

    3. RGSAA 1/10/1 (undated), pp. 15–30.

    4. PRS 1898: pp. 426, 442.

    5. SGM 14/10: Oct. 1898, pp. 505–534 inc. RS lecture and map facing p. 572.

    6. MD: 4.19.1899.

    7. GJ 14/5: Nov. 1899, p. 85.

    8. MD: 10.27.1899.

9. RSA: ms. 547–548, Papers of Sir A. B Kempe KC.

10. This had almost been the case at the June meeting, for the cost of the ship was already nearly £47,000 as against the £35,000 Markham had allowed when he drew up his first estimate in Norway in 1897. That brought the total to £2,000 more than the £90,000 available. However, a new estimate hurriedly assembled by Markham and Scott in November 1900 brought the total within the £91,000 by then available. Scott had returned from Berlin on October 26, and Markham had to have the budget approved by the Executive Committee on November 14 if it were to be agreed by the Joint Committee that year. Something had to be left unrevised, and Markham opted to leave the expenses at the £8,000 level included in the original estimate. When properly re-estimated they had risen by nearly half, which, with a further increase in the cost of the ship, brought the total to £95,000. The Royal Society treasurer added the expenditures and commitments in time for the first Finance Committee meeting on December 12, recording the figures against the estimated figures in the minutes of the November 14 Executive Committee. The cost of the ship had risen by a further £1,862, and the estimate for expenses for a two-season expedition had grown by £3,520.

11. RGSAA 1/10/3 (undated), pp. 9–11.

12. Ibid.; MD: 12.1.1900.

13. Borchgrevink (1901): p. 261.

14. GJ 16/4: Oct. 1900.

15. Ibid., 17/5: May 1901, p. 488; Bernacchi (1901): p. 244.

16. RGSAA 20/27: Minutes 12.19.1900.

CHAPTER 5

1. Kathleen Scott's diary: 6.14.1911.

2. SPRI 366/15/25: 6.3.1899; 26: 6.26.1899; 27: 6.28.1899; 28: 7.1.1899; 29: 7.24.1899.

3. Huntford (1979): p. 135.

4. MD: 3.31.1900.

5. Markham (1986): p. 14.

6. MD: 4.6.1900.

7. Ibid., 5.24.1900.

8. SPRI 366/15/46: 7.11.1900.

9. Ibid., 352/2: Scott's journal 10.10–26.1900.

10. RGSAA 5/2/36: 6.16.1900.

11. RGSAA 5/2/39: 4.12.05.

12. Nansen (1898), vol. 1: p. 116.

13. Ibid., p. 58.

14. Ibid., p. 97.

15. Ibid., pp. 462–463; vol. 2: p. 2721; Cook (1900): p. 24.

16. Markham (1986): p. 26.

17. Armitage (1925): p. 129.

18. MD: 5.27 and 5.29.1900; RGSAA 7/1/1.

19. Markham (1986): p. 15.

20. MD: 5.27.1900.

21. MD: 6.1.1900.

22. RGSAA 20/27: 6.8.1900.

23. MD: 1.16.1901.
24. Nansen (1898), vol. 1: p. 60.
25. SPRI 342/28/8: 10.28.1900 letter to Skelton.
26. RGSAA 7/1/4: 12.30.1900.
27. Scott (1905), vol. 1: p. 88: 1.6.1903.
28. Mawson (1918), vol. 1: p. 247.
29. Nansen (1898), vol. 2: p. 55.
30. Ibid., p. 53.
31. Ibid.
32. RSA: ms. 548, Sir A. B. Kempe's draft report of meeting.
33. RGSAA 20/27: 6.21.1900.
34. SPRI 342/28/8: 10.28.1900 letter to Skelton.
35. 3.20.1988 letter to author.
36. Doorly (1916): pp. 44–47.
37. Lecointe (1904): pp. 237–238.
38. Cook (1900): pp. 210, 277, 329, 364, 382.
39. Nansen (1898), vol. 2: p. 88.
40. Cook (1900): pp. 330-331.
41. Scott (1905), vol. 1: p. 79.

CHAPTER 6

1. MD: 10.12.1899.
2. Markham (1986): p. 133.
3. RGSAA 4/1/4: 3.16.1900. Something of the scale of this proposal, which assuredly did not figure in the conversation with Markham, can be gauged by comparing it with Lieutenant Prestrud's 385-mile journey, with Johansen and Stubberud, to King Edward VII Land in the last two months of 1911. Taking two sledges and fourteen dogs, the three men left Amundsen's 80°S depot with each sledge weighing nearly 600 pounds and took five weeks for the journey that was the out-and-back equivalent of, but for the most part less difficult than, that up the coast of Victoria Land to the far side of the mountains by the route the University of Sydney's Professor David was to take on foot, with Douglas Mawson and Dr. Forbes Mackay, a decade after Gregory wrote his letter. At that point there would have been 180 miles to go to the magnetic pole, and the total distance would have been 900 miles, or as far as that to the South Pole with no assurance of finding the head of a feasible glacier leading back through the mountains. If the route had been similar in difficulty to Prestrud's, it would have required three months and as much as 22 tons of laden sledges pulled by over sixty dogs, although a depot laid in the first season and seals killed on the way up the coast could have reduced that somewhat.
4. This copy of the March 16 letter (ibid. 4/1/4) contains no reference to Gregory's January 19 letter, so Markham must have added the remark as a post-script. The statement in his February Memorandum to the RGS Council "I *added* that his letter of January 19th was approved" (my italics) bears this out.
5. The cable read: "Formally appointed, wire when fully able to decide" (ibid. 20/1/105: 2.15.1900), confirmed in Markham's March 16, 1900, letter: "We telegraphed you some time ago that you had been appointed . . . if you can obtain leave of absence." Poulton's version, in a printed protest to the fellows of the Royal

Society the following year (Markham [1986]: appendix 2), has it that the June 15 Joint Committee instructed the secretary (Longhurst) to cable "Your letter of January 19 has been received and approved," but no such cable is copied in the Antarctic Letter Book, either after the February 14 meeting or after the one on June 15. In any case, the latter meeting did not discuss Gregory's appointment, dealing only with the appointment of a physicist, as can be seen in the minute book (RGS Minutes of Jt. and Exec. Committees). Poulton also claimed in his protest that Gregory "sent a decoded copy [of the cable] to Sir Clements Markham, who did not correct it." Markham endorsed his copy of Poulton's document: "Poulton sent it in cypher." But in the Letter Book, no. 487 is a copy of a February 5, 1901, request from Longhurst to Reuters Telegram Co. for copy of a coded June 14 telegram to Gregory reading: "soqquadra Scott venereus Armitage second 4 Koettlitz 1235 dedine venenum venicula." That same day Longhurst wrote to Gregory (no. 489), then staying in Stamford Hill, asking for the code "used by Poulton" in the cable. Perhaps Markham lost the decoded copy, and perhaps Longhurst misquoted the date, but the cable he quoted contained no reference to the date January 19, 1900.

6. RGSAA 4/1/5: 4.30.1900.

7. Ibid., undated, 1/10/1 (Markham's diary indicates he prepared it on 12.1–4.1900).

8. Ibid., 4/1/3: 1.19.1900.

9. MD: 12.15.1900.

10. RGSAA 4/1/9: 12.17.1900.

11. MD: 12.18.1900.

12. RGSAA 1/10/1: undated, p. 4.

13. Ibid., 20/27: 1.30.1901.

14. Markham (1986): p. 167.

15. MD: 1.13.1901.

16. Ibid.: 1.14.1901.

17. Ibid.: 1.16.1901.

18. Ibid.: 1.20.1901.

19. February 1901 Memorandum to RGS Council (SPRI).

20. RGSAA 1/10/11: 5.20.1901, p. 2.

21. Armitage (1925): pp. 134–136.

22. MD: 2.8.1901.

23. Armitage (1925): p. 140.

24. Ibid., p. 140; MD: 10.2.1901.

25. Markham (1986): pp. 139–140.

26. Markham (1986): p. 138.

27. Ibid., p. 140; MD: 2.16–19.1901.

28. RGSAA 1/10/6: dated "March 1901."

29. Markham (1986): p. 146.

30. RGSAA 1/11, 1/10: undated.

CHAPTER 7

1. MD: 2.6 01, 2.18.1901.

2. Armitage (1925): p. 129.

3. RGSAA 4/1/4: 3.16.1900.

4. *Times:* 3.23.1900.
5. RGSAA 4/1/5: 4.30.1900.
6. Ibid.
7. Ibid., 20/26: 9.24.1900, Jt. Com. Minute; 20/27 (PS to): 9.12.1900, Markham to Exec. Com.
8. Markham (1986): p. 12 (also Gregory's RGSAA 4/1/9).
9. RSA: ms 547–548, 12.31.1900, Longhurst-Kempe.
10. SPRI 1453/148: 2.10.1901.
11. Seaver (1933): pp. 53, 74–76.
12. SPRI 1122/1/2: 1.11.1901.
13. Markham (1986): p. 175.
14. RGSAA 20/29: 1.11.1901.
15. MD: 12.7.1900.
16. Armitage (1925): pp. 130–131.
17. Ibid., p. 141.
18. RGSAA 1/10/6: March 1901, tabled at 3.28.1901 council meeting.
19. RSA: ms 547–548, 1.2.1901, Scott-Kempe.
20. Armitage (1925): pp. 130, 142.
21. RGSAA 7/1/10.
22. Ibid., 9/1/3.
23. SPRI 1329: 1.21.1901, letter to Poulton.
24. *Nature* 73: 1.25.1906, p. 298. A testimony to Gregory's lack of communication with Scott was that Scott remained unaware of the basis of the hut's design, writing in *The Voyage of the* Discovery (1905, vol. 1: p. 215) that it was simply an Australian outback settler's bungalow with additional insulation. Peary's daughter Marie Ahnighito had been born in Anniversary Lodge on September 12, 1893, delivered by nurse Susan J. Cross, one of the fourteen expedition members.
25. RGSAA 7/1/10: undated; 7/3/6: 11.13.1901; 7/3/7: 11.16.1901.
26. SPRI 367/23/9: 2.24.1901.
27. Ibid., 2.26.1901.
28. MD: 15.2.1901.
29. RGSAA 20/1/585: 3.27.1901.
30. Ibid., 20/1/588: 3.29.1901.
31. Ibid., 7/1/6: 1.23.1901.
32. Ibid., 20/1/508: 2.18.1901 (p. 2 of letter).
33. Ibid., 7/1/9: 3.31.1901.
34. Ibid., 7/2/1: 4.6.1901 (dated 1900 in error); 7/2/4: 6.24.1901; 7/2/5: 6.26.1901; 7/2/6: 7.3.1901.
35. This was the Baldwin-Ziegler polar expedition aiming for the North Pole via Franz Josef Land. It was funded by American millionaire William Ziegler and led by Evelyn B. Baldwin, who acquired the Dundee whaler *Esquimau* (renamed *America*), the *Fridtjof*, and the *Belgica*. Trapped in the ice, the main party was rescued by the *Terra Nova* under Capt. J. Kjeldsen of Tromsö and brought back to Norway in August 1905. See Fiala (1907) in which a good picture of the *Terra Nova* appears facing p. 226.
36. RGSAA 7/2/1: 4.6.1901, letter dated 1900 in error.
37. Ibid., 7/2/2: 5.9.1901.
38. MD: 4.25.1901.

39. RGSAA 20/1/663: 5.20.1901, reply from Longhurst.
40. Ibid., 8/1/1: 1.18.1901.
41. Ibid., 8/1/2; MD: 5.10.1901, 5.14.1901.
42. *Dundee Advertiser:* 5.16.1901.
43. MD: 6.5.1901.
44. RSA: ms 547–548: Postscript in 11.12.1901 letter, Huggins-Kempe and Kempe's 12.4.1901 reply.
45. Ibid.
46. RGSAA 5/3/8: 2.28.1902, letter Dundee Shipbuilders to Secretary National Antarctic Expedition.
47. MD: 7.21.1901.
48. Ibid., 7.9.1901.
49. SPRI 342/1/1: undated, p. 4 (written between 7.25.1901 and 7.28.1901).
50. RSA: ms 547–548, 7.25.1901, letter William ShackletonBKempe.
51. Ibid., 7.26.1901, letter Huggins-Kempe.
52. Armitage (1905): p. 8.
53. RSA: ms 547–548, 7.25.1901, letter Kempe.
54. RGS: Scott Corresp. 4, undated letter to Keltie.
55. RSA: ms 547–548, 8.15.1901.
56. MD: 1.31.1901.
57. Ibid., 8.1.1901.

CHAPTER 8

1. RGSAA 12/1/2: 8.14.1901, letter to Markham.
2. GJ 19/4: April 1902, p. 417.
3. SPRI 366/14/31.
4. Ibid., 1329: 10.28.1901, Mrs. Gregory to E. Chaplin.
5. RGSAA 12/3/8: 12.22.1901, p. 6.
6. The only storage space outside the circle and aft of the first watertight bulkhead was in four small compartments reached through hatches either side of the galley. Each measured 9 feet by 3 feet 6 inches by 6 feet high. Beneath them lay a lesser area among the bow-reinforcing timbers.
7. Armitage (1905): appendix D.
8. Ibid., p. 303.
9. RGSAA 12/1/2.
10. Drygalski (1989): pp. 58–59.
11. Ibid., p. 78.
12. Scott was well pleased with the modifications to the winches based on Hjort's advice, but the risk of losing the advanced water bottle developed by Nansen was still enough to cause Mill and Scott to urge Markham to buy another. Two more were ordered from Stockholm, but to cover for any delay Mill lent his own to go out with Bernacchi on the *Cuzco.*
13. Markham (1986): p. 111.
14. Proc. Berlin Univ. Geog. Institute: Mar. 1902, p. 97.
15. SPRI 342/1/1: 8.14.1901.
16. RGSAA 19/2/1: 8.18.1902.
17. Markham (1986): p. 107.
18. SPRI 575/2: 8.16.1901.

19. Drygalski (1989): p. 59.

20. SPRI 342/1/1: 8.17.1901.

21. Ibid., 774/1/1: 8.20.1901.

22. GJ 19/4: Oct. 1903, p. 423.

23. SPRI 774/1/1: 8.24.1901.

24. RGSAA 12/1/5: 9.29.1901.

25. Drygalski (1989): pp. 59, 84.

26. RGSAA 12/1/5: 9.29.1901.

27. SPRI 342/1/1: 8.23.1901.

28. Armitage (1905): p. 19.

29. SPRI 595/1: 8.31.1901, p. 16.

30. WD: 9.1.1902.

31. PRO: BT100/145.

32. In his predicament he could not dismiss McNeish, the carpenter, and Able Seaman Vincent, and he eventually took them on his historic open-boat journey to South Georgia, because he wouldn't subject the Elephant Island Party to their behavior. Even their part in saving the lives of all the others failed to prevent him from refusing to recommend them for the Polar Medal, along with two other seamen (Stephenson and Holmes).

33. Cdr. C.L.A. Woollard in *The Last of the Cape Horners* ([1967], p. 36) describes how on his first voyage in the *Penrhyn Castle* the southeast trades carried them almost in sight of the Brazilian coast. The fair copy of the Deck Log (RGSAA 12/1/13) shows the course was S45W, changed sometime before 8 A.M. to S62W and an hour later to S68W. This was nearly 10 points off the wind, so it can hardly have been dictated by the SE wind. Scott's words ([1905], vol. 1: p. 93) can easily be mistaken to mean that the ship's sailing characteristics and the leeway it made were responsible for its course trending so far west. The dotted line south of the equator on the chart shows the course they could have followed had *Discovery* been able to sail as its commercial contemporaries could. It appears to show that the ship's sailing characteristics cost them three further lost days. However, it also shows that the wind did not back into the east in the usual 10°S latitude, which cost them one of those days, so the real penalty was just two days.

34. Scott (1905), vol. 1: p. 93.

35. According to Markham (RGSAA 12/1/13: 11.28.1901) and a note in Scott's hand (ibid.), the following went out by steamers: ss *Arcadia* (sailed 8.22.1901), with 1,054 packages of foodstuffs (another source speaks of 1,100 cases with another 400 going by other steamers) including 45 cases of bottled fruits "left [behind] for want of room," 27 cases of furs, and 5 tons of dog food; ss *Cuzco* (sailed 9.12.1901), with Louis Bernacchi with the Eschenhagen instrument; ss *India*, with magnetic huts and, most significant in light of their later fate, twenty-three dogs accompanied by AB Isaac Weller and "1 ton of [fish] sledging food for dogs." Scott also refers to 500 pounds of American pemmican and 30 pairs of Canadian snowshoes, probably aboard the first ship. Eventually there was also more than 4 tons of tinned Australian meat, 10 tons of Spratts flour, and the shore hut.

36. SPRI 342/1/1: 9.5.1901; WD: 9.5.1901.

37. They had left London with 245 (imperial) tons. On the leg to Madeira, steaming in favorable winds had required 5 tons a day. The stoking force had been sized for occasional steaming in Antarctic waters and was inadequate for continu-

ous steaming. Even though reinforced by ABs in the tropics, stoking efficiency must have declined sharply in such temperatures. Also there had been no time to adjust the HP cylinder bearings (SPRI 342/1/1: 9.9.1901). All these factors had cost perhaps 60 tons. With favorable winds they could have steamed twelve more days and might have gotten into Cape Town by September 26.

38. RGSAA 12/1/5: 9.29.1901.

39. SPRI 436/2: 9.23–24.1901.

40. Ibid., 595/1: 9.23.1901.

41. RSA: ms. 547, 11.8.1901 Markham-Kempe.

42. Ibid., 11.12.1901 Huggins-Kempe.

43. Ibid., 11.9.1901 Markham-Kempe.

44. RGSAA 1/1/5: 9.29.1901.

45. SPRI 595/1: 10.1.1901.

46. Ibid., 342/1/1: 10.4.1901.

47. Ibid.

48. Ibid.

49. SPRI 366/15/57: 11.8.1901.

50. Drygalski (1989): p. 95.

51. SPRI 753: 10.5.1901.

52. Scott did not know Else had resigned on account of his wife's illness, and they had sailed again before Markham wrote to tell him (SPRI 366/15/55: 10.29.1901).

53. Drygalski (1989): p. 96.

54. SPRI 774/1/1: 10.22.1901.

55. Williamson seems to have been confused about the date when entering the mileage as 207 because the log shows the twenty-four-hour run to noon on the 22nd was 172, with 203 miles achieved in the previous twenty-four-hour spell.

56. WD: 10.22.1901.

57. Ibid., 10.27.1901.

58. Harland (1987): p. 214.

59. DD: 10.28.1901.

60. WD: 10.28.1901.

61. Woollard (1967): pp. 42–43.

62. Drygalski (1989): pp. 84, 127.

63. RGSAA 12/1/13: 11.28.1901, pp. 7–8.

64. Woollard (1967): p. 43.

65. WD: 10.27.1901.

66. Armitage (1905): p. 25.

67. DD: 11.12.1901.

68. Scott (1905), vol. 1: p. 100. Naval stoker Frank Plumley's diary entry described the oil lamp as having set fire to the fore topgallant sail, whereas Scott heard what happened from the officer on duty. Such disparities show that the seamen's diaries cannot always be trusted to give the facts.

69. RGSAA 12/1/13: 11.28.1901, p. 10. The noon position for the 17th, given in the log as 62°21S, gives the impression that farthest south was achieved that day, but clearly it was on the 16th, with the course generally eastward until noon the following day.

70. Ibid., p. 15.

71. Ibid.
72. WD: 11.26.1901.
73. RGSAA 12/1/13: 11.28.1901, p. 16.

CHAPTER 9

1. RGSAA 12/1/13: 11.28.1901, p. 17.
2. Ibid., 12/3/8: Letter of Proceedings no. 4, p. 4.
3. Bernacchi makes it clear that the holds were emptied before docking, and from Scott's remarks that would have included stores in the lower deck compartments.
4. SPRI 654/1: 11.29.1901.
5. Ibid., 342/1/1: 12.3.1901.
6. Ibid., 654/1: 12.3.1901.
7. Ibid., 12.6.1901.
8. Ibid., 342/1/1: 12.9.1901.
9. PRO: BT100/145.
10. Markham (1986): p. 98; RGSAA 12/3/6: p. 1.
11. As the midships section shows, the rim of the bilge, formed by the heads of the fillings between the frames, would have made the ship's bottom a solid basin, even if the caulked joints in the inner lining were to leak. That rim was about eight inches above the floor installed by Dailey on the Atlantic voyage, so the water left in the holds musts have been entering from above that level. When the dock was finally drained, water was seen seeping from numbers of boltheads below the bilge line and also fron two holes found to be filled with shavings cemented in. One, only five inches deep, was of no significance at all. The other, some ten feet from the keel, was eighteen inches deep and holds the clue to how the water got in. It was halfway along the main bunker under the wardroom, but there was no suggestion of any excessive leaking into the bunker (which had been empty upon arrival at the Cape), though in London the water found in the hold had been thought to have come through the bunker from the sternpost leak. But if water could get into that bolthole and continue seeping through, it could only have come from the spaces between the frames and the inner lining and outer planking. If that was so, then as much as eight feet head of water could have built up above the rim of the bilge, ample enough to force water into any boltholes where the seal between frame and planking or lining was imperfect, especially if the twenty-inch-long clenched bolt was loose in any way. Many bolts below the bilge line were found to need tightening, which meant that many more must have been in similar conditions behind the sheathing.
12. RGSAA 5/3/11: 3.15.1902 letter.
13. This shows clearly when the picture of the ship in dry dock with the coaltar scraped off is compared with two later pictures in The Voyage of the Discovery (vol. 1, facing p. 196, and vol. 2, facing p. 352).
14. SPRI 654/1: 1.5.1902.
15. Ibid., 774/1/1: 1.11.1902. Dailey's second report speaks of the majority, but not all, of the screws coming out easily. That equates with the screws holding the bottom plates found to be less loose than those at or just above the waterline, which is what would have resulted from impact with pack ice. Six months later, when the ship was frozen in by ice 3'3" thick, with its surface at the 14-foot mark on

the bows, the leak stopped, showing that the water must have entered between 11 feet and 14 feet above the keel. As new screw bolts had been fitted, the continuing leaks bore out shrinkage as the cause, the bow timbers being all solid oak.

16. Ibid., 367/23/27: 1.9.1902.

17. The engine flywheels were usually splashing in water, which corroded piping submerged in it because they had not used seamless tubing. Attempts to caulk the leak at Kerguelen were only partly successful, and, as aboard the British ship, it disappeared only temporarily while the ship was frozen in.

18. SPRI 342/1/1: 12.3.1901.

19. Markham (1986): p. 98.

20. PRO: BT100/145.

21. DD: 5.27.1902.

22. Ibid.: 1.4.1902.

23. SPRI 654/1: 1.5.1902.

24. Ibid., 972: 1.6.1902.

25. Ibid., 744/1: 1.11.1902.

26. RGSAA 21/4: 1.8.1902.

27. SPRI 367/23/27: 1.9.1902.

CHAPTER 10

1. RGSAA 12/3/2: 12.17.1901.

2. SPRI 654/1: 1.10.1902.

3. DD: 1.10.1902.

4. SPRI 366/14/13: 1.15.1902.

5. WD: 1.15.1902.

6. Scott (1905), vol. 1: p. 148.

7. Ibid., p. 153.

8. Ibid., p. 154. Piecing the records together after the expedition, Lt. George Mulock, who would only see the coast from much further out on the voyage home, marked on his map a "low sloping shore" at the head of the inlet with a hill immediately to the north. When geologist Douglas Mawson, who later became Australia's leading polar explorer, could not find it during Shackleton's expedition in 1908, that and the subsequently established position of Evans Coves as in 75°S were among disparities that later cast doubt on the accuracy of the expedition's surveys. The entries in the logs for January 19, 1902, do not mention that shore (RGSAA 21/1, 21/4; SPRI 366/5/3). Yet it must have existed, for Shackleton was on the bridge when the ship had to turn eastward along the Drygalski ice tongue about 1:30 A.M. on the 20th, and almost seven years later, on his own expedition, he told the Magnetic Pole Party to look for "a sandy beach" (Jacka and Jacka [1988]: 12.11.1908) After crossing the ice tongue in 1908, they could find no trace of the beach north of it. Shackleton had instructed the *Nimrod* to search for them as far north as "the low beach on the north side of the Drygalski Barrier" (Shackleton [1909], vol. 1: p. 257). In his account of the journey, Prof. Tannat W. Edgeworth-David left a clue to what Shackleton had seen on January 19, 1902, describing a cone of solid ice covered in sand, mud, and gravel in the moraine of the Backstairs Passage Glacier (Shackleton [1909], vol. 2: pp. 161–162).

The *Discovery* was there at the same season as the returning sledge party, and clearly in 1902 the pack ice had gone out all along the coast from the ice tongue to

Cape Washington. Had it done so in early December 1908, Edgeworth-David and his party might never have reached the magnetic pole, for the ascent over the foot of Larsen Glacier instead of Backstairs Passage would have cost much time.

There was no time to do a proper running survey on the voyage south, and when Mulock laid out his charts he must have learned of the beach from Shackleton, for on the voyage home he could not have seen it when he passed as far out as the *Southern Cross*, a distance that had stopped Colbeck from charting any of that coast. If Mulock got this feature right, along with the position of Mounts Nansen and Baxter, something went very wrong with his positioning of the Mount Larsen/Mount Gerlache group, which along with others behind the ice tongue appear to have been rotated southward from his viewpoint. This is readily understandable, however, when the vagaries of the compass so near the magnetic pole are recalled.

Far less understandable is the total omission from Mulock's maps of what was later called Inexpressible Island by the Northern Party marooned there on Scott's last expedition. The "low bare foothills" Mulock shows correspond with Mounts Abbott and Browning (named after two petty officers in the marooned party). These are shown clearly in Wilson's previous panorama (CXXXII in the 1908 Album of Expedition Photos) on the 18th, drawn as the ship steamed toward them. Clearly, Mulock had not seen or had forgotten the detail of the panoramas, which eventually bore the names assigned to the mountains and on which Wilson used the same term, *low bare foothills*, to describe Inexpressible Island. Although Colbeck may have seen the island mirage up from his course about 15 miles closer to it, the fact that he placed the ice tongue too far south suggests the coastal land he charted in 75°S was the same as Mulock's foothills (e.g., Mounts Abbott and Browning about 20 miles further north) and that Colbeck's Markham and Oscar II Islands were, respectively, the then unnamed nunatak in the Campbell Glacier and Oscar Point. Both are clearly visible in the first panorama Wilson sketched on the 18th.

9. WD: 1.20.1902.
10. SPRI 972: 1.20.1902.
11. DD: 8.2.1902 (referring to 1.21.1902).
12. SPRI 366/23/27: 1.22.1902 report.
13. Ross (1982): p. 156.
14. Scott (1905), vol. 1: p. 171.
15. DD: 1.27.1902.
16. SPRI 366/14/13: 1.28.1902.
17. Like the first cul-de-sac, what they had seen was another hint of a permanent disturbance in the great ice shelf, and although the first was still there nine years later, this one had been replaced by another a few miles further east (in 167°W). Ross had been too far off to see anything in 167°W, but the semblance of the first inlet had existed in 169°W in his day, whereas for Borchgrevink there was only some sort of inlet a few miles west of 167°W. All were the westerly harbingers of land in the offing. The watercolor (no. 61/11 in case 18/3 at SPRI) gives their position as 78°24S 167°55E.
18. Ferrar diary 1.29.1902: "Came to the place Bernacchi landed . . . at 3am."
19. Scott (1905), vol. 1: p. 176; the reference to an inlet 300 yards wide "filled with hummocky ice" can hardly be equated to the 2-mile-wide inlet they steamed into five days later.

20. WD: 1.29.1902.

21. SPRI 366/15/56.

22. Ibid., 654/1: 1.30.1902.

23. RGSAA 21/1: 1.31.1902.

24. Scott (1905), vol. 1: p. 188.

25. RGSAA 21/1: 1.31.1902.

26. SPRI 654/1: 2.1.1902.

27. RGSAA 21/1: 1.31.1902.

28. SPRI 654/1: 2.1.1902.

29. Armitage (1905): p. 58.

30. SPRI 654/1: 2.1.1902.

31. Scott (1905), vol. 1: p. 189.

32. RGSAA 21/1: 2.1.1902; 0600 hours entry by Barne.

33. In Markham's address to the RGS May 26, 1902, Anniversary Meeting he asserted that Scott was prepared to risk loss of the ship because of the assurance of a second ship (GJ 20/1: July 1902), but Scott's December 17 letter from New Zealand (RGSAA 12/3/1) appears to contradict this. Scott, having discovered land at the eastern end of the barrier, must have banked on being able to get everyone ashore and back to a point the *Morning* could reach. To risk both ships would have been much rasher.

34. RGSAA 12/3/1: 12.17.1901 letter to presidents.

35. Ibid., 21/1: 2.1.1902.

36. WD: 2.1.1902.

37. SPRI 55/6/2.

38. Huntford (1979): p. 149.

39. SPRI 972: 1.20.1902.

40. WD: 2.2.1902.

41. SPRI 654/1: 2.2.1902.

42. Ibid., 366/12/56.

43. Bernacchi (1938): p. 32.

44. Armitage (1905), p. 59, said "3 miles," but as the log (RGSAA 21/4) records that it took them three hours to reach the end, clearly Mulock's chart is right in showing a bight 12 miles deep. 45. DD: 2.4.1902.

46. SPRI 774/1/1: 2.3.1902.

47. Ibid., 366/12/2: 3.4.1902.

48. Scott (1905), vol. 1: p. 202.

49. SPT 1: June 1902, p. 7; SPRI 342/1/2: 2.4.1902. Lashly's diary records that Skelton rather than Heald went up after Shackleton, but Skelton's diary entry shows that he himself did not go up. Wilson, Ferrar, and Duncan all wrote of two ascents, but as the *South Polar Times* describes Heald's ascent and the log records three ascents, it is clear, particularly in Ferrar's case, that they were at work elsewhere when the third ascent was made.

50. WD: 2.4.1902.

51. SPRI 753; DD: 2.4.1902. Plumley wrote of "about two dozen of the best" (SPRI 972: 2.4.1902). Six days later in Arrival Bay, he refers to "hundreds of seals . . . so we have no fear of starving." Such details are important to grasp the scale of Scott's campaign to amass seal meat for the winter.

52. Mulock's charts fail to show this part of the course.

53. WD: 2.8.1902.
54. SPRI 1264/1: 2.8.1902.

CHAPTER 11

1. Armitage (1905): p. 215.
2. Scott (1905), vol. 1: pp. 171-172.
3. SPRI 774/1/1: 2.1.1902, 2.8.1902.
4. WD: 2.19.1902.
5. Ibid., 2.20.1902.
6. SPRI 1264/1: Ferrar journal 2.20.1902.
7. Ibid., 753: 2.28.1902.
8. Ibid., 366/12/9: undated report to Scott covering 3.3-19.1902 Cape Crozier journey with copies of 3.8.1902 letter to Scott and instructions to Lieutenant Barne.
9. Ibid., 753: 3.2.1902.
10. Ibid., 3.15.1902.
11. Ibid., 366/12/9: attachment dated 3.8.1902.
12. SPRI 753: 3.15.1902.
13. Ibid.
14. Ibid., 972: 3.11.1902.
15. Armitage (1905): p. 75.
16. SPRI 342/1/3: 3.11.1902.
17. Scott (1905), vol. 1: p. 242.
18. DD: 3.11.02
19. SPRI 654/1: 3.19.1902.
20. Ibid.
21. This account comes from Hare's diary and differs from Scott's account of his ordeal. Curiously, Ferrar understood that Hare was buried in the snow somewhere beyond (i.e., north of) Castle Rock.
22. DD: 3.15.1902.
23. SPRI 366/12/10: 3.25.1902.
24. GJ 19/1: July 1903, report dated 2.23.1903.
25. SPRI 753: 3.15.1902.
26. It is unlikely they had only reached the outcrop beyond Half Moon Crater because after rounding the latter, the course to it would have been at almost 90° from that to Crater Hill. Although the rocks are very magnetic, the compass error would hardly have been that extreme.
27. SPRI 366/12/10: 3.25.1902.
28. Scott (1905), vol. 1: following p. 242.
29. Ibid., p. 257.
30. SPRI 366/12/9: 3.12.1902.
31. Ibid., 1264/1: 3.19.1902.
32. DD: 3.21-23.1902.
33. Armitage (1905): p. 81.
34. Ibid., pp. 81-82.
35. Jackson (1899): p. 253.
36. SPRI 774/1/1: 3.31.1902.
37. DD: 3.21-23.02.

38. SPRI 1254/1: 4.2.1902.
39. WD: 4.2.1702.
40. Scott (1905), vol. 1: p. 272.
41. WD: 4.3.1902.
42. Ibid.
43. Scott (1905), vol. 1: p. 439.

CHAPTER 12

1. SPRI 753: 4.13.1902; Ellis (1969): p. 36.
2. SPRI 654/1: 9.26.1902.
3. WD: 10.7.1902.
4. SPRI 1464/3: 7.18.1902.
5. DD: 11.6.1902; Scott (1905), vol. 1: p. 339.
6. Drygalski (1989): p. 68.
7. WD: 6.14.1902.
8. Ibid., 6.9.1902.
9. SPRI 972: 5.13.1902.
10. DD: 6.10.1902.
11. WD: 5.2.1902.
12. Ibid.; SPRI, 1464/3: 7.18.1902.
13. SPRI 753: 5.31.1902.
14. DD: 6.12.1902, 6.22.1902.
15. SPRI 654/1: 6.18.1902.
16. Ibid., 1464/3: 7.28.1902.
17. Ibid., 7.18.1902.
18. WD: 5.23.1902.
19. DD: 6.9.1902; SPRI 972: 5.14.1902, 5.16.1902.
20. The cast list in the "Royal Terror Theatre" program and pictured in Scott's book ([1905], vol. 1: fp. 376) was as follows: (*left to right* in picture) seated: Mrs. Aspen Quiver–Horace Buckridge; Mr. Aspen Quiver–Frank Wild; Mary Ann (housemaid)–Gilbert Scott. Standing: Joe–Arthur Pilbeam; 2nd policeman–Isaac Weller; 1st policeman–Jacob Cross; Thomas Muggetts–Thomas Feather; Bottles (butler)–David Allen (CMA: ms. 212, item 155).
21. SPRI 654/1: 9.25.1902.
22. Ibid., 972: 8.24.1902.
23. Ibid., 2.10.1902.
24. Bernacchi (1938): p. 47.
25. WD: 6.22.1902, 7.9.1902.
26. SPRI 1464/3: 7.17.1902.
27. Ibid., 1254/1: 6.16.1902.
28. Ibid., 1464/3: 7.18.1902.
29. Ibid., 753: 8.31.1902.
30. Ibid., 1464/3: 7.18.1902.
31. DD: 5.23.1902.
32. SPRI 753: 8.31.1902.
33. Ibid., 1464/3: 8.2.1902.
34. DD: 6.27.1902.

CHAPTER 13

1. WD: 6.12.1902.

2. Seaver (1933): p. 106: The extract quoted, apparently from a letter, goes on to refer to a debate "yesterday," clearly over sledging. Wilson's diary refers to such a debate on Tuesday evening, July 8, 1902.

3. WD: 6.12.1902.

4. RGSAA 7/1/8: 1.28.1901.

5. SPRI 1464/3: 10.26.1902.

6. FD: 8.31.1902; DD: 8.9–31.1902.

7. DD: 8.27–29.1902. Most of the foregoing is based on July/August entries in his diary.

8. WD: 7.15.1902.

9. Scott (1905), vol. 1: p. 306.

10. FD: 12.30.1901, 3.27.1902.

11. WD: 08.29.1902.

12. GJ 18/5: May 1901, p. 488: 3.11.1901 lecture on topography of South Victoria Land.

13. SR Physical Science 5: p. 132.

14. DD: 8.22.1902.

15. SPRI 654/1: 1.11.1902.

16. Ibid., 1464/3: 8.23.1902.

17. WD: 9.2.1902.

18. SPRI 1464/3: 9.5.1902.

19. Ibid., 9.12.1902.

20. Armitage (1905): p. 215.

21. SPRI 366/12/14: 9.9.1902.

22. Scott (1905), vol. 1: p. 518; 90 pounds per dog = 1,170 pounds total less two weeks' rations 142 pounds net and approx. 524 pounds fixed weight (calculated from SPRI 366/12/15) suggests only 500 pounds depoted.

23. Ibid., p. 522.

24. Ibid., p. 524.

25. Ibid., pp. 518–525; SPRI 366/12/15: undated.

26. SPRI 366/12/17: 10.3.1902, p. 6.

27. Ibid., p. 8.

28. Just over eight years later Griffith Taylor, geologist on Scott's last expedition, still described the southern side of the glacier as "cut up into gullies and pinnacles such as made sledging almost impossible" (Taylor [1916]: p. 121).

29. SPRI 1456/3: 10.4.1902.

30. Ibid., 654/1: 9.26.1902.

31. WD: 9.27.1902.

32. SPRI 366/12: Armitage-Scott report, 10.1.1902.

33. Armitage (1905): p. 139.

34. SPRI 353/3/1: 8.31.1902.

35. Wilson diary 9.30.1902. His October 5 entry makes it clear the bilge was pumped out.

36. SPRI 366/14/23: 10.3.1902.

37. DD: 9.10–11.1902.

38. Scott (1905), vol. 1: p. 534; SPRI 1464/3 (journal): 9.30.1902. Armitage makes it clear that the dog food would last for more than six weeks (Armitage [1905]: p. 141). Curiously Shackleton, in his journal entry on October 1, 1902 (SPRI 1456/2: 10.1.02), mentions only 1 gallon of oil, 225 pounds of dog biscuit, and the sledge sails. If the word *biscuit* was not a slip of the pen and there really was that much dog biscuit (and Wilson's references to the dogs preferring the fish suggest there was), then that biscuit was supplied by Spratts and incorporated cod liver oil, which would at least have provided the dogs with some vitamin C, yet another indication of the connection between the fish and their failure, as was Shackleton's journal remark (quoted in Chapter 14) testifying to their diet of seal meat throughout the 1902 winter.

39. DD: 11.9.1902; SPRI 366/12/13: 9.1.1902.
40. WD: 10.5.1902, 10.7.1902.
41. SPRI 353/3/2: 10.2.1902.
42. Ibid., 1464/3: 10.19.1902.
43. Scott (1905), vol. 1: p. 544.
44. Ibid., pp. 544, 547.
45. WD: 10.13.1902.
46. Ibid., 10.3.1902.
47. SPRI 1464/3: 9.30.1902.
48. Ibid., 353/3/1: 8.30.1902.
49. WD: 10.15.1902.
50. SPRI 1464/3: 10.19.1902.
51. Scott (1905), vol. 1: p. 547; *Polar Record* 1955: pp. 467–485.
52. Armitage (1905): pp. 104–106.
53. SPRI 366/12/25: Skelton-Scott report, 10.11–12.1902.
54. Ellis (1969): pp. 56–59.
55. SPRI 641/2: 10.25.1902.
56. Ibid., 366/12/26: 10.31.1902.
57. Armitage (1905): p. 153.
58. SPRI 1456/3: 10.9.1902.
59. WD: 10.4–7.1902.
60. Armitage (1905): pp. 153–155.

61. Barne turned back 28 miles south of Bluff Depot, which was almost certainly in 78°45S. That meant they had reached 79°12S on the 14th. Assuming less than the 8 miles a day Scott was banking on and exceeded, the extra six days would have brought the two parties to the 80th parallel on the course Scott followed. From there he could have reached a suitable position for Depot B in 80°33S by December 6 instead of the 13th. Shackleton in his November 14 journal entry says that after leaving enough for the return to Bluff Depot, they could take thirty-three days' provisions onward (SPRI 1456/2: 11.14.1902). Thus, getting to a point a few miles south of the actual Depot B seven days sooner, they could have started from there with at least forty days' provisions and traveled south for twenty days. At their actual average of 8.46 miles per day (110 miles in thirteen days), they could have traveled almost 170 miles, bringing them approximately to 83°10S 169°30E. At that point the mountains would have appeared to insurmountably bar the direct route to the Pole. Such a view would probably have deterred even Shackleton from mounting his expedition five years later. That

position, however, is no more than 18 miles from a point (83°17S 171°12E) at which the great gap in the mountain chain becomes visible.

62. Blanco, persistently slack on the trace, had been sent back with Barne. The eighteen dogs included Bernacchi's *Southern Cross* dog, Joe.

63. Armitage (1905): p. 156.

64. SPRI 366/12/29: 11.27.1902.

65. The only alternative explanation (and Scott's otherwise unintelligible November 12 postscript suggests it) is that the mid-October plan envisaged a four-sledge, three-tent, nine-man Southwest Party. But its reduction to six men, the eventual strength, would have overcome the sledge and primus problem, leaving no justification for delaying Barne's start until Koettlitz's party returned.

CHAPTER 14

1. SPRI 1456/2: 11.15.1902.

2. Ibid., 11.16.1902.

3. Ibid., 366/5/1: Armitage 12.1.1902.

4. WD: 11.19.1902.

5. The dating in Shackleton's journal has been adopted here, as it equates better with the meteorological record in the Scientific Reports. It is the first of several cases where the three men's journals differ in dating, strongly suggesting they were not always made up on the actual day. Wilson, in the copy he made back at the ship, simply wrote that there were clouds all along the land line. Scott's journal entry dates the sighting as on the 17th, while for simplicity, in *The Voyage of the Discovery* (vol. 2: p. 28), intended for popular consumption, he clearly consolidates this into the entry for the 19th.

6. SPRI 1464/3: 11.17.1902.

7. Ibid., 1456/2: 11.20.1902.

8. Starting off from Anniversary Lodge on April 1, 1895, Peary had failed to find his first depot the very next day. On April 6, when hours of searching failed to locate the main depot with 1,400 pounds of pemmican cached in it, Peary described it as a staggering blow. When they reached the farther side of the ice sheet 500 miles from base, with just eight dogs capable of pulling, their chances of returning alive depended on finding musk ox on the coast. Failing that, Peary reckoned, the dogs might last a third of the way back, and then at best they would have just twenty days' rations left for the 333-mile man-haul to safety—something he clearly regarded as a lost cause (Peary [1898]: pp. 442, 457).

9. WD: 11.21.1902.

10. Ibid.

11. Ibid., 11.23.1902.

12. Ibid., 11.24.1902.

13. Wilson's dating. Yet another case of the journals differing about the date of events. Shackleton's says they started seal meat on the 25th, the two going back for the second train eating their lunch cold on the way.

14. On parting company with Barne they had twelve weeks' rations for themselves, augmented by 70 pounds of seal meat, which gave them an outward range of forty-two days. With fourteen days' supply already consumed and ten more before they could reach the depot position, that would leave them an eighteen-day supply. For the dogs they only had forty days' food, intending to progressively feed ten of

the pack to the dwindling survivors and get back with nine dogs (Scott [1905], vol. 2: p. 104).

15. SPRI 1456/2: 12.13.1902.

16. Scott (1905), vol. 2: p. 19.

17. SPT 2: June 1903, p. 9.

18. Wilson's December 15 remark that they left four weeks' food must be a mistake. The report in the July 1903 *Geographical Journal* says they left a three-week supply. Both he and Shackleton had noted that they took on thirty-three days' food, and that equates with the lesser quantity depoted. Subtracting the thirty days expired and twenty-one days depoted from the eighty-four-day supply they had set out with, there would have been food remaining for thirty-three days. Scott later wrote ([1905], vol. 2: p. 58) that they had cut down from 1.9 pounds a day to 1.5 pounds from the evening meal on December 1, so they must have considerably overrun their rations up to that time. Scott hoped the savings would extend their range, but the amount they had left at the depot shows his hope was not realized.

19. According to the midnight sight. Scott was so exasperated at the waste that he wrote of only a 2° gain in his journal and missed the mistake when copying the entry into his book after the expedition. His midnight sight put the depot in approx. 80°29S, and he described it as in line with "a conspicuous rocky patch" and one of three distant peaks (ibid., pp. 47–50). Modern maps show such an outcrop on a line from Mount Hamilton and a position about a mile east of such a rift as stopped them from reaching the land. That would place the depot in about 162°15E 12 miles from the shore, compared with Scott's estimate of 10 miles in the June 1903 *South Polar Times* (p. 9).

20. Scott (1905), vol. 2: facing p. 68, "Coastline in Lat. 81°S."

21. SPT 2: June 1903, p. 16.

22. WD: 12.23–24.1902.

23. SPRI 1456/2: 12.16.1902.

24. Scott (1905), vol. 2: facing p. 63.

25. SPRI 1456/2: 12.25.1902.

26. SPT 2: June 1903, p. 20.

27. SPRI 1456/2: 12.25.1902.

28. According to Scott (SPT 2: June 1903, p. 11; Scott (1905), vol. 2: p. 70). Wilson in his entry for Christmas Day says they named it Christmas Height, and he still called it that in his sketch in Scott's article in the June 1903 *South Polar Times*.

29. SPRI 1456/2: 12.27.1902. Shackleton thought they were only 8 miles distant, but Wilson, passing them on the way back on January 3, wrote that they had passed 15 miles offshore on the way south (WD: 1.3.03). The cliffs can only be those in 81°57S.

30. Scott (1905), vol. 2: facing p. 76.

31. SPT 2: June 1903, p. 9.

32. WD: 12.31.1902.

33. Scott's statement (Scott [1905], vol. 2: p. 80) that they had approached the cliffs on the southern side of the strait and could see the irregular distribution of the black-and-red rock implies that they were far across the inlet, but as they believed it to be 20 miles wide (WD: 12.31.02) when it was only 10, Scott would naturally have believed they were approaching the cliffs. The farthest-south camp

was at best only 9 miles from them, and it would have been possible to see the bands of different colored rock at that distance, as had been the case when they passed the cliffs 10 miles distant on December 27.

34. This accounts for Scott's remark the next day that they had "less than 14 days' food" (Scott [1905], vol. 2: p. 79) and, given that an extra lunch was consumed the next afternoon, also for Wilson's remark the following evening (the 31st) that "we are so short of food" (WD: 12.31.1902). On the 30th they were in fact just one-and-a-half days' short at the most, and after the extra lunch the following day they cut down the daily allowance so that by January 7 they had saved half of the overrun (Scott 1.7.1903: "We have gained a day on our allowance" (Scott [1905], vol. 2: p. 90)). They did not cut further into the reserve, as shown by Wilson's January 9 remark "We ought to reach the depot on Tuesday (13th) with 4 days' food in hand," which they did (WD: 1.9.1903). It was a reasonable margin but clearly did not seem so to the man responsible for their lives. Despite the unfair implication that Scott had not taken a sufficient emergency ration, the risk loomed so large in Scott's mind, still befuddled by the aftermath of scurvy, that when he wrote his report after the return to the ship he mentally halved the amount they had left on arrival (GJ 22/1: p. 32).

35. Scott (1905), vol. 2: facing p. 82.
36. GJ 18/5: July 1903, p. 31; WD 12.31.1902.
37. Scott (1905), vol. 2: p. 71.
38. WD: 12.29.1902.
39. GJ 22/1: p. 32.

CHAPTER 15

1. Main sources are Sledging Journals SPRI 366/5/1 (Armitage), 342/1/4 (Skelton), 1264/2 (Ferrar).
2. Armitage (1905): pp. 158–160. C team's sledges were loaded with 287 pounds more than D team's pair, hence the extra man. The journals taken together leave some doubt about the Support Party tent occupants. There is also some doubt about the numbers of 11-foot and 9-foot sledges because of contradictory statements in Armitage's and Skelton's journals. The numbers given here and in subsequent pages have been adopted as most compatible with other statements and photos.
3. SPRI 1264/2: 12.9.1902.
4. Sk 244–247, three of these were reproduced in plates 16/1 and 17/1 in published album of expedition photographs.
5. SPRI 366/5/1: 12.3.1902.
6. Ibid., 342/1/4: 12.15.1902.
7. Ibid., 12.18.1902.
8. The glacier would not be descended again until the November 25, 1980, descent by a New Zealand party (Drs. Bob Findlay and Dave Craw, with Gary Ball and Drew Brown).
9. Given that they had set out with fifty-six days' rations and left food for fourteen days in depots, there would have been fourteen days' left at that point, but the fact that Armitage wrote that evening that they could go on another week suggests that they had gained two days by using the liver from seals caught at the Eskers.

10. SPRI 366/5/1: 12.28.1902.
11. Ibid., 1.2.1903.
12. Armitage (1905): p. 182.
13. SPRI 366/5/1: 1.13.1903.
14. Armitage (1905): p. 188.
15. According to Armitage's journal entry for 1.16.1903, but in *Two Years in the Antarctic* ([1905], p. 189) he says fog prevented observation.
16. Ibid.
17. SPRI 342/1/4: 1.17.1903; Scott (1905), vol. 2: p. 139.
18. SPRI 654/2: 1.19.1903.
19. Scott (1905), vol. 2: p. 141.
20. SPRI 342/1/4: 1.12.03–1.13.03.
21. Ibid., 366/14/25.
22. RGSAA, Admiralty N9088: 10.1.1903, to presidents of Royal Society and RGS.

CHAPTER 16

1. Principal sources are Barne's sledging journal (SPRI 366/6/1) and report to Scott (SPRI 366/12/34).
2. The bearing Barne noted was in fact that of the southern point of the first "island," 62° north of the point he steered for. As his watch had stopped on December 26 and he had had to guess the sun's zenith when resetting it, the error then affecting his calculation of compass variation would easily account for such a small angular discrepancy. Similar errors were likely in his position fixes, for he had no sledgemeter. Because his journey had not figured in the plan developed in the winter, Skelton's men had only made two—one for Scott, the other for Armitage.
3. SPRI 366/12/34: 1.5.1903.
4. Ibid., 1456/2: 1.14.1903.
5. Ibid., 1.15.1903; SPRI 1464/4: 1.14.1903.
6. SPRI 1464/4: 1.15.1903.
7. Ibid., 1.16.1903.
8. Ibid., 1456/2: 1.17.1903.
9. Ibid., 1.18.1903.
10. WD: 1.19.1903.
11. Ibid., 1.26.1903.
12. 20th, 25th, and 26th. On the second occasion Wilson sketched the entire coast. Scott had written in his journal on the 20th that they could see the land between Range A on the north side of the strait and the next range, with another gap between that range (b) and the next (c). The land between a and b appears barely continuous in Wilson's panorama, but the gap between b and c shows well and is clearly Mulock Glacier.
13. SPRI 1456/2: 1.28.1903.
14. WD: 1.29.1903.
15. Ibid., 1.30.1903.
16. SPRI 1456/2: 1.30.1903.
17. Scott (1905), vol. 2: p. 164.
18. GJ 22/1: July 1903, pp. 20–37.
19. SPRI 366/12/34: 2.1.1903.

20. Ibid. Eight months later he was writing to Barne "concerning the gaps [through which] from our very limited view no rise in level could be seen, and no background of elevated land" (Ibid., 366/12/44: 10.1.1903).

21. GJ 22/1: July 1903, p. 31.

22. Two days before, on December 29, Wilson had written: "We are rather surprised that we haven't come across any volcanoes, either active or asleep. All our mountains are in all probability granitic, simply a continuation southwards of the mountains of S. Victoria Land" (WD: 12.29.1902).

23. GJ 22/1: July 1903, p. 34.

24. SPRI 366/14/24-25: 1.19.1903. Koettlitz also listed Hodgson (who had volunteered to remain: "I have fully explained to him the risks he runs . . . if the responsibility rests with me I cannot but advise his return"); Macfarlane, who as Chapter 15 revealed was almost certainly the lucky survivor of a heart attack; and the cook, Brett, "owing to his condition through having contracted syphilis."

25. WD: 2.23.1903.

26. RGSAA 12/4/1: 2.27.1903.

CHAPTER 17

1. Principal sources are Drygalski (1989) and Expedition Scientific Reports.

2. GJ 21/1: Jan. 1903.

3. SR 1/1: p. 57; Drygalski (1989): p. 300.

4. Six months after the *Gauss* had left the base, two scientists in the party had developed symptoms of the deadly Japanese beri-beri fever that had killed two of the Chinese crew of the freighter *Tanglin*. Meteorologist Josef Enzensperger died, and the party's leader, Dr. Emil Werth, narrowly survived thanks to the patient nursing of his three surviving comrades.

CHAPTER 18

1. RSA: ms. 547-548, undated attachment to 5.12.1903 Kempe-Huggins.

2. Ibid., 5.13.1902 letter to Kempe.

3. GJ 18/1: July 1902, p. 215.

4. RSA: ms. 547-548, 7.8.1902 letter to Kempe.

5. Ibid., 2.23.1903 letter to Kempe.

6. SPRI 366/15/58: 2.28.1903.

7. The ship had been bought for £4719, and £8383 had been spent on alterations and repairs, as well as £615 for a suit of sails (Doorly [1916]: p. 58).

8. RSA: ms. 547-548, 3.25.1903 cable copied to Huggins and Kempe.

9. RGSAA 19/2/8: 3.25.1903. In 67°242S 179°552W. Doorly records that he later proposed naming the islands after Markham, but Borchgrevink had already named an island after Markham. Colbeck must have learned of this after meeting Scott, for Markham's May 20, 1903, reply to Colbeck's first letter from New Zealand includes the RGS Council's "congratulations on the discovery of an island in 67°40S and 179°E, and of a remarkable rocky islet, which you have named respectively Scott Island and Haggitt's Pillar" (CMA: ms. 212/box 4/item 100, Colbeck Papers). In the printed version of Colbeck's letter, which he must have known Markham would circulate to the Council, there is no mention of naming, so Colbeck must have expressed his wish in a private letter to Markham.

10. RSA: ms. 547–548, 4.2.1903 letter Markham to Huggins.
11. Ibid., 3.27.1903 letter Huggins to Kempe.
12. GJ 18/1: July 1902, p. 215.
13. RSA: op.cit: 3.27.03 letter Huggins to Kempe.
14. RSA: ms. 547–548, copy 3.28.1903 cable Colbeck to Markham.
15. Ibid., 3.27.1903 note to Kempe.
16. MD: 3.28.1903.
17. SPRI 1464/3: 3.11.1903; WD: 3.9.1903.
18. RSA: ms. 547–548, 4.2.1903 letter to Huggins.
19. Ibid., 4.24.1903 letter to Kempe.
20. Ibid., 5.20.1903 letter Markham-Kempe and reply.
21. Ibid., 5.22.1903 letter to Kempe.
22. Ibid., Treasury letter 9182/03 dated 6.20.1903 to presidents of Royal Society and RGS.
23. Ibid., 6.19.1903 letter to Kempe.
24. Ibid.
25. MD: 6.26–27.1903.
26. Ibid., 7.7.1903.
27. RGSAA 14/2/16: April 1903.
28. SPRI 1464/3: 3.11.1903.
29. Ibid., 753: 2.19.1903, 2.23.1903.
30. Clarence Hare understood that Page and Peters were being invalided home, but they were not so described in Scott's report, which, according to the covering letter to the Admiralty signed by the two Society presidents, stated that in contrast to Macfarlane, they were "not recommended." That winter Scott wrote in his journal that their messmates were "extremely glad to be rid of them" (RGSAA: 5.22.1903 letter to Admiralty from RS; SPRI 1464/3: 3.20.1903).
31. SPRI 1464/3: 6.24.1903.
32. FD: 6.22.1903.
33. WD: 3.7.1903.
34. RSA: ms. 547–548, 3.28.1903 cable (copy).
35. Scott (1905), vol. 2: p. 175.
36. FD: 3.11.1903.
37. WD: 6.23.1903.
38. FD: 2.2.1903, 6.25.1903.
39. WD: 7.1.1903.
40. Ibid., 7.18.1903.
41. Scott (1905), vol. 2: p. 201.
42. Armitage (1925): p. 132.
43. SPRI 342/1/4: 12.6.1902.
44. Ibid., 12.3.1902.
45. SPRI 342/1/4: 12.30.1902.
46. Ibid., 1.12.1902.

CHAPTER 19

1. SPRI 366/12/38: 12.22.1901.
2. Ibid., 342/2/5: 9.8.1903.
3. Ibid.; also 1464/3: 9.22.1903.

4. Ibid., 342/2/5: 9.14.1903.

5. Ibid.

6. Ibid., 9.15.1903.

7. The photo facing p. 206 in vol. 1 of *The Voyage of the* Discovery, entitled "Looking up From New Harbour," was taken at the lunch camp on September 16 on the glacier and *not* from the sea ice, which its title implies. Debenham's maps in *Scott's Last Expedition* (Scott et al. [1913]) show that in Scott's day the glacier proper extended beyond Herbertson Glacier. Today, the seaward face of Ferrar Glacier has retreated to the position of the hanging glacier behind the tents in the photo.

8. GJ 153/3: p. 365; Lot 250 Sotheby 12.18.1889 sale: 2.27.1904 letter from Scott to Mrs. Noble-Wilson.

9. SPRI 1464/3: 9.22.1903.

10. WD: 7–9.17.1903.

11. Armitage (1905): p. 244.

12. SPRI 342/2/5: 9.14.1903.

13. According to Skelton (SPRI 342/2/6: 10.26.1903) who makes no mention of cannibalizing the damaged sledges. Scott must have confused the intention with the actuality when he wrote over a year later that Dailey had made up the 11-foot and 7-foot sledges from the "wrecks" (Scott [1905], vol. 1: p. 233).

14. SR 2 (Meteo): p. 344.

15. SPRI 342/2/6: 11.1.1903.

16. Scott (1905), vol. 2: p. 258.

17. SPRI 342/2/6: 11.1.1903.

18. Ellis (1969): pp. 71, 75, 11.1.1903 and 12.1.1903. Royds's Southeast Barrier Party took 40 pounds for a thirty-day journey, so there would have been at least 65 pounds of seal meat aboard the two sledges, Ferrar's party having a separate ration.

19. Skelton says "just above the Inland Forts" (SPRI 342/2/6: 11.2.1903).

20. Ellis (1969): p. 72, 11.4.1903.

21. SPRI 342/2/6: 11.4.1903.

22. 1.31.1904 letter from Ferrar to family copied onto diary extracts sent home from New Zealand.

23. Scott (1905), vol. 2: p. 263.

24. FD: 11.11.1903.

25. Scott (1905), vol. 2: p. 251.

CHAPTER 20

1. SPRI 366/12/44: 10.1.1903.

2. Ibid., 366/12/38.

3. Ibid., 366/12/44: 1.10.1903.

4. Ibid., 1518/4: 10.6.1903 gives sledges used by both parties.

5. Progress was measured by Mulock's daily noon sights, here derived approximately from the positions given in the Meteorological Scientific Report Table 22, which equates to the 25 statute miles quoted by Armitage ([1905]: p. 252).

6. SPRI 366/12/46: 10.12.1903 and other dates.

7. Ibid., 11.17.1903. This point is approximately on the 161°E meridian, but as the map shows, for Barne to have described them as "level with Cape A" [Cape

Selborne] the party must have been at least 3 or 4 miles west of it. The mileage from October 28 to November 13 adopted here equates to that and is supported by Barne's November 13 diary remark that they "could see a disturbed surface about 2 miles inshore from us off the 'a' range snow slope" (ibid., 1518/4: 11.13.1903), which equates to the disturbed area of ice shown on modern maps. However, the position given for the last November 20 noon sight before they turned back is 12 miles short of the point they must have reached, given that on the 21st Barne described them as coming back across the ridge connecting the snow slopes of the two capes (of which there is no sign today).

8. SPRI 366/12/46: 11.17.1903.

9. Ibid., 11.20.1903.

10. A sketch map in Barne's report to Scott shows the tumulus "K" distinct from the Cape Kerr snow slope. This must have been part of what Landsat 1 photos have revealed as grounded ice that has now extended 24 miles northeast from Cape Kerr along the north side of the rifts at the edge of the glacier ice flowing into the barrier. The tumulus does not appear in Barne's November 25 panorama.

11. When the mountains were eventually precision mapped over sixty years later, every feature in Barne's sketches could be seen to match, even to the extent that from his position east of the 161E meridian, the view up the glacier, later named after Skelton, was hidden. By the time they had next seen the coast, they were too far east to see up it, and it remained undiscovered, to be named simply the Skelton Inlet until Sqn. Ldr. Claydon of the Royal NZ Air Force flew over the Royal Society Range on the Commonwealth Trans-Antarctic Expedition. He found it to be the great glacier highway, which Sir Edmund Hillary's tractors used to gain the summit plateau on their way to lay the depots for Dr. Vivian Fuchs's transpolar party. Dr. Margaret Bradshaw, the first New Zealand woman awarded the Polar Medal, who has sledged over the hinterland and across Mulock Glacier, pointed out to me that Michael Barne could not have seen the detail he shows of that glacier if he drew the panorama from a point that far west, suggesting that he must have modified it later in light of what he had seen on his 1902–1903 journey. What he showed in this panorama, however, does suggest there is an inlet there, and that is what it became on the maps published after the expedition.

12. What struck him was "a very prominent point on which were some bare rocks somewhere under 'c' range which, as we had never passed so close to this part of the coast before, was unfamiliar to me" (SPRI 366/12/46: 11.30.1903). This was probably a reference to Teall Island, missing from his 1.5–6.1903 panorama. This journal entry quoted in his report, as well as his eventual insertion of a view of the great Mount Dawson-Lambton column into his January 5-6 panorama of the coast showing its convex curvature, makes it clear that Mulock's eventual plot of their return route was as inaccurate as his position of the farthest point they had reached on the glacier.

13. WD: 12.13.1903.

14. Ibid., 12.1.1903.

15. Ibid., 12.13.1903.

16. Ibid.

17. Armitage (1905): p. 269.

18. FD: summary of events in his absence, p. 9.

19. SPRI 366/12/46: 11.21.1903.

20. Mulock's chart (published by RGS in 1908) mirrors the impression the others wrote of, showing Barne's November 19–20 camp 8 nautical miles short of the glacier mouth but 20 miles beyond Barne's January 1903 farthest. As with Mulock's positioning of their return route on December 1, east of Barne's 1.5–6.1903 camp, it is at odds with Barne's account in his report.

CHAPTER 21

1. SPRI 689/13: 11.12.1903.

2. Scott (1905), vol. 2: p. 453.

3. Paleobotanist Dr. W. N. Edwards, writing in the 1907 Scientific Report volume on geology, described them as "in all probability . . . of vegetable origin" (SR Geology 1: [1907], p. 48). Wilson (diary 12.12.1903) refers to the fossils being found in a band of coal shale.

4. Landed at Hope Bay to attempt to reach Otto Nordenskjöld's base on the Swedish Antarctic expedition after the *Antarctic* had failed to reach it, Andersson had discovered plant fossils from the Jurassic period in January 1903.

5. FR: 11.13.1903.

6. Ibid., 11.16.1903.

7. Ibid., 11.19.1903.

8. Ibid., 11.21.1903.

9. Ibid., 11.30.1903.

10. FD: 11.27.1903.

11. Ibid., 12.1.1903.

12. FD and SPRI 689/13 give date as 12.6.1903 (FR says 7th).

13. FR: 12.7.1903.

14. WD: 12.12.1903.

15. Captain Larsen, who was in command of Nordenskjöld's ship and at that moment fighting the pack in a vain endeavor to pick up the shore party, had discovered the petrified wood and some fossilized mollusks on Seymour Island off the Antarctic Peninsula. The peninsula was finally proved to be part of the mainland by the British Graham Land Expedition thirty-three years later.

16. Report in *New Zealand Times*, April 1904, in scrapbook compiled by Ferrar. The specimens were not unpacked in New Zealand, and Captain Hutton FRS, no doubt in harmony with other scientists there, concluded from Ferrar's description that one was a form of veronica and that all probably belonged to the Miocene epoch.

17. SR Geology 1: (1907), p. 48.

18. Ibid.

19. Gondwana was the district in India where similar fossils in coal seams were first found in the nineteenth century. The concept of the supercontinent had been proposed well before the expedition sailed. As late as 1973, despite the find in the central Trans-Antarctic Mountains (in 1967, by which time there was widespread acceptance of the continental drift and plate tectonics theories) of the fossilised jawbone of a Triassic age amphibian that had also lived in Africa, *Glossopteris* was still regarded in influential quarters as among the "best evidence" of the origin of Antarctica in the primeval land mass (Marvin [1973]: pp. 198–199).

CHAPTER 22

1. Scott (1905), vol. 2: p. 201.
2. Armitage (1905): p. 242.
3. SPRI 353/3/4: 11.23.1903.
4. Ibid., 641/1/3: 11.24.1903.
5. Ibid., 654/1: 11.23.1903.
6. Ibid., 641/1/3: 11.26.1903.
7. Ibid., 353/3/4: 11.24.1903.
8. Ibid., 641/1/3: 11.27.1903.
9. Ibid., 353/3/4 (Bernacchi's rough pencil drawing).
10. Ibid., 11.28.1903.
11. Ibid., 12.3.1903.
12. Ibid., 654/1: 12.10.1903.

CHAPTER 23

1. WD: 9.3–6.1903.
2. Ibid., 9.1.1903.
3. Ibid., 9.7.1903. That camp must have been extremely near the present-day Williams Field ice runway maintained by the United States, where all supply flights from New Zealand now land.
4. Wilson says they advanced a "couple of miles" (WD: 9.11.1903) by 11 A.M. on the 11th and camped "level with two dimly seen rock patches and a blue ice glacier on our left." The lower rock patch shows on the modern map as the eastern face of a 320 m knoll just east of the 169°E meridian. The glacier face lies 2 km SW of the rock face. That would make the three-day march from September 8–10 around 29 miles. The final camp must have been below what today is named Igloo Spur, and the "few" miles advanced on the 12th must have been about 5 miles.
5. The skeleton was brought home and tentatively identified as a "very large *Notothenia*" in the Natural History Science Report (vol. 2, Zoology, part 4, p. 1) on fishes. Absolute identification was difficult without the head, but the contributor described it as "apparently related to *N. Colbecki.*"
6. WD: 10.21.1903.
7. This is taken from Wilson's report on Antarctic birds in the same volume (SR: Natural History: Zoology, part 2), in which he highlighted the staggering mortality rate and inferred from Skelton's estimate that there had been a similar rate the previous year. But there is a curious arithmetic disparity between the chicks' absence on November 10, 1902, and his conclusion that eggs, laid the first week of July, hatched after seven weeks and that the chicks developed their feathers in four months, for that would mean the eggs were laid around Midwinter's Day, June 21. It seems equally possible that there had been 100 percent mortality in 1902, which accounted for the total absence of birds when Royds was there on November 20. Wilson next saw the rookery on July 20, 1911, when there were only 100 birds, some of which were incubating eggs.
8. WD: 11.15.1903.
9. Ibid., 11.20.1903.
10. Ibid., 9.13.1903.
11. Stonehouse (1975): Introduction, p. 4.

12. *Archaeopteryx* had teeth, and having written in the scientific report (Zoology 2: p. 31), published in 1906, of the probability that Emperor penguin embryos would show them to be the most primitive form of bird, his diary entry for June 27, 1911, records his belief that "if vestiges of teeth are ever to be found in present day birds, it would most likely be in the Emperor embryo." However, W. P. Pycraft, writing on the evolution of penguins in the same volume (p. 24), stated that other penguin embryos made it certain that penguins were descended from early *Steganopodes* (the diving family of birds). Wilson was unquestionably influenced by the view expressed in 1887 by Dr. M. von Menzbier (*Bulletin Soc. Imp. des Naturalistes*, Moscow 1887) that penguins were distinct from birds but shared the flying dinosaur as a common ancestor. The theory he expressed to Cherry-Garrard, however, was unquestionably his own, formulated as a result of his experience on the *Discovery* expedition. By 1933 birds and penguins were still held to descend separately from bipedal flightless dinosaurs such as *Ornitholestes* (a Coelurosaurian) (Proc. Zoological Soc. 1933 1: p. 483), whereas the modern understanding is that penguins are a divergent evolution from the late Cretaceous true birds, which preceded the dinosaur extinction (see Appendix 10) (Fastovsky and Weishampel [1996]: p. 314).

CHAPTER 24

1. SPRI 342/2/6 (Skelton's journal): 11.13.1903. Narrative is based on Skelton's journal; Scott (1905), vol. 2; and SR Meteo 2: table 20 to November 23 outward; then from Scott (1905), vol. 2 for Scott's party and SPRI 342/2/6 for Skelton's return journey.

2. Ibid., 11.17.1903.

3. Ibid.

4. Ibid., 342/2/6: 11.19.1903.

5. Scott (1905), vol. 2: p. 256. Scott learned this from Handsley's tentmates, but Skelton mentioned only the sore throat, not the other symptoms.

6. SPRI 342/2/6: 11.19.1903.

7. Ibid., 11.22.1903.

8. Ibid.

9. According to Mulock's chart, published by the RGS in 1908.

10. Scott (1905), vol. 2: p. 252.

11. Ellis (1969): p. 72.

12. Scott (1905), vol. 2: pp. 261–262.

13. Ibid., p. 264.

14. Ibid.

15. Ibid.

16. SPRI 342/2/6: 11.28.1903.

17. Ibid.

18. Scott (1905), vol. 2: p. 271.

19. Ibid., p. 274.

20. Ibid., p. 277.

21. Ibid., p. 286.

22. SPRI 342/2/6: 12.3.1903.

23. Ibid., 12.7.1903.

24. Scott (1905), vol. 2: p. 287.

25. Armitage ([1905]: p. 280) quotes Scott's letter to him describing the journey in which he speaks of arriving at the ship "with both sledges." In the last entry in Lashly's diary on December 15, he wrote, "When we started we had another nine foot sledge to pull."

26. SPRI 342/2/6: 12.9.1903.

27. Ibid., 12.6.1903, 12.14.1903.

28. WD: 12.17.1903.

29. Scott (1905), vol. 2: p. 290. The defile appeared much wider almost sixty years later when Dr. Colin Bull of Ohio State University walked through it.

30. "The English Nation, truly, has cause to be proud of them [the men of the Franklin period] . . . I bow in admiration," Nansen wrote in *Farthest North* ([1898], vol. 1: p. 404). Scott ([1905], vol. 2: p. 296) wrote of 725 statute miles for the main journey and 1,098 miles in all for the three journeys. When Skelton's estimates of the 144 mile and 170 mile round-trip distances on the depot journeys (SPRI 342/2/5 and 6) and the 389 he estimated for his own journey (SPRI 342/2/6: total of daily mileages recorded) are added to the distance Scott traveled west of Skelton's farthest (200 miles out and back), indicated by Mulock's 1908 chart, totals of 1,078 statute miles overall and 716 statute miles for the main journey result—close enough to exonerate Scott from any charge of exaggeration. Scott would hardly have questioned Skelton's depot journey mileages, partly confirmed by sledgemeter measurement on Armitage's glacier ascent.

CHAPTER 25

1. Armitage (1905): p. 281.

2. WD: 1.1.1904.

3. Wilson's words can be taken to imply that he was writing about a pyramid that seemed to him to be in the middle of the glacier. And despite the panorama photo (reproduced in vol. 2 of Scott's book) Armitage and Heald took that afternoon, that was where George Mulock took it to be in the map he produced to record the viewpoints and arcs embraced by Wilson's panoramas drawn in the area of McMurdo Sound and reproduced in a volume of panoramas published after the expedition. Contradicting panorama CXXXIV in that volume, Mulock shows the pyramid as a nunatak in the very center of the glacier and identifies an isolated peak to the southeast of it as Heald Island. That would equate with the 1,200 m+ peak (in 78°222S 163°422E) on the north side of Mount Morning. That, in turn, does appear in the middle of the glacier in Wilson's panorama, which, however, clearly shows the pyramid against the west shore of the glacier. And a photo taken from Hut Point in November 1995 by Tim Higham, the NZ Antarctic Programme Information Officer, confirms that the only peak corresponding to a pyramid is the 851 m cone on the western shore of the glacier, named "Pyramid Mountain" on modern maps. Wilson must have meant that it appeared in the middle *of the scene* in front of him. The height he reached on December 7, 1903, must have been the one in 78°102S 163°32E, about 3 km west of Armitage's, a position that equates well with his account of going "along the ridge top to another height" after lunch. From there and nowhere further east, the thaw pool on its upstream side would have been visible through the valley today named Pyramid Trough.

That the pyramid was then separated from the shore of Koettlitz Glacier by about 12 miles can be seen on the maps published after Scott's last expedition by Frank Debenham and in the sketch in his diary (reproduced on p. 84 of *The Quiet Land* [Bluntisham Books, 1992], edited by his daughter, June Debenham Back). From Debenham's account and Griffith Taylor's in *Scott's Last Expedition* and his own book *With Scott: The Silver Lining* (1916), it is clear that on March 1, 1911, Taylor, Wright, and Edgar Evans climbed the same height Wilson had reached, naming it Terminus Mountain. Debenham and Edgar Evans had reached the summit of Heald Island the day before. From there the two men would have seen the pyramid as the nunatak completely separated from the shore, which Debenham indicates on his maps. For that to be so, there must have been a significant decrease in the thickness of the glacier in the ensuing sixty years.

4. Almost certainly at 77°55S on the ridge along the south side of Hobbs Glacier.

5. Scott (1905), vol. 2: p. 427.

6. WD: 1.5.1904.

7. Scott (1905), vol. 2: pp. 349–350.

8. The inscription reads: "Sacred to the Memory of George T. Vince AB RN of the *Discovery* who drowned near this spot March 11 1902."

9. RGSAA 21/6, *Terra Nova* log: 2.16.1904.

10. Doorly (1916): p. 179.

11. WD: 2.17.1904.

12. If it had taken twenty minutes to drive the ship the short distance toward the port anchor against the force 10 midday storm, few could have doubted that even with both anchors out a force 12 hurricane would have made *Discovery* drag them sternward the few yards to inevitable destruction against that icebound shore. Scott must have had no way of knowing whether the ship might not also be smashed against it by storm-driven ice invisible in the blinding drift.

13. Scott (1905), vol. 2: p. 358.

14. Adjusting for the confusion in A.M. times by the transcriber, the *Terra Nova* log, having spoken of a sudden freshening to gale force at 10:35 A.M., records "heavy gale increasing" with thick snow drift at noon. An hour later, putting out an ice anchor, the engines needed to run at half speed to hold station against the ice edge, until at 2:30 P.M. a "squall of hurricane force" broke the ice anchor (RGSAA 21/6). This was much nearer to the head of the sound, and it appears reasonable that at Hut Point the wind had risen to at least force 10 by the time Scott made his run for the open water. His reference to the *engines* going ahead (Scott [1905], vol. 2: p. 358) must be wrong in its implication that full power was available.

15. Scott (1905), vol. 2: p. 358.

16. RGSAA 21/3: 2.16.1904.

17. Wilson, learning the story secondhand, clearly got the sequence of events somewhat confused in writing up his diary, saying the engines stopped on first grounding and that there was shallower water off the bow.

18. GJ 24/1: Jul. 1904, p. 27; GJ 23/6: Jun. 1904, p. 743.

19. SPRI 1329: 3.5.1904, letter Scott-Gregory.

20. GJ 23/6: Jun. 1904, p. 743.

21. Ibid.

22. Armitage (1905): pp. 289–290, 292.

23. SPRI 1329: 3.5.1904, letter Scott-Gregory.

24. GJ 24/1: July 1904, p. 29.

25. Scott (1905). vol. 2: p. 386.

26. Ross (1982): p. 103.

27. Joseph R. Stenhouse, master of the *Aurora* on Shackleton's trans-Antarctic expedition, drifting in the pack on November 23, 1915, saw what he believed was Cape Hudson on a bearing S60W true from 66°26S 154°16E, describing it as "a high bold headland with low undulating land stretching away southeast." The next day, from almost the same position, there was no sign of it, and he dismissed it as "a mirage" (RGS Archives, OBS153 file). The position of the USS *Peacock* (Lt. Hudson) when Midshipman Henry Eld saw the cape on January 19, 1840, was 66°20S 154½E. The position of Cape Hudson was finally established on February 21, 1959, when Dr. Phillip Law, leading an Australian National Antarctic Research expedition, discovered the Mawson Peninsula and recognized its northern point as the cape seen in 1840 (Bertrand [1971]: pp. 175–176).

28. Scott (1905), vol. 2: p. 393.

29. GJ 23/6: June 1904, p. 743.

30. MD: 4.1.1904.

31. It was more a sign of failing health than unfairness that Markham, who had worked tirelessly at keeping the men's families in touch with the news, omitted Macfarlane, whom he had all along acknowledged as invalided home. Later when compiling his *Dictionary of Antarctic Biography* he added "with a weak heart" (RGSAA Markham: Dictionary of Antarctic Biography).

32. PRO: ADM 1/7848.

33. SPRI 1453/171/1: 9.3.1904.

34. MD: 9.15.1904.

35. GJ 24/4: Oct. 1904, p. 380 (9.16.1904).

36. Ibid., p. 383.

37. Ibid., p. 384.

38. Pound (1966): p. 121.

39. Ibid.

40. Ellis (1969): pp. 89–90.

41. Only when the quotation was accepted two days later did Keltie mention the crucial requirement that the medals had to be ready for presentation at Albert Hall. Wyon had to reply that it was impossible, and the Society had to settle for presentation of a dummy gold medal to Scott. Duly received with the original inscription designating Scott as RN, MVO, FRGS, it was then realized that no one had told Wyon about the award of Scott's CVO, the royal warrant for which was dated October 11. Keltie sent a telegram to Wyon the day of the meeting, and Scott received the dummy with the original inscription. Photos of the dummy appeared in the December 1904 *Geographical Journal.* The actual medals were not received from Allan Wyon until mid-February 1905 (RGSAA Keltie-Wyon correspondence: 10.19, 20.1904, and 11.7.1904).

42. The fourteen men on the platform with the officers were Dellbridge, Ford, Cross, Smythe, Croucher, Dell, Handsley, Joyce, Pilbeam, Wild, Plumley, Whitfield, Gilbert Scott, and Weller (RGSAA Markham Collection, no. 43).

43. GJ 24/6: Dec. 1904, p. 619.

44. Ibid., p. 620.

45. SPRI 1453/140/1: 9.24.1904.

46. The only discordant note, harbinger of disputes to come, had been the Royal Society's objection to the scientists and officers lecturing on their scientific work, voiced two days before the Albert Hall meeting. The objection was withdrawn six days later (MD: 11.8.1904).

EPILOGUE

1. Besides George Vince and Josef Enzensperger, seaman Auguste Wiencke and Lt. Emile Danco, magnetician, on the Belgian expedition; Nicolai Hanson, biologist on Borchgrevink's expedition; Allan Ramsay, chief engineer on the Scottish expedition; and seaman Ole Wennersgaard on the Swedish expedition had all lost their lives in the Antarctic before the *Discovery* escaped from McMurdo Sound.

2. MD: 10.29.1905.

3. SPRI 1453/171/2: 10.20.1905.

4. MD: 11.14.1905.

5. Huntford (1979): p. 231.

6. The others who received their medals from the king were Bernacchi, Dailey, Feather, Hodgson, Mulock, Skelton, and Wilson (PRO: ADM 171/61; MD: 12.18.1905).

7. *Nature* 73: Jan. 25, 1906, p. 297.

8. Huntford (1979): p. 229.

9. SPRI 1453/48: Barne-Scott 10.1.1906.

10. Ibid., Barne-Scott 3.19.1907.

11. Pound (1966): p. 124.

12. SPRI 1456/23/2: Scott-Shackleton 2.18.1907.

13. Mill (1923): p. 103.

14. SPRI 1456/28/8: 2.16.1907, letter to Markham.

15. Ibid., 1456/24/10: 2.20.1907.

16. Ibid., 1456/24/8: 2.16.1907, letter to Markham.

17. Ibid., 1453/122/2.

18. Ibid., 1453/28: Barne-Scott 2.17.1907.

19. Ibid., 1456/23/1: 2.18.1907.

20. Ibid., 1456/23/2: 2.18.1907.

21. Ibid.

22. Ibid.

23. Ibid.

24. Ibid.

25. Ibid. He had also written to Markham, who was staying at the Grand Hotel in Palma, Majorca. Obviously assuming he had or intended to put Scott in the picture, Markham concluded his welcome for Shackleton's plan with the words "I hope you have kept Captain Scott informed of your plans" (Ibid., 1456/21/1: 2.26.1907, letter to Shackleton).

26. Ibid., 25/2: 2.28.1907, letter to Scott.

27. RGS Archives: Scott correspondence files, Keltie-Scott 3.1.1907.

28. SPRI 1456/26: 2.28.1907.

29. Ibid.

30. Ibid., 25/4; quoted in Shackleton-Scott 3.7.1907.

31. Ibid.

32. Ibid.

33. Ibid., 1456/23/3: 3.12.1907. The copy of the letter in the Shackleton family papers, made by his biographers, James and Margery Fisher, is dated March 7, which must be a misprint for the 12th, the earliest date Scott could have received Shackleton's March 7 letter, which he acknowledges in this one.

34. RGS Archives: Scott correspondence, Secretary to Scott, 3.8.1907, and Scott to RGS Secretary, 3.26.1907.

35. SPRI 1453/188/3: 3.8.1907.

36. Ibid.

37. Ibid., 1456/26/8: 3.8.1907.

38. Ibid., 1456/26/2: 3.11.1907.

39. Ibid., 1456/23/1: 2.18.1907 (postscript).

40. Ibid., 25/5: 3.8.1907.

41. Ibid., 1456/23/4: 3.26.1907. As in the case of the transcript mentioned in note 33, the date March 26 on this one was probably a misprint for March 16, as it is acknowledged in Shackleton's March 23 letter (in ibid., ms 25/6).

42. Ibid., 25/6: 3.23.1907.

43. Ibid., 25/7: 5.17.1907 (attached to 25/12: 5.22.1907 letter).

44. Ibid.

45. Ibid., 1456/23/5 (undated), 6: 5.23.1907.

46. Shackleton (or perhaps his ghost writer, Edward Saunders) speaks of "the inlet where Borchgrevink landed" on page 72 of *The Heart of the Antarctic*, vol. 1, but gives a map of "Balloon Bight" on page 73.

47. Dr. Jean-Baptiste Charcot had led the *Français* expedition (1903–1905) with the objective of getting ashore south of the Antarctic Peninsula. Repulsed by the ice at 66°S in February 1904, the following season he had sledged through De Gerlache's Lemaire Channel (the southern part of which is today's Penola Strait) to reveal that the Belgian's "vaste baie ou détroit" was not Eduard Dallmann's Bismarck Strait, which Nordenskjöld and others took it for. Later he had sailed south, to be repulsed off Alexander I Land, and then he nearly lost his ship off the coast of Adelaide Island, which he named Terre Loubet. Charcot mistook the coast for the mainland, so much vaster was it than the small island Biscoe had glimpsed, and named after William IV's Queen Adelaide.

48. SPRI 342/10/2: report compiled 3.17.1908, p. A1.

49. *Le Monde Illustré* (1908): p. 209.

50. SPRI 1453/3: 3.8.1908, letter to Kathleen Bruce.

51. Pound (1966): p. 167.

52. MD: 3.26.1909.

53. *The Times*: 9.15.1909.

54. SPRI 1453/64/2: 3.1.1910 letter Charcot-Scott.

55. GJ 25/4: April 1905.

56. Shackleton (1909), vol. 1: p. 73.

57. Ibid., vol. 2: facing p. 12 in English ed.

58. SLE 1: pp. 438–439.

59. British Antarctic Expedition (BAE) 1907–1909: SR Geology 1: pp. 241, 250–251, and BAE 1910–1913: SR Geology 1, part 1: p. 42, Prof. Seward.

60. From the Mount Buckley camp they covered 110 statute miles to the Granite Pillars (BAE 1910–1913: SR Maps in Report on Surveys), 4 statute miles

over the Gap to Lower Glacier Depot (WD: 2.18.1912), and 261 statute miles from there to the last camp (SLE 1: pp. 632-633)–a total of 375 statute miles in thirty-nine days on the move (tentbound in a blizzard on March 10). The 11 extra miles to reach One Ton Depot represented 2.9 percent of that distance, equivalent to about 490 yards extra per day on the move. Using the data in Cherry-Garrard's copy of Scott's draft plan (SPRI 763/2) and adjusting for a five-man party, the Pole Party would have been pulling an average load (the load halfway between depots), excluding the rocks but including the sledge with iron-clad runners weighing about 90 pounds, amounting to 350 pounds. The rocks increased that load by 10 percent.

APPENDIX 3

1. Markham (1986): Intro. by C. A. Holland, p. xxiii.
2. Fuchs and Hillary (1958): pp. 88-89.
3. Markham (1986): p. 12 (evidently referring to 1897).
4. RGSAA 5/2/2: 4.26.1899.
5. Ibid., 1/10/3: 6.9.1900.
6. GJ 14/5: Nov. 1899, p. 479.
7. RGSAA 4/1/3: 1.19.1900.
8. Ibid., 1/10/3: undated.
9. SPRI 366/15/42: 6.19.1900.

APPENDIX 4

1. Scott (1905), vol. 1: p. 314.
2. Bernacchi (1938): p. 43.
3. Scott (1905), vol. 1: p. 300.
4. RGSAA 5/2/8: 10.26.1899.
5. Bernacchi (1938): p. 23.
6. Markham (1986): p. 38.
7. SPRI 595/1: 10.1.1901.
8. Scott (1905), vol. 1: facing p. 343.
9. Bernacchi (1938): facing p. 47.
10. DD: 9.30.1902.
11. The *Sphere*: Sept. 1901.
12. WD: 8.1.1902.

APPENDIX 5

1. SPRI 366/12/2: 3.4.1902.
2. WD: 2.19.1902.
3. SPRI 366/12/9: 3.3.1902; 10: 3.25.1902.
4. Ibid., 774/1/1: 3.31.1902; GJ 22/3: Sept. 1903, pp. 304-305.
5. WD: 9.2.1902.
6. SPRI 366/12/15: undated.
7. Ibid., 366/12/17: 10.3.1902.
8. Scott (1905), vol. 1: p. 518.
9. Armitage (1905): p. 134.
10. Scott (1905), vol. 1: p. 525.
11. SPRI 366/12/24: 10.4.1902.
12. GJ 22/3: Sept. 1903.

13. Scott (1905), vol. 2: facing p. 10.
14. GJ 22/1: July 1903, pp. 20-37.
15. SPRI 641/2: 11.3.1902.
16. Armitage (1905): p. 158; ibid., 366/5/1: 12.18.1902.
17. Armitage (1905): p. 159.
18. SPRI 366/12/34: 12.20.1902.
19. Names per photo 458 in Royal Society Albums.
20. SPRI 366/12/43: 9.7.1903.
21. Ibid., 342/2/5: 9.9.1903.
22. Ibid., 366/12/46: 10.6.1903.
23. WD: 11.16.1903, 11.26.1903.
24. SPRI 342/2/6: 11.22.1903.
25. Ibid., 366/12/38: 11.10.1903; 366/3/4: 12.7.1903.

APPENDIX 7

1. SPT: June 1903 (map).
2. *The Charts of the* Discovery *Expedition*, published by the Royal Geographical Society, 1908: p. 5.
3. Scott (1905), vol. 2: p. 104.
4. Ibid., p. 47.
5. SPT: June 1903, p. 7.
6. Worsley (1931): p. 281.
7. SPRI 1456/2: 12.8.1902.
8. Scott (1905), vol. 2: p. 252.
9. SPRI 342/2/6: 12.11.1903.
10. Scott (1905), vol. 2: p. 257.
11. SR 2, Physical Observations: p. 343.
12. Scott (1905), vol. 2: p. 263.
13. Ibid., p. 267.
14. Ibid., p. 287.
15. Ibid., p. 267.

APPENDIX 8

1. PRO: ADM1/7848, Palace Nov. 28, 1905, file.
2. Ibid., February 17, 1905, letter to secretary.
3. Ibid., February 24, 1905, memo.
4. Clearly, that should have included Macfarlane and above all Vince, who had died in the cause of exploration. The May 22, 1903, letter from the presidents of the Royal Society and the RGS to the secretary to the Admiralty (forwarding Scott's commendations, which resulted in reinstatement of William Smythe to PO 1st Class rating and promotion of Dailey, Dellbridge, Ford, and Quartley) refers specifically to Macfarlane as "invalided." Sent with the letter was a copy of Scott's Letter of Proceedings, posted from New Zealand by Colbeck, which had fully described the loss of Vince. However, if the Admiralty failed to insist that both men be included on the list of those qualifying for the silver medal, Scott must bear some of the responsibility. When asked after he returned to England for a list of those who served on *Discovery* and "particulars of discharge of any who may have left the ship" and any not recommended for the award, Scott included Macfarlane

on the list of those "discharged at their own request" and omitted Vince altogether. The Naval Branch secretary, W. Graham Greene, a month after the conditions of award were finalized, "presumed that the late G. T. Vince, AB *Discovery*, whose case was dealt with in N11886/04, is only to be regarded as having qualified for the Bronze Medal" (PRO: ADM1/7848, Palace Nov. 28, 1905, file). That was on May 19, 1905, and when the final list was sent to Scott the following October he made no comment on the inclusion of both men in the list of five *Discovery* men to receive bronze medals. It all smacked of an official attitude toward the lower deck that eight years later resulted in Edgar Evans's posthumous RGS 1913 Memorial Medal being bronze rather than silver.

    5. The conditions for this issue were described in the author's article, "The First Environmental Campaign Medal," in the British magazine *Medal News* in April and May 1989, amplified by letters in the July and October issues that year.

    6. PRO: ADM1/7848, 4.4.1905, memo by V. W. Baddeley.

    7. RGSAA and Library ms files.

    8. RGSAA 21/6: 11.8.1902.

    9. SPRI 342/28/59: 10.12.1909.

    10. PRO: ADM171/61, BT100/146.

    11. RGSAA 16/3/1: undated.

    12. Ibid.

    13. PRO: ADM171/61, BT100/50.

APPENDIX 9

    1. 8.14.1908.

    2. GJ 32/2: Aug. 1908, p. 191.

    3. RSA: ms 547–548, Scott-Geikie 10.10.1908, pp. 8–9.

    4. SPRI 641/1/3: 11.26.1903.

    5. RSA: ms 547–548, Scott-Geikie 12.11.1908 attachment, p. 4.

    6. Ibid., Scott-Geikie 11.23.1908.

    7. Ibid., Chree-Geikie 10.11.1908.

    8. SR Meteo 1: pp. 489–490.

    9. RSA: ms 547–548, Scott-Geikie 11.20.1908.

    10. Ibid., Scott-Geikie 12.11.1908 attachment.

    11. Ibid., Scott-Geikie 1.9.1909.

    12. Ibid., Scott-Geikie Nov. 1908.

    13. Proceedings of Physical Society of London, 2.14.1908.

    14. RSA: ms 547–548, Field-Geikie 12.7.08.

BIBLIOGRAPHY

Amundsen, R. *My Life as an Explorer.* London: Heinemann, 1927.

Armitage, A. B. *Two Years in the Antarctic.* London: Edward Arnold, 1905.

——. *Cadet to Commodore.* London: Cassell, 1925.

Bernacchi, L. C. *To the South Polar Regions.* London: Hurst and Blackett, 1901.

——. *Saga of the "Discovery."* London: Blackie and Son, 1938.

Bertrand, K. J. *Americans in Antarctica 1775–1948.* New York: American Geographic Society, 1971.

Borchgrevink, C. E. *First on the Antarctic Continent.* London: George Newnes, 1901.

Cherry-Garrard, A.G.B. *The Worst Journey in the World.* London: Constable, 1922.

Cook, Dr. F. A. *Through the First Antarctic Night.* London: Heinemann, 1900.

Doorly, G. S. *The Voyages of the "Morning."* London: Smith Elder, 1916.

Drygalski, E. von. *The Southern Ice Continent* (tr. Raraty). Huntingdon: Bluntisham Books, 1989.

Ellis, Cdr. A. R. *Under Scott's Command.* London: Gollancz, 1969.

Fastovsky D. E., and D. B. Weishampel. *The Evolution and Extinction of the Dinosaurs.* Cambridge: Cambridge University Press, 1996.

Fiala, A. *Fighting the Polar Ice.* London: Hodder and Stoughton, 1907.

Fisher, M., and J. Fisher. *Shackleton.* London: J. Barrie Books, 1957.

Fuchs, Sir V. E., and Hillary, Sir E. *The Crossing of Antarctica.* London: Cassell, 1958.

Gerlache, Cdt. A. de. *Quinze Mois dans l'Antarctique.* Brussels: Imp. Ch. Bulens, 1902.

Harland, J. *Seamanship in the Age of Sail.* London: Conway Maritime Press, 1987.

Hayes, J. G. *Antarctica.* London: Richards Press, 1928.

Hobbs, W. H. *Peary.* New York: Macmillan, 1936.

Huntford, R. *Scott and Amundsen.* London: Hodder and Stoughton, 1979. Published facsimile in New York: G. P. Putnam's Sons, 1980. Also abridged as *The Last Place on Earth* (next entry).

——. *The Last Place on Earth.* London: Pan Books, 1985.

——. *Shackleton.* London: Hodder and Stoughton, 1985. Referred to in text as Huntford (1985 #2).

Jacka, F., and E. Jacka. *Mawson's Antarctic Diaries.* London: Unwin Hyman, 1988.

Jackson, F. G. *A Thousand Days in the Arctic.* London: Harper Brothers, 1899.

Lecointe, G. *Aux Pays des Manchots.* Brussels: Schepens, 1904.

Linklater, E. *The Voyage of the Challenger.* London: John Murray, 1974.

Marvin, U. B. *Continental Drift: The Evolution of a Concept.* Washington, D.C.: Smithsonian Institution Press, 1973.

Markham, Sir C. M. *The Life of Sir Clements Markham.* London: Smith Elder, 1917.

——. *Lands of Silence.* Cambridge: Cambridge University Press, 1921.

——. *Antarctic Obsession* (ed. C. Holland). Huntingdon: Bluntisham Books, 1986.

Mawson, Sir Douglas. *The Home of the Blizzard.* London: Heinemann, 1918.

Mill, H. R. *The Siege of the South Pole.* London: Alston Rivers, 1905.

——. *The Life of Sir Ernest Shackleton.* London: Heinemann, 1923.

Murray, Dr. G. (ed). *The Antarctic Manual.* London: Royal Geographical Society, 1901.

Nansen, Dr. F. *The Crossing of Greenland.* London: Longmans Green, 1890.

——. *Farthest North.* London: George Newnes, 1898.

Neumayer, G. von. *Auf zum Südpol.* Berlin: Vita Deutsches Verlagshaus, 1901.

Nordenskjöld, Otto. *Antarctica.* London: Hurst and Blackett, 1905.

Peary, R. E. *Northward Over the Great Ice.* London: Methuen, 1898.

Pound, R. *Scott of the Antarctic.* London: World Books, 1966.

Priestley, R. E. *Antarctic Adventure.* London: C. Hurst, 1974.

Ross, Rear Adm. M. J. *Ross in the Antarctic.* Whitby: Caedmon of Whitby, 1982.

Royal Geographical Society. *Report of 6th Int'l Geogr'l Congress.* London: John Murray, 1896.

Savours, A., and Deacon, M. (in) *Starving Sailors.* Greenwich: National Maritime Museum, 1981.

Scott, Capt. R. F. *The Voyage of the Discovery.* London: Smith Elder, 1905.

Scott, Capt. R. F., et al. *Scott's Last Expedition.* London: Smith Elder, 1913.

Seaver, G. *Edward Wilson of the Antarctic.* London: John Murray, 1933.

Shackleton, Sir E. H. *The Heart of the Antarctic.* London: Heinemann, 1909.

Stonehouse, Dr. B. (ed). *The Biology of Penguins.* London: Macmillan, 1975.

Taylor, G. *With Scott: The Silver Lining.* London: Smith Elder, 1916.

Thomson, D. *Scott's Men.* London: Allen Lane, 1977.

Wilson, E. A. *Diary of the "Discovery" Expedition to the Antarctic 1901–1904* (ed. A. Savours). London: Blandford Press, 1966.

——. *Diary of the "Terra Nova" Expedition to the Antarctic 1910–1912* (ed. H.G.R. King). London: Blandford Press, 1972.

Woollard, Cdr. C.L.A. *The Last of the Cape Horners.* Ilfracombe: Stockwell, 1967.

Worsley, F. A. *Endurance.* London: Philip Allan, 1931.

INDEX

For sledge journey participants, crew members, and medal recipients, see appendixes. Index does not repeat this information, or chart detail.

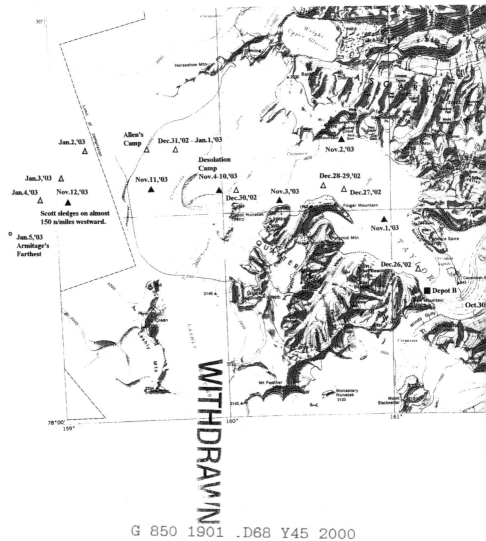

30'

Wright
Upper Glacier
940±

Fleming

Horseshoe Mtn

Jan.2,'03
△

Allen's
Camp
△

Dec.31,'02 - Jan.1,'03
△

Nov.2,'03

Jan.3,'03 △

Desolation
Camp
Nov.4-10,'03

Dec.28-29,'02
△   △ Dec.27,'02

Jan.4,'03 Nov.12,'03
△   ▲

Nov.11,'03
▲

Nov.3,'03
▲

Dec.30,'02

Finger Mountain

**Scott sledges on almost
150 n/miles westward.**

Depot Nunatak

Nov.1,'03

○ Jan.5,'03
**Armitage's
Farthest**

Pyramid Mtn

Dec.26,'02
△

Depot B

Oct.30

2140 △

Mt Crean

Mt Feather

Monastery
Nunatak
2133

Mount
Blackwelder

78°00'
159°

160°

161°

WITHDRAWN